RESTORING
MUSEUM
AIRCRAFT

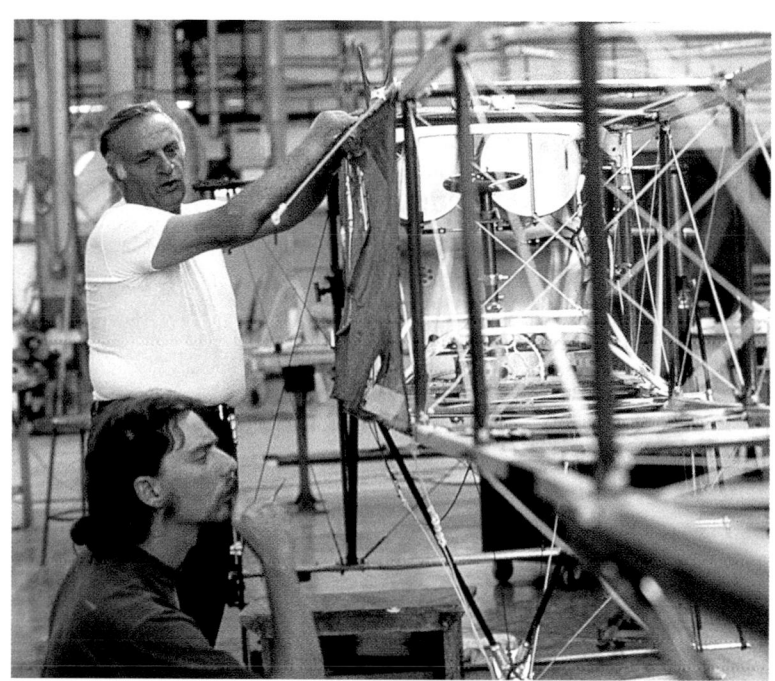

ROBERT MIKESH

RESTORING MUSEUM AIRCRAFT

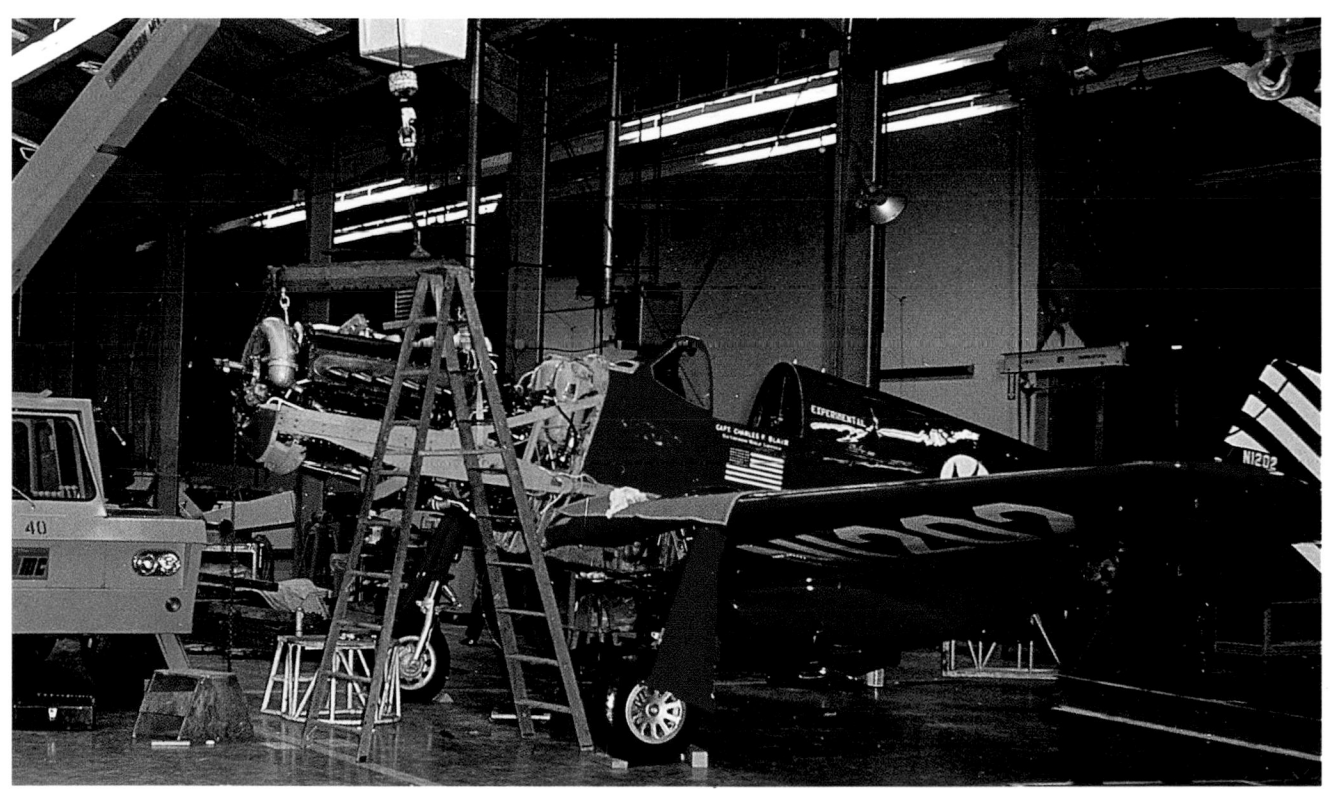

Airlife
England

Copyright © 1997 Robert Mikesh

First published in the UK in 1997
by Airlife Publishing Ltd

British Library Cataloguing-in-Publication Data
A catalogue record for this book
is available from the British Library

ISBN 1 85310 875 8

Typeset by Phoenix Typesetting, Ilkley, West Yorkshire
Printed in Singapore by Kydo Printing Co. (S'pore) Pte Ltd.

Airlife Publishing Ltd
101 Longden Road, Shrewsbury SY3 9EB, England.

CONTENTS

Acknowledgements   6

Introduction   7

Chapter:

1. **Considerations; Where to Begin**   9
   How Far?   10
   How it Began   12
   The Conservator   17
   The Restoration Technician   19
   The Curator   20
   I'll Be Back!   21

2. **Collection and Restoration Decisions**   22
   Restoration Planning Concepts   22
   Matching Museum Mission   24
   Marking Decisions are Critical   25
   Levels of Exhibit and Preservation
       Condition   31
   Curatorial Guidelines   36
   Technical Materials   37
   Programing   37
   First and Last Restoration   38
   Suspending Exhibit Aircraft   41
   Cutaways, Sectionalized and
       Segmented Aircraft   42
   Price vs. Value   44
   Will it Fly?   45

3. **Before the Teardown:**   49
   Photography   53
   Work Log-books   55
   Parts Identification   56
   Parts Storage   56
   Racks and Trunnions   57
   Marking New and Repaired Parts   58
   Documenting the Past   58

4. **Wood-and-Fabric Aircraft:**   61
   No Half-way   63
   Replace or Repair?   64
   Restoring the Albatros D.Va   65
   Aircraft Fabrics   76
   Wright Flyer   77
   Early Dopes and Clear Finishes   79
   Spad XIII   82
   Successes and Failures   86

5. **Lozenge-Pattern Fabric:**   87
   The Availability Problem   88
   Developing NASM's Lozenge Fabric   90
   To Achieve Exactness   92
   Halberstadt Lozenge Fabric   93

6. **Metal Aircraft:**   95
   History within the Paint   95
   Chemical Processing   100
   Restoring the J1N1-S 'Irving'   105
   Cockpit Detailing   111
   Electrical Wiring   113
   Little Surprises   114
   Polishing   115
   Steel Tube Fuselage Frames   117

7. **Aero Propulsion:**   119
   Change in Approach   120

When Disassembly is Necessary   121
Protective Coatings   122
Ignition Harness   123
Engine Openings   124
Propellers   126
Wooden Propellers   127

8. **Aircraft Tires:**   129
   Tire Development   129
   Replacement Tires   130
   Aeronca C-2   134
   Kawanishi N1K2-J 'George'   135
   Arado Ar 234B-2 Blitz   136
   For the Long Term   137
   Tire Care While on Exhibit   137
   Tire Storage   139

9. **Colors and Markings:**   141
   P-51C *Excalibur III*   142
   Documenting Color   144
   From Those Who Know   145
   Exterior Markings   145
   Arado Ar 234B-2 Blitz   145
   F-100D Tail Markings   149
   Lockheed XP-80 *Lulu Belle*   151
   At the Fly-Ins   152
   Reversible Painting and Markings   154
   Two-for-One   156

10. **Finishing Up:**   159
    Mini Record   159
    Truth in Labeling   160
    Concluding Check List   160
    Publish the Knowledge Gained   160
    'Smithsonian Quality'   161

11. **Contracting the Project:**   163
    Advantages and Disadvantages   163
    The Contract   163
    Planned Visits   164

12. **Preparing Unsheltered Exhibit**
    Aircraft   167
    The Preparation   167
    Exhibit Placement   169
    Recurring Maintenance   170
    Window Tint Film   174
    How Long Can it Last?   174

Footnotes   175

APPENDICES: 177
   A. Wood-and-Fabric Aircraft, Sample:
       Curatorial Guidelines (Benoist
       Type XII)   177
   B. Metal Aircraft, Sample:
       Curatorial Guidelines (Arado
       Ar 234 B-2 Blitz)   187
   C. Concluding Report, Sample   197
   D. Restoration Contract, Sample   200
   E. Man-hours for Restorations   202
   F. Sources for Technical Information   203
   G. Vendor Information   205
   H. Propeller Markings   208

GLOSSARY   213

INDEX   215

Acknowledgements

A book such as this which covers a large variety of technical skills and philosophical areas cannot be written by just one person expressing a single viewpoint. For that reason I am greatly indebted to many people who have willingly helped me in gathering and consolidating this material and have contributed their thoughts on aircraft restorations in the hope that others may benefit by this collective effort.

When mentioning the names of individuals who have helped with the creation of this book, it is not intended to imply that they endorse the concepts expressed here. It is safe to say, however, that where differences in methods and opinions became evident, they have either been included here, or were basically a matter of semantics. At first I thought that there would be numerous differences, but this was not the case.

From an early stage of this project, one person in particular became interested in this work and remained a steadfast supporter and adviser throughout its gestation. Dr Kevin McCartney, a professor at the University of Maine at Presque Isle, and long-time aviation enthusiast and friend has helped immeasurably in assisting to organize this material. His constructive comments, editing, and knowledge of aviation has been of tremendous help in reaching this final form.

I placed heavy emphasis on the opinions and guidance of conservators because of their importance in preserving these valued aircraft. David Hallam, former Senior Conservator at the Australian War Memorial in Canberra, now Senior Scientist, Materials Conservation, Queensland Museum, has been a positive influence for many years and has contributed many constructive thoughts contained here. Edward McManus, Conservator at the National Air and Space Museum has been a willing participant with his guidance and help on many technical matters. James A. Burnham, formerly the Chief Conservator for the Henry Ford Museum, now Director of Sloss Furnaces National Historic Landmark, Birmingham, Alabama, originated stability condition categories of aircraft that help to determine various levels of preservation. His classifications expressed in this book may well become a standard for terminology in aircraft restoration and preservation usage.

Dr Michael A. Fopp, Director of the RAF Museum at Hendon, London, has been very helpful throughout the development of this book. His concepts for safeguards of our aircraft collections and individual objects, as seen through the eyes of a museum director, have been conveyed in many places throughout this book.

Mr Leonard E. Opdycke, publisher and editor of *World War I Aero* and *Skyways* magazines gave willingly of his time and good counsel. His editing suggestions give a broader perspective to much of the material contained here.

Space does not permit listing all the individuals or their areas of expertise as it pertains to this book. All have contributed material and knowledge, and others have reviewed portions or all of the manuscript as it was developed. Among those deserving my individual thanks and great appreciation are, in alphabetical order:

Dan-San Abbott: aviation historian
Peter M. Bowers: aviation historian, photographer, and sport aircraft designer/builder
Richard Brown: vintage tire specialist
Herbert S. Brownstein: aviation consultant and author, NASM
Ralph A. Bufano: Executive Director, Museum of Flight, Seattle, Washington
Louis S. Casey: former Curator of Aircraft, NASM
Dale Crane: aviation training consultant
Air Vice-Marshal Ron Dick, RAF (Ret'd): aviation historian
Thomas Dwenger: vintage tire specialist
Jeffrey L. Ethell: aviation historian and writer
Joseph Fichera: restorer of vintage aircraft, formerly with NASM
David L. Goss: restorer of vintage aircraft
Peter M. Grosz: aviation historian and writer
Captain William T. Hardaker, USN (Ret'd): aviation consultant, NASM.
Ken Hyde: restorer of vintage aircraft
Harry A. Jay: propeller specialist and historian
Paul Lake: restoration shop foreman, US Air Force Museum, Dayton, Ohio
Air Commodore David F. Lawrence, RAF (Ret'd): Keeper of Aircraft and Exhibits, RAF Museum, London, England
Richard A. Leyes II: Curator of Aero Propulsion, NASM
Harvey Lippincott: aviation historian, archivist, United Technologies (Ret'd)
Kenneth M. Molson (deceased): former Director, National Aviation Museum, Ottawa, Canada
Stephen R. Payne: Curator, Aeronautical Technology, National Aviation Museum, Ottawa, Canada
Dr. Walter Rathjen: Deputy Director, Deutsches Museum von Meisterwerken der Naturwissenschaft und Technik, Munich, Germany
William C. Reese: restoration shop foreman, NASM
Alfred J. Shortt: Director, Collection and Research, National Aviation Museum, Ottawa, Canada
Dr. Dr. Holger Steinle: Deputy Director, Deutsches Technikmuseum, Berlin, Germany
Christopher J. Terry: Director-General, National Aviation Museum, Ottawa, Canada
Alan D. Toelle: aviation historian and writer
Colonel Richard L. Uppstrom, USAF (Ret'd): Director, US Air Force Museum, Dayton, Ohio
Larry Webster: restorer of vintage aircraft
Max Widmer: Technical Supervisor, Swissair
Henry Wydler: Vice-Director, Verkehrshaus der Schweiz, Luzern, Switzerland

Special thanks too for the excellent photographic assistance obtained for so many years from NASM photographers, Mark A. Avino, Dale E. Hrabak, and Carolyn J. Russo.

To all these who gave so freely of their time towards this book, and to others that have inadvertently been overlooked, I extend my sincere thanks and appreciation.

INTRODUCTION

The title of this book is actually a misnomer. It could really be titled 'Preserving Museum Aircraft', for in truth, the work that is about to be described places more emphasis on preserving the original integrity of the airplane in question than in the mechanics of a restoration process. Normally when working with a museum aircraft, the intention is to change its current state and bring it back to an earlier condition, be it factory-fresh and operational, or as it might have been when involved in a historical event. In many cases, considerable work must be done on the airplane to achieve this goal through restoration, yet at the same time preserve as much of its original materials as possible. The word 'restoring' was chosen because it has understanding for most people.

For this reason the word 'restoration' will be used more often than the more correct 'preservation'. Museum technicians should be accustomed to including preservation as a continuing part of the restoration process of static museum aircraft. It is not uncommon, however, to view some restorations taking place that have little or no thought given to preservation of original materials. The differences between these two terms will become more clear as this subject evolves throughout the book.

This is not simply a textbook that tells technicians how to preserve and restore aircraft. Instead, my objective is to put into words and illustrations some of the many restoration and preservation concepts, many of which were formulated during my 21 years at the National Air and Space Museum. It was during most of that time that I was the curator responsible for that wonderful collection of historical aircraft. This task and honor included directing and monitoring the preservation and restoration process of some of these aircraft. No two aircraft restorations were alike, and therefore there is no set plan that applied across the board. This book is intended to cover major aspects of this process, while interjecting unique personal experiences that will be of help to some, and interesting to others who enjoy reading about airplanes and their structures.

The subject to be addressed in this book is relatively new in one sense of the word. There has been very little written about philosophies and solutions used in preserving and restoring large technological objects, particularly aircraft. Aircraft seem to be especially susceptible to damage, mostly because of the effect of neglect and the elements on their lightweight structures. Only in recent years has museum aircraft preservation taken on a more serious and scientific approach. Initially, 'restoration' meant a new coat of paint. As awareness of our need to preserve aviation technology in its original form increased, more effort was directed at long-term preservation of components and internal systems to make an airplane complete. Acceptance of an airplane as complete when cockpits are partially empty of instruments and knobs is no longer passable in today's higher level of museology.

In perspective, aviation is relatively new to the vast world of museums. A mere half a century ago at the end of World War II, for instance, museums dedicated exclusively to aircraft were almost non-existent. In the US there were some collections of 'old planes' such as the privately owned Jarrett collection of World War I armor and aircraft rotting in the outdoors at Atlantic City, the beginnings of Ed Maloney's The Air Museum 'Planes of Fame' in California, an assortment at the Smithsonian Institution in Washington, DC, and aircraft in the Air Force Technical Museum at Wright Field, Dayton, Ohio. There might have been one or two other collections of aircraft in the US at that time. In Europe there was the Musée de l'Air near Paris, the collection at the Imperial War and Science Museums in London, a grouping of rare airplanes in Italy and perhaps one or two other large collections worldwide. The magnificent collection held by the Deutsche Luftfahrt Sammlung in Berlin had been partially dispersed but largely destroyed during World War II bombings. It was not until the 1950s, when World War II airplanes were being sent to many locations when asked for, that the term 'Air Museum' began to take hold. Initially, visitor satisfaction was gained by merely walking along rows of airplanes, the more fortunate specimens having labels that identified them.

Times have changed in the development of aviation museums. Missions for air museums are now being more focused with a specific theme and purpose. This brings selectivity to the collection and display of the aircraft and related objects. This is reflected in the purpose and configuration for which an aircraft was acquired and prepared to support the museum's mission. Along with this, the rows of airplanes within museums are beginning to give way to placing airplanes with supporting artifacts in habitat environments or full-size dioramas which help to tell the story of the airplane and the people who used them. The visitor then becomes a vicarious participant in the event.

With greater awareness being given to meaningful exhibit surroundings for the airplane, along with the impact that each has made in aviation, more attention is rightfully given to the airplane as the focal point of planned exhibits. It is hoped therefore, that this book will contain ideas, suggested materials, and new ways to use restoration skills that can improve the quality of the museum aircraft preservation and restoration process, now and for the years to come.

Robert C. Mikesh
Washington, DC, 1996

In the 1970s, major governmental air museums worldwide opened new buildings to exhibit their collections. Among these was the National Air and Space Museum in Washington, DC, a birthday present to the Nation marking its 200th year in July 1976. (NASM, SI 83-16825)

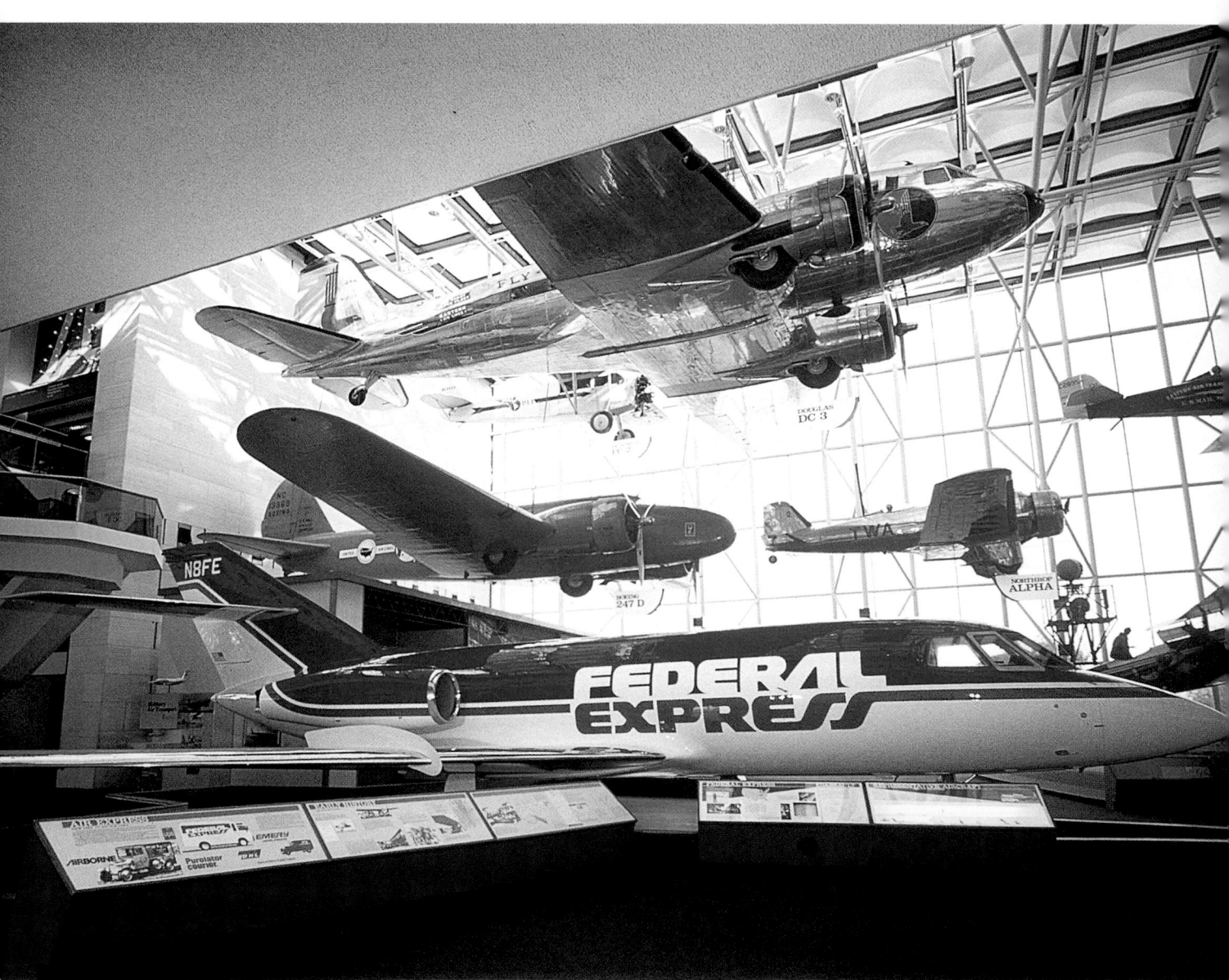

CHAPTER 1
Considerations; Where to Begin

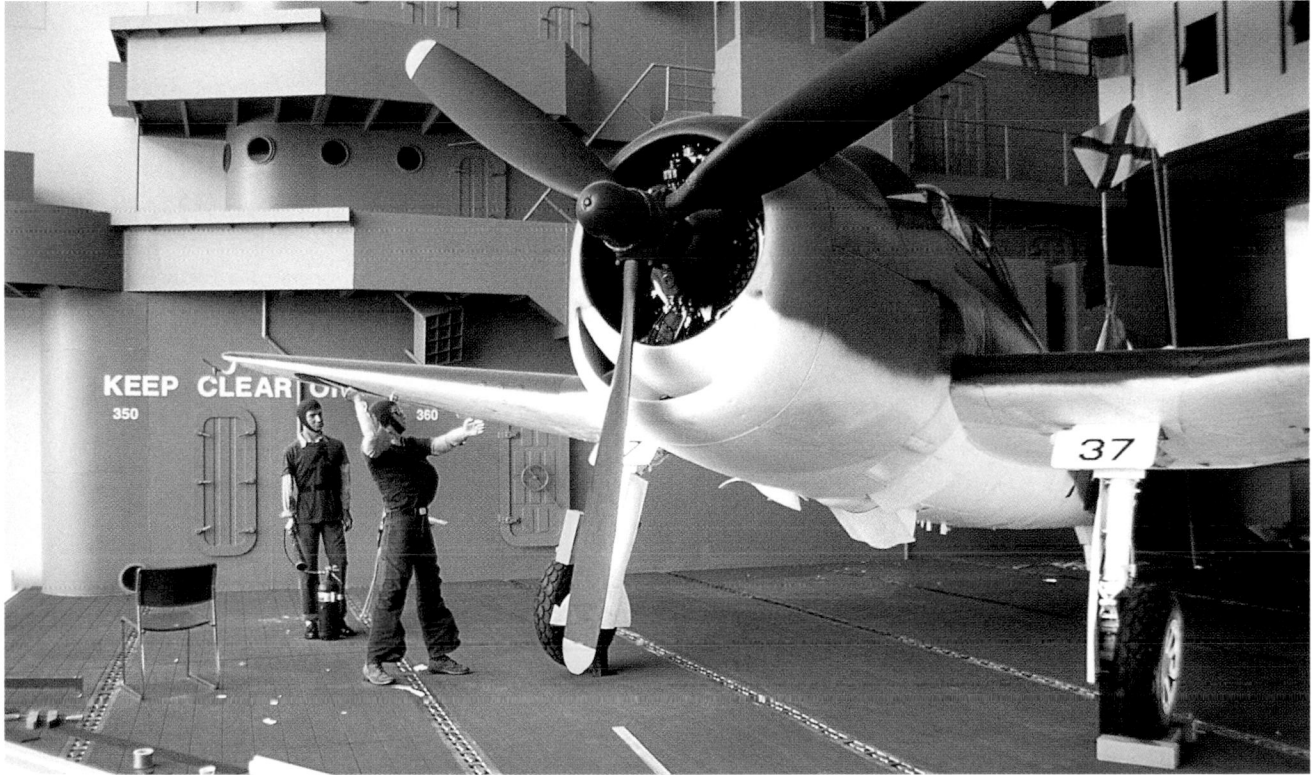

On the main floor of the National Air and Space Museum (NASM) a few years ago there was a Grumman F6F Hellcat, an important American naval fighter of World War II vintage. It rested on a mock-up of a carrier deck, suggesting that it was poised for take-off into battle. Mannequins in proper attire for their duties were positioned to suggest a strong wind was blowing across the deck. However, despite all this realism, the appearance of the Hellcat was puzzling. Anyone who looks out onto the wing of a modern commercial airliner will see the sort of spots, stains, and scratches typical of a well-used civil airplane let alone a warplane engaged in daily combat. The Smithsonian's Hellcat is, however, perfectly pristine — no dents, scratches, oil streaks, or chips in the paint that would suggest that the aircraft had ever been used.

Simulated live action is captured in this diorama of a carrier deck scene of a Grumman F6F Hellcat at the National Air and Space Museum in 1985. For an aircraft engaged in combat, this one looks too new. (NASM, SI)

The Hellcat's appearance is valid only because it was received by the museum in a degraded, non-exhibitable condition, and restoration was imperative for exhibition as a museum object, a purpose considerably divorced from its original reason for being. Ideally, had this airplane been removed from combat while still in an operational state — and preserved in that condition — that 'used look' would have enhanced its value as a museum exhibit depicting a combat airplane. Post-war modifications to this Hellcat followed by neglect made a restoration imperative. But as Karl Heinzel,

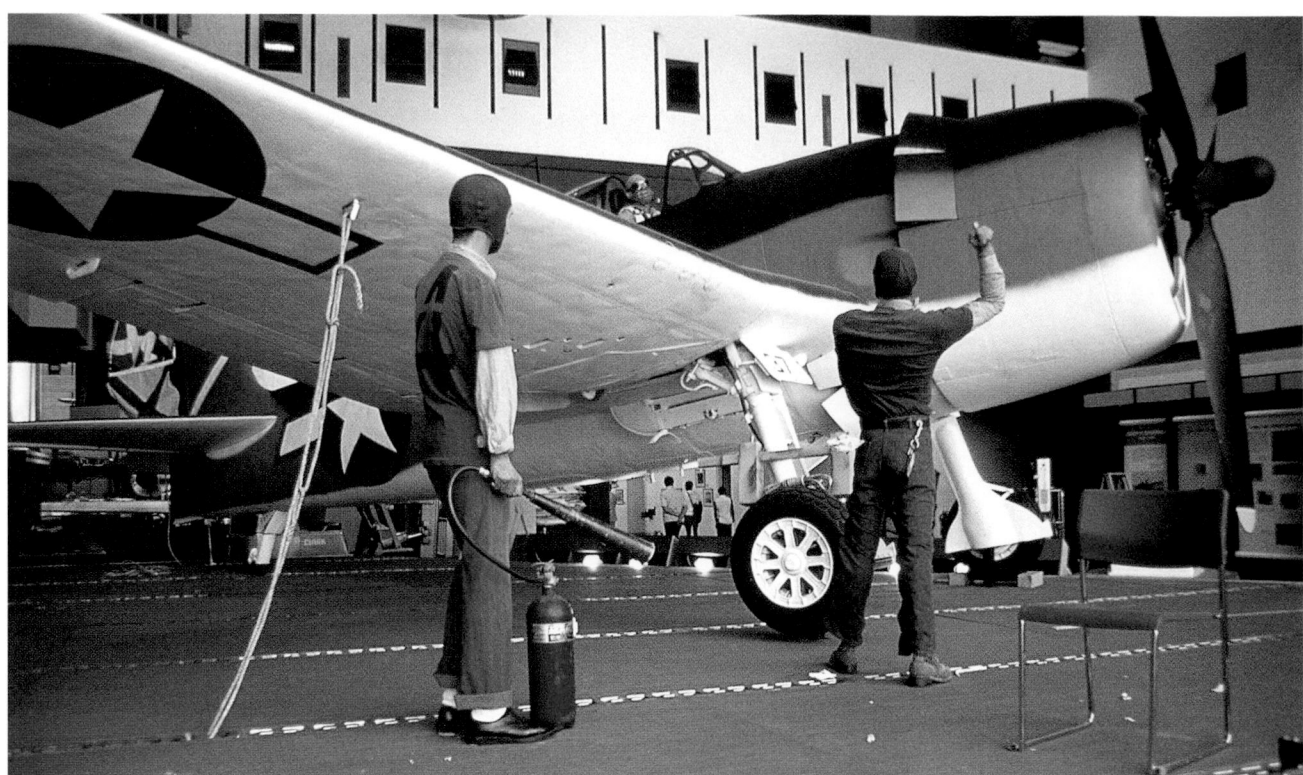

To be exhibitable, this F6F Hellcat required restoration and preservation. Unless painted with falsifying marks of wear, a 'like-new' appearance is unavoidable when total restoration is required as in this case. (NASM, SI)

a restoration technician at the museum's Paul E. Garber Preservation, Restoration and Storage Facility, described the situation: 'It is hard to make a repainted airplane look used without using it.' And using it would defeat the preservation purpose of restoring the Hellcat.

How Far?

This observation about the Hellcat, although overly simplified, serves as an example for studying the problem of how far a museum should take a restoration. What are the options and alternatives that curators have in making restoration decisions about an artifact? When does an exhibit lose its originality through excessive restoration?

Such questions concerning the museum restoration of aircraft are not new to those involved with the collection at NASM. Acknowledging the existence of these problems and being able to do something about them are two different things, a statement well recognized by most museum curators. This can be underscored by a *Restoration Philosophy and Policy*[1] statement drawn up as early as May 1969 by Louis S. Casey, who was then the Curator of Aircraft at the NASM. In part, his words describe quite closely the way that the same problems are viewed today:

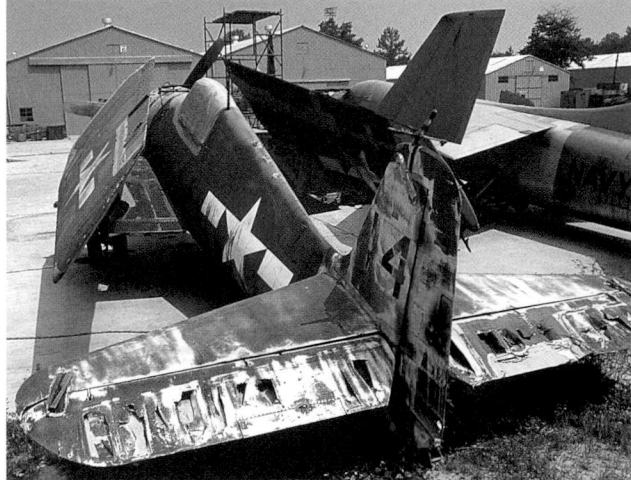

This view of NASM's F6F Hellcat when received leaves little doubt that its deteriorated condition made restoration inevitable. The red finish is an indicator that the airplane had last served as a drone aircraft. (Jeffrey L. Ethell)

'During the restoration process extreme care should be taken to preserve, intact, existing fabric and other materials. In making the specimen "like new" we can destroy the research value of the specimen. Try as we may, it is difficult, if not impossible, to restore a specimen to its former or original condition. The general tendency for laymen to 'restore' vintage aircraft to like-new condition should be resisted at all costs. As a national museum we should expend the time and energy necessary to preserve the original materials and details. There has to be a first time for each process of preservation. We should intensify our efforts in this direction as hopefully other museums will look to us, NASM, for guidance in these matters. We should prepare ourselves for this challenge and eventuality.'

Many will applaud these objectives, yet some may say that museum restoration efforts have not changed, since the aircraft still take on that 'new look' appearance. One may then wonder if those who make such comments actually understand the underlying problems associated with aircraft that must undergo restoration? For example, over-restoration gives an unquestionable 'new look' with no evidence of aging and the appearance of having never been used. 'Restoring' or 'preserving origi-nality' retains evidence of usage and aging while returning the aircraft to its operational appearance.

From another curatorial perspective, after years of having dealt with restoring aircraft while striving to retain that 'original used look,' I realized that goals in certain areas have often been too simply stated. Some have referred to this *like-new* appear-ance as 'Imagining'. Museum visitors are accustomed to cleanliness and the 'well-cared for look,' ranging from glistening floors to pristine arti-facts. One conservator asks if the public's aesthetic appreciation for this look is inherent, or if visitors develop it by exposure to only this kind of restora-tion treatment and appearance? As a curator I must ask if an old and tattered airplane that truly shows

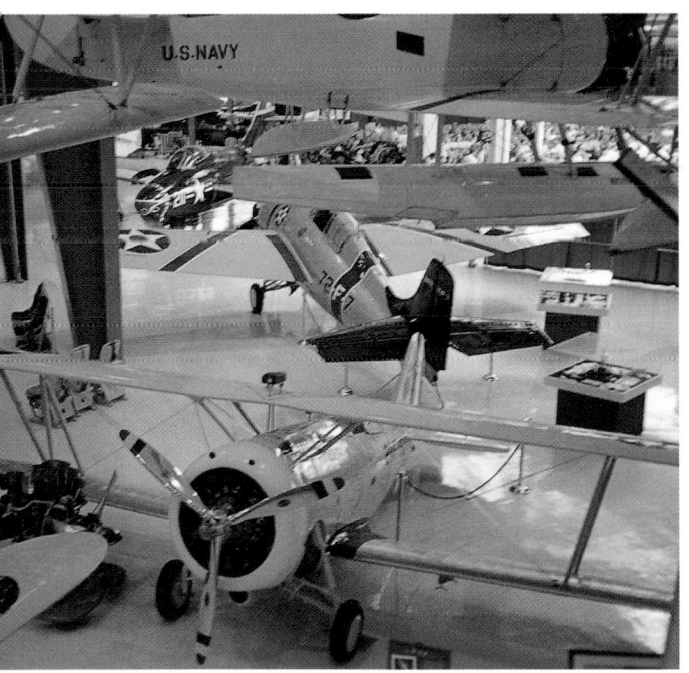

Museum visitors relate to the clean, well-kept conditions of the museum building as well as the artifacts. This is a typical view inside the National Museum of Naval Aviation, NAS Pensacola, Florida. The hallowed Grumman F3F-2, retrieved from the ocean floor and restored by the San Diego Aerospace Museum, is in the foreground.

neglect and decay will convey the importance for which it is in the museum? Concepts and limitations expressed in the following chapter will give clearer meaning to many of these problems.

Since conservators and curators will voice different opinions over these matters, some quali-fying terminology is needed for the discussions that follow. Combining terms used by some major museums with those of *Webster's Dictionary*, as they apply to aircraft and related objects, some of the often-used terms are defined here. (See Glossary, page 213, for examples and additional definitions.)

Original: A specimen that can be shown to be in the original as-built configuration, or as modified by the user, that remains unaltered from the time it ended operational service.

Restored Original: An artifact composed of at least 50 per cent original components (by surface area or volume), and the remainder returned to accurate early condition made with the same materials, components and accessories.

Reproduction: A reasonable facsimile in appearance and construction of an aircraft made with similar materials, and having substantially the same type engine and operating systems.

Replica: A reproduction built by the constructor of the original artifact in part or in total and having substantially the same type engine and operating systems.

Preservation: The act of sustaining and maintaining cultural and natural resources that have been iden-tified as significant and/or threatened and that warrant protection.

Conservation: As the technology of preservation, conservation is the scientific investigation of materials, the environment, and those things responsible for the deterioration of cultural resources.

From these definitions, we can say that preserva-tion and conservation are similar activities designed to keep an object in its existing condition while halting further degradation, whereas restora-tion is a more active process which attempts to undo changes caused by past deterioration.

Conservators will often insist that doing nothing to alter the object, except to stabilize further dete-rioration, is the correct approach. This works fine for placing the object in museum-quality storage with controlled humidity and temperature, away from light, to be used only as part of a study collec-tion. However, a curator may find the aircraft in its present condition unacceptable for exhibit, espe-cially if the object experienced serious deterioration during active service, or through neglect and mishandling. Rather than expect an untrained

11

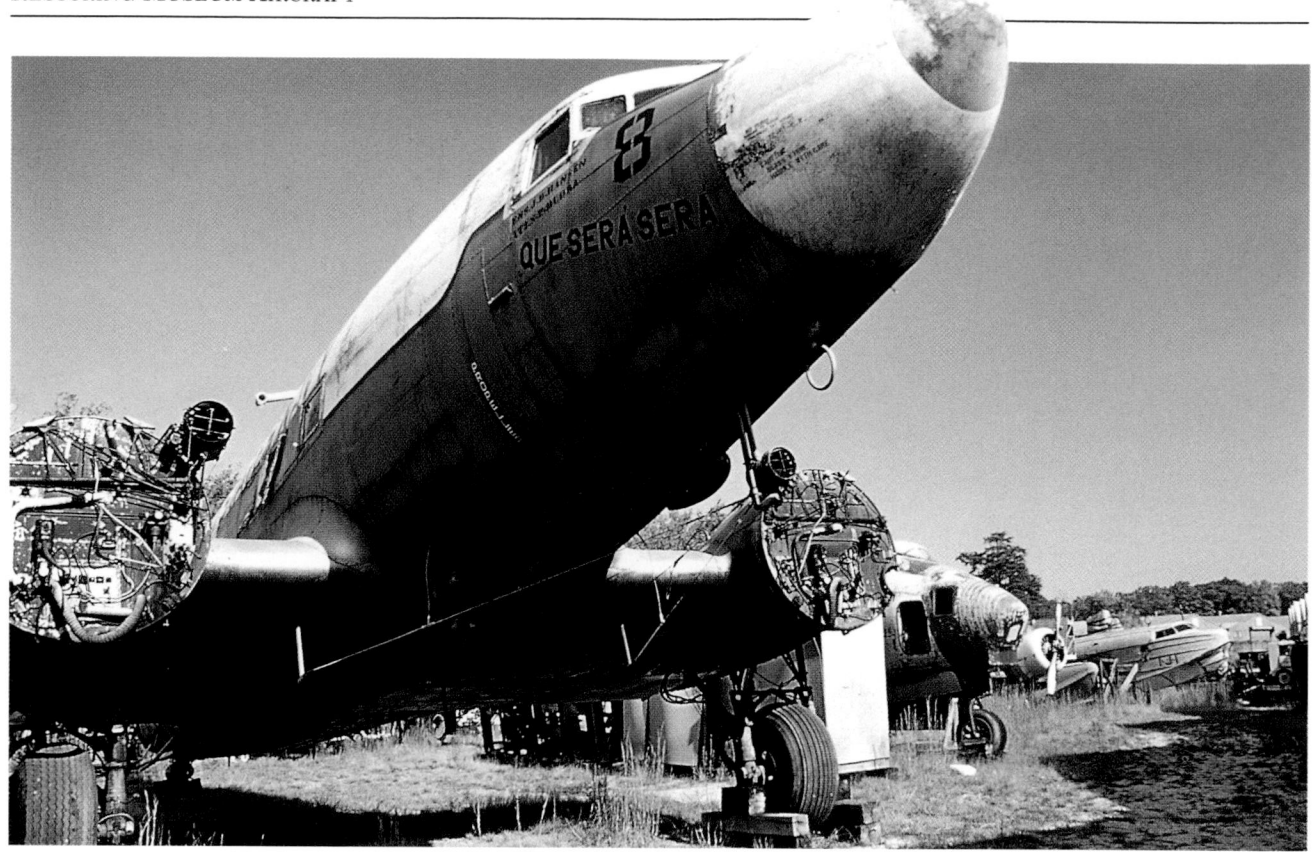

*Exhibit aircraft for museums must often come from sources such as these in outdoor environments. It is often only when aircraft are fully expended that they are turned over to museums who must then undo the neglect. (*Robert S. Harding*)*

visitor to interpret what the airplane looked like when functional, these interpretations must be made by the curator. This becomes the reason for which airplanes must be restored.

As my colleague, Dr Michael A. Fopp, Director of the Royal Air Force (RAF) Museum in Hendon has written:

'It is important to understand that an object (aircraft or anything else) is in itself a document which can be read in the future. Some people will only need to look at the cover (the external airframe) others may want to see the contents page (flight deck), the index (engineering panel) or even the bibliography (the Flight Manual). There will, though, always be the people who want to devour the document from cover to cover. If they find pages missing, or worse still, [dissimilar] pages from another document, their understanding of the original will be compromised.

'If the curator does his/her job, provision should be made for each type of "reader", so that the object carries with it, its whole story into the future. In the "real world" pages fall out of documents (they even get torn out) and others are inserted in their place; in the restoration of aircraft it is particularly impor-

tant that "bookmarks" in the shape of restoration notes are comprehensively maintained to document these omissions.'

To achieve this, it will become evident in the early planning stage of a restoration that a number of compromises, or insertion of 'missing pages,' must be made, both in the interest of preservation of originality and restoration to exhibit condition. However, at this point in the discussion, it is too early to make generalizations. Each artifact must be evaluated separately, and there are rules that can be applied to help make the best decisions in formulating restoration plans for each specific object. These help in deciding how far one should go, how far is enough, and how far is too much.

How It Began

Aircraft restoration procedures have gone through several phases of change over the past four decades. In general terms, when the very small number of existing air museums were recognized in the 1950s as a new and separate form of museum, restorations applied to their aircraft were more like making repairs than a restoration in the more modern sense. By the 1960s, as more air museums were established, the majority of the aircraft from World War II, for instance, were beginning to show their age. Repainting became a necessity and this was termed a restoration. In this process it became popular in some instances, to change color schemes as far from military markings as possible. Recall as

An early trend with post-World War II 'Warbirds' was to move as far away from combat markings as possible. When the Confederate Air Force was first formed, their colors were all-white with red and blue trim as seen with this FG-1 Corsair and P-38 Lightning. (Frank Stranad via Jeffrey L. Ethell)

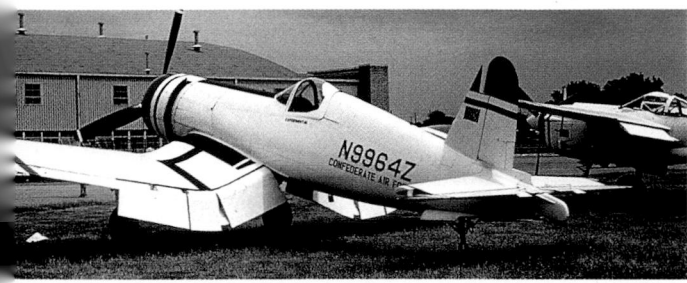

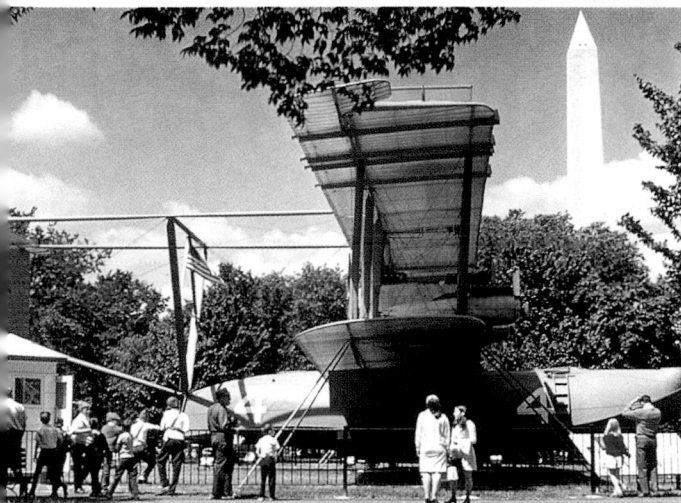

In 1969, to commemorate its 50th Anniversary of the first Atlantic crossing, this Curtiss NC-4 was restored and placed on the Washington Mall for the occasion. Placing such a historic object as this in the open would be unheard of today as appreciation of such artifacts increase. (NASM, SI)

especially to house museum aircraft for the major collections of the US Air Force Museum at Dayton, Ohio (1971), RAF Museum at Hendon, England (1972), National Museum of Naval Aviation at NAS Pensacola, Florida (1974), and NASM in Washington, DC (1976); and others followed in short order. With these came the need for the museums to have their aircraft more exhibitable to fill the new galleries. In most cases, these were more thorough undertakings in terms of aircraft restoration, which in the process formed a more professional approach towards the preservation of airframes. This was a trial period in many ways. Mistakes were made, but valuable experience was gained.

Of the three major governmental air museums in the US, the Air Force Museum was the first to celebrate the opening of its new building in 1972. Continued and growing interest has caused it to double in size from the time it was first opened. (USAF Museum)

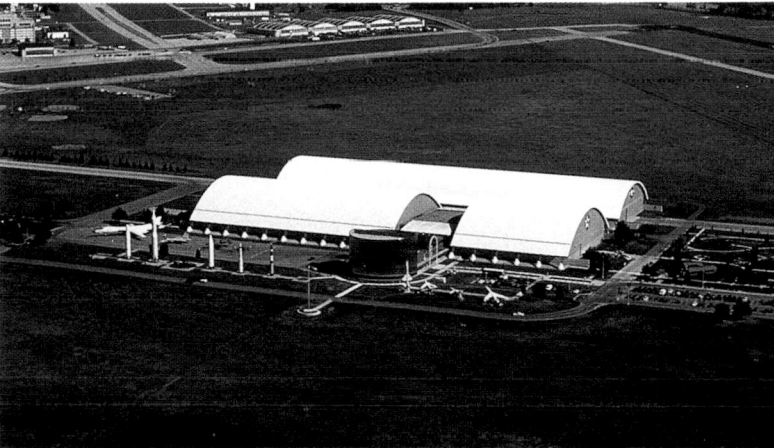

examples the all-white Confederate Air Force aircraft with red and blue trim.

Also during the 1960s, considerable interest was being expressed by dedicated volunteers to the idea of recreating some of the very early aircraft types. In the US, for instance, while taking great pains to work with original drawings, reproductions like the Curtiss A-1, Wright Flyer, Wright Model B, Sperry Messenger and others were created and became museum artifacts. The three US Government-sponsored aviation museums[2] began paying closer attention to care for their more significant airplanes. At the National Air Museum, for instance, historic aircraft such as the Lockheed Vega 5C *Winnie Mae*, Wright EX *Vin Fiz*, Curtiss R3C-2, NC-4 and others were brought back to exhibit condition. However, the completion of these time-consuming restorations was slow because of the small work-force and limited budget.

The 1970s were a major growth period for air museums, worldwide. Buildings were constructed

From this came a more formal method directed towards restoration and the preservation process. Instructions (generally called 'Curatorial Guidelines') were written as curators took a more active part in the work process. Research for relevant information was no longer conducted by those working in the restoration shop, left on their own to decide what was needed.

By the 1980s, restoration and preservation practices for museum aircraft became more professional. The need for trained conservators was gradually recognized to be an important partner in the overall process. New cleaning and preservative materials along with improved procedures were developed by conservators to assure greater longevity for the airframes and engines. They were tried, used, and some were laboratory-evaluated within the museums to achieve the best results. Accuracy in recreating aircraft markings and colors took on a greater appreciation because of the historic significance they represented. No longer were these aircraft judged by their exterior appear-

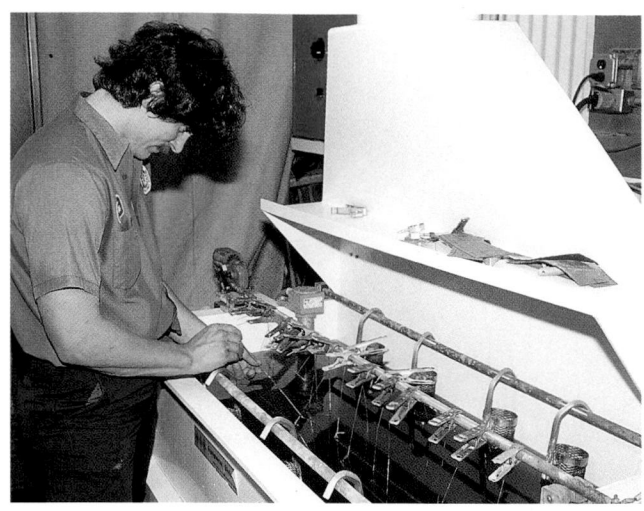

A major breakthrough surrounding the restoration of museum aircraft was improving their life span with new techniques of cleaning and preserving metals and materials within the aircraft structure. Bayne Rector at NASM prepares to cadmium plate metal parts as they were originally.

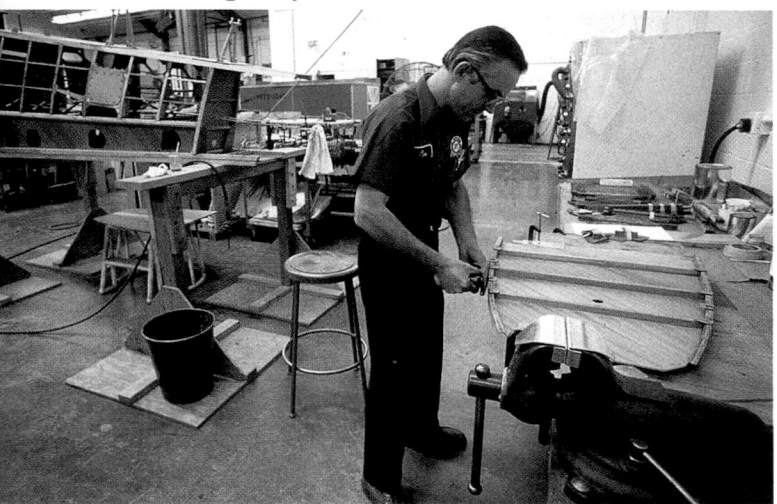

Where possible, original nails should be carefully removed then treated for longevity so that they can be used again in the structure after repair. This is far more time-consuming than the simple solution of using new nails that depart from originality. Garry Cline repairs a wing rib of NASM's Northrop N1M1 Flying Wing.

ance alone, but consideration was given to the way an airplane would relate to the collection as a whole when it might be assembled in a meaningful presentation.

Also in the 1980s, increased attention was given to completeness of aircraft interiors. A full set of instruments and a set of controls no longer sufficed for a finished restoration. Greater emphasis was given to having the smallest detail in its place, including systems that were not even seen from outside the airplane. If sections of the interior did not match a period photograph of that area, it was clearly incomplete. These details were actively sought from collectors. New parts were fabricated

Unfortunately, most museums are grateful for even having a building with a sound roof in which to store aircraft awaiting exhibit. For many, temperature changes, humidity, dirt and rodents take their toll while in this condition, which makes a restoration and preservation process essential before stored aircraft can be exhibited

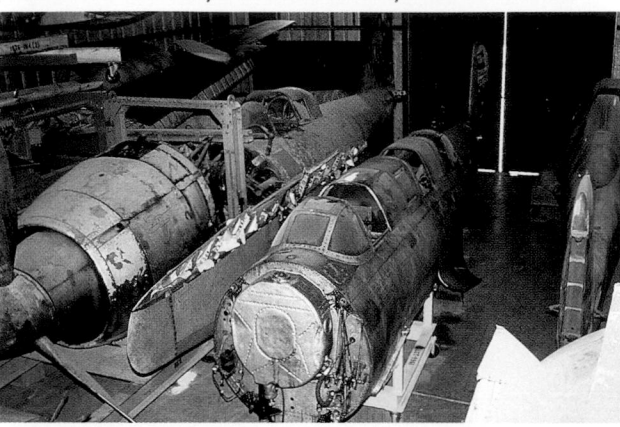

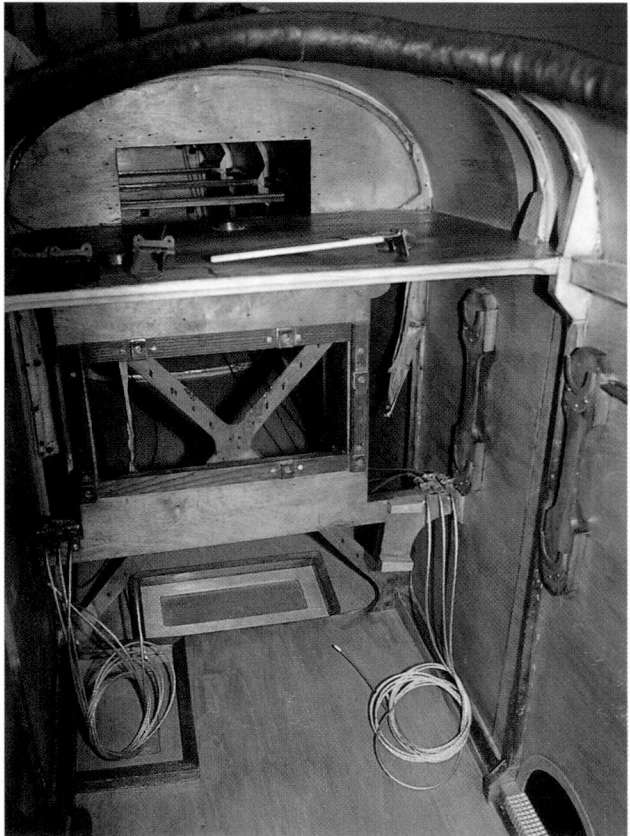

This Halberstadt CL.IV restored by the Museum für Verkehr und Technik in Berlin shows in this view looking aft, the mix of old and new wood used in an attempt to save as much of the original material and workmanship as possible. New and repaired parts are stamped and dated as such. This essential practice of preserving the old is far more labor-intensive than making new parts.

OPPOSITE PAGE:
This restored cockpit of the DH.4 belonging to NASM was returned to its original operational configuration. It had been flown by the factory with unrelated test equipment which has been removed. It now reflects the first type of combat aircraft built in the US during World War I.

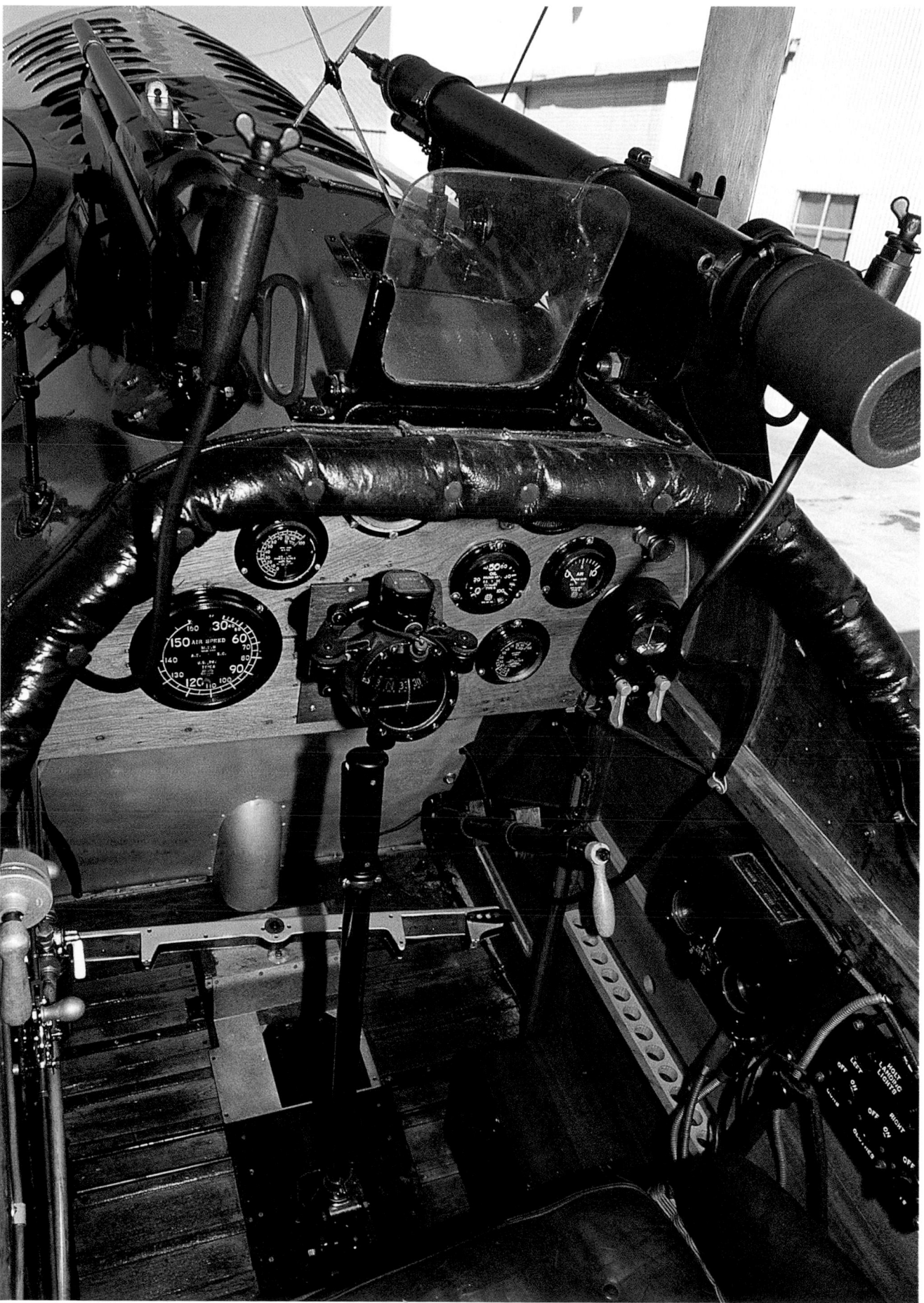

(marking them as such), provided the technical information was available. Recapturing the technology of the time for a given airplane became the goal. This attention within growing museums ranged from completeness of passenger compartments, to having all the tubing and cabling that was originally found throughout the structure, particularly those items that could be seen in cockpits and wheel wells. This degree of detail was not always attainable, but in many restorations it became the objective. There was greater awareness of the need to preserve originality, such as parts, painted surfaces and related materials, as opposed to the previous method used by some museums who removed, replaced and/or repainted.

As aircraft rework efforts within museums reached these higher levels of quality, a new and more accepted concept and understanding for the term 'restoration' came into being. Projects falling short of these higher standards could be described more correctly as rebuilds, look-alikes, mock-ups, or perhaps merely a repainting.

Some conservators believe that adding missing components to an aircraft during restoration dilutes the originality of the object. The same is expressed with the changing of fabric and other short-term

An aircraft restoration is not necessarily preservation, yet a preservation of an aircraft can include a restoration. A prime example of both is this Curtiss F9C-2 Sparrowhawk belonging to NASM. The overhead structure allowed the aircraft to be launched and recovered from the USS Akron and Macon airships of the 1930s.

materials. It must be recognized that there is no way of stopping the aging process, only of slowing it through proper care. The removal and loss of original components of the aircraft has already taken away its originality. By making these needed replacements, either with or without original parts, the aircraft can continue to serve the museum for the purpose for which it was intended.

Some critics casually label the more time-consuming work on details for these restorations as fanaticism, their focus being on assembly and painting of the aircraft so that it can be placed on exhibit as quickly as possible. Survey teams, often comprised of people outside the museum profession, are known to have made comments suggesting that standards were too high and the work could be done more cheaply if sights were set a bit lower. It would not take much for this type of 'throw-away' comment to be converted into 'positive action' to lower standards. Fearful of such happenings, Dr Michael A. Fopp reminds us that:

'If there is belief in our role as stewards of property for future generations, then there is ample justification for maintaining the highest standards. If, on top of this, you have inherited these standards from colleagues who have gone before, how can you possibly be a party to anything which would marginalize their efforts and mark yours forever? It would, in my view, take an insensitive fool to consciously accept that there are half measures in conservation and restoration.'

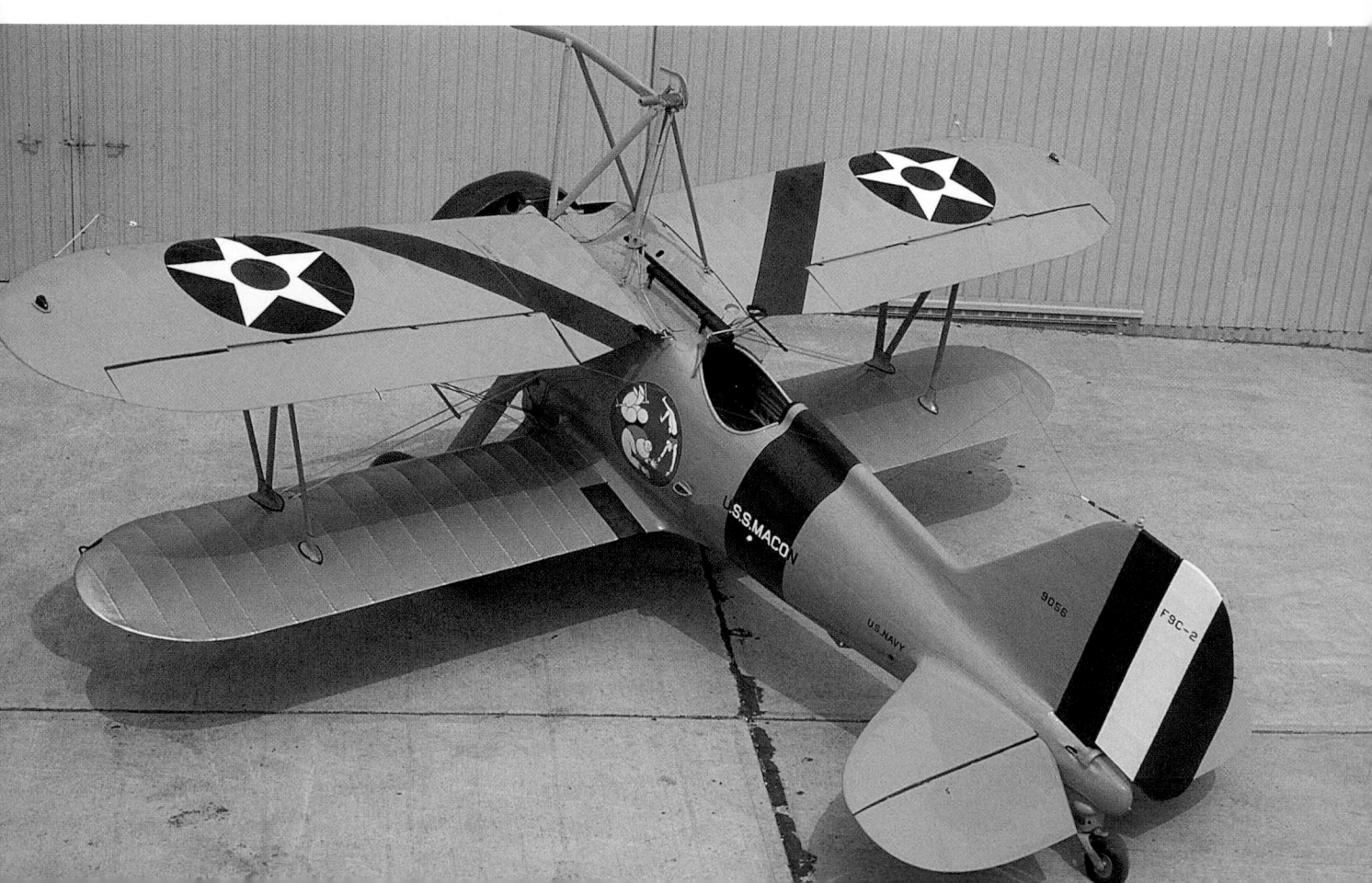

The professional view of museum care for these airplanes in our collections is to document their technology for the time period in which they were built. Heavier-than-air manned flight has not yet celebrated its first 100-year anniversary. Future generations will one day regard all of today's modern airplanes as 'early flying machines!' It is our mandate today to ensure that these airframes are not only preserved with an extended indefinite life span, but that they exhibit as completely and accurately as possible the technology of their time.

These are marvelous ideals that few will find fault with. But in the hope of not sounding hypocritical, all curators, directors and overseers who are placed in positions of artifact responsibility do not necessarily feel that these objectives are achievable — and therefore such efforts are often defeated before making the attempt. Cost factors and time consumed are often named as reasons.

I am not so sure that this is always a valid reason. For example, one institution voluntarily restored an aircraft for NASM, achieving excellent results and the satisfaction of NASM curator. This same institution undertook a second aircraft for NASM with the same work-crew and shop, but new leadership. That person in charge had an entirely different and unchangeable attitude towards this restoration and preservation project, and the results were disappointing. Perhaps the real reasons for compromise for less-than-desired quality in some restorations are not cost and time, but attitude, lack of job knowledge, poor leadership by the responsible curator and weakness in management on the part of the team leader.

The Conservator

The profession of conservator is not new to museums. They have been generally associated with art museums, and perhaps most conservators prefer that association. The profession has migrated into other forms of museums, and perhaps lastly — unfortunately — is only now being recognized as a necessity for air museums.

The end of the 1980s brought a realization to museums that the collections for which they were responsible were deteriorating at a faster rate than restorations were taking place. It had been thought that the process of restoration, with preservation measures included, would prove to be the cure-all. However, collections were getting larger and items not on exhibit in the controlled temperature and humidity areas of the museum were deteriorating at an increasing rate.

The term 'conservation' refers to the process of retaining the object's culturally significant qualities and to minimizing deterioration. Preserving the originality of the object in the first place is the primary objective. When that cannot be achieved

because an aircraft or any object has already deteriorated to a non-displayable condition, certainly some original materials can be preserved in the course of a restoration project. To be more specific, the mere cleaning of metal surfaces can remove original metallic coatings that could otherwise be preserved if proper procedures were used. For example, encouragement and direction by conservators is needed to also retain original painted surfaces of components, often on the interior, that might not need to be disturbed if properly cleaned and given a protective invisible coating.

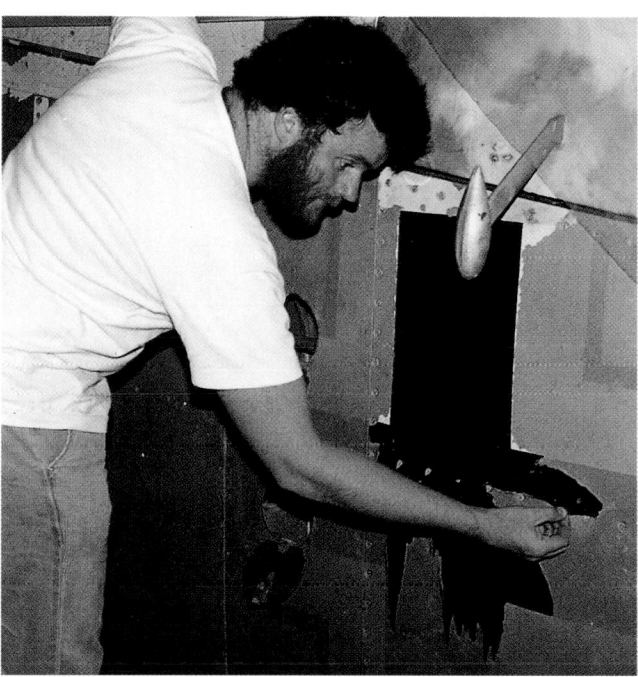

David Hallam, Senior Conservator at the Australian War Memorial in Canberra, peals away the protective coating applied to the wing of a Messerschmitt Bf 109. This may well be a Condition Level 2 airplane and therefore able to retain this original finish after the cleaning and preservative process is completed when preparing the airplane for exhibit.

The need for a trained conservator did not become apparent to those of us at NASM until the arrival of an energetic red-haired and bearded fellow from Australia who was serving an internship at NASM's Paul E. Garber Facility. Observing his work, we began to take note of the relationship that conservation had with aircraft and the restoration process. This was David Hallam, Senior Conservator at the Australian War Memorial in Canberra,[3] who wanted to gain experience working outside his institution in his field of material conservation. As he went about his work in researching restoration and preservation methodologies employed at NASM, we began learning more from him. Our need for a NASM conservator became more and more apparent. Some of what was learned from his extended visit is included in later portions of this book. Recognizing its importance has brought about a full-time conservator to NASM staff.

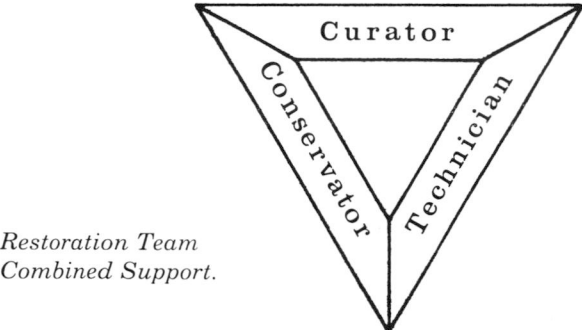

Restoration Team Combined Support.

This new appreciation for conservation aspects has resulted in a working team of three on museum restoration projects. There is the curator who in layman's terms can be looked upon as the architect of the project. He or she determines the final form to which the restoration is aimed and oversees the project to that end. The conservator evaluates the condition of the materials found in and upon the airplane and establishes methods to keep selected parts original and to stabilize others. The restoration technician possesses the working skills with which these objectives can be met in the restoration process. The desires and capabilities of each team member cannot always be met for a given restoration, and it is here that discussions take place and all three must reach certain compromises. The curator must always be the team leader and is responsible for the decisions made.

To provide a clearer distinction between conservation and restoration, Ed McManus, Conservator at NASM, provides two definitions that may make the primary objective of each more clear.

Conservation treatments are carried out in accordance with specific preservation ethics and standards that are intended to protect the history and integrity of any object, be it great or small, complex or simple. Often the successful treatment results in no perceptible change in appearance. In other instances, a change in appearance results when later accretions, such as green corrosion on bronze sculpture is removed.[4]

Restoration's main objective is returning the object to an earlier appearance or to working condition. Restoration and conservation can be one and the same but are not necessarily the same. Restoration treatments generally present a greater risk to the integrity of an object than do conservation treatments. In the restoration process, it is often desirable to replace damaged or missing parts, refinish entire surfaces, or eliminate later modifications. Restoration treatments

are generally more extensive and more intrusive. Risks include the misinterpretation of physical evidence and the removal of historically significant modifications or materials.

For example, a yellowed and damaged canopy or cockpit clear panel would be far simpler to replace than the laborious task of repair and surface polishing. A new piece would look far better. But this is original material to this aircraft, perhaps formed in a far different manner than as processed today with newer materials. It is far better to restore the original panel if structurally sound albeit may look old, yet the visitor knows and accepts that it is old — and most likely original.

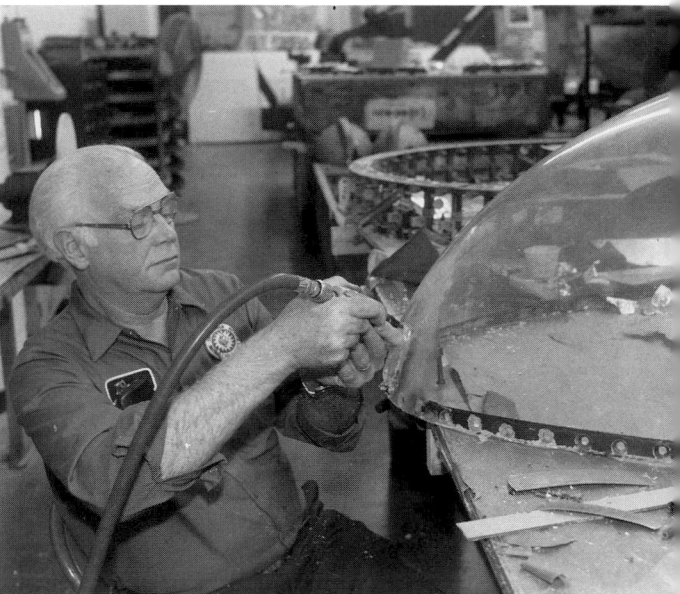

The cockpit nose enclosure was unusually large for curved plexiglass which was made in two major halves. Damage which consisted mainly of discoloration, cracks and lost chips was repaired by Reid Ferguson in NASM's shop. A canopy of this type was quite advanced at this point of wartime manufacture. (NASM, SI 86-3792-42A)

Tremendous advances have been made in recent years with materials for corrosion control, cleaning agents, preservatives such as coatings, electrolytic phase inhibitors and waxes. It would be impossible for the curator, without professional specialized training, to remain abreast of these rapid changes. Qualified conservators logically step in and make these trained observations by selecting the appropriate chemical materials. They provide the guidance needed for these treatments relevant to the objects being restored. Working with product technical-representatives and conducting in-house tests, the conservator can then make decisions for selecting which products best suit the restoration need.

The Restoration Technician

An important member of the team of three in the decision-making process of aircraft restoration is the restoration technician. There are major differences in concepts between a flight-line airplane mechanic and a museum aircraft technician. As an Airframe and Powerplant mechanic, there is the demand for flight safety. It is better to replace a worn or damaged part than to trust a repair that might suffice for the expected operational life of the airplane or extend it to the next periodic inspection. Surface corrosion in a slow but advancing state is acceptable, as is a rusty aileron hinge when not detrimental to safety of flight. There is no need for immediate attention. This will be attended to in time, for appearance sake, before it becomes damaging.

In aircraft restorations, the intent should be to preserve originality regardless, generally speaking, of the amount of operational wear that appears on any given part of the aircraft. (Thought would have to be given on an individual basis to such things as tire wear, aged opaque glass, etc.) Admittedly, in most cases, it requires more time to repair a deteriorated or damaged part than to make or replace it with a new one. An experienced restoration technician will be aware that by saving and preserving the original or worn part in the structure, it shows how that portion of the aircraft performed and therefore, it must be retained as part of the airplane and its history. Signs of active corrosion, albeit slow, must be addressed during an aircraft restoration. Every process must be geared to making the airplane last indefinitely, not for the normal life expectancy manufactured into the airplane. This difference in philosophies becomes the major identifying features between these two highly technical fields.

I was interested to learn what the Restoration Shop Foreman at NASM's Paul E. Garber Facility had to say about qualities that he looked for in selecting Restoration Technicians. This was Bill Reese, a man with 18 years of experience at the NASM and who knows what qualities are desired based upon his first-hand knowledge.

Uppermost on his list of qualities is having a broad base in mechanical aptitude on one side and an avid interest in aviation and its history on the other. Everything and anything is expected from museum restoration technicians from sheet metal work, machining, welding, painting and adhesives, woodworking, knowledge of fabric application; the list goes on. Naturally some technicians excel in some fields while some are more skilled in others. This makes for a good team of technicians.

There must be a bond between the technician and the field of aviation — something more than just the job. That 'something' is generally an appreciation of history and a commitment to preserving the past. A

Missing parts that must be fabricated for a restoration reveal no history of how well each part performed in operational service. This adds to the original shape of the aircraft and eliminates this interpretation for the viewer. Here Bill Stevenson fabricates an engine cowling for the Bellanca CF at NASM.

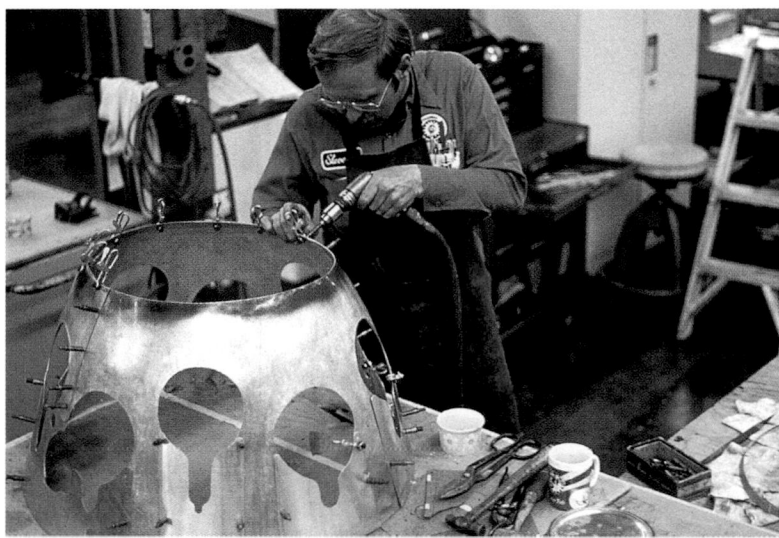

relationship must be established with the aircraft being worked on, not merely to be looked upon as just another machine or work effort. A technician interested in this particular field of work will have an increased awareness of what is found in the structure of the airplane which may have more significance beyond what the uncaring may see. An understanding and special sensitivity in this field of aviation brings out that ability to recognize these significant elements when they are encountered.

Other desired elements in technician qualities are a logical approach to the work, a tidy work place, and a flexible attitude. This attitude relates to an absolute willingness to commit and listen to the curators assigned to the project. Flexibility means a readiness to assist colleagues when another pair of hands is necessary.

Many of the good aircraft restoration technicians that I know are fellow pilots, some of whom have their own aircraft. While this certainly is not a requirement for this field, it shows an avid interest. 'This is what some call a "gut feeling" about an airplane which is so important,' says Bill Reese, 'often expressed in other ways, such as a general interest in aviation history or building model aircraft. All this leads to the essential caring part of the work that is being put into the aircraft being restored.'

Another aspect of the restorer's craft is having a basic understanding of chemistry. The interaction of the many products and chemical applications upon the varying materials used in aircraft structures comes with experience. There is a greater appreciation for conservation through having this

Airworthiness should not be a consideration when restoring museum aircraft. Instead, the procedure to be followed is to retain the original part to the greatest extent possible, make necessary repairs and mark them as such. The often simpler method of making a new part must be avoided. After repairs on this bulkhead, Karl Heinzel at NASM prepares to install matched rivets to the originals.

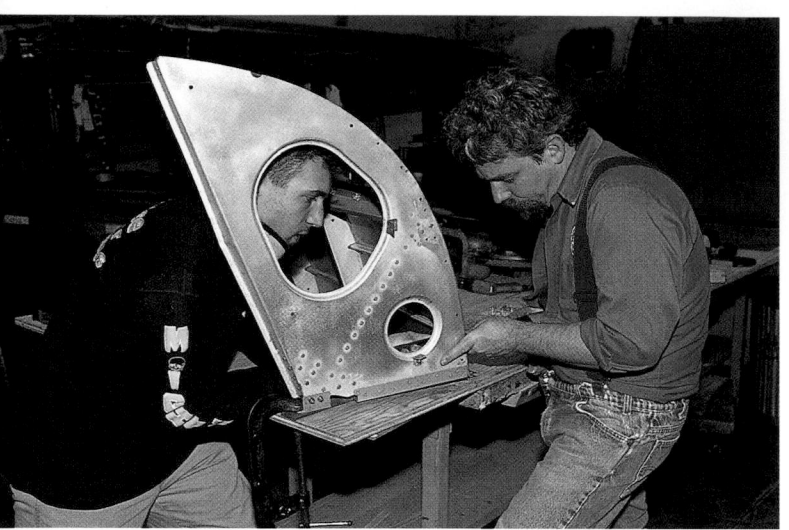

fundamental knowledge of chemistry and electrolytic action and reaction. This is an essential quality in preserving and restoring museum aircraft.

As if these qualities were not enough, Bill Reese had a secondary list that he threw open for discussion. An aptitude for photography is important in being able to record on film the work process. After all, the work of restoration is a major chapter in the history of the subject aircraft.

And there is yet another aspect of recording the restoration process; an ability to write about one's work that was just performed on any given airplane. If the work log is not adequately filled in, or related reports about the work being accomplished are not well-constructed, no one will accurately know what has taken place. This is not a task that can be passed to others. The technician knows what work process he used, and no one can better record these details. Being keyboard-literate with a word processor is also helpful but not essential.

While all these skills and qualities apply across the board in many technical and mechanical fields, the love for airplanes stands out as one essential element an aircraft restoration technician must have. That care and attention will become as apparent with the aircraft restoration technician's finished and preserved product as the identifying final brush stroke made on a painting by an artist.

The Curator

An obvious quality needed when matching a person to an aviation curatorial position must be that

strong feeling towards aviation. The person most likely has had a lifelong affair with airplanes if he or she is seeking such a position. Without that bond (it is obvious in those who have it, namely serious museum visitors and scholars who make contact with curators), much credibility can be lost when that emotion is not conveyed.

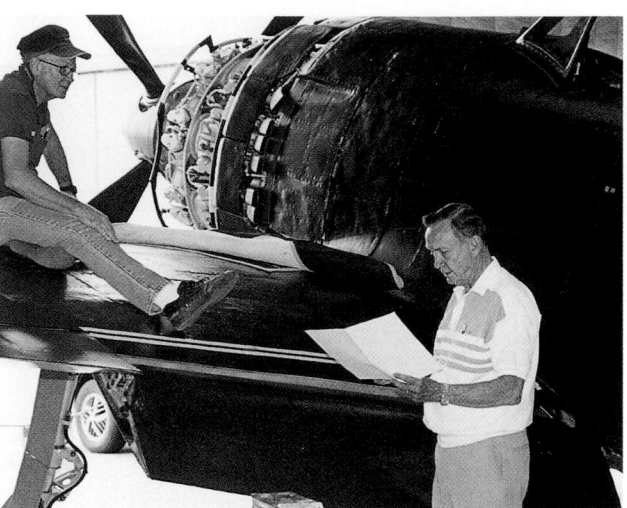

A curator must remain aware of all aspects of an airplane during the restoration process. Here the author reviews with restoration technician Jack Reiser, various locations for stenciling during the final phase of restoring the Kawanishi N1K2-Ja Shiden Kai (Modified) fighter, codenamed 'George'. (A. Gruening)

Throughout my career I was often asked what qualities I would consider important for one considering the field of aviation curator. What special talents or skills would be ideal to have for such a position?

When addressing young groups at the museum on this subject, I was never hesitant when saying that I drew upon my experience as an avid model airplane builder for perhaps 80 per cent of that job knowledge. So much is learned from this type of hobby. To begin with, the ardent enthusiast learns of the many types of airplanes throughout the world by this mere association with the variety of models available. This adds perspective in recognizing the part played by each of these airplanes. Aviation history is transmitted in such an easy form and in so many ways when it stems from this contact with what the model represents.

Of great importance with this hobby is the process of learning the many details that go into an airplane and how they relate from one airplane to another. Most of this knowledge has to be gained from personal research. Here again, experience is gained by using the research aids available to help complete a special model that also apply to actual aircraft. There is that appreciation for detail that becomes apparent with serious model-building that is so essential for a curator.

Only recently have I realized another quality for curators that was expressed to me by a fellow curator. Someone who has personal collections of meaningful objects and systematically groups and identifies them is demonstrating an interest in history and technological change. This type of interest is very desirable for the curatorial field.

From the academic aspect, there are new courses being created that deal directly with museum functions. Selected ones would be helpful. A background in history and the ways in which this research is conducted, aspects to look for that weigh against one another, would be useful.

In this type of work, there is a need to document objects. If a curator candidate shys away from recording the vital aspects of what is learned, those who follow will not have access to the knowledge about the object that preceded him or her. This type of documentation is a vital function in the curatorial field, one that is obviously associated with the process of restoring museum aircraft.

I'll be Back!

Whether the person is a curator, specialist or technician, related to museum work of any kind, there must be that ever-present thought of doing what is best for the objects over which he or she has control. One experience comes to mind which happened when I first began working as a curator with restorations at NASM in the early 1970s. I noted one particular technician often taking certain shortcuts in his work habits. When I questioned him about his methods of doing certain aspects that would affect the preservation, he would respond, 'Don't worry about it, Bob, this will outlast both of us.'

After being confronted with this response several times, I had to take a stand:

'[So-and-so], when we die,' I began while struggling to keep a straight face, 'we are all going to purgatory first. After 300 or so years, I am going to be sent back to check on the condition of everyone's work here. For those that have failed — you know what is going to happen!'

This brought about general laughter of disbelief. After about the second or third time I made these threatening remarks, I noted a marked improvement in this person's attitude and quality of work. Perhaps the reason he made this change was — just in case I might be right!

Aircraft received by museums in this condition can serve little purpose until restored to their operational appearance and configuration. In the meantime, neglect is often their greatest hazard. Shown here is one of four Convair XF2Y-1 Sea Dart fighters.

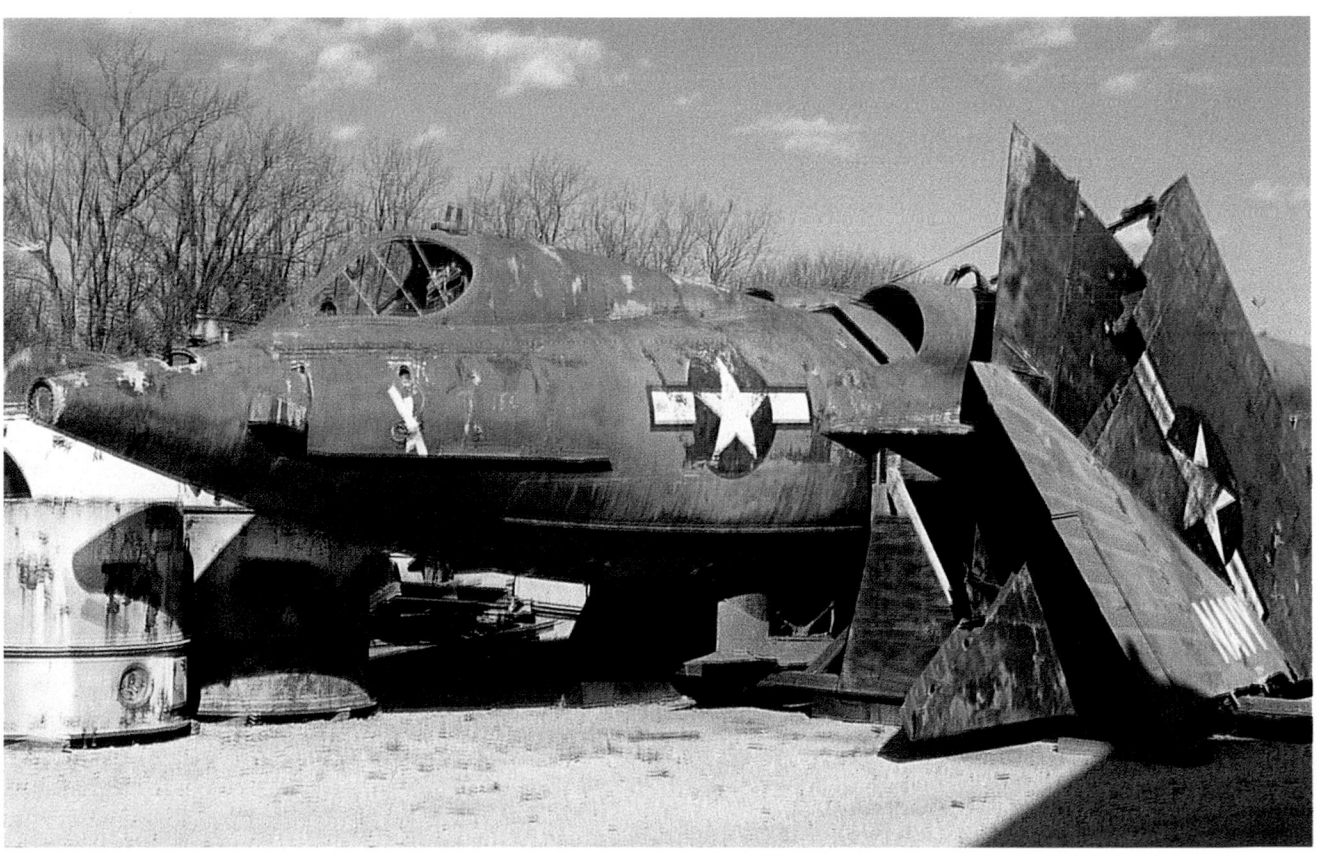

CHAPTER 2
Collection and Restoration Decisions

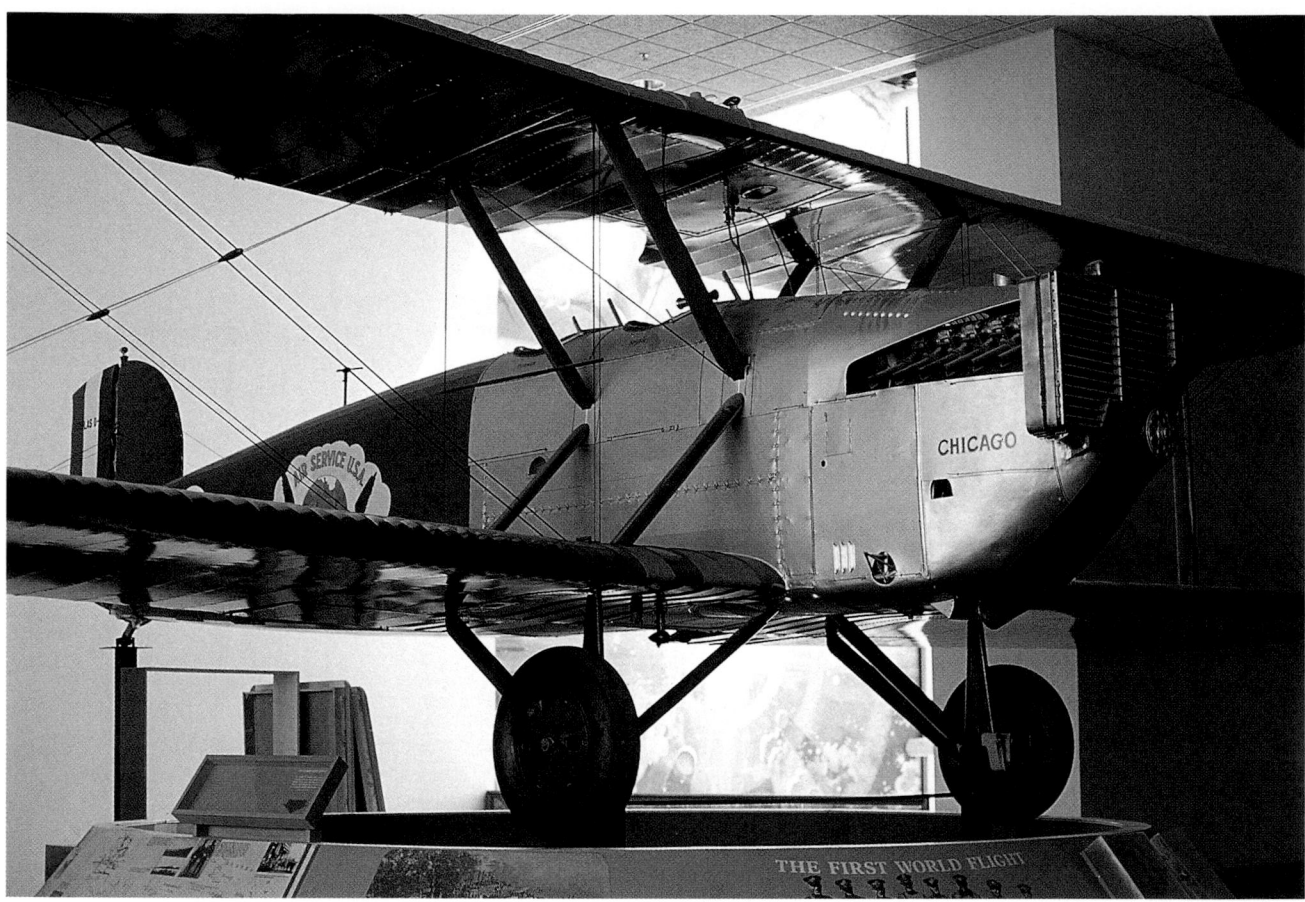

Restoration Planning Concepts

When the planned building for NASM on the Washington Mall was to become a reality in 1976, a major undertaking was needed to restore many airplanes needed for these galleries. Plans and guidance had to be enacted before this work could begin. In 1973, Director Michael Collins and Deputy Director Melvin Zisfein formed a **Vehicle and Power Plant Restoration Planning Committee** of 12 aviation notables brought in from all parts of the country.[5] They addressed these issues and the results became museum policies that remain valid today.

Generalizations with regard to the extensive collection of NASM were not practical, so they identified the types of aircraft by three categories in order to define and differentiate treatment. They are noted here verbatim:[6]

NASM has three classifications for aircraft to identify their purpose. A historic airplane like this Douglas DWC-2 World Cruiser is Category I, and therefore will not be altered from its original configuration and markings.

Category I:

Aircraft which are historically significant by virtue of taking part in an historic event (e.g. Wright Flyer, *Spirit of St Louis*, World Cruiser)

Aircraft in this category will be restored to represent the event for which they are most famous.

Other examples that may further clarify types of historic aircraft in NASM collection include Admiral Byrd's Fairchild FC-2W2 *Stars and Stripes* (first plane to fly in Antarctica), the Piper Super Cruiser *City of Washington* (first in its 100 hp engine class to fly around the world), the Curtiss NC-4 (first aircraft to fly across the Atlantic), and the Wright EX *Vin Fiz* (first airplane to make a transcontinental United States flight). NASM's Spad XIII *Smith IV* would be considered historic because of its World War I combat record. The same holds true for the Boeing B-17D *Swoose* for its unusual combat record in the early part of World War II.

Category II:

Aircraft which are technically significant due to technological features (e.g. XP-55, Pitcairn AC-35), participation in aeronautical research (X-15, *Winnie Mae*), or being prototypes or advanced developmental steps for aircraft which became historically significant (P-51C *Excalibur III*).

Aircraft in this category will be restored to represent the event for which they are most famous.

Additional technically significant aircraft would be the Lockheed XC-35 (produced for the specific purpose of conducting experiments in cabin pressurization and engine supercharging for high-altitude flight), the Herrick Convertoplane (having a second stationary wing that, when disengaged, would spin like an autogiro's rotor as an escape method upon engine failure), and the Northrop HL-10 (a lifting body essentially without wings). Some aircraft can be classed as either

Category I or II, but in both cases, treatment is the same. Examples that might fall into both classes are the Gossamer Condor (first to fly a defined course to demonstrate the technical aspects of manpowered flight) and the Rutan Voyager (combining technologies that allowed for this first unrefueled round-the-world flight). *Excalibur III* in the above quote of NASM document is a modified P-51C that was used to prove the technical concept of navigating across the polar regions by the use of sun lines, yet was also historic for this same reason and other records this aircraft set.

Category III:

Aircraft which are not significant in their own right but which represent a type of historically significant aircraft (e.g. F4F Wildcat, Piper J-3 Cub, Boeing 707)*

Military aircraft should be restored to represent their most widely-known operational role. Markings and configuration historically known to have been on the aircraft are preferred.
Private (civil) aircraft should be restored to represent the standard factory delivery paint scheme or markings known to have been on that aircraft.
Commercial airliners should be marked in the colors of the airline which donated the aircraft to the Collection, or in the colors of the airline which first accepted delivery and used that type of aircraft, or an airline or operator (perhaps now defunct or merged) famous for using that particular type.

*The Boeing 707 mentioned here refers not to NASM's Boeing 367-80 prototype, but to the importance that the 707 as a type had in early jet commercial aviation.

Another issue raised for the committee's action was the choice of military markings for Category III aircraft that were in the collection as representative types, and not in themselves historical airframes. Their intense study of the situation resulted in the following:

In the case of military aircraft it is necessary to select a set of markings which designate the theater of operations in which the aircraft type was used. The main objective should be to display the aircraft in markings which are representative of its major role and most desirable if the aircraft was at one time marked thus. It is best not to use the markings of a famous individual on a general aircraft but to try to make a more general identification. An average P-47 should be restored as a typical P-

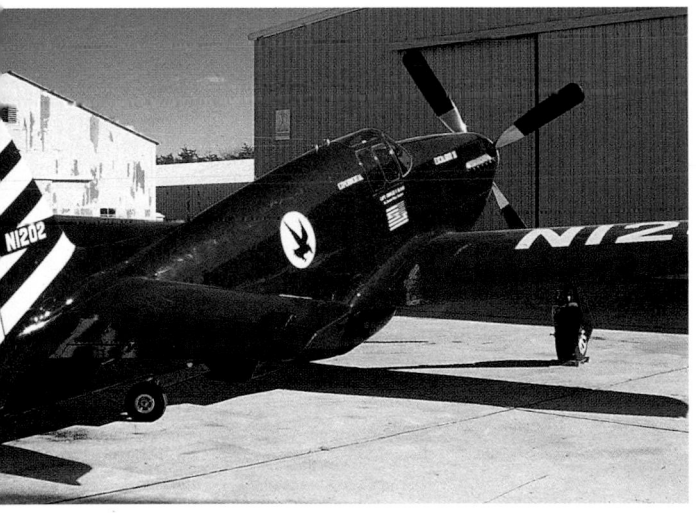

North American P-51C Excalibur III *gained technological as well as historical significance flown by Captain Charles F. Blair in 1952 to prove a means of polar navigation. The technology gained through this Category II airplane brought about a major change in northern defense measures for protecting North America.*

An early example of twin-engine corporate transports of the late 1930s was the Grumman G-21 Goose. That being the purpose for which this airplane was restored as a Category III aircraft of NASM's collection, it was appropriate that it be in the factory paint scheme of the time and for that purpose.

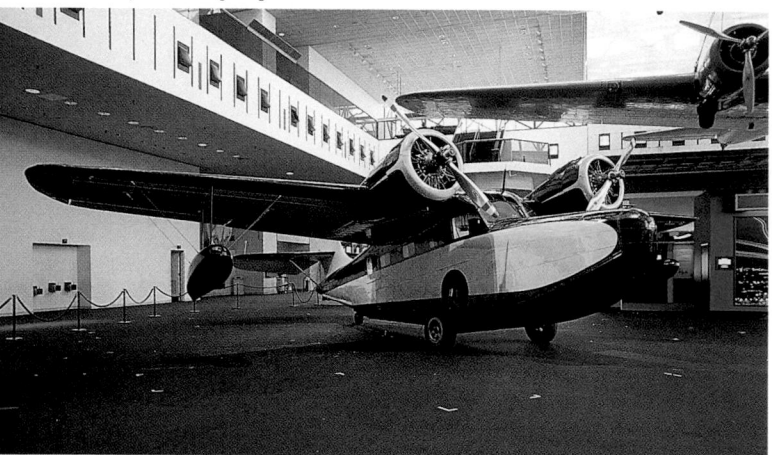

47 (preferably in one of its former sets of markings) and not as, say, the P-47 of Gabreski. Whenever possible, military aircraft should be represented in the markings of the branch of the service to which they were actually assigned. Careful research must be done to assure authenticity of the markings once chosen. If an individual nickname is painted on the aircraft it must be one that was used with the squadron markings chosen. If possible, a military airplane should retain its original identification numbers, but these numbers must not negate the authenticity of the markings.

The committee was obviously made up of very perceptive members. Aside from the obvious, the details in the above criteria have been applied to many NASM restorations and have proven to be practical and appropriate.

An airplane's identification can sometimes become blurred because of component replacement during its operational life. It has been a long-standing practice, however, that the accepted identity of such aircraft, be it by serial number, registration number, or other types of identification, comes from the fuselage, which is the primary component of an airplane.

Match Museum Mission

A factor in planning the markings for a Category III aircraft is that of the mission or objectives of the museum. Because of the ever-growing number of air museums, the general trend now is to focus more on a specific theme of aviation, avoiding an accumulation of aircraft and planning a meaningful collection. Examples of theme museums are the Strategic Air Command Museum, Champlin Fighter Museum, and Flying Farmers Air Museum. Regional examples include the New England Air Museum, Cradle of Aviation History and others that record the history within their geographical areas. Aircraft collections in theme museums should be

As a Category III military aircraft with no significant history, this Grumman FM-1 was restored in the configuration and markings typical of many Wildcats that served aboard escort carriers during the Pacific War. (Grumman)

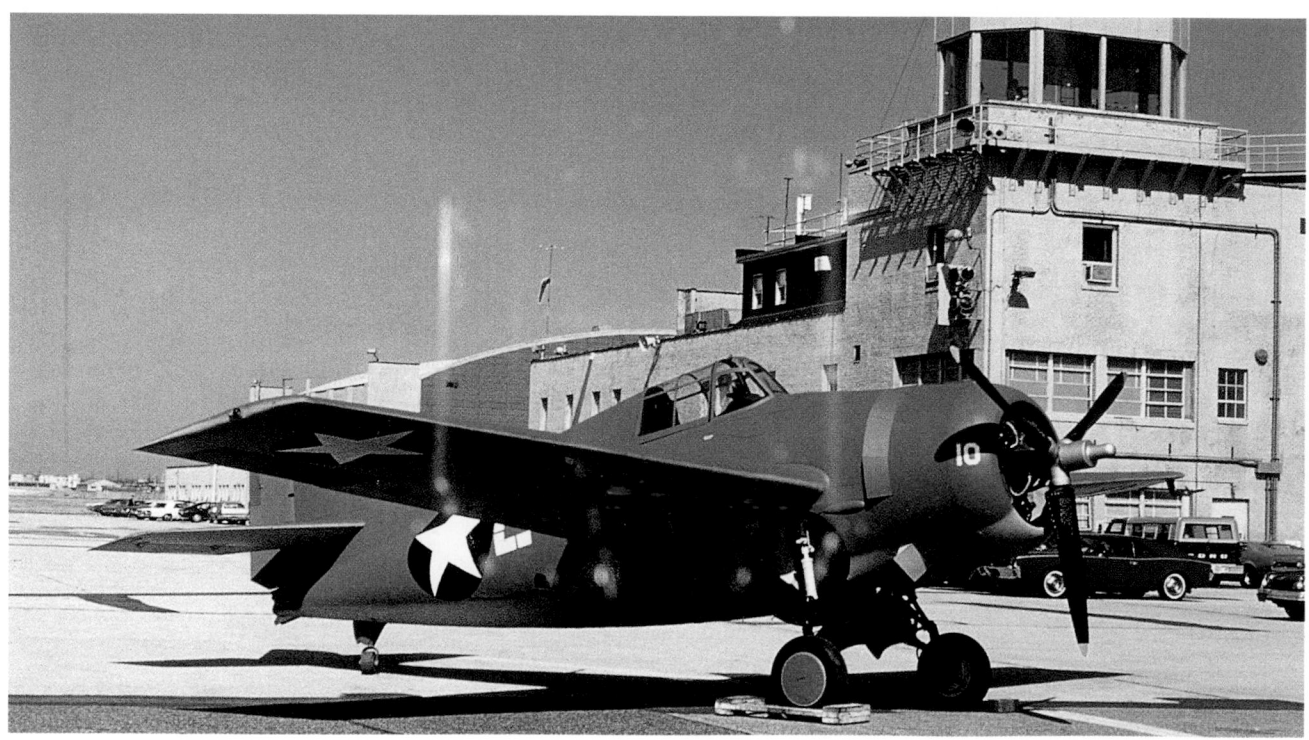

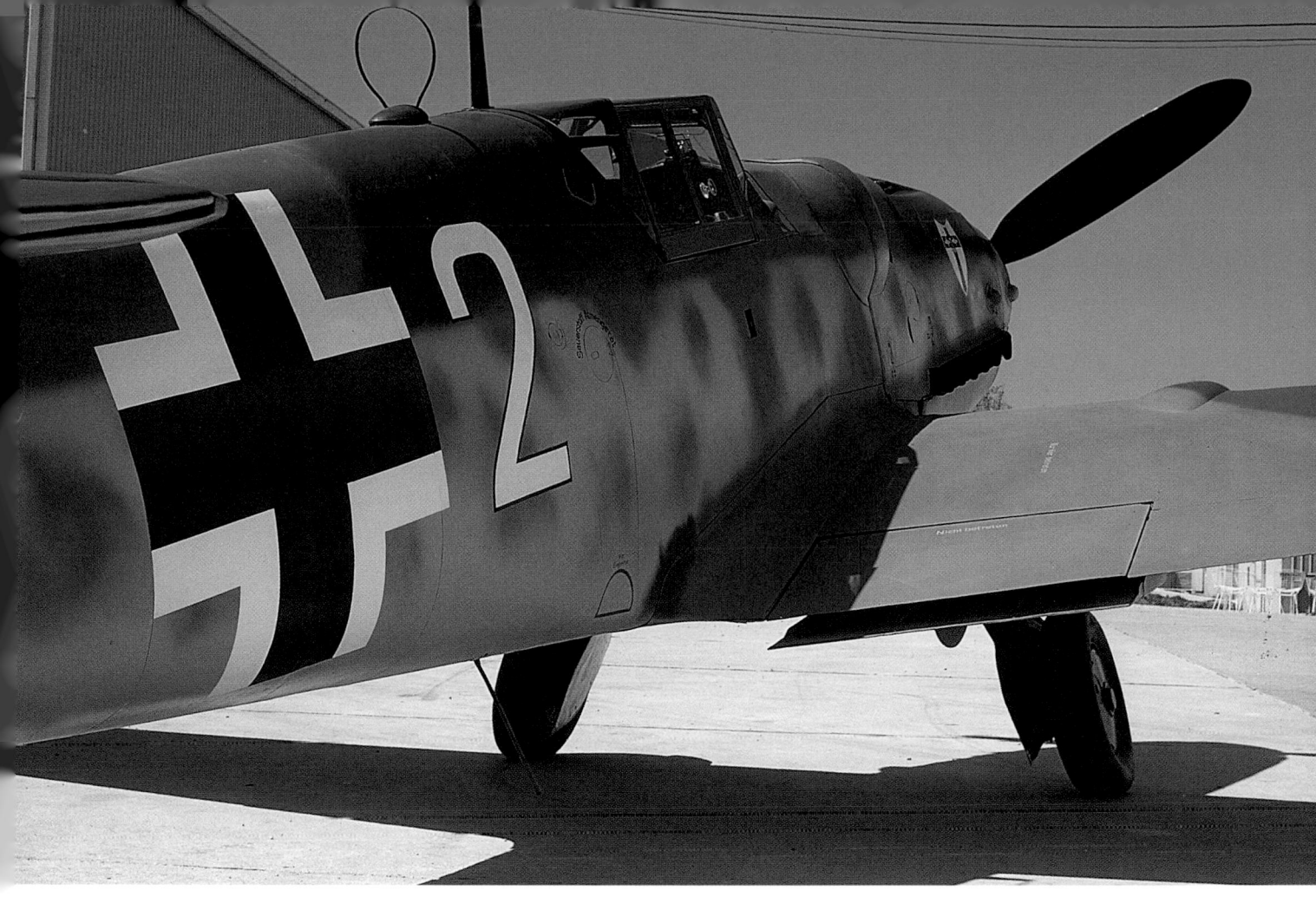

Foreign aircraft are included in the collection of NASM in order to compare the opposing technologies. In this case the Messerschmitt Bf 109G-6 / R3 that came to the museum without a trace of its identity or war history was restored with the markings of III / JG 27, a Luftwaffe unit that opposed American forces in the Eastern Mediterranean in late 1943.

limited to those that have a role in supporting the museum's mission.

When NASM was formed by Public Law 722 in 1946, it was initially called the National Air Museum and its mission was to:

> ...memorialize the national development of aviation; collect and display aeronautical equipment of historical interest and significance; serve as a repository for scientific equipment and data pertaining to the development of aviation; and provide educational material for the historical study of aviation.

To fulfil this mission both the civil and military collections are necessarily comprehensive and large. To collect one of every type of aircraft is counter-productive, if not impossible, but representative types of technically or historically significant aircraft are important. Samples of foreign military types are included to show the state-of-the-art of friendly and opposing countries in comparison with American aircraft.

Marking Decisions are Critical

In developing the military collection at NASM, as an example, US Navy aircraft include significant types used during World War II. Their restorations were planned so that if all were grouped together for exhibit, there would be a representative example of each camouflage scheme for the time period that respective aircraft were in service. Since the national insignia also changed frequently during that wartime period, each airplane was assigned to wear one of these insignia to show this aspect of history.

Another part of this World War II collection belonging to NASM are four British aircraft to represent the RAF. When planning the appearance of these airplanes as a collection, a major factor considered was the camouflage scheme to be used for the Hawker Hurricane IIC undergoing restoration. NASM's Supermarine Spitfire VII was already in the post-Battle of Britain gray and green scheme that it actually carried while in service. The Westland Lysander III as well as the de Havilland Mosquito B.35 came to the museum in schemes that had their lower halves painted black and will probably remain unchanged. Since Hurricane IICs were known for their effectiveness in the night intruder role, this Category III aircraft was destined for a scheme of such a unit. Many of these Hurricanes were painted overall black; but before this, the standard brown and green shadow camouflage scheme was common for the Hurricane and representative

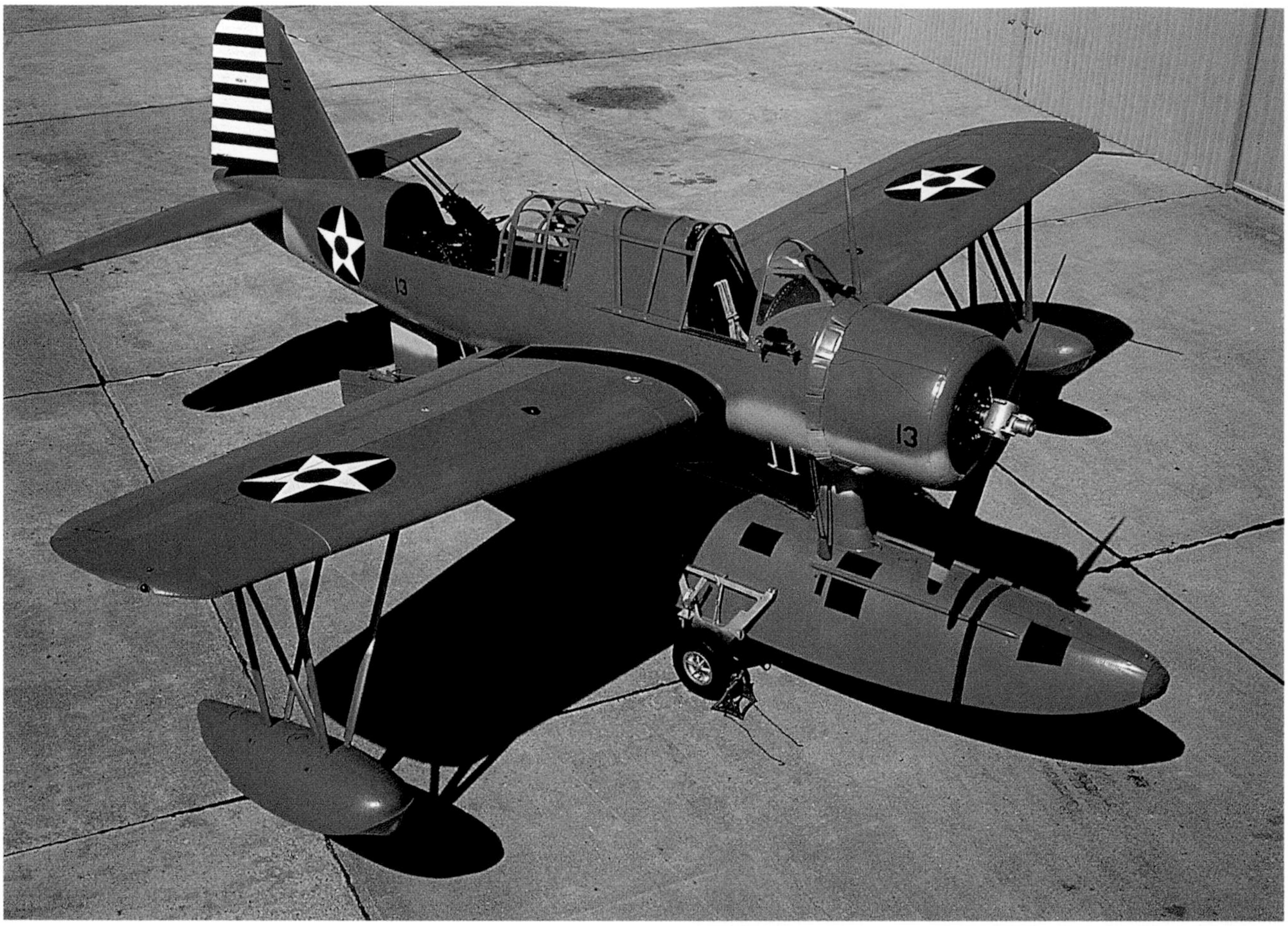

Prolonged outside exposure brought about the need to restore and preserve this Vought OS2U-3 Kingfisher of NASM. The camouflage and markings scheme selected is that in which the aircraft was delivered from the factory. This helped NASM complete a sample of each of the World War II naval camouflage schemes within this one collection of US Navy aircraft.

of the wartime RAF. This was considered more appropriate for this airplane within this collection, rather than to have another dominant black color, not typical of the overall RAF.

Take for instance NASM's collection of World War II bombers and fighters. In the current plan, when each is restored there will be a balanced representation of the different US Army Air Forces covering the major war theaters. Only four of these airplanes (three bombers and one amphibian) have seen combat, and thus are Category I (historic) and will retain their most noted configurations and be identified with their respective unit markings.[7] Since all the others are Category III aircraft, meaning they have no significant backgrounds, they will be configured to represent the combat role for which they were intended, and have markings of a specific unit for various combat areas of the world.[8]

The North American P-51D Mustang in NASM's collection was the first in this series to be restored

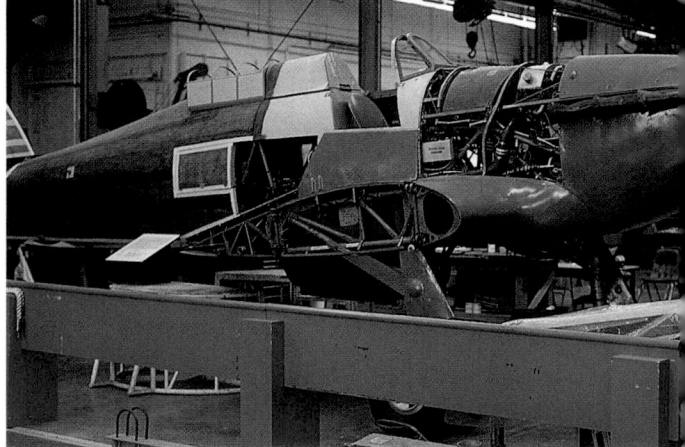

When the Hawker Hurricane IIC came to NASM in the late 1960s, its pristine exterior condition made it appear ready for exhibit. However, its cosmetic restoration concealed the severity of its deteriorated structure. This made it difficult to work the aircraft into the restoration schedule ahead of others less exhibitable in appearance. When finished, its camouflage and markings scheme should balance the collection with other RAF types on hand.

for this purpose. When developing the overall plan, the 'D' was selected to represent the most prevalent European theater type since this model was specifically developed as a bomber-escort and became significant for long-range missions deep into

Europe. But the P-51D in the collection was never in a combat unit. It went from its place of manufacture to a training unit in the US and in its post-war markings carried the peacetime slogan 'ENLIST IN THE AAF, GUARD THE VICTORY' on the side of its fuselage. If left in these service markings, this would hardly be representative of the combat role for which it was designed and brought into the collection to represent. (Some argue that an airplane should be restored to the condition in which it left the factory or was received by the museum, and to use photos and graphics to illustrate how it may have looked in combat. The right solution is the one that best suits the museum's mission, depicting the airplane for which it was brought into the respective collection.)

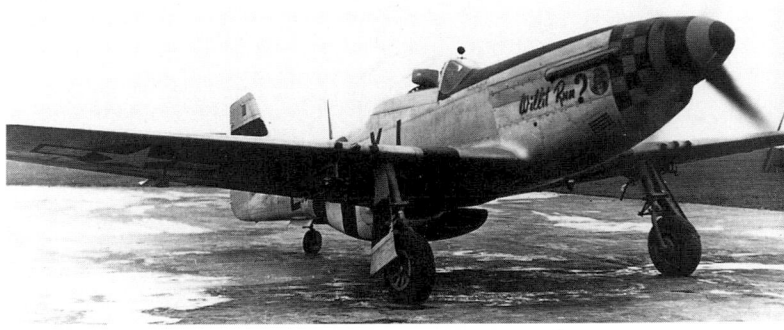

This photo of a P-51D was selected to become the pattern to which the restoration markings would be copied. By selecting such a photograph to be copied as closely as possible, there is the assurance of accuracy in duplicating an actual aircraft. This airplane belonged to the 351st Fighter Squadron, 353rd Fighter Group, based at Raydon, Suffolk, England. (USAF)

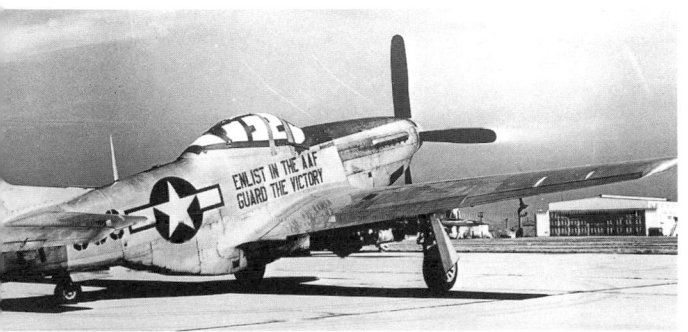

In the case of NASM's Mustang, a photo was selected of a P-51D to use as a pattern for combat markings depicting a unit based in England and assigned to long-range bomber escort missions. The photo was ideal because at the angle at which it was taken, the wing blocked the serial number from view. Thus, when painting NASM Mustang to match the one in the photo, there would be no potential mismatch between the real serial number

ABOVE:
This is NASM's P-51D as received by the museum. It bears post-war markings adding no significance or purpose to the collection. If restored as delivered from the factory, its appearance would convey none of the wartime unit codes or colors which were so prevalent throughout the war. (USAF)

BELOW:
The North American P-51D Mustang belonging to NASM had been used as an operational advanced trainer before becoming a museum aircraft. As a Category III aircraft, having no historical background, it depicts an aircraft of the 8th Air Force based in England during World War II. As such, it reflects the purpose for which the airplane was designed. (NASM, SI 74-7247)

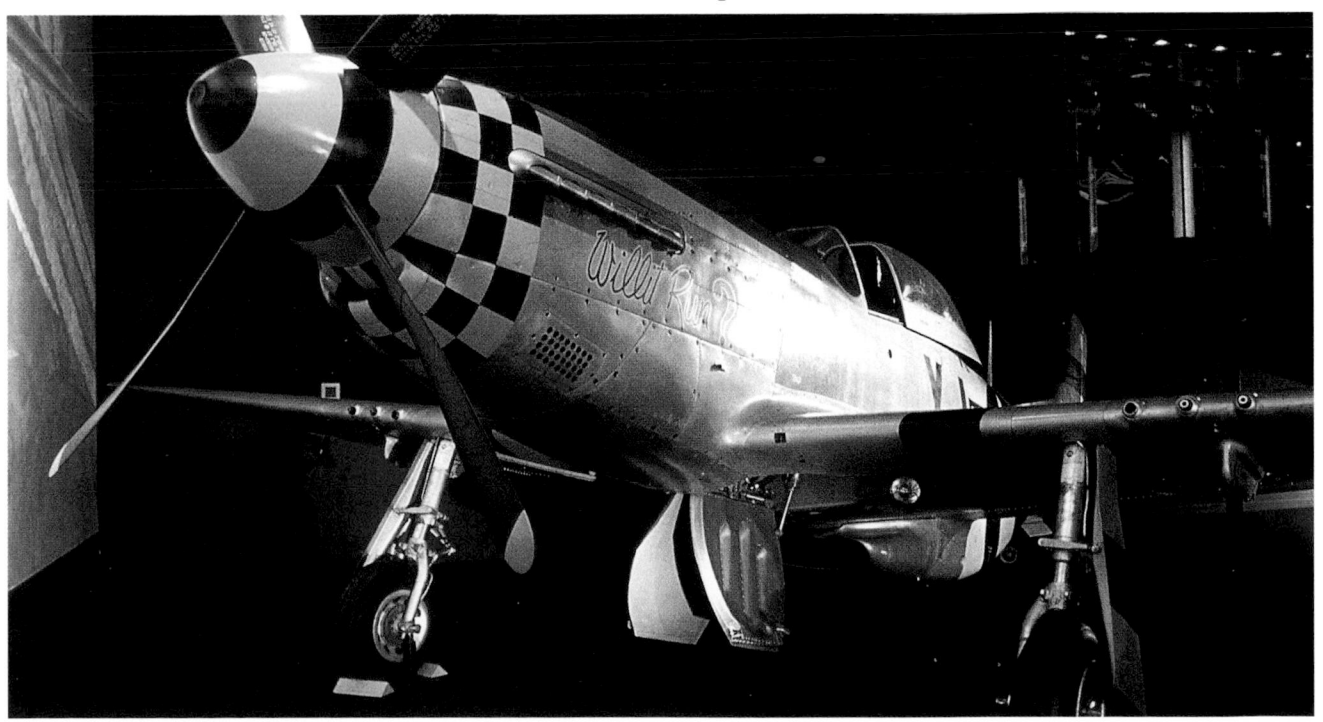

of NASM aircraft and the one in the photo. No specific airman was identified with this airplane, so that aspect also fits the established museum criteria for selecting unit markings for a Category III aircraft. The museum's Mustang now has the nickname *Willit Run?* on its nose, an exact duplicate of a known typical P-51D that had flown in combat over Europe. The exhibit label explains these imitation markings.

If the airplane is historically or technologically significant (Category I or II), there are fewer decisions to be made regarding its final configuration. That should be self-evident. A review of photos of the operational airplane will help to determine the specific time period to which the airplane is to be configured and for this restoration to be focused. A mix of markings and components covering different times is not acceptable.

A case in point is the recent restoration of the NASM B-29 *Enola Gay*. The plan initially called for the airplane to be configured as it was on the day of the historic bomb-drop on Hiroshima. This seemed like a logical decision. But in subsequent studies of photographs of the airplane taken at various times, indications were that within the first six days following the Hiroshima mission, the name on its nose had been intensified by over-painting and serifs were added. Names of crew members on board the historic flight were also added, as were bombing score markings painted on the nose showing four black Fat Man figures that represented the four practice drops of nuclear bomb shapes. Two of these missions were over Japan, and a fifth Fat Man painted in red recorded the actual and historical drop.

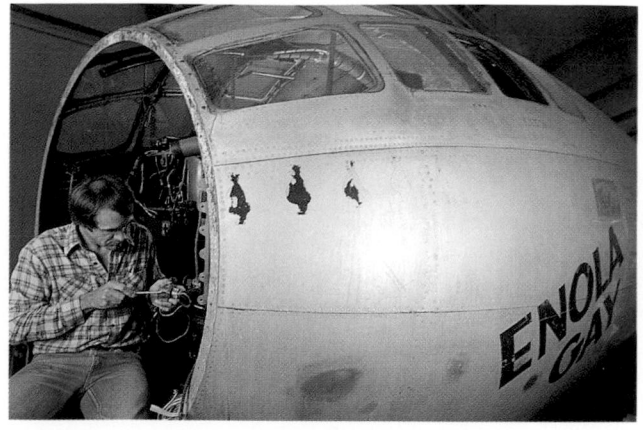

Of the five mission markings painted on the nose of the B-29 Enola Gay, *only parts of three can be seen here although an earlier tracing of the five was made for eventual replacement. The name in this configuration shows the addition of serifs added at a later date. Sufficient information is therefore on hand at NASM to reinstate these historic markings for this restoration.* (C.H. Phillips)

To have depicted the airplane on the day of the drop, these historic markings that have been recognized as part of this airplane all these years would have to be eliminated. By writing this plan in advance of painting final details, time was available to adequately research a consistent set of markings for a given time period for the airplane. The time selected for the *Enola Gay* to be restored to was six days after the bomb-drop, so that the historic markings added by that time period could be carried on this airplane and retain the history they record.

Museum aircraft in Category III that do not have a historical connection with their colors and markings as received, are best exhibited in the way that the factory produced them. There were many variations, yet factory and FAA records often record their original configuration. This Beech C-17L at NASM is an example of duplicating factory colors and trim.

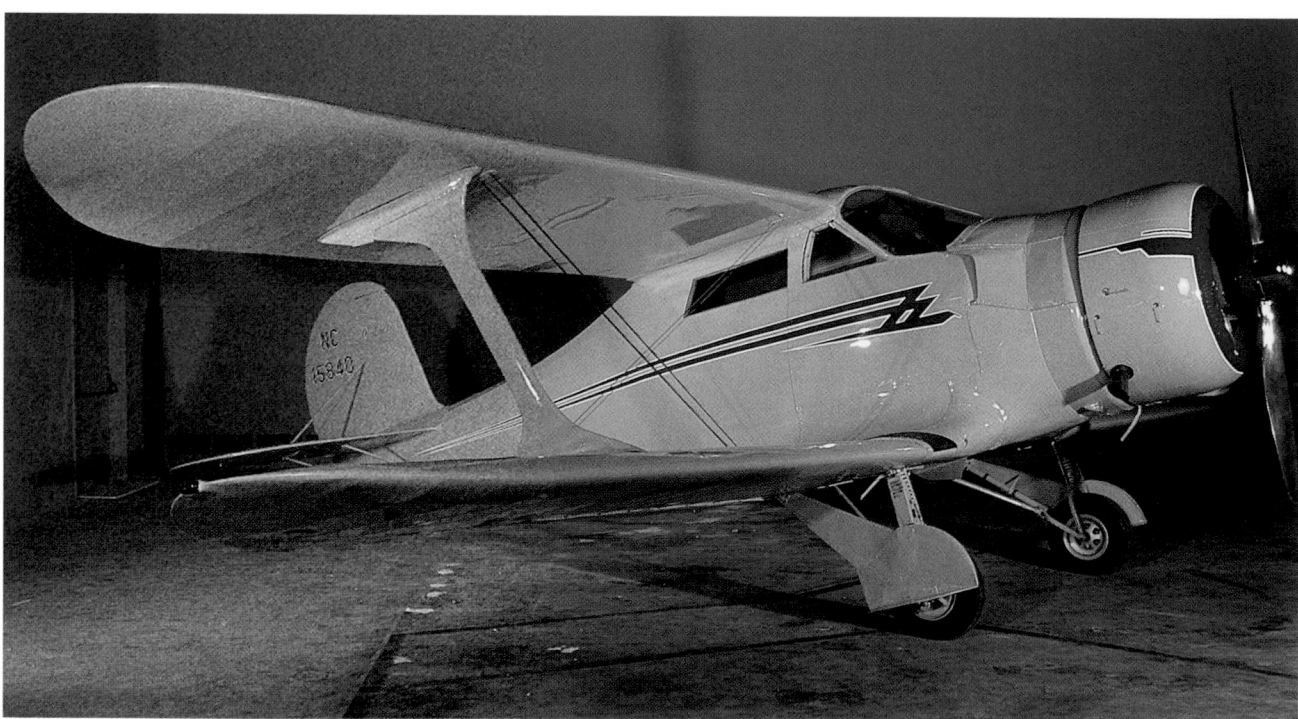

For Category III aircraft, the decision as to what the final configuration should be becomes more involved. For civil aircraft, there are often records held by the Federal Aviation Administration (FAA) or the manufacturer that describe the original colors and markings that applied to that particular aircraft. This is often the best configuration to follow for restoring originality if the aircraft is to be a rather generic type representation.

For military aircraft in Category III, particularly those of the World War II period, there are a number of factors to consider when deciding upon the external markings configuration. To begin with, the reason for having this type of aircraft in the collection is probably to preserve that portion of visual representation and mechanical technology of the combat role for which it was designed. Most surviving combat-type aircraft in museums never saw combat. To fulfil the purpose of representing a type of combat airplane in the museum, markings and colors typical of the type that would have been used by a combat unit fulfil the historical significance requirement.

By evaluating a number of photographs taken of this type of aircraft assigned to a combat unit or operational theater, one particular view must be selected to serve as the master photograph for this restoration. It should not be such a well-known picture of a given airplane that visitors may identify it with similar significance as one flown by a

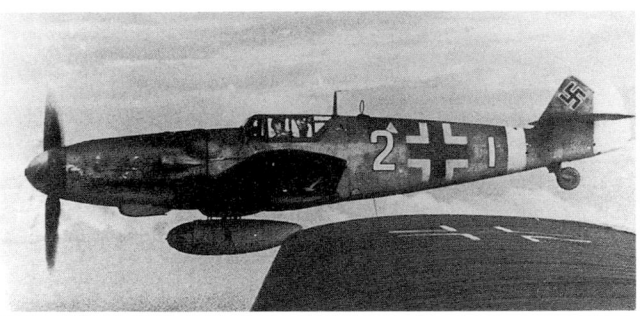

When selecting colors and markings for NASM's Messerschmitt Bf 109G-6/R3, it was surprising how few photographic examples there were to select from for this particular model. This is the view selected of an airplane from III/JG 27 to use as marking pattern. (T.H. Hitchcock)

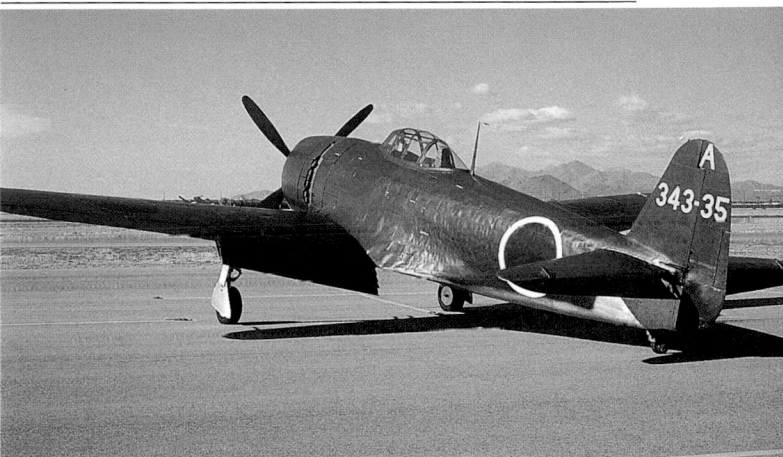

The Japanese Navy Kokutai to which this Kawanishi N1K2-Ja 'George' of NASM was assigned was easily determined but not its ship number. From a list of ship numbers assigned to the 343rd Kokutai to which pilots were not identified, the number '35' was selected. To do otherwise would imply that this airplane belonged to a known pilot.

A curatorial decision regarding NASM's Bf 109G-6/R3 was to add the III/JG 27 insignia on the nose that was missing from the pattern photograph. This was done to illustrate operational markings for completeness of the type that were carried on other aircraft of this unit. (T.H. Hitchcock)

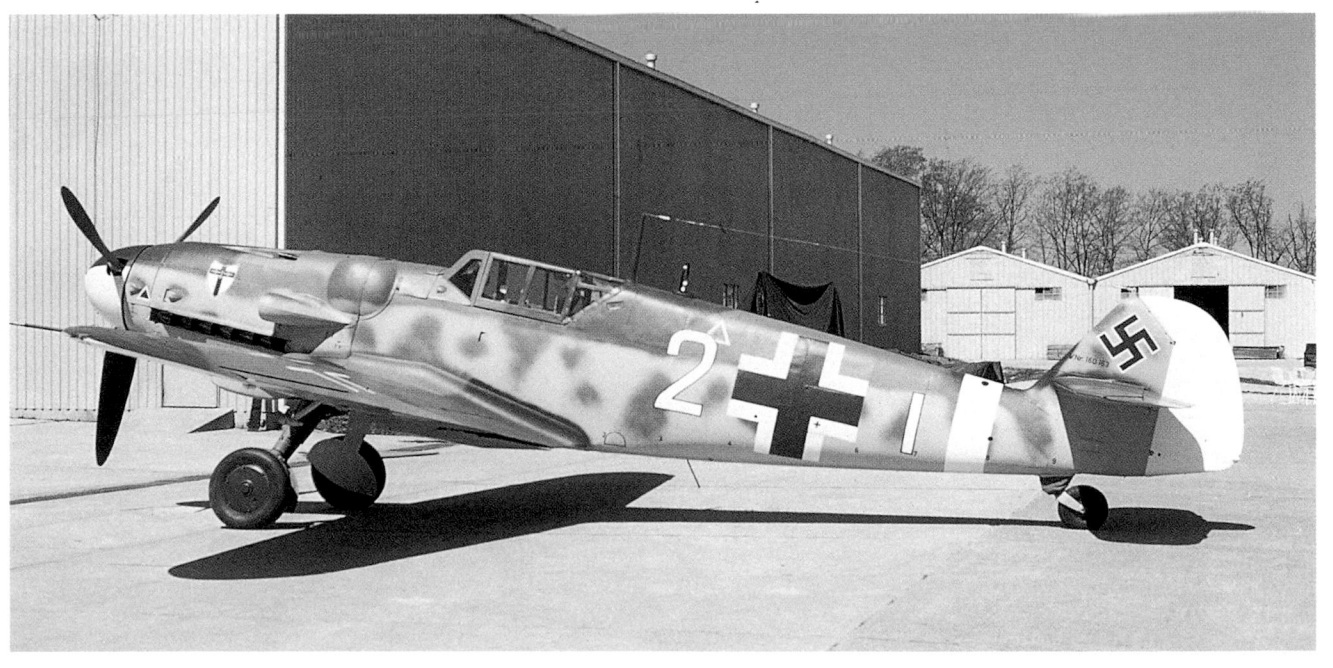

well-known pilot. To copy a plastic model airplane marking scheme is equally as bad. A very typical marking scheme is the most appropriate, and the photograph should support related curatorial decisions if questions over accuracy arise in the future.

Take for instance a photograph of a German aircraft that is selected as a master from which to work. This shows the camouflage lines on one side only. Information for the opposite side would have to be obtained from other photographs showing the style and appearance of a similar aircraft. Make certain that the pattern photograph is of the same type-model airframe as the airplane being restored — you will hear about it later from airplane buffs if they are not the same airplane model! This photo is ideal as part of the label authenticating the patterned aircraft when it was operational.

NASM abides by its policy of not personalizing aircraft that are of the Category III variety. Instead, a pattern aircraft is selected that is not associated with any particular pilot or event. Associating an airplane with a pilot or incident may confuse the viewer and give the impression that this is the same airplane. As expressed by Walter J. Tuck, of the Science Museum in London, 'To do so compromises the airplane being imitated and degrades the airplane before us to the level of a full-scale reproduction.'[9]

One museum with a considerable number of military aircraft has a pilot's name painted on each one. That pilot may have only flown that type of aircraft, but not that particular example. Many times when there is a change in the membership of a museum's board of directors, a pilot's name must be changed to appease a new board member. What effect does this have on the museum's reputation for authenticity? It is safer not to become involved in this fictitious personalizing of museum aircraft since it does become misleading.

When planning a new exhibit that would require the use of a Category III aircraft, it can become a temptation to paint for a second time these aircraft in new markings to suit changes in exhibit themes. This, however, allows an exhibit requirement to dictate a change to the original purpose of the airplane in the collection, degrading its significance, and altering the collection plan. The reverse should be the case in that exhibit planning should be aligned to support the significance for which any given airplane is in the collection. Museum airplanes *should not* be treated as exhibit props! They are the primary objects collected by the museum for the significance they represent and should be regarded as such to protect the integrity of the museum. Once their museum identity or personality has been established within the collection, the artifact takes on a significance and image

This is an example of changing identity. As a stock, yet damaged Lockheed 10, its repair includes converting it to the configuration of Amelia Earhart's aircraft in which she was lost at sea. Is this replication of a historic aircraft an ethical museum practice? Although it will be neither its former self or the Earhart airplane, similarly the Wright Flyer and Ryan Spirit of St. Louis *have been replicated for museum exhibits.*

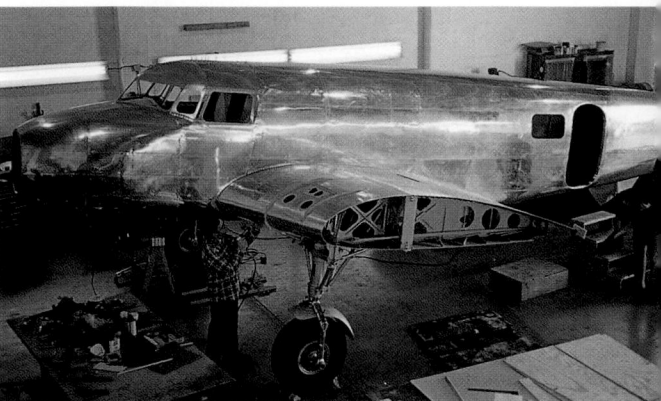

that should remain unchanged (except to correct an earlier error).

This leads us into another area of restoration that by necessity is filled with compromises. It has to do with determining which changes are appropriate for an aircraft, knowing that making these changes will leave dissimilarity in time periods of different parts within one aircraft. There are many situations where this degree of compromise becomes an issue, so let us take a specific example, the McDonnell F-4 Phantom II acquired for NASM collection.

The Phantom II's purpose as a museum object is to be part of the collection of aircraft of the Vietnam War time period. Since the F-4 was originally designed as a US Navy carrier-based fighter, it was appropriate that the Phantom II selected would be a US Navy aircraft, and one that had served in the Vietnam conflict with a US Navy unit. The aircraft eventually picked had a degree of history in that it had a victory to its credit. However, when the aircraft was retired from service 20 years after its combat tour and delivered to NASM, it came in a different overall paint scheme and in US Marine Corps markings of the last unit in which it served. It was no longer an F-4B as it was in Vietnam, but highly modified to F-4S configuration. What changes to be made, if any, would be valid for this Category III aircraft? Of several, there are two distinct courses of action to follow.

Repaint the airplane to the 1960s color scheme and US Navy unit markings in which it served, complete with its victory credit mark. The authenticity of its existing painting techniques would be lost, but the earlier appearance would be renewed. Interior components and structural changes would remain as received. These changes were generally made at depots or when returned to the factory and would be beyond the technical capabilities of a restoration shop. The latest technology for this aircraft is therefore retained and components of the earlier time period that would have been installed can be exhibited as separate items alongside this aircraft. This leaves an ambiguity problem, however, between general outward appearance of an earlier time, as opposed to internal structural changes and upgraded cockpit and other components for a later time period.

Or, as an alternative:

Leave the aircraft in its received condition. This documents many technologies such as techniques used in its last painting with authentic colors, markings and placards. Its structure and components remain unchanged as described above and therefore are compatible with its existing appearance. The compromise, however, is that it does not represent to museum visitors the time period for which the airplane as a type was selected for a collection with other aircraft. A photograph showing the airplane in service in the war zone could supplement the exhibit label explaining the earlier appearance of the airplane.

By evaluating the needs of the museum and the ground rules that apply for meeting the mission of the museum, the right decision will be reached. A mix within one system, such as markings and colors that encompass different time periods on the same aircraft, would not be acceptable. But a modernized cockpit, or upgraded power system that does not affect the exterior appearance of appropriate colors and markings for another time period seem to be reasonable compromises if documented in the aircraft's records and explained on the exhibit label.

To have a better understanding of any given artifact or airplane after determining the Category in which it belongs and agreeing upon the rules that govern respective museum restorations, some additional questions should be asked when developing restoration and reconfiguration plans:

1. Is the full history and significance of the airplane adequately documented and understood, beyond hearsay and legend, that may affect the work plan?
2. What secrets might this structure hold that should be looked for after considerable thought; e.g. German metal found in structure of Japanese airplane, other foreign parts used, what is learned from study of cross-section of paint sample, and does pollen found in structure indicate where it was manufactured or flown?
3. What maintenance problems will be encountered for safe-guarding this airplane after being restored; e.g. internal illumination, scuff-mark protection when there is visitor entry, strut and tire inflation, etc?
4. What effect, if any, will a restoration have upon enhancing or degrading the aircraft's historic or technological significance; e.g. deleting special markings applied that were intended to commemorate an event, repairing damage which occurred as part of the event, etc?
5. Will the aircraft at some time be the primary subject of an exhibit, or will it be a supporting element that relates to a group of aircraft?
6. What time period is it to represent; e.g. a certain event, the beginning of its service life, the end, or a selected time in between? Is it to be tailored to blend within a group?
7. Do the original, and perhaps quite mundane, markings of the aircraft permit the museum to explain or interpret a facet of its mission which would not otherwise be possible? Example:

The RAF Museum has a Category III Hawker Tempest V late World War II fighter that as a type was quickly relegated to second-line target-towing duties. While the Tempest was an important World War II RAF fighter, the Museum's plan is to restore this machine to target-towing configuration and markings in order to interpret this very important training role.

8 In what way does the artifact add educational value and strengthen the collection? What technical details need special attention for this function; e.g. cutaway and exhibit graphics?

Levels of Exhibit and Preservation Condition

We have described the three categories into which aircraft of a collection can be placed, and therefore have established some guidelines by which to manage them. There is an additional identifying system that will describe the condition of an aircraft that becomes very useful when planning restoration needs within a given collection.

James A. Burnham, former Chief Conservator at the Henry Ford Museum & Greenfield Village, in Dearborn, Michigan, has conveniently described four Levels of Aircraft Condition.[10] This not only has to do with an airplane's condition for exhibit, but also the stability in preservation of its structure. Once an aircraft has been identified as belonging to one of these levels, the type or degree of restoration work required becomes easier to understand. Dr Burnham uses these examples to describe the Levels of Condition:

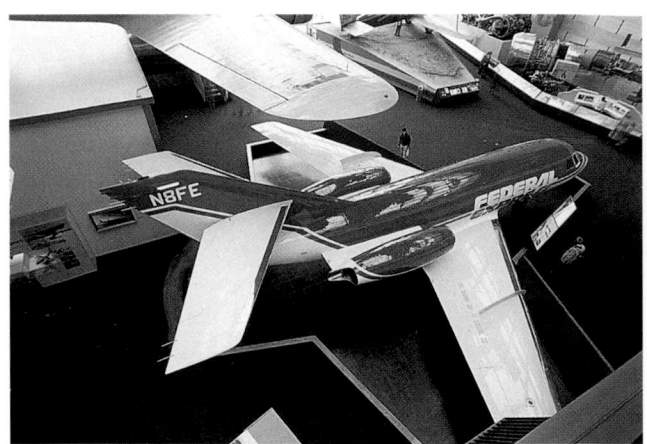

This example of a Level 1 Condition aircraft, a Dassault Falcon 20, shows little sign of wear because it was freshly painted before being donated to NASM, therefore revealing little of its operational history.

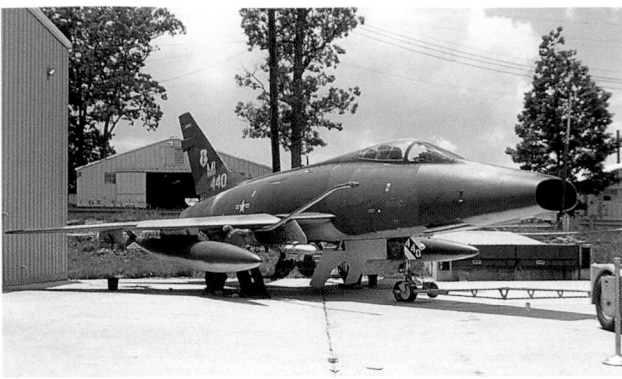

This North American F-100D Super Sabre left operational service in such good condition that it is classed as Level 2 Condition. Deserviced and with markings changed to represent its Vietnam War service unit, it is ready for exhibit. Its service is evident by its scrapes, scratches and oil stains.

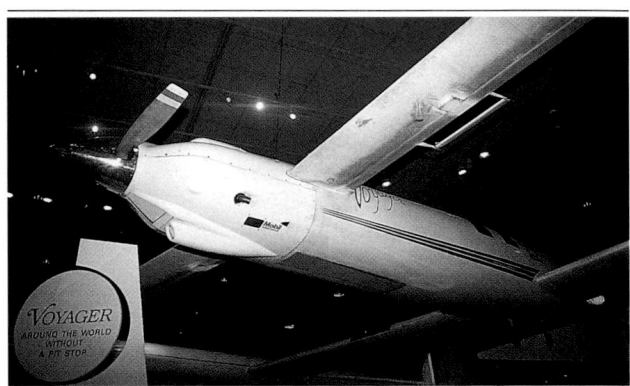

Historical aircraft must not lose their importance as a result of repairs that would erase an event. The Rutan Voyager is historic for making a non-stop, unrefueled flight around the world. Fortunately, the Voyager was obtained by NASM while still in its unchanged Level 2 Condition soon after the conclusion of the flight.

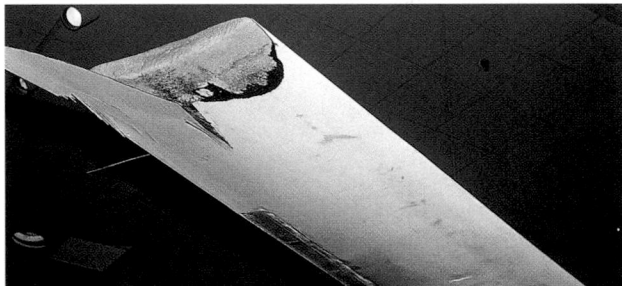

The Voyager is on exhibit in NASM displaying its broken wing-tips and loss of winglets. This occurred at the time of take-off when these tips dragged on the runway. To make repairs would degrade the importance of this incident as part of the flight.

An aircraft (including its engine) in **Level 1 Condition** will almost always be in pristine condition and ready for exhibit. It will not be deteriorating, meaning it is in a stable condition, since it will either be new or will have undergone a total and complete restoration with preservation safeguards. If the aircraft is new and set aside at the time of manufacture as a museum piece, the aircraft would show no indications of a service life or reveal technical points of wear or failures. Conversely, when restoring an aircraft to this level, great care must be taken to retain evidence of usage that has occurred to the aircraft as a result of its past service.

To have an aircraft in this condition, however, it must be maintained in a stable environment. It would require preservation of its engine(s) and various systems. This can be done by removing liquids and lubricants that over a long time could accelerate deterioration. Interior surfaces of these systems should then be coated with protective materials. Filling some systems with nitrogen under slight pressure is often recommended in this process. To receive and process an aircraft in this condition would certainly eliminate a lot of museum restoration problems.

Level 2 Condition is the 'in recent use, well cared-for' look. Aircraft in this condition are also suitable for exhibit, but often require some clean-up, markings changes to return it to its significant role, and may require minor preservation attention. At this level the aircraft materials will also be in stable condition, but will also have the scratches, little bumps, a chip of paint missing, stains, patches, and other surface flaws incurred during its service life. These will still be evident although not distracting, even though the aircraft was well maintained while it was operational. In the conversion treatment and stabilization process required to prepare the aircraft to become a museum specimen,

these blemishes will be stabilized and preserved to serve as documentation of the aircraft history. The observer, upon seeing this evidence of operational use, should be able to differentiate this appearance from museum neglect or abuse. Again, further restoration would not be appropriate for second-level aircraft, avoiding the 'new look.'

(There are exceptions to every definition. Take for instance a helicopter that may have been submerged in sea water. When retrieved and washed down, it certainly has the unchanged appearance of being ready for exhibit as Level 2 Condition, but the sea water has rendered the structure unstable as described for Level 3 Condition.)

Another example of historical damage can be seen on NASM's Northrop Gamma Polar Star. *Famous air explorers Hollick-Kenyon and Ellsworth charted new land features while using this airplane. In so doing, several landings were necessary because of ice, fog and high winds. One hard and memorable landing caused this wrinkling of the nose which must remain as historical evidence.*

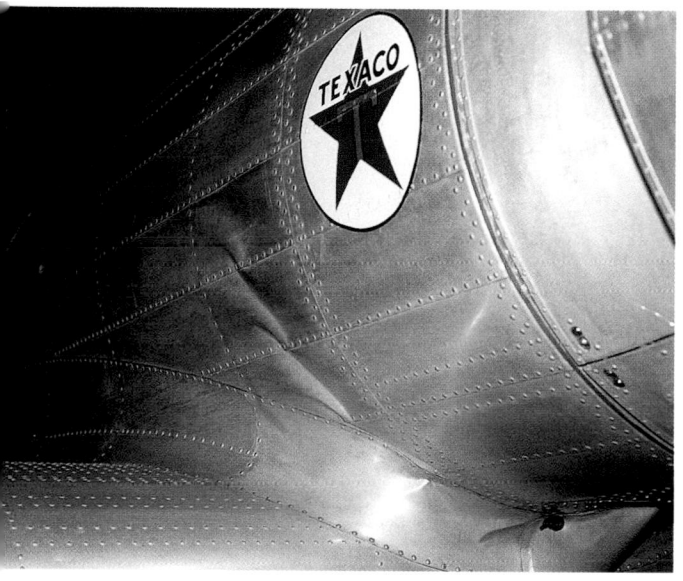

Level 3 Condition might simply be called 'deteriorated and unstable condition.' Aircraft of this description are not suitable for exhibit purposes without a complete or nearly complete treatment involving preservation and restoration. This condition may have resulted from heavy usage or poor care. Unfortunately, this condition is often influenced by neglect and even abuse within the museum itself. These aircraft, seldom in stable condition, are fragile, brittle, torn, and probably incomplete. That the aircraft were no longer serviceable is probably the reason they were passed along to a museum in the first place. Unfortunately, this is the way many aircraft come into museum ownership. Aircraft in this state are not exhibitable for the purpose of conveying, without interpretation, the nature of the aircraft while it was operational. It is this condition of instability and deterioration that will be examined to determine how far a restoration of such an aircraft should be taken. Before beginning, however, the fourth level of aircraft condition should be described.

Level 4 Condition includes those aircraft that are derelict and virtually destroyed. It may be

possible to conserve them in their present condition, and some museums have used them very effectively as exhibitions in a diorama effect that shows how the aircraft was discovered. An excellent example is what the National Aviation Museum in Ottawa did with the recovered remains of a noted Curtiss HS-2L flying boat, G-CAAC. Rather than disturb what originality was left with these fragments, the hull and other components are exhibited as received. To rightfully represent the airplane as a complete unit, a new hull was built, some factory-built components were gathered from locations throughout North America, and others were built from factory drawings. Now on exhibit alongside the recovered remains is a reproduction of this significant flying boat.

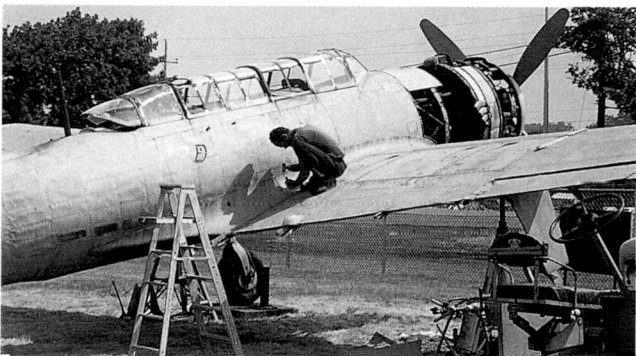

It is usually through neglect that aircraft such as this Nakajima B6N Tenzan codenamed 'Jill', at NAS Willow Grove, Pennsylvania, degenerated to a Level 3 Condition aircraft. Because of years of exposure, a complete breakdown is necessary, corrosion control measures need to be taken, and the restoration must use as many as possible of the original-type components added to replace those stolen and vandalized over the years.

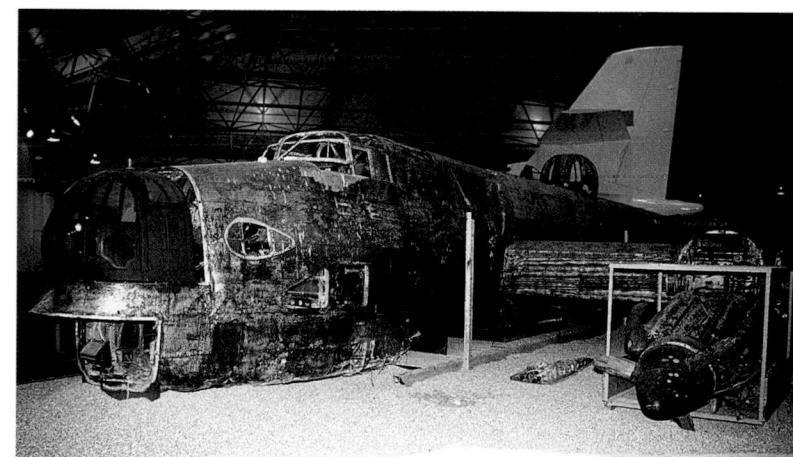

All need not be lost with a Level 4 Condition aircraft. Soon after the RAF Museum began a restoration of this sole remaining Handley Page Halifax bomber, it became apparent that to make it a complete aircraft again would destroy its authenticity and produce, effectively, a replica. Instead, they converted the project into a diorama that depicts how the bomber was discovered resting on the bottom of a lake.

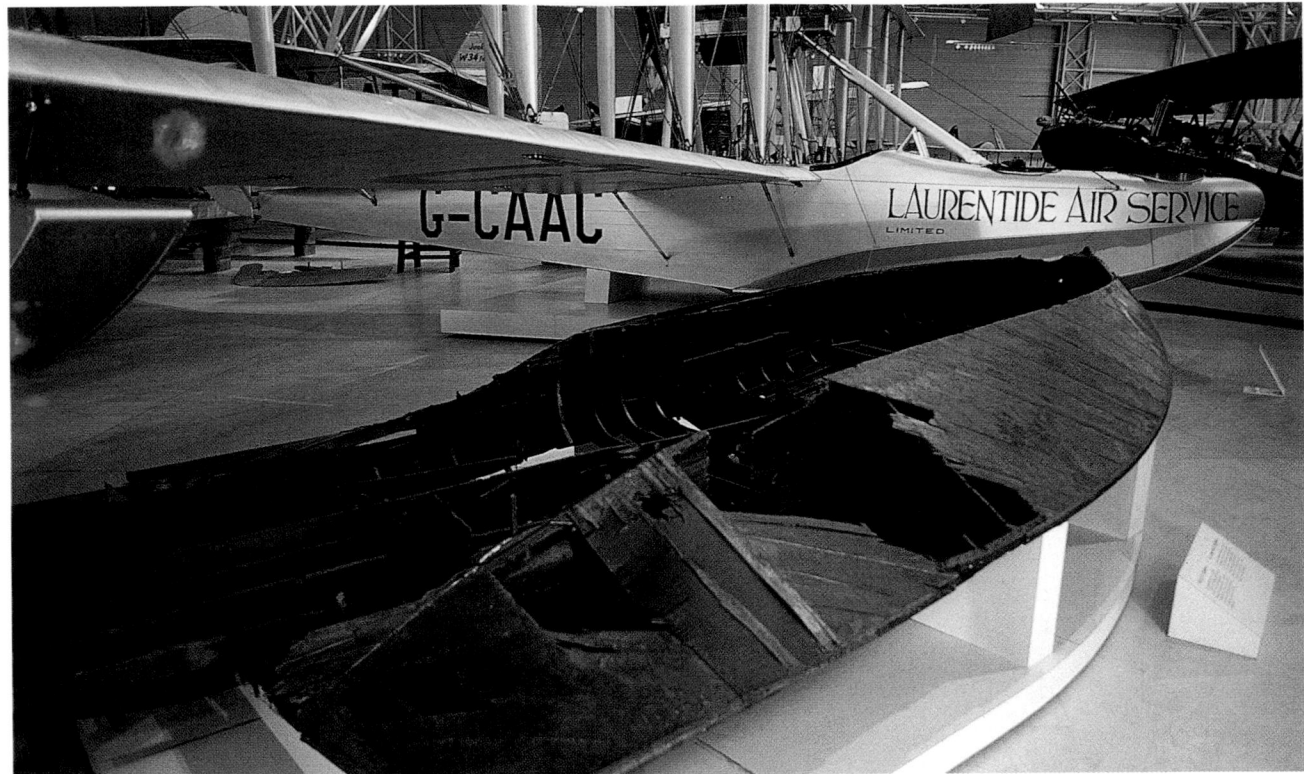

*There are situations where it is best not to disturb what is left of rare aircraft, but instead to preserve surviving evidence of the past. These parts of a hull and other components of this Curtiss HS-2L flying boat in the National Aviation Museum in Ottawa, Canada, are exhibited unrestored in front of a representative aircraft. (*National Aviation Museum*)*

From the foregoing Levels of Condition it is evident that there is a wide range in appearance, as well as preservation stability of museum aircraft between the second and third levels; i.e. those that were in good operational condition as opposed to those having suffered neglect and deterioration. Further, to bring a derelict aircraft from the fourth or third level, to the first (pristine) level — the act of restoration — requires a total treatment of the entire aircraft.

Senior Conservator David Hallam warns against undue tampering with aircraft that can be satisfactorily retained in a Level 2 Condition if in fact they are received in that condition. He points out[11] that what is needed is a conservation program based on scientific fact, beginning with an assessment of the traditional means of caring for a particular functional object. If we plot the wear rate of a functional object against time, a common pattern develops (see adjacent graph). The initial wear period is followed by a plateau, which equates with the object's economic life, followed by failure. If an object in this pre-failure state is placed in a museum without any preparation or maintenance, it will begin to deteriorate to Level 3 Condition (failure) and an intrusive restoration becomes essential.

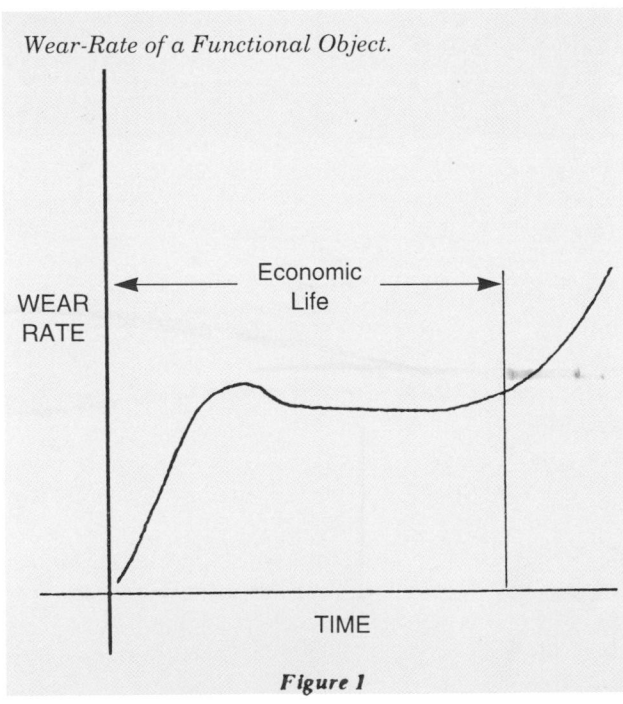

Wear-Rate of a Functional Object.

Figure 1

There is a wide variation in people's perception of what 'restoration' of an aircraft really means. As mentioned in the Introduction to this book, the term is being used here very specifically in this regard for museum-restored aircraft, intending the usage to include all necessary action that will preserve the structure indefinitely. Not only is the exterior complete in every detail, but internal systems are also complete to preserve the technology of their design. All parts for that airframe are original in design to the best extent possible.

Others may use the term 'restoration' quite liberally. Quite often this refers to 'cosmetic restoration' by repainting, yet giving limited attention to extended structural preservation and duplicating original technology with components, structure and completeness throughout the aircraft. More appropriately, other terms such as 'modified original,' 'reconstruction,' or 'reproduction,' with or without original parts might be appropriate. To owners of these aircraft, this terminology is a sensitive issue, so make certain when referring to issues discussed in this book that these pertain to static museum aircraft only.

When a museum is faced with the task of having to restore an aircraft that is defined as being in Level 3 Condition, there are certain aspects that must be recognized and accepted at the outset. A restoration is bound to bring an external 'like-new' appearance in the form of new fabric, new paint, or new wooden veneer skin, and in the case of natural metal surfaces, a cleaned and often polished appearance. There is no middle ground. If it is new paint, an old and used appearance does not come out of the can. New fabric that is artificially made to look old is therefore not representative of the original. Metal surfaces that over the years have darkened with oxidation (a form of corrosion) will no longer resemble their appearance when in service. There is

no point in painting exhaust or oil stains on a museum aircraft to make it look less than factory-fresh, or bead-blasting all leading edges to simulate erosion caused by flying. This we call 'Hollywooding' the airplane. This is the real airplane and nothing need be falsified in the restoration process. To add 'make-up' destroys a museum's integrity and confuses the observer as to what is authentic about the airplane and what is cosmetic. Perhaps 'Hollywooding' can be defined as acceptable for airplanes flown or used for movie purposes, but not when displayed as an authentic museum specimen.

It is obvious that engine exhaust and leaking oil have not muted the repainted surfaces of this Curtiss P-40E Warhawk. This had been a Level 3 Condition airplane and required a full restoration and preservation. Operational marks and blemishes need not be faked because this is a real airplane. Indoor museum aircraft are expected to look clean and be clean with a cared-for appearance.

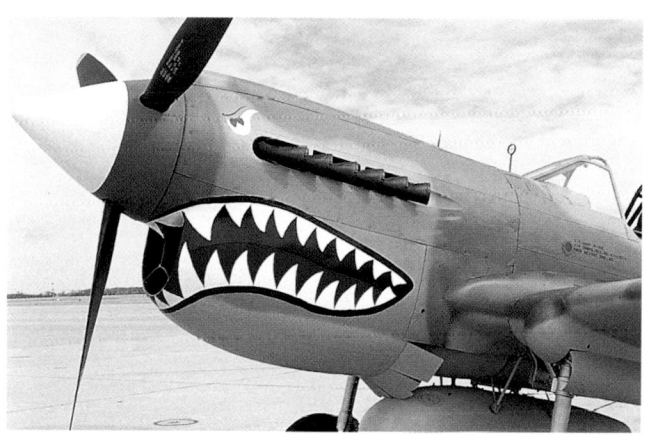

Considerable artwork can be added to an artificial appearance of wear and operational service as applied to this Boeing B-17 Flying Fortress. This is essential for movie-making and looks good on warbirds that are flown.

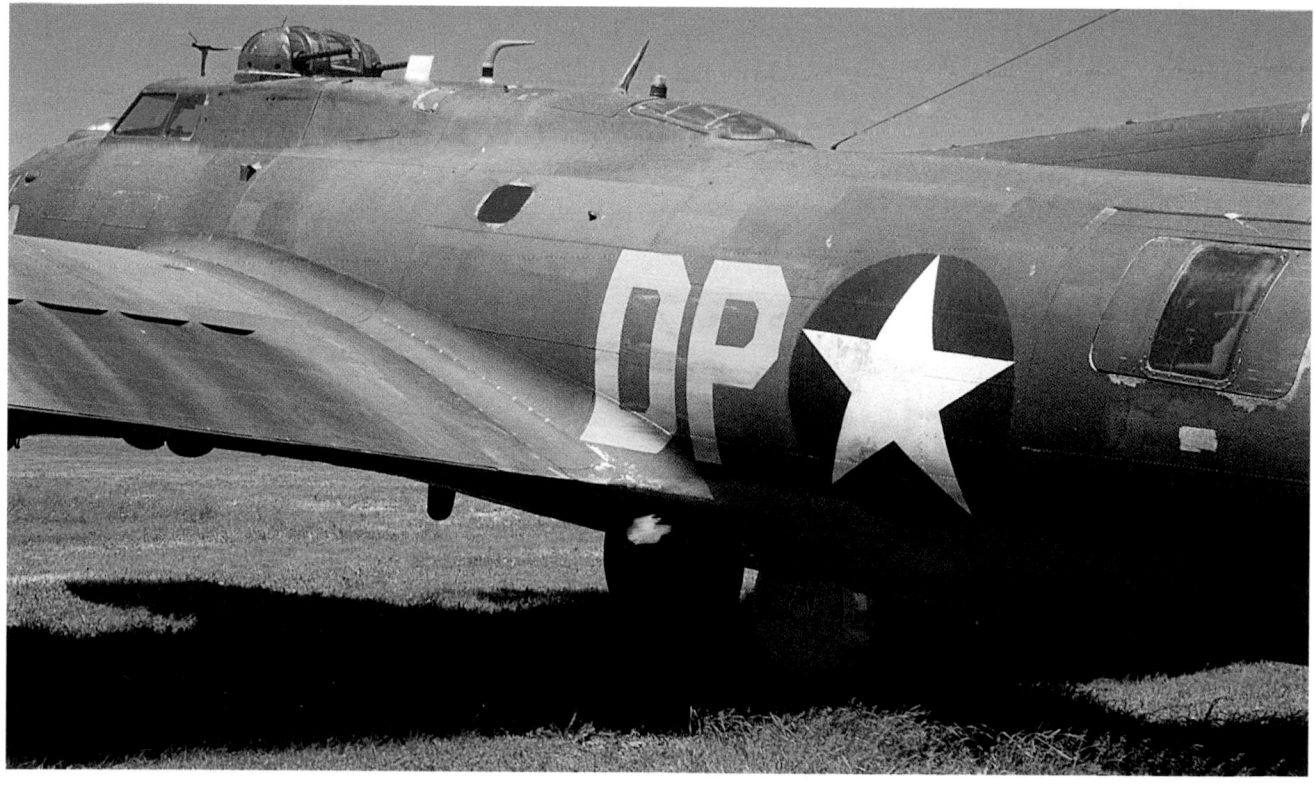

Antique cars, to use a different example, are expected to look clean and crisp in museum settings, but when seen on the screen (as when filming vintage aircraft) they carry 'make-up' to suit the setting.

The goal for each aircraft in a collection need not be to achieve a 'like new' appearance, nor be left as received, in order not to disturb evidence of its origin or background. There are compromises in the case of each aircraft, and these must be defined as to their Level of Condition before any work is attempted. Work of any kind is deliberately avoided until the 'level' is established by the curator which then defines the scope of the project.

A case in point: NASM has a Lockheed P-38J Lightning that has been in storage since being received in good condition after World War II. It is unaltered in every way except for telltale marks of disassembly and reassembly on its discolored paint. Two or more courses of action can be followed when the aircraft is scheduled for reworking:

Treated as a Level 2 Condition airplane, it could be carefully cleaned on the outside in order to disturb as little as possible of what is original. Major components would be disassembled so as to reach as much of the internal structure for cleaning and preserving. This is difficult without a total disassembly. When exhibited, the airplane would be as original as possible despite the fading and reddish cast that US west coast wartime green camouflages acquired after time.

Treated as a Level 3 Condition airplane, a more extensive teardown could be undertaken in order to reach all of the internal structural areas for preservation. In doing so, this would disturb more of the external paint that has been unaltered from the time of manufacture except for paint deterioration, handling wear, and color shift. A repainting to its original colors would be called for.

The making of such a Level of Condition classification becomes a joint effort on the part of the curator and conservator since this involves both appearance and preservation. Once the Level of Condition has been determined, the direction of the work process can more logically be defined based upon definition of the two. The final choice must be that of the curator. But most importantly, a condition report of the airframe and reasons why one Level was decided upon over the other must be adequately documented within the aircraft's records. This, again, becomes a co-ordinated effort on the part of the curator and conservator.

Curatorial Guidelines

Now that the overall condition and external configuration of the airplane to be restored has been

determined, writing of the Curatorial Guidelines can begin. This document becomes the baseline of reference from which all those concerned with the project can work. Its function is as essential as a blueprint is for building a house. It is written for the restoration technicians, not to tell them how to do their job, but to define the objectives to be attained when the work is finished.

There are certain subject elements that I have found work well around which these guidelines are written. Others can be added when and where appropriate, but for basics, these major headings are:

Identification
  Name of the aircraft
  Aircraft identifying numbers
  Museum accession and/or catalogue number
Significance of the Type of Aircraft
  Magnitude of overall use and primary purpose
Background of the Specific Airframe (to include):
  Date of manufacture
  Where manufactured
  Assignment location(s) and/or used by whom
  Donor of the aircraft to the museum
  Date received by museum
  Total flying hours
  Summary of previous restorations, preservation treatments and/or storage conditions
Current Condition and Configuration
Final Appearance Configuration
Individual Component Discussion
  Fuselage
  Cockpit
  Wings (can include landing gear if attached to the wing)
  Empennage
  Engine(s)
  Color Scheme and Markings
Concluding Comments

The purpose of beginning with Significance of the Type of Aircraft and Background of the Specific Airframe is for the information of those who will be working on this airplane. By knowing details surrounding its past, clues discovered while working on the structure can be linked with other aspects that may add more meaning to the airplane's history. For instance, by knowing of the Atlantic crossing made by Amelia Earhart in the Lockheed Vega being worked on, the chewing gum wrapper with a notation on it found under the floor took on far greater personal significance. The same was true with the stone found inside the cowling of the Messerschmitt Me 262A; this became more significant when recalling that forced labor was used in manufacturing many of these airplanes and the stone may have been placed there in the hope that it would dislodge and cause rotor damage to the engine and destroy the airplane. Pure supposition, of course, but the stone remains a part of NASM's collection.

These written and agreed-to Curatorial Guidelines must be at hand at the start of the restoration work. While not receiving all my attention during this development time, I found that drawing up a thorough plan often took three or more months. Time-consuming research, query letters, waiting for replies, followed by more research into new avenues that became apparent all took more time than expected.

Many people will avoid writing at any cost, especially a document as involved as a Curatorial Guidelines plan. To make this task simpler by providing a sample from which to work, two that were actually used in restorations at NASM are included in the appendices. Appendix A pertains to a wood-and-fabric aircraft, the Benoist Type XII, and Appendix B describes a metal aircraft, the Arado Ar 234B-2 Blitz. Keep in mind that there is no standard to which a plan must be matched. It is up to respective museums to design a plan format that works best for them. *It is very unprofessional* to embark upon work of this magnitude without a written plan, for to do otherwise is bound to lead to mistakes and disappointments brought about by a lack of mutual understanding! These issues would normally be recognized and identified during the thought process while writing the plan and could therefore be resolved *with the best choice of solutions* well in advance of the actual work. There are no assurances that the same technicians will see the task through to its conclusion. The Curatorial Guidelines provide the needed direction and continuity.

As in the case with the Australian War Memorial and perhaps other major museums having conservators on staff, Conservation Guidelines are prepared after the curator completes the Curatorial Guidelines. A treatment proposal for the object is developed by the conservator with the aid of the crafts-person. The Curatorial Guidelines combined with the Conservation Guidelines then become a complete package referred to as the **Restoration Guidelines**.

It is not uncommon that as the restoration progresses, changes to the original plan become necessary. A notation to this effect should be marked at that location in the plan, calling attention to a correction memorandum that must be prepared and attached to this plan.

Technical Materials

While the Curatorial Guidelines are still in draft form before they are circulated, they should be used as a point of discussion with those who will become involved in the work. That is the best time to resolve possible problems, or to bring to the fore issues that have been overlooked. After all, the curatorial viewpoint on a particular matter could be unachievable from the perspective of the restoration technician. At this point, the technician may suggest the type of technical drawings, manuals, etc., that will be needed. It should be the responsibility of the curator to locate and provide this material, relieving the technician of this research burden that would otherwise be directed to the restoration itself.

Reference materials are key in putting together a complete Curatorial Guidelines package. Determine what drawings will be needed for missing or heavily damaged parts. Response time by those who can provide this material could cause delays if not recognized early enough in this thought process. Plan well ahead.

There will be times when a part is needed, yet no drawings can be found from which to make or fabricate the part. If the curator is not capable of making these drawings, he or she should be responsible for having these drawings made by others. A restoration technician should not be expected to create the object without something more than an overall dimension. Examples of drawing development in cases where working drawings were not available are shown in Appendix A.

Knowing the various archives that may have the technical materials needed is essential. See Appendix F for some of these archival sources.

For every aircraft there seems to be a specialist who can answer questions about that particular airplane. Search for that person and get his or her help with your project. That person may have already written on the subject, and a library may be of help in locating a list of relevant authors and titles. A curator at a major air museum may know who that specialist is!

Programing

Ideally, as painfully learned from experience, a project should not be planned beyond a three-year program except on very large and complex aircraft. To go beyond that, it becomes a love/hate relationship of not wanting to look daily at the same heap of parts strewn on the floor. This is particularly true with a volunteer force. After the first year, if one-third of the effort is not apparent as having been accomplished, a high drop-out rate within the volunteer work force begins. Paid help may stay on the job, but morale and effectiveness suffers.

Naturally, there are exceptions. For larger aircraft with complex interiors, there is no restoration staff large enough to complete major projects in a three-year time period. NASM's B-29 *Enola Gay* is still in the process after 13 years, and the RAF Museum's Supermarine Southampton required 15 years. By making separate projects of major components, such as the cockpit, fuselage, wings, etc. and assigning these to separate work teams will help solve the monotony problem.

Enthusiasm for any restoration project of this nature is highest at its beginning and end. Expectations and realization are major factors. It is the inbetween time when the project and the workers suffer. This is a time spent preparing all the little parts to have them ready when the assembly phase begins. In the meantime, there is the appearance that nothing is happening — not only might the boss have this impression, but also those who periodically stop by to see the project.

A 'fake' solution has been to reposition the major components so that the view is not the same for months on end while the finer components are being restored, yet not seen as visible progress. Laugh if you wish, but this has a positive effect. Have the fuselage face the other way for a while; join temporarily two major components — anything to alter the appearance of the project area that otherwise conveys the impression of being stalemated. It gives a fresh perspective that something is

happening — which it is — and everybody feels better about it.

There are sufficient records now that have established actual man-hours expended on the restoration of major components of an aircraft and the completed project (see Appendix E). Using these figures, make a man-hour estimate for the project being contemplated. Once an overall time estimate has been made for the project, dividing that number by 2,000 man-hours per person per year, full-time, will tell you the work force in numbers of technicians needed to complete the project in the time allotted. This planning is necessary if any sort of schedule is expected to be maintained. At NASM, try as we may to reach this figure before beginning the project, an overrun of 10-20 per cent developed in nearly every case because of unexpected problems. As skills and techniques improve, one would think that fewer man-hours would be required for a given project. The reverse is true, however. The reason for this seems to be that the tasks were being accomplished more thoroughly in terms of stabilizing materials for greater longevity as techniques improved.

First and Last Restoration

There are several points that cannot be emphasized enough when doing a first-time restoration on an airplane. First, any intrusion upon the structure is removing evidence of originality. Therefore, when this becomes necessary, particularly on Level 3 Condition aircraft, it is essential that originality be duplicated in every way possible during the rebuilding phase of this restoration.

To maintain an active appearance while doing time-consuming, tedious work is not conducive to the morale of those involved. Merely repositioning major components gives the impression that the project is progressing, even when the labor-intensive details are not apparent. In this view, Charlie Parmley stitches fabric on the wing of NASM's Corsair.

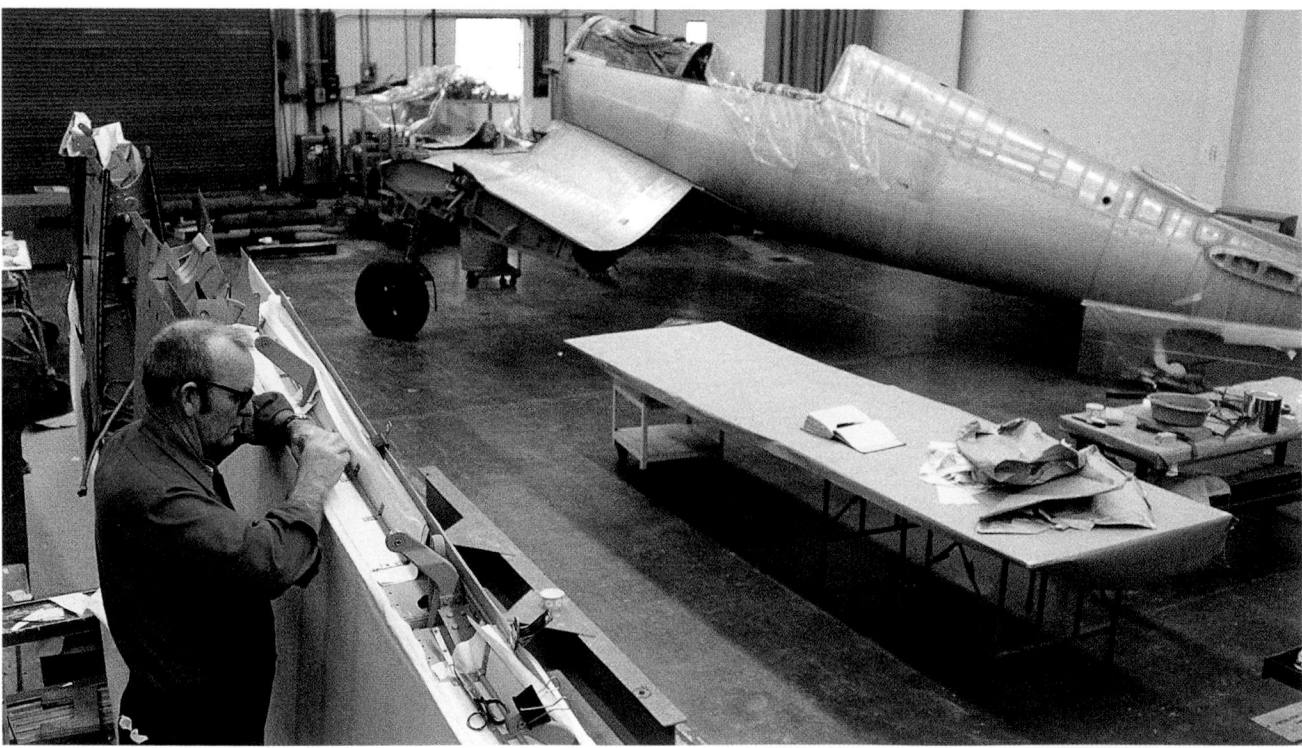

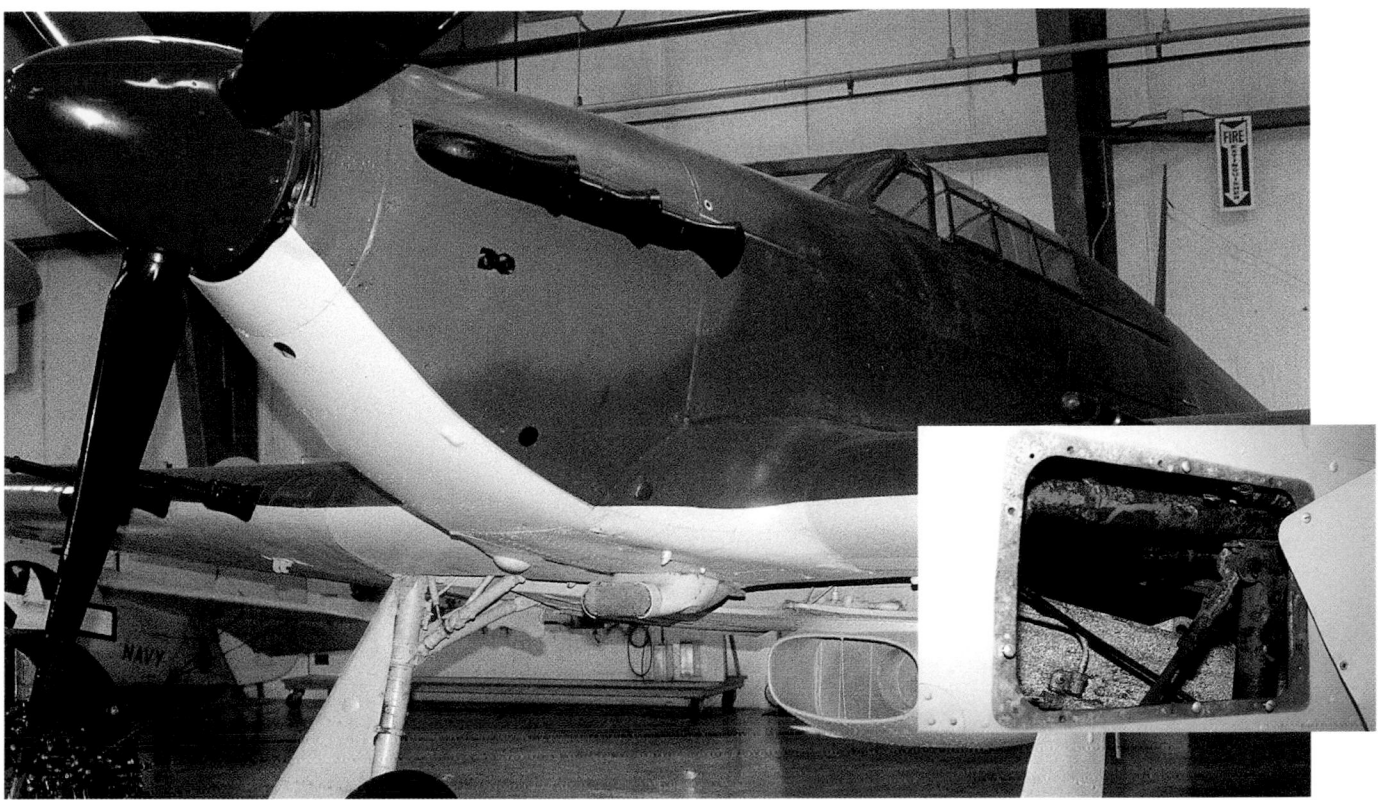

Take for instance cockpit details. Originality is often easily perceived by noting the remains of original chipped decals, traces of color marks that were once used as a form of reference, as well as other subtle details still in evidence. Once these details are cleaned away, the surface repainted and not reinstated from accurate notations, the reference to cockpit technology these details once documented may be lost. A complete restoration of these areas is so essential while details of what was found and notes made are still fresh in the mind of the technician. To do this work in part, thinking that these details will be added later, usually doesn't happen.

Anything short of a complete treatment becomes a cosmetic restoration. However, it is far better to leave areas just described in their present state, still reflecting aspects of how they were originally, than to paint over for cosmetic purposes and destroy confirmation of markings, colors, position where evidence of removed components, etc. Otherwise, when the interior can be restored, there is a lack of original information that cannot now be duplicated for lack of evidence. However, it is highly essential that these areas of deferred restoration are cleaned and stabilized against corrosion and further degradation, making sure that indicators of originality are not lost in the process. Having to exercise these precautions, one can see that half-way restorations of this type become overly complicated merely by having to work around the problems rather than resolving them in what should be this one-time work process.

This is an excellent example of the harm that a cosmetic restoration can do to an aircraft. Because of its pristine outward appearance, this Hawker Hurricane IIC remained an exhibit aircraft for more than 20 years before a preservation and restoration project for it began. The photo shows the condition of the engine mount (as seen through an inspection opening) compared to the outer painted surface.

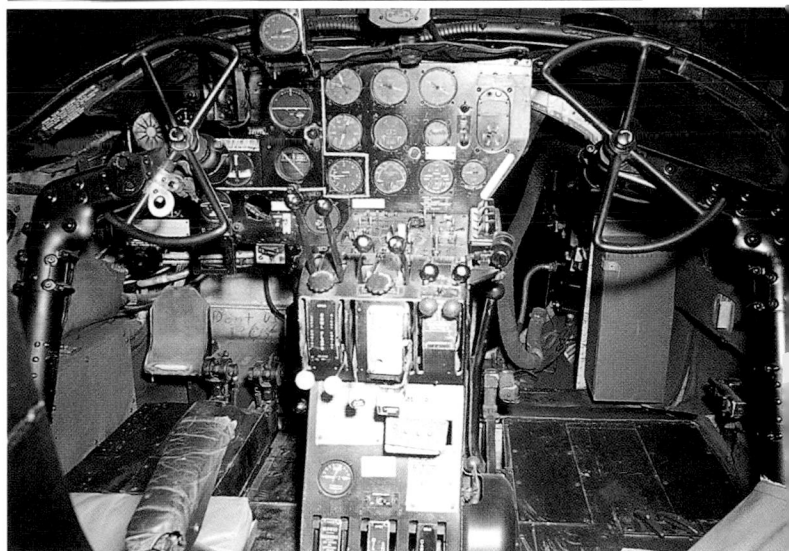

There are few examples of a Category I aircraft (historic) that are received by a museum in a Level 2 Condition. This is NASM's Martin B-26B Marauder Flak Bait *which upon completing its 202nd bombing mission over Europe, was flown to a port in France, disassembled, crated, and shipped back to the US for museum purposes. The cockpit reflects that unchanged condition.*

To be brutally honest about this, if the restoration of hidden components of the aircraft such as interiors and engines is deferred, will they ever be properly treated to safeguard their technology? If these aspects do not affect its general exhibit qualities, moving back to the project at a later date would be both a monumental and psychological effort. Who is the one person willing to accept this responsibility for a so-called half-way preservation and restoration that in the course of time becomes so damaging to the artifact? This should be established beyond all doubt.

The most damaging thing that can be done to an airplane, thus ending its original state, is to interrupt the work process for a lengthy period of time or perhaps even place the airframe and parts in storage until some point in the future. Technicians change jobs, and even if they do not, so much is dependent upon memory to determine how something appeared at the time it was disassembled. Do not stop the project until it is fully completed and accomplished according to the original plan. Do not change configuration plans in mid-stream. This surely will affect something that has already been accomplished according to the original plan.

Simple things like installing new fabric boots for which only fragments of the originals remained, or leaving a wiring bundle until another time, eventually depart from originality. How could a replacement boot be matched to that of the original by a technician different to the one who can remember how the rotted original fragments that disintegrated in this process were fabricated and attached? The same goes for reinstalling a complex electrical wire bundle. Nothing less than a complete restoration must be accomplished on the first effort.

In any first restoration, originality intended to be copied is bound to be disturbed. If intended to be renewed on subsequent work efforts, what then is the correct technique to follow? Normally, only the workmanship of the previous technician is available to be copied. One good example: sewing stitched-on fabric surfaces. Work from the original piece may have been available when replaced for the first time, yet it is possible that the person doing the work the second time used another sewing technique for expediency. How does the technician really know, and then how is originality matched? Careful record-keeping is therefore essential. If the new work is identical, say so. If deviations occur because of machine work and materials, be specific in descriptions. This is not as painful as it may sound, but it is so very essential as part of a restoration! See more on this in Chapter 10.

Before proceeding further, for reasons just stated, I must make it clear that a second or subsequent restoration should not even be considered at the time of this work process. You have heard it said, 'Do it right the first time, and it will not have to be repeated.' This is good advice to follow. But we must also be realistic. No matter how hard we may try, some of the materials used on aircraft, and those reapplied during the first restoration, have a limited life span. While the basic airplane structure can be preserved in the restoration process to last for hundreds of years, or better still, indefinitely, certain supportive materials are bound to degrade or disintegrate. These will be discussed later; but for up-front planning, let's take a look at what we can expect to deteriorate first. Here is a list of materials that, if kept in the average museum environment, may last 100 years, hopefully more, depending upon the material composition and the care given:

Rubber parts: tires, seals, grommets, hoses
Lubricants: mineral and organic
Fabric: surface coverings and interior appointments
Leather: coaming covers and interior details
Plastic: particularly clear panels
Composite metals: e.g. ESD[12] in Japanese aircraft
Paint, exterior: color shift, handling and dusting abuse
Wood veneers: exterior skin surfaces if degradation had already begun before being placed in a museum environment

By recognizing that there are limitations, we can plan more effectively other restoration work. For example, when tacking new fabric to a wooden aircraft frame, how many times can this process be repeated along an edge before irreversible splintering will occur? Go easy on the number and size of the tacks used for recovering. Remember, it is not going to fly, but instead it must last. Or should sticking to original methods, sizes and numbers of tacks be adhered to for accuracy, come what may? Whichever path you select, make well-written reasons to support your decisions, accompanied by descriptions and sketches of how the original was found at the time of disassembly. Save samples of the original fabric with stitches and hardware in protective covers with the written record.

There is a time-honored saying that I learned early in my experiences involving the restoration of museum aircraft, from my mentor Louis S. Casey, former Curator of Aircraft at NASM:

> Preserve rather than restore
> Restore rather than replace
> Replace only when necessary

This very clearly states what museum care concerning aircraft is all about. The preservation aspect is the most vital part of museum work. Proper storage and care is far less expensive and damaging to an aircraft than to have to change its original form through restoration brought about by museum neglect.

Suspending Exhibit Aircraft

A critical element of any museum is having sufficient space. If there is vertical clearance within the museum, there is a natural temptation to suspend one or more aircraft. Generally this is described as having the airplane in its natural environment simulating flight. The fact that it is surrounded by at least four walls and a stilled propeller is thought to be of little importance. What cannot be denied is that to follow such a practice allows more aircraft to be exhibited within the museum if the building's structural loads permit.

Accepting that suspending aircraft is going to be one possible choice, there are factors that should be considered at the point when planning the restoration process. Are there suitable suspension points within the aircraft structure? If not, now is the time to engineer hanging points into the structure for safe suspension of the airplane.

The Curatorial Guidelines should describe in detail what modifications, if any, are to be made to the structure. Generally this will require removal of some specified skin panels or cowling in order to reach selected points of the structure for attaching lift fittings. It would be very inappropriate to modify these original panels; instead, make replacement pieces for use while the airplane is suspended. Be sure to adequately tag these parts, then safely store them for future replacement on the airplane when returned to the ground.

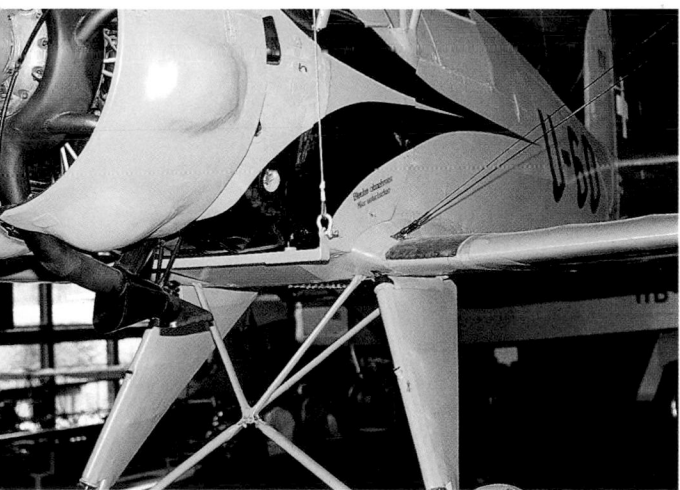

When suspending an aircraft for exhibit, great care must be taken to ensure that the structure does not have to take stress loads for which it was not designed. Here is a case where the Swiss Transport Museum placed safety first and added an exterior structure under the Bücker Bü 131B Jungmann to serve as the main lift points.

As an example, when planning to suspend the Mitsubishi A6M5 Zero belonging to NASM, one skin panel of each wing just above the landing gear attachment point of the wing spar was removed. In their place were new and temporary wing skin sections having the desired openings through which cables could pass from suspension fittings fabricated and bolted to the wing spar. In this fashion, the load of the structure rested where the ground load was designed for the airplane.

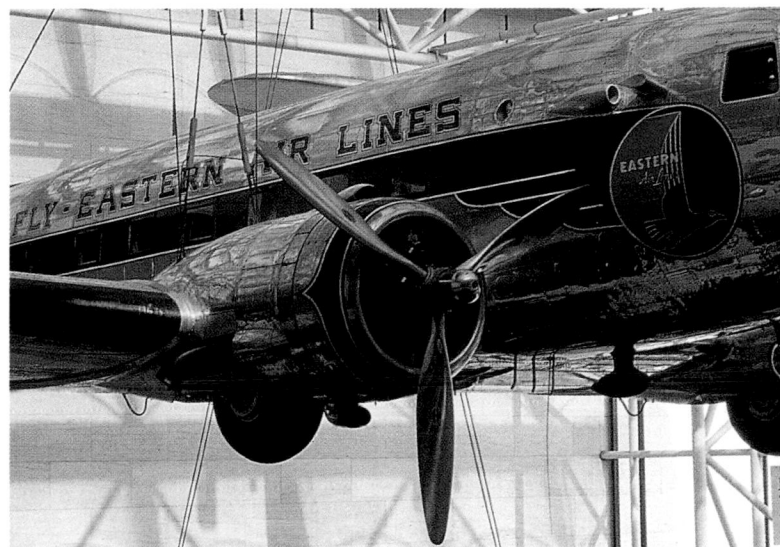

A double and balancing cable arrangement supports this Douglas DC-3 at NASM. Two plumb bobs (not visible) serving as gages are suspended from the ceiling above each wing-tip. Their weights hang free within cups glued to the wings. Should settling occur, the brightly-painted weights would begin to appear above the cups.

There is a tendency to suspend aircraft in an other-than-level attitude. Once an airplane is suspended, it will undoubtedly remain in that attitude for a very long time. It should not be surprising to realize that because of the designed light structures of aircraft, basically only flight and static load stresses are incorporated into the design, not sustained side loadings. The point is that nothing beyond a slight variance from a level attitude should be placed upon the structure for extended periods of time.

As a curator, there was always one major drawback that I saw in suspending an aircraft. Once in place, access to its cockpit, interior components, engine and the like was no longer possible. Try as we may to photograph these details for reference that may arise, there was always that certain angle, instrument serial number, or color sample that was not recorded beforehand. In a very definite way, the suspended aircraft becomes little more than a decoration. Its technology is kept from researchers until well into the future when it may again be placed on the ground for the access it deserves.

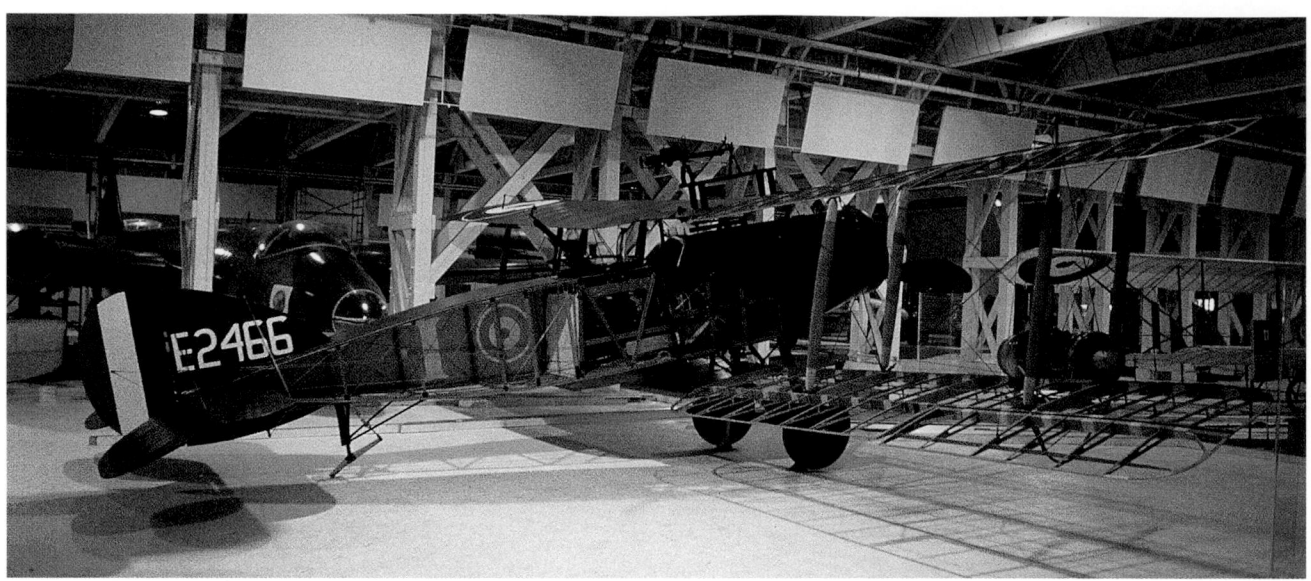

Cutaways, Sectionalized and Segmented Aircraft

To some, the dismemberment of an aircraft for the purpose of exhibiting a certain point seems sacrilegious. To others, it has great educational value as it permits the observation of selected technology. Walter Tuck, formerly with the Science Museum in London, has said that if only a part of the aircraft shows the technical advance made, then the whole of the airplane is not necessary to make the point. But for a collection to be attractive to the general visitor, it requires complete examples to illustrate its subject, so a 'bits and pieces' policy followed to extremes can be overdone.[13]

A mix of both is desirable, a balance that directly relates to the mission of the museum and the purpose of the aircraft in the collection. A good example can be found at the Deutsches Museum von Meisterwerken der Naturwissenschaft und Technik (German Museum of Achievement in Science and Technology), in Munich, Germany. Having limited gallery space (as do most air museums), among the complete aircraft the museum displays segments of aircraft showing technical aspects of certain structures.

Certainly a passenger jet transport could never be placed in the Deutsches Museum's exhibit building; yet by displaying a fuselage cross-section of about two passenger seats deep, showing the detail of the structure that surrounds the passengers and the cargo hold below the floor makes an interesting and educational exhibit for even the casual visitor. Added to this is the landing gear in the adjacent wing section that periodically retracts, something that an inquisitive passenger would never see, but only hears as a thump from inside. At NASM is the separated nose section of a Douglas DC-7 transport which visitors can enter. This is one of the more popular visitor attractions.

Younger generations sometimes do not appreciate that early airplanes were merely covered with fabric. The RAF Museum exhibits this reproduction Bristol F.2B in half-uncovered condition. This unnatural state has some distracting drawbacks since several museum visitors have offered to contribute financially towards its completion.

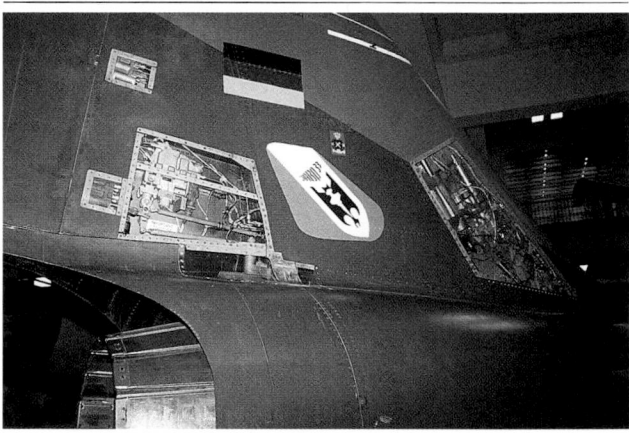

On display in the Deutsches Museum in Munich, this Lockheed F-104G Starfighter has had many of its inspection panels removed in order to show the complexity of supersonic fighters with all their systems, servos, and actuators crowding every available space.

This prototype Airbus A300 fuselage cross-section housed in the Deutsches Museum, reveals to visitors the structure of the fuselage around passengers and the baggage compartment. This type of exposure to the technical aspect of aircraft is an excellent teaching device.

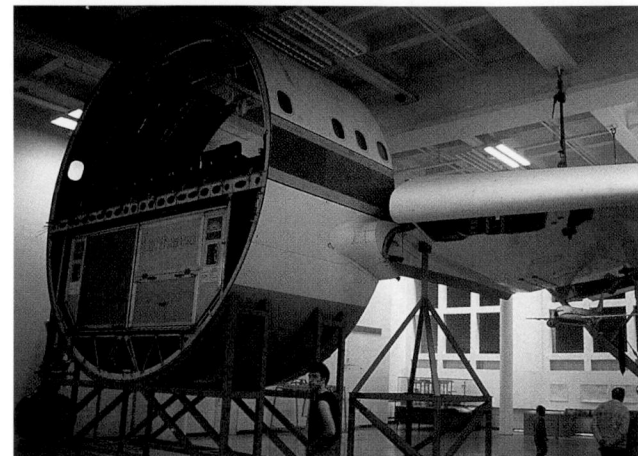

The danger, however, is that segments and cutaways may destroy the whole artifact as the disassembly of the airplane is often non-reversible. In my estimation, segmentation should never be carried out with a Category I (historical) aircraft. Recognizing that Category II (technical) aircraft were collected for their technical aspects, there are dangers in permanently removing parts in anticipation of special displays. For example, NASM's Douglas XB-42A, known as the Mixmaster because of its two contra-rotating propellers mounted behind the tail, is the sole survivor of the two that were built. To facilitate the movement of this airplane by truck from storage in Park Ridge, Illinois, to what is now the museum's Paul E. Garber Facility at Silver Hill, Maryland, its wings were cut from the fuselage and discarded. The airplane was looked upon merely for the technology it could impart by showing its landing gear retraction geometry, and the unusual engine installation which used two sets of five Bell P-39 driveshafts to turn the two propellers. This became an irreversible disassembly, making it impossible for current and future curators to have the option to ever exhibit this XB-42A as a complete airplane.

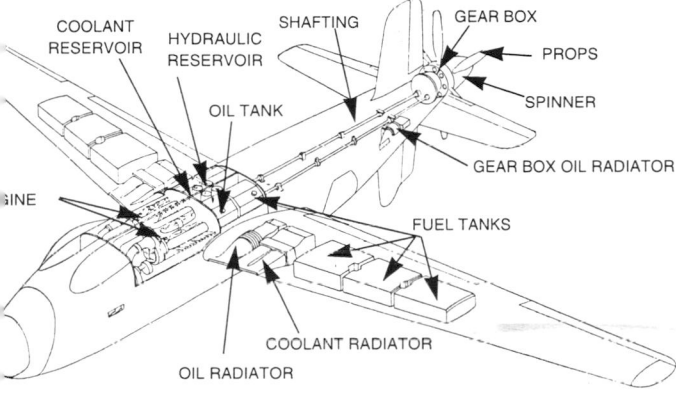

Quite novel in design was this Douglas XB-42A Mixmaster, saved for museum use only for the technology of its engine installation and landing gear retraction mechanism. There is no second chance of exhibiting this as a complete aircraft because its wings were discarded, a decision now irreversible.

In the case of segmenting, a safe solution is to restrict this procedure to Category III (i.e. generic) aircraft only. In cases where skin is to be opened, or even major structural sections removed for exhibition purposes, the process need not become irreversible. Remove the parts at attaching points and retain them for possible reattachment if needs change in the future.

To be even safer in respecting the preferences of future curators for safeguarding the collection, retain a second but complete example of the same type of airplane if the luxury of space permits. A good example of this is a Beechcraft center-section wing assembly that was common to several Beech-Twin models. This assembly could be a separate technical exhibit showing part of an aircraft structure. This wing center-section was first used for the Model 50 Twin Bonanza, borrowed for production of the Model 65 and Model 80 Queen Airs and the U-8 Seminole, and naturally was used in certain Swearingen refinements of these models. Attached to this common assembly were different fuselage shapes, various size engine mounts, wing spar extensions and main landing gears for these respective models; an efficient aspect which saved engineering costs in such a competitive market. To give greater impact to this exhibit would be to have one of these aircraft nearby in complete form so that visitors can relate the exposed structure to the real aircraft and the related importance.

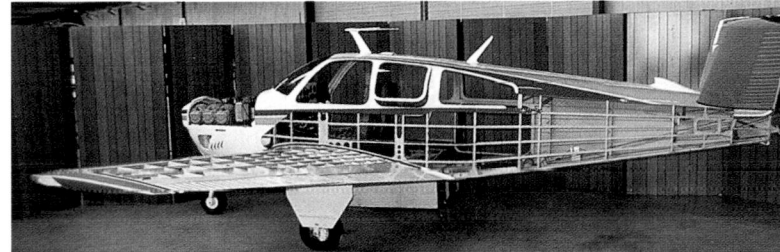

This is a factory-prepared cutaway example of a Beechcraft Bonanza that is ideally suited for educational purposes to show the basic structure of an aircraft.

What was once only a portion of a derelict Bristol Beaufighter has been wisely turned into a cutaway exhibit which clearly shows cockpit details and structural technology of World War II. This is a RAF Museum exhibit.

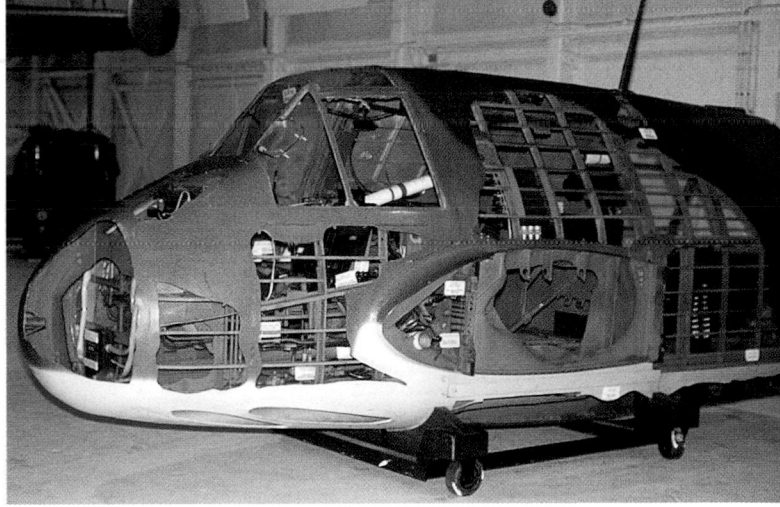

While serving as an NASM curator, decision-making about displaying museum aircraft was always a vital function of the job, one to which I gave considerable thought and attention. The correct decision often seemed to be weighted in favor of reversibility. This applies to conservation measures (taken or not taken) as well as restoration configurations. ***Don't make irreversible decisions now***

with which curators in the future are left to cope! The logic is simple. With aviation still in its infancy as compared to other technologies, what might appear to be irrelevant today could be very important in the future. The airplane dissected now in order to exhibit its structure could be far more important in the future as a complete aircraft.

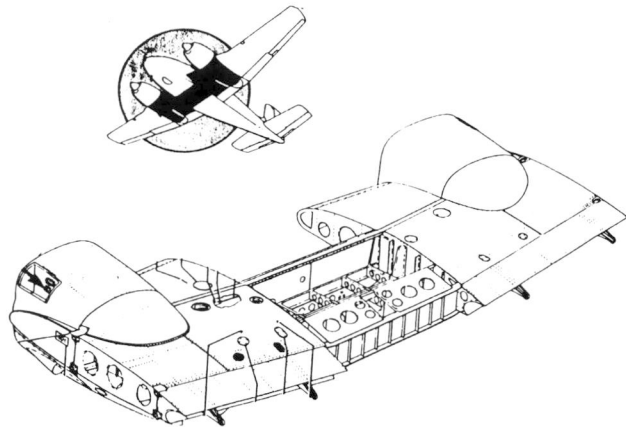

Parts of aircraft demonstrate technical advances as well. For example, this portion from the Beech Twin main wing-section would illustrate how this well-engineered component was adapted for use in several similar-designed aircraft.

Just so much junk in the eyes of the unknowing are these remains of an RAF Handley Page Hampden recently recovered from Russia. Since no other evidence of this significant RAF bomber remains, the cost to prepare it for exhibit will be great, but its value will be far greater. (RAF Museum)

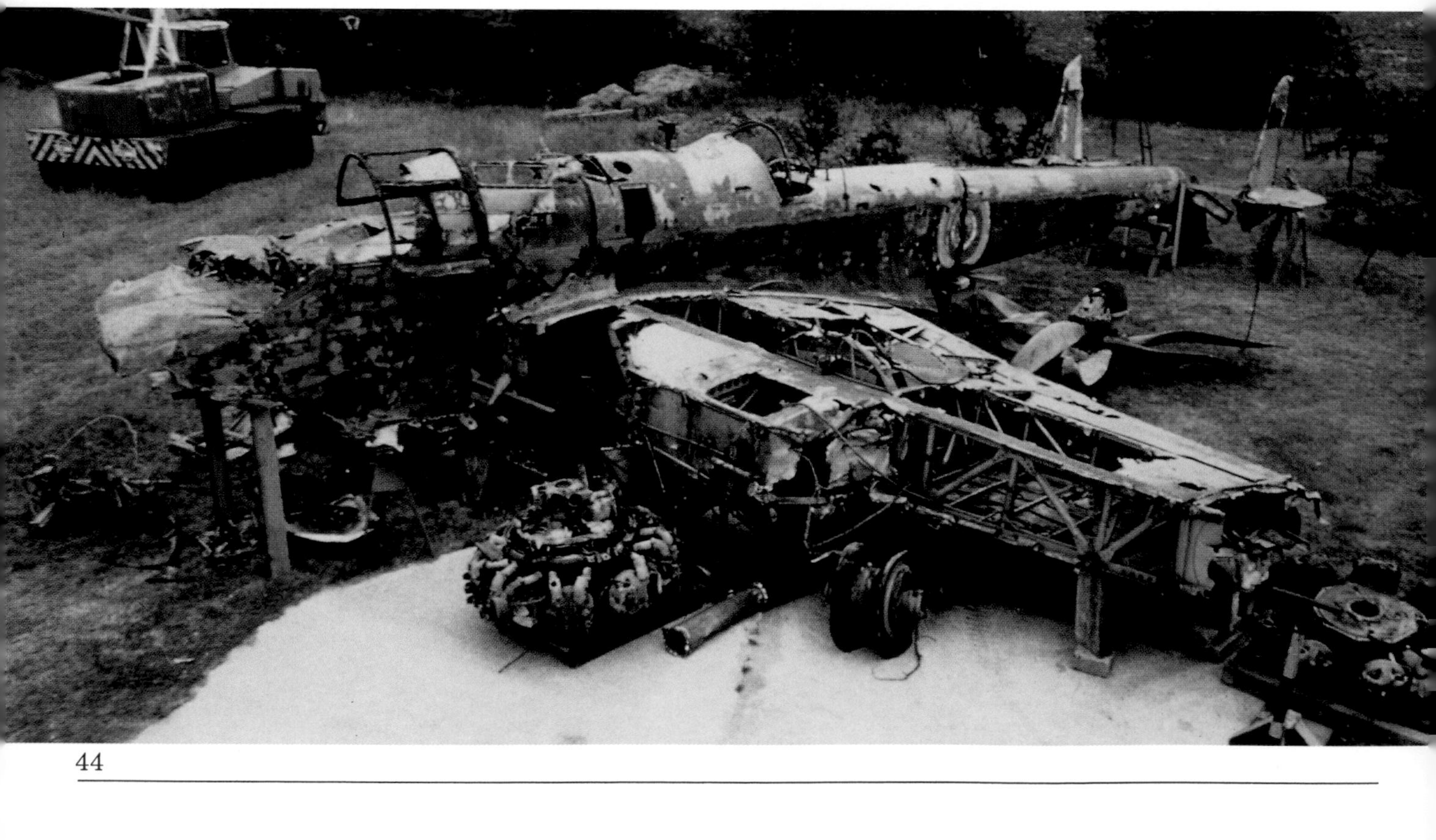

Price vs. Value

There is another museum factor that is not always looked at in a practical sense. What comes to mind are fledgling museums that, when groping for a start, will bring in truck-loads of aircraft wreckage, with magnificent plans for rebuilding this scrap into museum artifacts, yet they have limited resources. Here are a few thoughts in this regard that may be useful guidance.

Museums should be run with the same degree of care and professionalism as any other organization.

At the start of World War II in Europe, the Handley Page Hampden was one of three types of twin-engine bombers that equipped the RAF until the four-engine varieties came into service. Today, not one complete Hampden survives. Photo is reversed for comparison purposes. (RAF Museum)

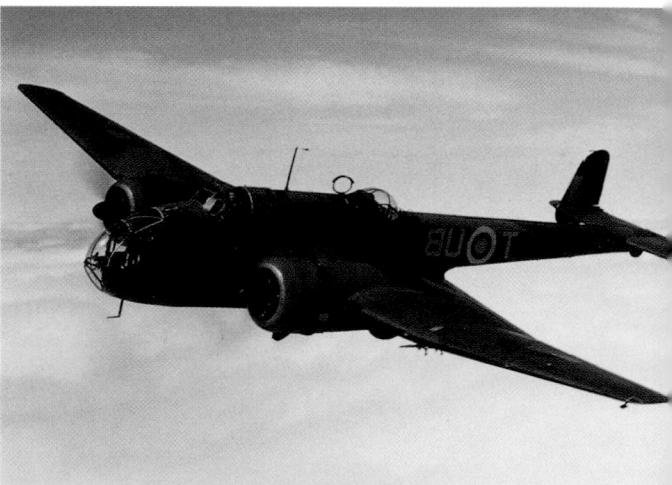

However, we differ from many organizations in being 'not-for-profit' and for having as our main 'product' objectives which can be 'priced' but which in many (if not most) cases are also of exceptional value. We must be aware of the cost of what we do and the price of the objects we care for. However, we need to balance these tangible elements with that most difficult of judgments — 'value.'

Michael A. Fopp, Director of the RAF Museum, gave me an example of museum 'value'. The museum had recently recovered a crashed Handley Page Hampden from Russia. This machine is a Category III aircraft and in Level 4 Condition, yet these are the only remains of a Hampden in Europe. The recovery was costly and the restoration will take many years and huge resources. In simple business terms, Fopp explained, the price is not right; but as an addition to the UK's national collection the 'value' is huge.

The reason for raising this issue is to point out that curators need to be skilled in differentiating between price and value. Traditionally we have tended to let value rule our decision-making, but this will leave us vulnerable. We must be aware of the costs (all of them!) so that we may argue our case in a more business-like manner with those who have grown up with the monetaristic attitude which has become fashionable in recent years. Accountants and lawyers now make a disproportionately high number of decisions for organizations. They can only be countered by thoroughly professional and business-like responses from museums.

Will it Fly?

There are diverse viewpoints about flying museum aircraft that must be considered. The debate appears to rest on a definition of terms. What is a historic aircraft? Those unique airplanes that are famous for historic flights or other singular events leave little doubt. Once that unique airplane is destroyed, it is gone forever. Its historic significance cannot be replaced by another airplane. For an airplane type of which more than one survives, these should not be classed as 'historic'; perhaps the term 'classic' is more appropriate. The argument against flying a classic where more than a few exist becomes weak.

In the case of NASM, a number of individual types without specific histories (Category III) for which others exist elsewhere and perhaps are still flying are looked upon as being future sole survivors. The fact that these airplanes have flown is a recorded fact. Airplanes being flown for today's generations will ultimately deplete the supply. Therefore, aircraft held in non-flying collections are those which will be appreciated in the future when all vintage or classic flying aircraft cease to exist.

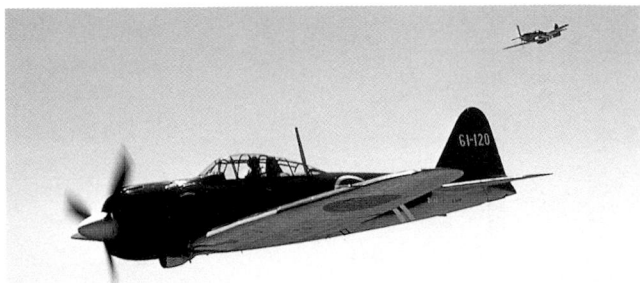

Few people born after World War II have the opportunity to see or hear a Japanese Mitsubishi A6M Zero in flight. This is one of two flyable examples of this famous fighter, yet there are approximately 33 examples of various models of the Zero that are kept safely in various museums. Shown here is the 'Planes of Fame' A6M5 being chased by a P-51D Mustang. ('Planes of Fame')

Static display remains the most effective form of conservation! Until this mishap, this Bolingbroke (Canadian-built Bristol Blenheim) was the only flying example of its type.

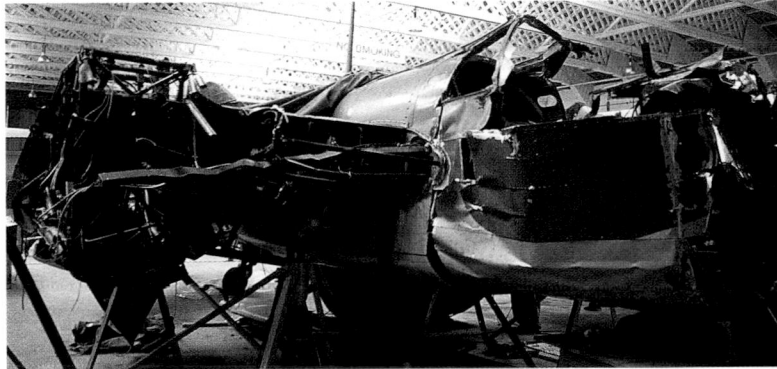

There remains the question of how 'original' are the vintage aircraft that are still being flown, a virtue perhaps already lost? Consider, for example, a Vought F4U Corsair. This is regarded as an 'all-hydraulic' airplane, and its safety would certainly be jeopardized if flown with 50-year-old hydraulic hoses, connectors and seals. To remain airworthy, these parts would need to be replaced with newer items made from far better materials than the originals. Aging electrical wiring would not be deemed reliable, and would have to be replaced. These alterations and replacements reduce originality. To find original, functional, vacuum tube avionics of an operational airplane today would be very rare if not possible. To maintain functional reliability, modern solid-state electronics would be the only safe way to go. A quick glance at the instrument panel would probably reveal some modern instrumentation. In some cases there are government standards that would dictate modification of the original structure before the airplane could be licensed for flight. Viewed from the outside, the airplane structure appears to be 'original,' but how much original technology, particularly in systems, has been lost on the inside?

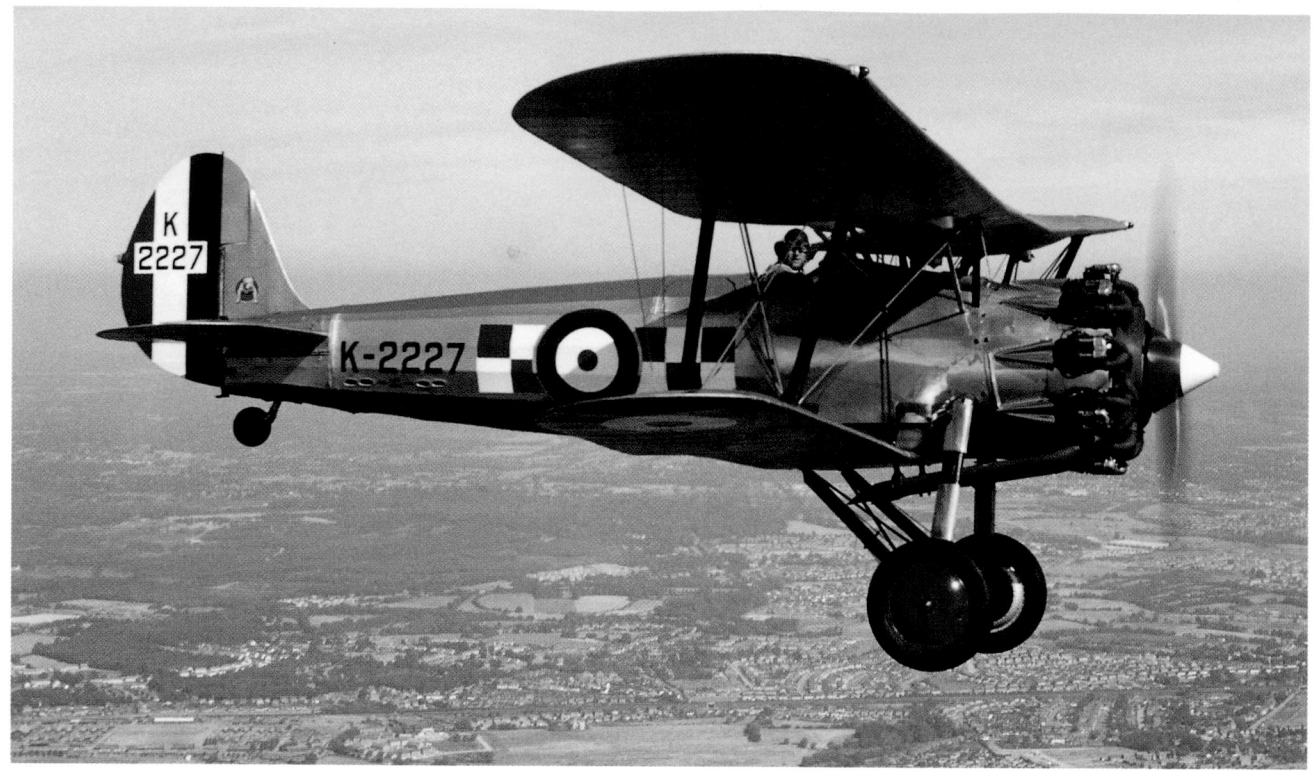

We can concede that flying vintage aircraft has some educational value. But how that is looked upon in the museum's charter must be the deciding factor. Many collections and privately-owned vintage aircraft are flown for the rightful enjoyment of flying them and watching them fly. I am among those who share that enthusiasm. How fulfilling the sound and smell of the engine and actually seeing in flight that familiar shape normally only seen in pictures and videos.

Within the museum community little argument is heard when deciding not to fly a sole survivor of a type, yet this has and does happen. A prime example often used is that of the Bristol Bulldog, one of the most famous RAF fighters of the inter-war period. By the 1960s this machine was the only surviving example in the UK, with another modified variant in Finland. The original manufacturer restored the aircraft to flying condition and donated it to one of the very few (in those days) collections of aircraft which actually flew their airplanes.

A few months after the Bulldog's first flight since the restoration it went to the Farnborough Air Show as a star attraction. In front of a huge crowd it spun in during one of its displays. The pilot survived but the aircraft was damaged beyond repair. The remaining parts were dispersed to other museums and private owners.

Recently, an inventory was made of surviving Bulldog parts which by now included a couple of undamaged (unused) wings from RAF stores and those parts purchased back from owners or donated to this cause, and it seemed feasible to consider

The sole surviving flyable Bristol Bulldog, a significant between-the-wars RAF fighter. The thought of loss, should it occur, was not as appreciated in the 1960s and before as has become the case in more recent years. (RAF Museum)

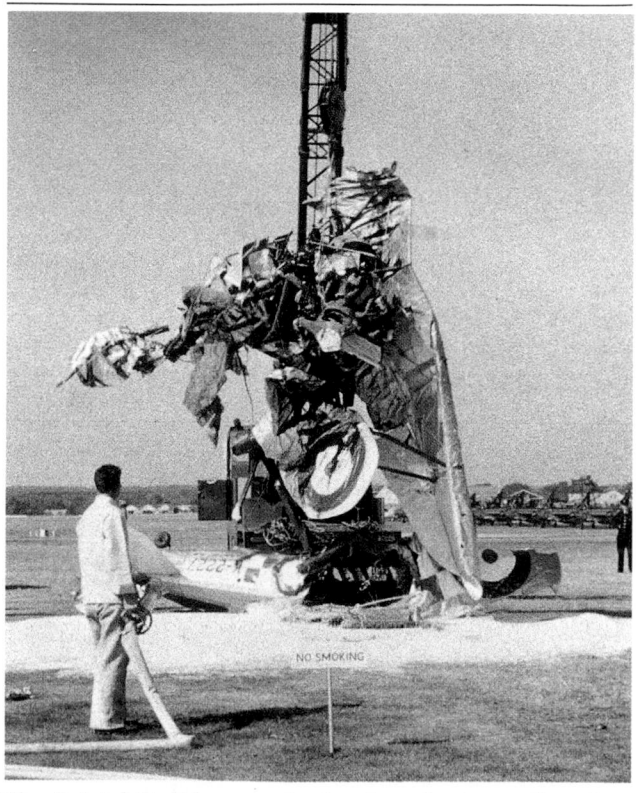

The Bristol Bulldog survived a few short months after restoration to flying condition before this mishap occurred at a Farnborough Air Show. This loss was a hard lesson that brought about a greater appreciation for not flying sole survivors. (RAF Museum).

rebuilding the Bulldog. A contractor has now commenced the work, and one day new life might be found in a Bristol Bulldog for exhibit in the RAF Museum at Hendon. To preclude such events happening again, it may be that countries should have a mechanism for compensating owners of rare aircraft and drawing them into safe public ownership.[14]

Another viewpoint on this matter was expressed to me by Air Vice-Marshal Ron Dick, CB, RAF (Ret'd), an avid aviator and historian. His feelings are that certain artifacts must be 'embalmed' for posterity, but it is also true that something equally valuable is being lost in the process. Movement, sound, feel, smell — the sorrow is that we cannot always have it both ways. We need to preserve these aircraft, but they are dead creatures, as dead as the elephant in the entrance to a museum of natural history. If all live elephants were gone tomorrow, he would be an invaluable record of an extraordinary beast; but anyone who has seen an elephant, alive and in its natural environment, could not but say that he is the merest shadow of his former self. There is no substitute for the living, breathing animal.

On the other hand, Stephan Wilkinson has written[15] that the Science Museum in London displays a Spitfire IA and a Hurricane I that still bear the oil, cordite, and dust of the day they were taken off the flight-line. They haven't been touched since, and they are vastly more legitimate artifacts than all the world's chromed and re-engined, Imroned and Loraned[16] 'restorations'. You'll never hear their Rolls-Royce Merlins make the sound of ripping gingham — the inevitable rationalization of the 'you gotta hear 'em fly' crowd — but it doesn't matter. These airplanes were really there, truly part of history.

So the different concepts go on, each totally correct from their respective point of view. One thing for sure seems apparent, however. Through the major holdings of such museums that do not fly their aircraft, generations ahead will be assured of having so-called 'embalmed' aircraft to look at and feel that will help them imagine the excitement long after flying examples become extinct. When completing a major restoration of an aircraft at NASM, with the normal preservation safeguards taken in the process, I could not help but feel with great satisfaction that I was looking at what one day would be the sole survivor of its type.

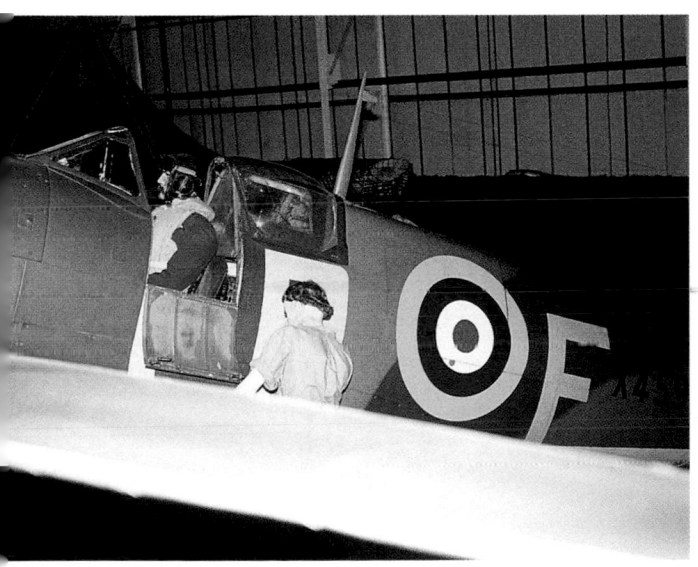

This Spitfire I, along with a Hurricane I in the Battle of Britain Gallery of the RAF Museum, Hendon, is displayed in a diorama presentation complete with pilot ready to start, being helped by a female member of the groundcrew. Such settings bring life and realism to the otherwise static aircraft.

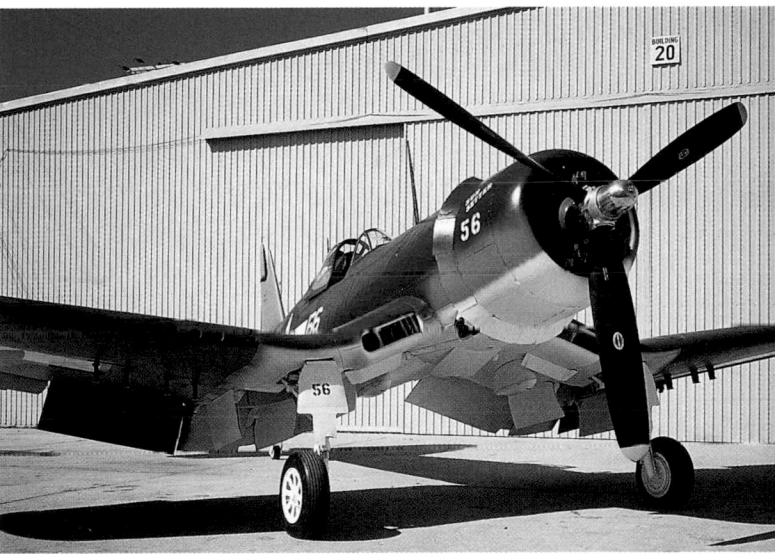

As many original components as possible were retained in this Vought F4U-1D Corsair restoration by NASM. Since it was not to fly, hydraulic hoses, electrical wire bundles and the like are original. These would have to be replaced if it were to be flown.

Dry rot, rusted metal, and fragmented pieces are what stand out the most with this Albatros D.Va belonging to NASM. It would seem easier to build an all new airplane than to restore. But with time, effort and ingenuity, the greater share of the original material was saved. (NASM, SI)

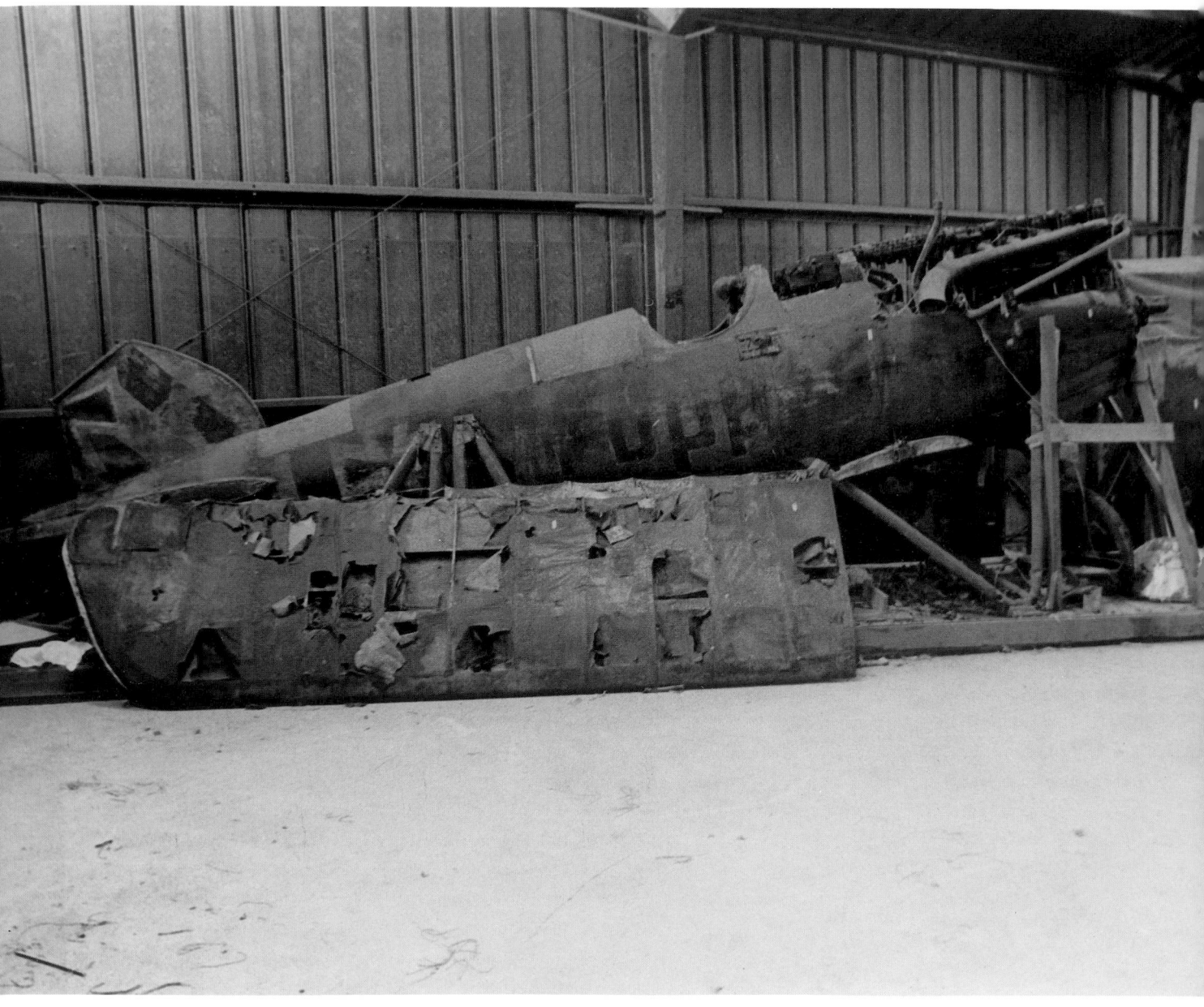

CHAPTER 3
Before the Teardown

Some of the most remembered aspects of any restoration are the days in which the project is just beginning. In some cases it may seem an impossible task to reform the broken and decayed pieces that once were an airplane, to bring it back to its restored original self.

I recall the opening days of the Albatros D.Va restoration. Nothing could be more intimidating than its deteriorated and crumpled appearance. How could these broken parts become a real airplane once again? The task would be one of the most intensive that NASM had ever undertaken. Here was an airplane, one of the few in any museum collection, that actually saw combat during World War I. We knew nothing of its wartime history, yet as this project continued we would unearth from its structure enough details of its past to formulate and document its story. During the restoration process, we learned that the airplane had been shot down; a bullet had passed though its fuel tank. This single bullet hole allows us to reconstruct an important part of the aircraft's history — how it came into Allied hands. Fuel systems of this type had to be pressurized in order to force-feed fuel to the carburetor. The bullet hole caused the tank to lose pressurization and the engine failed immediately. The airplane was thus forced to land while flying behind enemy lines.

Continued examination of the aircraft parts as the restoration progressed helped piece together the workings of the throttle system. A lever on the control stick was identified as the throttle during early inspection of what remained of this aircraft. It was not until the many details belonging to this airplane were restored and placed in their original positions, however, that an auxiliary throttle was recognized on the left of the cockpit that, when engaged, provided an emergency linkage in case the stick-mounted throttle handle failed.

With each day of working on this project, as with so many other aircraft undergoing restoration, these details continue to become evident and when

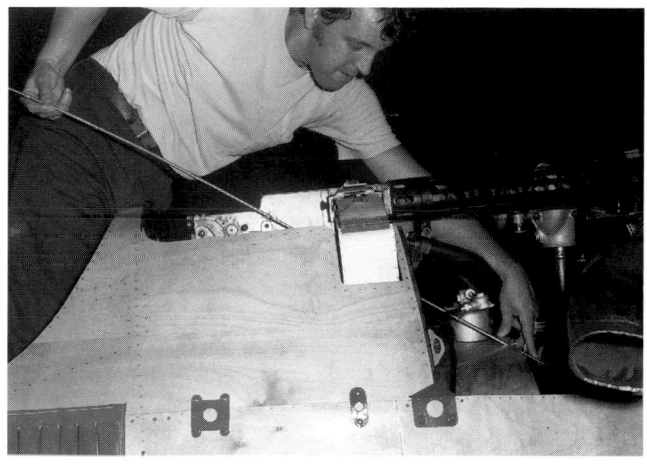

The trajectory of the bullet that brought this airplane down is illustrated by Restoration Technician Richard Horigan with this metal rod. The puncturing of the pressurized fuel tank, beneath Rich's left hand, brought about fuel starvation to the engine. Damage of this type is left unchanged.

added together bring greater importance to these functional objects. They not only take on more meaning as an aircraft of the past, but have a personal storyline of their own. What better way to preserve this knowledge than in a book about the airplane? Such was the case with this Albatros D.Va[17] along with other well-deserved books of this type that focus on restored aircraft and the unique information newly revealed in this process.

Across the Atlantic Ocean, one of the recently completed restorations of the RAF Museum is a rare Supermarine Southampton. Here the original objective of restoring a complete airplane changed to the objective of displaying only the restored original parts. With even that reduced effort, more than 10 years were spent on the project.

The Southampton was one of those monstrous yet graceful multi-engine flying boats that emerged after World War I. Designed by Reginald J. Mitchell

Cockpits of these early aircraft were quite austere. This left-side view of the cockpit shows the poker-like handle which serves as the emergency throttle linkage. This is only engaged when used instead of the throttle on the control column.

This view shows the left side of the gutted cockpit at the start of the restoration. When comparing the completed project with 'before' pictures, a great feeling of accomplishment is justified. (NASM, SI 83-16452-27)

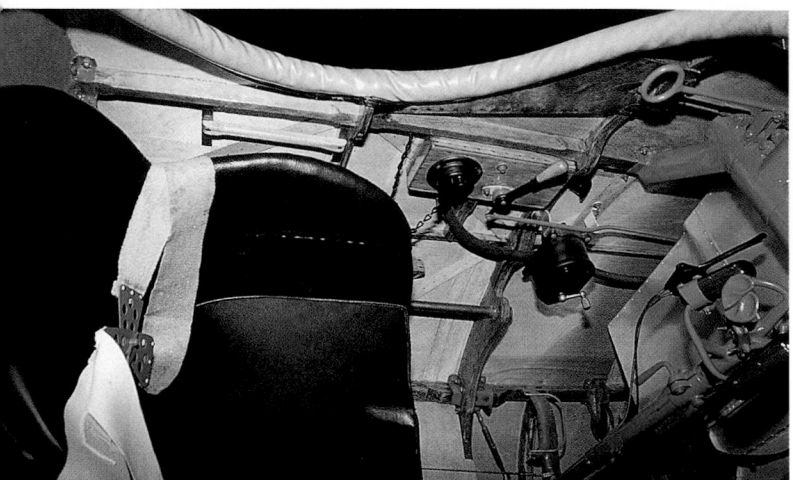

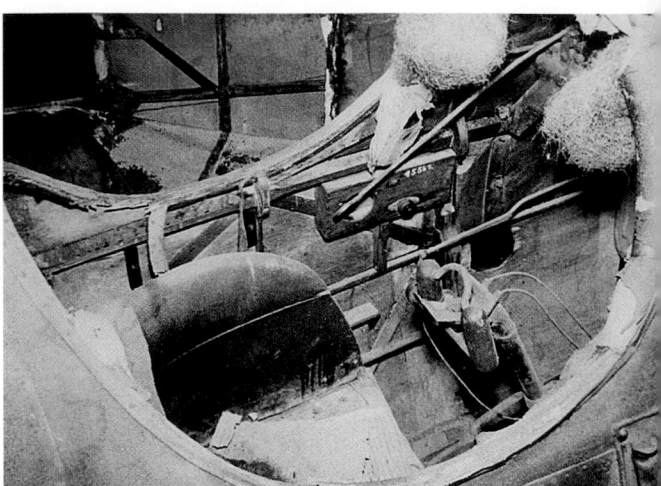

of Spitfire fame, it was used by the RAF in the inter-war years to 'police' the British Empire. The boats ranged over the whole world, principally to the British colonies in Asia and the Far East. The original Southamptons were made of wood, but after a few years of operation, the wood became waterlogged and aircraft performance deteriorated. They were then refitted with metal hulls. Before this happened, the RAF Museum aircraft was seriously damaged in a gale in home waters and scrapped. A man bought the hull and turned it into a houseboat by adding a roof, windows and a front door!

In the late 1960s the yet-to-open RAF Museum received a call from a local council informing them that they were about to take an old man into care because he could no longer look after himself and that, as he had not paid his mooring fees, his house-

Having served for many years as a houseboat, this Supermarine Southampton hull was retrieved by the RAF Museum in 1967 with the intention of making a full restoration. This is the only wooden-hull flying boat relic that survives in the UK. (RAF Museum)

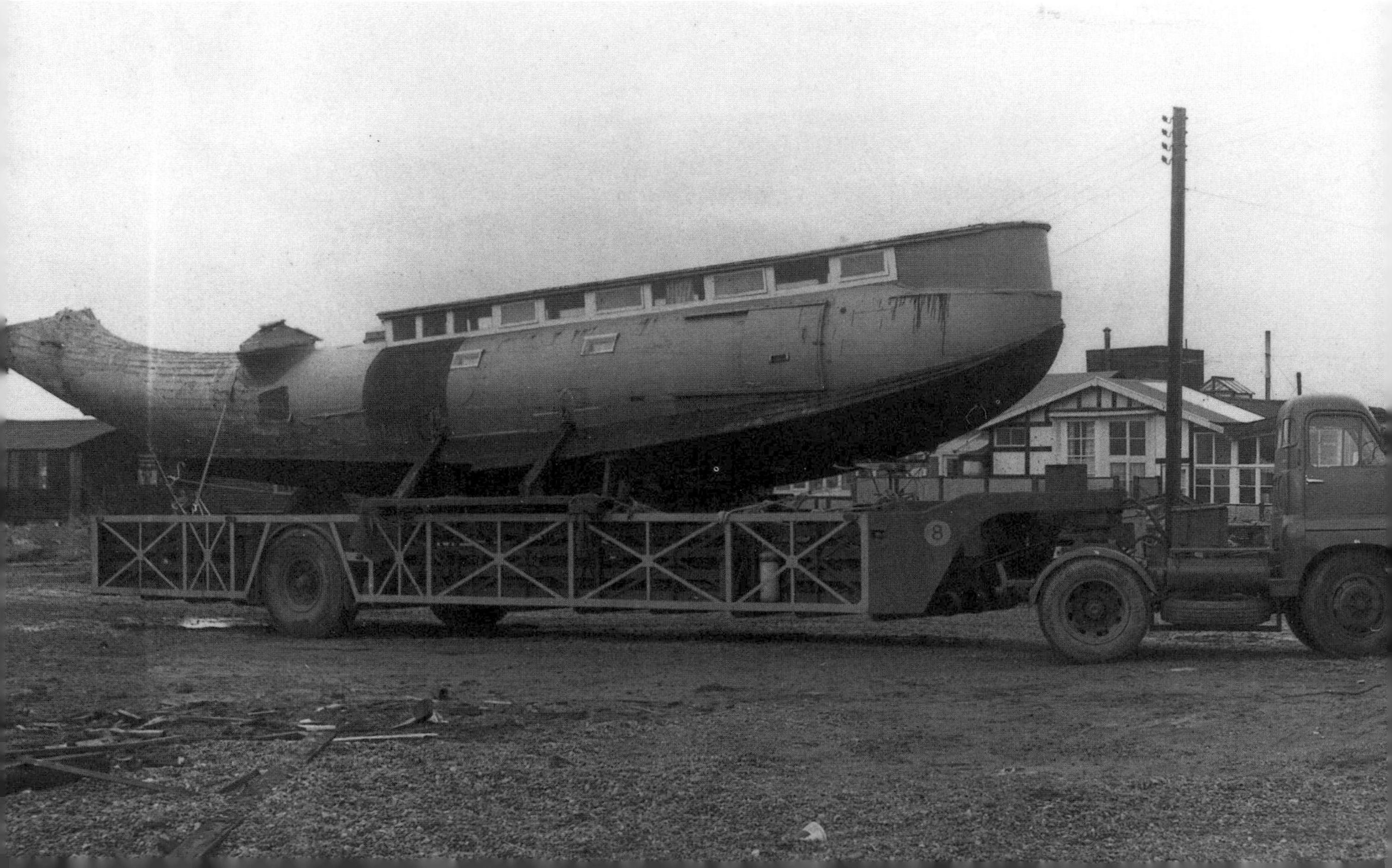

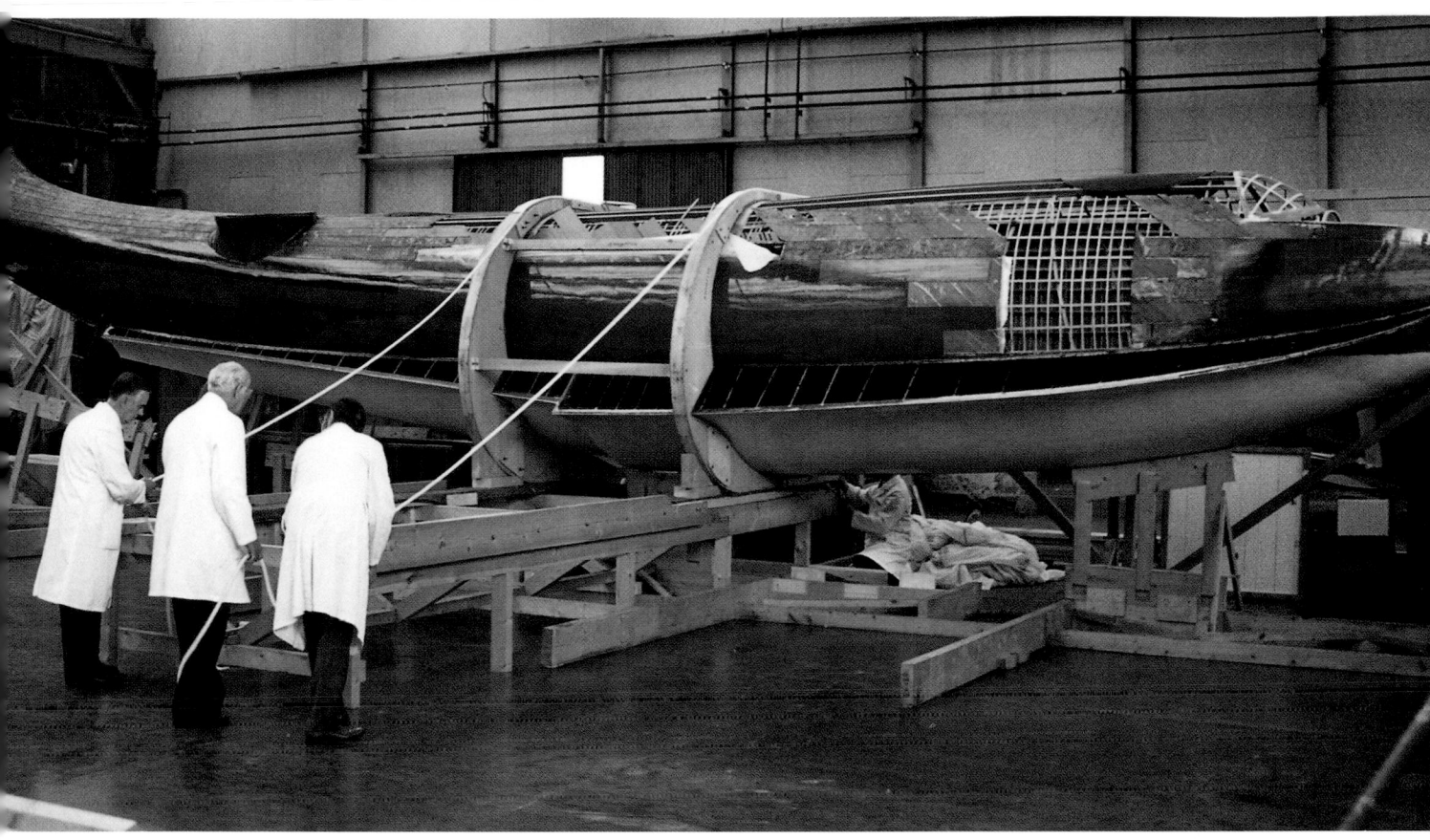

After seven years of drying, the hull of the Southampton is shown here in the RAF Museum's shop at RAF Cardington. Following restoration and conservation of the 'planing bottom' in 1989, the hull was rolled over for final work on the upper surfaces and interior. (RAF Museum)

boat was to be scrapped. However, some intelligent and knowledgeable person thought perhaps the museum staff might wish to inspect the house. Imagine their surprise when this was discovered to be the last surviving wooden-hulled British flying boat!

The first difficult task was to remove the house additions and to stabilize the stressed-skin wooden structure in order that the hull could be stored for the drying-out phase of the conservation. The drying-out took seven years. The restoration took a further 10 years of painstaking attention to detail. The hull alone required 75,000 No. 2½-inch (12.7 mm) brass countersunk wood screws and 150,000 ½-inch (12.7 mm) copper nails. The techniques for laminating the two layers of ¼-inch (6.35 mm)-thick mahogany boards between linen had to be rediscovered. The original fish glues had to be analyzed and remanufactured. Mistakes made by the original shipwrights were discussed to determine whether these errors should be rectified or not (they weren't, by the way) and the damage carried out to convert her to a houseboat had to be repaired.

It was during this project that the RAF Museum's philosophy of 'restoration vs conservation' changed.

The project had been so lengthy that during the process, three generations of curators had passed through the staff. The initial intention was to restore the hull and build new wings and tail surfaces to produce a complete aircraft. As the restoration developed, the resources needed for an all-new replicated set of gigantic wings were better appreciated. A new concept was considered and enacted. As a result, the hull and tail are now exhibited in the Hendon Main Hall. The huge dimensions of the complete aircraft will be demonstrated by laying a 'shadow' of the missing 72-ft (22m) wings, full-size, on the floor around the hull.[18] The decision to depart from the original plan is justified because of the effort needed. It is a decision that at some future time could be reversed, since reproduction wings and available engines can be added.

These finished projects, the Albatros D.Va and Supermarine Southampton, are the rewards for arduous and painstaking aircraft restorations. As discussed in the previous chapter, the overall objectives for projects such as these have already been formulated in the Curatorial Guidelines. Now is the time to look at more tangible objects for reaching restoration objectives. Prior to beginning the disassembly of the airplane beyond its present condition, there are certain shop details that should be prepared for. Let's pause a moment and consider these before getting too anxious to start work on the airplane.

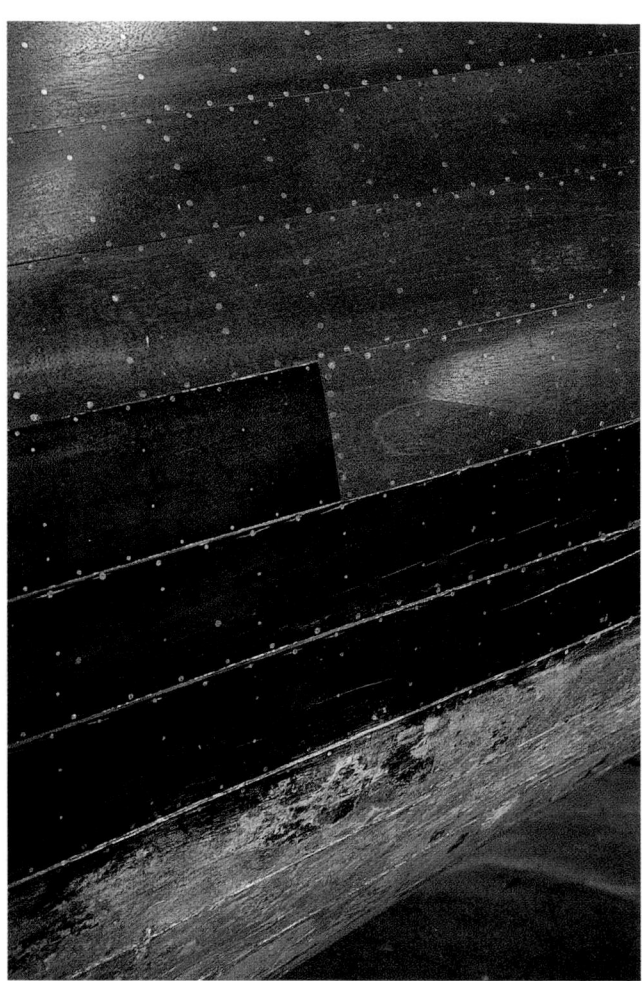

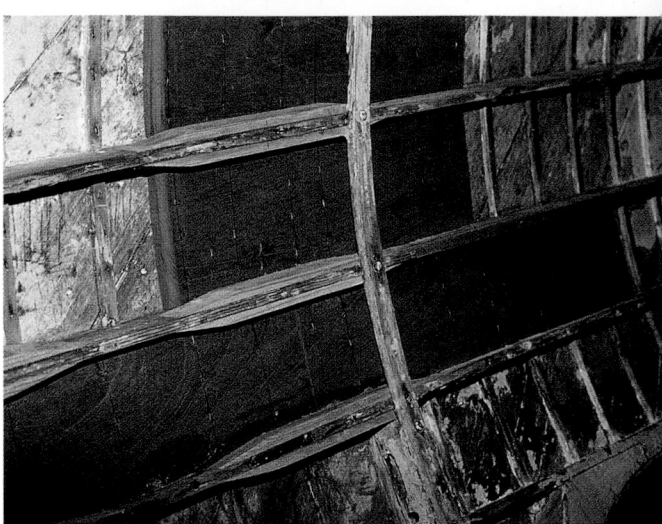

Extremes of the hull structure of the Southampton are apparent in these two views. To the left is the exterior showing visual differences in restored and unrestored areas. Dark wood is restored original. The interior view at right leaves little doubt as to original and new material. Note the splices over fractured stringers.

BELOW:
Only the restored hull and all-new triple tail will represent the twin-engine Southampton biplane flying boat of the between-wars period. To build the complex wings as reproductions only was not considered effective in man-hours and money. This curatorial decision is sound yet safely reversible. (RAF Museum)

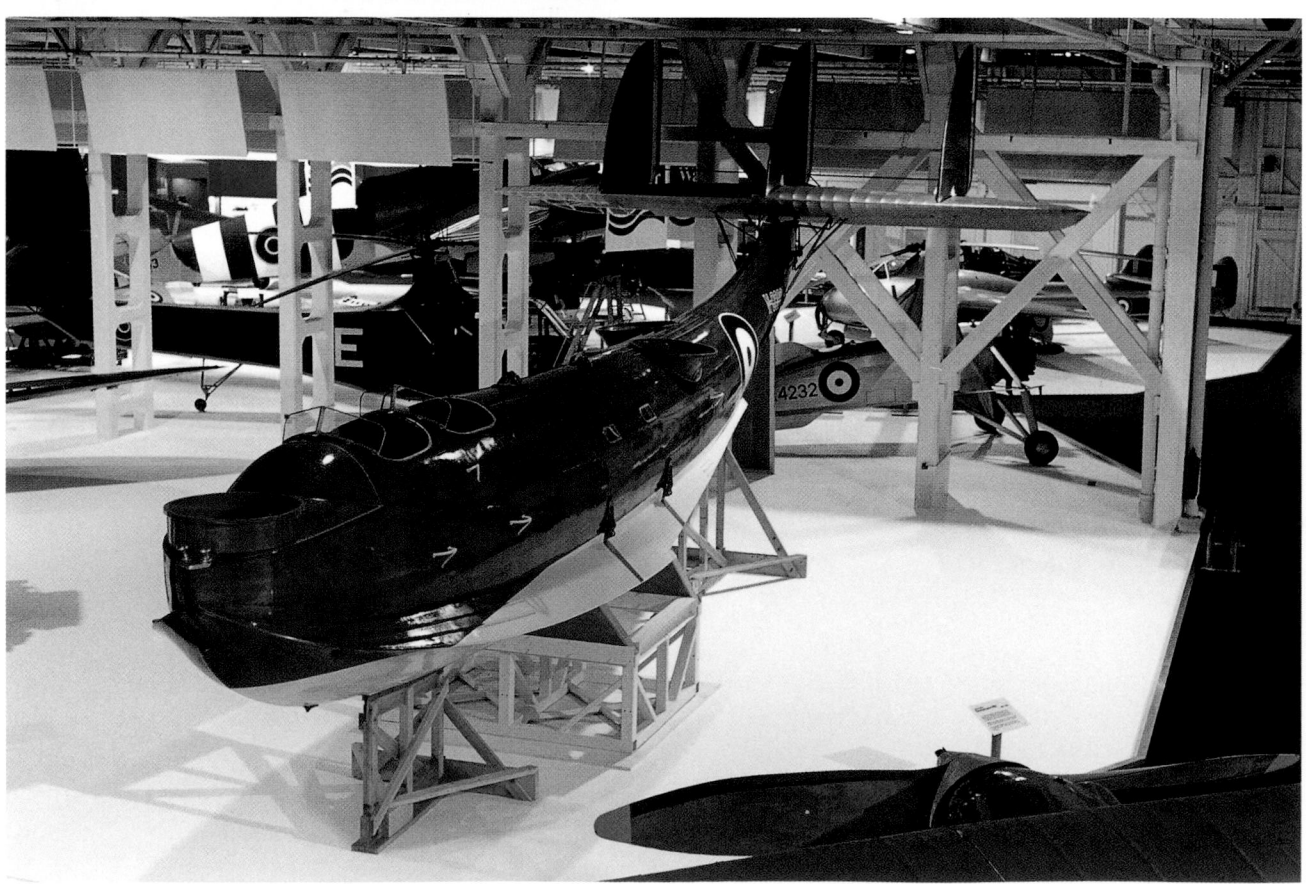

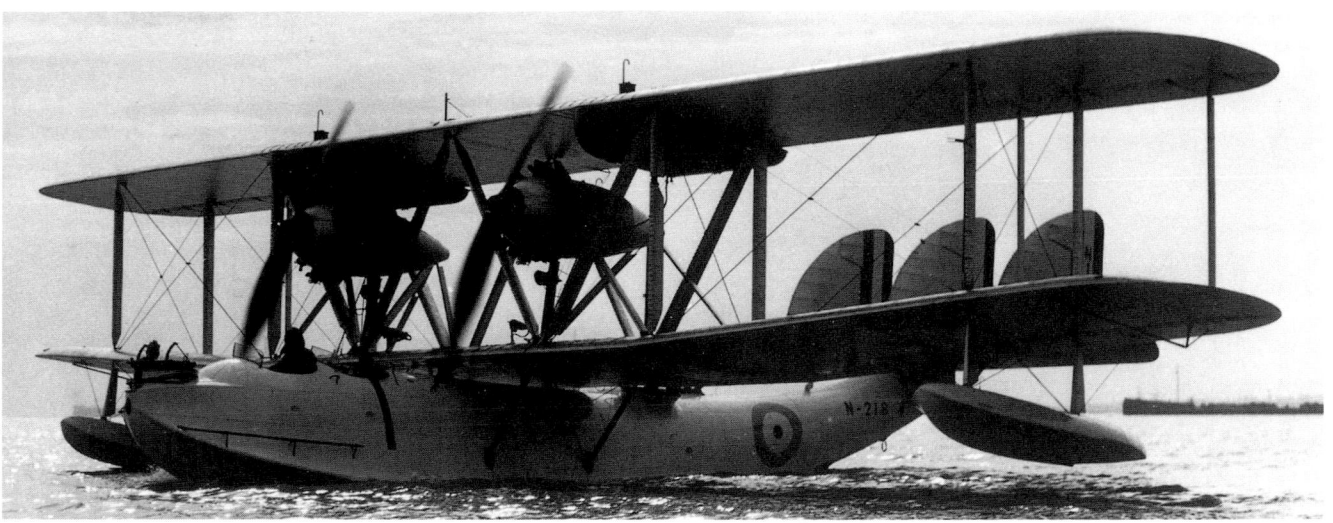

One of the Supermarine Southhamptons in operational service with the RAF in the late 1920s. (NASM, S.I. 96–15450)

Photography

If the restoration is being done under contract, the requirement for progressive photographs will probably have been covered in the contract for reporting purposes. But there is more to be considered.

To begin with, baseline photographs taken at this early point to document the overall condition of the aircraft and its parts are of major importance. Questions may arise at a later date such as, was there an antenna mast or missing panel when this project began?

A case in point: When the recently restored Kawanishi N1K2-Ja 'George' fighter belonging to the National Museum of Naval Aviation entered the restoration shop, it lacked a canopy, windshield, and major components of the propeller hub. Early photos of this airplane taken when it first left US Navy hands nearly 20 years ago for several aborted restorations show these items were in place. Knowing that these parts existed at a given time, the airplane's travels were traced and eventually the missing parts were located in the personal shops of those who intended to restore these components.

These baseline photographs are the source from which to find many similar answers. There will also come a day when there will be a need for these early photos to compare with the finished work and to complement a very transformed airplane. Consider what those final photo poses for the aircraft may be, and take similar perspectives of current conditions for later comparison.

Progress photos should be taken on a scheduled basis. Some restorers have engaged a photographer to appear at a designated recurring time to document the progress made. Depending upon the

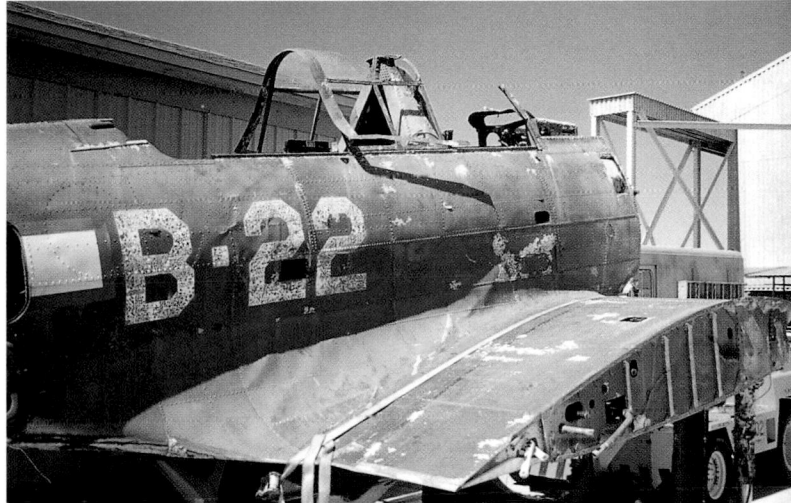

Baseline photographs are essential for documenting condition and missing parts at the earliest moment of acquiring an aircraft. This Douglas SBD Dauntless recovered from Lake Michigan, having just arrived at the National Museum of Naval Aviation, has already been partly disassembled for transport. This and other photos record condition of the canopy, missing panels, etc. — so essential to know during the restoration.

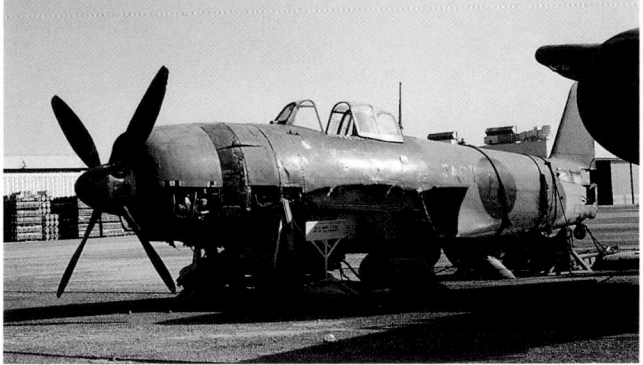

This ramp view of the Kawanishi N1K2-Ja 'George', s/n 5128, at NAS Norfolk around 1978 shows a relatively complete but disassembled airplane. Several components were lost during the restoration process which were later found after their existence was verified by dated photos such as this.

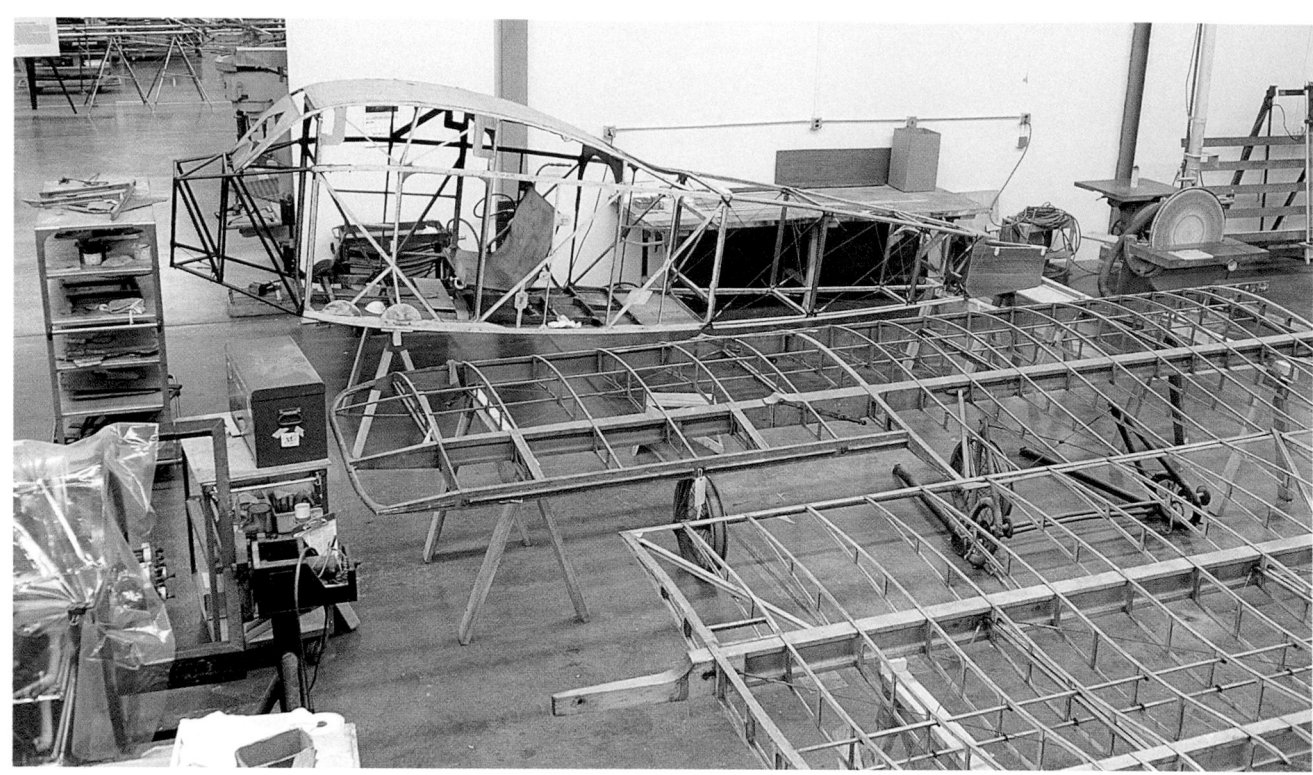

This photo of the Bellanca CF at NASM summarizes the progress being made by a given date marked on the photograph. Photos of this type not only serve as a 'how-goes-it' *illustrations, but reveal considerable details about the aircraft once it is covered and completed.*

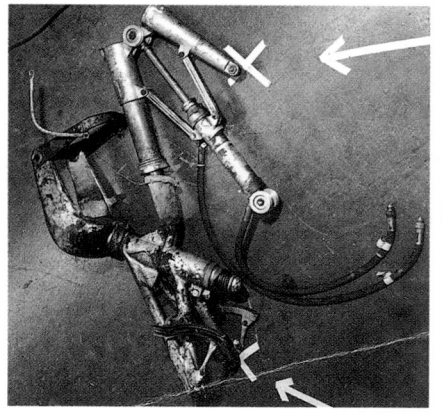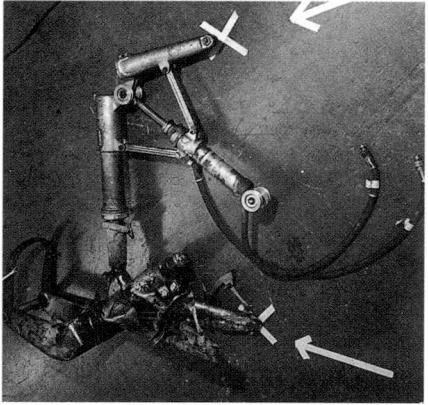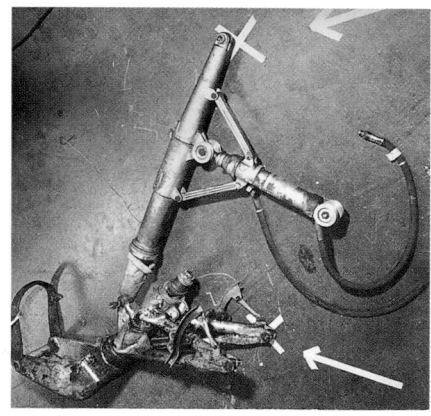

intensity of the project, twice a week would be effective, but weekly or bi-weekly may suffice. The problem here is that if the photographer is not on the restoration staff, that person is often not there when it is time to document or record a specific event taking place with the project. It would be best to augment the scheduled pictures with impromptu photographs taken by a staff member. Pictures from this grouping of photographs will be needed to support periodic reports that cover restoration progress. Emphasis must be placed on dating each photograph! Some photographs justify having a description written on the back as to what is seen and who the people are if shown. This information should also be kept with the negatives in case the original prints are lost.

There are also photographs taken to record the

Photographs taken of various components can be of value in many ways. As a means of documenting the operation of a system being restored, sequence photographs become quite valuable. These three views show the retracting sequence for the Nakajima J1N1-S 'Irving' night-fighter's tail wheel as it would fold into the fuselage. Arrows point to what would be the fixed pivot points within the fuselage.

location of parts before their removal to use as a guide when it is time to reinstall each part. Memories play tricks when it comes time to reinstall a strangely curved piece of tubing, or a wire bundle and its routing. For this aspect of photography, a Polaroid camera in the hands of a restoration technician should serve the purpose. Photographs need to be clear enough so that numbers on marking tags can be legible.

Ensure that a photo library is developed in such

a way that it is not only accessible for use by the technician, but later as a historical reference that can be cross-referenced against completed work entries. Quick access in finding a particular subject photo is also important. A file by date may work best for one restoration, while a file by various components would be best for another. Properly arranged it will help the technician immensely, not only as a visual reference but for properly recording and tabulating events. Dating each picture is so important.

One recording aid used at NASM is a video camera kept in the shop for immediate use. It has proven to be valuable when removing complex parts in complicated areas of the aircraft. A voice recording made at the time gives added information as reminders for the time when these parts have to be returned as they were when removed. These video tapes are not considered to be kept as a part of the aircraft files when the project is completed.

Work Log-books

This aspect of documenting the work that is done during a restoration, or for that matter, the continued life of the airplane as a museum object, is often treated very haphazardly and with little or no standardization. Far too often it is either not done, or when accomplished it may be after the event by 'relying upon corporate memory.' This is a professional aspect of restorations that needs far more attention than given in the past.

Recognizing this shortfall, two staff members at the RAF Museum at Hendon, Air Commodore David F. Lawrence, RAF (Ret'd) and Bruce James have produced an excellent paper on this subject.[19] Encapsulating the importance of complete and regular documentation, they point out that work performed on an aircraft to be flown must be well-documented in order to receive a Permit to Fly. Yet for restorations of historic museum aircraft there is no governing body to dictate rules of record-keeping for aircraft on static display. It is up to the individual organizations to produce their own method of documentation and to make certain that its goals are accomplished. Part of a solution to this problem pointed out by Lawrence and James has to do with standardized and well-designed forms that should be capable of directing the technician to record the necessary information and to place any cross-references in their rightful places. Here is the place to record the unique discoveries about the aircraft as well as the various materials used, where and how applied, vendors from whom special parts and hardware were acquired, telephone numbers, etc. Sketches of how a part was made or attached to the airplane should be part of this log. This documentation can be designed such that entries must be made at least once per day; thereby ensuring that

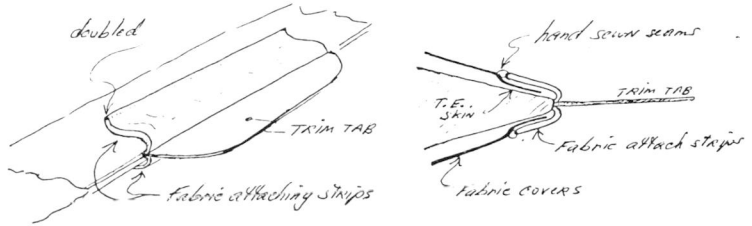

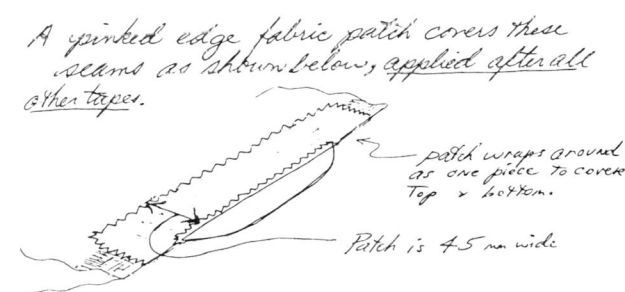

This sample page from a restoration technician's log book leaves little doubt as to how fabric was formed around a trim tab of the Kawasaki Ki-45 Toryu fighter, codenamed 'Nick'. When the time comes to apply new fabric, these instructions will make the process very clear. This serves a second purpose in that it records on paper the technology of the time it was originally applied.

there is no opportunity for the technician to leave work unrecorded for periods of time and rely on his or her memory to update the record at some later time. Careful printing of notes made by the technician is essential. Handwriting styles change over a century, even if legible in the first place. Electronic documentation is a far better means of record-keeping.

An excellent method pointed out by David Lawrence and Bruce James to solve part of this documentation problem has to do with a form of bar chart showing progress. I first saw this being used at the Experimental Aircraft Association (EAA) Museum a number of years ago. Quoting from their paper:

'For a major project such as the Hawker Tempest V, a simple restoration plan is being used; in essence,

RESTORATION SHEET NO. 8/1.

AIRCRAFT *HAWKER TEMPEST T.T.5 NV778*

MAIN ASSEMBLY *FORWARD FUSELAGE*

SUB ASSEMBLY *ENGINE SUPPORT STRUCTURE*

Ser No (a)	Rectification Reqd (b)	Rectification, Adjustments, etc carried out (c)	Date Complete (d)	Remarks (e)	Photo/ Drg No (f)	By Whom (g)
1	DIAGONAL BRACING STRUT BELOW FUEL TANK IS BENT AND CORRODED	STRUT DE-CORRODED AND STRAIGHTENED REPROTECTED & PAINTED 'COCKPIT GREEN'. ANTI-CORROSIVE PX-32 COMPOUND APPLIED TO STRUT.	15 JAN 93	STRUT NOT HEAT TREATED ON COMPLETION. NOT SUITABLE FOR FLIGHT USE. (REFITTED AT ITEM 4, BELOW)	M/CS/057 TO M/CS/059 INCLUSIVE	E. FREEMAN P. WATERHOUSE I. MASON
2	RADIATOR, REAR SUPPORT STRUT DISTORTED/ CORRODED	STRUT REMOVED, MOUNTING BRACKETS STRAIGHTENED AND WELD REPAIRED. ALL ITEMS REPROTECTED AND PAINTED 'COCKPIT GREEN'. ANTI-CORROSIVE PX32 COMPOUND APPLIED TO STRUT	15 JAN 93	WELDING NOT CHECKED FOR FLIGHT USE. (REFITTED AT ITEM 5, BELOW)	M/CS/057 TO M/CS/059 INCLUSIVE	E. FREEMAN P. WATERHOUSE I. MASON
3	RADIATOR, REAR SUPPORT STRUT, ATTACHING BRACKETS CRACKED AND DISTORTED	BRACKETS REMOVED, STRAIGHTENED AND WELD REPAIRED, REPROTECTED AND PAINTED IN 'COCKPIT GREEN'. ANTI-CORROSIVE COMPOUND PX-32 APPLIED TO BRACKETS	15 JAN 93	WELDING NOT CHECKED FOR FLIGHT USE (REFITTED AT ITEM 5, BELOW)	M/CS/057 TO M/CS/059 INCLUSIVE	I. MASON E. FREEMAN P. WATERHOUSE
4	DIAGONAL BRACING STRUT TO BE REFITTED	DIAGONAL BRACING STRUT REFITTED	19 FEB 93	STRUT REFITTED USING 5/16" BSF HTS BOLTS AND NUTS, LOCKED BY PEENING. (ORIGINALLY ATTACHED BY TUBULAR RIVETS AND BUSHES)	M/CS/160 TO M/CS/162 INCLUSIVE	I. MASON H. SAGE
5	RADIATOR, REAR SUPPORT STRUT AND BRACKETS TO BE REFITTED	RADIATOR REAR SUPPORT STRUT AND BRACKETS REFITTED	2 APR 93	REASSEMBLED USING JC5 JOINTING COMPOUND, AREA TREATED WITH ANTI-CORROSIVE COMPOUND PX 32 ON COMPLETION	M/CS/160 TO M/CS/162 INCLUSIVE	I. MASON

This sample aircraft log-sheet used by the RAF Museum serves as a record in many ways. A formal log like this, easily monitored by a supervisor, makes for good record-keeping. (RAF Museum)

a bar chart to show an estimate of the project time and the progress being made. The project was split down into main assemblies, starting with the initial dismantling and a full survey. Only after the survey was it possible to produce the remainder of the chart. Bearing in mind that there will probably be only one or two technicians working on the aircraft, a bar chart rather than a more complex network analysis was deliberately chosen.

'In addition, a separate chart is used to show the progress of each main assembly. For individual tasks, a simple work sheet is used, again by main assembly, and showing the defect, rectification and the serial number of any drawings or photographs. This sheet is particularly important as it confirms that the work has been carried out, and is a long-lasting record of the restoration.'

Parts Identification

To tag and mark every part that is removed is a must. This not only identifies the part in photographs just mentioned, but also serves as reference in the work log which describes what actions have been taken in restoring or preserving

the various parts. Naturally, these tags will be removed when the part is reinstalled, therefore the photographic reference remains important.

String-tied paper and cloth tags are excellent for this type of identification. Not only can a highly visible mark such as a number be placed on this tag that can be easily recorded by the camera, but handwritten notes can be added as further identification and instructions to assist in the work process.

There are other considerations as well. Quite often these parts must be passed through chemical processing, and therefore these tags will easily disintegrate in the process. One technician at NASM had his own nail board with a series of round metal disks, drilled, and metal-stamped with numbers and his personal mark. These tags would be wired to the parts and recorded on his daily work log as to their disposition; e.g. chemical processing, placed on certain numbered shelf, etc. When going through chemical baths, the tags and wire were not affected. This method for marking works well, and serves many purposes.

Parts Storage

There is nothing worse than having many parts lying about waiting for reinstallation in the airplane. Metal racks with multiple shelves work well, and are even better if mounted on casters. Shelves can be dedicated for objects from certain areas of the aircraft, or going even further, logged in and assigned to a shelf and rack number in a more realistic cataloging system. Once these parts have a protective dust cover such as polyurethane sheeting placed over them, such methods will eliminate a frantic search under these covers for one item among the hundreds that will be generated over many months. Part location accountability is highly recommended.

There will always be visitors to the workshop areas. A major problem can be the souvenir collector/thief. I painfully recall an incident during the restoration of NASM's A6M5 Zero fighter when the newly-processed gunsight left on the workbench over the weekend was gone the following Monday. Parts cannot always be locked away while conducting a restoration project that utilizes these parts. Polyurethane sheeting placed over unattended workbenches and draped over the front of storage shelves gives some semblance of security.

With this pre-planning and procedures worked out ahead of time, the disassembly work can begin in the knowledge that there will be accountability of parts and how each part is to be returned to its original place.

Racks and Trunnions

Man-hours spent in building substantial racks for supporting the main components of the aircraft will be saved through easier access to the component being worked on. Ideally, a trunnion for supporting the fuselage nose and tail will facilitate the work process. This arrangement will allow one man to rotate the fuselage to any angle without requiring lifting equipment and additional help. Work on the underside, often difficult to reach if merely placed on a stand, can be made easier by rotating the fuselage to a comfortable angle. Cockpits especially are more easily reached from a standing position when the fuselage is placed on its side, rather than having to climb inside from the top and work within cramped quarters. (Make note of the previously-described Southampton with the circular frame attached to the hull sides, able to be rolled on the platform provided. Since this circular frame was segmented, portions could be detached over areas being worked on.)

Wing supports of the same type can allow rotation and positioning of the wing in an upright position, far easier to work on than having to reach across horizontal surfaces or work from the bottom. Even if a trunnion-type arrangement becomes too complicated, a rack on which to hold the wing upright will save considerable effort by placing the wing in a more easily workable position.

These racks can become even more serviceable if placed on wheels. For metal components, this allows freedom to move to cleaning areas of the shop or into paint booths. Often it is ideal to work outside if only the component were more mobile. Above all, these

It takes time to fabricate a holding jig and trunnion for the major parts of an aircraft undergoing restoration. Time is saved, however, by providing easy access to otherwise difficult-to-reach areas. Convenient access to the cockpit of this Focke-Wulf Fw 190F-8 is appreciated by NASM's technician Joe Fichera.

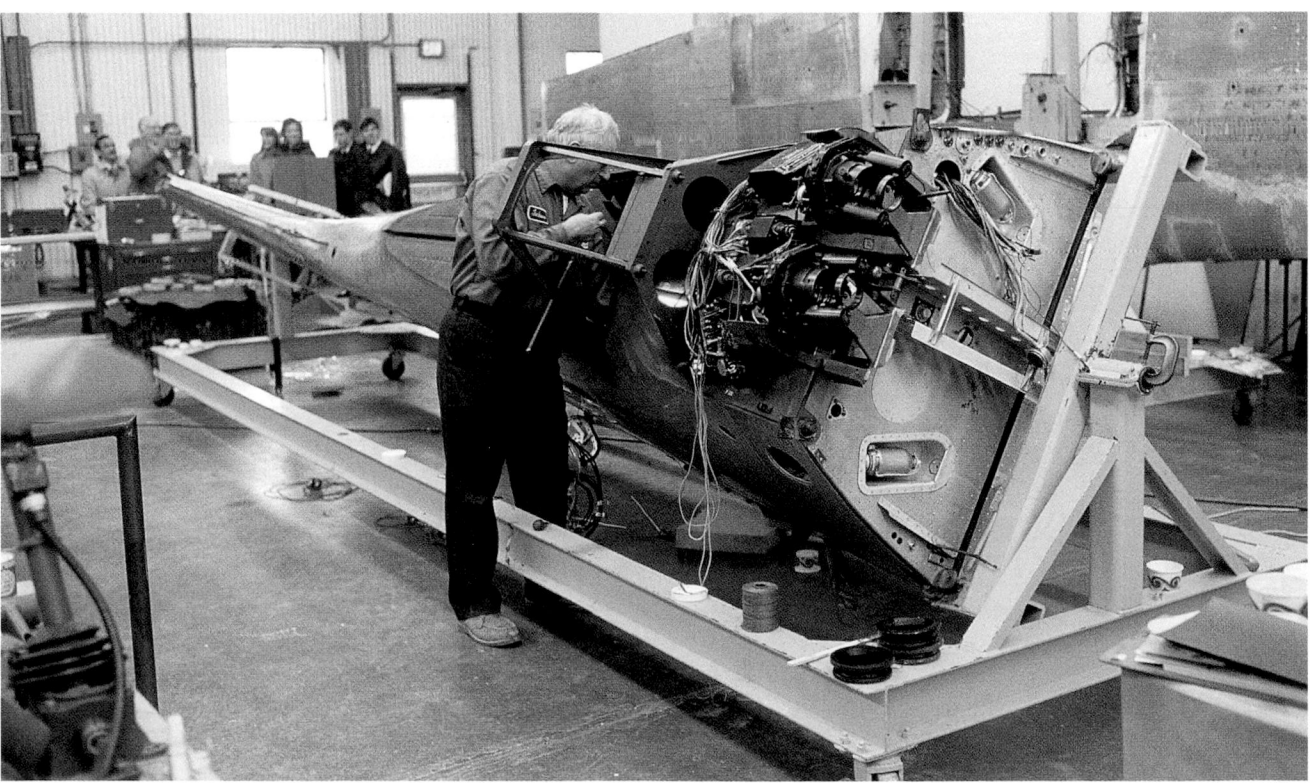

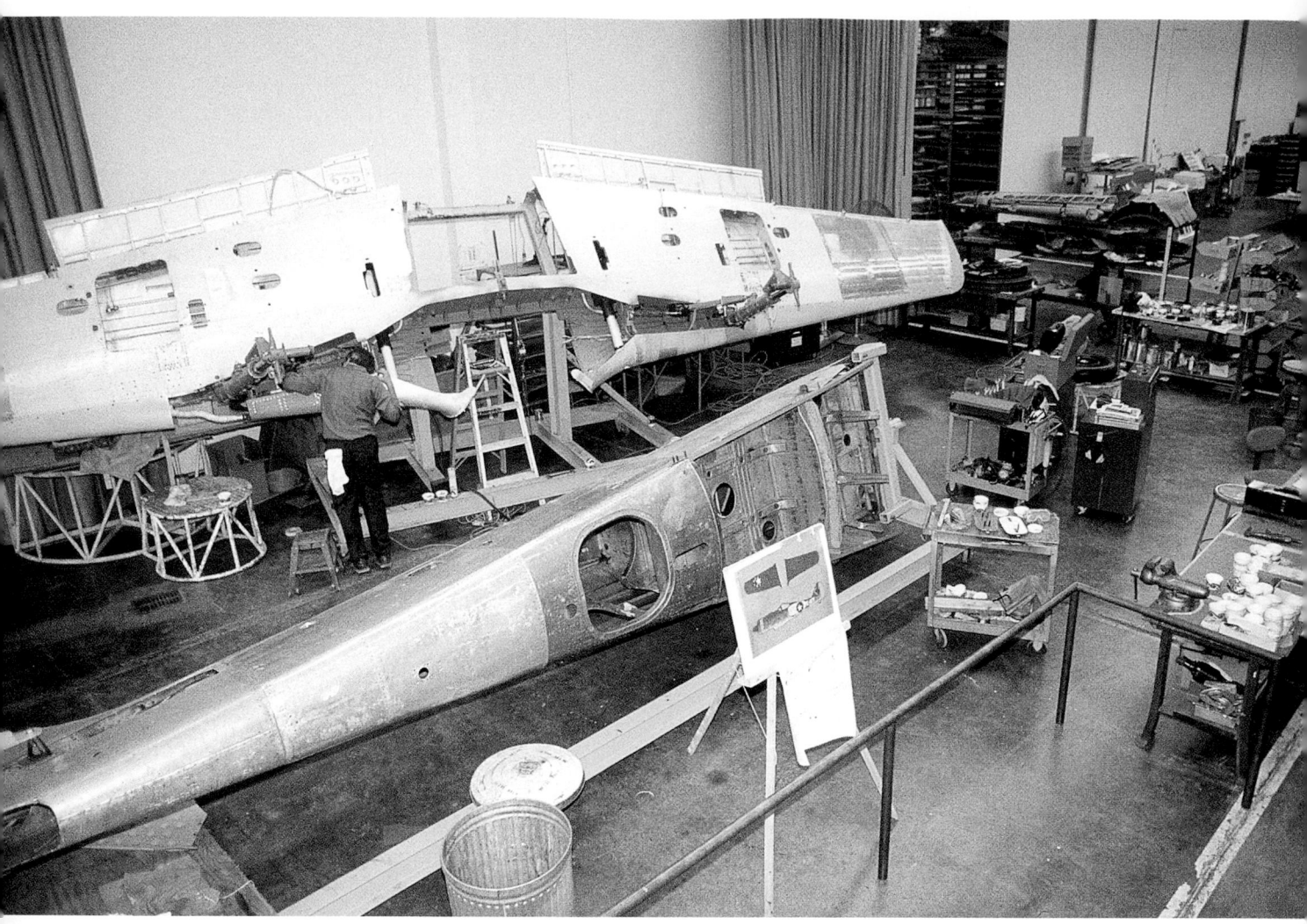

A special rack to support the wing of the Fw 190F-8 in the background was also fabricated for this restoration. It could be tilted towards whichever side was being worked on in a standing position by the technician. The inverted fuselage of this airplane is in the foreground.

racks must be durable in order to provide safety for the worker as well as the component it supports. Time spent on building substantial and functional racks will be returned in time and money saved.

Marking New and Repaired Parts

This early planning stage is the best time to custom-order two marking rubber stamps and indelible ink pads and pen for marking parts that will not be original to the airplane. The permanent identification of these respective parts is essential in any restoration project. The examples shown here indicate what museum did this work (NASM), one stamp being for a repaired part and one for a replacement part. The date line is filled in by hand with an indelible pen.

These stamps should always be kept close to the project for ease of application. The impressions usually go on the inside surface of the part so that

> NOT AN ORIGINAL PART
> REPRODUCTION DATE 2/15/79
> NASM
>
> REPAIRED ORIGINAL PART
> DATE 11/24/76 NASM

These are samples of rubber stamps used at NASM for identifying parts that are not original to an aircraft being restored. The make-up of these stamps can be altered to suit the restorers and the facility, so long as they identify the nature of deviation from being original.

they will not be conspicuous or painted over. For even more permanency, a clear coating is brushed over the imprint on either wood or metal parts.

Documenting the Past

The degree of originality desired of the restoration should be decided on before work begins. Let us take for example an airplane of Level 3 Condition; that is, an aircraft demanding a complete restoration. Generally, for metal aircraft, the structure has visible signs of corrosion, badly dented and torn skin, and many missing parts. For fabric and frame aircraft, the fabric is spent, the structure is in need of repair with rust quite prevalent, and parts are missing. But what in its original state can be saved in addition to the structure?

All three guiding hands of this restoration — curator, conservator, and restoration technician — should go over the aircraft together and determine what can be saved that will enhance the originality of the airplane. Many items in the cockpit, for instance, by their very nature of being sheltered inside the fuselage, may not need to be repainted, but merely cleaned, preserved and returned to their rightful place. Damaged metal skin can either be repaired or when agreed upon, replaced for various reasons. Wooden parts that show lamination separation, splitting or rotting can be repaired and retained as original parts. The emphasis during this walk-around should be on saving as much of the original structure as possible, and also making written notes for later review. More on this will appear in later chapters.

The purpose of this marking of parts is an obvious one: in years to come, there may be some reason that

This early stage for planning the restoration of NASM's Aichi M6A1 Seiran by the curator, conservator and technician, identifies areas which require special attention. Shown at the tail are bags holding hardware that was removed during part of the disassembly for storage.

an airplane structure must be opened up again. Eventually, even new wood or shiny metal that is so obviously different from the adjacent original material when the repair is made will take on the same appearance as the old material. In order to avoid any misidentification by those examining the structure, repaired or replacement parts can easily be identified.

The use of methods for distinguishing original parts from replacement parts is not new in aircraft restorations. The earliest known example is that of Orville Wright, for he is credited with distinguishing replacement parts as early as 1927, when he restored the Wright Flyer for eventual shipment to the Science Museum in London where it stayed until 1948. In the meticulous notes that Mr Wright made for any project undertaken, he pointed out that ash parts were used for spruce replacements, and spruce was used for ash replacements. This dissimilarity of wood parts became quite evident when the Wright Flyer was being restored at NASM in 1985.

There are other ways in which this identification between new and old parts can be accomplished. The use of modern materials not conceived of at the time the original part was made becomes a way of identifying a replacement or repaired part. Replacements for wheel pants and spinners might be made with fiberglass instead of aluminum as were the originals. After all, lack of the original forms and dies prevents making an exact duplicate

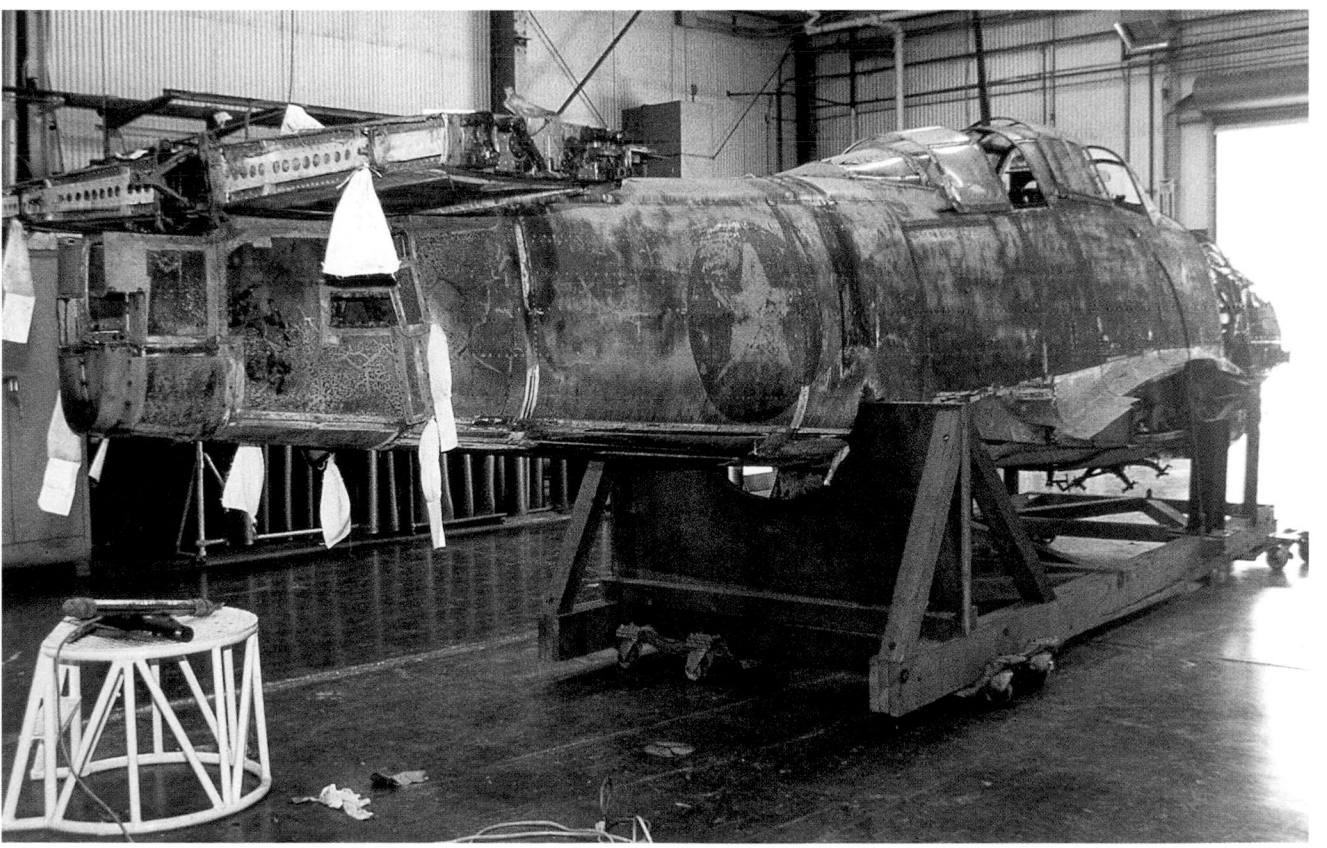

even when using the same type of material.

The Nakajima J1N1-S 'Irving' provides an example of a restoration where original and new materials were used on a single aircraft. Rather than making an extreme alteration in an engine heat shield that had sustained extensive corrosion damage from outdoor storage, fiberglass was used to fill in the rusted-out area. This kept the design of the part original and intact without a questionable-looking patch made with the same metal. After all, this damage was caused through neglect, not operational use that would otherwise have an appropriate type repair. The part was obviously repaired, should an evaluation ever be warranted. Yet throughout the rest of the airframe, repairs were made with similar materials, stamped and dated. Here was a mix of both methods on one aircraft.

This must be a curatorial decision, and the decision might vary from one situation to another. There is no true solution to such problems. Written documentation made at the time that gives reason for the decision resolves any future questions.

Now is the time to record certain things about the aircraft that will be needed as the restoration progresses.

Fabric sample: This is sometimes historic in nature, but usually there is a fragment of fabric that can be removed as a sample for selecting replacement material, often appropriately sent to a laboratory for a better analysis. Ideally, an 8½ x 11-inch (21.6 x 28 cm) piece that is placed in a clear vinyl sleeve for inclusion in the final report is desired. Mark the location where this was taken from the aircraft.

Paint colors: Methods used in recording paint colors are discussed later in this book. However, now is the time to record these and to consider equivalent colors and materials to be used in the restoration if not already described in the Curatorial Guidelines. Make certain that color

readings are taken from the most protected areas, often found under fairings and covers when removed.

Original paint sample: If the situation warrants, it is ideal to retain a part of the airplane that has a sample of original paint color(s) on it that is not to be reused. This is usually a badly-damaged piece of metal, wood or fabric that must be replaced, yet retains a good sample of the paint. Ideally, this would be about 8 x 10 inches (20 x 25 cm) and can be placed in a clear plastic envelope, identified, and kept with the aircraft record file. There may be some future need for a laboratory analysis of the original paint, either for technological or historical purposes or the state-of-the-art at the time of application.

Materials: Gather, bag and record samples of unusual materials that were found on this airplane such as composition materials, a fragment of unusable window and various fabrics in addition to skin coverings. Samples of hardware that cannot be used — types of nails, screws and bolts — should also be retained.

Missing parts: Begin listing missing items that will have to be acquired to complete this aircraft, e.g. instruments, radios, tires, and special materials that cannot be reused, but need replacement.

There will be instances where missing parts cannot be replaced. For instance, an empty radio rack once held a component, yet records or photographs may not be available to identify what the original object was. Is it better to leave the rack empty, or to fill it in with an item that could be close. I feel that the former is the correct way when an item does not affect the visual appearance of a complete cockpit, for instance. Otherwise, since history cannot be recorded by including original parts or duplications, history is not being created by the input of guesswork that others will believe are true copies of the original items. Do keep in mind that good documentation makes either choice the right decision.

CHAPTER 4
Wood-and-Fabric Aircraft

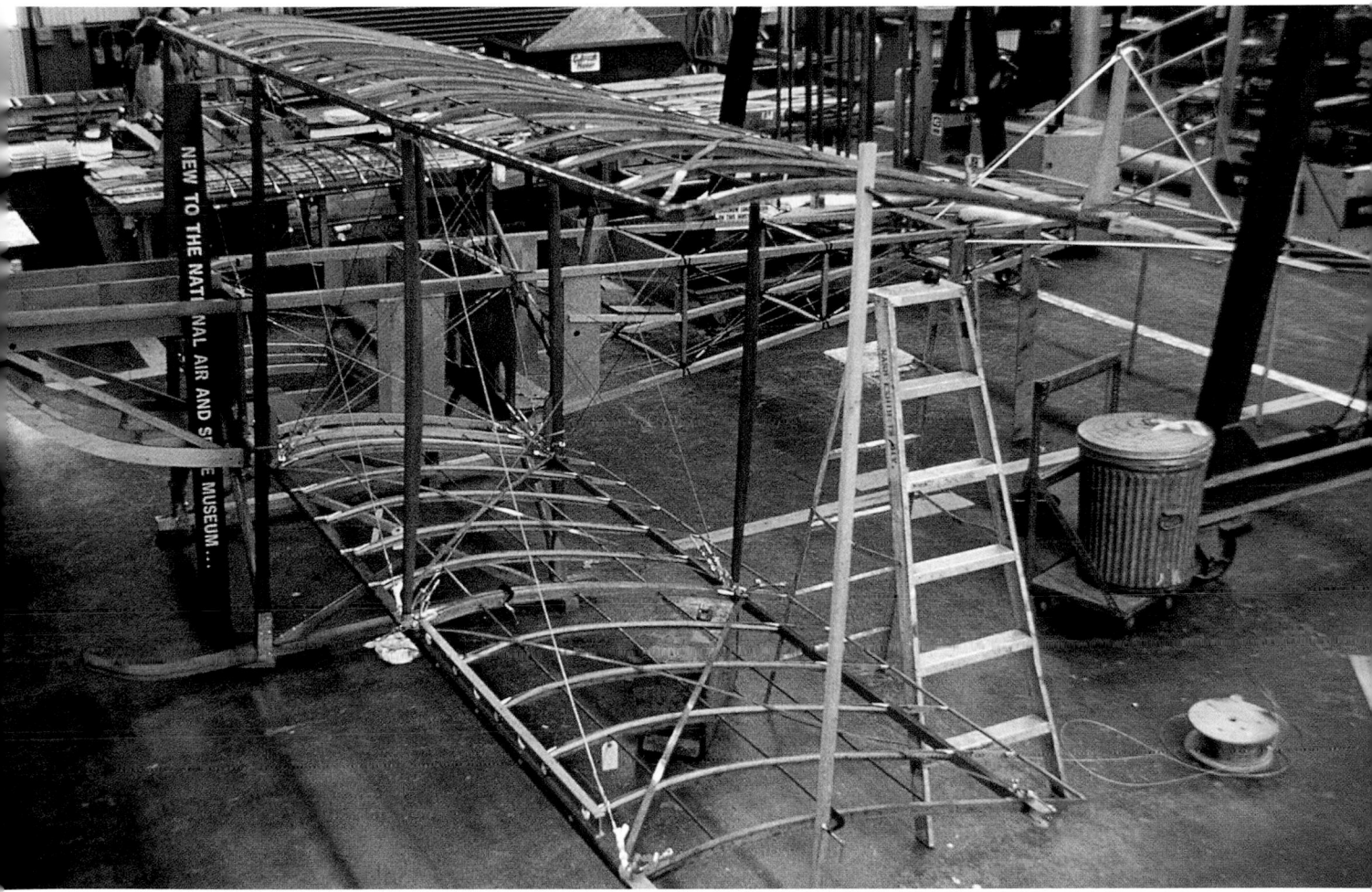

With the passing of time, the art of aircraft woodworking and fabric application is becoming an unused skill. Examples such as this Benoist Type XII when accurately restored become physical examples of techniques once used. The Benoist is the subject of restoration in Appendix A.

Decisions about restoring frame and fabric aircraft are often based upon the condition of the fabric covering, regarding the structure only secondarily. I recall quite well our considerations with respect to the Domenjoz Blériot XI at NASM. This airplane was to be prepared for exhibit in the planned Early Aviation Gallery because of its significance as the most commonly-used monoplane of its era. In a machine of this type, Louis Blériot was the first person to cross the English Channel in 1909, covering the 25 miles (40 km) between Calais and

Dover in 36 minutes and 30 seconds. The museum's Blériot XI is historic in that it was flown by the well-known flight exhibition pilot John Domenjoz in many events. Flying in Buenos Aires in April 1915 in this specially strengthened model, he performed 40 consecutive loops in 28 minutes, a feat that earned him the name 'upside-down Domenjoz.' In New York the following year, he and this airplane made headlines with a series of loops over the Statue of Liberty.

When undertaking the preparation of this airplane for exhibit in the late 1970s, we found the fabric in relatively good condition despite its age and discoloration. This early fabric gave the airplane the desired appearance of being old and historic, which was truly the case. It appeared that with the addition of tires, a general clean-up would suffice for the structure as well as the fabric, and therefore the aircraft would retain its original unrestored condition.

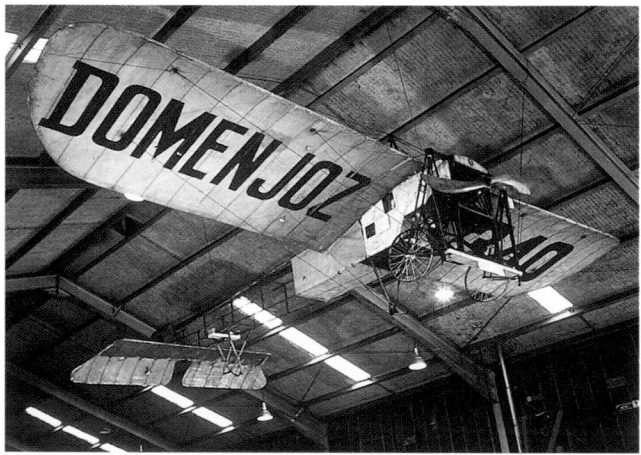

Upon cursory observation, the Blériot XI at NASM seemed only to need a general cleaning and replacement tires to make it fit for exhibit. The general opinion was that the airplane was old, and therefore it should look old.

When monitoring the cleaning of the open fuselage structure, however, I noted during my periodic visits that metal fittings from one bay would be missing, only to reappear for my next visit in well cared-for condition, and vacancies appear elsewhere. It became obvious why these fittings were being removed since there were significant traces of rust where they had been, particularly in the area of holes where bolts passed through the wood. Wood rot in these areas was becoming apparent. When I asked Joe Fichera, the restoration technician, how much of this removal and cleaning might be expected for this 'so-called' minor clean-up, he replied that all these fittings should be removed and treated. By doing so, they could be chemically stabilized so that further rusting would not take place, and therefore further deterioration of the wooden members would also be curtailed.

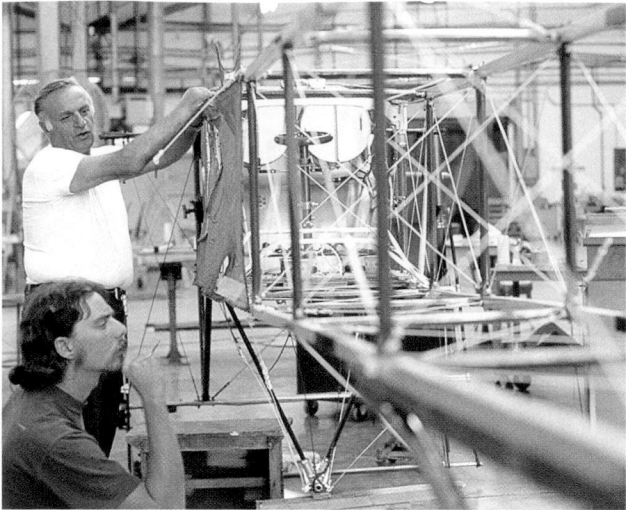

Metal fittings against the moisture-holding wood longerons were causing wood rot that was otherwise out of sight. Joe Fichera (standing) and Karl Heinzel soon realized that the metal parts had to be separated for cleaning and vapor barrier inhibitors had to be applied to prolong the life of this Blériot XI.

Although the fabric gave the Blériot XI the desired appearance of an old museum piece, it hid from view the rust and deterioration that was beginning to take place inside the wing and tail surfaces. Once the tension was released on this varnished fabric, it was not practical to put back in place.

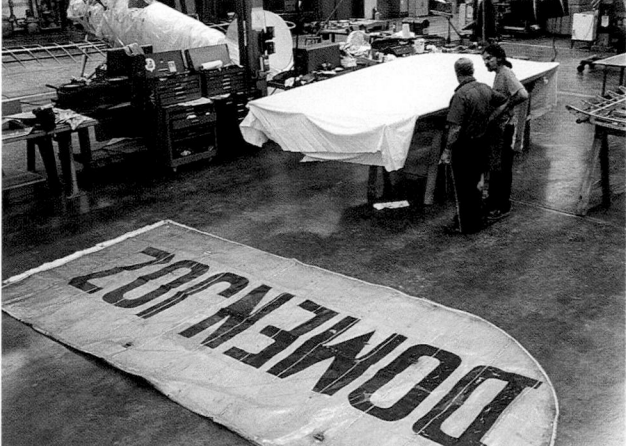

After further discussion, it became clear that what was being attempted was a half-way restoration rather than a general clean-up. It was taking more time to work around the problems, piece by piece, in doing a clean-up than it would be to go all the way. At this point we changed our approach and decided to do a complete restoration after all. Not only was this simpler, but the life expectancy of this valued artifact was greatly improved.

With this decision, we called for the removal of the fabric on the wings and tail although the cloth appeared to be in relatively good condition. This was a very fortunate move, because where the metal components touched the wood structure inside the wing there were signs of even greater deterioration.

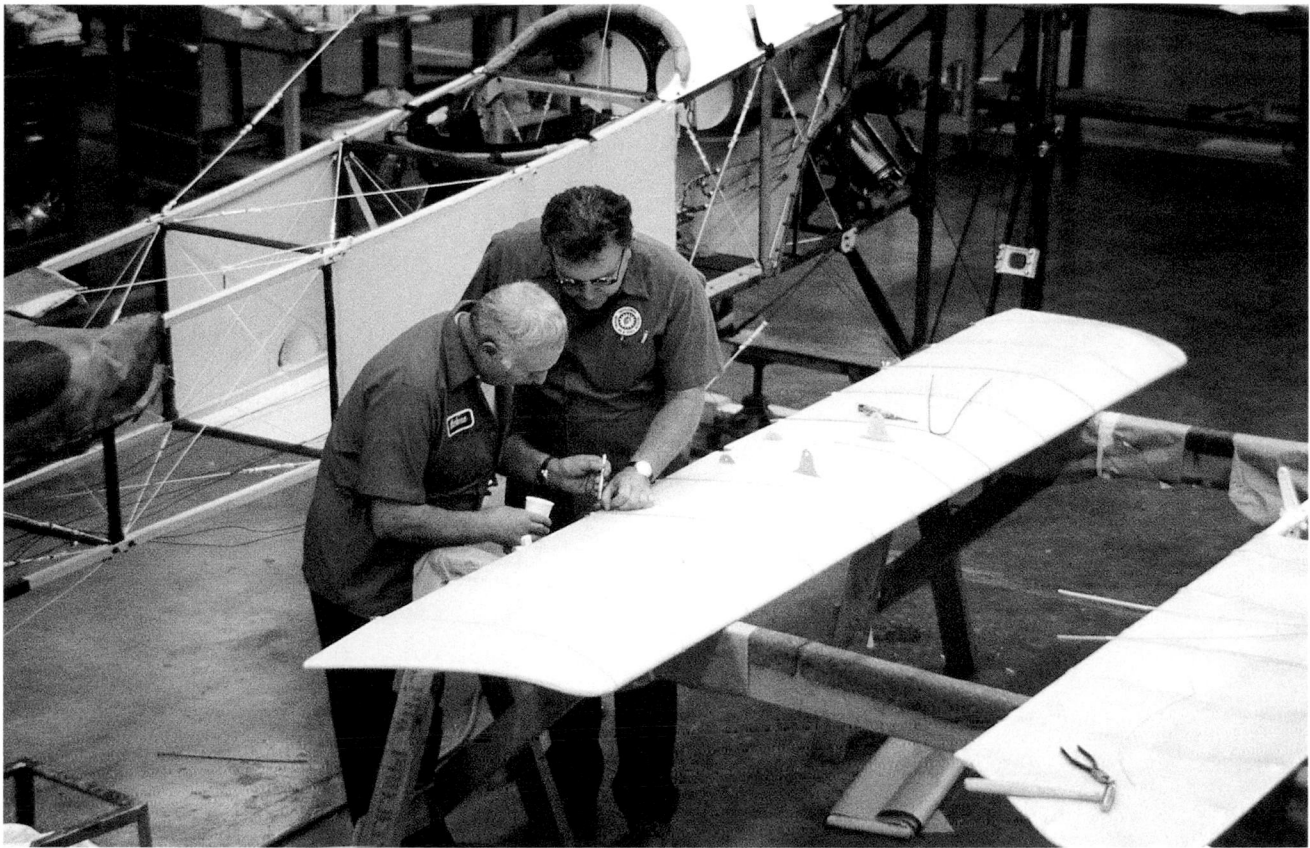

Grade-A cotton was found to be the closest match to the original fabric on the Blériot XI. The unique methods of fastening the original covering were duplicated here in the greatest detail as a form of documenting this early technology. Strips of reed split in half were tacked over the fabric to the rib as the attachment method.

The cause may well have been that the fabric not only drew moisture but also trapped humidity within the structure. We lost the originality and 'museum object' look by not having the original fabric in place, but by doing so, the structural deterioration had been abated. In retrospect, what we thought was a Level 2 Condition aircraft was actually a Level 3.

No Half-way

Experience such as this has proven that there is no half-way method for a restoration. Airplanes, when built, are made to serve an immediate functional purpose without thought being given to a longer life as a museum artifact. However, it is imperative that this conversion from an operational aircraft to museum artifact be made at some point before extensive deterioration takes place, and that it is backed up by a maintenance and monitoring program.

Conversion to a museum artifact requires considerable explanation, so here are some of the major points. Functional components such as engines and hydraulic, fuel and oxygen systems require their own special forms of preservation. This aspect is

covered in later chapters of this book. Metal components used on wood-and-fabric airplanes require a special preservative treatment not only for their own stability against corrosion, but to protect adjoining materials such as wood parts. When the Blériot XI was manufactured, there was no concern for future rust on metal fittings or their effect upon adjacent surfaces that needed a protective barrier. Their life expectancy was not a factor.

There are other reasons for avoiding the pitfalls associated with half-way restorations. In these hurry-up processes, what is often touted as a restoration is actually a cosmetic undertaking. Aircraft interiors receive the least attention with the promise of doing these areas later, yet if this work is undertaken at a later date, the problem that develops is the harm that can be caused to the exterior while working on the interior. Cleaning agents and chemical treatment used on the inside of the structure will certainly stain the new outside finish through seams and openings. Even more apparent is the effect of wear on the outside when accessing the inside during the work process. It is often more difficult to work on interiors when the aircraft is in an assembled state. Naturally this is dependent upon the type of aircraft as well.

The advice given here is to not attempt a partial restoration, but to do the task completely and do a one-time restoration correctly. This is not to imply that everything must be repainted. Cockpit areas, for example, have sometimes survived well enough

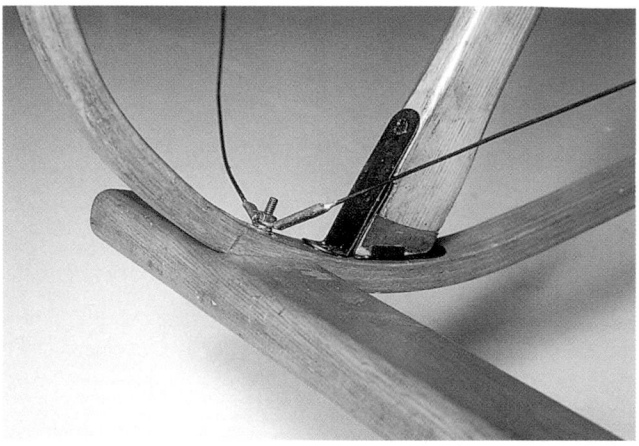

The original wood finish of varnish on the Wright Flyer was retained after a thorough cleaning. As a reversible protective coating, Butcher's Bowling Alley Wax™ was applied to all exposed wood surfaces.

There have been more difficult cleaning problems for wood than those encountered with the Wright Flyer. In the case of the Spad XIII *Smith IV* at NASM, there were heavy build-ups of grease and oil resting on parts of the wooden structure. If not removed, these would affect the fibers of the wood and perhaps induce dry rot. These areas were first soaked with a detergent applied with a sponge. When dried, the grease that had lifted was removed with acetone and ethyl alcohol. After about three applications of this process the grease stains were hardly visible.

The most damaging effect found within the structure of the Spad XIII *was the build-up of grease and oil in the nose section under the engine. This was laboriously cleaned with several applications of detergent to lift the grease which was removed with acetone and alcohol.*

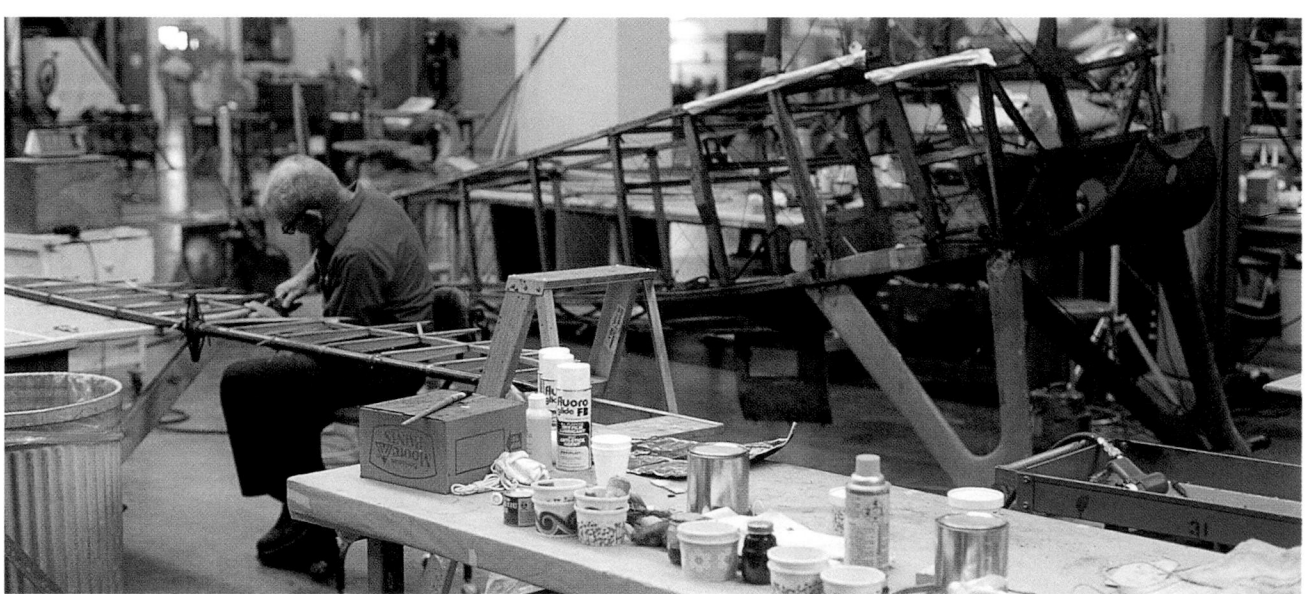

that small but important details such as instructional placards and original paint on components can be cleaned and preserved. If this process of preserving originality presents an operational-appearing cockpit, that is the course to follow.

Hopefully in this process much of the wood is in a condition whereby a good cleaning is all that is necessary. In the case of the Wright Flyer, its exposed structure had been varnished, yet the years of exposure to dust and humidity produced a dark film over the wood members. Excellent cleaning results were obtained with a light scouring with methanol, rubbed with 400/500 sandpaper which removed the stain. This did not remove the original varnish, but restored a clean, well cared-for appearance. There were no new coatings of varnish applied, but instead, a protective coating of Butcher's Bowling Alley Wax™ was added as recommended by conservators of the Smithsonian Institution's Conservation Analytical Laboratory.

Replace or Repair

How often is it said that 'I can make an entirely new piece in far less time than to repair the old one.' No argument there, but what is the objective? The intent is to preserve the original airplane with its original parts and materials, not to be so perfect that a new airplane evolves. There is an undefined line of demarcation here, but for the sake of preservation, the repair of the original piece is the ethical approach. While this goal has merit, too many patched-in areas create other problems. Should it no longer have the appearance or structural integrity of the original part because of many pieces, then it is appropriate to duplicate that originality with a new part. This must be determined by the curator with the aid of the restoration technician at the time the situation is encountered. This type of decision can seldom be foreseen and covered in detail in the Restoration Guidelines.

A typical example is a wooden wing rib. It is not uncommon for a gusset to be missing or, for that matter, portions of the fragile rib cap strips. It is often simpler and less time-consuming to build an entirely new rib, using the old one as a pattern. However, there are prescribed and time-proven methods for scarfing[20] in these missing pieces, thereby retaining as much of the original structure as possible.

There is another extreme to consider. A museum technician was taking great pains to steam and straighten a stringer on the fuselage of a Spad XIII. This even required a few stiffeners that were obviously added parts that were needed for alignment. A fellow worker mused, 'Wood still grows the same today as it did 40 years ago — cut a new piece and begin with a straight piece.' Our critical technician replied that much has changed in the world since that original piece of wood was grown. Air chemical content as well as changes in the soil make it impossible to find an exacting composition of wood from the same type tree as the one used to produce the original piece. Well, he had a point, but then to what extremes must this be taken?

It would be difficult to define hard-set rules other than what has been described here. Perhaps the success or failure of retaining the originality of an aircraft can best be measured by a look in the waste container at the conclusion of the restoration and evaluating *how much of the original and highly-valued aircraft has been thrown out with the trash.*

Restoring the Albatros D.Va

At the time the Albatros D.Va was acquired in 1947 by Paul E. Garber, Curator of the aeronautical collection, it had already been reduced to nearly unrestorable condition because of outdoor exposure and abuse in California. This was such a rare aircraft that Garber acquired it for the collection, anticipating a future restoration. How fortunate, for this is one of only two original D.Vs that survive, the other being in the Australian War Memorial in Canberra. By describing the work process in restoring this Albatros, many of the principles already discussed will be put in clearer perspective. Perhaps this will be helpful to others when undertaking similar projects.

This restoration was extremely demanding and required continual effort by two museum craftsmen assigned to the task for 26 months from 1977 to 1979. Richard Horigan and Garry Cline, both experts in woodworking fabrication, devoted 7,401 man-hours to this project. Supporting this work was the on-call assistance of other shop technicians when their specialized skills were required. Their efforts accounted for an additional 1,228 man-hours, making a total of 8,629 man-hours for the

The Albatros D.Va that had spent many years exposed to the outdoor elements presented one of the more challenging restorations at NASM. This was one of two survivors of the type and had considerable historical and technological significance for aircraft of the World War I time period. (NASM, SI 76-8473)

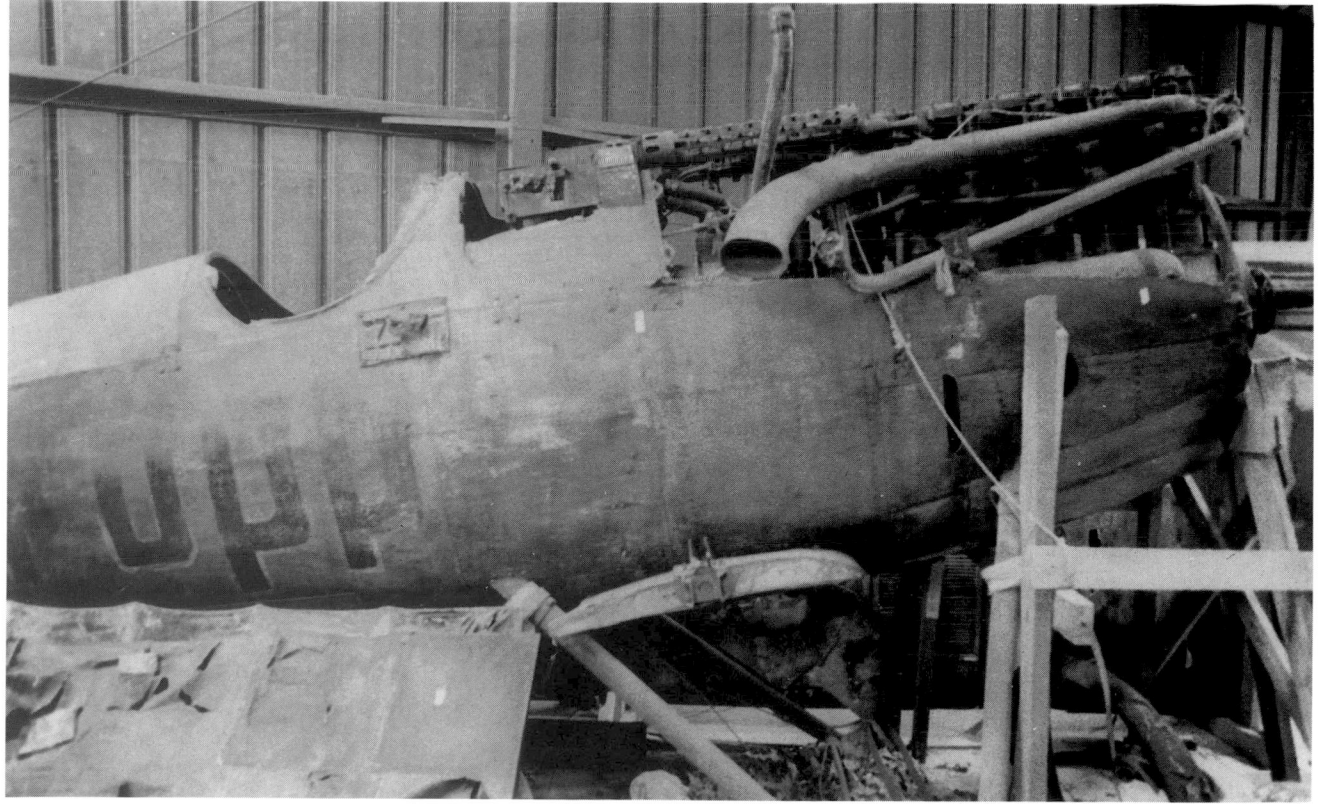

entire project.

Fuselage: At the outset, this fuselage was a literal basket case. It appeared there was little that could be done except to use its parts as patterns, retain and use some of the best components, and start anew. But, this would defeat the purpose of preserving the original structure. Richard Horigan, well-skilled in aviation woodworking techniques, took on a fuselage project which challenged his ability to accomplish the virtually impossible.

For several months, the work continued with little visible progress. Rich's time was absorbed in pattern-making and in the building of forms and molds to match the original contours for the replacement skin. In this case, the fuselage of the Albatros D.Va was a semi-monocoque construction, made up of concave formed sheets of plywood, all having to be pre-shaped before being attached to a series of formers.

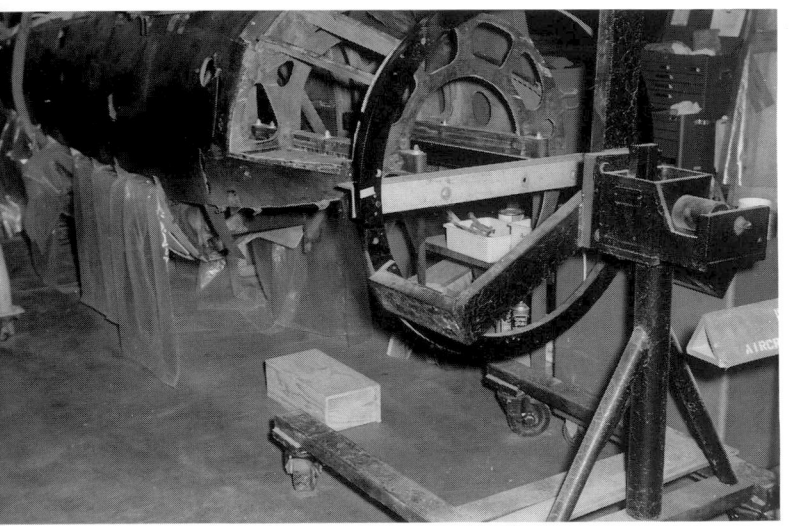

To begin the project, a trunnion was fabricated that would hold the nose of the Albatros so that it would not only be steadied, but able to be rotated as the work area dictated. An overhead sling supported the aft section of the fuselage.

These 0.08-inch (2mm)-thick plywood sheets of fuselage skin proved to be most deteriorated part of the Albatros. In the years preceding this restoration we had considered the possibility of removing the many plywood panels separately and impregnating them with Wood Rot Cure™, an epoxy penetrant, to strengthen and preserve this original, yet deteriorated, wood. Areas of the skin panels that had literally rotted away could be built up with this epoxy material. Although this was possible, it was recognized that the finished fuselage would not look as it did originally, but instead would be a patchwork of old material in contrast with new and filled-in skin areas. How 'original' would the original wood actually be after this epoxy-fill process? Having to be left in its natural, unpainted wood finish, this left little choice but to reskin the entire fuselage.[21]

Here was an airplane built 60 years earlier and in another part of the world. Where would plywood of this grade and metric size be found? After a search of aviation products that covered many parts of the world, thin plywood in metric measurement and similar grade of birch were found to be produced in Finland. An order was placed for this material, a nearly perfect match to the plywood found on the fuselage. An obvious difference was it being almost white, compared to the age-darkened original fuselage wood.

In reworking the fuselage, there was no way that all the skin could be removed and replaced at one time. Typical of monocoque construction, the alignment and rigidity of the fuselage were dependent on the strength given to it by the skin. Therefore, only a few sections at a time could be removed and replaced with new panels before moving on to the next area.

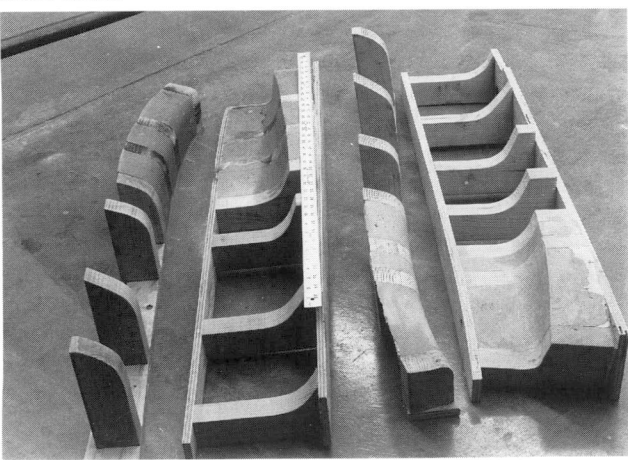

Left and right male and female molds had to be made for 15 one-of-a-kind compound curved pieces of plywood. In the making of these molds, formers establish the inside and outside contours as copied from the actual fuselage formers. The areas in between these molds were filled with plaster of Paris to complete the desired contour.

During this process, a feature of the fuselage construction was discovered that was not apparent when looking at photographs or even fuselage drawings, which are usually incorrect. The skin mating lines do not fall at the location of the fuselage formers as the drawings imply and as would naturally be expected. The reason was first revealed while viewing a rare motion-picture film that was made at the Albatros factory during World War I.[22] In a brief glimpse there appeared to be entire fuselage sides being carried to production areas. A study of the original Albatros skin showed that the top, bottom, and two sides were pre-shaped and glued as four major units and then attached as large panels to the fuselage frame. This forming of the skin may well have been accomplished through the use of large molds possibly cast from cement, just as Lockheed did with the Vega. In the process, steam-softened rectangular plywood skin panels were pressed into the mold and glued together with two-inch (50 mm) scarf joints with the splice reinforced by a strip of heavy-weave linen cloth glued to the inside.

While Roland and Pfalz, companies that also manufactured the Albatros D.Va, employed convex molds for this process, details on the inside skin face of the Albatros-built fuselage imply that concave molds were used. On NASM's Albatros, many edges of this cloth were found sandwiched between the bulkheads and the skin, offering further evidence that the cloth was attached over the splice while held in the concave mold before the skin was secured to the fuselage structure.

This technique complicated the restoration of the Albatros. Since the molds could not be recreated with the assurance that they would produce the original contours accurately, the skin pieces had to be fitted separately to the fuselage structure. Since the skin splices were located in areas away from the support of formers, this often required the temporary insertion of a false former to provide stability and shape when joining the panels.

This reskinning process had to be started at the rear of the fuselage due to the direction of the scarf laps. Unfortunately, this area was the most difficult as 15 differently-shaped pieces in this tail-section had to be molded individually to their separate contours. The question was asked whether plywood could be formed into compound curves. 'If the Germans could do it, I can do it,' Rich commented — and he did.

At the left is the condition of the tail cone of the Albatros D.Va at the beginning of this project. The structural formers provided evidence of shaping new skin covering. Most of the fuselage structure was able to be retained which supported the new covering at the tail as shown at right.

Before removing the old skin in this area for molding new pieces, templates were made of the curves. These were transformed into wood diaphragms and attached in a box-frame arrangement, for both a male and female form. The areas between these diaphragms were then filled with plaster of Paris to make a continuous contoured form. The plywood to be formed was then placed in a steam box for five to 10 minutes to be softened. It was then clamped between the two halves of the mold for four days, then clamped on the fuselage frame for one day for final drying.

After a few necessary alterations were made to the molds to compensate for hidden stresses, the desired compound shapes were obtained. This was a slow, arduous operation, but this insistence on perfection got the repair of the fuselage off to an excellent start. The other panels forward of this aft-section, cut to the exact dimensions of the originals, could then be formed directly on the fuselage.

As in the original manner, most sections were attached with screws at their corners. Rows of nails and glue were used to further hold the skin to the formers and longerons. For this restoration, the skin was first held in place by the screws positioned into the original screw holes with the aid of a blind rivet-hole locator. The structure outline was then traced on the inside face of the skin before the panel was removed. A centerline for the nails was drawn within the penciled lines of the structure and evenly marked for the nails at 0.79-inch (2 cm) intervals. A #60 drill-size hole was made at each mark. Glue was applied to the fuselage formers, the skin again screwed back to its earlier location and ½-inch (12.7 mm) #18 steel cement-coated aircraft nails were driven through each hole which resulted in a perfect alignment of the nails. New nails had to be used for attaching the skin, for to have restored the old metric-size nails in these small quantities for this

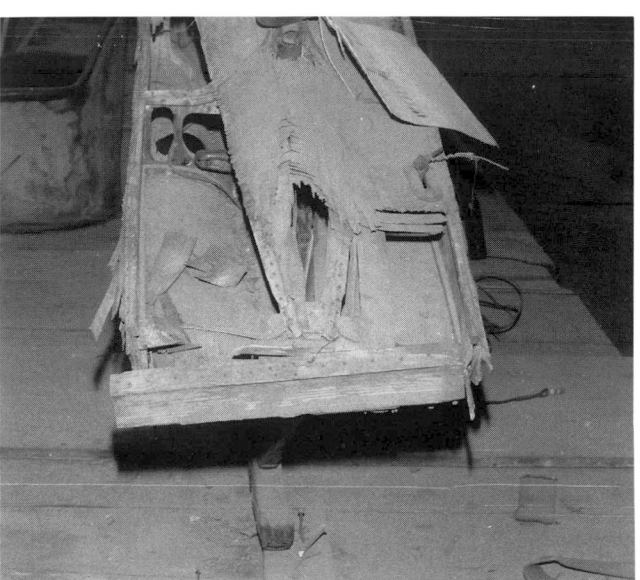
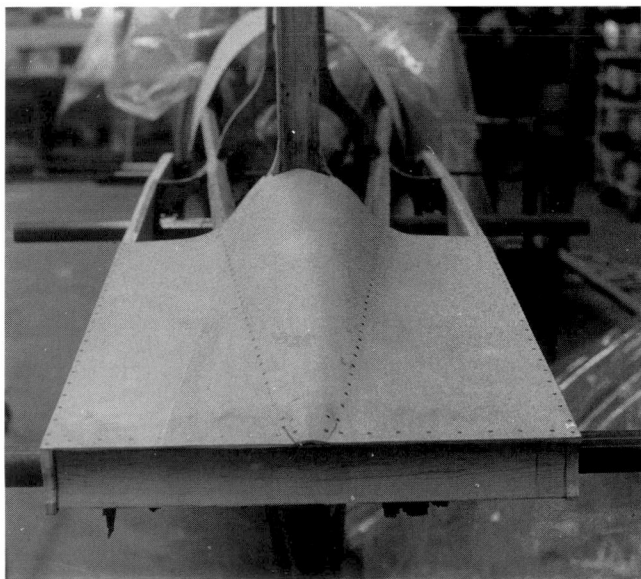

Glue was the primary skin application method, supported by light screws and nails. Garry Cline backs the structure while Richard Horigan nails the pre-formed skin in place at the bottom of the fuselage forward of the ventral fin.

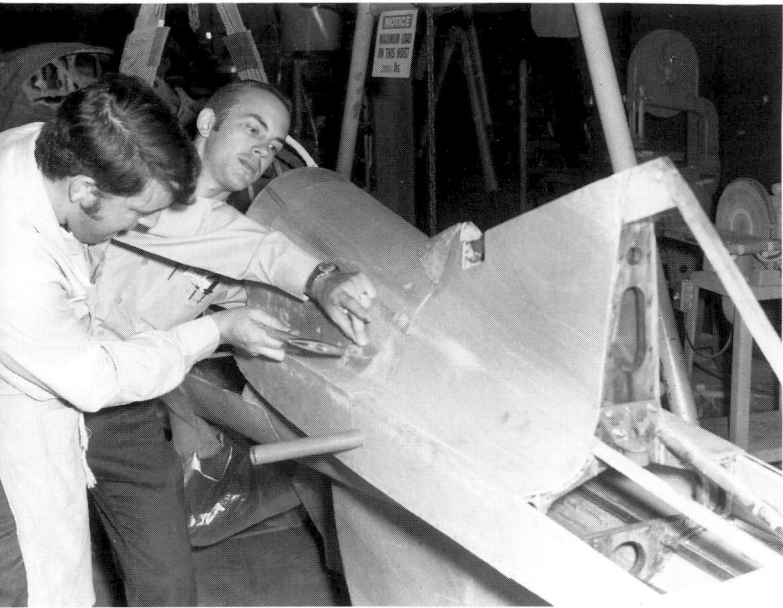

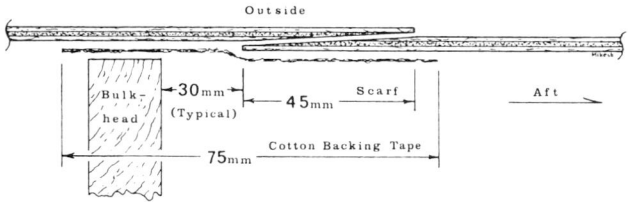

Since original production of the Albatros had the skin panels pre-shaped and lapped together before they were applied to the fuselage structure as a shell, the mating lines did not necessarily fall across fuselage formers. This is a cross-section view (not to scale) showing this skin scarf joint.

As the skinning process moved forward, this view shows a skin lap near a former. This presented problems of having the fabric reinforcement tape already in place around the former before applying the skin panels which it was to support.

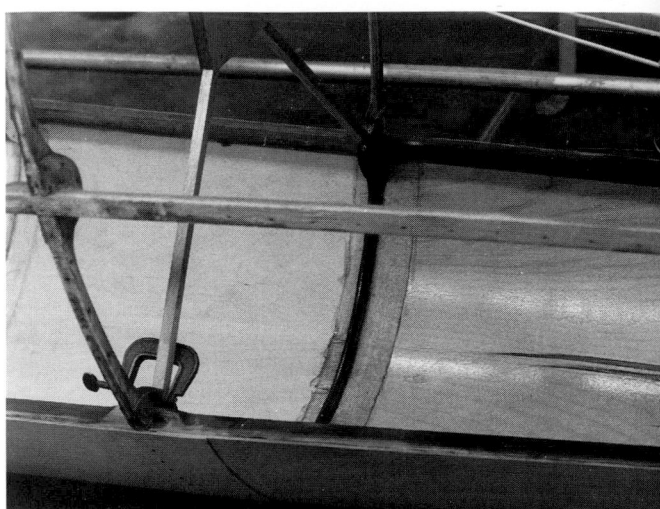

long derusting and preservation process would have been impractical.

Trying to duplicate the original and less effective adhesives would not have added technical value. Instead, modern adhesives, such as Weldwood™ plastic resin glue, were used in this restoration for greater strength and durability. Gluing had obviously been the primary method for joining materials, while screws and nails were secondary.

For proper overlapping of the skin panels, the application of panels began at the rear and moved forward. Removal of the old skin was limited to only that area needing to be worked on in order to retain the structural shape.

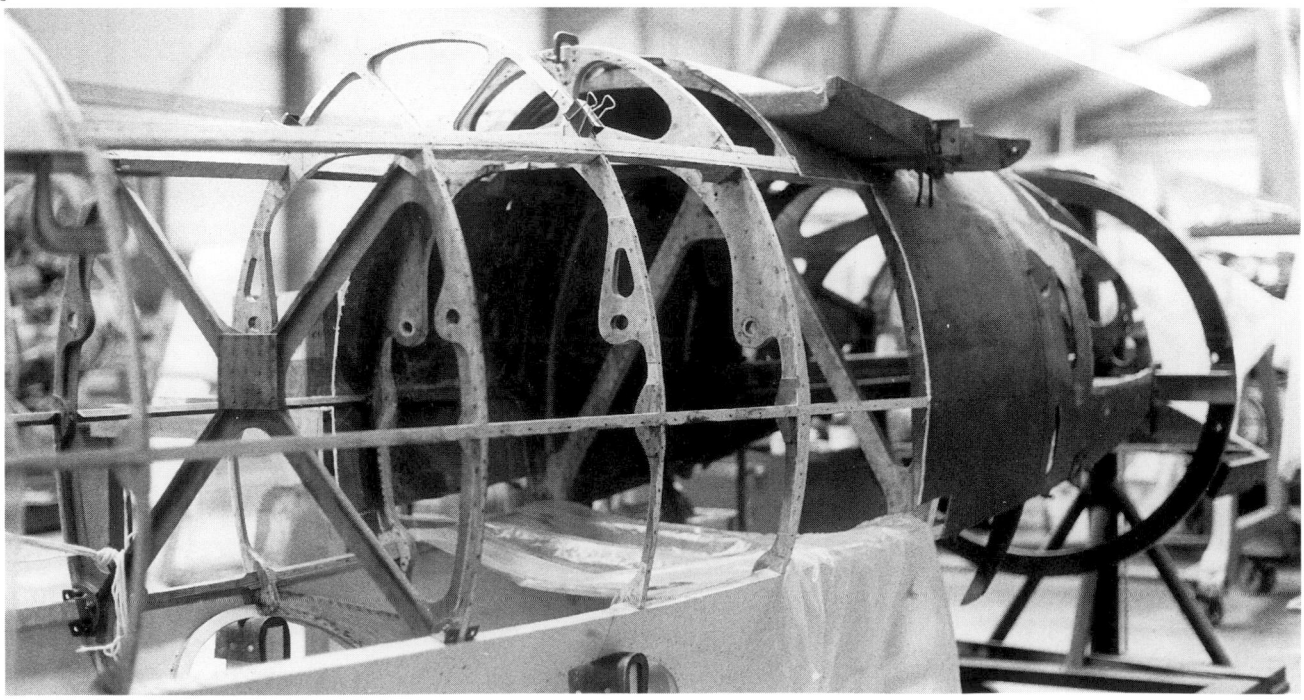

Restoring the interior structure of the fuselage was nearly as demanding as the reskinning. Ideally, this work should have been done with the fuselage completely unskinned. Instead, only small sections at a time could be cleaned and repaired where longerons and formers were exposed by the removal of single panels of skin. Some of the formers at the belly of the fuselage were completely rotted away, while others had been poorly patched for exhibit purposes many years ago; all the rotted wood had to be replaced.

The restored interior of the skin and structure was covered with two coats of spar varnish. As each section was completed, it was brush-painted from the outside through the next newly-opened section.

It was interesting to discover ground wires literally imbedded into the fuselage structure. They were placed in grooves along the outside of the upper and lower longerons so that when the skin was applied, they were concealed in the structure. The ground wire routing was from the engine mount, along the longeron to the lower wing-spar reinforcements and on to the tail-post tube and horizontal stabilizer. The wire along the upper longeron connected to the top wing-strut fittings and the ground was carried by the metal struts to the top wing which also had a ground wire.

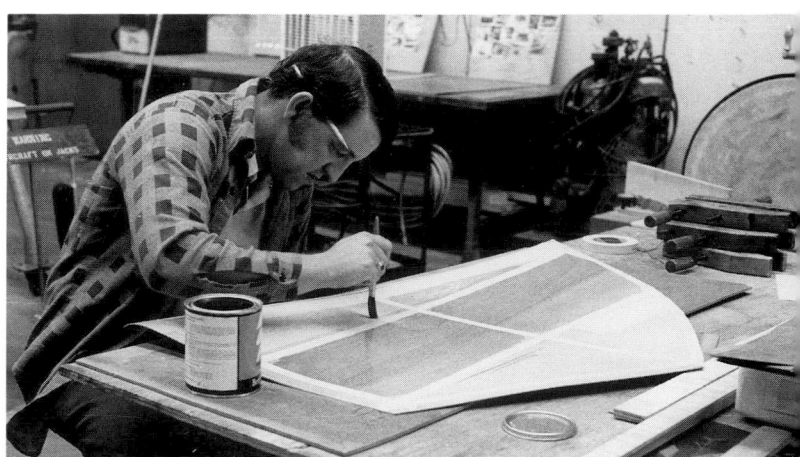

Like the originals, the new skin panels carried a coating of varnish on the interior. This skin panel for the fin had to be marked as to where glue would be applied for attaching to the structure and then varnished in the open areas. Glue would not adhere as well to a varnished surface.

Weeks turned into months, and piece after piece of precisely-sized plywood replaced the old, moving from the tail to the nose. Before dirt or discoloration could taint the new material, several coats of spar varnish were applied to the completed plywood surface as was the practice in German production. Early forms of varnish had a yellow cast which resulted in a warm transparent straw color for the fuselage, while modern varnish with less discoloration had left this fuselage a little lighter perhaps than when originally manufactured. Experience gained in finishing this fuselage indicates that we should have added a tint to the varnish with raw sienna or burnt umber to darken the plywood slightly. This would have been an alteration for purely cosmetic reasons, but the fact must be accepted that modern varnishes differ from the earlier ones and we expect them to provide better protection.

Cockpit: Restoring a cockpit is usually an unpleasant task due to the cramped working space and the many wires, tubes, and accessories that make cleaning so very difficult. In the case of the Albatros D.Va, however, this section was quite different. To begin, there were very few components compared with later cockpit interiors, and all were able to be easily removed for restoration. Also, with the fuselage skin removed, the internal details of the fuselage structure were easily accessible for cleaning and necessary repair. When new skin was attached to the fuselage, this naturally gave a clean, like-new interior.

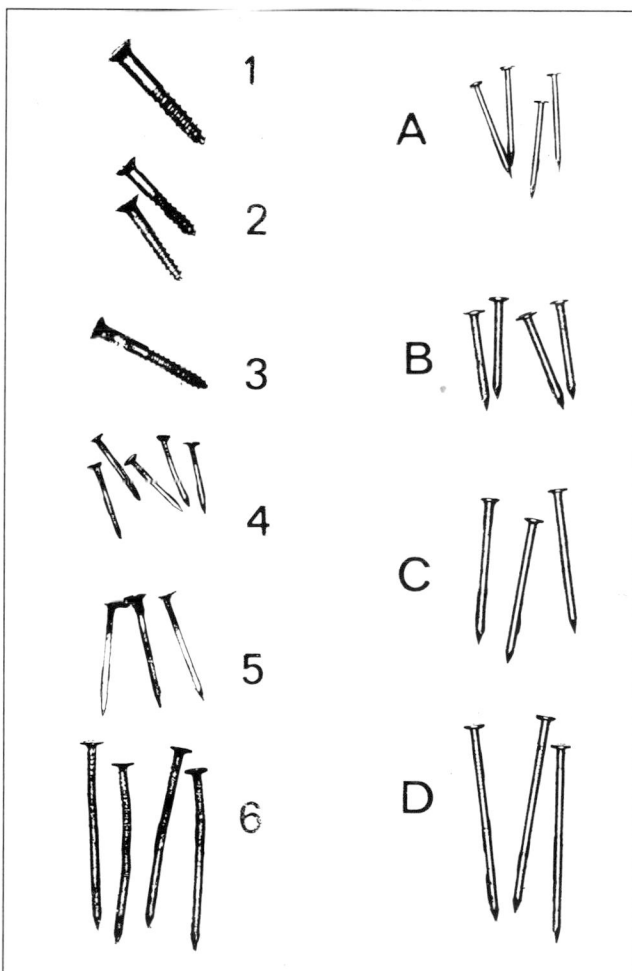

For a more positive record, samples of old and new nails and screws were glued on a card and covered with plastic. They were further described as to their composition and where within the structure they were generally found.

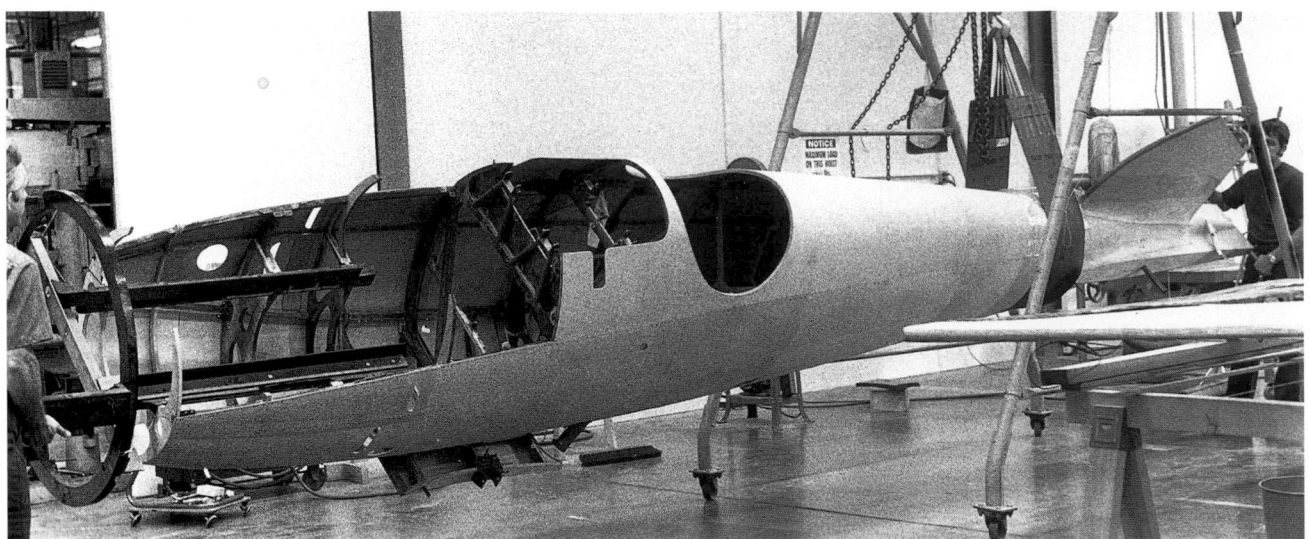

The newly-skinned Albatros D.Va fuselage is turned over for adding further details. The metal gun mounts are visible forward of the cockpit. A metal cowling and protrusion of the engine will fill the forward open areas.

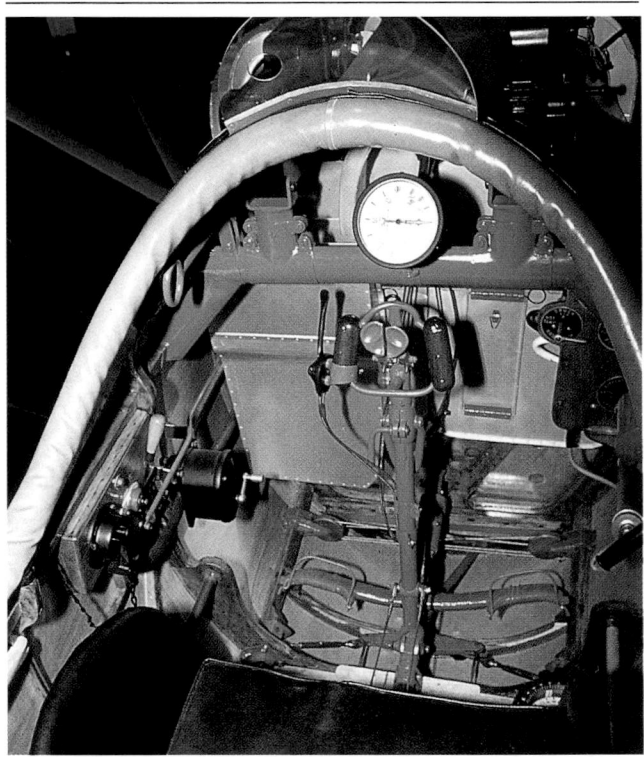

Cockpits of these early aircraft were quite austere. Noticeably lacking in this completed view of the cockpit is an instrument panel since the only instrument in front of the pilot was the tachometer. The throttle lever is on the left side of the left-hand grip on the control stick.

The cockpit and its equipment are of vital concern to NASM in the restoring of any aircraft. It is here that the technology available to the pilot for the operation of the aircraft can be observed and studied. In the case of this Albatros, researchers can now find every detail in its place, just as it was when the airplane was combat-ready in World War I.

A study had to be made of how the various systems components operated so they could be properly connected and restored to like-new and workable condition. These components and their functions are very different from those used in later years.

A number of cockpit items were missing and had to be replaced — no simple task for an airplane out of production for such a long period. Fortunately, a replacement booster starter magneto was obtained from the late Joseph M. DeFiore, an expert restorer of early aircraft in his own right. When doing a restoration of an obscure type, it is essential to locate a person who is an expert on that type of airplane, either directly or through the history of the type. Each airplane seems to have such an expert, perhaps there are several. Such experts know where to find what is needed, be it parts, drawings, or information, and must be brought into the project for this reason.

A fuel gauge was located within the museum's collection of vintage instruments to replace one of the missing items. Although the size and mechanism of the instrument matched the original type, the dial was graduated differently. John Siske of the museum's Exhibit Department undertook the task of recreating a new face. He photographed the old dial which contained many items such as the manufacturer's stylized name and other markings common to the required face. He used these details to develop a new dial face to match pictures showing the correct design. The museum's Exhibit Department is often called upon to apply its myriad capabilities to small details of this type.

Ammunition cans and their feed chutes located in front of the pilot's knees were cleaned of corrosion and repaired; however, a new expended cartridge belt container had to be fabricated. Details like this container and other missing parts were often provided by Bob Waugh of Australia, who made frequent reference to the D.Va in Australia to sketch these details. Over the years preceding this restoration, Francis P. Garove of Baltimore, Maryland, had taken a deep interest in the museum's Albatros and had gathered this type of material from such friends of the museum as Bob Waugh, Peter M. Grosz, Peter M. Bowers, Ed Ferko, the late William Puglisi, the Australian War Memorial Museum, and others. This combined effort provided many of the needed details for ready reference in the fabrication of parts, and saved considerable research time for the museum staff.

One of the embossed identifying valve placards located in the cockpit was also missing from the museum's Albatros. To replace this, David R. McMullen, who was in the process of building his own reproduction Albatros at the time, offered a spare example that he had cast for his project. Going one step further at the museum, Rich Horigan used this casting as a mold and made an aluminum impression that more closely matched the originals in the cockpit. A look inside the cockpit reveals little evidence that one of these placards is not an original. Museum records on this Albatros restoration, however, list this item as a replacement and not an original piece.

Wings: While the foregoing was taking place, Garry Cline undertook the restoration of the wings. As the rotted fabric was carefully removed and set aside for future reference and pattern needs, the structure took on the appearance of a mass of disjointed sticks. At this point, the wings appeared to pose an impossible task, much as the fuselage had done earlier. They appeared suitable only for patterns. With the confident smile that never

seemed to fade from his face, Garry began the 14-month task of restoring these three wings: upper, lower left, and lower right.

Starting with the lower left wing, the plan was to complete it before the lower right wing was altered in any way. Thus, one wing could serve as a pattern for the other. As glue seemed to have deteriorated at all joints, the entire wing structure had to be fully disassembled, each rib repaired, and the wing reassembled. The one advantage of this time-consuming task was that it allowed for the thorough cleaning and repair of each part, particularly the box spars whose 0.1-inch (3 mm) birch plywood webbing had delaminated in many places. In fact, the top wing spars were broken at approximately the mid-point of the wing. In this disassembly, the original nails were removed; most were able to be restored and used again during the rebuilding process. The restoration of the nails consisted of soaking them first in a hot alkaline rust stripper and then a hot phosphate solution, followed by a dipping in linseed oil as a preservative.

All wood used in the restoration of the wings was in metric sizes. Ash, basswood (linden) and long-leaf pine were used in the original wing, and the same type of woods were used for replacement parts. According to Joe Fichera, one of the senior restorers at the museum's facility, the current FAA Manual 43.13-1 contains good repair procedures to follow, for few changes have been made in wood repair methods since World War I. All splices that were needed for inserting new and replacement structural members were overlapped 10 to 1.

Almost every wing rib required some type of repair, from merely regluing loose portions, to

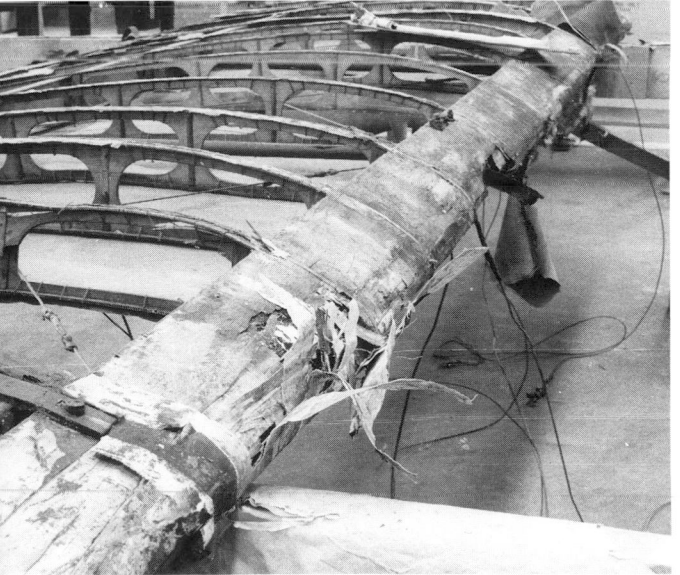

The fabric covering of the wing helped prevent the loss of many broken parts of this structure. Its poor condition necessitated a full disassembly for repair of the many parts before being aligned in the reassembly process.

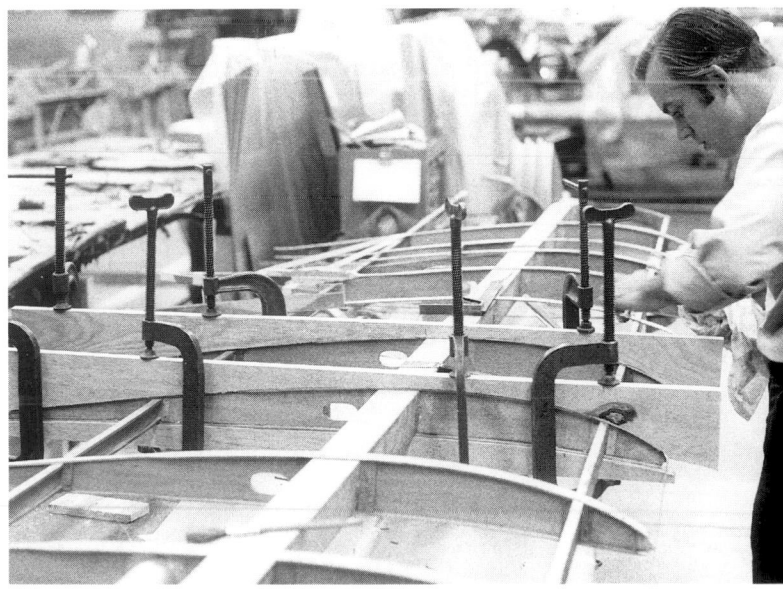

The wing was constructed in such a way that the nose ribs had to be assembled after the main part of the rib was in place. Garry Cline had to be ever mindful of the alignment during every step of this assembly process.

building new ribs where so much of their structure was broken or missing. No completely new rib was used, for each one had some original piece included. Garry Cline fabricated jigs for this work to ensure accurate and constant contours. This worked well for the lower wings, but to everyone's surprise, a number of ribs on the upper wing had variations in camber, especially in the area of the radiator. It seemed apparent that this could have been done to compensate for the radiator which may not have matched the intended airfoil. Since this was an unrecorded structural technical find, Garry made tracings of the various rib forms from which I made formalized drawings for any future reference needs.[23]

Reassembling the wing became an arduous task: care had to be taken not to induce a warp into the structure as the wings were rebuilt. Instead of completing each rib with its numerous small pieces, complications arose on the top wing which required assembling each rib around the two spars. Otherwise, fittings and glued reinforcement blocks that were permanently attached to the spars would have to be removed in order for the ribs to be slipped down the spars to their proper locations. Some ingenious jigs, templates, and methods evolved from this unorthodox reassembly.

The Germans were very methodical with their own marking of these wing ribs. From the center rib on the upper wing, and the butt ribs of the lower wings, each was numbered consecutively outward to the wing-tips. Ribs left of the centerline were marked on the left side, and conversely so for the right.

The wing-tip bows had become badly damaged over the years, but their outlines could be traced for use in making templates and fixtures to reconstruct them to their original shape. At first it was thought that these bows were made of three laminations of wood. Instead, two parallel cuts were made lengthwise in this wing-tip member, forming what appeared to be three separate strips. This made the bend much easier, and the strips were then glued together. This was only done in the area of the wing-tip bow where the bend was to take place. When glued and set, they were then routed on the inside of this curved area to reduce weight.

As with many aircraft designs of that period, the wing trailing edge consisted of a piano wire approximately 0.004-inch (1 mm) in diameter, attached to the back tip of each rib by a simple aluminum box-like clip. Normally, this wire was stretched to about 100 lb (45.4 kg) tension according to Joe Fichera, who found this reference in a manual for repairs on Curtiss JN-4 Jennys. Since this Albatros was not to fly and was to last indefinitely, this tension was lowered to 30–50 lb (13.6–22.7 kg) to reduce structural stress. This wire had to be taut enough that

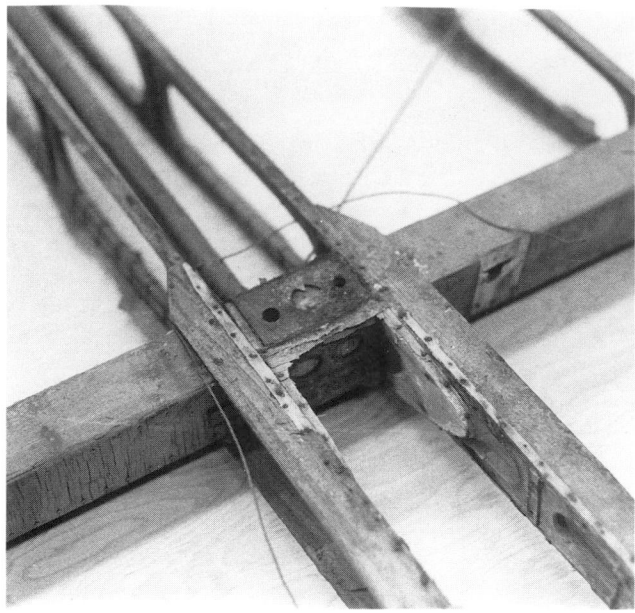

In this area of the aileron-horn cut-outs, the wing spar and wing rib caps had deteriorated badly. Many of the rib cap strips had to be replaced with new ash wood, all finished to metric sizes. Original and replacement gussets were 3 mm (0.1 inch) 3-plywood. New parts were stamped as replacement or repaired parts and then dated.

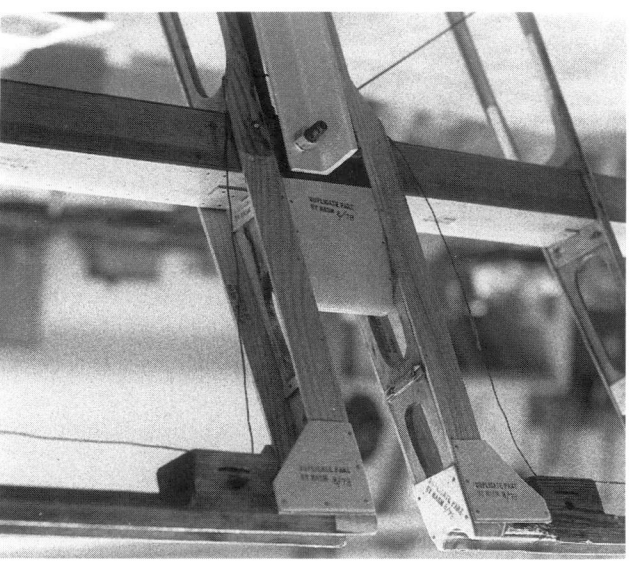

when the fabric was applied and tightened, the scallops would be even with no tendency to bend upward or downward.

Shortly after starting the project, Garry Cline discovered that the two lower wings were not a matched set. They appeared to have been made at the same factory, but at widely-spaced times. The left, for instance, had two metal compression stiffeners between the main spar and the leading edge, while the right had three which is believed to have been the standard. The butt ribs were constructed differently on each side of the two lower wings. In addition, rib-strip lacing with black thread was used on one wing while white thread was used on

This right rear view of the lower right wing-tip shows the restored structure ready for fabric covering. A slot in the wing rib where it butts against the wing spar fits over the small wood block for the correct vertical alignment. Fabric strip from the rib cap forward was 22-mm (0.87 inch) cotton tape, and a 150-mm (six-inch)-wide strip was doped to the wing leading edge as chafe strips. (NASM, SI 78-16523-20A)

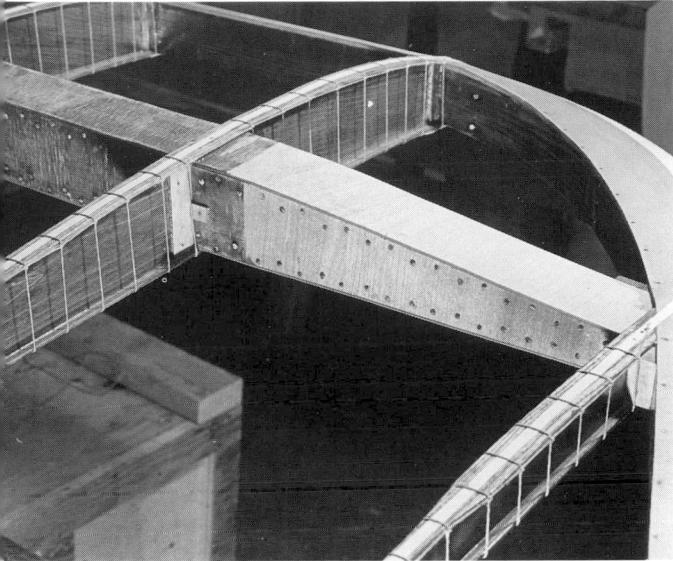

the other. Most noticeable was the red tint varnish on the left wing, while the other was nearly clear. All of this had little effect on the finished restoration, but it was interesting that no two of the three wing panels were of a set for this Albatros.

All metal fittings were cleaned, repaired, and painted in their original color. Internal fittings on the top wing were generally black, while the natural color fittings on the lower wings were coated with Water White[24] for the purpose of this restoration. There was so much reconstruction and repair of these wings that what aged varnish remained was removed and the structure revarnished. (Polyurethane epoxy varnish should not be used on aircraft structures. This material becomes hard and non-porous, and the wood cannot breathe properly or expand with environmental changes. These stresses eventually will weaken the wood fibers and reduce longevity.)

When the three wing structures were completed, 2,226 man-hours had been devoted to their restoration. Included in this time was the fabrication of a new right aileron out of metal tubing using the left aileron as a pattern. Although the new tubing nearly matched the material originally used on the left aileron, the new structure was noticeably heavier since the tubing walls were thicker. Thin stock to match the 60-year-old tubing could not be located.

Empennage: Restoring the tail presented few problems that were not anticipated. To begin with, all that remained of the rudder was the forward hinge post. The remainder had been removed years before the airplane was taken from exhibit at the De Young Memorial Museum in San Francisco. Why someone had torn away the rudder behind this structure member is hard to explain, for it would have been far simpler to merely remove the hinge pins. Fortunately, drawings prepared with reference to the Albatros in Canberra had been acquired several years before, and a new rudder was fabricated, beginning with the existing hinge post.

The wooden stabilizers were in as poor condition as the wings. Nearly every member had to be reglued; however, a full disassembly of the structure was not necessary. Much of the cracked wood needed splices for repair. Two coats of dope-proof varnish completed the structures and made them ready for fabric covering.

The metal structure of the elevator was in poor condition. It was rusty, bent, and broken in several places. After chemical processes were completed to remove rust from both inside and outside of this tubing structure, routine methods of repair were used. When completed, it was painted, as it was originally, a light bluish-green (Munsell Color code 10G 7/1).

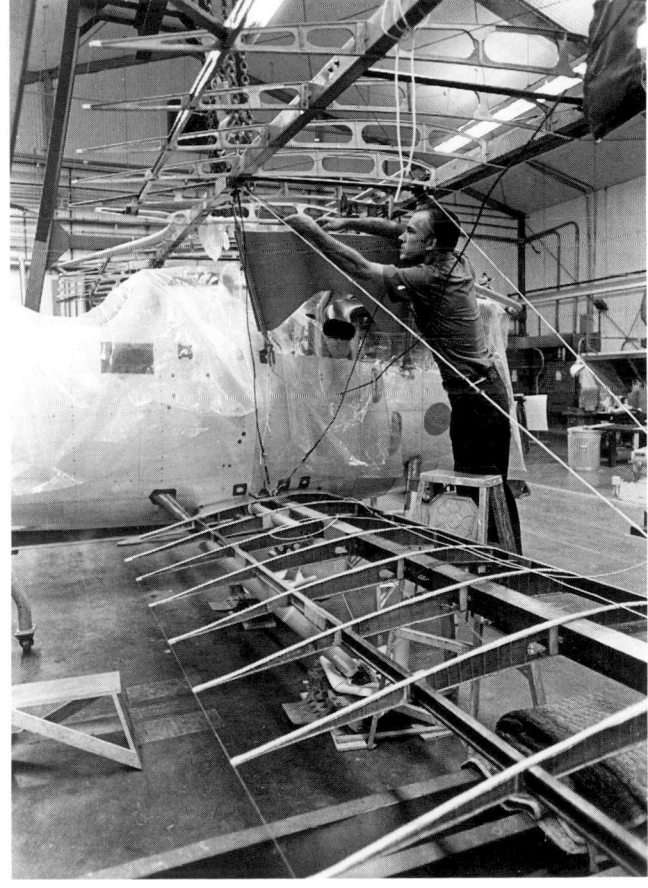

Neither struts nor bracing wires had adjustment points on the Albatros D.Va. Components had to be rigged and properly fitted at this early stage before fabric covering could be applied. Garry Cline attaches temporary cabine struts for proper alignment. (NASM, SI 78-16190-8A)

Final Assembly: When the components were restored, final assembly began. This is always the phase that is eagerly anticipated after the many months spent preparing the individual parts and assemblies. The main effort for this phase had already been accomplished several months earlier when the Albatros was assembled for a fit-check and before the wings and tail were covered with fabric. None of the original struts came to the museum with this airplane, nor were adequate drawings or rigging diagrams available. There was but one way to do this, according to Garry Cline, and that was to position and align all components in their proper location in relation to the fuselage, and make the struts to size.

Using the little dimensional information that was available, plus a few key dimensions and detailed photographs obtained from the Albatros in Canberra, the parts were put in place much like a model-builder would set up jigs to use in attaching the top wing to a biplane model. The fuselage with its lower wings in place was rigidly fixed in a horizontal position. Using an A-frame to hold the upper wing, it was meticulously aligned above the fuselage. Plumb lines were hung from many points to check alignment. Once all parts were in their correct location, temporary wing struts were fabricated from sections of electrical conduit tubing by having the ends of each section flattened and holes drilled for bolting into position. Cardboard templates confirmed proper angles. When all seemed to properly align, each strut assembly was fabricated — one at a time — in the form it was originally, and put in place. What seemed unusual was that none of these struts had a method of adjustment, they all had fixed bolt holes or pin attachment points. Perhaps some trimming was accomplished through the external bracing wires.

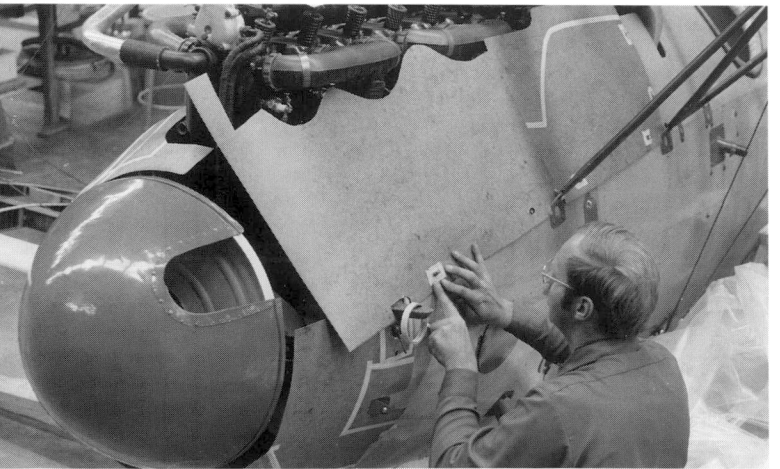

The Albatros was received by NASM *without cowling. Metal specialist Bill Stevenson fabricates a cardboard template to make and form the metal component that when finished will have compound curves. Note the cowl fasteners already in place. (*NASM, SI 78-18298-11*)*

All this rigging was a very time-consuming and difficult task, yet it was accomplished as accurately as the available information permitted. One questionable matter was the dihedral used on the bottom wings, for no reliable record of this angle could be found. Measuring from drawings presumed to be accurate, a dihedral of two degrees was used.

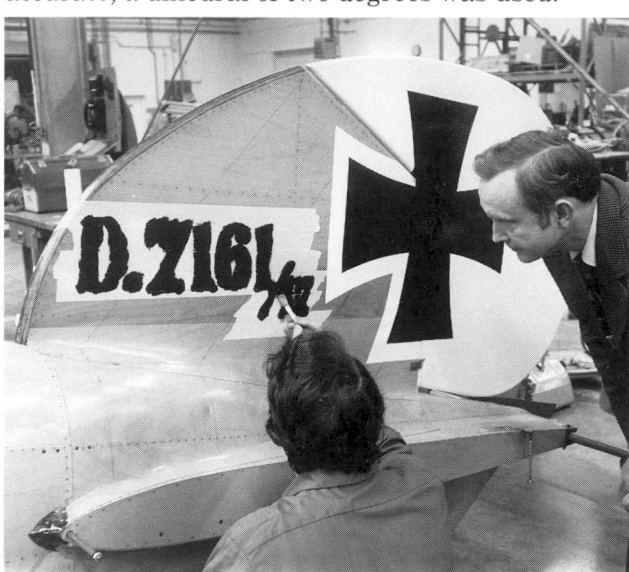

Not until this restoration was the serial number of this Albatros D.Va discovered when the green and yellow tail stripe paint was removed from the fin. Project curator, Bob Mikesh watches Rich Horigan repaint these numbers as they were originally. Masking tape allowed a paint build-up so that the numbers could be slightly detected when the striping was again applied over this identification.

Structural twisted stranded cable-bracing between the wings presented other problems. Originally these were of metric size, but this type of cable was not available in the US, nor could it be located in Europe. In desperation, Garry discovered a standard cable in stock in the US that contained a core very close to the original unbraided cable size needed. Unraveling this large cable to obtain only the core strand consumed a lot of cable, but for the sake of exactness, this was the solution that was pursued. Cables cut to the desired length were prepared with a woven tuck splice at each end securing them to turnbuckles and fittings. Some original cables came with the airplane which did help with the assembly process to some degree, and a difference can be detected between the original and replacement cables, primarily by the number of wires in the strand and lay, but there are only slight differences from the original diameter. The original standing rigging (drag wires) are 1 x 38 (inner core of 19 wires twisted in one direction, covered by 19 wires twisted in the opposite direction), while the running rigging (flying wires) are 7 x 12 (seven strands consisting of 12 wires each). Replacement standing rigging became either 1 x 19 or 1 x 38, while running rigging is 7 x 19. In all, 13 cables are original to this airplane and 23 are of new material.

Once all rigging was checked for proper alignment, the Albatros was disassembled so that the wings could be covered.

Long before this stage, the landing gear had been restored and put in place. This phase was not an easy task, for about all that was on hand were the main axle and two rusty landing gear V-struts; both struts had their streamline tubing bent. Missing was the spreader bar to hold the struts in place while the axle floated on bungee shock cords. Using dimensions obtained from the Albatros in Canberra and checking against the length of the cross-tie cables, a spreader-bar assembly was reconstructed.

Even the wheels that came with the airplane were a mismatch; the rims were of the same size, but one hub had a babbitt bearing while the other had brass bearings, and both had slightly different grease fittings. It was presumed that the wheel covers would have been of spun aluminum. Not having this capability within the shop, these were made from flat .025 soft aluminum cut to become conical in shape, and the seam was Heliarc-welded. With a stroke of luck, one wheel cover mounting block remained wedged between the spokes of one wheel which served as a pattern for the rest. Ten blocks per wheel provided support for a 0.18-inch (4.5 mm) bolt through these blocks to hold the aluminum wheel discs in place.

Tires for these wheels were obtained from Universal Tire Company stock for classic car restorations; however, these did not fully satisfy the

design that was used and the search continues for more accurate tires. Those that were put on the airplane after its arrival in the US were 'Harburg-Wien' 760 x 100s, but they had hardened with age and were unusable. Other sources show the proper tires to be 700 x 100s.

When the fabric covering was complete, the final assembly of the entire aircraft proceeded quickly. Marking details had already been accomplished as each major component was finished. Therefore, when the components of the Albatros were assembled, the project came to a swift, anti-climactic, conclusion. Details that still remained incomplete at that time were the centerline fuselage stripe for field alignments and the few metal instructional placards to be attached to the main components. These details required additional research that could best be accomplished after the aircraft was assembled, and were added to the airframe a few months later.

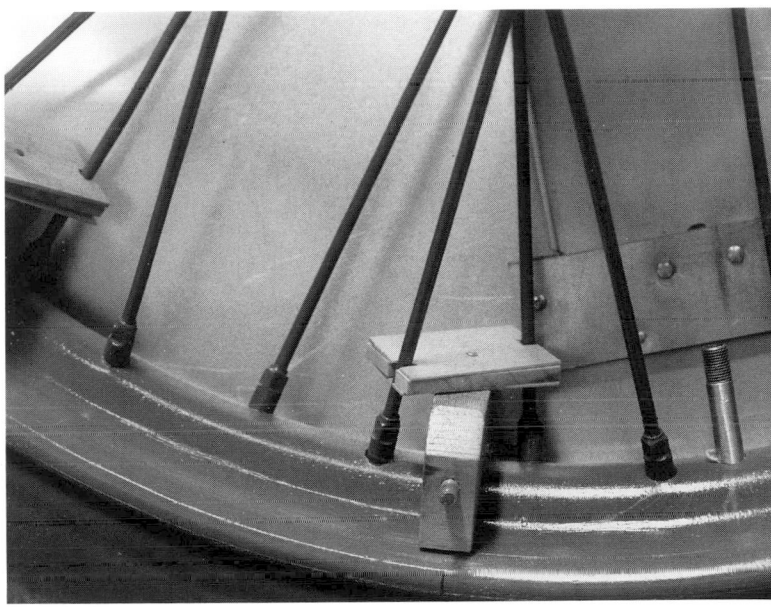

Wheel covers for the spoked wheels of the Albatros D.Va consisted of a block having studs on each side, held in place by a wedge block between the spokes. Two original blocks are all that remained to serve as patterns from which to fashion this early technique.

Although real bungee cords were used on the Albatros D.Va landing gear restoration, a steel cable underneath these windings absorbed the weight of the airplane that would eventually overstress the bungees. (NASM, SI 79-4783-31)

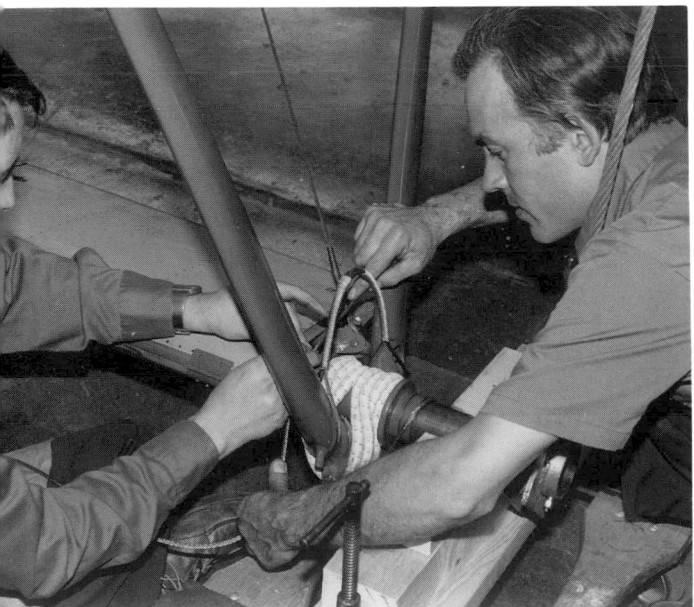

Aircraft Fabrics

The selection of a new material for the recovering of fabric aircraft is often a perplexing problem. If the airplane in question was originally covered with Grade A cotton, there is no problem. This duplication of originality can be resolved with the purchase of new Grade A cotton[25].

The use of Dacron or similar modern materials as a substitute for cotton is a dead giveaway to the knowing eye. They simply do not look right on vintage aircraft. Added longevity should not be the reason for using these materials on museum-type aircraft. Cotton should last to the point where the

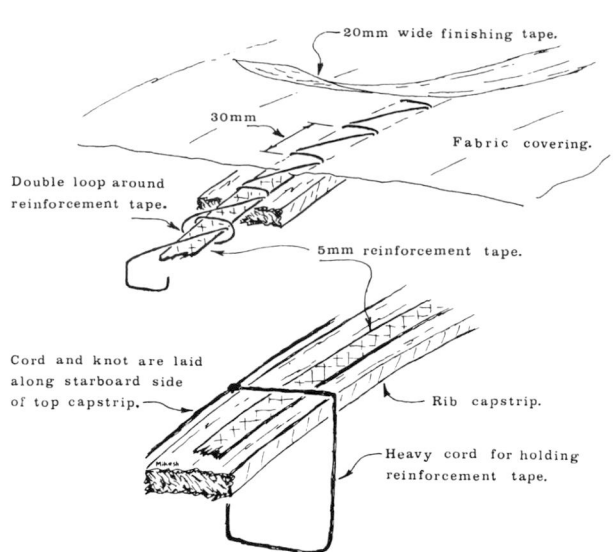

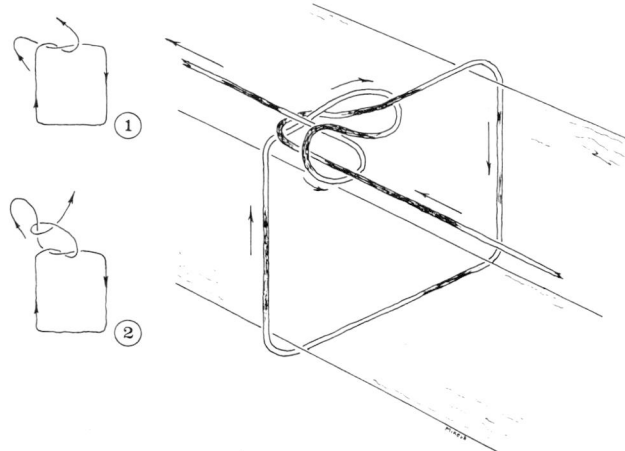

This is the method by which the wing fabric was attached to the wing rib.

This is the rib stitch knot for the Albatros D.Va that holds the reinforcement tape to the cap strip. This knot was first an overhand loop (1), secured by a half hitch (2). Loop ties are approximately 30 mm (1.2 inches) apart along the rib.

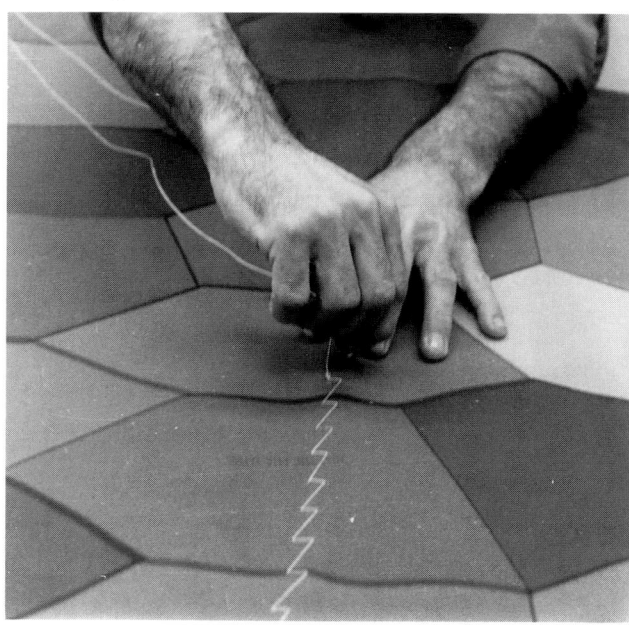

A curved needle was used to catch the reinforcement tape that was laced along each rib cap strip. Stitches were 30 mm (1.2 inches) apart. The dark border around the polygons is a deliberate overprint of the adjacent colors so that white lines would not show.

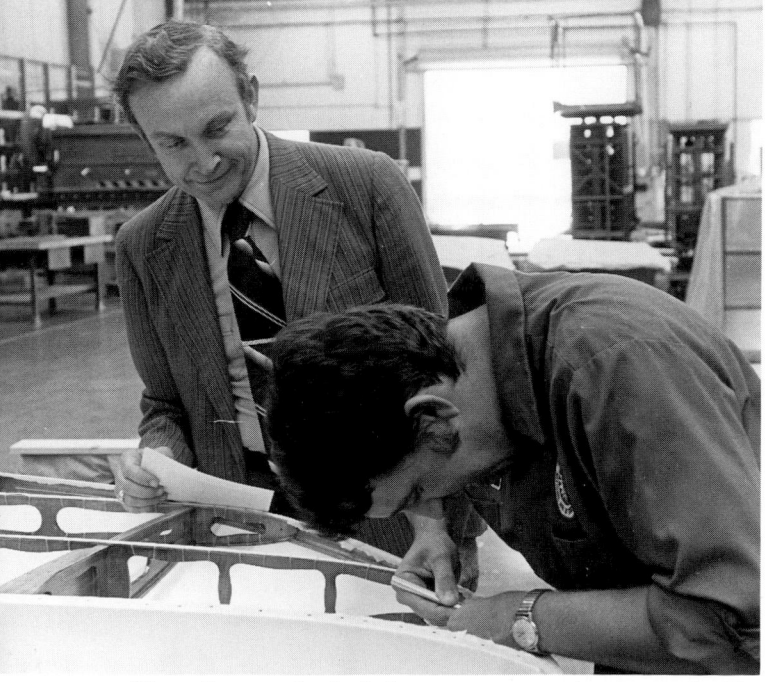

The tedious task of reinforcement tape-tying is watched by the author and curator for this restoration. Richard Horigan uses one of several tools specially fabricated for certain functions of this project in order to match original techniques. (NASM, SI 78-16524-4)

structure would need preservation attention that would require the material to be removed anyway. Examples of cotton durability are seen on the 1909 Wright Military Flyer and 1917 Caudron G-4 at NASM, both with original cotton fabric.

For the very early type of aircraft built before the introduction of Grade A cotton, the problem is compounded. In aircraft restorations, there is that strong desire to acquire exactly the same material that was used originally. The problem is that you usually cannot get there from here!

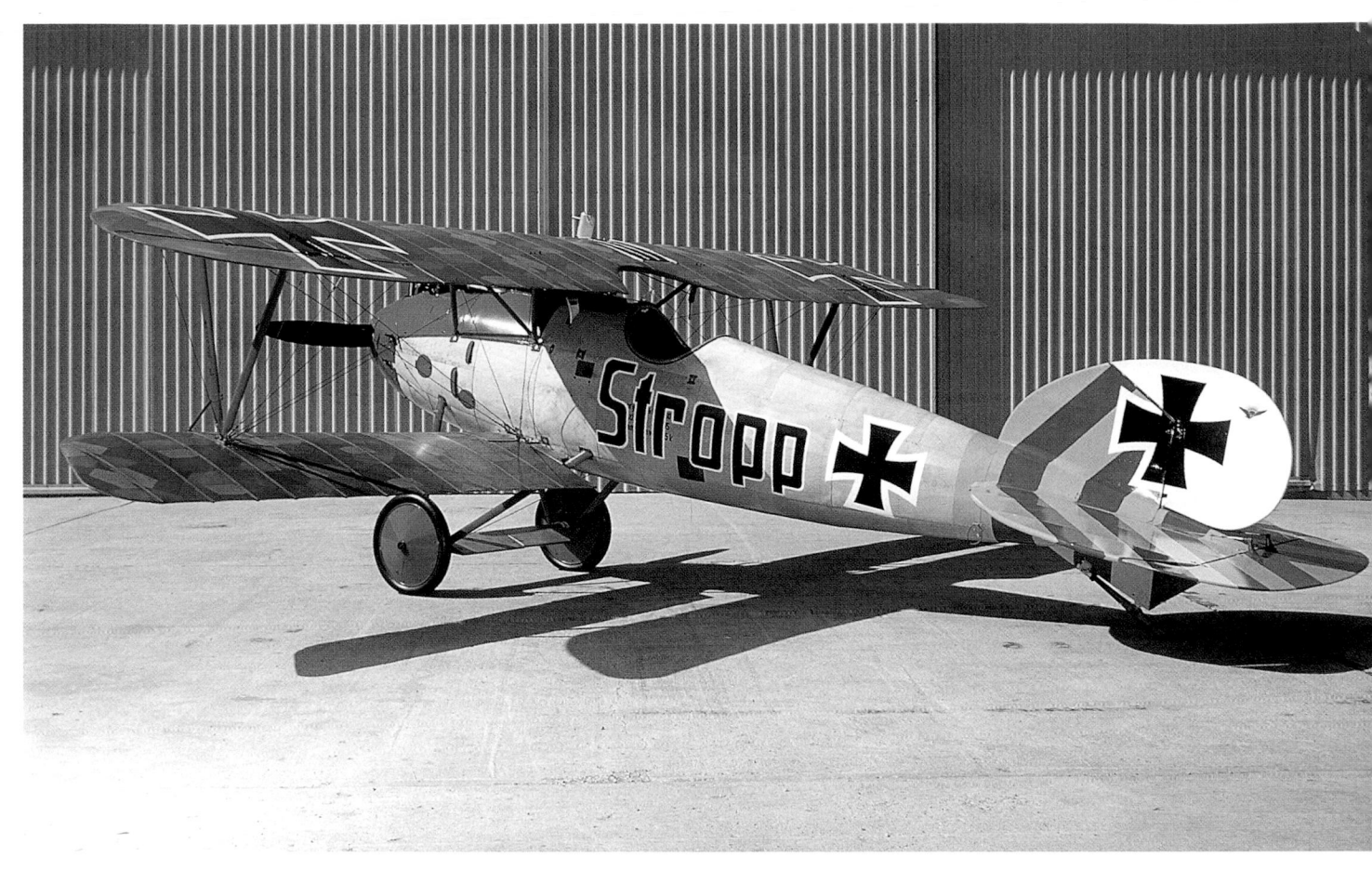

The completed Albatros D.Va as it appeared on roll-out at NASM when completed in March 1979.

Wright Flyer

This realization became apparent when we had to select new material for recovering the Wright Flyer during its 1985 restoration at NASM. The existing fabric was beginning to fail and was too fragile to withstand the rigors of cleaning and spot removal of the many water stains. When Orville Wright undertook the first restoration of this airplane in 1926-27, his meticulous records showed that he too wished to acquire from Pride of the West™ once again the identical plain-weave cotton fabric that he had used originally. He was able to do so, although the new material was three inches (7.62 cm) wider.

For the 1985 restoration a search for a fabric company that would match the original material like that of either of the first two coverings revealed that few modern manufacturers produced the pure cotton fabric required for this duplication. Even Pride of the West™, the original company that made the Wright Brothers' material, was now owned by Fruit of the Loom™, and no longer made a similar fabric.

One company, J.P. Stevens & Co., of New York, came to the rescue in wishing to help with this historic work. After studying a sample of the orig-inal 1903 fabric, Stevens & Co. experts identified a very similar material in current production. With a count of 118 threads per inch in warp and woof in the new fabric, as opposed to the count of 102 warp and 107 woof for the original 1903 material, the difference would be virtually undetectable to the naked eye or to the touch. The fabric was accepted. The coarser fabric that formed the interior rib sleeves designed to draw the lower fabric surface up against the bottom of the ribs was not available anywhere. Once again, J.P. Stevens & Co. came to NASM's assistance, weaving a special fabric of identical thread-count especially for this restoration. Few restorations of this historic value can acquire such outside co-operation. In this instance, the restoration specialists trimmed the new fabric to the original 37-inch (94 cm) width, and used detailed photos and the single surviving wing of 1903 fabric as a guide to the position of the seams.

We were quite pleased with what was accomplished, for there was a generally-held feeling that this near-duplication of original fabric would provide another 65 years of exhibition before the fabric would again have to be replaced. My words were no sooner overheard by a textile conservator who was observing our work, than I was quickly corrected. I received a short lecture describing why today's modern fabrics are far less resilient than the materials that we had hoped to have duplicated.

The differences are in production methods, the stability of the fibers, and even the finishing has changed. 'You may remember your grandmother, Bob, who would hand-scrub your grandfather's white shirts on a scrub-board,' the conservator reminded me, 'and yet they lasted for years. Try that on a white shirt today and see how long it will last.' She made a good point.

Although not intended for the purpose of enhancing longevity of the wing fabric, the method by which the Wright brothers attached their cotton fabric to the airframe had an effect. Instead of the common practice of attaching fabric squarely to a rectangular frame such as their wing form, the Wrights applied it diagonally. This diagonal or bias placement on the wing allowed for more stretch with less tension on the fibers. This was done to facilitate their wing-warping method of lateral control while at the same time, intentional or not, it placed less strain on the fabric while at rest. Perhaps the most famous use of this diagonal or bias construction is that of 1930s screen star Jean Harlow's form-fitting evening clothes where contours were not confined by rectilinear restrictions of fabric weave. That is, she could wear an extremely tight dress, sit down, and not split the seams.[26]

It is pointless to anticipate finding a perfect match to original fabrics of the early years of the 20th century. Changing techniques in manufacture makes this near impossible. When restoring the Wright Flyer in 1985, an attempt for exactness was made but a compromise became a necessity.

The duplication of early fabric to the correct widths to the selvage edge for the Wright Flyer restoration became impossible since looms had changed over the years. The search for 100 per cent cotton expected to be found in clothing of the 1980s, the time period of this restoration, was also futile. Most had a durable press finish. This was said at the time to lessen the durability of the cotton by 30 per cent. On the other hand, cotton blends without this finish were more durable than 100 per cent cotton. Of these, the most common are 50/50 cotton polyesters. They retain the same appearance of pure cotton, yet are more resilient to light, water, insects and fungus.

Material having a longer life can be attained with 100 per cent synthetics; yet these synthetics are more opaque, and therefore do not have the appearance of the original cloth. They often have a reflective glossy finish. Cotton blends, therefore, make for a better appearance and life expectancy while still looking like the original material. When aircraft having fabric blends are examined in later years, it will be apparent that this fabric was a replacement since this type of material had not been developed during the flying times of these early aircraft. This was the reasoning used when tying a protective sleeve of Gore-Tex™ over the metal cap at the leading edge of each wing rib of the Wright Flyer. This will prevent any transfer of rust stain from showing through the outer covering, as happened with the earlier covering.

It is difficult to select from modern materials the right fabric covering and proper coatings for use on these early aircraft. For aircraft of the unpainted

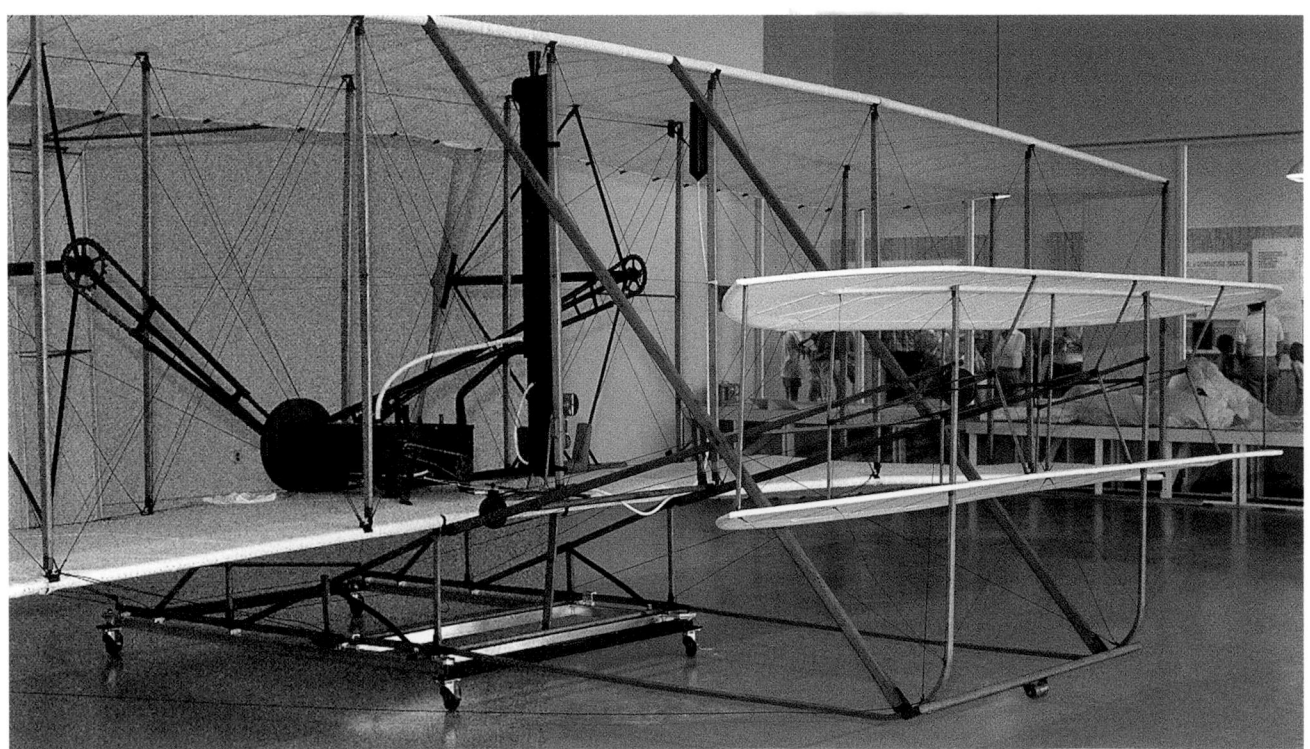

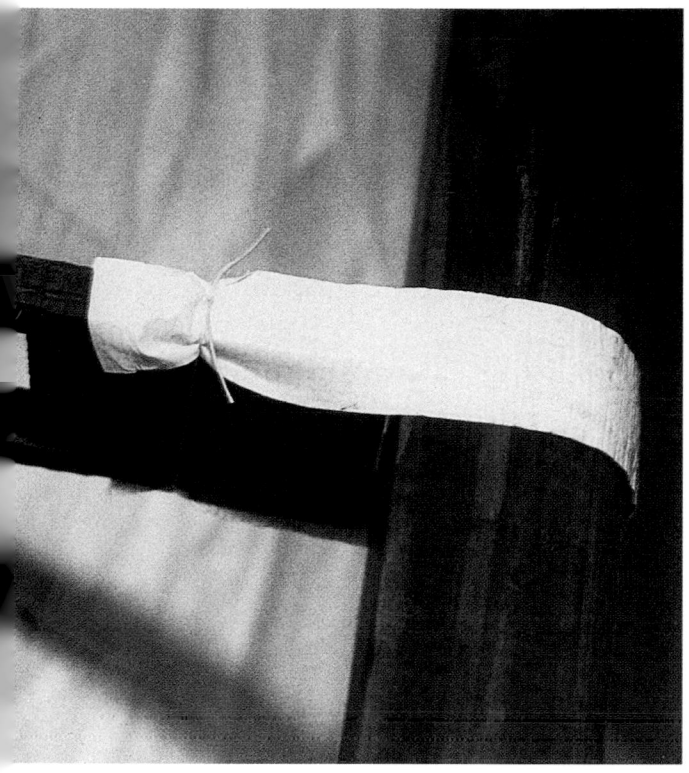

To shield the new fabric covering from possible rust stains when it rested against the tin fasteners of the wing rib, a Gore-Tex™ mit was tied over the end as a moisture barrier. This modern fabric mit and string will not be confused during future recoverings as having been 1903 material or a preservation technique.

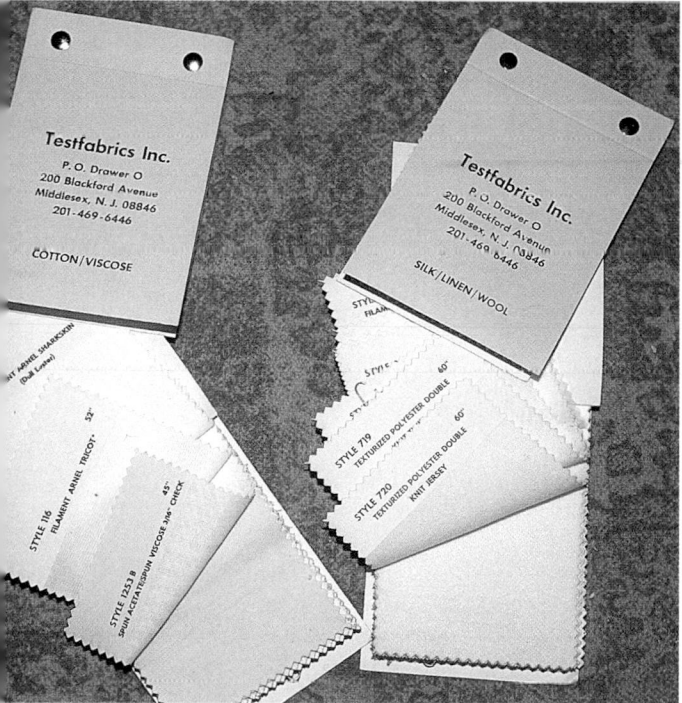

When restoring early aircraft that used unpainted fabric for coverings, it can be difficult, if not impossible to find an exact match. Fabric material companies can supply samples from which to match to the closest visual appearance and obtain greater longevity with the more modern blends.

variety showing the natural material, much will depend upon the intent of the restoration or mock-up project. If the airplane is to be a flying reproduction, this aspect falls outside the coverage of this book. If the aim is to have the airplane *look* as it did in its earlier and newer state, the word look gives us the needed guidance.

This search for a suitable fabric covering can be focused on one of several fabric supply houses that can furnish sample books of their materials (see Appendix G). Select a fabric that looks like the original with regard to thread-count and appearance. This largely has to do with the see-through qualities when compared to photographs of the original or actual covering.

Before making the final selection of material, obtain about a yard (0.9 m) of each of the samples being considered with which to make a few tests. Determine each material's contouring and shrinkage qualities. To do this, build frames upon which to stretch and mount these fabric samples. These frames should also have contours such as wing rib curves. One fabric we selected would not shrink adequately in one direction and therefore retained undesirable sags, resulting in having to make another and hurried last-minute selection. On the fabric that appears to be the best at this point, apply the clear coatings planned for the restoration and see how well the material responds.

Early Dopes and Clear Finishes

The application of a suitable finish to these early unpainted fabric-covered aircraft presents another problem. We must interject here this hard-to-accept word *compromise*. Some of the gelatin solutions, linseed oil, flour paste, and thinned rubber coatings of the past, as examples, may approach the original methods and materials used, but would certainly lessen the life span of the fabric material.

The Wright brothers used no filler or sealer on their fabric; if used it would have improved the flying quality of the Wright Flyer considerably. For the 1985 restoration of this airplane, a liberal coating of 3M Scotch Guard™ was applied to the unsealed fabric for easier cleaning and protection of the fabric.

The late Kenneth M. Molson, aviation historian and former Director of Canada's National Aviation Museum, conducted considerable research on this otherwise obscure subject of early aircraft fabric coatings. He learned that the Wrights advanced to adopting a rubber-coated fabric, probably cotton, thought to be at the time when they made their first sales. The Aerial Experiment Association's first aircraft, the Red Wing, was covered with red uncoated silk; the next, the White Wing, used uncoated cotton; the third, the June Bug, used cotton treated with paraffin wax dissolved in

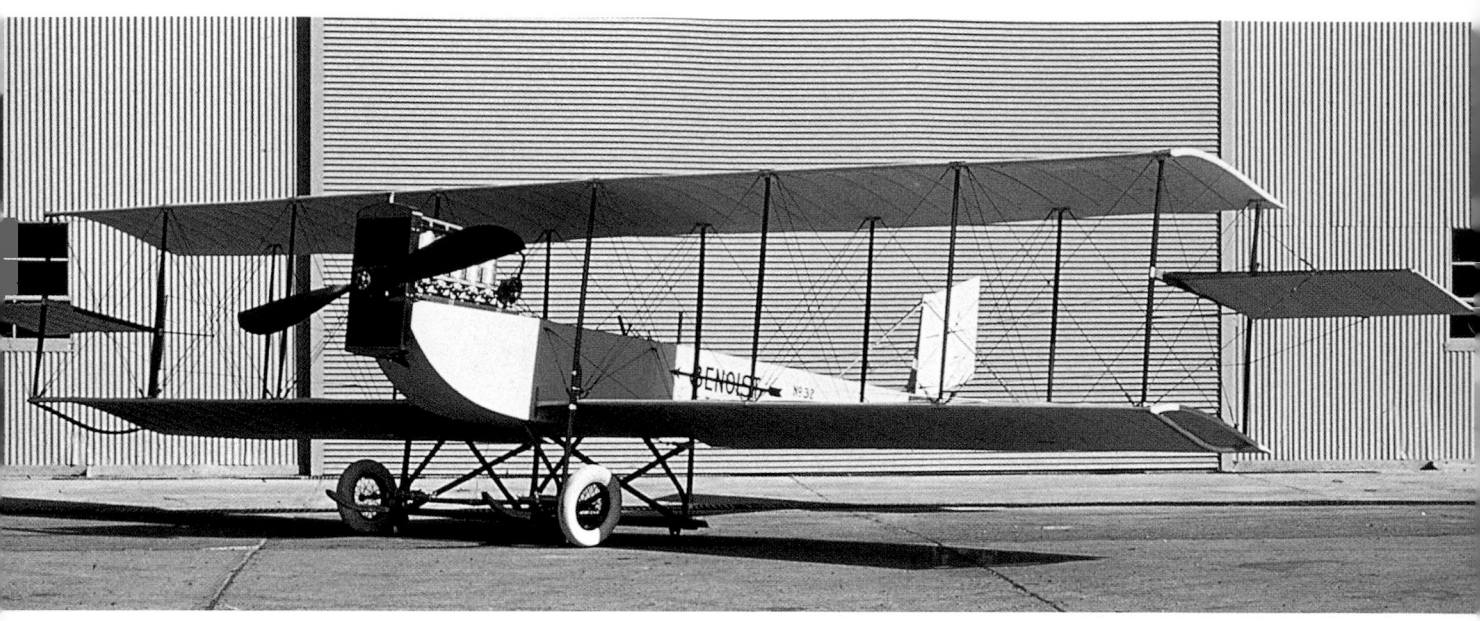

While exactness was attempted by covering this Benoist Type XII with original-type balloon cloth consisting of a coating of latex over the fabric, longevity of the fabric was lost. The latex has changed color to a dark parchment and another recovering process lies in the near future.

gasoline; and their last machine used rubberized silk. When Glenn Curtiss established his own manufacturing business he standardized the use of rubberized silk until summer 1913.

It may be wise to elaborate a bit more on this early history of aircraft coverings and fabric sealers for those who may have need or the good fortune to have aircraft of this early period to restore. According to Molson's extensive research, what appears to be the first dope to be offered in the US was announced in the September 1912 issue of *Aeronautics*; a new fabric varnish which would dry quickly and tighten up the fabric. The July 1913 issue first carried the term 'dope,' but this word did not quickly become widespread. A better cotton fabric for aircraft was first used in the US in April 1917. This marked the beginning of what is now known as aircraft cotton.[27]

Various methods were adopted for making aircraft fabric weather-proof and air-tight. In addition to applying water to tighten the fabric to the structure by shrinkage, a coating of vulcanized rubber was the usual practice in early days. This was superseded by flexible paints or dopes, oil or other varnishes.

Of the three classes of varnish used, the spirit varnish consisted of dissolved resins, such as shellac, in alcohol or methylated spirit. Oil varnishes were composed of drying oils, such as linseed, walnut, and poppy, which readily oxidized in thin films when exposed to the air. A third class of varnish was a blend of oils, resins and turpentine.[28]

When restoring vintage aircraft that pre-date World War I and used these clear finishes, it is generally impossible to precisely duplicate the materials used. Even if the name of the fabric or coating materials are known, their duplication with today's manufacturing differences and changes in chemical products would make these attempts impractical.

The National Aviation Museum's restoration staff in Ottawa was faced with this problem when restoring their 1915 McDowall Monoplane in 1983. This airplane is of considerable importance because it is the oldest Canadian-build airplane that survives. In this restoration they wished to duplicate the use of materials as much as possible. The early use of linseed oil treatment on this and many airplanes of its time period was never very satisfactory for a number of reasons, but nevertheless was used extensively in the pre-World War I days. The use of dope on the McDowall Monoplane would probably provide greater longevity for the fabric but it would not look or be right historically. The difficult decision was made to go with the original use of linseed oil.

Now finished and in its tenth year, Mr. A.J. 'Fred' Shortt, Director, Collections and Research at the National Aviation Museum reports that so far, the finish has proved to be as durable as any of the other fabric (doped) aircraft on display. There was concern that the linseed oil would remain tacky and collect dust or other particles. This did not become a problem. It is surviving well with its original-type coating and honey-like color. This is believed to be the only museum specimen to be restored with this pioneer finish.[29] So far, according to 'Fred' Shortt, there is no evidence of the oiled fabric becoming brittle as the original did. This was removed after 70 years, having been in far less than a museum environment for many of those years. We must wait a bit longer before reaching any definitive conclusions.

If we were to assume that there are shortcomings in longevity with this type of duplication, serious consideration should be given to using the proven Grade A cotton and clear dope for as long as supplies of this material last. Unfortunately, the application of fabric covering is quickly becoming a lost art, and airplane Grade A cotton is no longer being produced yet remains available without the 'airplane' qualifier. This type of cotton fabric surface is on the 1918 Curtiss JN-4 trainer that has been in the collection of NASM since leaving operational military service in 1919. Kept within buildings all this time, even though in unstable temperature and humidity conditions, the original cotton covering with varnish is still on this aircraft at the time of writing with no significant signs of failure. This longevity negates the argument that Dacron-based fabrics are needed to enhance the survivability of museum aircraft.

At NASM, we ran an accelerated test program on Grade A cotton panels to evaluate various coatings. For our study, we 'carefully *tossed*' panels with different coatings out behind the shop where they were exposed to sunlight and weather for 38 months. The butyrate-doped surface with spar varnish showed the least color change and deterioration. This test was made at a time when nitrate materials were not being used within the shop; but

in practice today, nitrate dope would be used to provide control over fabric shrinkage as opposed to using butyrate dope. (See illustration of test results of various coatings.)

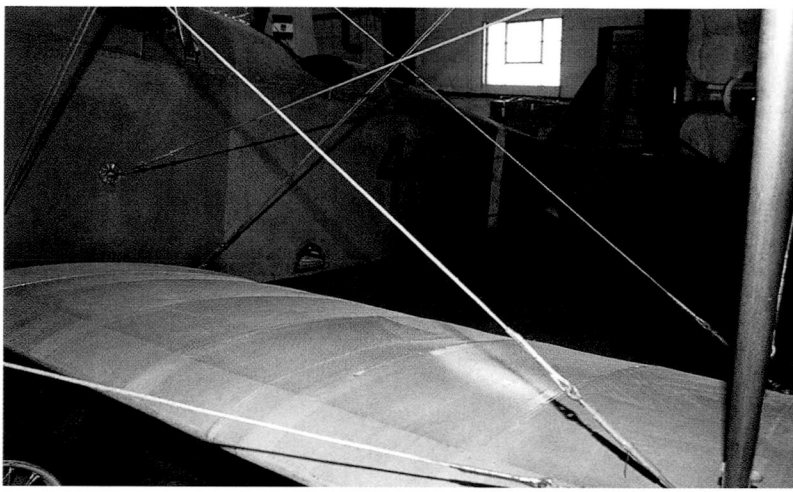

When Grade-A cotton was the original fabric and needs to be replaced, that may be the best material to use again. This Curtiss Jenny has its original 1918 fabric after 75-plus years because the airplane spent all but the first few years indoors despite uncontrolled atmospheric conditions. When cotton fabric must be replaced, the inner structure will probably need attention as well.

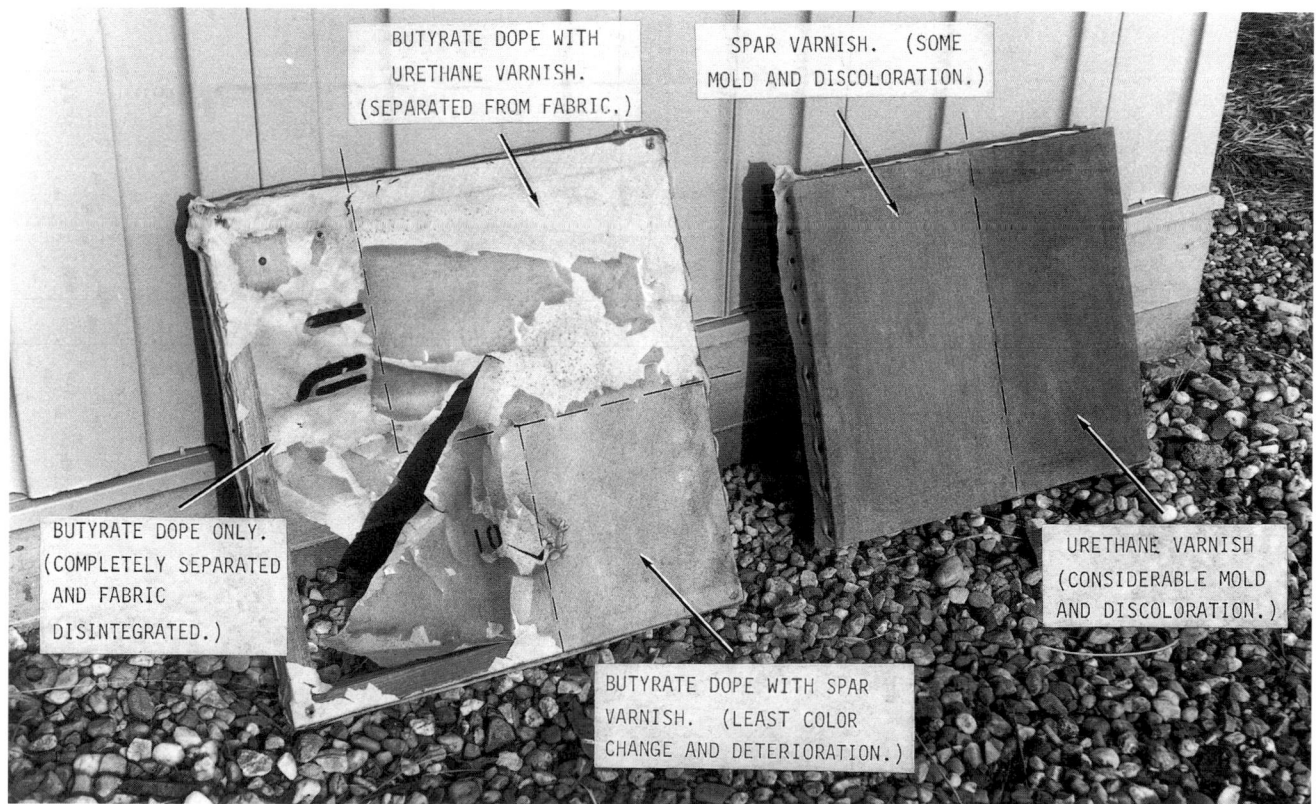

Accelerated test of clear coatings on fabric with continual exposure to sunlight, weather and changing temperatures for 38 months.

Always keep in mind the need to reduce the number of future restoration operations for an airplane to as near zero as possible. Therefore, fabric longevity is desired, as well as replicating the attachment method as was used originally. When this new covering fails — and in time it will — those tasked with its replacement in the future will wish to be as exacting in application as the recovering work taking place. What more can those future restorers use as a sample to duplicate originality than the current work on the airplane? Think of the questions and questioning that would come to mind in this regard. Therefore, it is not only necessary to retain well-preserved samples of original fabric, stitching and attachment techniques, but to prepare a narrative as well, to be retained with the aircraft record permanent file. If you are proud of your work in following the same technique as you found in the original work, write it down and say so, giving confidence to those that follow to use your work as a positive guide.

As previously mentioned, painted fabric surfaces add far less problems than clear finishes once the fabric to be used has been selected. Here again, pigmented dopes and paints, as well as the media have changed, and will continue to change, making it more challenging to duplicate originality. Therefore, it may be best to concentrate on duplicating the original color and texture of the painted surface as long as a sample of the original paint material is saved and well-documented. (More will be said about paints and colors in Chapter 9.)

When applying color finishes to newly-restored aircraft, there is a tendency to apply too many coatings in order to obtain a showroom appearance. More than likely, the airplane being restored was manufactured during the Great Depression, when very few coats of pigmented dope were applied. The weave of the fabric would be visible except for special-order finishes having more coats of dope.

Spad XIII

One of the more challenging paint surface replications for an NASM aircraft took place when restoring the Spad XIII *Smith IV*, which saw combat during World War I. Although always retained and exhibited indoors after being acquired as a museum artifact in 1920, the museum environment of fluctuating humidity and temperature had taken its toll. Sometime before 1956 the fin and rudder damage caused by a falling ladder had been repaired and was conspicuous with contrasting fresh new paint. By the 1970s, repair stitches over other parts of the airplane became more frequent in helping to hold the brittle and breaking fabric to the structure. The airplane's appearance was clearly departing from how it looked while in operational service. It left too much interpretation up to the

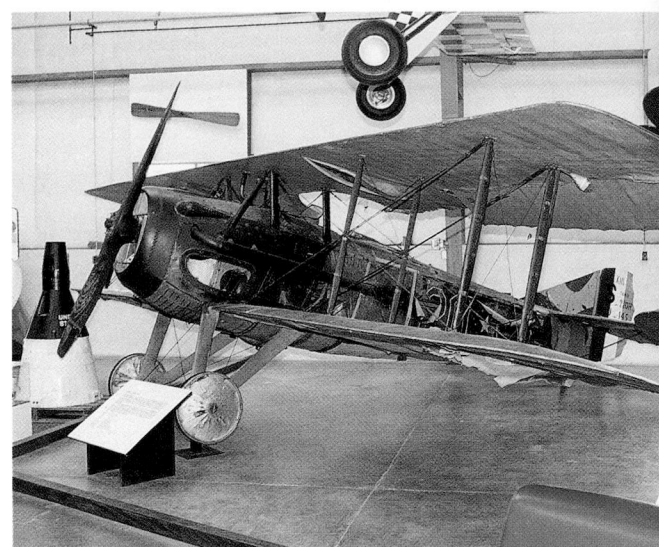

This Spad XIII in the collection of NASM was proudly displayed as being an original combat aircraft of World War I. It had a well-known and documented history which added greatly to its value.

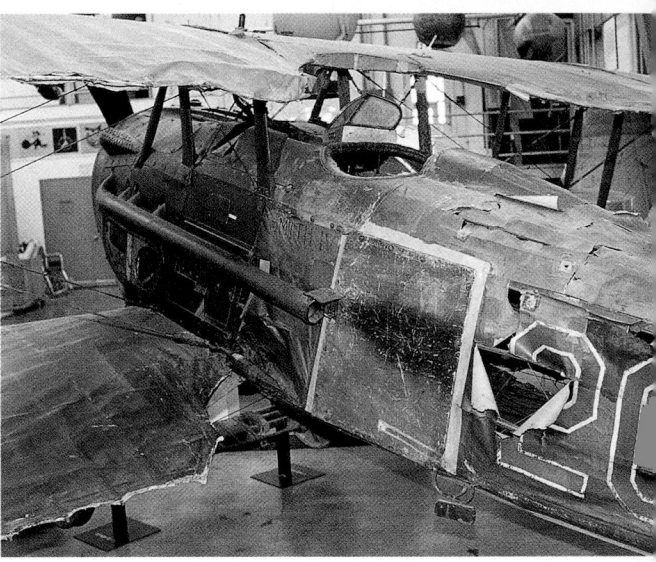

The Spad XIII at NASM, however, had deteriorated to such an extent externally that in truth it could hardly be said to be representative of a combat aircraft of its time. The fabric covering was literally falling off of the aircraft, calling for major attention.

visitor who had limited knowledge of combat machines of World War I. To retain the airplane's value to the collection, something had to be done.

The Musée de l'Air et de l'Espace in Paris had already addressed this same problem when restoring their Spad VII, once flown by the flying ace Lieutenant George Guynemer. After restoring the structure, and with the aid of art conservators from the Louvre, the original fabric was attached to a new supporting fabric that held it in place on the aircraft. Areas on the supporting fabric where original fabric was missing were filled in with matching paint.

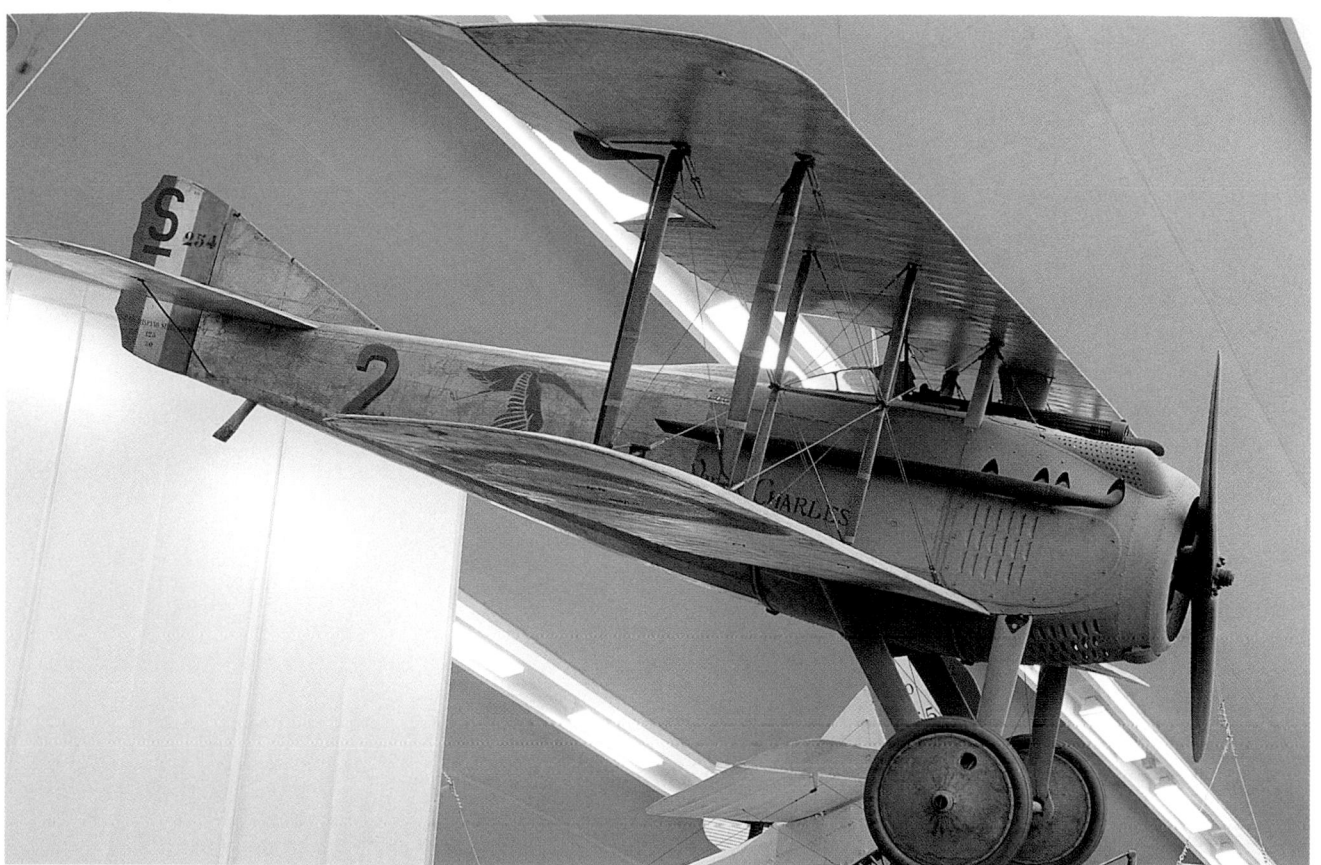

The Musée de l'Air in Paris used a different technique in the restoration of their Spad VII. This airplane too, had a noted wartime history, having been flown by flying ace Lieutenant George Guynemer. Its appearance is that of a well cared-for original machine.

This method can be looked upon in two different ways. First, this is an excellent preservation, in that the old fabric is retained in place and is original to the aircraft. Second, when this aircraft was in wartime service it did not look as it does now, because of its patchwork appearance and its color, which had darkened over the years. I found this appearance to be distracting from what the airplane itself was meant to convey to me as the viewer. With two layers of fabric on this Spad instead of one, attachment techniques had to have been altered, or at best, covered with a non-standard second layer of fabric. Both views have merit and the curator in charge must decide between them.

At NASM we were faced with making such a decision when planning our own restoration of the Spad XIII beginning in March 1984. For many years this restoration had been delayed to avoid destroying the Spad's originality. But was it original with the fabric merely string-tied to the exposed structure? Its darkened colors and camouflage demarcation lines were difficult to determine because of age.

Recognizing that the structure was in serious need of stabilization for preservation, we began the

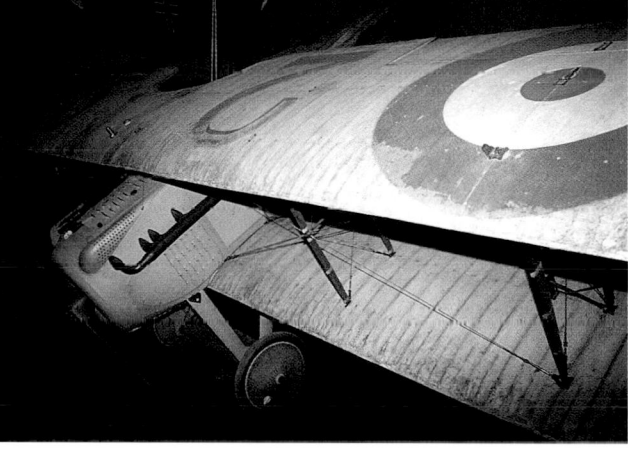

To retain as much originality as possible of this Spad VII, the French restoration team, with the aid of art conservators from the Louvre, attached the original fabric to a new supporting fabric that held it in place on the aircraft.

restoration. The brittle fabric was carefully removed. Great care was given to the structure and the engine to return both to good health and enhance their longevity. But the real test of this restoration was to duplicate the original covering, camouflage coloring, and unique markings.

A new covering material of linen was matched in thread-count to the old as closely as possible. Paints of matching color and texture were the next challenge. The bits and pieces of painted fabric that had fallen off the airplane were prized samples to be analyzed and tested by a specialist on this subject,

Areas of original fabric that were missing from this Spad VII were painted-in to match the surrounding fabric. This technique produced the results that were expected, yet it does raise a number of issues, one being that of duplicating original appearance and fabric application techniques.

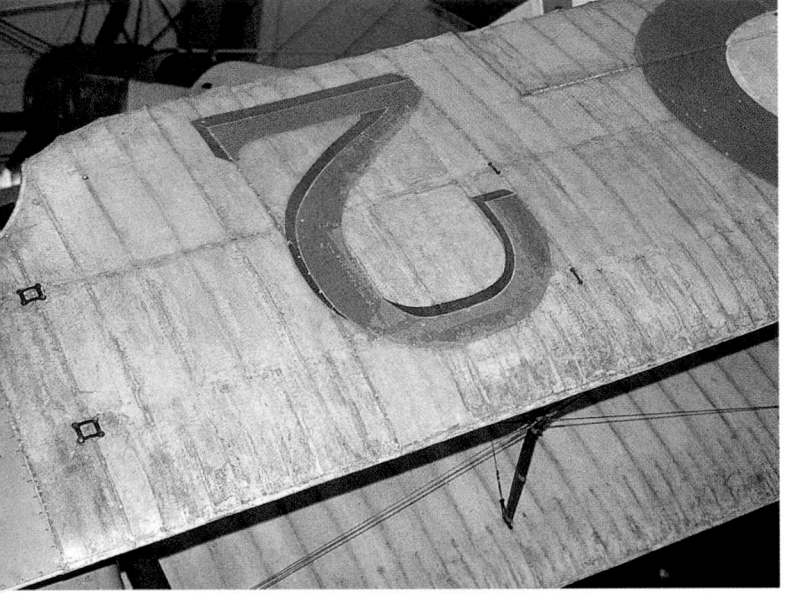

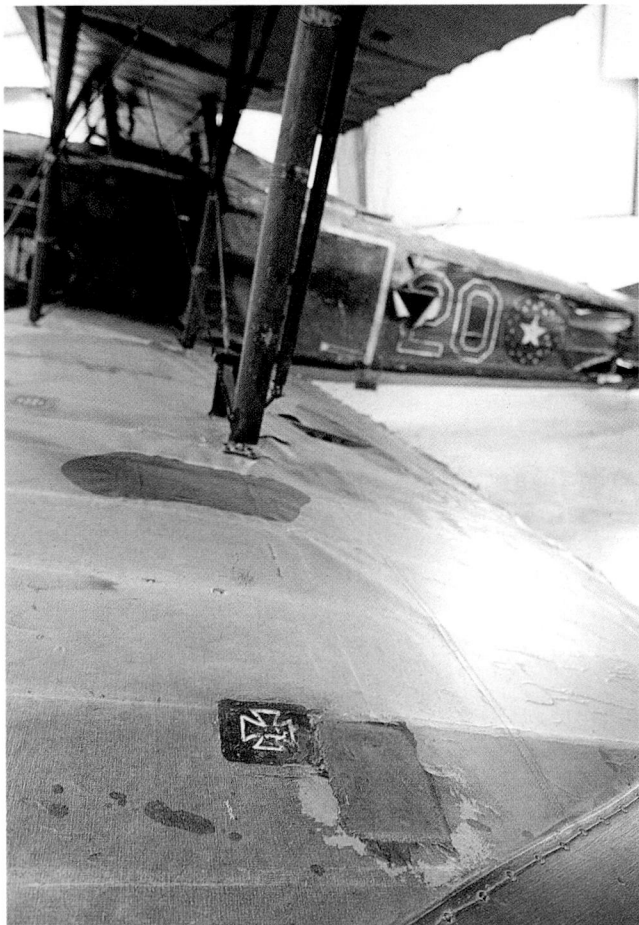

There was speculation with NASM's Spad that many of the patched bullet holes with a German mark were fake, but this point was difficult to prove without an inspection of the underside of the fabric covering. Regardless, this made the artifact more appealing.

Alan D. Toelle, of Seattle, Washington. Over the years, he had gone to great pains to have a laboratory analysis made of these paint samples from which to determine their composition and pigmented colors. From this came the various formula that were used when it came time to having these finishes prepared for NASM Spad XIII. Going a step further, we at NASM asked Mr. Toelle to supervise the mixing of these colors and paint content to his satisfaction at his location before sending the material to the NASM.

Here again, we all had to recognize that the chemical make-up of the pigment suspension agent was different from that of 1918 as well as the dope. A unique feature of these near-duplicated layers was that they included an aluminum powder mixed with the pigmented dope, an early form of protection against ultraviolet light.

Every effort was made to duplicate the original application techniques of fabric and dope as closely as possible. As such, the colors were painted on with a brush, since that was how the paint was originally applied. Even the described 'wet look' for newly-manufactured aircraft that is noted in early accounts was well duplicated by the prescribed application of a final clear coating.

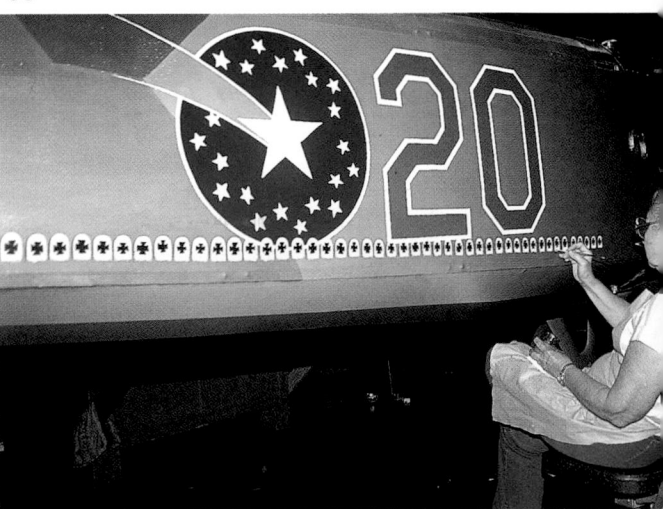

The original fabric retained with the Spad XIII Smith IV, although spent, served as a pattern for reproducing the colors and markings as close to original as possible. In this final phase of restoration, Mary Feik at NASM reproduces the unit's combined victory markings on the right side of the fuselage.

As a result, the aircraft looks too new to have been a combat airplane. Were the engine to be run for perhaps 30 minutes, spewing out its oily haze and exhaust smudge along the fuselage and portions of the wing, and the airplane placed in the rain and sun for a few days, its appearance would be softened. But this defeats the purpose of the restoration, because the aircraft and engine would likely begin to deteriorate again.

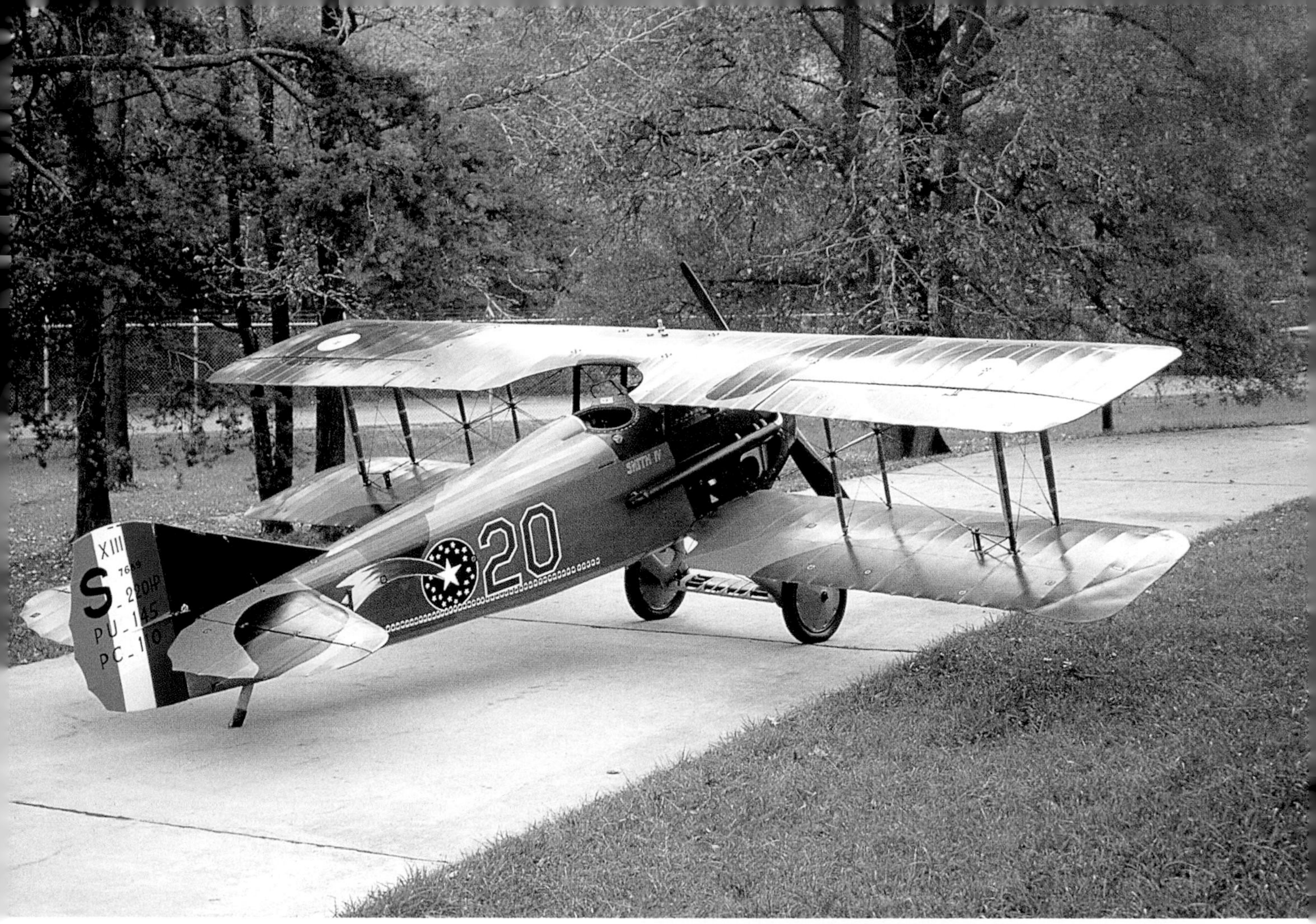

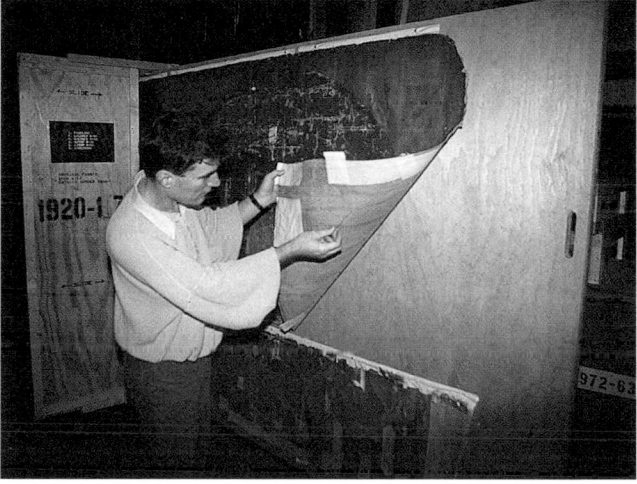

To save the structure of the Spad XIII, a total restoration took place. This included all-new fabric and repainting, all of which was done to duplicate as near as possible the techniques employed at the time of manufacture.

To preserve the original fabric from the Spad, a special box was built with six sliding panels consistent with the largest piece of fabric removed from the airplane. Screws through reinforcement fabric glued to the top edges suspended each panel separately. To have these panels lying flat would be better since this would cause less strain on the fabric. Such a method of lying flat with double the number of panels would require more storage space, generally a limiting factor. This original fabric is readily available for inspection of not only the outer surface, but the inside surface as well. This examination capability was not possible while the fabric was attached to the aircraft. Oddly, the removal and inspection of this wing fabric revealed that very few of the thought-to-be original bullet holes, with their Teutonic cross-marked patches, were actual holes. Wings for this Spad were replaced after combat on 30 October, 1918, and little action followed until the Armistice of 11 November, 1918. The impressive but often questioned signs of combat because of the excessive bullet-hole patches can now be examined.

Compromises had to be made during both the French and American restoration projects. These decisions were difficult, and were not made lightly in either case, yet different courses of action were

Following the restoration, the fabric removed from the Spad XIII was mounted on specially fabricated and coated vertical slides. This picture shows one of the wing panel boards drawn from the storage box, with an inspection being made of the back side of the fabric.

chosen. Here were two classic examples of viewing the same problem with two similar aircraft, and two different solutions. One method was in taking the conservator's approach (the French) while the other followed the line of reasoning of a curator (NASM). Thus, the world has two configurations of Spads for study, which should satisfy either philosophy of how a restoration should be accomplished. It was recognized at the start that neither was a perfect solution, nor could one be achieved.

Successes and Failures

Not all restoration efforts achieve the desired results. One of the few failures occurred with the restoration of the Piper PA-12 Super Cruiser *City of Washington* belonging to NASM. This airplane was being readied as an exhibit in the new museum building. It was historic in the fact that this was one of two Super Cruisers that made the first round-the-world flight by aircraft in the 100 hp engine class.

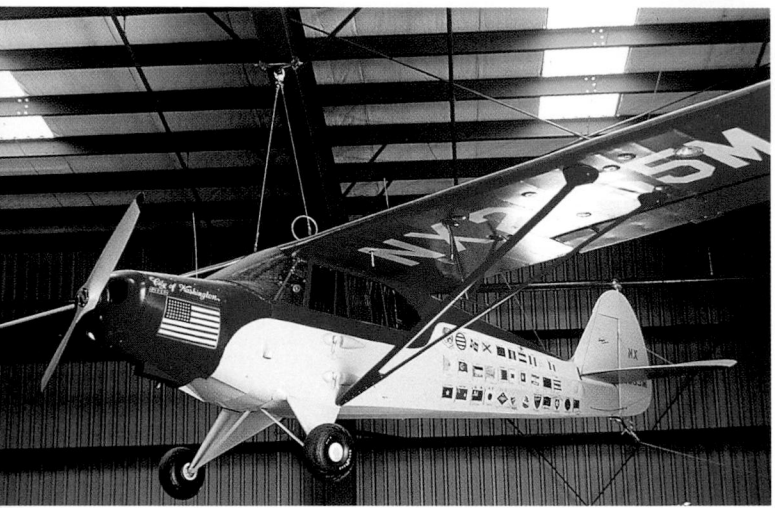

One of two Piper PA-12 Super Cruisers that made the first round-the-world flight in aircraft of the 100 hp class was City of Washington, *now belonging to NASM.*

At each country visited, the flag of that nation was painted on the sides of both airplanes. These flags became a significant feature, yet with a new fabric covering, this uniqueness would be lost. The detached fabric panel by itself, framed and hanging on some wall, had little significance without being on the airplane. So as not to separate the two, the plan was to attach the panel with flags to new cotton fabric backing by using art-painting conservator's techniques. The new covering would be put in place in the process of recovering the entire aircraft.

When the restoration was completed, the desired results were achieved. The significant historic features of this airplane were intact — but for only the first few years. What was not taken into account was that restoration technicians were directed to use butyrate dope exclusively in the process as a new museum policy (later amended). The continuing tightening of the fabric caused the binding of the old fabric panel over the new fabric to fail. To make matters worse, when taken off exhibit, the airplane was suspended in a building where ceiling heat in the summer reached the melting point of the special adhesive for the flags.

This was a case of too many hands managing the one object. The intent was sound, but all the underlying factors that caused this to fail were among varying and unco-ordinated responsibilities.

Of historic significance were the hand-painted flags of countries visited by City of Washington. *Their value was retained by once again applying this portion of original material on to the aircraft over grade-A cotton material.*

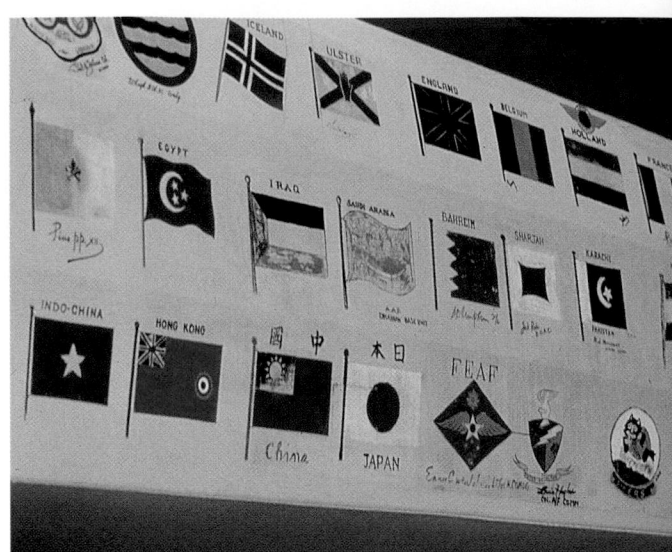

Having used butyrate dope exclusively, the shrinking process continued beyond the strength of the adhesive holding the original fabric to the cotton backing. The two decisions made here were not compatible with the methods and materials used.

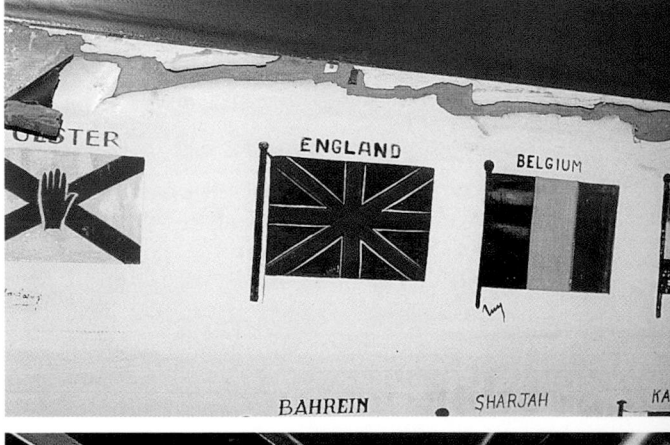

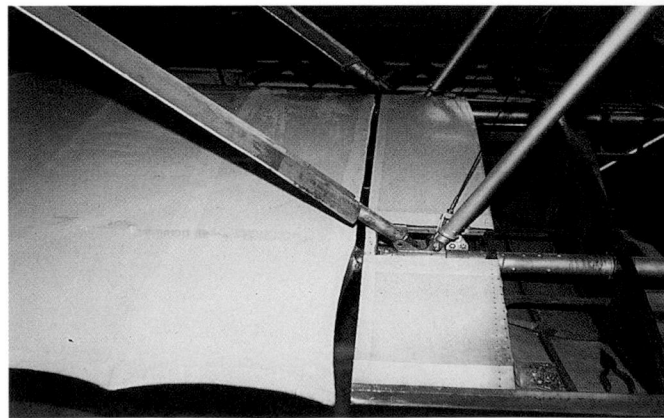

Here is another example of using fabric-tautening materials that bring stresses beyond the strength of the aircraft structure. This newly-covered wing had to be recovered using amended coating techniques.

CHAPTER 5
Lozenge-Pattern Fabric

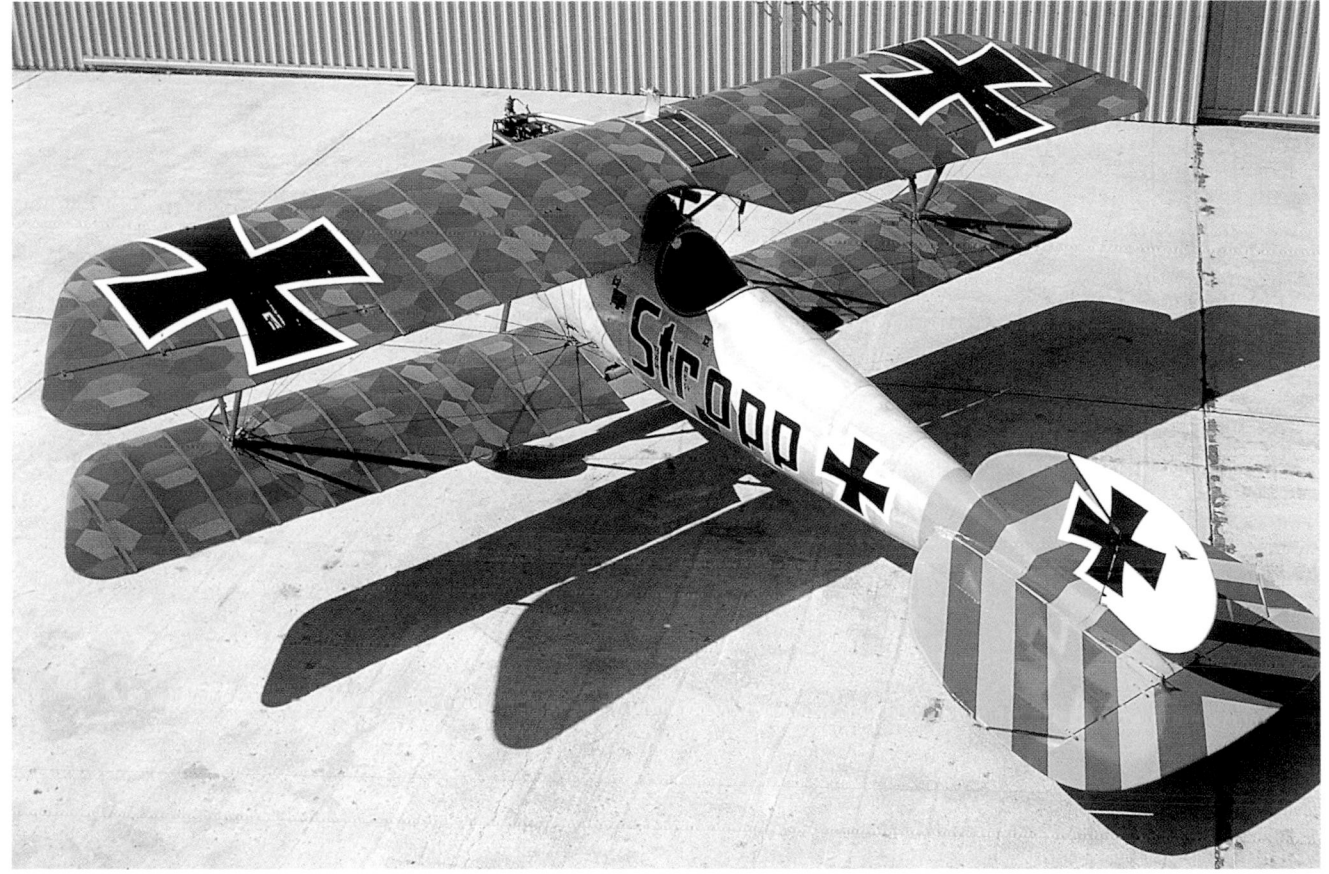

Aircraft having the lozenge camouflage pattern have always made interesting subjects, setting them apart from all others because of this exclusively German camouflage system. Shown here is NASM's Albatros D.Va when newly-restored. (NASM, SI)

Fortunately, there is basically only one situation in which fabric to be applied to an airplane must be printed or dyed to certain colors and patterns before being put in place. This happens when restoring German World War I aircraft with lozenge camouflage fabric.[30] Decisions that relate to using this fabric cannot be arbitrary since those aircraft manufactured after 21 April 1917 were to use the new printed material.[31] One can readily see that obtaining this pre-printed fabric for a restoration becomes quite troublesome since this is not an item on the market. How this pre-colored fabric was adopted for use on German aircraft is a story all its own, but a brief background of this method of camouflage is worthy of note at this point.

Prior to the introduction of camouflage, the majority of German military aircraft simply had the unbleached linen fabric coated with clear dope. Over this was a final protective varnish, resulting in a 'white' appearance which was often used to describe German aircraft in early Allied combat reports.

This finishing practice continued until the early summer of 1916, at which time Terrain/Sky

Camouflage was introduced, using large irregular handbrush-painted patches of varying shades of greens and reddish-browns. This was applied in a pattern similar to the 'shadow shading' that was used on USAF aircraft in Southeast Asia commencing about 1964. The undersides ranged from a pale bluish-white to sky blue to grayish-turquoise, and yellow was known to have been used. Beginning in April 1917, the red or reddish-brown patches on the top surfaces were eliminated in exchange for lilac. With what seemed to be continual changes in camouflage patterns and colors to the end of the war, very little standardization was in evidence.

In an effort to save the valued coating materials that were in short supply, a pre-printed fabric having a pattern of irregular polygons was introduced. This is commonly called the 'lozenge camouflage pattern,' although this is a misnomer as the figures are not four-sided or of equal length in diamond shape as the word is defined.

The first mention of printed fabric was in a German order dated 27 October 1916,[32] calling for the return of all cloth held by plane manufacturers to the fabric mills in exchange for newly-processed printed fabric. This does not firmly identify an effective date for the adoption of this printed fabric except for a directive dated 21 April 1917, stating that all new aircraft would be covered with the printed colored fabric. Aircraft already in production, obviously, would not be stripped of painted fabric and recovered with new printed material. It was a case of new aircraft replacing old or lost machines; therefore, the change was gradual during 1917, and for a time airplanes with both types of camouflage, painted and printed, were assigned within the same air units.

The Germans adopted several basic geometric designs for these printed colored patterns. The first printed camouflage pattern was the Five-Color Day Camouflage scheme which provided a set of five dark colors for the upper and side surfaces. The undersurfaces were covered with the identical geometric pattern in five lighter colors. The first recorded appearance of this pattern was on an Albatros D.V delivered in 1917. In the year following the introduction of printed five-color fabric, a Four-Color Pattern appeared for the first time on a Fokker D.VII which was delivered in March 1918.[33]

Linen fabric manufactured in Europe for covering airplanes was prepared in bolt widths of about 50 x 54 inches (127 x 137 cm)[34]. When the printing of the lozenge design and colors took place on this material, the camouflage pattern was identical for both widths, but for the 50-inch (127 cm) material, the outer two inches (51 mm) of the overall design were deleted. The printing was from selvage to

selvage through the use of rollers suitably cut with the desired design. Each design had two sets of dye colors: a darker set for fabric to be used for top and side surfaces, and lighter colors for bottom surfaces. There is seemingly no correlation of color values between the two pattern designs.

The Availability Problem

Having to provide fabric covering for German airplane restorations of the World War I time period is truly a challenging project. With nearly every endeavor, the effort of having to acquire this unusual-patterned material seems to start at ground zero. There are many reasons for this.

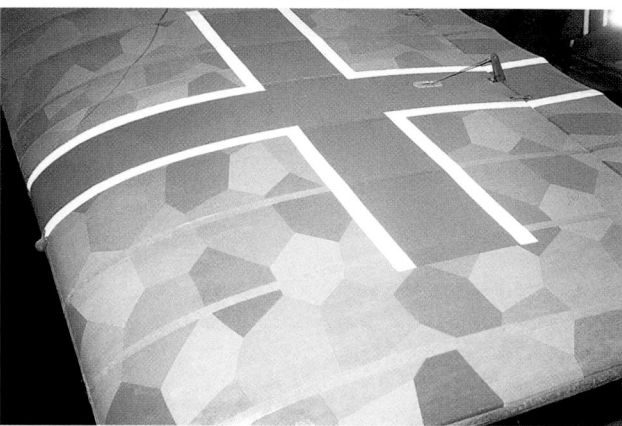

The Musée de l'Air have this example of lozenge fabric on their Fokker D.VII. Note the unusual exactness of matching the color patterns without color overlap. Rib tapes are light blue.

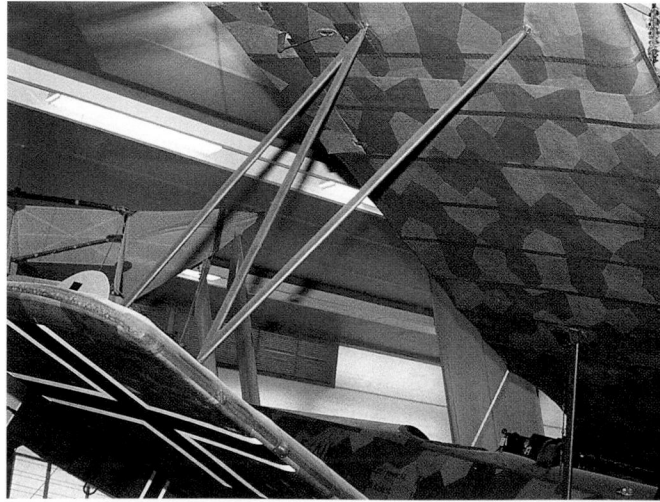

This is a bottom view of the Fokker D.VII at Musée de l'Air. Colors shown here may be exaggerated because of improper lighting for this photograph. Rib tapes appear abnormally dark compared to the more normal color in the top view of the same wing.

First, there is no ready source for this fabric. Because of the cost, hardly more than enough is ever printed to cover a given project, leaving perhaps enough for one or two additional aircraft. Generally this disappears over time to become custom

This is a sampling of lozenge fabric reproduced for the LVG C.VI at the Shuttleworth Collection, Old Warden, England. This is the upper surface of the lower wing. Note the light blue, unpinked rib stitch tapes.

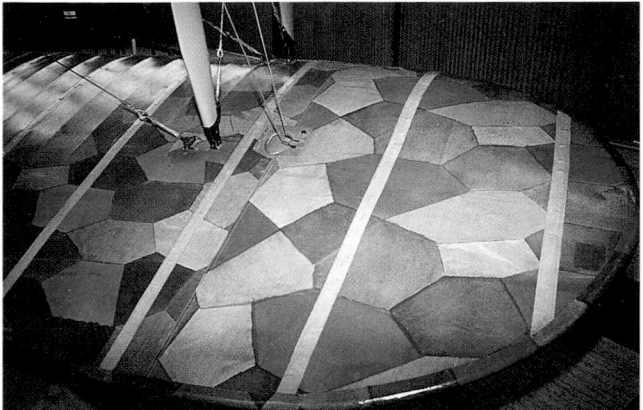

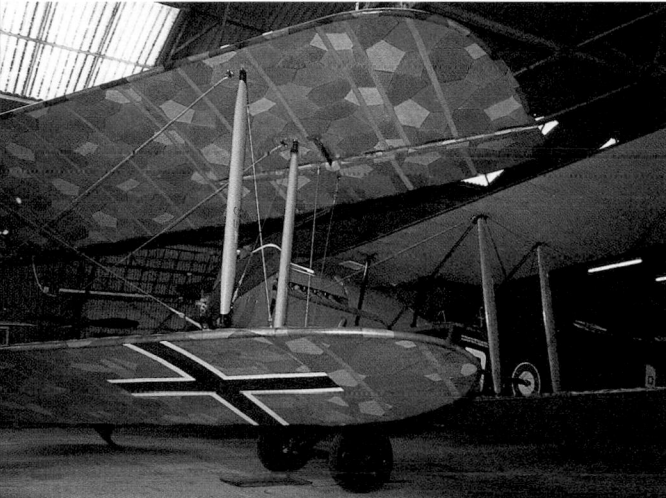

This view shows the bottom colors of the LVG C.VI at the Shuttleworth Collection. The wraparound of the upper fabric over the leading edge is of interest for application.

draperies or mere souvenir swatches. One source in Germany has a limited supply at the time of writing (see Appendix G).

Second, restorers are generally not satisfied with evidence of previously-printed fabric techniques and results, and therefore start at the beginning each time in the hope of achieving perfection. This begins with studying a piece of original fabric, identifying what are believed to be true colors, and devising ways of having it reproduced.

It is here that different opinions appear in the analysis of what has already been done and the separation of what could be fact from fiction. Strangely, little of this research about colors has been disproved, yet what is seen is seldom perfectly matched with the old fabric or between each new effort. With each new plotting of the design patterns, there are variations, although their differences are minuscule.

Which evaluations are correct and which ones are incorrect? More than likely, they are all correct — but perhaps correct only for the sample of fabric that was the subject of the study. The greatest problem appears when placing the old fabric against the new. Patterns may match, but the values of colors that are seen on the new print have a crisper, more vibrant look.

Having been closely involved with obtaining lozenge fabric for NASM, I feel that I can speak with some experience on this matter. Realizing that printed lozenge fabric would be needed for what were then undecided future restorations, acquiring such material became a museum project. This became so time-consuming that the restoration of the Albatros D.Va got underway before this project of printing fabric came to an end. Like other attempts, the results of this printed fabric left us knowing we had not achieved perfection. The perfectly reproduced lozenge fabric has yet to be printed to fully satisfy all critics as to the 1918-produced lozenge-printed fabric colors and geometry. What are thought by some to be correct reproductions of lozenge fabric appear to be so when compared to early samples that could have changed over the years even though well-protected.[35]

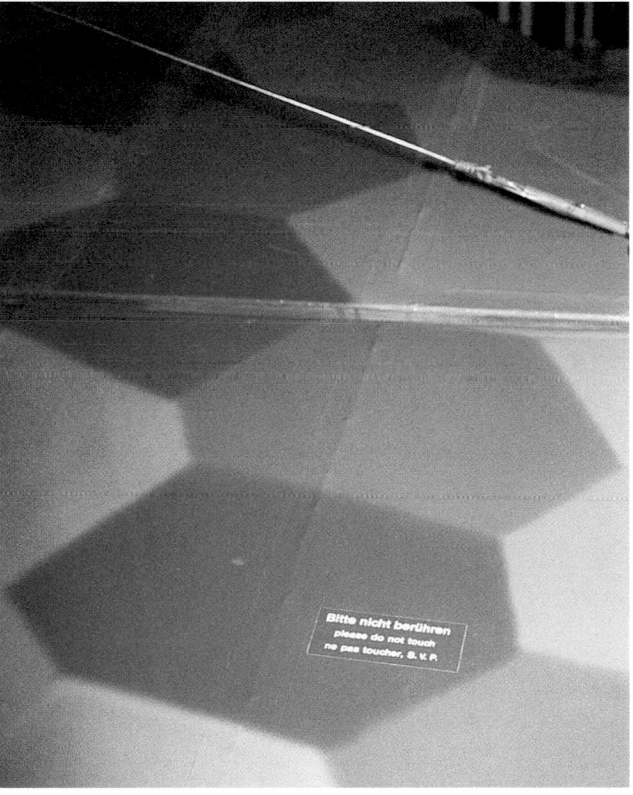

This is the lozenge fabric detail found on the Fokker D.VII at the Deutsches Museum in Munich. For lack of a more practical method for creating lozenge fabric at the time of restoration, these patterns were spray-painted on the fabric after being attached to the wing. Note the intended overspray for color overlap and the lack of contrasting rib tapes.

89

Also at the Deutsches Museum is this Rumpler C.IV with lozenge fabric, some of which is original, some replicated. Rib tapes in this case are of the sometimes-used remnant made into strips of the lozenge-patterned material. Irregular color overlap is a good representation of original fabric.

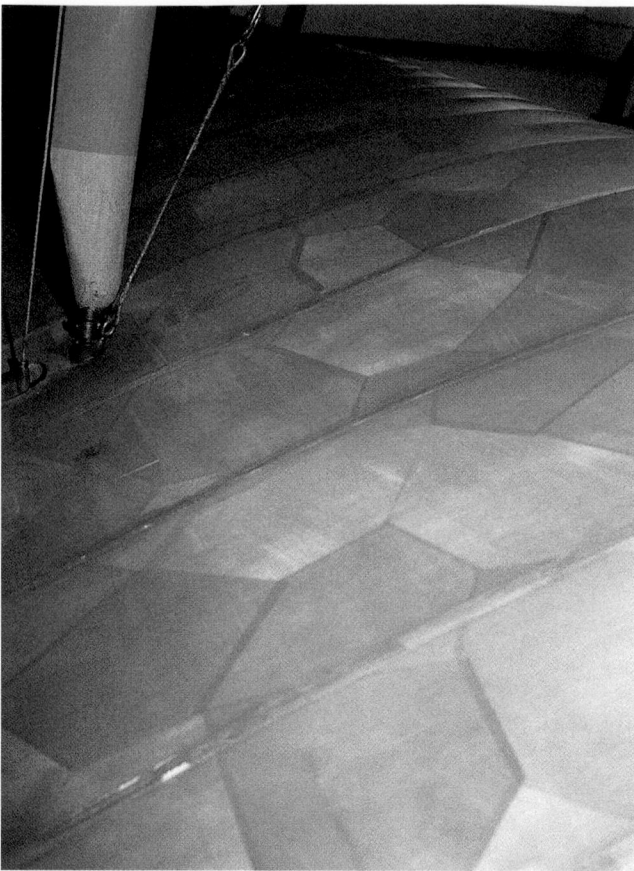

Unfortunately, the surviving examples of original fabric with colors and designs vary with each sample. Normally each piece being evaluated had been protected over the years from sunlight and other elements, but each under a different environment depending upon location. This being the case, we can imagine that there would have been some color variations at this juncture, assuming that they were identical to begin with. Going a step further, the examiner's results recorded depend upon the method he used in determining the color, be that under a microscope or with the naked eye while matching to a color on a card, spectroscopy systems, and others.

Then there is the matter of light source, such as artificial or natural, with variations of each, and how standard these colors were in the first place. There was little color consistency during World War II (take the common Olive Drab ANA 624 with numerous inconsistencies, for example). Are we even to assume that the color dyes used during the earlier World War I were more consistent? I doubt that they were any closer than meeting descriptive names such as purple, ochre, green, lilac and others.

No other descriptions or formulas for standards are known to me. Most will agree that approximations were very likely the case when mixing these original colors to match a sample on the wall as reference for the various German fabric mills. If so, then we do not have a chance of standardizing something today that was not precisely controlled in the first place. Therefore, matching to colors found on any documented original piece of fabric considered to have survived well should satisfy judging and reproduction requirements.

Developing NASM's Lozenge Fabric

The biggest problem in creating the fabric that is now on NASM's Albatros D.Va was that even though the colors are as correct as possible, the conditions of creating this printed fabric were entirely different. Our fabric was printed on Grade A cotton before we even considered that one day it would be used on an aircraft that had used linen. As a joint museum effort, Robert Bradford, then Director of the National Aviation Museum in Ottawa, Canada, with the assistance of (then) museum curator A.J. 'Fred' Shortt, labored for many hours over this project, as I did at NASM. Under a strong magnifying glass, Bradford pulled fibers of the same colors from different areas of the cloth to determine these color values as a group from this one piece of light-protected cloth. I am satisfied that these color sample readings match the original fibers as closely as humanly possible by this noted artist, well experienced in working with colors. Mr Bradford could not take into consideration that with these thin dyes applied to this linen, all of the fiber does not take the color. Capillary attraction within the weave caused the liquid dye to draw to inner parts of the weave, leaving other parts of each thread uncolored. Therefore, this makes for a much softer presentation than with a fabric like cotton that more readily takes the color.

The co-ordination for this project became my responsibility. Much of the way had been cleared on an earlier and similar printing of lozenge-pattern fabric for the Fokker D.VII by Louis S. Casey, Curator at NASM at the time. Greeff Fabrics, Inc., in Port Chester, New York, which had printed fabric for these museums in the past was asked again to help. As before, Albert Zellers, director of the Design Department, willingly undertook the task of having the cloth printed, even though such a small project was unprofitable and very time-consuming. The entire process had to be started from the very beginning — the silk screens from before had disintegrated and disappeared. Since the original German rollers were non-existent, silk screens were prepared again for the hand-printing process. Five colors for each pattern required five screens.

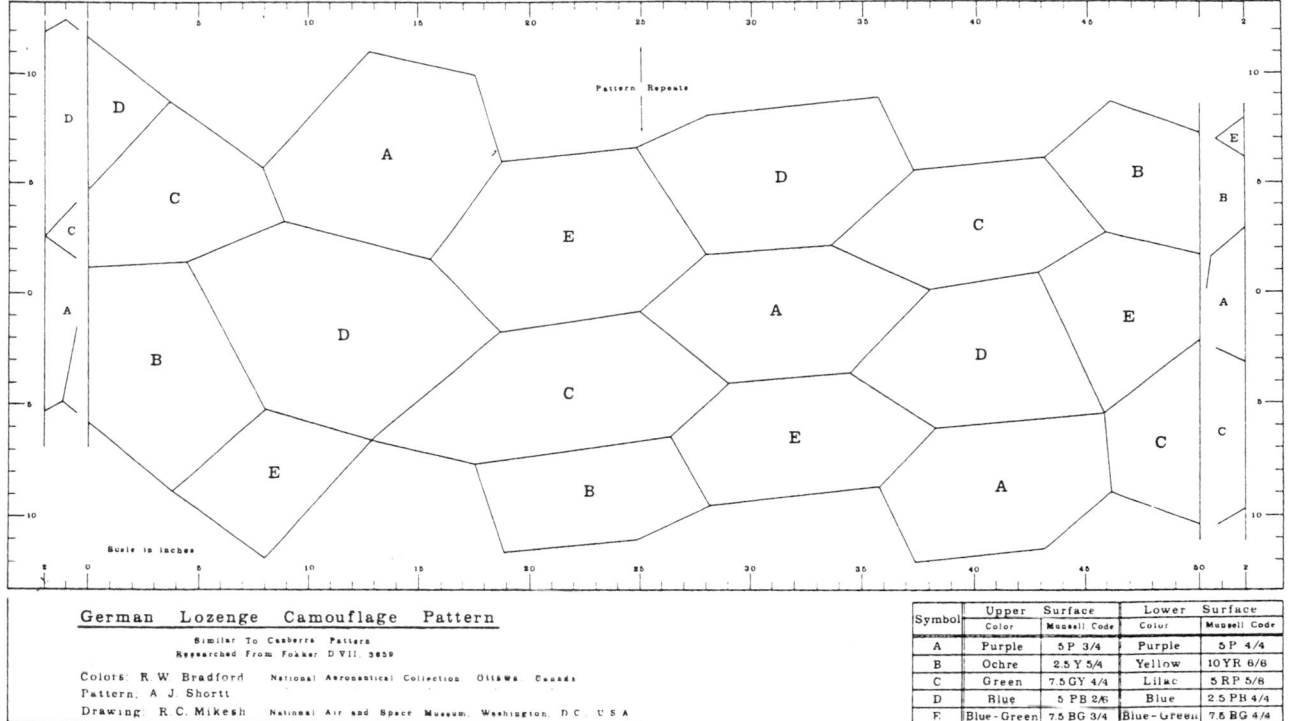

Symbol	Upper Surface		Lower Surface	
	Color	Munsell Code	Color	Munsell Code
A	Purple	5 P 3/4	Purple	5 P 4/4
B	Ochre	2.5 Y 5/4	Yellow	10 YR 6/6
C	Green	7.5 GY 4/4	Lilac	5 RP 5/6
D	Blue	5 PB 2/6	Blue	2.5 PB 4/4
E	Blue-Green	7.5 BG 3/4	Blue-Green	7.5 BG 4/4

German Lozenge Camouflage Pattern

Similar To Canberra Pattern
Researched From Fokker D VII, 3659

Colors: R. W. Bradford   National Aeronautical Collection, Ottawa, Canada
Pattern: A. J. Shortt
Drawing: R. C. Mikesh   National Air and Space Museum, Washington, D.C., U.S.A.

Typical lozenge camouflage pattern and color notations. This interpretation (copied from original material) was made for the Albatros D.Va, D.7161/17 belonging to NASM.

Sample swatches were printed on material supplied from the bolt provided by NASM, reviewed for color accuracy by those involved at the participating museums, and the go-ahead given for production. So far, the operation has been presented as though no problems had been encountered, but there were many. Each participating museum supplied 200 yards (183 m) of its own 60-inch (152 cm) Grade A cotton fabric, but this material from varying sources turned out to have differences in its ability to accept the dyes without color change. The dyes printed evenly on the material supplied by NASM, as it did with the early test, but the material obtained by the National Aviation Museum in Ottawa produced a blotchy effect due to the

different fabric fillers. There were even problems and delays with passing the fabric across the Canada-US border and back again without undue Customs charges. For NASM, the results were very satisfactory, and the fabric was on hand by the time it was needed in the restoration process of the Albatros D.Va.

When it came time to cover the top wing, a decision had to be made as to the direction the fabric pattern should run. For this airplane, all known references described the materials as running spanwise with a 12-inch (30 cm) strip sewn at the rear to extend the fabric to the trailing edge between the aileron cutouts. This method was used on the Albatros at the Australian War Memorial which

---

This is a broad comparison of upper and lower lozenge camouflage colors. This composite pictures shows both top and bottom of the wings of NASM's Albatros D.Va.

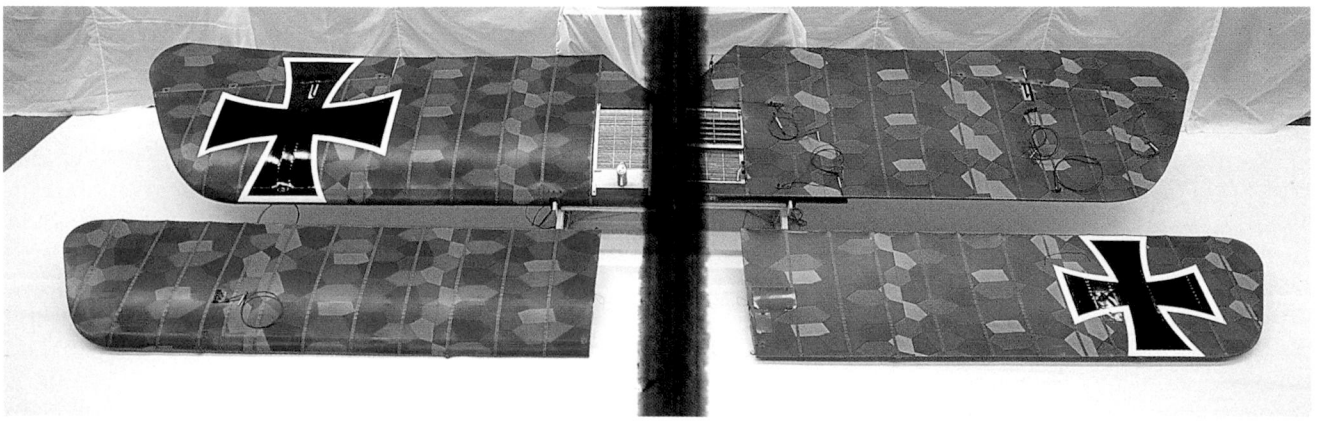

Original fabric is the best source of information for application methods that were used. This picture shows restorers examining original fabric that had been rolled in corrugated acid-free paper for storage. Details such as seam direction, reinforcement tape application and distance between rib stitching, are but three examples that can be studied.

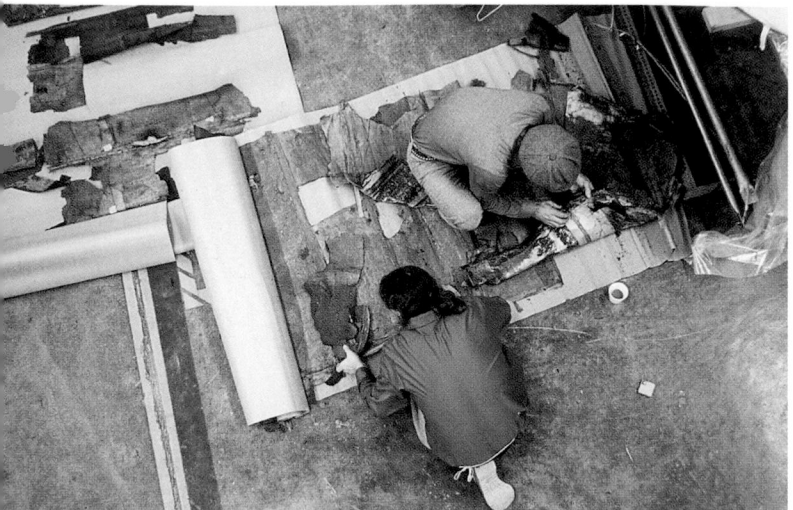

had its original fabric. It is plausible that the only recorded descriptions for attaching Albatros fabric have been based on this one aircraft.

Of the 23 photographs of operational Albatros fighters that were clear enough to show the direction this fabric was laid, all showed it to be laid fore and aft. Obviously either method was correct, but since the original fabric on NASM's Albatros wing ran fore and aft, even though this was not lozenge-printed fabric, the new fabric was attached in the same manner. In support of this decision was a German directive which stated that aircraft were to be covered with the colored fabric in exactly the same way as with the earlier white fabric.[36] The unprinted edges of the 60-inch (152 cm) material were trimmed off to achieve the 50-inch (127 cm) pattern.

There is no denying that the dope application on the restored Albatros used different dope and more coatings than in wartime 1918. This was of little consequence when considering the preservation benefits that were gained in using modern, longer-lasting materials and techniques. Butyrate dopes which are fire retardant were used on all the fabric surfaces.

The first coatings, thought not used originally, were brushed-on fungicidal clear, followed by two coats of non-tautening dope. Surfaces were lightly sanded, followed by rib stitching over which were placed one-inch (25 mm)-wide tapes with four pinks to the inch as per the original. One source states that these tapes were blue; however, salmon-pink-colored tapes are frequently recorded and were found throughout the original lozenge covering on

the lower wings, so the replacement tapes were made to match. Three more coats of non-tautening dope were sprayed on and again sanded, followed by two heavy coatings. The final coat was non-tautening clear flat. This was in accordance with a German directive that stated the final coating would be matt lacquer.[37]

NASM restoration technician John Cusack places reinforcement tapes on the underside of the top wing of NASM's Albatros D.Va. Fabric on this wing runs fore and aft as found on original covering. Photos of other Albatros aircraft show that fabric running span-wise was an application also used.

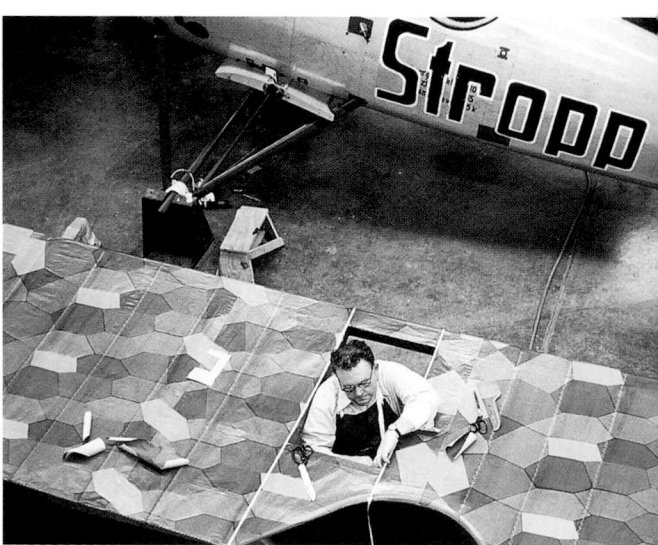

To Achieve Exactness

Like the Spad XIII described in Chapter Four, the finished Albatros D.Va had that new look that cannot be avoided with Level 3 Condition restorations. The colors look too new and crisp. In the case of the Albatros, if the pattern had been printed on linen so that the color dyes would have adhered less well, the results would have been better.

Unfortunately, even if linen had been used, this would not have solved the problem of reaching exactness. Today's linen is processed differently than it was then which would again produce a difference, as would the intensity of the color within each of the dyes. There are other variables as well to prevent duplication of the original, and which there is no way to control.

Therefore, to have achieved a closer resemblance of the original fabric colors, I would suggest today a new but time-consuming method. Color card samples at least 3 x 5 inches (7.6 x 12.7 cm) in size for each of the desired colors, to be compared at a distance of 20 to 30 feet (6 to 9 m) alongside the original cloth color, blanking out all other colors of the fabric while matching. In this way, the softening of the tones that the original fabric presents would be more closely identified when viewed at a distance. That card sample corrected to the likeness of the fabric color sample could then be said to be the color of the fabric being compared. But then once the shade of color has been resolved, the second half of the problem is that of transferring that color value seen on a card as a Munsell, Methuen, or any other color system equivalent, on to the fabric and still managing to duplicate the impression of the original.

However that is done, the results are something of a compromise of the true color, the same as what is called the 'modeling effect' when creating miniatures with softer, more realistic-looking colors in the form of a haze placed over the true color. But what will not happen is that a true color value will result from this technique, only a simulation of the original color will be achieved. This seems less desirable than using exact color matches and accepting the more intense shades. Some will disagree for good reason.

Halberstadt Lozenge Fabric

Years later, in 1989, NASM again needed to duplicate lozenge fabric, this time for its Halberstadt CL.IV, *Werk Nummer* 8103. The Museum für Verkehr und Technik, now the Deutsches Technikmuseum, Berlin, wished to restore this airplane for NASM in exchange for parts of another Halberstadt. For the needed stock of lozenge fabric, the silk screens for the earlier fabric were considered: but curator for the project, Dr. Dr. Holger Steinle wished to improve even further on this reproduction technique of fabric. After all, the original fabric was manufactured in his country.

A group of visiting members from other air museums evaluate closely the newly-printed lozenge fabric for NASM's Halberstadt CL.IV. This work was done with great care by the Museum für Verkehr und Technik in Berlin under the direction of Dr. Dr. Holger Steinle (center, profile).

The company that Dr. Dr. Steinle found to be interested in producing the material was located in Konstanz, southern Germany. Original print pattern rollers were long gone, but the company felt that they could duplicate the rolling method of printing. The one thing that they could not do was to have irregularities in the overlap margins of the colors that were so apparent with original lozenge fabric. Modern fabric-printing machines do not allow this type of deviation.

Having to begin all over meant starting with the print pattern. An enthusiast on lozenge fabric design was a graphic designer from Zuelpich who wished to become involved in the project. This was Manfred Thiemeyer, who introduced yet another variable in the design that he had studied and felt had not been previously considered. In a demonstration at the restoration site, he showed how the alignment thread pattern was seldom a straight line, having been influenced by how sample material was either folded in storage or if mounted on a wing was influenced by shrinkage stresses. He proposed making a new drawing of the design based upon selected thread lines as base lines and straightening these lines as they would have been in the printing process. Previous efforts had generally established a base line by laying a straight-edge over the flattened material and discounting any curves to the weave. From this evolved yet another drawing of the lozenge pattern. Like others, differences were apparent only when overlaid, and like the others were slight.

From this, the new linen fabric with lozenge design was manufactured and used for the Halberstadt CL.IV to our satisfaction. With assured certainty, this process of production will be repeated as the need arises, with each effort striving for perfection in matching original 1918 stock for which there is no stable and exact standard because of the passing of time.

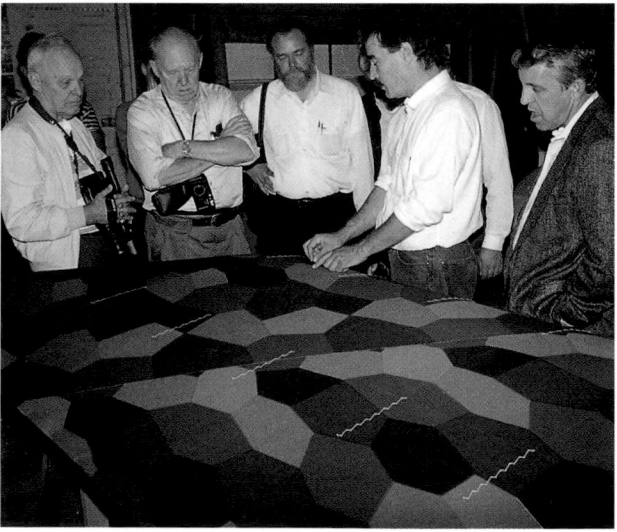

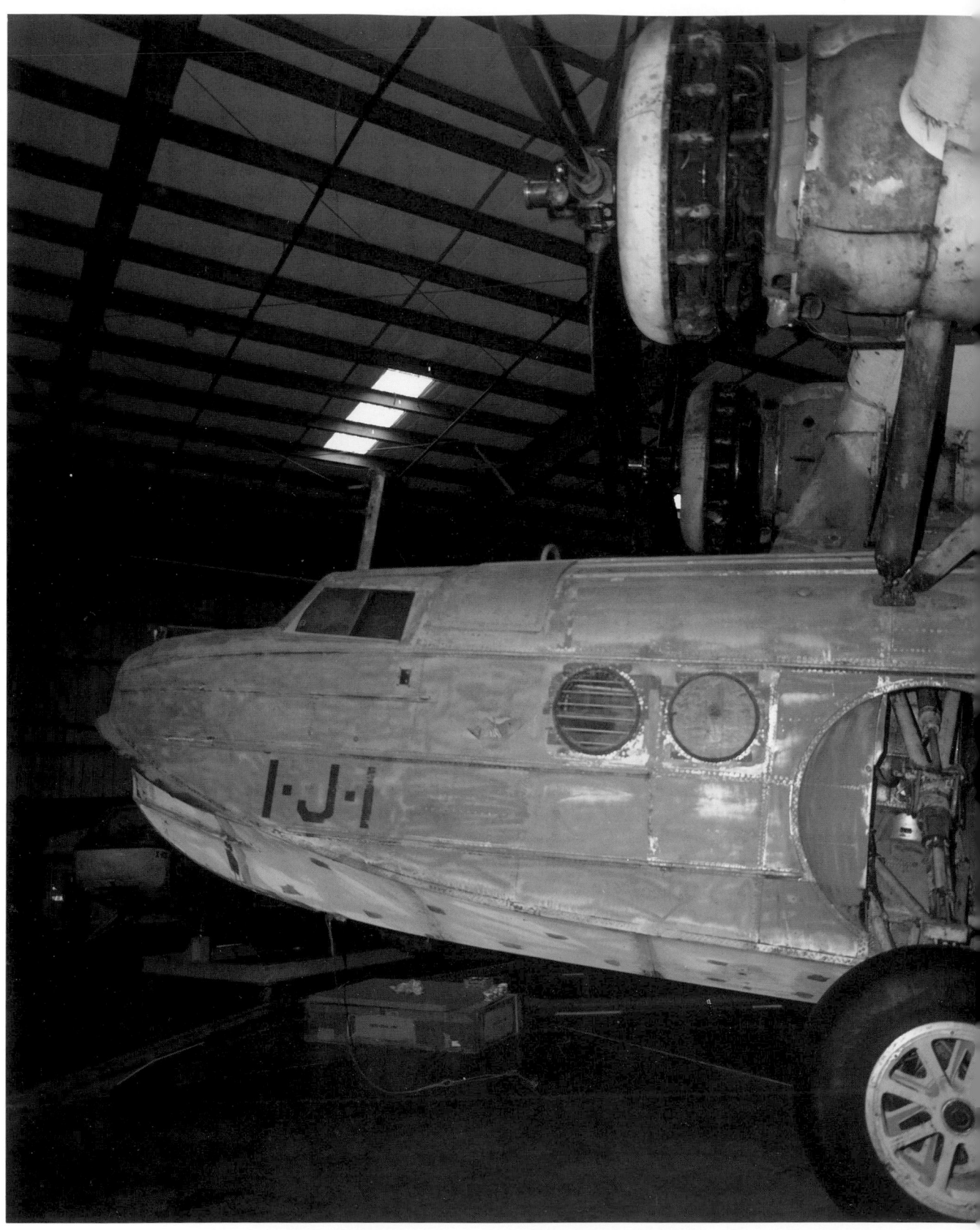

An aircraft positioned like this Sikorsky JRS-1 belonging to NASM, makes a walk-around inspection far simpler than when disassembled. All of the JRS-1's exterior can be examined and full access to the hull interior is possible. Missing parts are readily identified. (NASM, SI 84-5332-7)

CHAPTER 6
Metal Aircraft

Treatment of metal aircraft judged to be at Level 3 Condition must obviously follow a different restoration process from those described for wood-and-fabric aircraft. The objective for extended longevity as well as other principles are common to both, but the processes for reaching these goals are as different as the materials themselves.

To begin this process an inquisitive look at the airplane and its components must be made before commencing work. As with wood-and-fabric aircraft, this walk-around is made by the team of three: curator, restoration technician, and conservator. The intent here is to study and discuss what parts of the aircraft can be treated without altering their current and seemingly original condition, and which components will require partial or full restoration.

In restoring the Fw 190F-8 belonging to NASM, curators and technicians were fortunate in having all layers of the original paint still on the aircraft. In this view, color chips (foreground) were used to catalogue the various colors of camouflage and markings that were found. (NASM, SI)

For Level 3 Condition aircraft, it is very likely that the exterior paint, if there is any, is already spent and should be removed so that corrosion control processes can assure the best chances for greater longevity. Some conservators recommend that the original paint be left in place if the paint is adhering well to the surface. This may have merit, for if paint removal requires severe treatment, why not use that paint as an adhering surface for the replacement overcoat? However, paint is not a perfect sealant against oxygen and moisture, so corrosion might be taking place underneath. If the paint is not removed and the surface fully treated, the question of active corrosion underneath remains unresolved. Does corrosion under paint in the early stages produce blistering or make it less adhesive? I think not. The decision to remove this paint is best left to the circumstances and closer inspection of the airframe in question.

History Within The Paint
Ideally, it is best to encounter this airplane with its original paint in place, regardless of the number of

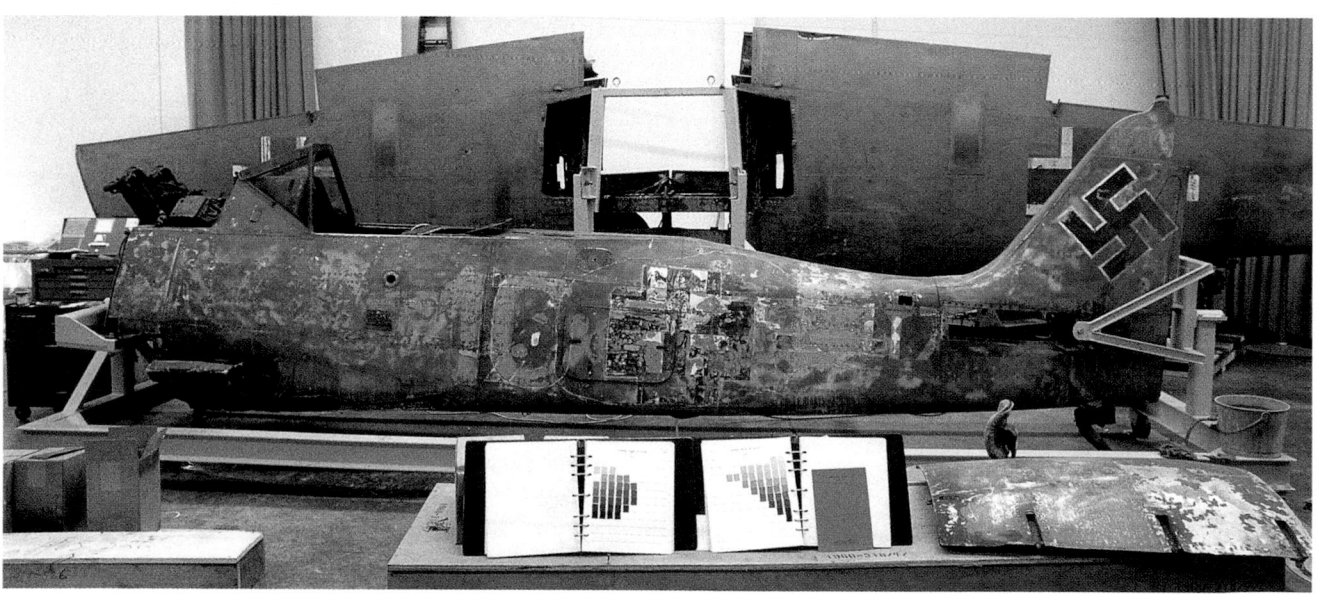

overcoats that are present. Once the original paint layers have been removed, much of the airplane's history goes with it forever — a good argument for retaining the original paint even though it is to be painted over. Whether the decision is to remove or retain, every effort to document what history this paint holds is a critical element in any restoration. I will point out a few examples shortly.

What is also important is to save a fragment of the airplane that contains a good sample of the original paint. This is often a damaged part of the skin that must be replaced. Mark it as the master paint sample and place it safely in an acid-free envelope with the permanent records for this aircraft. It records the current state of the original paint and may have some unforeseen laboratory value in the future. This relatively accessible sample for reference will provide what others wish to save under a newly-applied finish.

One unfortunate situation involving exterior paint — or the lack of it — was found during the restoration of NASM's Messerschmitt Bf 109G-6/R3 in 1972. All exterior paint was usually removed from captured aircraft during wartime evaluation by the US military. The airplane was then released for museum use in this condition. Every clue as to the Bf 109G-6/R3's unit markings, including its *Werk Nummer*, had been removed or souvenired during this process. Since its history had not been recorded at the time of its capture, these details are difficult to recover with any degree of certainty.

On the other hand, the Focke-Wulf Fw 190F-8, also received from the military, had not been 'Americanized' for evaluation purposes and still had

every layer of paint on its surfaces from the time it was first manufactured, later processed through a German modification depot, to having its final coat of paint applied here in the US. From a close inspection of the major components, the history of this aircraft could be reconstructed by evaluating these layers of paint.

When the restoration process was begun in NASM's shop, the late Mike Lyons, restoration technician on the project, very carefully sanded through each layer of paint with 800-wet sandpaper and made a record of each color by layer. This was done at pre-planned as well as random locations over the entire aircraft. The camouflage demarcation lines were transferred to four-view drawings of the airplane so that they might be used when repainting the aircraft. Areas where unit numbers, insignia and identifying marks were found on the various layers were directly traced, as were structural skin location marks so that any or all could be accurately positioned and reapplied.

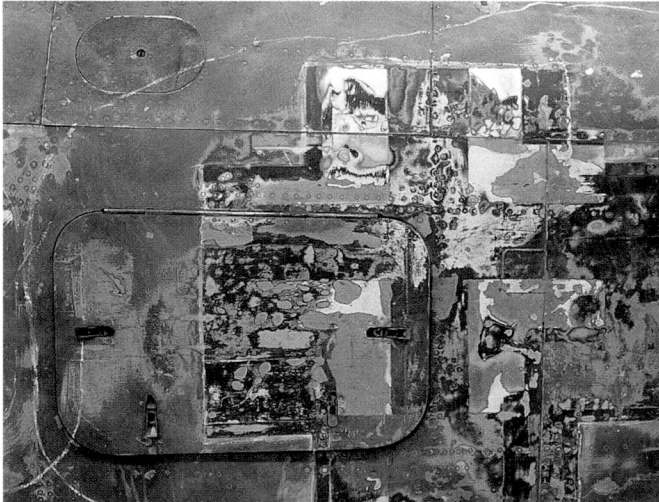

When markings and camouflage lines became identifiable by sanding off outer layers, they were outlined in chalk and then photographed as a permanent record. The left-side hatch was an obvious field replacement by virtue of the yellow paint under the insignia on the door only.

With so much uncertainty existing as to what might be found throughout the paint layers, infra-red photographs were taken of the areas where markings were usually placed. Extra care was taken in removing paint from those areas where something could be seen or was suspected from these photographs. The *Werk Nummer* that became visible at the top of the rudder was revealed in this way. The complete number was found on the left side, though only the last three digits remained on the right. Until this discovery the identity of the aircraft had been a mystery.

After evaluating these colors, markings and their locations, seven separate camouflage schemes were reconstructed from the findings gathered. By

Painstakingly, Museum Restoration Technician Mike Lyons lightly sands through each layer of paint on the Fw 190F-8 in order to reveal color demarcation lines. In this case, the '7' discovered here was later reapplied as it had been when the aircraft was in use during the 1944–45 time period.

Infra-red photography was used on several areas of the Fw 190F-8 in order to determine if markings could be below other paint surfaces. This simulation view of infra-red photography with color film reveals the serial number 931884 across the top of this film after some of the paint layers have been removed.

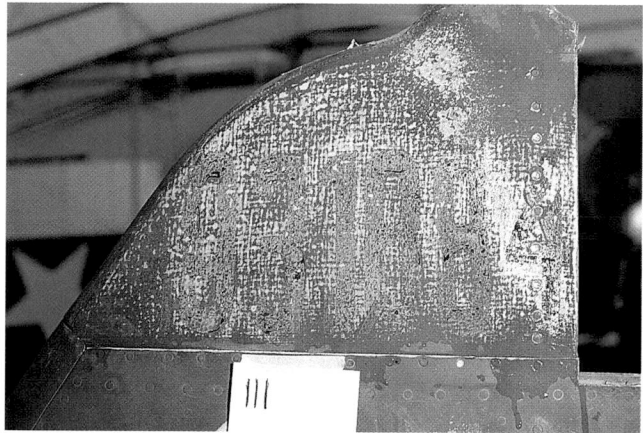

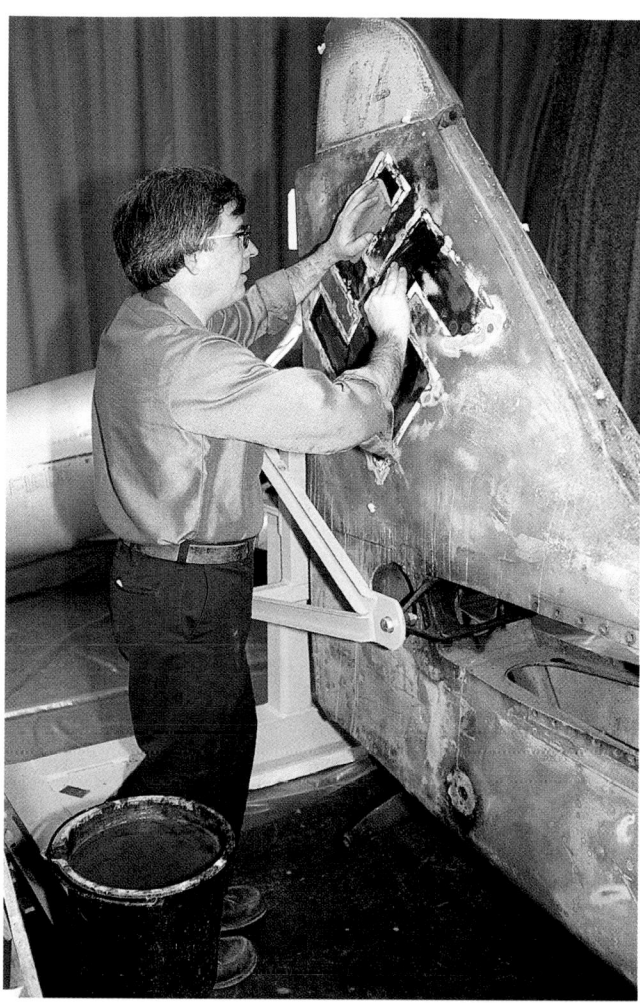

RIGHT:

Wet sandpaper and careful rubbing brings out the details of the swastika on the vertical fin. All markings were carefully traced not only for record but for exact reapplication when painting the restored aircraft.

This exhibit graphic displayed alongside the Fw 190F-8 shows, from the most recent (top left), the various color schemes and markings found on this airplane during the restoration process. The views at right without wings depict the aircraft before it was sent to a depot for conversion to a ground attack configuration.

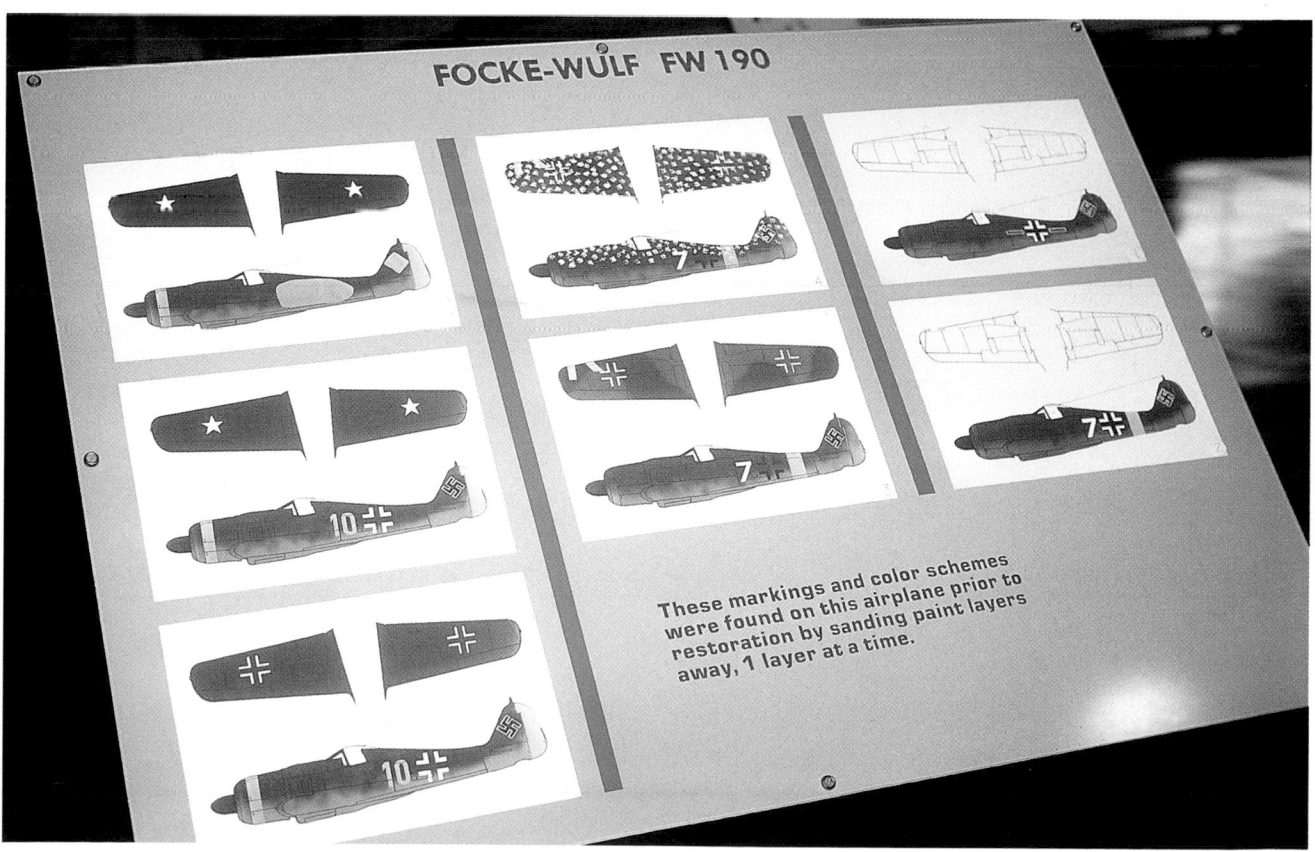

FOCKE-WULF FW 190

These markings and color schemes were found on this airplane prior to restoration by sanding paint layers away, 1 layer at a time.

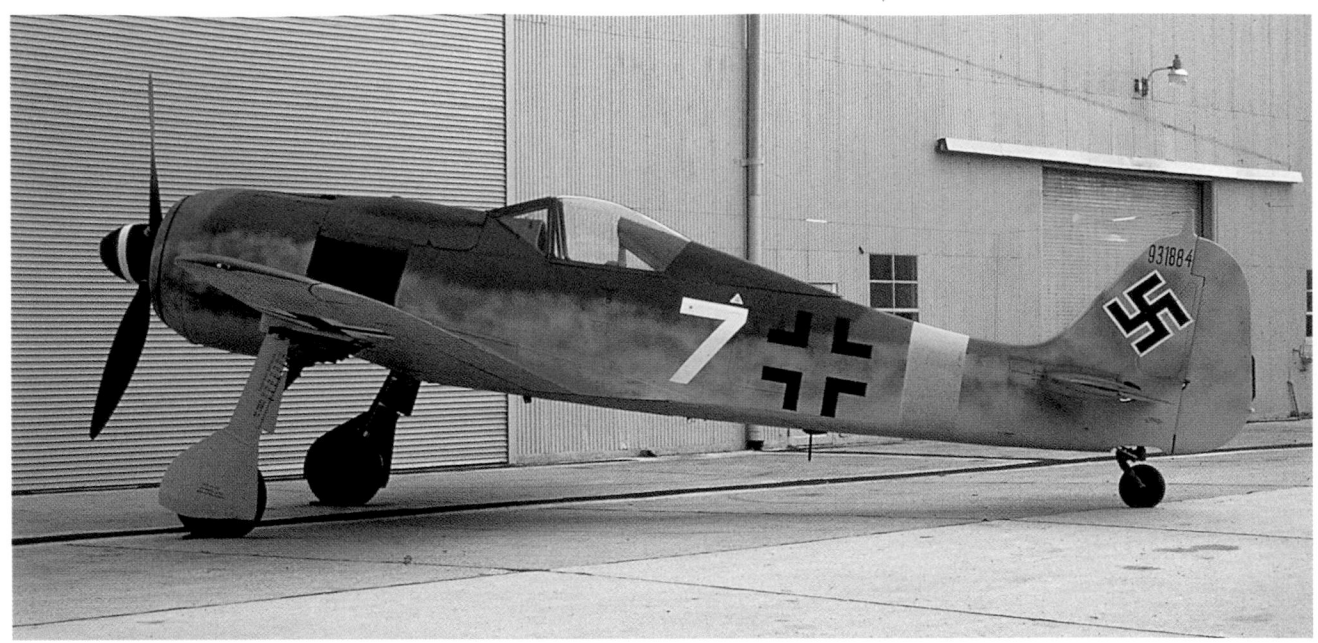

The repainting and marking of this Fw 190F-8 were done with confidence from knowing the patterns used had been traced from one of several sets of markings and camouflage demarcation lines found on the aircraft when removing the paint.

knowing that certain camouflage schemes were created for specific geographical locations, these became clues to theaters of operations. Coupled with identifying aircraft numbers, the colors for respective camouflage patterns showed that at one time the airplane was assigned to *Schlachtgeschwader* (Close-Support/Ground Attack Wing) 2 on the Eastern Front. This is thought to be part of the Wing's *erste Gruppe*, commanded by Major Heinz Frank, recipient of the Knight's Cross, in the spring of 1944. Had this paint been removed early on, or had its first restoration been done haphazardly and not fully recorded and illustrated, none of this history could have been reconstructed.

The same consideration should be given to all aircraft at this initial phase. Now that we have the technology to accurately record colors by use of chroma meters, readings should be made while the paint layers are being sanded to expose this information. The best samples of paint are those that may have been hidden under wing fairings or the edges protected by cover plates.

Aside from the paint, consideration should be given to what hidden details the aircraft structure might reveal before the work process begins. Advice on what to look for should be clearly stated in the Curatorial Guidelines. This would normally be addressed in the *Background* section describing this airplane or placed at the end of the Guidelines in a specific section which would describe quite clearly what details to look for. If the airplane is foreign, was it ever retrofitted with equipment of another

country for evaluation? If so, what has been found? Can elements within the structure confirm the serial number, known or not known? Where identity is really a problem, note should be made of every part number or unusual mark that might later be useful in revealing information about the airplane. This is not unlike an intelligence-gathering review of a captured enemy aircraft during wartime!

Such information-gathering is one reason for having an experienced and responsible museum curator close at hand when this type of work is in progress. Generally, a well-versed curator will know where certain identifying marks might be found on specific parts of the airframe. If painted on a part of the aircraft, and perhaps already only faintly visible, they can be inadvertently lost by just the initial surface washing. Other details of similar importance might also be overlooked easily.

NASM's Kawanishi N1K2-Ja Shiden Kai (Violet Lightning, Modified), code named 'George' 21, had an identity problem during all the years of its outdoor display at NAS Willow Grove, Pennsylvania. This Japanese fighter also had been stripped of its original paint, leaving no clue to its manufacturer's serial number or unit identity. During the restoration process, the hand-painted number 5340 was found inside the right wing, and 5341 was found inside the left wing. Initially these were thought to be part numbers until 5341 was repeated on additional parts. This was the true serial number of the airplane which had had a right wing substituted during manufacture. A review of a known recovery list of Japanese airplanes gathered after the war for shipment to the US for evaluation revealed that 5341 was among four of this type of aircraft brought to the US in this group, and came from Omura Air Base on Kyushu. The only unit in

This is the Kawanishi N1K2-Ja 'George' fighter that stood for many years at NAS Willow Grove, Pennsylvania. When acquired by NASM, it was disassembled and stored indoors so that its deterioration could be stabilized until restoration was possible. The external paint provided a degree of protection, but interior surfaces show the effect of outdoor exposure.

In addition to discovering the serial number hand-painted on major parts inside the structure, evidence of combat was also found. When the skin was removed from the wing in order to remove corrosion, a bullet was found lodged in one of the ribs. It was photographed, recorded, and there it remains.

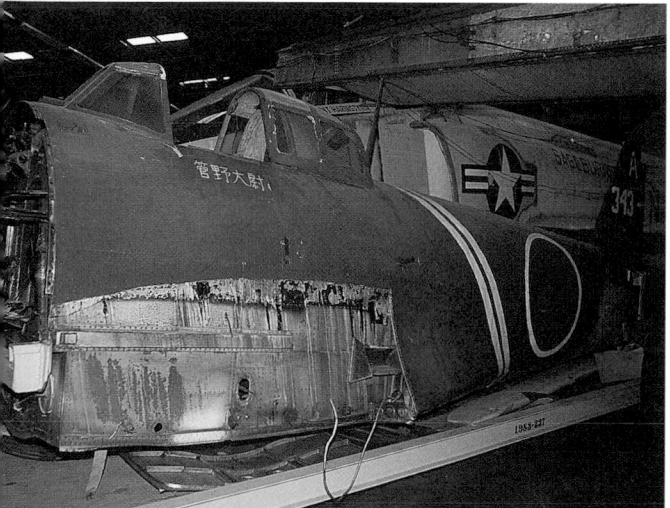
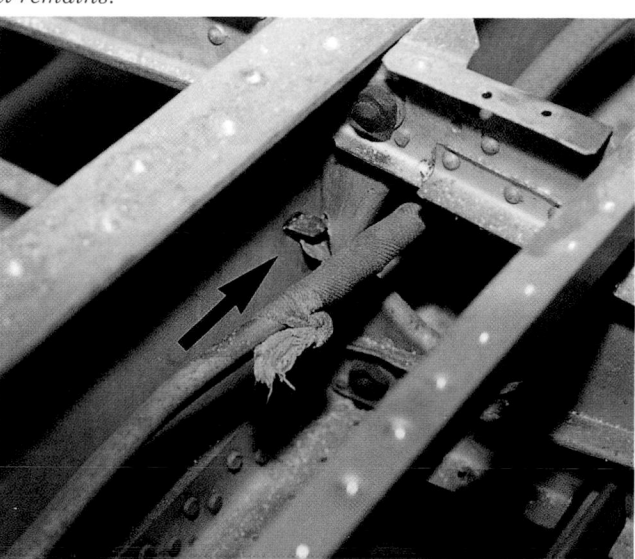

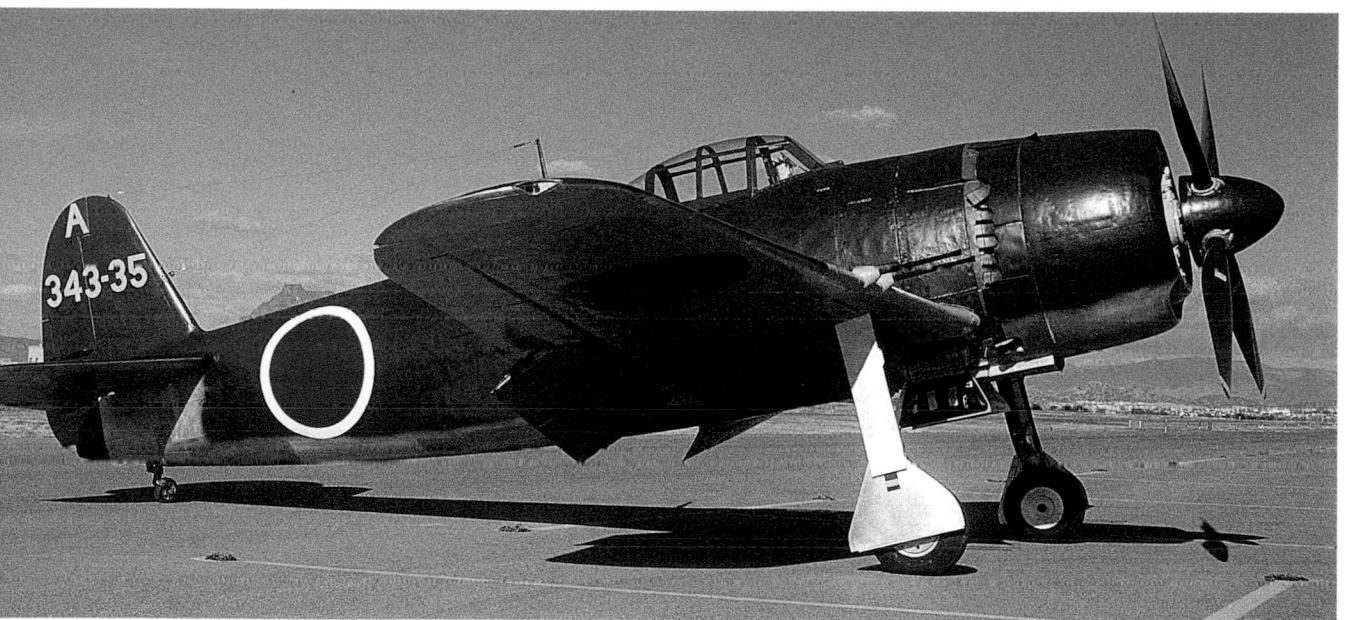

All identifying markings on this Kawanishi N1K2-Ja 'George' fighter were removed and lost during its years on exhibit at NAS Willow Grove. With the finding of '5341' on the interior of components during its restoration, this established the aircraft's serial number, allowing its history to be traced to the 343rd Kokutai on Kyushu. This confirmation of identity had much to do with the selection of tail markings appropriate for that unit.

that area of Japan to use this type of airplane was the 343rd *Kokutai* (Naval Air Corps), Imperial Japanese Navy, and thus, much of the history of this airplane could be tied to that unit through this obscurely-painted number.

During one of my visits to the Champlin Fighter Museum at Mesa, Arizona, where this aircraft was being restored, a skin patch on the right side of the fin was pointed out to me: this was a field repair of a bullet hole. Since the fin was a closed structure and therefore not accessible from the back side and not conducive to riveting, the hole had been cut a bit larger, nut plates added to the back side of the hole, and the patch screwed in place. Had this find not been properly recorded at the time of the first restoration, those studying this structure in the future would never know if this was accomplished as part of the restoration, or a field repair during time of combat.

A patch on the engine cowl confirmed that a bullet had entered the engine section. This view of the firewall shows the damage that remains from that bullet across this engine-mount stiffener.

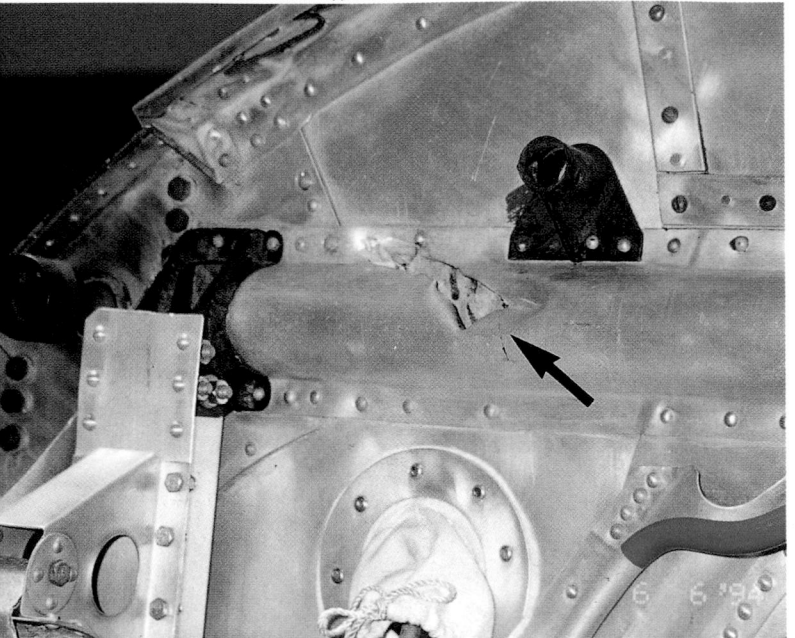

For this reason I was not too willing to relocate NASM aircraft for restoration elsewhere. Without a frequent watch over the project, clues of this nature could be lost during restoration, and with them would go the knowledge of the aircraft's earlier history. In the absence of a frequently present curator, a well-written Restoration Guidelines package will identify critical elements to watch for — but to be of value it *must be read* and adhered to

by those working on the airplane. Restorations for aircraft are becoming more intense than in earlier years. Technicians working on any of these historic aircraft projects must be made aware by the curator of the importance of uncovering these points of history and — so important — recording these findings in the work log. These discoveries must also be photographed for a visual record.

Chemical Processing

The chemical processing treatment is not limited to metal aircraft, for it has to do with nearly all metal parts, including those on fabric-covered aircraft. I always take visitors to the chemical processing department of NASM's shop first in order to emphasize the importance of this aspect of any restoration. This should not be a makeshift aspect with a temporary one-time set-up in the restoration process. Its function is continuous.

There are three major steps to be taken in the preservation of airplane components. They are *cleaning*, which prepares the part for the technicians who restore the structure; *chemical treatment*, to remove corrosion and inhibit future deterioration; and *protection*, which shields the structure for the future from outside elements. Protection is

The importance placed upon chemical treatment and corrosion control is evidenced by the completeness and spaciousness of NASM's Chemical Shop shown here. Because these chemicals are always ready they are more likely to be used at the moment of need rather than substituting a lessor procedure in an attempt to save time. (NASM, SI 96-15254-14A)

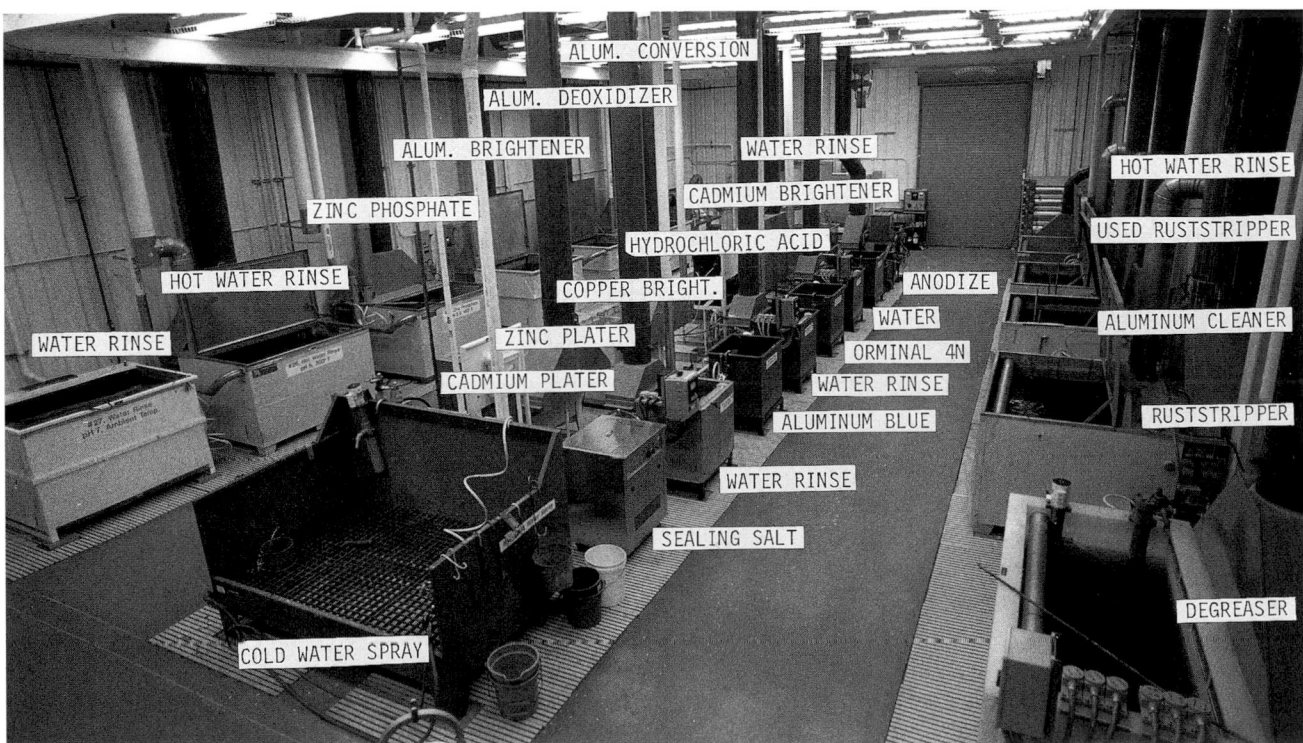

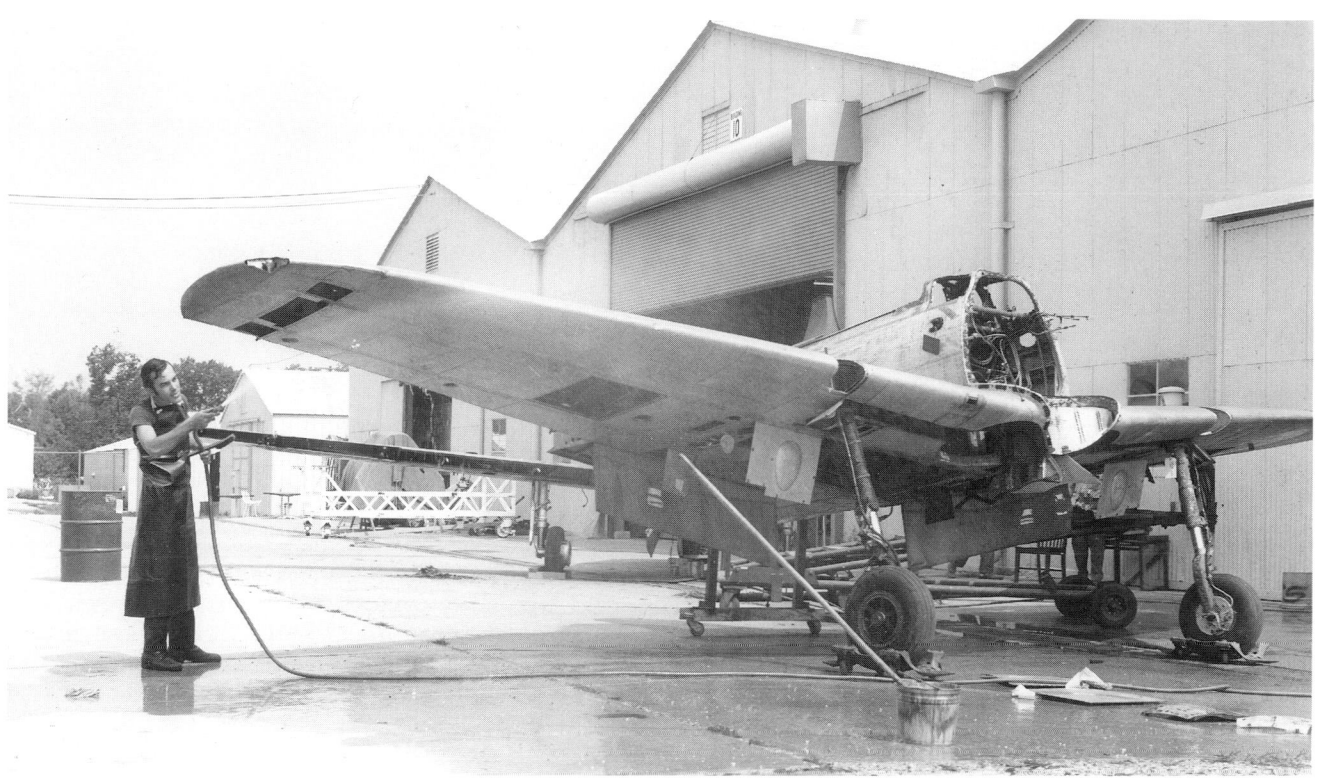

When the condition of the structure warrants chemical cleaning as opposed to using the dry method, a large structure such as this wing and fuselage section of the A6M5 Zero is cleaned at NASM over a drain area where chemicals can be gathered. A fresh-water rinse, being applied here by Garry Cline, is repeated for several days to ensure the drawing out of all the corrosion control chemicals from the structure.

usually surface painting or coating, for both the inside and the outside of the structure. The first two of these major steps are the responsibility of the chemical processing section of the restoration shop. This chemical treatment process makes the difference between truly preserving an aircraft for museum longevity, and lesser restoration efforts that only remove the visible rust or corrosion and paint over potentially active deterioration.

The importance of cleaning cannot be over-emphasized. While its importance is recognized its vigor tends to dissipate over time. For example, I recall a crafts-person going to the needed trouble of opening a wing section of a P-51 Mustang in order to make certain there was no corrosion or foreign matter inside. When his work was done, the interior was sparkling clean, even though it was to be closed and not seen. The preservation coating applied would protect the inner surfaces indefinitely. Yet the same crafts-person a few years later when working on a similar aircraft structure merely fogged the interior with preservative material without cleaning, thinking that this treatment would adequately handle the preservation aspect. Why the change in thinking on his part?

Dirt of any kind, be it loose dust or encrusted material, can be a potent source of deterioration because it can give rise to an alteration product if a chemical reaction occurs between the dirt and the object. Oxygen and moisture is all it takes. Even if nothing so harmful does occur, it is unwise to assume that loose foreign matter (dust) is innocuous, or that it can be safely left on metal surfaces. Over a period of time, dust (if left inside a wing structure, for example) can cause corrosion and chemical change to an object.[38]

In recent years there have been two methods used for the *cleaning* phase of aircraft structures. One has been with chemical wash and the other has been by dry abrasive blasting with plastic or glass beads. Since debate continues over the relative merits of wet and dry methods for cleaning, it is best not to interject too much discussion here that may describe obsolete methods and materials. New materials are continually being developed for this purpose.

The importance of corrosion control must not appear to be minimized here for lack of extensive discussion. As an example of how critical this can be, consider the trailing edge of an all-metal wing. On a fabric-covered aircraft, this is where fabric rot will often occur because of the gathering of water. Without arresting the presence of inside-surface corrosion in an all-metal wing and without applying an inhibitor against further deterioration, in time the airplane will be like so many automobiles with a nice exterior finish, but with the metal eaten away from within.

After a record was made of all the colors found on the fuselage of the Arado Ar 234B-2 (almost all American applied), paint stripper was used to remove the paint. In this case, corrosion was suspected under the paint and body filler which warranted complete paint removal for corrosion control.

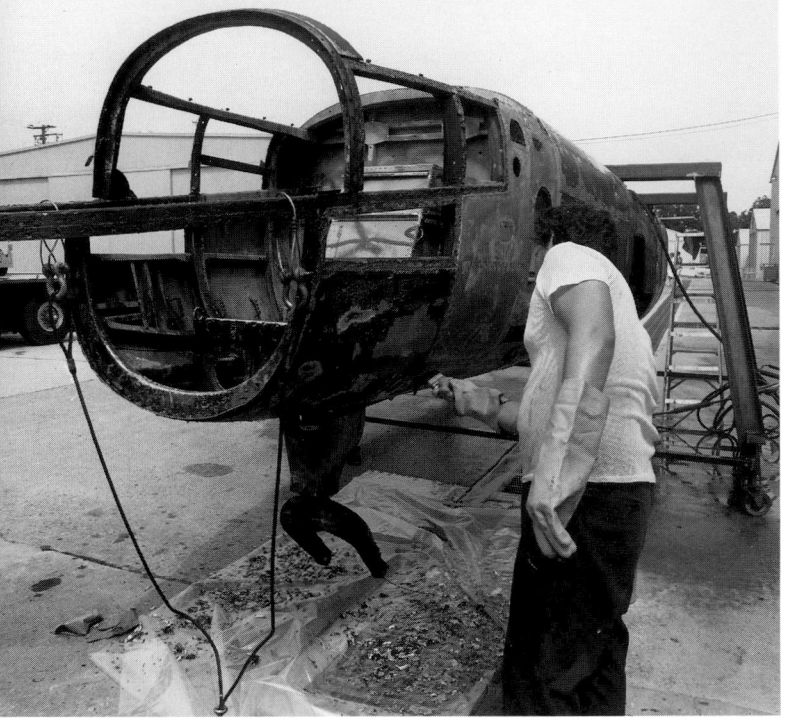

To reach these hidden areas of aircraft structures, it is often necessary to remove some of the skin panels by drilling out rivets and replacing them. This is a radical procedure and alters the originality somewhat, but it is safer to sacrifice several rows of rivets in order to thoroughly clean and stabilize the structure. This is one of the many compromises that must be addressed throughout a restoration. It is time-consuming, but important.

There are some areas which require chemical cleaning. Oily surfaces are cleaned with solvents such as varsol and trichloroethane, and exhaust stains can be removed with Magnusol 728™. Special care must be taken in the use of paint and rust strippers, and aluminum brightener. These chemicals, if left behind in crevices or allowed to act too long, can cause irreparable damage by eating into the metal. Only study and experience can prevent this damage from happening. When chemical cleaning is used for both ferrous and non-ferrous metals, heavily-pitted areas can be cleared by hand-brushing using steel or aluminum wool, or blasting with plastic, glass beads or walnut shells as the situations warrant.

The second of the three processes, *chemical treatment*, is a very important operation in the preservation of metals. Surface coatings for metal that are produced by chemical action should be duplicated as nearly as possible to that of the orig-inal surface coating. This forms a protection against corrosion as well as serving as a base for organic finishes. Corrosion and rust are relentless enemies of metal surfaces. No matter how high the quality of paint used, corrosion can form under the paint unless protected by a conversion coating. A smooth-appearing metal surface is actually a series of microscopic peaks and valleys which are electrically anodic and cathodic in relation to each other. When moisture is present, these combine to form electrolytic cells, and as with any battery this release of energy is a process of deterioration. This is why aircraft exhibited outdoors will not survive for long periods, no matter how frequently their exteriors are painted. With some paints, alkalis form certain metallic soaps that affect the adhesion between paint and metal, creating an adverse reaction.

To prevent this deteriorating action, a synthetic layer of phosphate and oxide crystals is formed on the surface. This is done by applying a solution that 'converts' the surface from oxides to the phosphate crystal structure of the 'phosphate conversion coating.' The process modifies the metal surface, removing evidence of previous treatments and use, but will ensure (if correctly applied) enhanced corrosion resistance in less-than-perfect environments. This conversion coating also serves as an excellent surface for paint adherence.

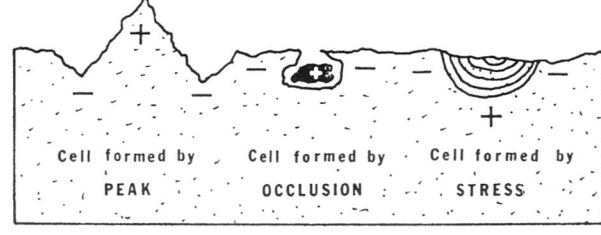

Unprotected Metal Surface

Preserved Metal Surface

Highly magnified view of a metal surface which generates deterioration through electrical differences. This is present with all untreated metals. Chemically-applied phosphate crystals neutralize this action.

'Corrosion, often as not,' according to Conservator David Hallam, 'is like a cancer which has to be dug out, the surface then resealed so that moisture cannot get in again. The truth of the matter is that you can never seal a surface with paint, and even epoxies are permeable. A more effective approach would be to treat an object with a process that will guarantee its preservation for a known time, such as a wax, after which it will have been retreated. This is far better than using an unmeasured-time material like epoxy, and having to monitor its preserving qualities more closely.'[39]

There is still much learning and experimenting to do in the field of extending aircraft life through chemical treatment. With new products becoming available, it would be improper to make any brand name recommendations in this regard. Chemical companies are eager and many sales representatives are qualified to give advice and literature about their various products. Therefore, for those restorers who lack assistance from a staff conservator, an initial step in learning more about the use of these chemicals is to contact local representatives of these chemical companies. Be aware, however, of exaggerated claims. Representatives are also salespersons.

To begin this process, stainless-steel tanks for various washes are necessary. Any degree of ingenuity is welcome in regulating temperature control, water flow, and various forms of chemical agitation. This can become expensive and involved. For one-time chemical use, a simple wooden box constructed to the size to fit the parts to be immersed will suffice. A polyurethane sheet as a liner will complete the fabrication of this form of inexpensive, disposable chemical tank.

Unfortunately, each basic type of metal requires its own form of processing. Regardless of how two dissimilar pieces of metal are joined, they must be separated and practical for their respective chemical treatments. Steel is given a phosphate coating; aluminum receives aluminum brightener plus a corrosion control treatment; and magnesium is given a cleaning, conversion coating, and other chemical treatments. Cadmium plating when used originally for preserving aircraft parts is also an essential element in restorations. Care must be taken to maintain the original type of surfaces.

The third step of the preservation process is *protection*, which is done in the painting phase. This is usually accomplished by the restoration team irrespective of the chemical aspect of the work. Painting the outside is an obvious function. For metal aircraft that have lost their protective Alclad coating and are to be left in their natural metal finish, we have found at NASM that Rhom and Hass Acryloid™ and Okite Clear Coat™ finishes work well. These not only protect the surface, but give the soft reflective qualities of the original Alclad aluminum.

When restoring NASM's P-51D, a situation

This is the undersurface of the Messerschmitt Me 262A wing. Its steel spar against aluminum skin and ribs caused excessive corrosion, so zinc chromated panels were removed in order to reach the interior. Now in place so as to keep the wing rigid, the adjacent panels were removed to ensure complete treatment of the interior.

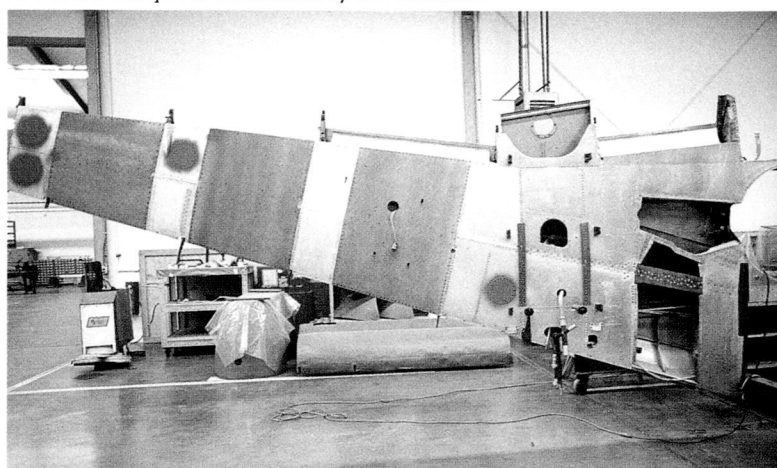

occurred where surface protection worked against a restoration project. The post-war slogan painted on its side, 'ENLIST IN THE AAF, GUARD THE VICTORY,' had to be removed. In so doing, the Alclad coating under the painted letters was bright and shiny, while the surrounding skin surface showed the normal dullness of having been exposed to the elements. This slogan thus remained apparent despite the paint removal, and had to be eradicated. (See illustration on page 27.)

To remove this distraction, aluminum wool was used to lessen the reflective surface until it matched the surrounding area. Once obliterated, the entire surface was polished and coated with protective Clear Coat™ by Okite, which was in standard use at that time. This was a severe treatment to the natural finish of the aluminum but had to be addressed, since our goal was to represent an operational fighter of World War II.

Sometimes things work in favor of the restoration process. US Navy aircraft of the World War II period had factory-applied paint on their interiors at the time of manufacture. This has proven to be a very protective coating that has lasted on these airplanes for years. On the other hand, almost all other metal aircraft interiors were not painted originally. During the restoration process it is tempting to coat over these corrosion-stained interior surfaces with zinc chromate or color paint for protection, but this should not be done since it deviates from the original appearance at the time of manufacture. Instead, there are two types of action that should be followed after the completion of the corrosion control process.

For lasting protection against corrosion of closed structures such as wings and empennage, water-displacing corrosion-preventative materials are

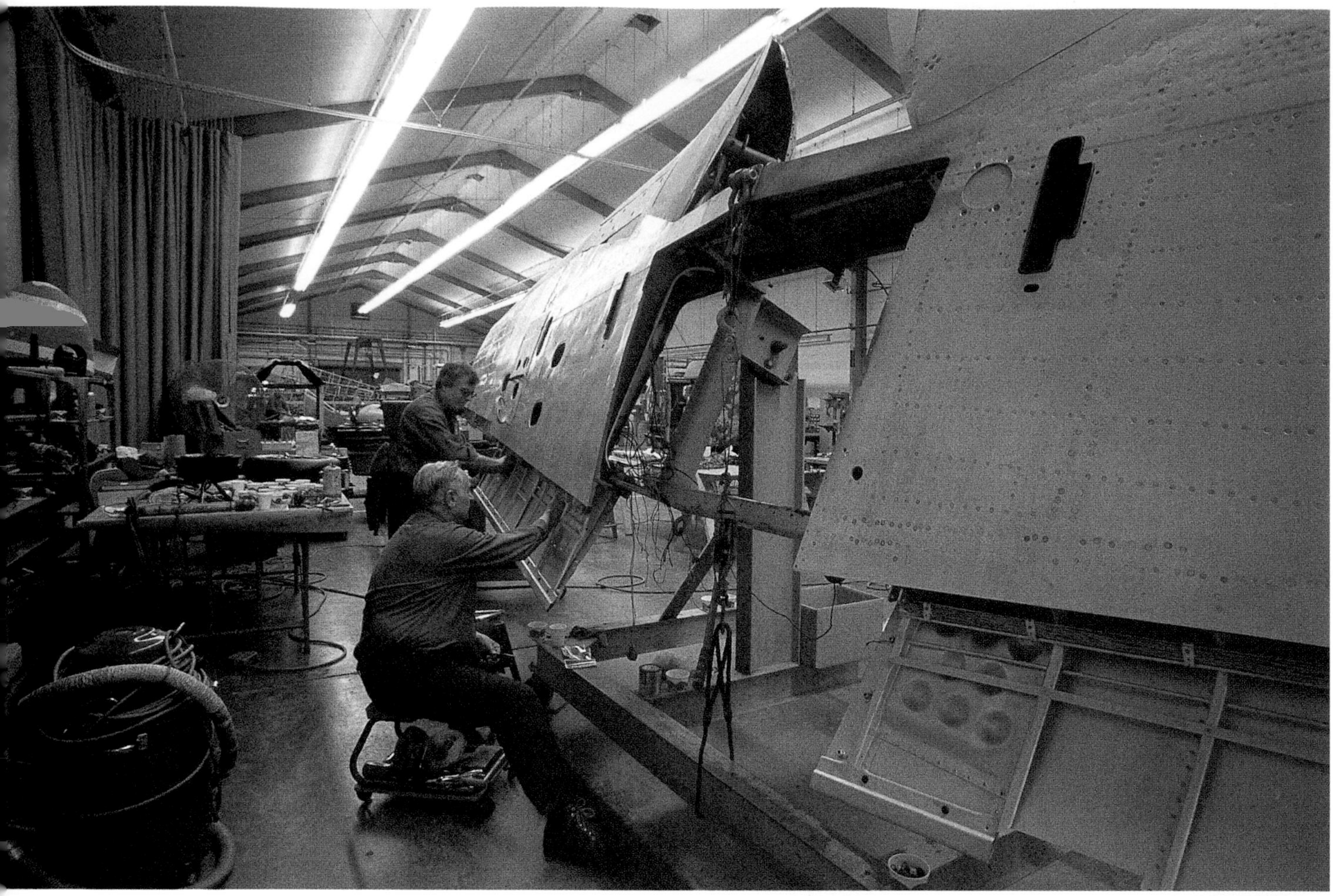

Areas of the structure to be left exposed but not originally painted are given a coating of clear Acroloyde™ for surface protection. Here the wing flap area is being prepared for this clear coating during the restoration of the Fw 190F-8.

constantly being developed and improved. Select one that seems to be working the best for providing a thorough coating to reach all interior surfaces of the structure. Currently, this is applied to the structure with a special spray wand (fogging). The carrier in the form of a fine mist is often a wax in itself, and also provides a protective film which retains the inhibitor. Once the fog appears at the far end of the structure, the coating is considered complete. Recall once again what sections of the structure must be opened to reach possible corrosive areas. While open and when assured the cleaning process is thorough, apply this form of preservative material before resealing.

Normally unpainted internal areas such as wing flap recesses and aft fuselage cavities should be coated with a clear coating such as Rhom and Hass Acryloid™ or similar proven protective materials. Resist the temptation to use paint, but instead do the job right by treating those inner surfaces to eliminate the stains and bring back the original appearance. This eliminates any question of active corrosion being present.

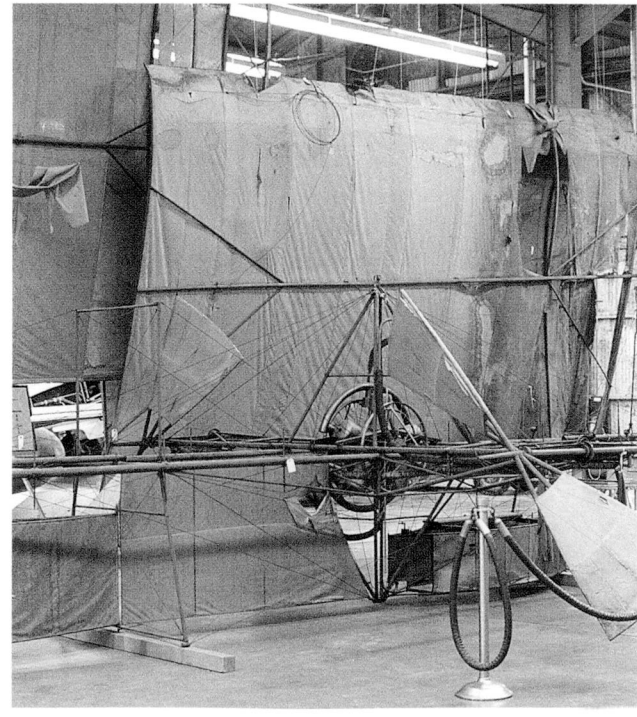

The steel-tube fuselage frame of the Langley Aerodrome rests in front of its wings. An auto body dip tank was used for the chemical cleaning of this one-piece, oversize fuselage. When thoroughly cleaned and washed, it was painted with a clear coating for protection.

A smaller assembly of the Langley Aerodrome fuselage is seen being worked on by restoration technician Bob Padgett of NASM. Here was a case where protective coatings first applied to the steel tubing would not prevent rust. Alternative materials and methods had to be used.

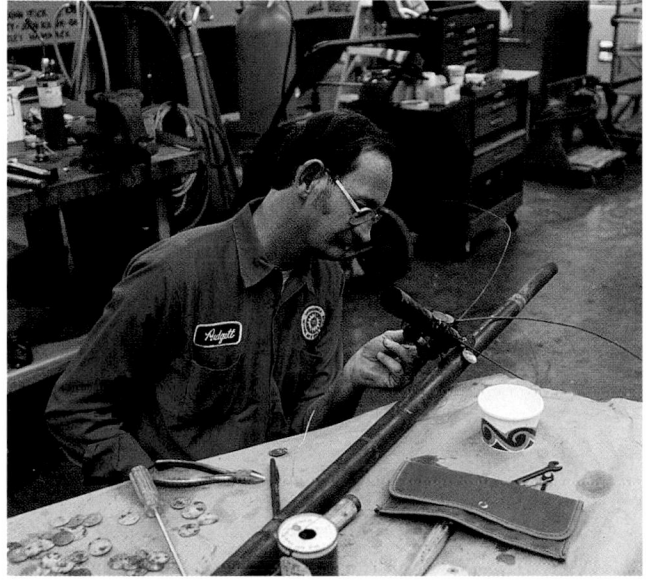

When using any type of coating material on metal, it is essential that the surface be perfectly dry, not just look dry. Steel shows corrosive effects faster than aluminum. At NASM an interesting experience occurred: when coating the freshly-cleaned steel tubular structure of the Langley Aerodrome in 1980 with Water White™, another clear protective coating, rust showed through this coating in a matter of only a few days. Tests were made on a similar piece of steel tubing to determine the cause. We discovered that the acetone, due to its rapid evaporation qualities, chilled the tubing when used to assist in wiping off the dust before spray coating. The resultant condensation allowed moisture to dwell in the finely-pitted surface of the tubing, which caused rust that was sealed underneath the protective coating. The use of a hair dryer or other drying device over the area just prior to painting solved the problem. This rust (corrosion) damage to steel and aluminum can take place under paint as well but unfortunately goes undetected.

While restoring the Langley Aerodrome, another interesting process developed. The fuselage was a large all-steel frame that had rusted, yet the tubing walls were too thin to be sandblasted to remove the rust. To use a rust stripper by hand would have been very time-consuming. In the Washington area was a dip-tank used for immersing an entire automobile body to chemically remove rust. What better solution to a major time-consuming effort? This worked well, but because of the length of the frame, only half could be immersed at a time. I must add that considerable care followed to ensure that the entire tubular structure was well-flushed and neutralized before continuing with this restoration. This process might be considered for similar application when encountering rusted steel tube fuselage frames for non-flying museum aircraft restorations.

Restoring the J1N1-S 'Irving'

The Nakajima J1N1-S Gekko twin-engined night-fighter, codenamed 'Irving', was one of the many enemy aircraft brought to the US from Japan for

When beginning the restoration of the Nakajima J1N1-S Gekko night-fighter, codenamed 'Irving', the exterior looked in fair condition. With a closer look, it was obvious that its unprotected skin had suffered from dirt while in storage, causing obvious corrosion. These parts just brought into the shop are having holding racks fabricated for them.

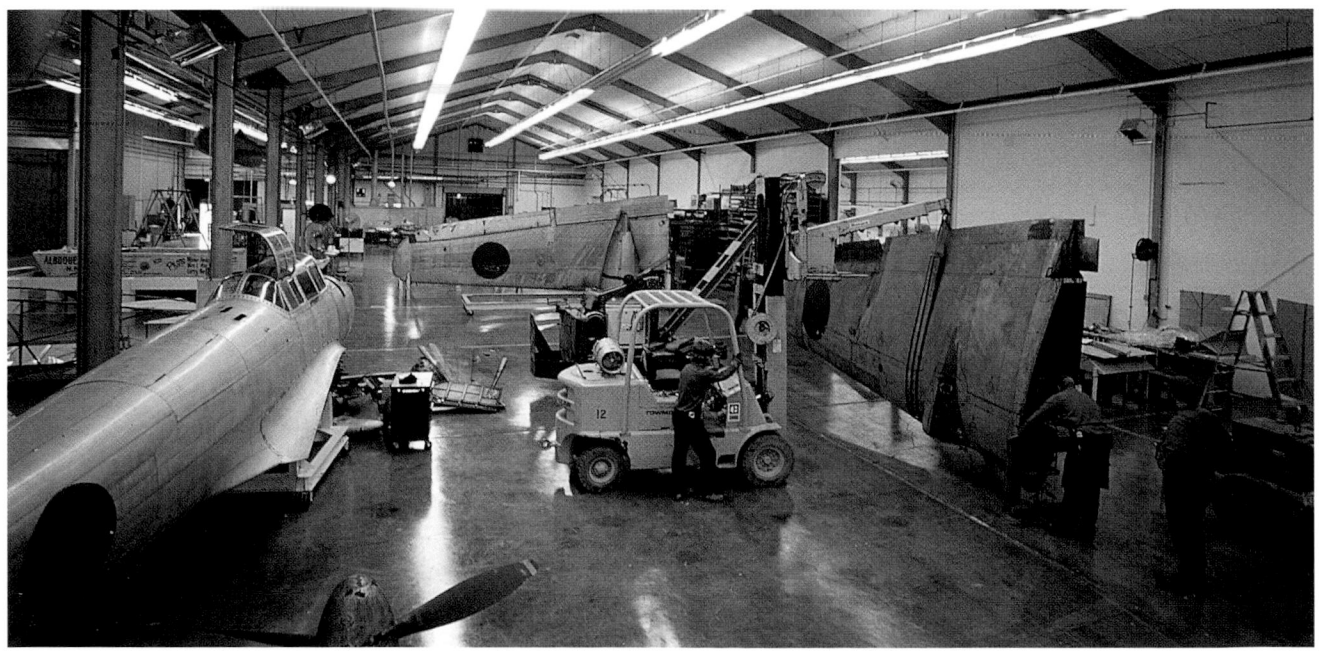

evaluation after World War II. Like many of these airplanes, it too had had its paint removed and therefore little or no surface protection over the years while in storage. For that reason, it was selected by NASM for restoration and to also facilitate its preservation. This is a significant Japanese airplane in its own right, offering night-fighter weapon system comparison with that of the US Northrop P-61C Black Widow and German Heinkel He 219A Uhu, both of which are in NASM's collection for that purpose. Despite the 'Irving's' development problems, first as an escort fighter, then reconnaissance aircraft, it later became a lethal night-fighter of the Imperial Japanese Navy. Obliquely-mounted cannon were behind the crew compartment to fire up into night-flying bombers. This low-firing position for the attacker was in the darkest part of the night sky and therefore difficult to detect from the bomber. The Germans developed a similar night-fighter system at the same time called *Schräge Musik* (Oblique or Jazz Music), neither country knowing of the other's efforts.

The restoration of the 'Irving' was started in September 1979, and consumed 17,247 man-hours by the time it was completed in December 1983. By comparison, this was the equivalent of two men working 40-hour weeks for four years. In actuality, however, a number of technicians were involved at different times depending upon the skills needed for the many aspects of this restoration. From start to finish, George Genotti, a licensed Aircraft and Powerplant (A&P) mechanic since 1952, nursed the aircraft through months of time-consuming details. Bob Padgett, also an A&P mechanic and assigned to the project, was often called away to assist with other unscheduled tasks, which extended the restoration of the 'Irving' over a longer time period than originally planned.

The greatest amount of restoration work on the 'Irving' was devoted to the fuselage and cockpit — a matter of 6,544 man-hours or 38 per cent of the entire project. This was understandable because of the many systems and components needing restoration. Every part was removed from the interior until only an empty shell remained. This meant the removal of the canopy, instrument panels, seats, floor-boards, and flight-control system. Their removal not only allowed every corner of the structure to be freed of corrosion and given a protective coating, but the removed components themselves to be processed more thoroughly.

The separation of dissimilar metals in contact within the structure was of major importance. Fortunately there were not too many instances of this, but the unions that did occur resulted in electrolysis action that caused considerable deterioration. Often the joining rivets had to be drilled away so that the contrasting metals could be

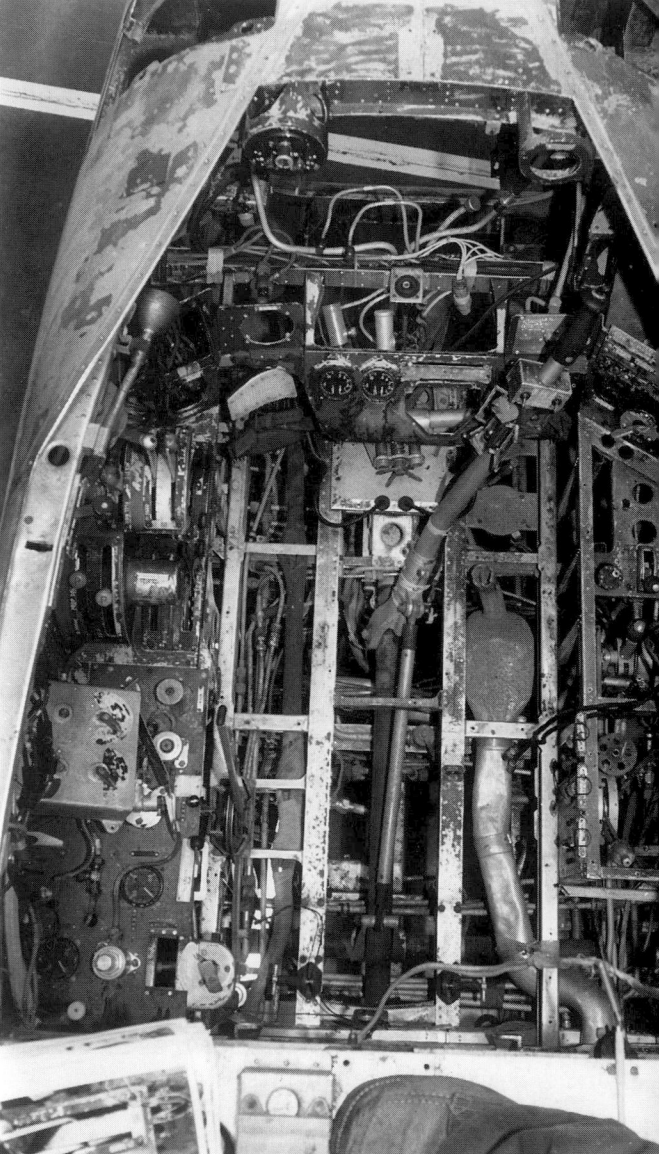

The most difficult work with the fuselage of the 'Irving' was the removal of all the components from the cockpit. Tagging each part and recording where it was to be returned as well as accounting for them in the meantime became labor-intensive in itself. The removal of all these parts was essential not only for their respective cleaning, but for complete access to the fuselage interior walls. (NASM, SI 81-3626-27)

given their respective chemical treatments for cleaning to prevent further rusting or corrosion. When rejoining them in the original fashion, a protective barrier, generally a generous coating of paint, was placed between them.

Before any of this removal was begun, photos were taken of the interior to show the location of the numerous parts. In addition a numbered metal tag was wired to each part and a log was kept to show the location of each item as an aid to reinstallation. It appeared to anyone viewing the pile of tubing, cables, components, instruments, and brackets that it would be a lengthy task to find their proper locations, let alone to reinstall them. All went back into place, however, without even a single washer being left over.

The most trying aspect of the fuselage work was the removal and replacement of the control cables. After these had been routed through guide holes within the structure at the time of manufacture, their ends had been spliced around their respective fittings. There was no possible way that these cables could be removed without cutting off one of the ends at a strategic point to facilitate reinstallation. When placed back into the structure, the cut ends were then swaged together; hardly satisfactory for being airworthy, but the technology and original cabling was retained. This was a drastic measure, but it was also the only way these steel cables could be treated for preservation, leaving the aluminum fuselage clear for its appropriate corrosion control treatment.

Because of the corrosion and resultant pitting of the structure, considerable attention was given to the chemical treatment of these major structural elements. This was done outside NASM's shop over the drain area specially constructed for the recovery of these corrosion control chemicals.

While new methods are always being tried and old ones improved upon, the earlier methods were not always that bad when done properly. For that reason, I will describe here the actual methods that were used upon the main structure of the 'Irving' airframe.

For those areas of the major components with a minimum amount of corrosion, a mild alkaline solution such as Oakite Aluminum Cleaner NST™ was sprayed over the surface. This was kept wet by further spraying for about 30 minutes. The affected surfaces were scrubbed with a brush, 3M Scotch Brite™ pads, scalpel or scribe as severity called for in order to remove deposits. An extensive water wash followed.

For areas that might be described as moderately corroded with blackened pits, a phosphoric acid-based solution was used, such as Turco™ W01, for 30 minutes to two hours, depending upon the severity of the corrosion. This was followed by a rinse in a suitable deoxidizer such as Oakite Deoxidizer™ LNC for 30-40 seconds before being rinsed with large amounts of water and high-pressure steam.

For the very severe areas of corrosion, plastic and glass bead blasting were used. A pressure of 20-25 psi was used; 15-20 psi is less likely to cause warpage, but with care, this can be avoided with the higher pressure which is necessary in severe cases. After this blasting the areas were washed with a mild aluminum cleaner using a 3M Scotch Brite™ pad to remove the unsightly haze that the blasting produced.

Once the fuselage was stripped of all its components, cleaning became a routine process. Because of the nature of the encrustation both inside and out, liquid chemical cleaning was selected. When properly managed and the parts thoroughly cleaned, this method has advantages over dry methods. (NASM, SI 81-10626-3)

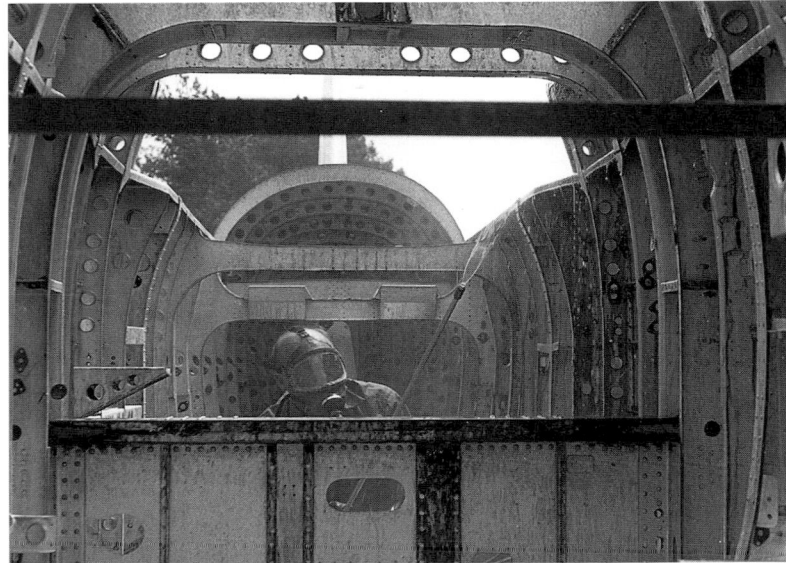

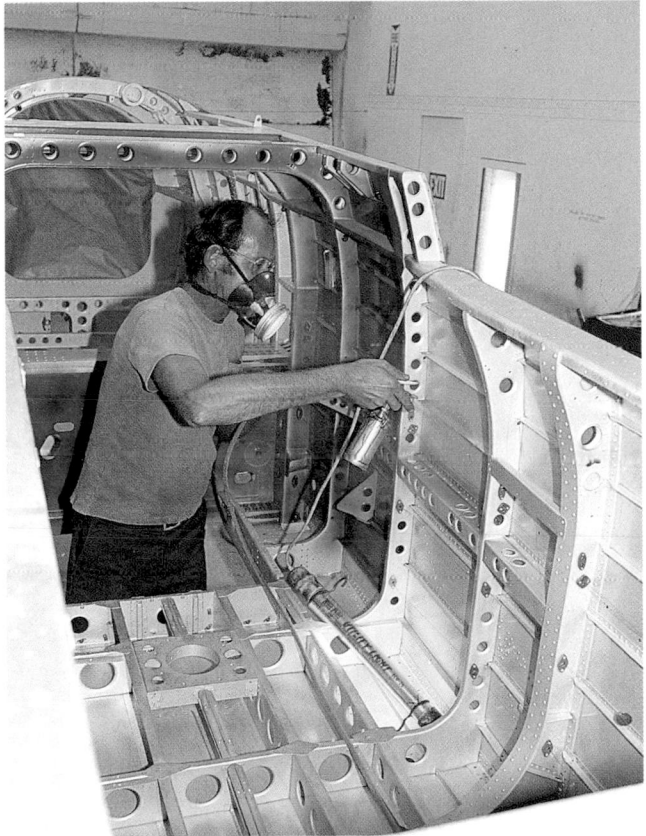

Bob Padgett begins the arduous process of reassembly within the fuselage. A nearly transparent coating of blue-green coloring was applied over the areas of the fuselage interior where this color had been previously. The original material could not be located in Japan and had to be simulated by adding a blue-green color to the clear protective material that the museum otherwise used over unpainted surfaces.

In all these processes an abundance of water and pressure was used to make certain that all crevices were clear of any chemicals. Nothing further was necessary for surface preparation, since the exterior was to be painted. More than a decade has passed, and the structure shows no signs of instability that may have been caused by any of these treatments. Three hundred years from now would be a better test of these methods, for only time can tell.

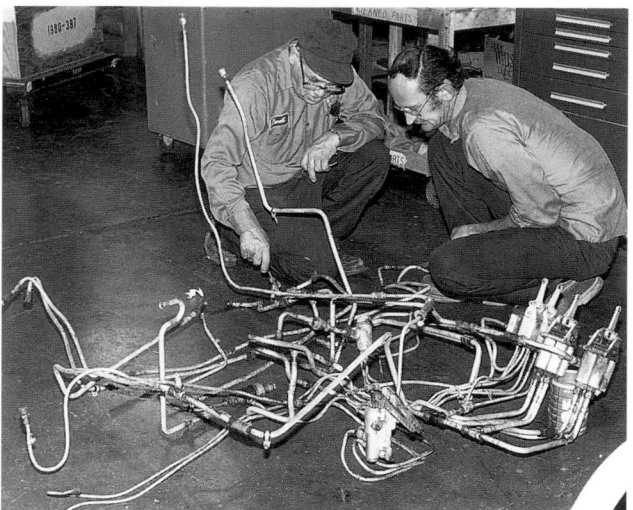

Hydraulic lines are placed on the shop floor to confirm where each piece fits before reinstallation is attempted. In keeping with Nakajima's position as the Japanese aircraft manufacturer with the greatest experience in hydraulic systems, the design of the J1N1-S 'Irving' had every major moving component powered hydraulically except for flight controls. (NASM, SI 81-4486-5)

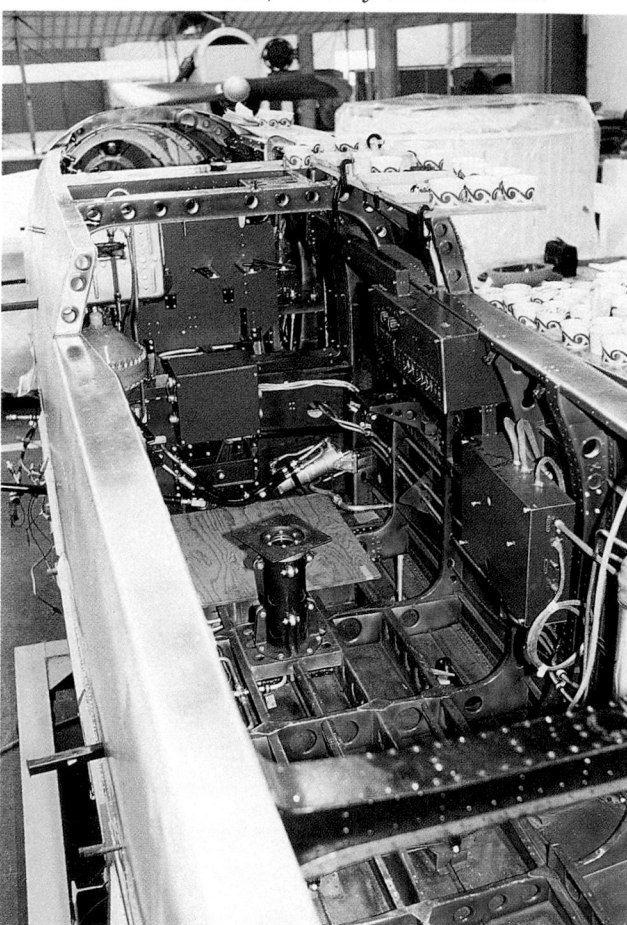

Having been in the protected cover of the fuselage, many parts merely needed a cleaning and preservation wax before being reinstalled. The rear cockpit of the J1N1-S 'Irving' begins to take on new interest as components are reinstalled.

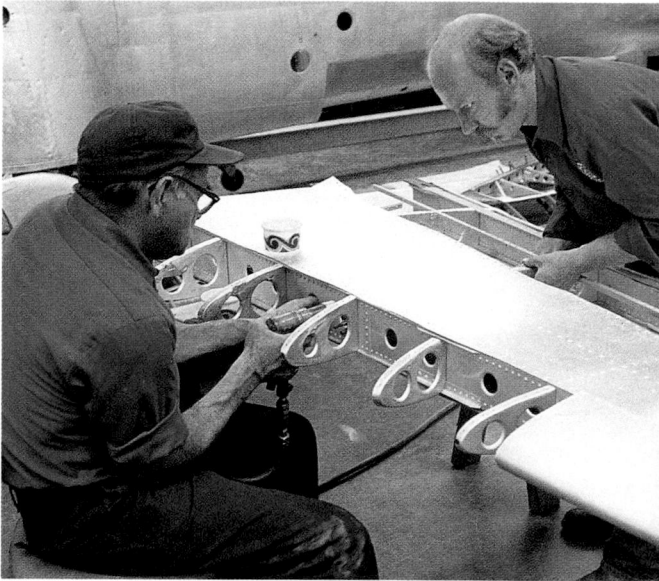

Access from the outside to the internal structure was very limited in the case of this Japanese fighter. To thoroughly clean away all traces of corrosion as well as deposits that would eventually induce corrosion, much of the skin panels had to be removed. Here Dale Bucy and George Genotti reattach the stabilizer skin.

Restoring the wings held no unusual surprises, but these were the largest all-metal wing panels to undergo restoration by the museum up to that time. The network of wires, cables, and tubing in each of the wheel wells made these wings nearly as complicated as the fuselage. The wings, however, offered the same advantage as the two engines: while the first wing was stripped of all its components, the untouched wing served as a direct reference. When the first was completed, it served as that pattern for the second.

The most severe structural damage within the wings was caused by a heavy side load that had been placed upon the right landing gear. The structure

holding it had been stressed and wrinkled as though from a ground loop.[40] Rivets were drilled away from the surrounding supporting members, damaged areas were straightened and then were secured together again. In the restored 'Irving,' there is hardly a trace of this early structural damage, which if left would have served no technical advantage as no history was connected to this accident.

Lubricating such moving parts as control systems, flaps, and slats could prove to be trouble-

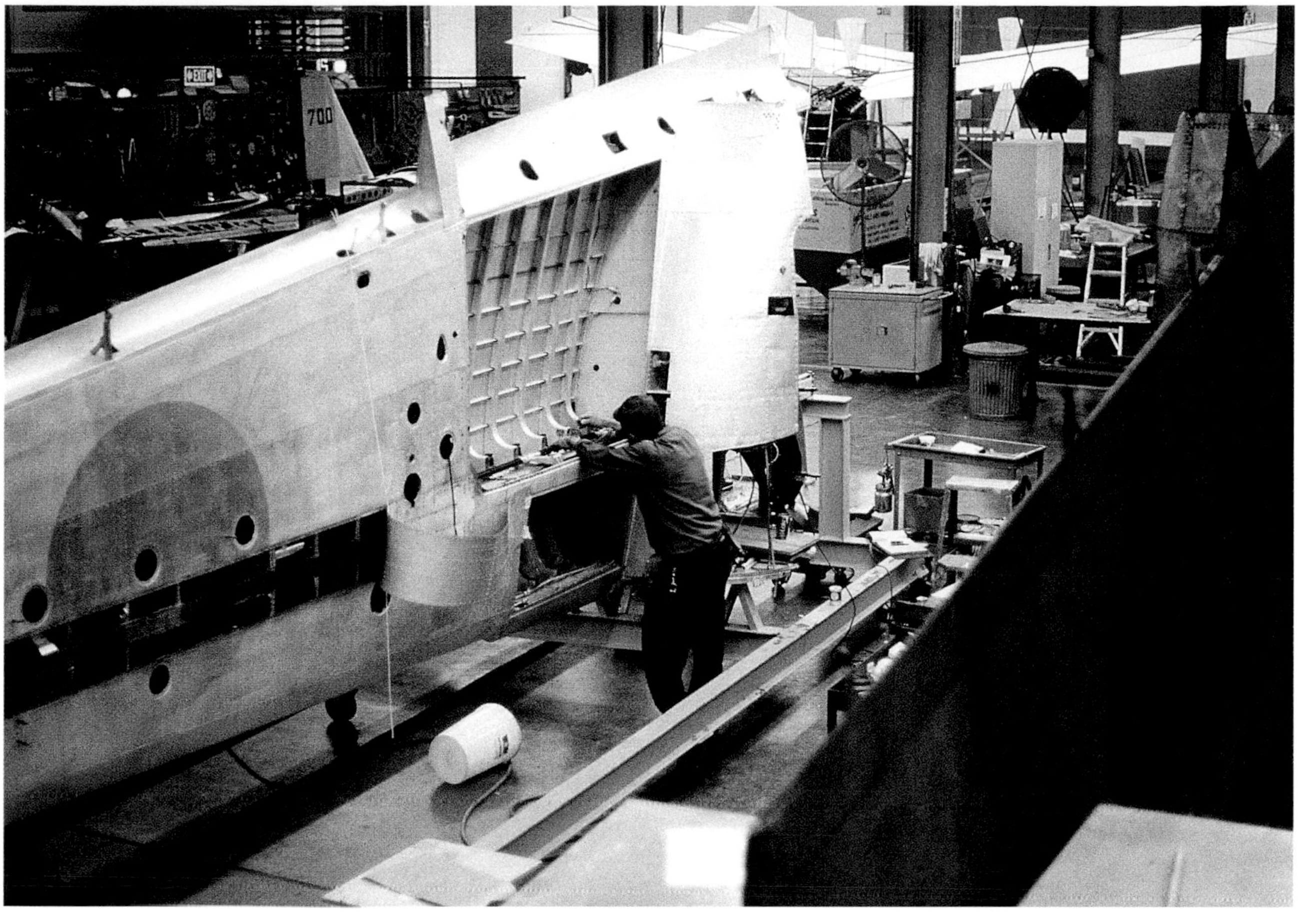

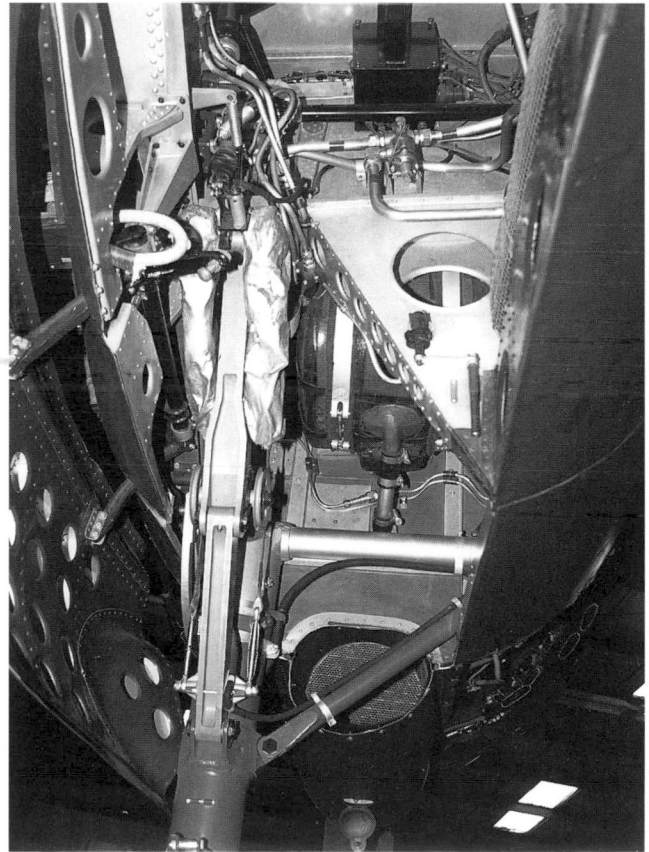

George Genotti prepared the wing fuel tank bay for the installation of the tank. The area had been wired for fire-warning detection, all of which was put in place after cleaning as it was originally. The special rack holding the wing allowed for easy access for the work process.

some in the future. These bearings needed no lubrication for the expected life of a combat aircraft, so no access panels for reaching these points were provided. From existing examples, grease appears to last about 50 years before becoming so hard that it can be pulled away from the surface it was protecting. A silicone grease which has a far greater life and longer-lasting protection was used during this restoration.

Cleaning, preserving, and restoring the two Nakajima Sakae Ha 35 Model 21 engines were no minor tasks. Each was totally disassembled and every part was coated with a preservative for lasting protection. This was a vital necessity, since the Sakae engine incorporated a number of magnesium parts that were heavily corroded. Up to that time, the residual engine oil had done a good job of preserving the walls of the engines, but we concluded that this protection of 40 years could not have lasted much longer. (See Chapter 7 for more information on engine preservation.)

These engines played another, unrelated, part in the restoration of this airplane. In reassembling the aircraft after a quarter-century of disassembly, it became virtually impossible to align the wing attachment brackets with those of the fuselage. George Genotti concluded that if the engines were placed on their mounts, the weight might provide enough 'twist' to the wing to make this alignment. His assumption was correct, for it brought the desired alignment results.

The right wheel well has the usual amount of lines and wires for an aircraft of this size; all of them received the same attention as other parts of the airplane. On the triangular strengthening panel is the removable hand crank used for pre-oiling the engine before start-up. In the other wheel well is the hand crank, if needed, for manual engine start.

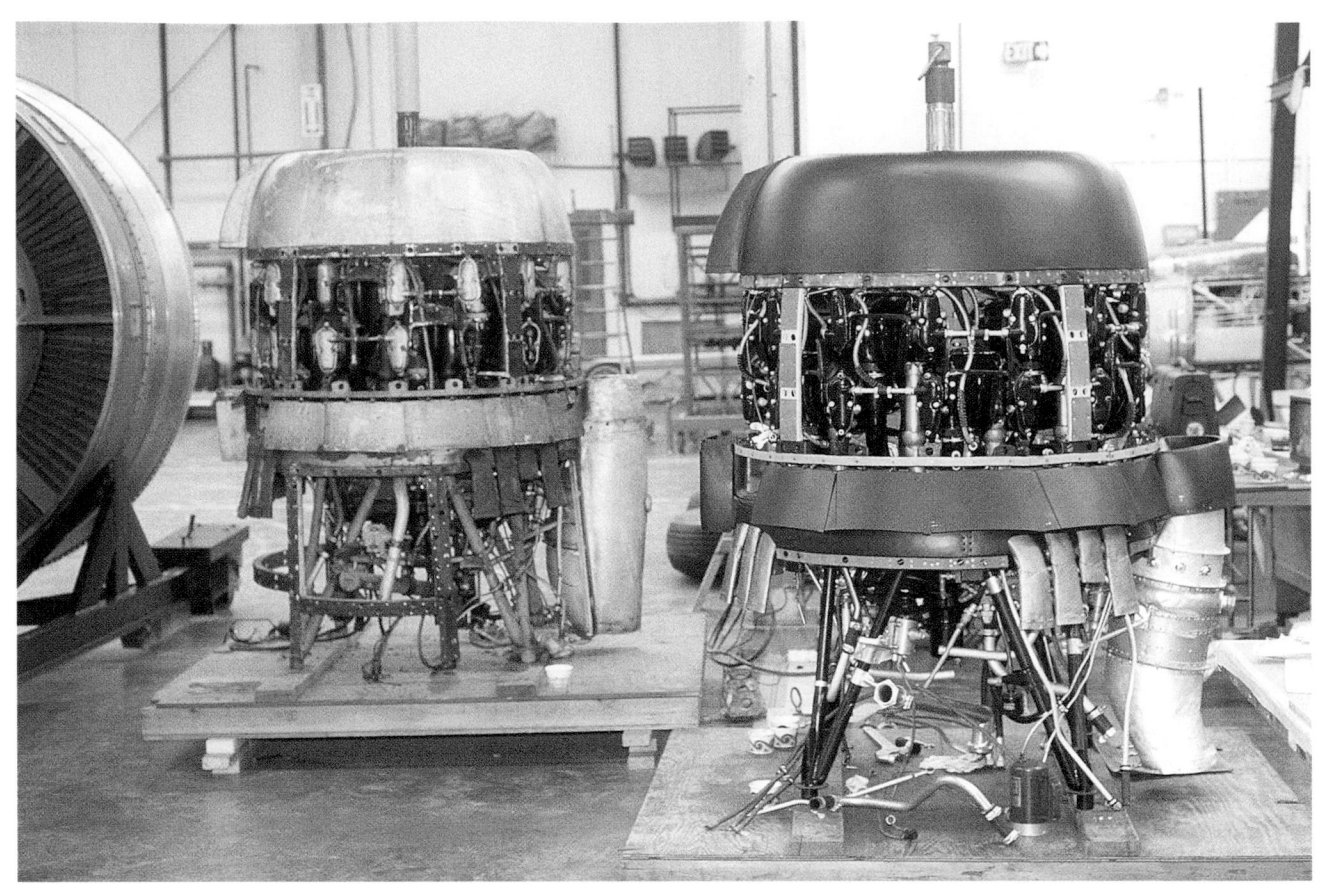

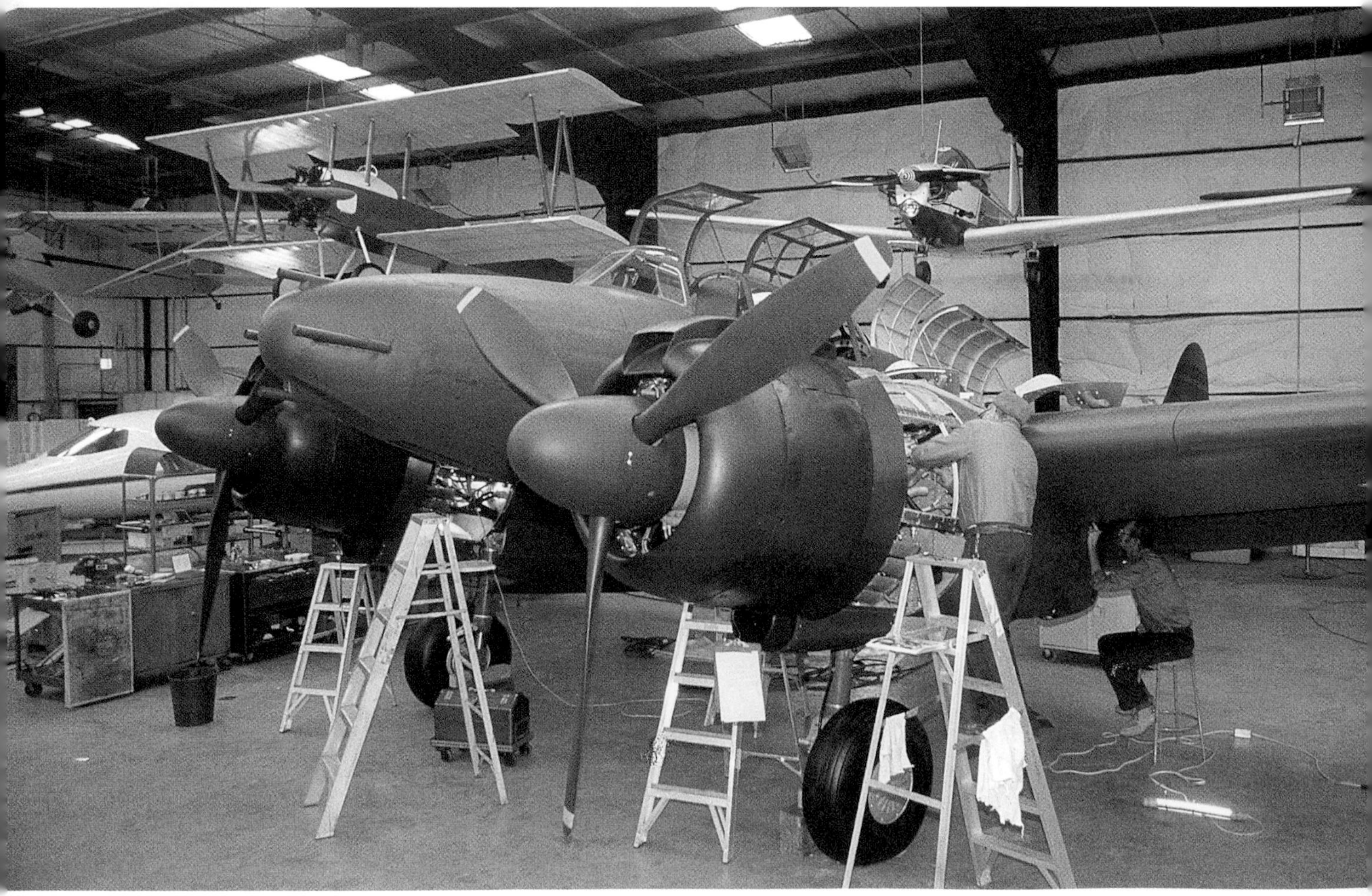

TOP LEFT:
Although double the work, restoring two-engine aircraft has an advantage. Shown here are the two Nakajima NK1F Sakae engines of the J1N1-S 'Irving'. While one is being restored, the other serves as a pattern for reattaching the many accessories. When the first is completed, it then serves as a pattern for the second.

BOTTOM LEFT:
The full realization that the J1N1-S 'Irving' was a big airplane became evident once the wings were attached to the fuselage. All the wing-attachment bolt holes would not align until the engines were attached which redistributed the wing load. Here George Genotti adjusts an engine accessory while Bob Padgett connects the wing flap hydraulic lines.

The finished airplane serves as an example of World War II technology in night-fighter aircraft. Note the two obliquely-mounted cannon that would fire upwards into enemy bombers from the darkness below. The pilot's gunsight was fixed to the same angle. The cockpit further documents the technology found in aircraft of this time period.

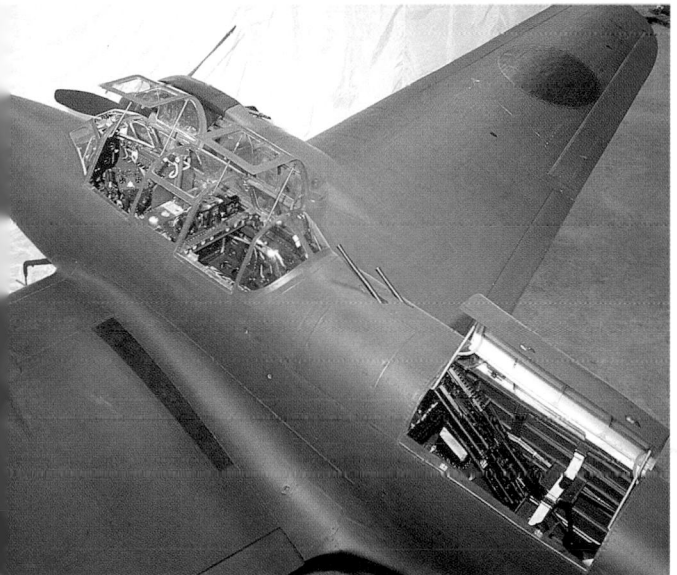

Time and money prevented completely restoring the cockpit of this N1K2-Ja 'George' fighter, serial 5312, therefore it was wisely left in this 'as received' state. An over-painting for appearance sake would have covered technically important color fragments and cockpit labeling. Cleaning and corrosion control are very difficult when electing to choose this deferral of restoration, but these are two vital elements that cannot be overlooked.

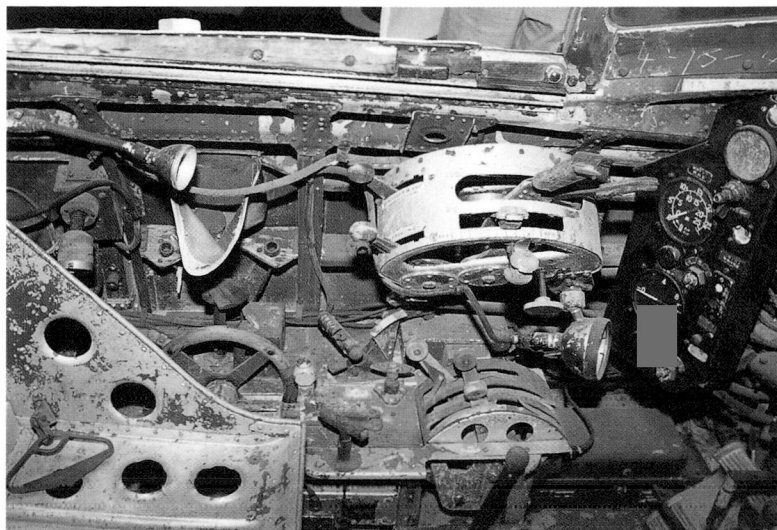

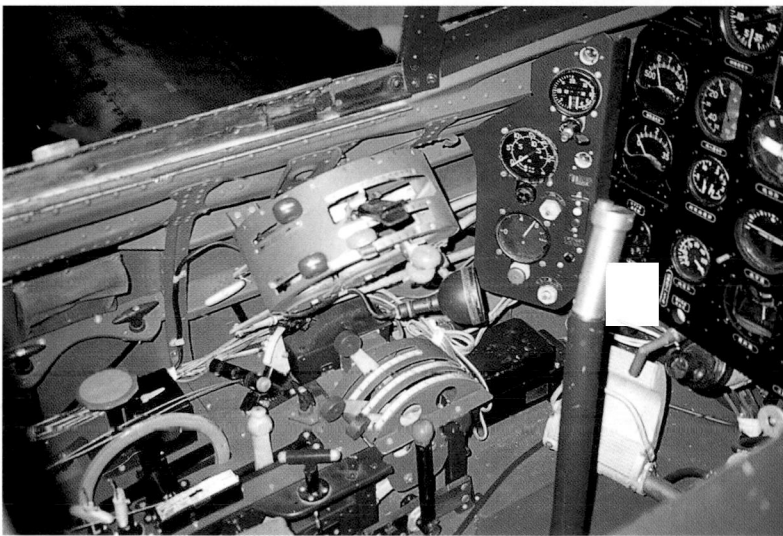

Meticulous care was given to restoring the cockpit of the N1K2-Ja 'George'. Detailed photographs and a record of colors and markings had been made before the project began. In spite of this degree of record-keeping, the unrestored cockpit in another museum provided answers. Accurately detailing cockpit technology is of major importance in any aircraft restoration.

Cockpit Detailing

Cockpits reflect much of the aviation technology of the airplane's time period, and this relates directly to the men who flew them. For that reason, cockpits must be given special attention in a restoration.

When two Japanese Kawanishi N1K2-Ja 'George' fighters were recently restored, we faced two different situations concerning their cockpits. For the airplane belonging to NASM, and being restored by the Champlin Fighter Museum at Mesa, Arizona, a major part of the overall project was to have as complete a cockpit as possible. This was achieved. In the case of the other aircraft, restored elsewhere, limited time and money became a governing factor, and therefore, what should be done about the cockpit? The degree of detail and time needed to complete the cockpit could not be met because of these restrictions. In this case, it was best to do nothing more than clean the interior and make certain that the corrosion had been cleared. To have repainted the interior just for appearance would have been a mistake: this would cover visible traces of colors that were once used, significant markings either made by the Japanese crew or manufacturer, and many other signs of originality.

This undisturbed cockpit actually served to confirm details needed in the reconstruction process of NASM's aircraft. If and when time and money will allow for the unrestored cockpit to be completed, the NASM aircraft would then serve as the record copy. This is not to imply that cockpits are best left unrestored. When they no longer reflect the condition level at which they were when operational, they should be brought up to that standard, recognizing that once committed to the project, it must be complete and thorough in every detail.

In the operational lifetime of an airplane, changes are often made in these cockpits with the addition of equipment or the upgrading of outdated components. In some, an entirely new instrument panel design may have been installed, often confusing the issue. One photograph of the desired cockpit to follow for a given time can aid much of the decision-making. Otherwise, manuals and other technical documents must become the primary source.

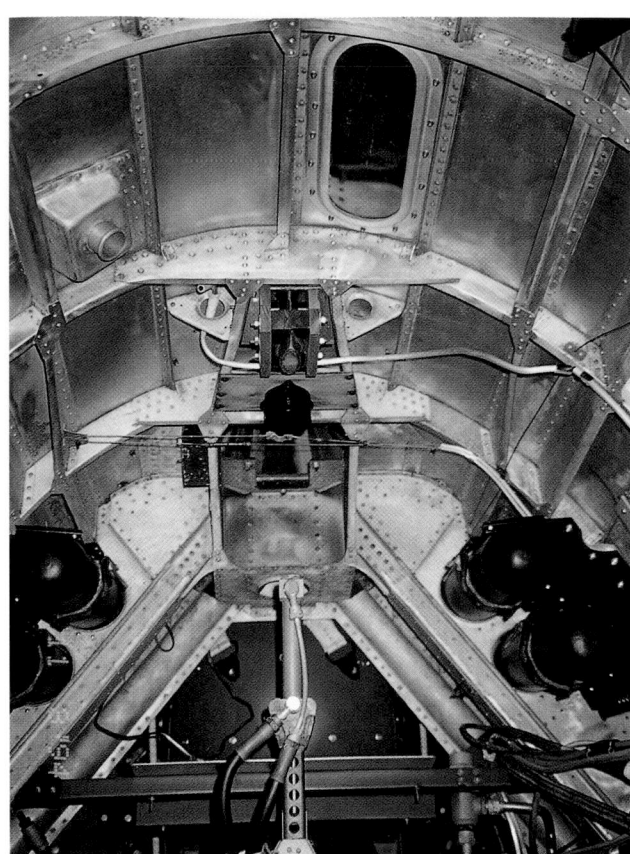

Other systems vital to this airplane were restored or reproduced as accurately as possible. Looking forward behind the green seat-back of this restored N1K2-Ja 'George' are two mock-up black oxygen bottles of the four that replicates the complete system. Note the cleaned skin interior and skylight in this aft fuselage section.

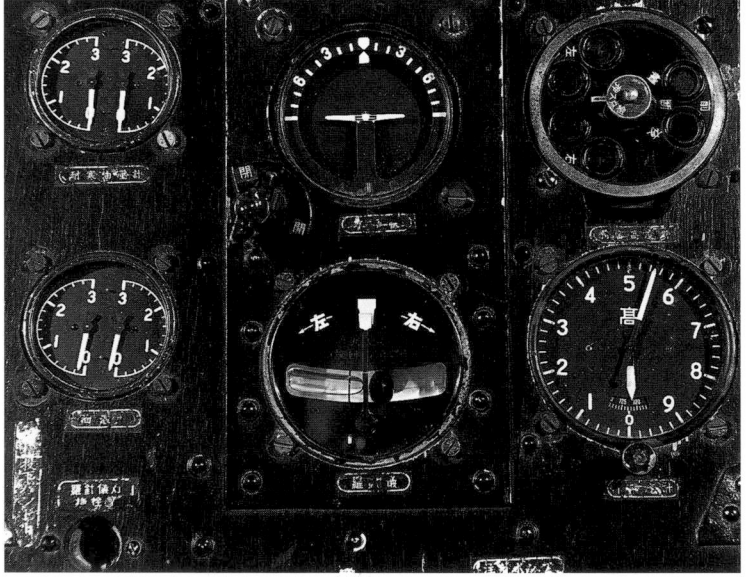

This instrument panel from an N1K2-Ja 'George' was made available for photographing its many details. A reader of Japanese characters and knowledgeable of aircraft was able to duplicate the original form of the damaged placards from this photograph. From that, decals were made as direct copies of these originals.

To find the correct model and type of instrument, radio equipment and other components suited to a particular airplane can become a major problem. There are collectors of these components, especially for World War II aircraft, both foreign and domestic. Trades or outright purchases from these collectors can sometimes be very helpful. New instrument faces have been known to have been created for use in instruments that could be spared in order to provide the correct dial appearance.

This leads to the question of whether to use a substitute instrument when the actual type cannot be found, or to leave it out and blank-in the hole?

These are difficult curatorial decisions for which there is no one right answer. A position somewhere in the middle may be the best solution. And there are degrees. Certainly an American instrument in a Japanese cockpit would not be acceptable. Yet as a substitution, a different model of the same type instrument with nearly the same appearance would seem acceptable, since such an exchange could have been made in the field. Of great importance is to thoroughly document these decisions in the aircraft records by noting what substitutions have been made. Having a ready list of desired items may lead to locating what is needed at a later date.

In earlier restorations at NASM, flight instruments were disassembled, repaired, coated on the inside with Soft Seal™ preservative and re-assembled. As time went on, we soon realized that instruments not visibly damaged were tightly-sealed units and were in good condition on the inside. Rather than disturbing internal adjustments and sealing grommets (which usually caused them to break), instruments in this condition are now merely cleaned externally, given a wax coating and installed. Whenever in doubt, instruments are opened for the treatments that are necessary.

When installing instruments, leads that are present are connected. Others for which leads may be missing and no reference is available as to how they may have been originally and with what type material are left disconnected. Power is never applied to a restored aircraft so there is no real purpose in making connections that are not original to the system.

So often, the finer details normally found in cockpits are overlooked in the restoration process. Decals and placards are so necessary in this regard. Some can be purchased for the more modern aircraft, while those of vintage aircraft must be created from whatever photographs and documents are available. In the case of the placards for the N1K2-Ja 'George' instruments and panels, little evidence remained. Close-up photographs were taken of the fragmented details that existed in the three surviving 'George' aircraft and of other Kawanishi N1K Kyofu floatplane fighters (code-named 'Rex') for lettering style. Supporting documents were gathered that listed these instruments as a guide to nomenclature. Layouts showing size for each placard were drawn, often based upon the attachment hole separation dimension that revealed their size. This data was sent to a Japanese friend of NASM's staff who was knowledgeable of this technology and able to reconstruct the proper lettering. From the resulting artwork, decals were made by NASM's exhibits department and installed in the aircraft to complete the project.

Instruments and panels are only one aspect of cockpit detailing. Seat belts, oxygen bottles and system, fire retardant containers, to name only a few components, are necessary in making a cockpit complete. In the case of the 'George' fighter missing so many of these components, like items were borrowed as patterns from which to make reproductions. There was no mistaking a wooden model for that of the real object (close up), but these items served well in achieving the desired appearance and completeness to document the technology of the time.

Electrical Wiring

Worst-case situations are often found when dealing with old, worn and deteriorated wiring associated with Level 3 Condition aircraft, especially of the World War II period. This wire has an outer fabric braided cover, often in rotted and frayed condition if not missing entirely. The rubber insulation by now is generally hardened and easily breaks away. Wire strands are often broken where exposed. These become so troublesome that the restorer is tempted to throw the tangled mess away and begin with new wiring. But the retention of original material is desirable, and there is a way to do this.

Any instrument that shows traces of deterioration, needs repair, or gives any indication that its case may no longer have a tight seal, is opened and restored. George Genotti is seen giving the necessary attention to a flight indicator for a cockpit restoration. (NASM, SI 82-5779-27)

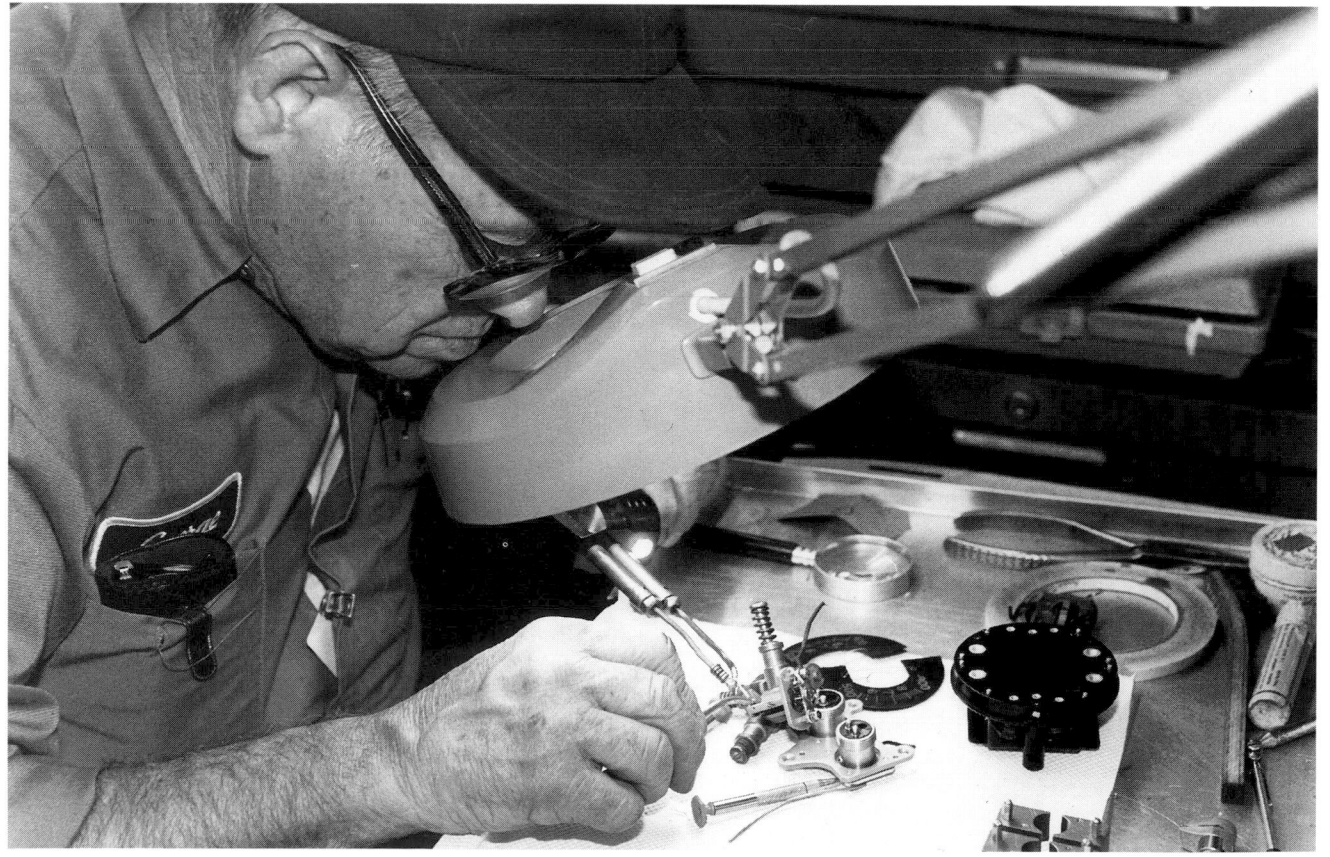

To begin with, I have never felt that there is a need to have a continuity check on such an old wiring system. This would require replacing much of the old wiring of a type that is no longer available as new wire. For a static display museum aircraft for which originality is wanted, this exchange of new for old is not required. There are cases, however, where individual wires and bundles are missing and being in a conspicuous location, must be replaced, usually for completing exposed wiring in the cockpit. Since this new wire is so different from that of the earlier time period, this different material replacement should be obvious to future researchers. My preference for a museum approach in restoring aircraft for static display is to retain the old wiring, preserved in one of several ways and returning all of it to its original locations. This is where photos, tags and diagrams are necessary.

So often, wire bundles come from junction boxes in the cockpit and are exposed as they spread out to their intended separate locations. In many cases, I have seen that these bundles can be retained in their original form with their ribbon ties left intact. At this point, spread out on the floor, the process looks pretty discouraging — but have faith.

With an air jet, blow off the excessive dust and loose dirt. Rinse as singles or a bundle in a tank of varsol in order to wash away remaining dirt and oil. This leaves a residue, therefore the wire(s) should be given an alcohol rinse and allowed to dry. A one-step operation by washing in trichloroethane would be even better, but this is sensitive material to work with and requires the technician to take extra precautions.

For preserving the insulation, again there are at least two options. A brush-coating of glycerin serves as a good rejuvenator of wiring insulation. This returns some semblance of flexibility to the insulation which reduces breakage of the material. After application, this must be wiped off to some degree since it will otherwise remain in its slimy form. A disadvantage with glycerin is that its longevity as a preservative agent is not fully known, and remaining in this tacky form will attract and hold dust.

Another method is to coat the individual wires or bundle with microcrystalline wax thinned to a brushing consistency with CRC 3-36, which will soon evaporate. Using a heat gun, the wax will further penetrate the fabric outer wrap and also coat the inner rubber insulator surface before the excess will drip away from the wire. When cooled, this leaves a slight gloss which in time will disappear and also consolidate the frayed ends of the fabric liner and other fragile parts in a more stable condition. The problem here is that the wiring loses some of its flexibility if the coating of wax is too

thick, and when reformed during installation it will naturally open micro-crevices. Once in place, however, these openings will close with quick application of the heat gun.

Little Surprises

When preparing the Curatorial Guidelines for any given airplane, we need to be aware of anything that looks unusual or something that may have a bearing on the history of the aircraft; not surprisingly, the unexpected does appear.

In the case of the 'Irving' restoration, George Genotti found a number of apparently deliberate scratches in the metal on the inside of the left engine cowling. As more of the caked grease was removed, it became obvious that it was Japanese writing. The adjacent photograph and caption describe what was found.

Some wartime markings of a personal nature have been scratched on exteriors. When the fuselage of the 'George' belonging to the National Museum of Naval Aviation was cleaned, John Neal of Low Pass, Inc. in Griffin, Georgia, who was doing the restoration, discovered an inscription scratched in the metal, forward of the left stabilizer. Its literal translation reads: 'If I should die over the South Pacific Ocean, I am just thinking of how many times the spring has passed away.'

Similar inscriptions were found inside the tail cone of the Mitsubishi A6M5 Zero belonging to NASM as well as inside the engine cowling of the Arado Ar 234B-2 Blitz. All surprises are not in the form of graffiti, however. Still wedged between the wing spar and a wing rib in the Messerschmitt Me 262A was a bullet, even though the pierced skin had a field repair. A similar lodged bullet was found in NASM's 'George' fighter during its restoration. Both projectiles remain in the aircraft structure, documented by photographs of each, taken when the skin was removed. These conclusively prove that the aircraft were used in combat.

One of the more lively discoveries came as an entirely different type of surprise when restoring the Focke-Wulf Fw 190D-8. During initial disassembly, the restoration team found that someone had forgotten to remove the German explosive shell used for emergency canopy jettisoning. A military demolition team was asked to assist with the removal of this potentially unstable explosive device and dispense with it, which they did. A similar situation occurred in Oberpfaffenhofen, Germany, when volunteers at the Dornier factory were restoring the Dornier Do 335A-1 Pfeil (Arrow) for NASM. The explosive charges that were to jettison the rear propeller in the event of an emergency were still in place. Fortunately in both cases, accidental discharge did not occur.

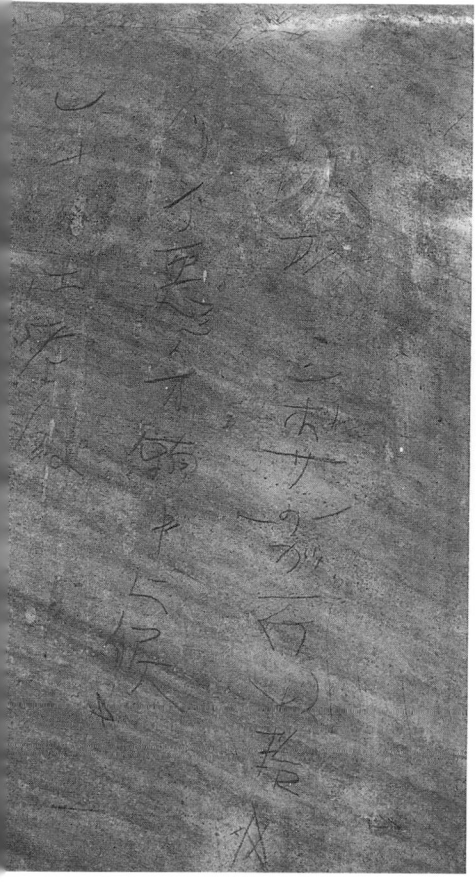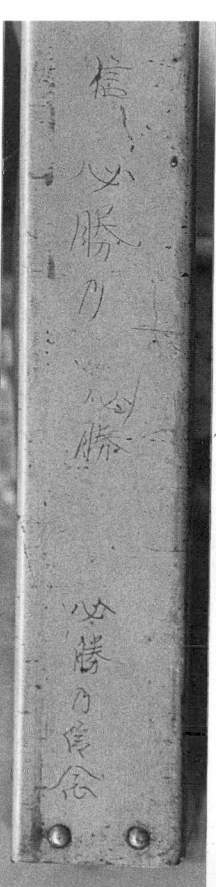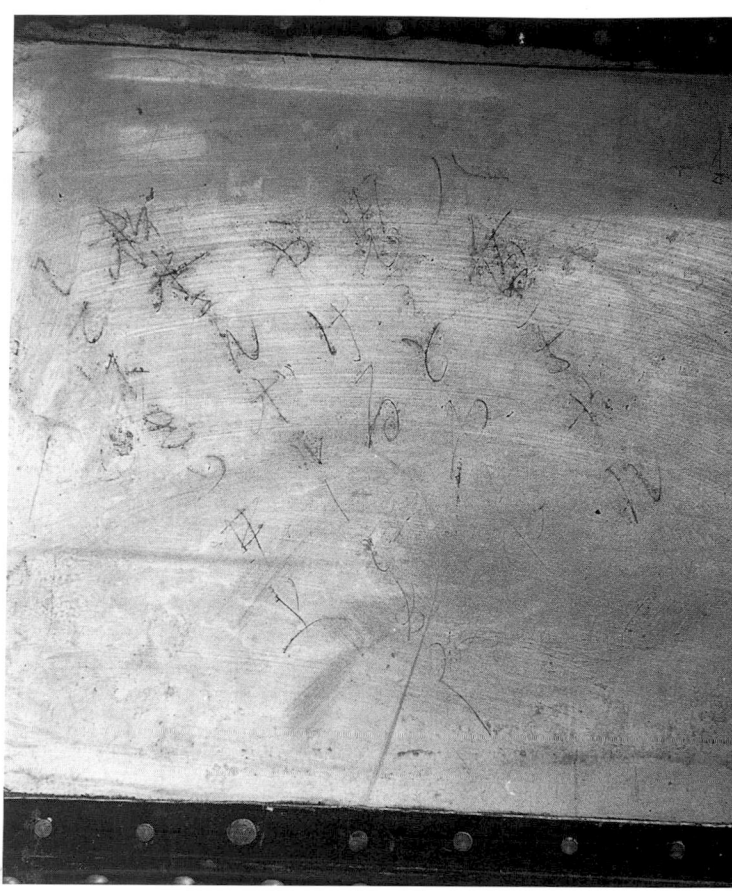

Here are three examples of graffiti found during the restoration of the J1N1-S 'Irving'. The one at left, on the aircraft's left engine cowl, translates roughly as, 'We kindly beseech you for your best efforts on our behalf!' — probably a sincere message addressed to the good fortune of the crew. At center, located at the right of the observer's station, was the message, 'We shall attain the ultimate victory, victory, victory!' A Mr Inoue, author of the sample at right, found in the right wing, wrote the note: 'Matsumoto-san, please tighten the bolt,' followed by his descriptive words about the virtues of a Miss Yueko, which would cause most translators to blush.

Polishing

Polishing is possibly the most labor-intensive and dreaded task in any aircraft restoration where unpainted surfaces are involved. So often it is a task started with uncertainty as to how the surface will look when finished. After all, the degree of luster to be attained should be appropriate for the aircraft and the time period to which it is being restored. The process of polishing goes according to the manufacturer's directions, but over the years I have witnessed some innovations in the way the polishing can been done.

To begin with, in most cases the aircraft surfaces are Alclad aluminum. This describes an aluminum alloy that has a very thin (approximately .001 inch/.025 mm) coating of essentially pure aluminum that is added for durability. It is this coating that allows the very highly-polished appearance that otherwise could appear more like aged lead. Too much polishing can wear away this protective surface, as can extensive exposure to the elements of weather. What has surprised many polishers is the luster that can be brought back to the surface despite the loss of this protective Alclad coating.

While visiting the USAF Museum in Dayton, Ohio, I could not help but be impressed with the gleaming luster of the Douglas C-54C *Sacred Cow* that had been completed for a year or two, yet looked freshly polished. My inquiries led me to Paul Lake, Restoration Supervisor for the museum. He had been the team leader for *Sacred Cow* at that time and the overseer of this polishing project.

According to Paul, the effort for this 50-year-old airframe consisted of four polishing applications over the period of the restoration. To begin with, window frames and doors were not in place, which relieved some of the effort in having to work around these troublesome details. Paul realized that this polishing task would be intensive, and rather than do it all at one time near the end of the restoration — and hate every minute of it — the effort was spread out at one-week intervals interspersed with the routine parts of the restoration.

Visitors from another museum were observing the project and expressed some concern that from the effort being expended a brighter finish should appear. After the visitors learned that the brand of polish being used was the accepted and most popular for this type of work, they said that they had better success with Matchless Metal Polish and sent them a sample. The museum tried it and the differences were noticeable. This brand does not require the use of flour, needed with the earlier polish to reduce the friction, and does not leave the black smut that is so difficult to remove from seam lines and scratches. (See Appendix G for nomenclature and source.)

Another trick that may not be known to all polishers is that the friction-heating of the metal with the polisher brings out the luster more rapidly than more rapid back and forth motions which some polishers adhere to. When surveying the large areas of *Sacred Cow* that would have to be polished, Paul Lake recalled an earlier incident of a similar nature. 'When I was in a VIP flying unit, there was this beefy crew chief, built like an ox, who would hoist a floor polisher up on the wing of his C-54 and have at it! The results of his polishing were remarkable, but I don't know how well the wing held up!'

Paul figured that if done carefully, the same method of large-area polishing could be covered in far less time than with hand-held orbital buffers. The softest grade of 3M pads were fitted to the broad rotating disks. Since the wings had yet to be attached to the fuselage, both top and bottom surfaces could be done in this horizontal fashion by turning the wing. Paul says that six months were saved on each wing by using this method of polishing. Hand-held angle buffers were used around the engine nacelles and fuselage.

The third application of polish was primarily to bring all the airframe surfaces up to a common luster. The fourth and final application was a coating of silicon polish for a protective finish. This was applied as one would polish a car: using a dampened cloth to apply the polish, waiting for the haze to develop and wiping off.

On another huge airplane restoration, the B-29 *Enola Gay*, the staff at the Paul E. Garber Facility of NASM were often asked about their polishing process and the material they used in this major undertaking. Perhaps the mere fact that normal practices were followed satisfied the many inquiries. Air-powered dual-action hand-held sanders and rotary drum polishers were used, fitted with the mildest of abrasive pads. These pads were fabricated in the shop by gluing a Scotchbrite™-type pad to a circle of stencil board (lightweight cardboard) with contact cement. The pad was then attached to the sander with feathering disk adhesive.[41] The caution here was to use the least abrasive pad available. Pads used were purchased from an auto-body materials supplier, having a white color code identifier. Generic pads are available, but there is no adequate substitute for reputable name-brand pads for the best and least damaging results.

As if still in service for President Roosevelt, the recently restored Douglas C-54C Sacred Cow *at the Air Force Museum poses on Wright Field, Dayton, Ohio in the summer of 1995. Its highly-polished surface, as it was when in Presidential service, does not reflect its age of 50 years. (David W. Menard)*

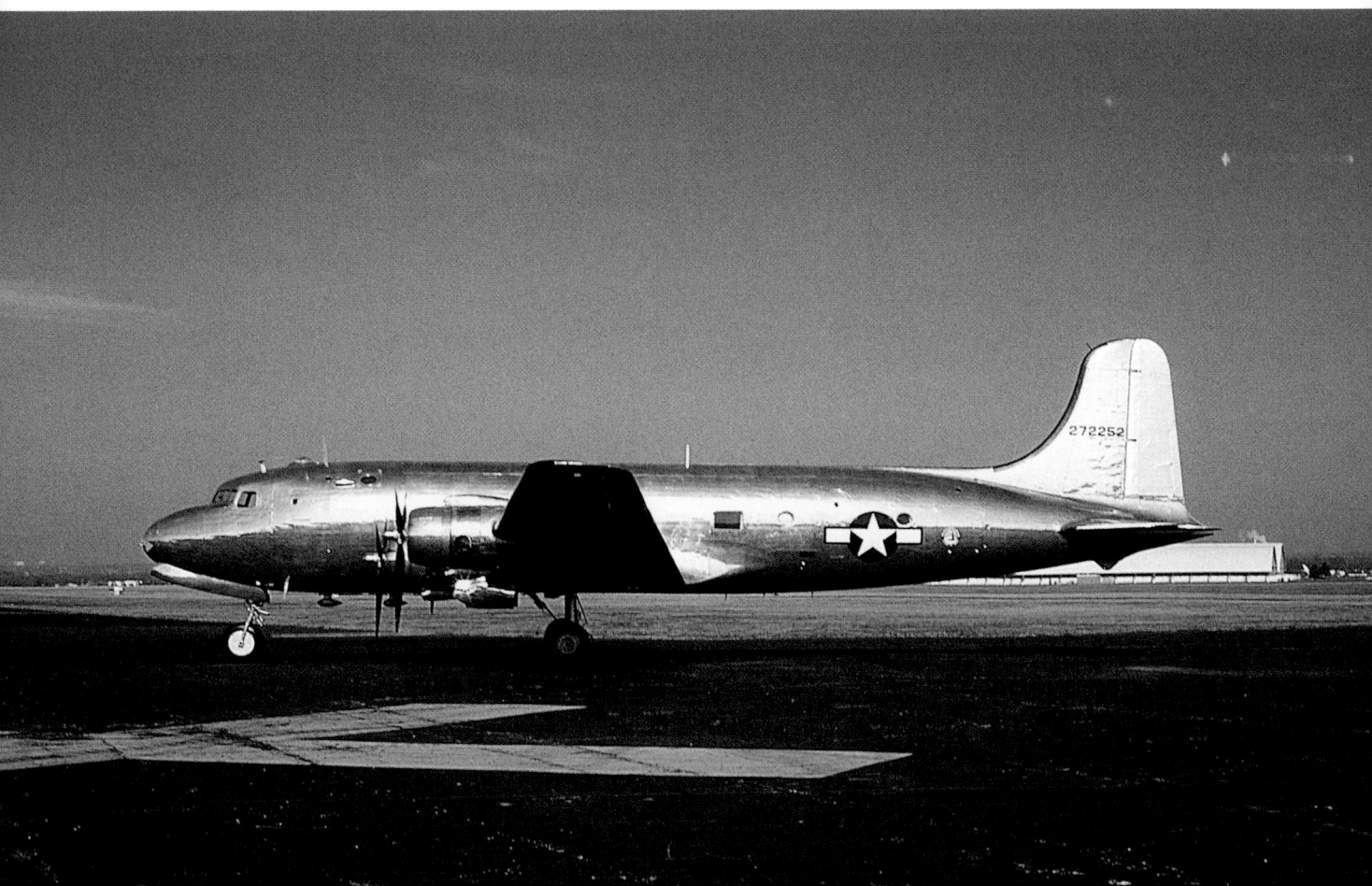

Steel Tube Fuselage Frames

There is more to tell about steel tube fuselage frames than space will permit. So that this aspect of preserving tubular structures will not be forgotten, here are a few generalizations worth telling.

Two types of steel tube fuselage frames were constructed, open tubular interior and closed end interiors. The open tubular interior was found on the more expensive airplanes such as Birds, Wacos and Staggerwing Beechcrafts. Airplanes in the smaller Cub classification usually had closed interiors.

The open tubular interior types were fabricated so that there was a 1/16th-inch (1.58 mm) oil-access hole drilled in the longeron at each point where the weld was made for the cross-tubing. Slag that forms at each weld could easily be sandblasted off from the outside, but this acid-producing material remained on the inside and began the deterioration process if not treated.

To counter deterioration, either raw linseed oil or lion oil was injected into the tubular structure. This oil would be pre-heated to at least 160°F (71°C) and inserted under pressure into the steel tube frame through holes drilled for this purpose. The pre-drilled 1/16th-inch (1.58 mm) holes allowed free passage across the structure. Others were drilled so that air could escape and to assure there were no air cavities. A feel of the tubing would indicate where the hot fluid had passed and where there might be blockages. When filled with this oil, self-tapping screws or drive pins were used to seal the holes. The fuselage frame was then rotated into many positions to ensure full interior coverage, the pins removed, the tubing then drained. Once this draining was complete, the holes were again closed with the screws or drive pins.

When restoring any steel tube fuselage frame, this same process must be repeated. A critical area is near the rear of the fuselage where water could collect inside and pool at this lowest point. It was not uncommon to have to replace rusted-out tubing in this area. To finish the process, the exterior was then given the usual cleaning and red oxide paint or zinc chromate followed by a color coating.

Preserving the technology of each engine is as important as preserving the airplane which it propels. In addition to the engine, there are many systems that deserve equal attention along with the technical instructions for their servicing. Here at NASM's restoration shop is the restored Rolls-Royce Merlin V-1650-9 engine being placed into the P-51C Excalibur III.

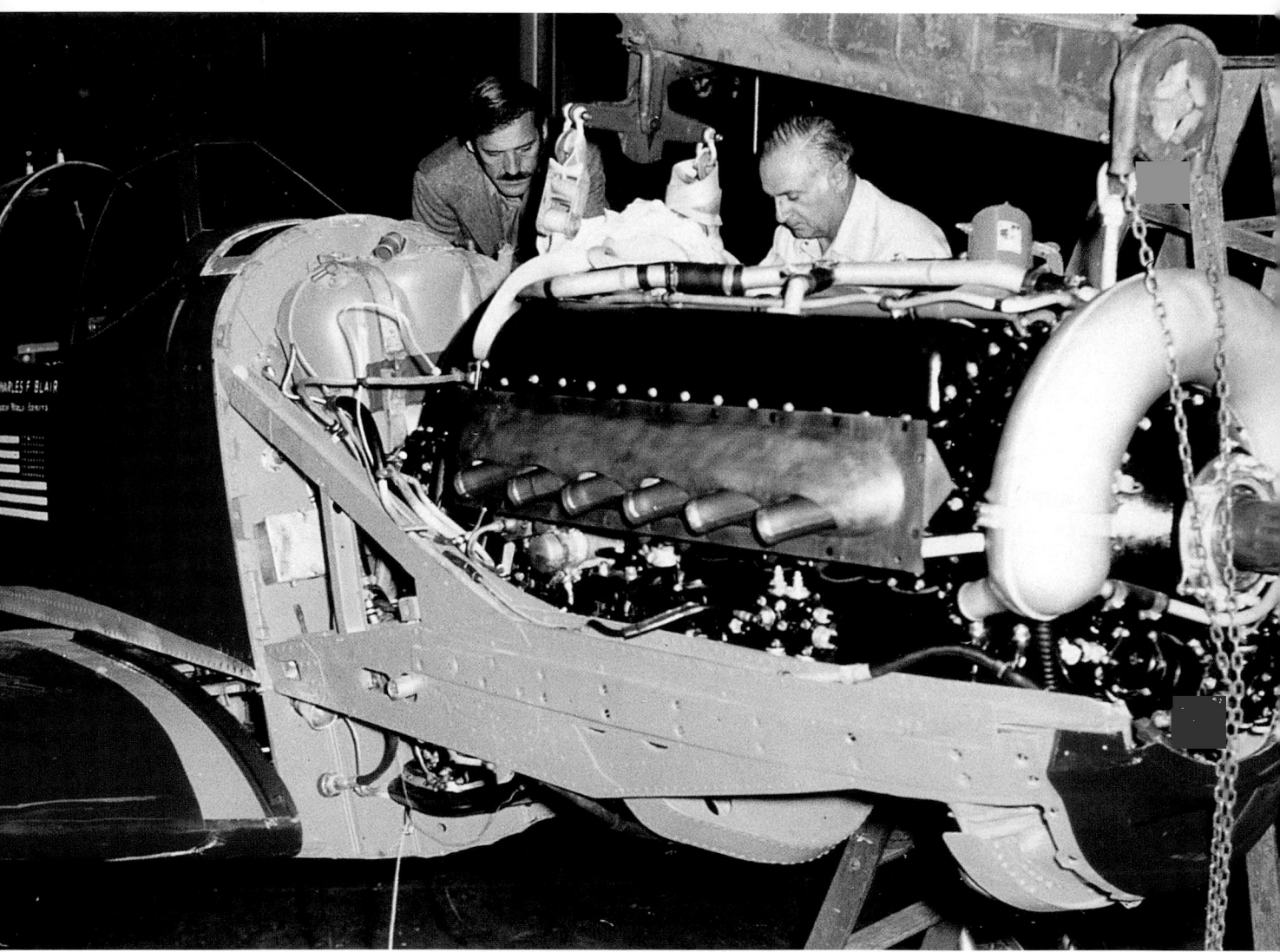

CHAPTER 7
Aero Propulsion

Some restorers of display aircraft have looked upon the engine as merely something on which to hang the propeller. Nowadays, a realistic museum approach is far more reaching. We have already seen the end of major development in piston engines, but it is these engines, most of which are no longer in production, that will remain to document this technology. Like the airplanes of the same time period, there will be a day when only a few record copies will survive. It is with this thought in mind that long-range preservation of each engine restoration should be approached.

Recognizing the rapid change in this technology, generations to come will wonder what an 'internal combustion engine' really was, how it operated, and what it sounded like. For a restoration, we should think that the engine being restored and preserved may be used for some technical purpose 200 or 300 years from now, possibly even to be operated.

There are several schools of thought when it comes to preparing engines during a restoration, be it the engine by itself, or as part of the entire aircraft. Both the engine and airframe are different in their technologies and materials, and therefore justify separate considerations.

The traditional approach to restoring an engine has been to disassemble the parts to their smallest denominator for cleaning and corrosion control. Every nook and cranny becomes accessible and therefore able to be cleaned both mechanically and chemically for prolonged preservation. The different metals and their surfaces can be treated separately and appropriately for their respective functional purposes. Main castings and other parts are often magnesium and are subject to severe corrosion and deterioration if they do not receive their separate and unique treatment that is not appropriate for other metals if not disassembled.

During reassembly, each part can be coated with a preservative. Coatings of protective barriers can be applied that will lessen the electrolytic activity between different metals. On the outside, because of this cleaning and repainting of separate parts,

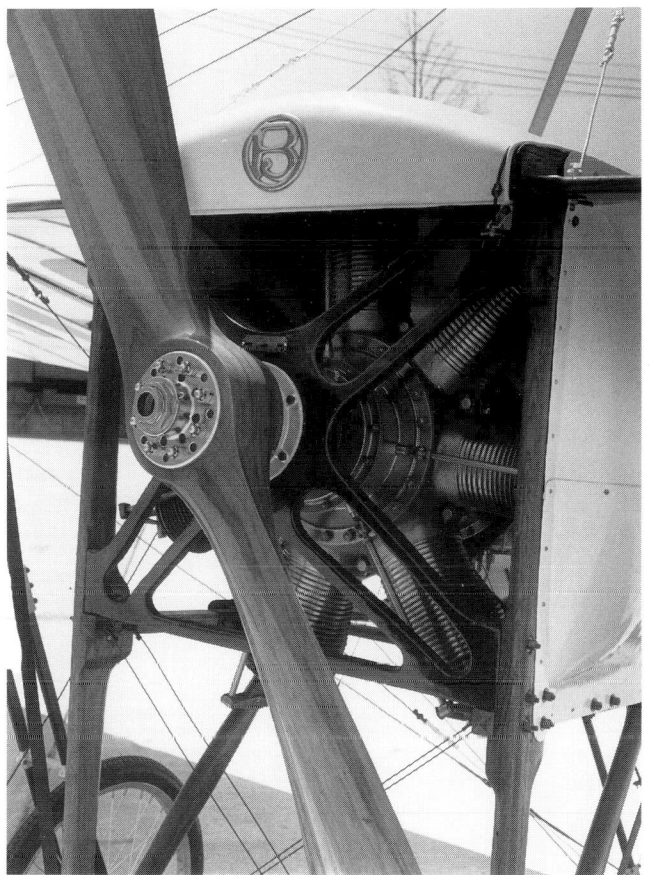

Rotary engines have a uniqueness brought about by their turning directly with the propeller. The temptation to demonstrate this feature is too great for many to resist, so the propeller-to-shaft key has been left out so that the engine will not turn and scrape preservative coatings from the engine wall. Shown here is NASM's Blériot XI with a 50-hp Gnôme engine. (NASM, SI 79-4616-12)

the assembled engine has nothing less than a right-off-the-production-line appearance. This is not the intent however, because after all, this has been an operational engine with some service life. But like the Level 3 Condition airframe being restored, a preserved and fully-restored engine cannot help but assume the like-new look in the process.

The other approach is to leave the engine in its undisturbed built-up state and to make an inspection of the internal walls and parts through openings with a baroscope in search of rust or corrosion. If not found, the engine oil and grease were working as well as preservatives. Further treatment with preservatives for coating interior walls is thought to be sufficient when made through small openings from the outside. An exterior cleaning with parts in place completes the outside. In this process, bolts and thrust bearings with torques preset by the factory have not been disturbed. Seals and gaskets remain original and untouched. Some argue that the combustion deposits on the piston, cylinder walls and exhaust ports reflect part of the engine's history with regard to its operation. As carbon deposits, they are thought not to be harmful to the surfaces if inhibitors are used, and used correctly. This concept is thought to be justified because it is less obtrusive to original fabric (metal), saves man-hours, and preserves factory assembly condition. Others look upon these stains as combustion acids which, despite claims made for inhibitors, in time will attack the metal and seriously pit these surfaces. I for one find little argument with cleanliness if not overdone by altering the metal surfaces.

Change in Approach

This brings to mind the experiences we encountered at NASM in the mid-1970s. Engine preparation for the most part was being handled in the form of the minimum teardown just described. Fluids from these engines were drained, interiors were checked for rust, and when the rust was not found, preservatives were sprayed inside the cylinders and crank-case walls. Internal lubricants had been working well as preservatives. After the exterior was cleaned of residual grease and oil, and final details added, the engine was then installed on the aircraft.

I recall the day that one of NASM's senior technicians, Joe Fichera, was doing this with a Wright R-1820 still on the engine mount of the Douglas SBD-5 Dauntless being restored. The outside of the engine had already been steam-cleaned of caked sludge and it looked quite good. This was followed by removing all the spark-plugs, and a thorough visual check was in process through the plug holes with the borescope, a handy, time-saving device. It showed the inside to be as clean as a whistle on all counts with residual engine oil working just fine — or so it seemed.

The most difficult cylinder to be checked was left until last. Since all the others were clear of corrosion, chances were that this one was like all the rest. But Fichera was persistent in not finishing without a look in all the cylinders. This final one revealed a trace of rust on the cylinder wall adjacent to the cylinder head. Nothing would do for Joe's satisfaction but to pull the cylinder. There he found more than the trace of rust that first met the eye! Another cylinder already declared to be clean was also pulled, and what was feared became reality along the cylinder wall between the piston rings.

A complete teardown of the engine followed, revealing that three cylinders had serious rust. Where magnesium parts were bolted against steel there was active corrosion — an electrolytic action was taking place right through the original seals, yet was not apparent on their outer edges. The porous material of these seals, although proper at the time, was no longer a protective barrier between the two metals. We realized that such a chance could no longer be taken with museum engines. From that point, NASM engines have been completely disassembled, cleaned and preserved.

It has been said by many an aircraft mechanic that for every pint of oil poured into an engine, two pints leak out! Must be true. For instance, there is the case of the A6M5 Zero belonging to NASM that

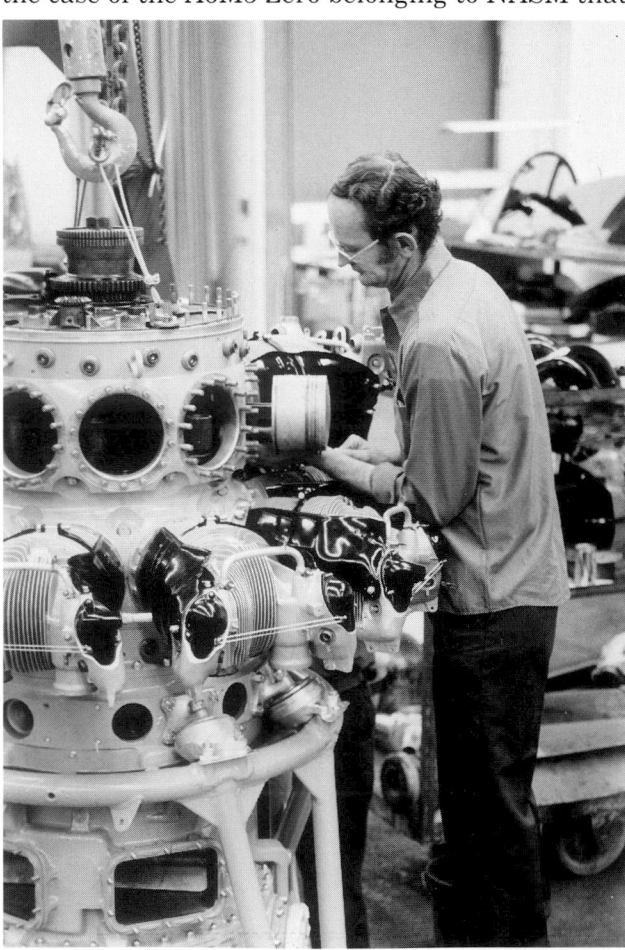

The complexities of the internal combustion engine for the horsepower they generate make it an engineering marvel. To preserve these flying wonders, each part has been cleaned of corrosion and given preservation coatings so that they will last indefinitely. Bob Padgett adjusts one of the pistons to this R-2800 before attaching the cylinder head. (NASM, SI 79-4617-24)

preceded by a few months the restoration of the Douglas SBD-5 just described. It too was checked internally, drained of (what was thought to be) all fluids, a preservative coating sprayed on the inside walls, and pronounced completed, as were its engine components. It wasn't until the museum had a lady's dress-cleaning bill to pay caused by a drop of oil from the Zero's oil cooler that the staff took note of the ever-growing oil stain on the carpet. Corrective action for this hanging aircraft: stuffing wadding into the oil cooler and changing this periodically as it absorbed the pooling oil. (I wonder if that wadding is still there and needed for oil seepage after 20 years?)

When Disassembly is Necessary

For long-term preservation, the need for complete engine disassembly becomes evident. The basic reason is that organic and mineral lubricants remain within the engine, displacing any protective coatings that may be applied. Once these break down — and they will — surfaces are exposed and susceptible to damaging corrosion.

Ideally, the engine manuals should be consulted when preparing this aspect of engine teardown, saving a lot of frustration caused by improper sequencing of functions or encountering opposite-threaded machined parts. Naturally, it is essential that these manuals be retained for future reference along with the records pertaining to this engine, normally kept with the respective aircraft's permanent records.

Once the engine is disassembled, the cleaning of these parts now becomes the major issue. As new products are continually being developed, so are methods of accomplishing certain tasks such as those involving the cleaning and preservation of engine parts. Here then are some current practices being followed at NASM — always subject to change because of improved materials and techniques.

The old adage *if it ain't broke, don't fix it* must be applied first. Almost all chemical and mechanical methods of clearing corrosion will change the original surface of an object. If only small areas on a part are affected, treat only those areas for clearing and arresting corrosion. Protect the remaining surfaces in an undisturbed state. This can be accomplished by masking off the undamaged areas, and by careful application of mechanical and chemical treatments to the affected surfaces. A complete disassembly is necessary, not only to reach all surfaces of the part, but to ensure that there are no trapped chemicals that were used in this cleaning process.

As is often the case with Level 3 Condition engines, the steel barrel will be heavily rusted and the aluminum cylinder head will be pitted with corrosion. Usually after the cylinders are removed

from the engine block, they would be degreased by immersion or brushing, using a solvent with a high flashpoint such as safety solvent or varsol. Where there is adequate ventilation, 1,1,1, trichloroethane is an excellent degreaser, but there can be severe dangers to the technician even when using an aspirator.

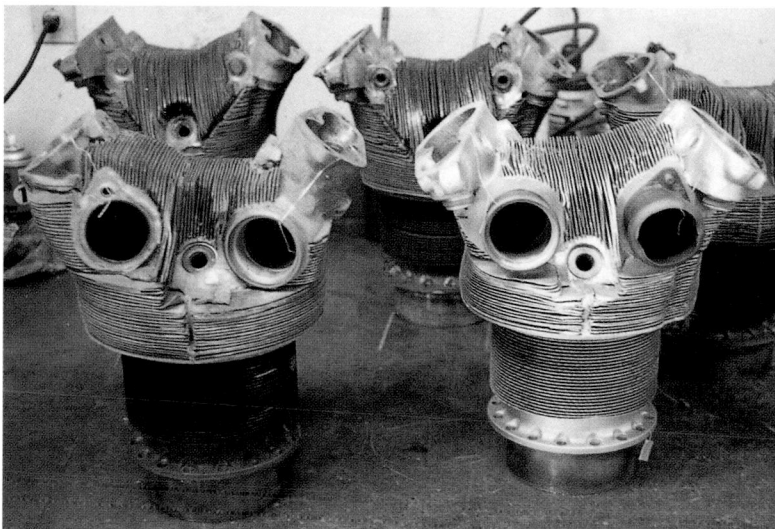

Further damage can easily occur to the fragile cylinder fins during the cleaning process. This before-and-after view of two cylinders from the Nakajima NK9H Homare 21 engine shows the one on the left before bead blasting, and on the right after cleaning and painting.

Larger parts such as the body of the engine can be cleaned by using water-soluble products such as Magnus Foam Degreaser™. This would be sprayed onto the part, then after 10-20 minutes rinsed with high-pressure water.

The exteriors of aluminum cylinder heads would be blasted with glass beads at about 15-20 psi. The fin areas may require from 20-25 psi in order to reach the more difficult areas. This is done after taping off the ends of the barrel so as not to disturb the interior wall of the cylinders. The application of Extend™42 to the rust on the steel sides and fins of the outside retains the protection that a rust build-up may provide. The entire unit can then be coated with Aluma Blast™ on the outside. This is a protective paint coating that resembles the Japanese plating that has eroded away. This action is reversible since it can be stripped off, and would have no effect upon the running of the engine for demonstration purposes if there should ever be a need.

Treatment of the interior of the steel cylinder walls, or any other machined steel or highly polished surfaces, requires extreme care. An abrasive cleaning will destroy or greatly reduce the corrosion-inhibiting qualities possessed by this type of surface. Rust on polished steel should be dealt with in the most delicate manner. Once treated, the polished steel surface should never be further treated with any type of conversion coating process such as phosphate, bluing, or blacking. This type of surface must retain its original polished condition.

The reason for separating magnesium parts from other materials is that they require their own special treatment. To remove the presence of corrosion, the part is first immersed in a caustic solution such as Oakite Superruststripper™ for two to three hours. The part is then blasted with glass beads at 25-30 psi, making sure not to touch the part with unprotected hands that would transmit body oils. The current process at NASM is to immerse the part into a boiling solution comprising ¾ lb (340 gm) of sodium chromate per gallon (3.8 ltr) of water with ¾ oz (21 gm) of calcium fluoride added to the solution. Treatment of the magnesium part in the boiling solution should be for 30 minutes. This is followed by a rinse in cold water for 15 minutes, then a final rinse in hot water of one to two minutes and drying.

Protective Coatings

As each part is processed, it should immediately be coated with a preservative. For the internal walls of these parts, NASM has been using several kinds of protective coatings which include products by CRC and Dow Corning Corroless™ thinned with CRC™ 3-36 (some prefer naptha), so that it can be sprayed until a liberal coating is applied. After the thinning agent evaporates, this material will not run, yet in the case of cylinder walls, if the pistons are moved while being reassembled or for repositioning the propeller for instance, it will not be fully scraped away from the cylinder wall because of its self-healing, migrating quality.

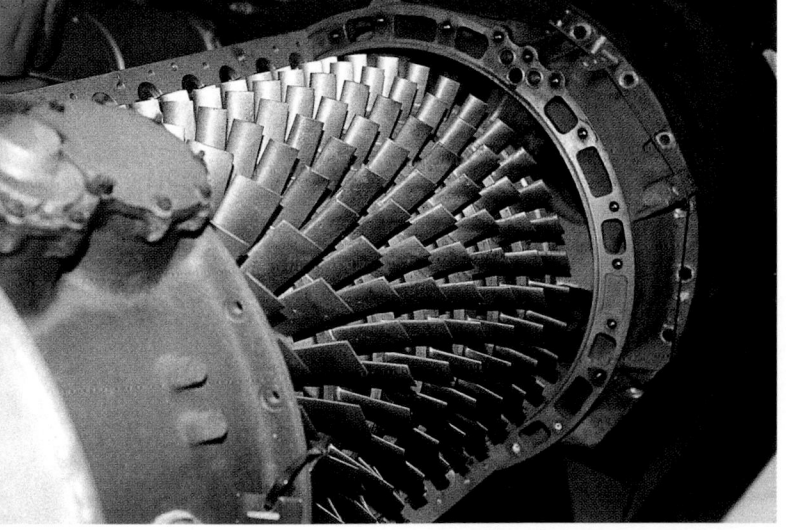

This restored Junkers Jumo 004 engine for NASM's Messerschmitt Me 262A has a portion of its engine case removed for final assembly inspection of its components. Note the golden sheen of the Soft Seal protective coating on the starter blades of the impeller.

While on the subject of moving parts, this leads to a discussion of lubricants used in engine build-up and moving airframe parts. The protective qualities of mineral and organic petroleum products are good, as when opening the older engines like those described. Accelerated laboratory tests, however, have shown that there is a continuing drop-off in this protective quality when these materials eventually turn to varnish with age and hardening. When this happens, they crack and separate from the surface, leaving those areas of exposed metal unprotected. What was once a lubricant now tends to draw moisture to these areas. Corrosion soon follows.

The solution is to remove that type of petroleum product through the process just described by a full disassembly and thorough cleaning of parts. Replace this petroleum with a synthetic grease, since laboratory tests show that such materials have a much longer life and protective quality (see Fig. 1). A suggested lubricant for bearings and similar parts requiring grease (including airframe systems) is Amsoil™ Multipurpose Synthetic Grease or similar products.

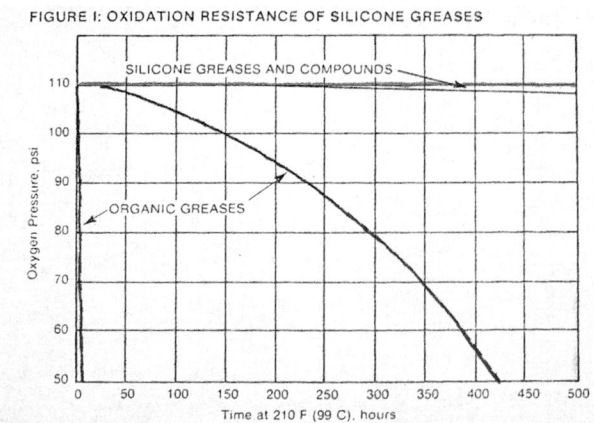

Fig. 1: Oxidation Resistance of Silcone Greases.

It is not uncommon to find broken parts such as piston rings within the engine. Knowing that the engine must be disassembled again if it is to be made to run or studied for some purpose, broken parts should be left in place. This records the history of the engine's failures. Only if a defective part will cause damage to adjacent components or is completely unsuited should another part be substituted. This is cause for a very detailed written record, and retention of the broken parts for future study. If damaged or broken parts are installed in the engine and noted in the records, serviceable replacement parts should be acquired when possible and set aside for future use.

When reassembling these engine components, one way to reduce points of contact is to have new gaskets fitted, since the old ones surely would have failed in the disassembly process. When joining the parts with a gasket separator, coat both sides of the gasket with Soft Seal™. This will penetrate the pores of the gasket material and become a more lasting barrier between these two metals than the original, which was designed exclusively for a running engine.

While Garry Cline was reassembling an early Roberts engine at NASM with its many parts already coated with a preservative material, I could not help but ask what it would take to make this engine operable once again:

'If engines were to be made operational in the future, I believe they should be given a teardown and rebuilt at that time. Our shop is not set up to properly overhaul engines,' according to Cline, 'but we can preserve them. We could make them run, no doubt, but not bring them to airworthy specifications. We have no need. Also, it might be difficult to ensure that all soft seal and preservative materials were removed which could block critical orifices without a thorough disassembly and inspection.'

Seeing that I was really pressing for more answers, Garry continued:

'Normally we time magnetos and set valve clearances to specification. Sometimes I wonder about crankshaft-to-camshaft timing being close enough to factory settings. Because of this closeness to operating settings, it's not a bad idea to ground mags so they could not "zap" someone if turned through, or to leave valve clearances as loose as possible so as to lessen their movement.'

It is just as important to apply the correct painted surface colors to the engine as it is to the airframe itself. On severely deteriorated engines it is not uncommon to find little or no trace of original colors, if any were applied. As a guide, it might be possible to locate an engine of this type in another museum from which to match original paint colors. External unpainted surfaces must have some sort of protective coating applied. Currently, NASM is using a clear acrylic such as Rhom and Hass™ B-48S Acryloid™.

Ignition Harness

These electrical wires with their fragile thin wire-braided shielding exteriors are difficult to restore because of their usually degraded condition. When reviewing the standards to which an engine in Level 3 Condition is to be restored, the treatment given to these harnesses can be either preserving original materials, used as a fabrication format, or duplicating original appearance only.

An ignition harness in this condition appears impossible to restore and use again. Such was not the case with this harness belonging to the NK9H Homare 21 engine for NASM's Kawanishi N1K2-Ja 'George' fighter. It was cleaned, then brightened, followed by a coating of microcrystalline wax to consolidate the frayed material.

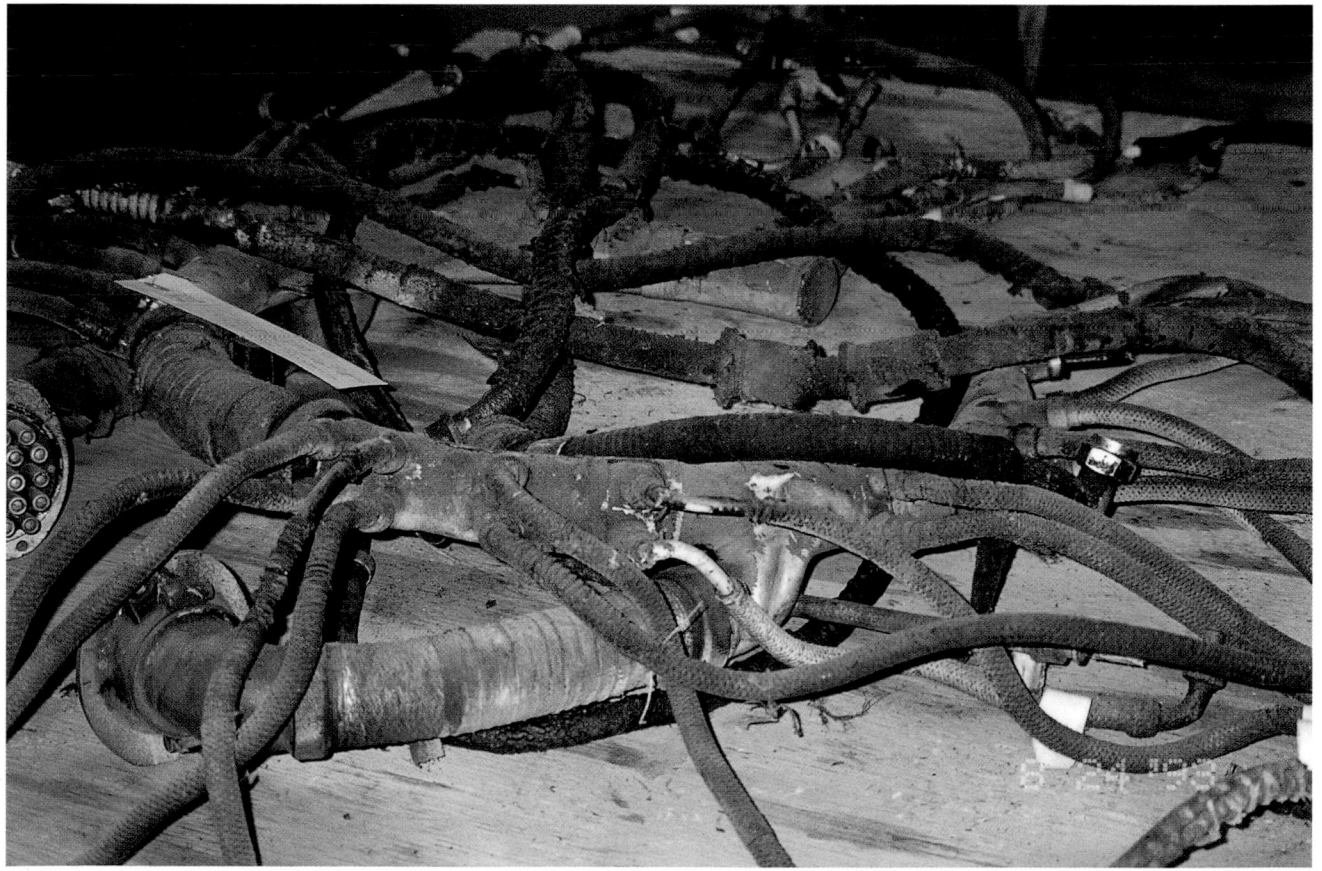

The neatly-cowled NK9H Homare 21 engine in this Kawanishi N1K2-Ja 'George' has the appearance of new condition. Note the restored ignition harness, compared to its unrestored condition as shown overleaf.

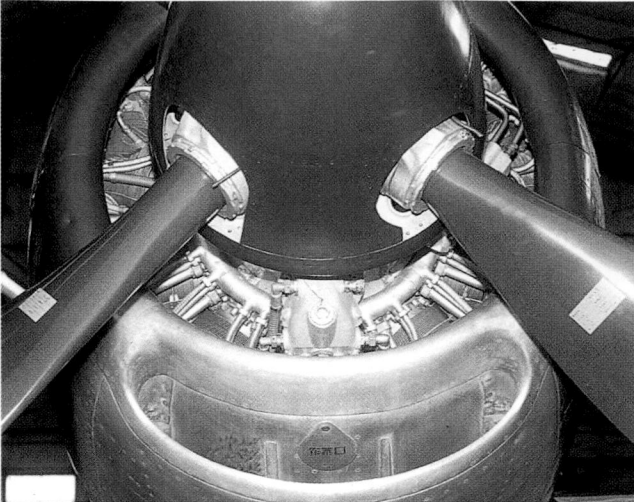

The initial cleaning of these assemblies is the hard part. The assembly should be dipped and rinsed in a solution of mild solvent, washed with a mild detergent and allowed to drip-dry or be blown dry. If the shielding is a steel mesh which is now rusted, coat with Extend™ or a similar product, then paint (if appropriate) with a natural-looking paint. If this shielding is brass, it should be cleaned with a soft brush and solvent followed by a Brasso™-type product that may produce the desired appearance. With the return of the original appearance of the materials and signs of active deterioration removed, many ragged edges of the worn and frayed metal shielding can be expected. The rinse-cleaning already given to the shielding is the extent to which the ignition cabling itself can be cleaned.

After the cleaning has been done to the best degree possible, the procedure is to hang the assembly off the floor so that a coating of micro-crystalline wax can be brush-coated over the entire assembly. This wax can be thinned to a paste-like consistency by heating to the melting point at which time petroleum spirits or naphtha (or CRC™ 3-36 brand) to thin, can be added and mixed in to retain this consistency.

When the assembly is fully-covered, a heat gun then melts the wax into the innermost portions of the harness and is applied long enough so that excess wax will drip away. This coating will be thin so that the wires can be properly positioned and reshaped when being attached to the engine. When installed, a slight reheating of the ignition harness will fuse any cracks that may have opened in the wax. Initially, this wax will give the harness an unusual low-luster appearance that will vanish in a short time.

Such a process with ignition harnesses is not as simple as just described. Leads will often be broken away from elbows to the spark plug connectors, and some leads will lack shielding of any kind. Since these harnesses will have deteriorated beyond any future use should the engine be made operational, appearance and the saving of original materials are the key factors when deterioration has developed to this degree. Having to use some new and similar harness materials is usually a final solution.

The temptation to use dehydrator spark-plugs (filled with silica gel) in place of original or even substitute plugs should be avoided. While this does allow the detection of moisture within the cylinders, it should not be necessary for an airplane engine kept in a museum environment. Dehydrator plugs are time-change items and installing them is time-expensive. This generally requires the uncowling of the engine. Multiply 28 plugs in one 14-cylinder engine, times the number of engines on one airplane, times the number of engines with plugs to be changed, plus removing and replacing cowlings, and the task becomes formidable. Chances are that the plugs will not be changed when they should be because of inevitable manpower shortages, and the plugs then draw rather than extract moisture, defeating their intent. The correct type of plug or a suitable substitute makes for a better seal against moisture in cases of museum aircraft and inherent limited resources.

Engine Openings

For static engines, exhaust ports and exhaust pipes are a natural for drawing insects in to nest, or as targets for spit-balls and other foreign materials. For the exhaust valves that are open, there can be a free flow of moist air to enter that cylinder. There are several ways of reducing this access, depending upon the exhaust pipe configuration. A plug for each exhaust stack shaped from cork, wood or preferably hard foam which will form to the contour, inserted a few inches into the pipe is hardly noticeable when painted black. For short stacks where a plug might show, it may be wise to leave the center of the gasket in place at the exhaust stack attachment. A 1/16th-inch (1.59 mm) hole drilled in the center will prevent an air lock should the propeller need to be turned (slowly) for repositioning, yet will guard against foreign materials.

There are many similar and reversible methods in blocking this passageway to the engine openings, and all precautions in closing these openings should be taken.

One objective to keep in mind is the possibility that this engine could be made to run again. Although it is very unlikely that this will be the case, it does provide a base-line from which to work with regard to achieving completeness by having all the accessories and fittings. Of vital importance, yet easily overlooked, is having all the pertinent tech-

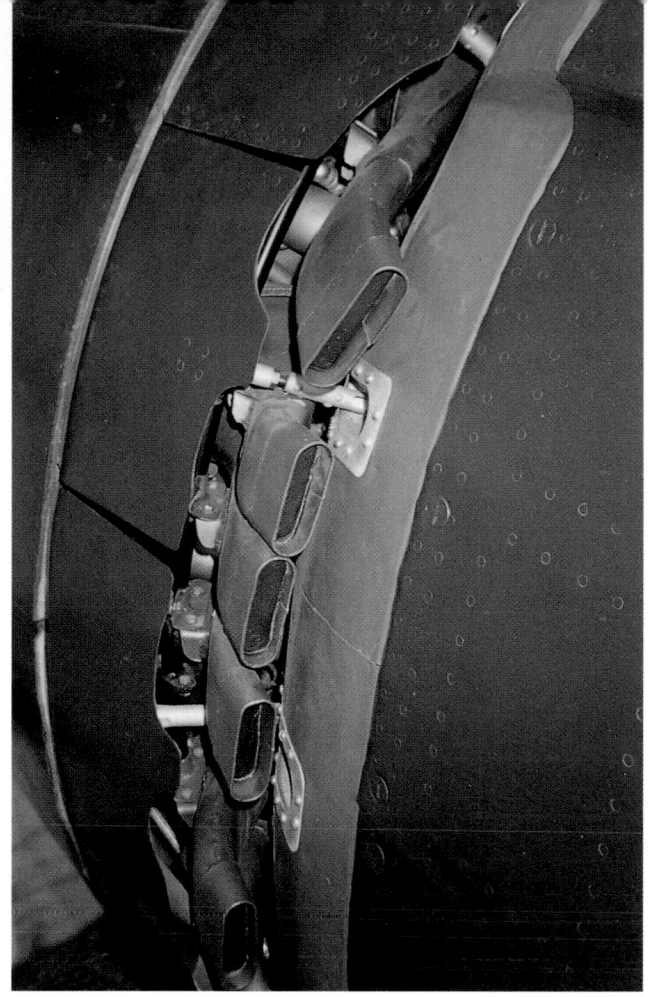

LEFT:
Certain precautions must be taken with restored engines placed in aircraft to prevent moisture and foreign objects being inadvertently or purposely inserted through engine openings. Plastic sponge plugs have been pressed into the exhaust stacks of this Kawanishi N1K2-Ja 'George' primarily to prevent insects from nesting.

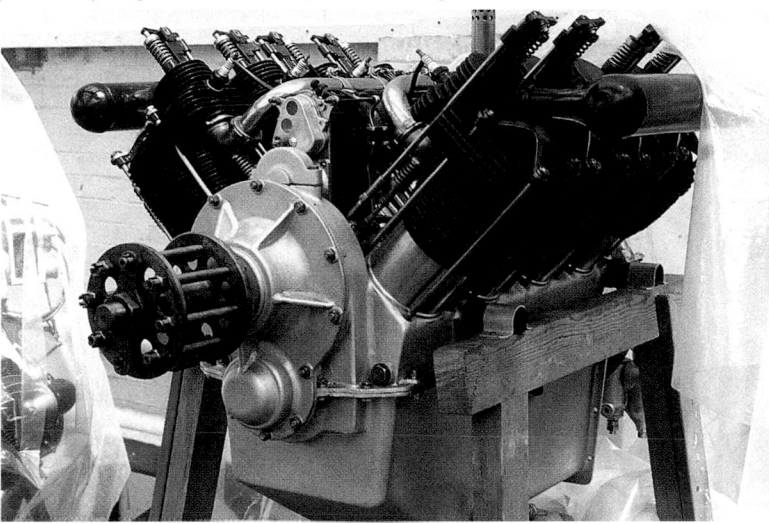

Occasionally an aircraft restoration calls for an engine of which none are available. A simple, but time-consuming solution is to build a look-alike. This replica of wood and metal accessories of an 80-hp Renault engine was created for the RAF Museum's Royal Aircraft Factory BE.2c for which no engine was available. Only very close inspection can reveal that it is not real.

Another look-alike engine of wood, plastic, Masonite and metal nuts and bolts was this ABC Scorpion built by Pat Packard of Oshkosh, Wisconsin. NASM's Flying Flea, restored by Packard at the EAA was without engine. To make the airplane appropriate for exhibit, the engine was built for the airplane. To simulate the texture of rough castings, sawdust was mixed in with the paint.

nical manuals saved with the engine. Without these, much of the technology that this engine would otherwise reveal will not be known. Needed would be information on various valve clearances, timing, thrust-bearing tensions, torque on nuts, as well as fuel specifications. This information must be kept safely as a permanent file that pertains to this engine. For those engines installed in aircraft, this reference material should be kept with the aircraft record files.

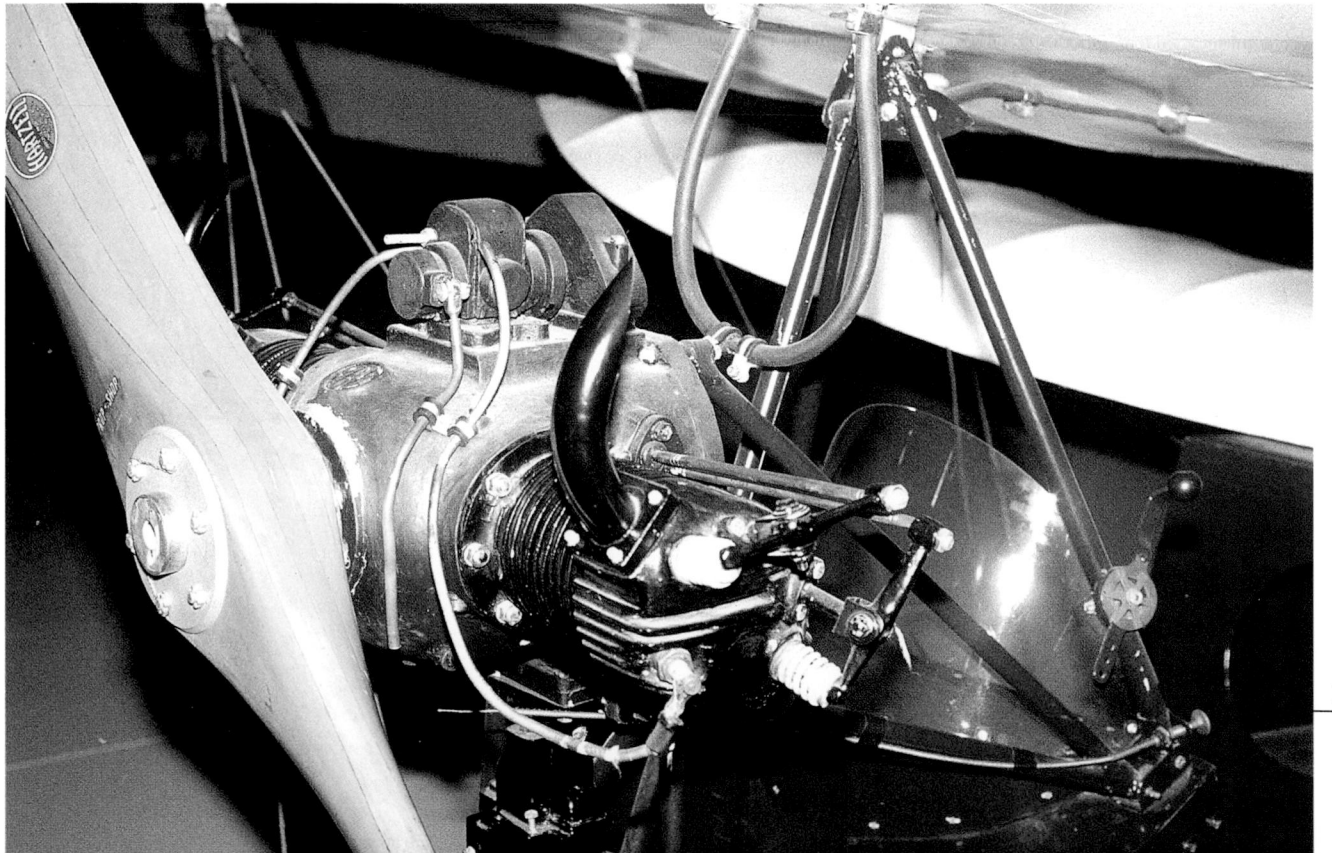

Propellers

Perhaps one of the most glossed-over parts of airplane restoration is the propeller. This is understandable because until now much of the technical detailing that goes into the propeller has been sparse, scattered and not readily understood by most of those restoring airplanes.

Nothing will be said here about the mechanical part of propeller restoration such as teardown, polishing and repairs. This is looked upon as strictly an application of job skill and requirements that should need no further explanation. This section mainly covers the final detailing of the propeller.

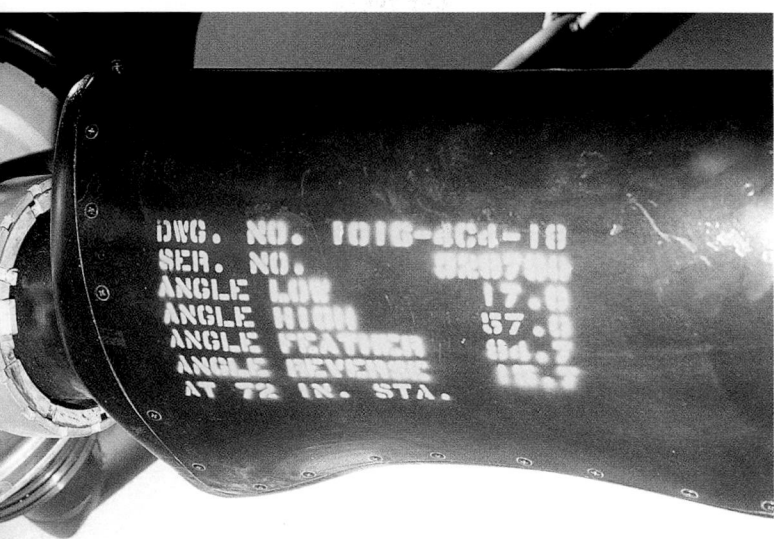

Shown here is a close-up of the original stenciling found on one of four propellers belonging to the B-29 Enola Gay. Note the reverse pitch angle given, a new feature on these late-war B-29s.

General Appearance: This is perhaps the easiest portion of the restoration process. To what degree the propeller is to be painted, or painted at all, as well as the inclusion of trademark decals and blade-tip warning colors, are all dictated by the selected photograph of the airplane to which the restoration is being patterned. Should that photograph show the propeller rotating but not seen, comparable photos of similar aircraft of the same time period can serve.

Described here are some basic points that will help confirm the findings from the photograph of the airplane being followed. For this section (and the technical content in Appendix H covering metal propellers), I am indebted to the wealth of knowledge conveyed to me by Harry A. Jay of Williamstown, Vermont, one who was inspired by the precision and design of propellers as a young man, to one who has made the repair, maintenance and installation of these vital airplane components a lifelong profession and study. I value his input highly on this subject.

For all natural metal-finished propellers there is little to be said except for tip markings established by respective users. Some hubs, not including the dome, had an olive drab iridite plating, this being a zinc and cadmium combination.

The most prevalent painted propellers are those of the military. This practice began during World War II on metal propellers and once established after subtle changes at first, the standard remained fairly consistent, but with the expected exceptions. It is the exceptions that require a close examination of photographs of the airplane type being restored that must be the guide.

When it became common practice for the propellers of camouflaged airplanes to be painted black, the four-inch (10 cm) yellow tip on the front and back of blades remained consistent. This provided a warning circle when the propeller was turning. Later on, for propellers that were 14 feet (4.27 m) or more in diameter, this yellow tip was extended to six inches (15.2 cm).

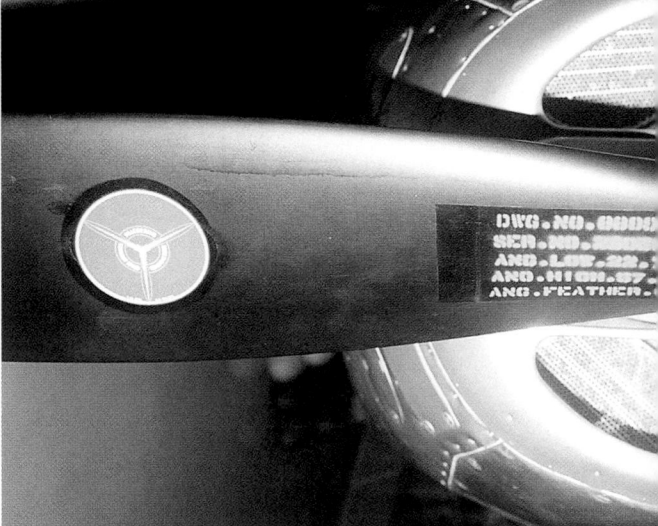

This propeller blade example is that of a Curtiss Electric mounted here on a Lockheed P-38 Lightning. Repainting during restoration included masking off the original data stenciling to be saved.

Markings: Restorations of US wartime aircraft sometimes overlook the identifying alpha-numeric markings that adorn the propeller hub and cambered side of the propeller blades. There is good reason for this. The application of this data differed with nearly every type of propeller, producer, and from new to depot-processed propellers. More importantly, few people understand the numbering system for this information.

The restorer must first make a decision as to whether to restore the propeller to factory-new condition, or like one that has been processed through a depot. Stenciling of the type often added at a depot can complicate the restoration. If there is a choice, it will be far simpler to restore to factory-fresh, but only if company decals are available — and of the correct style for the time period. If these trademarks are not available, there is little choice other than to treat the project as though the depot repainted the blades and did not apply the trademark, as might be the case. Propeller blades certainly look more complete with these decals in place.

Conspicuous on all operational military propellers were stenciled data varying from neatly applied, to lines with underspray that were hardly legible. Photos of the airplane being restored when operational will help with content and positioning of this stenciled data that may be reconstructed from the information described in Appendix H. Propellers on non-military aircraft can vary in marking and color configuration as much as the owners that used them.

Manufacturer's Trademark Decals: Use of an improper decal on a restored propeller is a mortal infraction of the restoration to those that know this compromise has been made. To assist in some way, samples of trademark design differences and time periods are illustrated in Appendix H. This assortment among collectors may never be complete because variations in designs show up regularly.

Wooden Propellers

For wooden propellers as part of a non-flying airplane under restoration, a surface refinishing may be tempting, but may not be appropriate. Propeller collectors and connoisseurs can spot a restored propeller, including those that are new and made to look as though they are old. Usually it is the smell of the varnish that gives this away.

As part of an aircraft restoration, the action to take with the propeller will depend upon the condition and appearance of the airplane to which it is attached. Often, this dictates a restoration of the propeller, especially for one with alligatored varnish, areas of which have turned to ugly black ridges of Bakelite. A propeller in this condition would most likely call for refinishing to bring it up to the level of the restored aircraft.

As a used propeller, it may have the expected surface abrasions, nicks and gouges that need repair. It is rare that an early propeller was carved from a solid piece of wood. Generally, propellers were a glued-up lamination of wood ranging in thickness from ½ to one inch (12.7–25.4 mm). This lamination method was not only for added strength, for each section is laid in the opposite direction of growth to that of the adjacent board. The reason has to do with retaining better balance of the propeller. The denseness of the board varies in vertical direction of the tree growth, so the wood's moisture retention is different from one end to the other, and therefore affects the balance. It is often these glued

seams that must be repaired during restorations.

Since this type of repair is so often visible when completed, one needs to know the accepted method of work for a vintage propeller. A wartime technical manual[43] of the 1940s regarding wooden propellers had this advice on repairs:

When advisable, appreciable dents, scars, etc., having surfaces or shapes that will permanently hold a filler and will not induce failure, may be filled with a mixture of the proper glue and clean, fine sawdust. This mixture will be thoroughly worked and packed into the defect, dried, and then sanded smooth and flush with the surface of the propeller.

To refinish the propeller the old varnish must first be removed. The use of paint remover is the best method, followed by denatured alcohol to wash away the residue. If some delamination has taken place, the most difficult part is to scrape away glue that remains. Generally a thin blade, perhaps custom-made, will make the best tool for this work. Once the particles have been removed as best they can, gluing and tight clamping follow.

An original propeller trademark decal is better than a replacement. When sanding the surface of the propeller for refinishing, take very good care to avoid further damage of the decal. Clean its surface as best possible without causing harm, and include it when resurfacing the rest of the propeller.

A minimum of two coats of varnish is recommended.[44] Synthetic or solvent-based acrylic varnishes are good, alkyd varnish is even better if the propeller is known to be kept indoors. It is unwise to use a polyurethane varnish since this seals the wood too tightly and does not allow it to breath sufficiently. These stresses upon the wood fibers will cause them to break and therefore reduce the life of the wood. Polyurethane varnish becomes unstable and is difficult to remove.

The older the airplane being restored, the more likely the chance that it lacks a propeller because of the mishap that put the airplane out of service. This happened at NASM when restoring the Benoist Type XII. Any photograph of this 1912 airplane showing the propeller would suggest that this nine-foot (2.7 m)-diameter, gracefully-curved lamination of wood was almost unique to this airplane. No propeller in NASM's extensive collection even came close. A new propeller had to be made.

Knowing the diameter, and scaling from photographs, a fairly accurate outline of the propeller was laid out. What remained were the cross-section details. Surprisingly, this was not as difficult as first thought. In the early days of flying, the time period for this airplane, there was a sudden and keen interest in all matters aeronautical. There was a large amount of material written about the design and construction of these airplanes. One such book was titled *Building and Flying an Aeroplane*.[45] In a chapter describing early propeller construction, the book suggested a 3½-foot (1 m) pitch[46] be used for the power of the Roberts engine being used. The blade pitch angles being worked out for sections at one-tenth propeller radius apart were conveniently shown on an adjacent page. Included were the 10 blade airfoil cross-sections and the angle of incidence at each of these stations. It was merely a matter of adapting this information to the width and thickness of the blade at these points.

Carving the propeller for the Benoist Type XII was another matter, and NASM contracted with a firm that was better equipped to carry out the work (see Appendix G).

Trademarks for these older propellers are another matter. For the most part, none were used. However, the wooden propeller for NASM's Albatros D.Va was in need of this finishing detail. After a search of early aviation magazines and books, the correct design for the Garuda Feldpropeller was found, and graphics were made for color separations needed for creating decals.[47]

See Appendix H for further details on propellers.

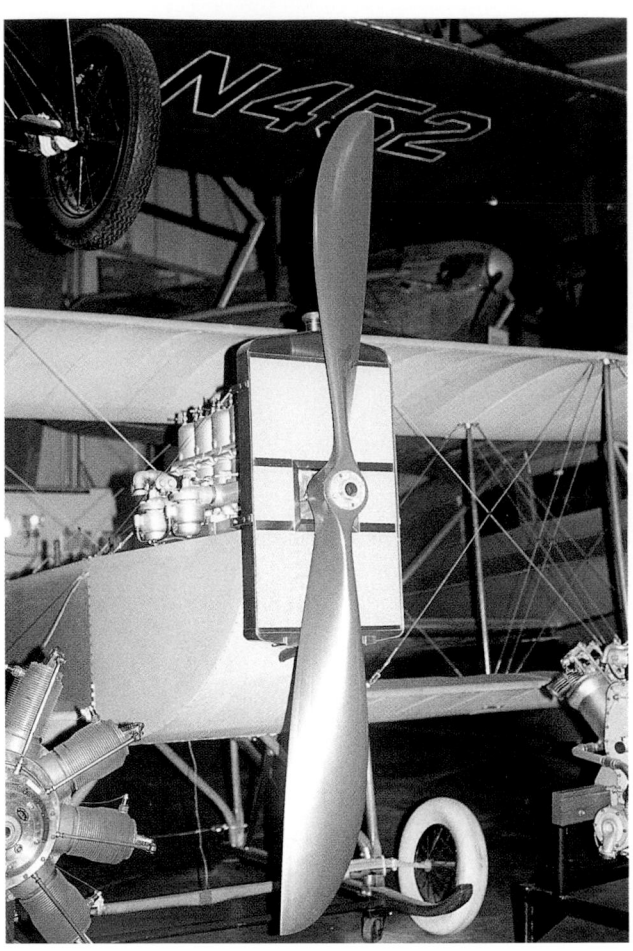

For lack of an original propeller for the restoration of this Benoist Type XII, a propeller was drawn and newly manufactured. Proportions and size were scaled from photos of the original aircraft.

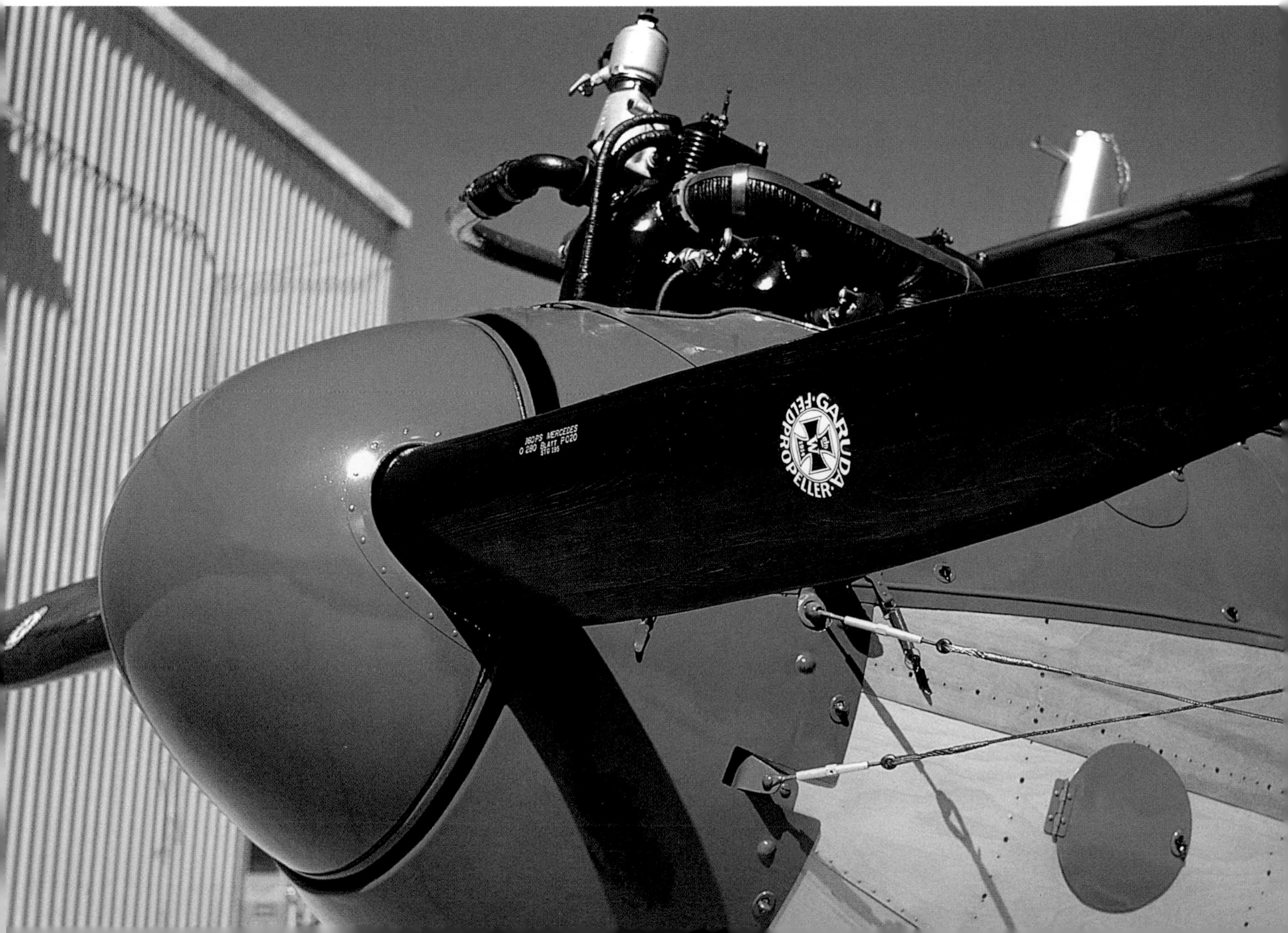

Refinishing in a standard fashion the propeller that came with the Albatros D.Va parts belonging to NASM. The trademark for the Garuda propeller was newly-made for this project.

CHAPTER 8
Aircraft Tires

The most difficult replacement problem while restoring vintage aircraft is finding the correct tires. It can also be said that tires and rubber parts degrade more rapidly than any other materials used with exhibit aircraft. Because of this difficulty in finding replacements for rubber parts, they must be given special care while on the aircraft in order to extend their limited life expectancy.

Tire technology in itself is a rapidly-changing subject. Because there is such a variety of aircraft tires, many of which were specially designed for a specific aircraft type, these tire designs only remain available as long as that aircraft is in service. There is a limit to a tire's shelf life, therefore stocks of serviceable tires are sometimes very limited.

Tire Development

The history of rubber tires is about as limited in time as the airplane itself. The large-scale use of rubber as a material only began as late as the 1890s with the manufacture of bicycle tires, followed at the turn of the century by what became the rubber industry's most important single item, automobile tires. Aviation was slow to develop the use of rubber tires on a large scale; early experiments in heavier-than-air craft, including the Wright brothers' early aircraft, generally resorted to launching rails and landing skids. Langley's early attempts at the turn of the century relied upon ditching in the water as a method of stopping.[48]

When wheels appeared on some early aircraft, they were of the bicycle variety. Weight loads of these craft were light, and the wheels served this purpose nicely. As weights increased, new designs for wheels and tires had to be made that were more suited for aircraft. It wasn't until 1909 that the first pneumatic tire was built specifically for an airplane, that being the Wright Military Flyer.[49]

As speeds of aircraft began to exceed 100 mph (161 km/h) in the 1920s, a narrow tire referred to as a 'streamline' tire was produced to reduce wind resistance of wheels that had yet to become

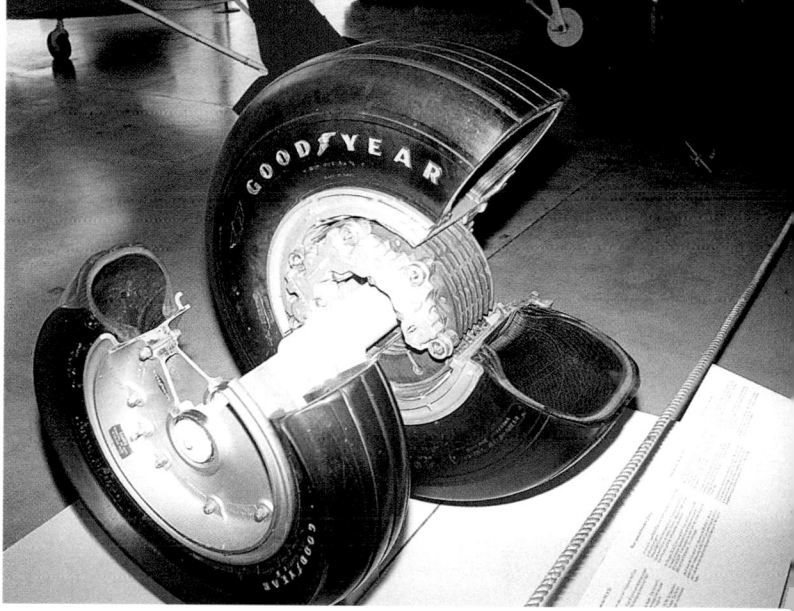

This is part of an exhibit showing aircraft tire and wheel development at the Swiss Transport Museum, in Luzern. Shown here in cutaway form are two Goodyear wheels and tires used on DC-9-30 transports; (smaller) 26 x 6.6, 10-ply rating, 225 MPH Deflector Type B for nose gear, and a 40 x 14, 24-ply rating, 30 SKID, 225 MPH which includes a very compact multiple disk-type brake for main wheel.

retractable. These were replaced by 'balloon' tires with ultra-low-pressure airwheels which were designed for operation from unimproved and often rough dirt fields. These were doughnut-like tires mounted on very small-diameter wheels. The wheels soon incorporated multiple-disk brakes which gave the pilot control while taxiing. These tires were generally of smooth contour, having no need for a gripping tread since ground speeds were quite low.

As more runways were developed, allowing inclement weather to be less of a factor in aircraft operations, tire treads of many designs appeared, all of which were intended for better gripping and braking action at higher speeds on runways. An improved and *all-weather* tire soon appeared, having a wider format and larger footprint on the runway or turf fields. As take-off and landing speeds continued to increase, particularly with the introduction of jet aircraft, wheels and tires became smaller, producing less forces upon rotating masses and limited storage space for a wheel retracted into the wing.

All of these phases of tire development included different-size wheels, treads, ply ratings, manufacturers, and some used tubes; others were tubeless. When restoring vintage aircraft for museum exhibit, a curator is fortunate if a tire of the right category can even be found to fit the original wheel. This part of the restoration calls for considerable compromise; others call it ingenuity.

Replacement Tires

It would be wonderful if this chapter could provide simple solutions for identifying and locating tires that would suit the restoration need. Unfortunately, each restoration presents its own set of requirements, and each solution is unique, especially if a certain tire design is no longer available. Too often, an original wheel for an airplane undergoing restoration must be set aside because existing tires will not fit. In such cases, a substitute wheel must be found as well as a compatible tire.

When beginning a search for a vintage tire, more than just a diameter or rim dimension is needed. One must know the correct tire design when beginning the search. If the old tire or specification is available, much can be learned by the format for which the tire is identified. One of several tire clas-

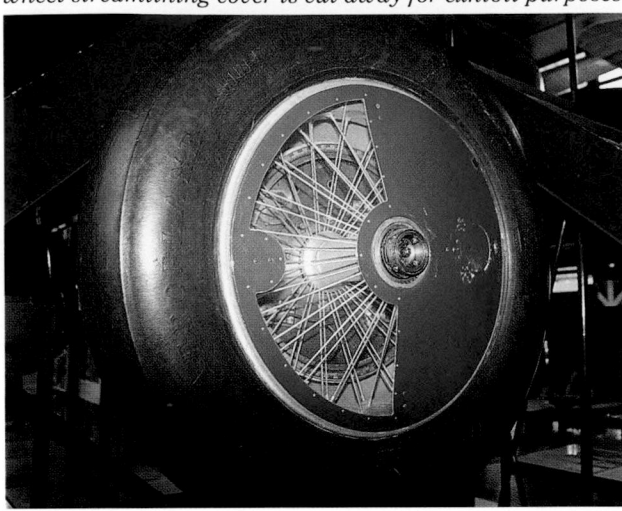

Shown here is a Dunlop™ Aeroplane tire, Wire Type, 1100 x 220 mounted on a Fokker F.VII at the Swiss Transport Museum in Luzern. It has a raised but smooth tread. The wheel streamlining cover is cut away for exhibit purposes.

sifying systems was by *Type* followed by a Roman numeral. This was developed in the late 1930s or early 1940s, but is not used today with modern tires which primarily uses dimension and ply rating for identification. (Only some Types I, III and VII are listed in current Goodyear catalogues.) Nearly all of the vintage tires described by *Type* have a uniqueness in purpose and measurement system. Here are examples for matching that *Type* description with a measurement **format** that may be found on the tire:

Type I: **Smooth contour** tire, often marked 'SC'
Example: Outside diameter 14½ inches (37 cm)
Identified as: 14.5 tire

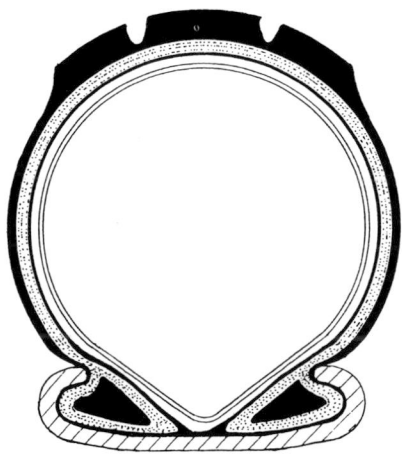

BEADED EDGE TIRE
This early clincher-type tire was created for bicycles and most cars up to 1924, and most motorcycles up to 1927. Some are known to have been adapted for airplane use during this period.

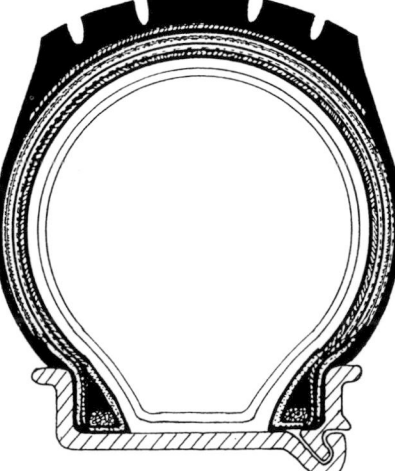

STRAIGHT-SIDED TIRE
This was the forerunner of wired-on tires. It had non-extensible wire beads and employed either rims with a detachable flange or rims that could be reduced in diameter for fitting and removal.

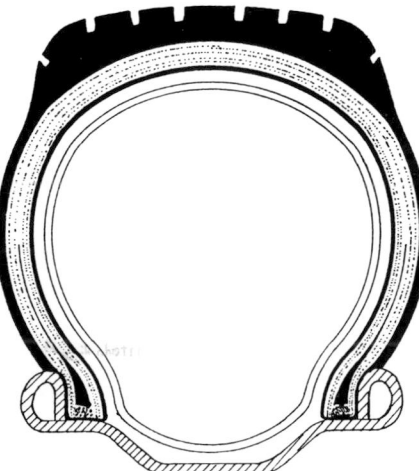

WIRED-ON TIRES
A further development of the straight-sided tire, this one-piece rim had a center well to facilitate fitting the tire into place. This concept of tire attachment remains in practice today, but not for aircraft tires.
(Drawings provided by Lambrook Tyres)

Type II: **High-pressure** tire
Example: Outside diameter 26 inches
(66 cm)
Section width 6 inches (15 cm)
Identified as: 26 x 6 tire

Type III **Low-pressure** tire
Example: Section width 9½ inches
(24 cm)
Fits a 16-inch (40 cm) wheel
Identified as: 9.50-16 tire

Type IV: **Extra-low-pressure** 'Airwheel' tire
Example: Outside diameter 35 inches
(89 cm)
Section width 15 inches (38 cm)
Rim diameter 6 inches (15 cm)
Identified as: 35 x 15-6 tire

Type V: **Streamline** tire that with the wheel
cover makes an exterior surface without
indentations. A standard dimensional
format is uncertain.

Type VI: **Low-profile** nosewheel applications only
Example: Outside diameter 15 inches
(38 cm)
Section width 6 inches (15 cm)
Rim diameter 6 inches (15 cm)
Identified as: 15 x 6.00-6 tire and now
classed as three-part name size (new
design) tires

Type VII: **Extra-high-pressure** and high-loading
tire usually for jet aircraft
Example: Outside diameter 24 inches
(61 cm)
Section width 7½ inches (19 cm)
Identified as: 24 x 7.7 tire
(Also two sub-categories: low- and high-
speed)

Type VIII: **Extra-high-pressure, low-profile,**
designed for military jet aircraft
having high-speed runway
requirements
Example: Outside diameter 30 inches
(76 cm)
Section width 11½ inches (29 cm)
Rim diameter 14½ inches (37 cm)
Identified as: 30 x 11.5-14.5
(At one time there were two sub-
categories: low- and high-speed)

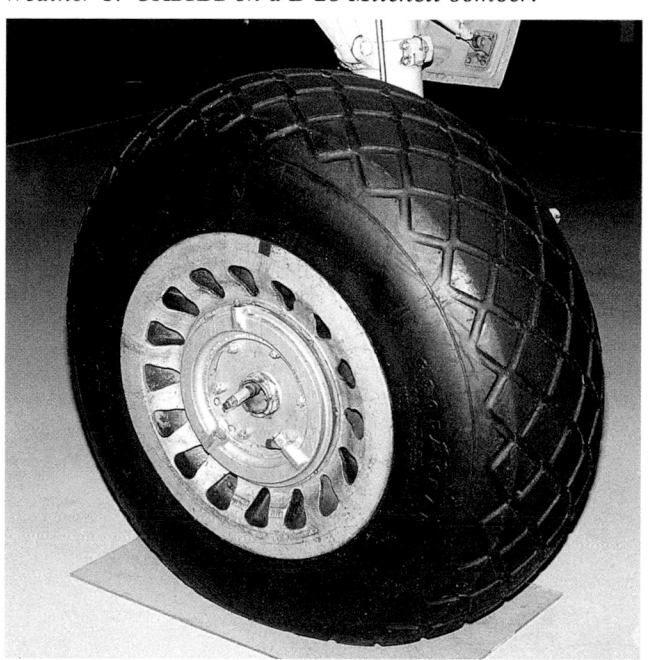

Type I, Smooth Contour Tire: *This tire was considered standard for aircraft of the World War II time period. Its design was used particularly on larger aircraft. Known as the SC (for Smooth Contour), it developed into an all-weather tire having treads (diamond shown here) yet retained the designation SC. This tire is a Goodyear All-Weather 47-OA21B2 on a B-25 Mitchell bomber.*

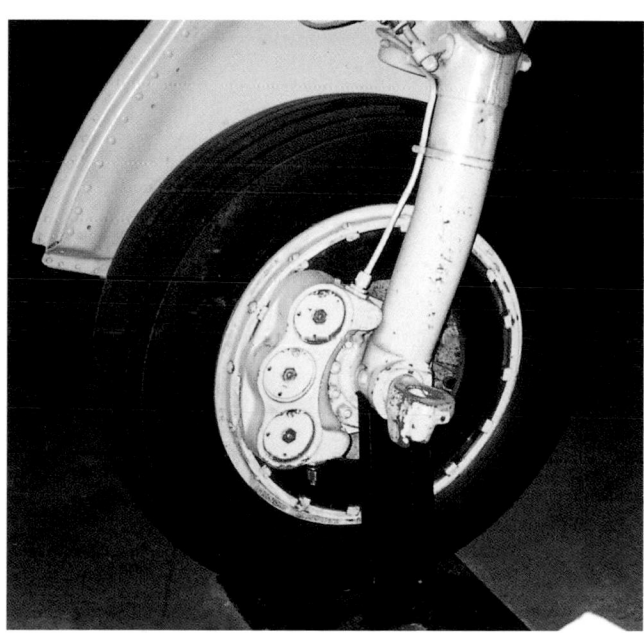

Type II, High-pressure Tire: *When aircraft landing gear became retractable, a much thinner and smaller-diameter tire needed to be fitted into aircraft wings. This tire was high-pressure to compensate for the smaller size. This tire is a BF Goodrich Silvertown 26 x 6.6 Tubeless, mounted on a Grumman F8F Bearcat.*

Type III, Low-pressure Tire: *Sport aviation brought the need for a tire with a large footprint for unprepared landing fields. This type of tire was closely associated with Piper Cubs, as illustrated here by an 8.00-4 Air Flight tire. Earlier aircraft such as Aeronca Cs of the 1930s proved the practicality of this type tire.*

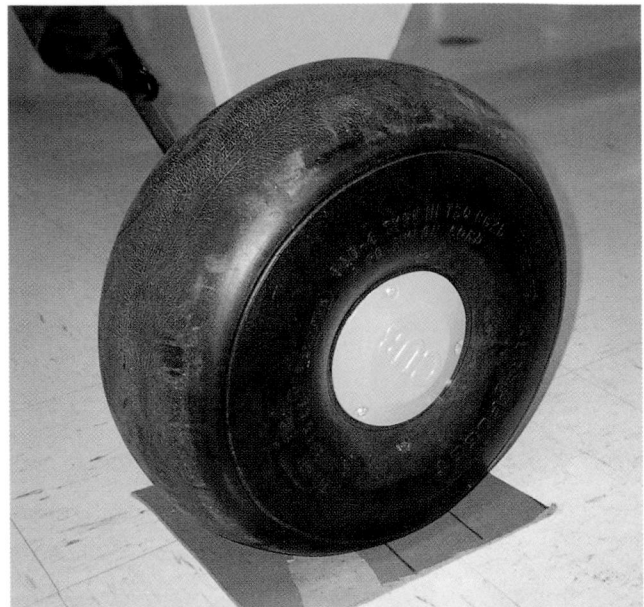

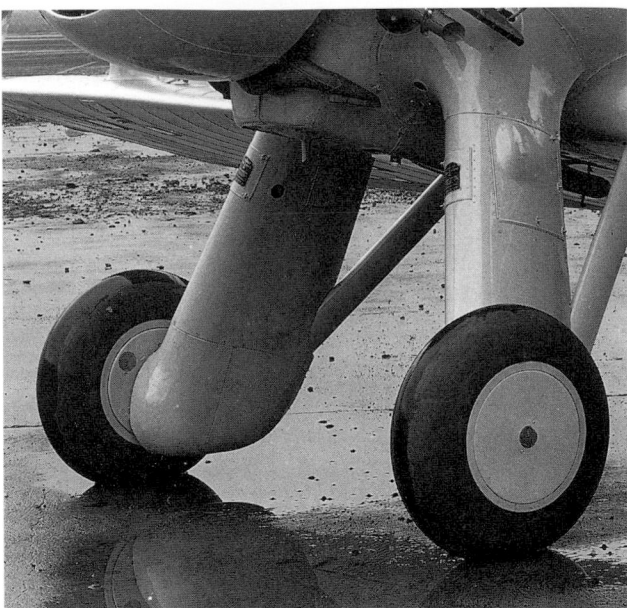

Type V, Streamline Tire: *This design was short-lived in the mid-1930s as a main landing gear wheel and tire. The tire side-walls flared smoothly to a sometimes slightly domed wheel cover. Fixed tail wheels of this type remained popular well into the 1940s. Streamline tires are known to have been used on Seversky P-35s, early Northrop A-17s, Douglas O-46As and others. Shown here is its use on the Boeing XF6B-1 in 1933.* (Peter M. Bowers)

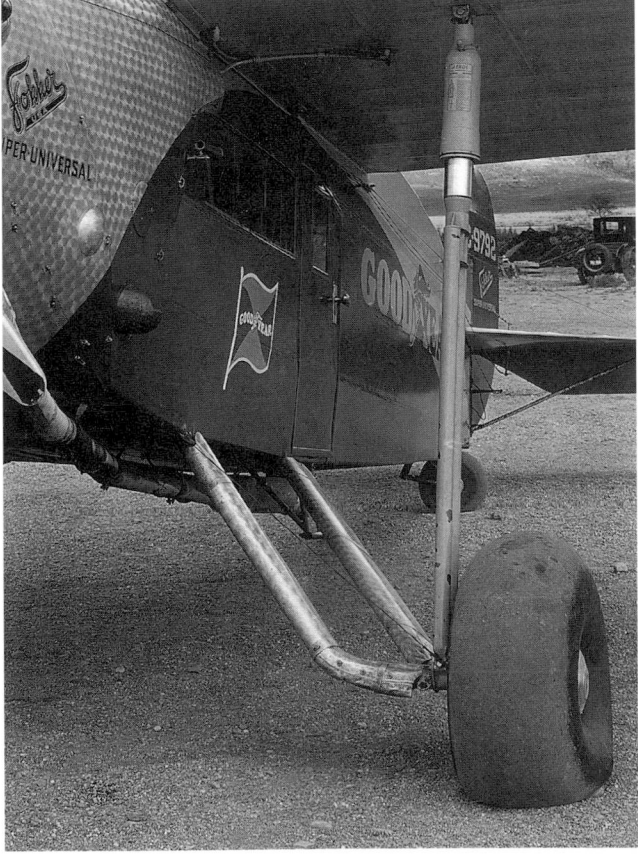

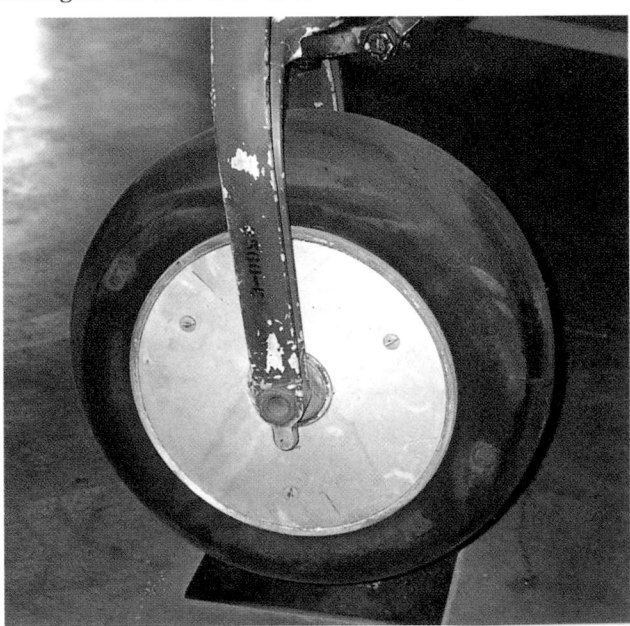

Type VI, Low-Profile Tire: *Tires of this type are designed specifically for aircraft nose wheels. In case of deflation, the low-profile would give minimum nose-down deflection. This 22 x 7.25-11.50 tire is mounted on a Bell P-63 King Cobra, the same size nose wheel tire used on Lockheed T-33A Shooting Star jet trainers. The Type VI designation is now called 'three-part name size'.*

Type IV, Extra-low-pressure Airwheel Tire: *This tire has been out of production for many years. It is an extra-low-pressure Airwheel tire designed especially for operations from rough and unimproved fields. Examples of its early use included bush-type aircraft; it is shown here on a Fokker Super-Universal in 1930.* (Peter M. Bowers)

New Designs: Tires of today have a general tire size system, identified almost exclusively by dimension
Example: Outside diameter 52 inches (132 cm)
Section width 20½ inches (52 cm)
Bead seat diameter 23 inches (58 cm)
Identified as: 52 x 20.5-23 tire

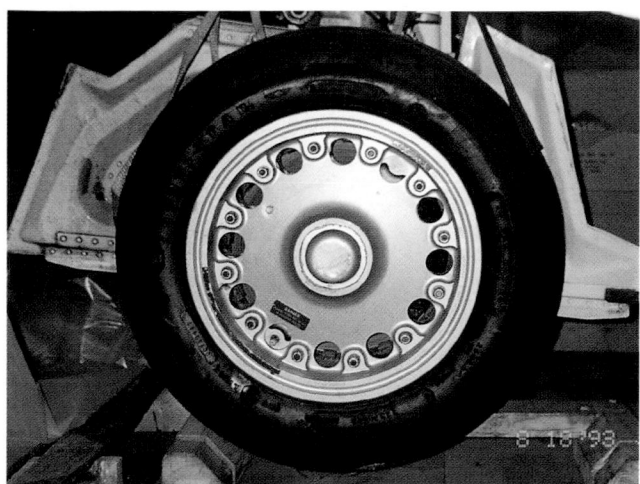

Type VII, Extra-high-pressure Tire: *This tire was designed especially for jet aircraft. It has a high load-carrying capacity and generally has tread-reinforcing plies for high runway speeds. Tread-reinforcing ply ratings go as high as 38-ply equivalency. Shown here is a 26 x 6.6 main landing gear tire and wheel of a Lockheed T-33A Shooting Star.*

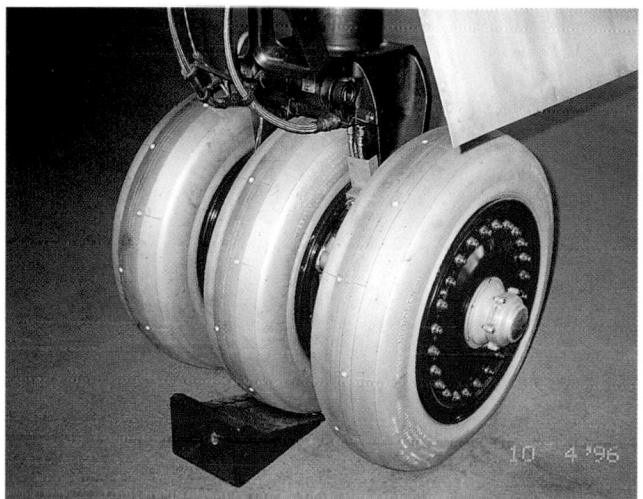

Type VIII, Military Tire: *Although military is not part of this nomenclature, the Type VIII is used almost exclusively for that purpose. These silver-painted 27.5 x 7.5-16 main tires and wheels are mounted on Museum of Flight's Lockheed SR-71 'Blackbird' in Seattle. They are inflated to 400 psi with nitrogen to be less volatile than oxygen-filled when at high cruise temperatures.*

The World War I aircraft restorations seem to present the biggest problem for acquiring tires, probably because of the abundance of actual and reproduction aircraft that generate this need. Most of these early tires were for clincher rim wheels, a method of tire-mounting long discontinued. (See Beaded Edge tire illustration.) It is not possible to utilize a tube tire casing with this type of rim even for exhibit purposes. All of us faced with this replacement problem have considered asking tire manufacturers to produce new tires to fit existing original wheels for greater authenticity.

The problems with such a plan to remanufacture tires tend to multiply from this point and eventually alter the course of action to follow. To begin with, tire companies recognize the liability issues with respect to making tires for an aircraft. *Promising* all you will that the tires will never be used on a flying aircraft has little effect on obtaining a yes from a manufacturer. Their liability risk is said to be too great for what they have to gain.

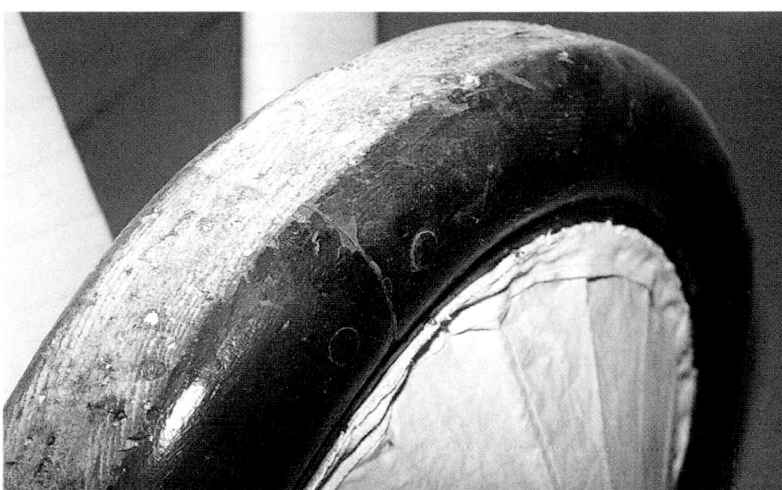

Restorers of the Royal Aircraft Factory BE.2c at the Imperial War Museum at Duxford solved their difficult tire problem many years ago with wooden replicas. A brushed-on rubber coating once covered the entire tire, but is now partially worn off through usage. It provides effective realism.

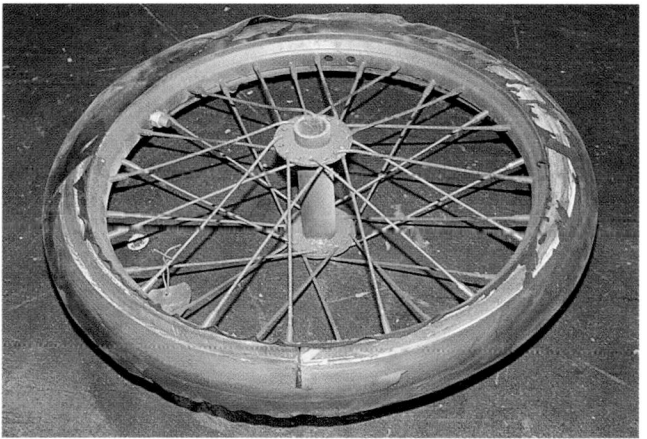

Another attempt at fabricating substitute tires is this aging example. A wooden form was made to the desired size and rim-fit of the original tires. Around this was placed a rubber inner tube. With the two wooden halves left unattached, the rubber tube held the assembly together and allowed for enough stretch in separating the halves for the whole assembly to be slipped over the rim.

If able to proceed further with intent to remanufacture, the next step is to have the tire molds designed and fabricated. These two functions may be done separately or through one provider, seldom directly with the manufacturer. Unless there is a great demand for a specific size, the unit cost even at this early stage of design engineering becomes prohibitive. At NASM on two occasions, we have had to terminate such prospects at this stage, for the estimated costs could not be justified. But if continued, there is the next and final phase, the manufacturing of the tire, adding still more cost to the project.

There have been cases where the tire manufacturers have become interested and therefore involved themselves in providing the needed tires. Michelin, for example, provided tires for the Jeannin Stahltaube of 1913 and three Halberstadt CL.IVs of World War I for the Deutsches Technikmuseum Berlin (at that time the Museum für Verkehr und Technik). Of the three Halberstadts, one was for the USAF Museum and one other for NASM. Few of us asked many questions as to why and how, thankful that this difficult task was being resolved by the manufacturer of the original tires.

In the US some tire manufacturers who have become involved have been able to modify existing tires or tire molds to meet certain requirements. But because of extreme size differences and design profiles compared with today's tires, this is a rare occurrence. An example that comes to mind is that of the Blériot XI that for years following its restoration was exhibited with bicycle wheels and tires. Goodyear was eventually able to modify an existing tire design to fit the original wheels.

(To provide a potential supplier with essential information, Lambrook Tyres has provided the rim measurement format showing needed dimensions. See graphic below.)

Every replacement tire has been a new experience and often with different solutions. A few cases are given here to give some idea of the variety of possible solutions.

When inquiring about vintage tires that may have to be modified from existing molds or stock, it is essential to have all the dimensions correct for the essential points. This drawing shows critical dimensions. A and B are diameters. (Provided by Lambrook Tyres)

Aeronca C-2

The National Air and Space Museum collection includes the first production airframe of the famous Aeronca C-2 series. Some rightfully describe this late 1920s airplane as a major step in opening sport and private aviation for the public at an affordable price. At some time while this particular airplane was operational, it had been upgraded by having a split axle tripod-mounted landing gear with airwheels fitted, replacing the straight-through axle with large-diameter wheels needed to provide ground clearance for the fuselage. With this change to the more modern landing gear went the pilot's ability to remove his own wheel chocks while seated in the cockpit and provide braking action with his gloved hand gripping the tire!

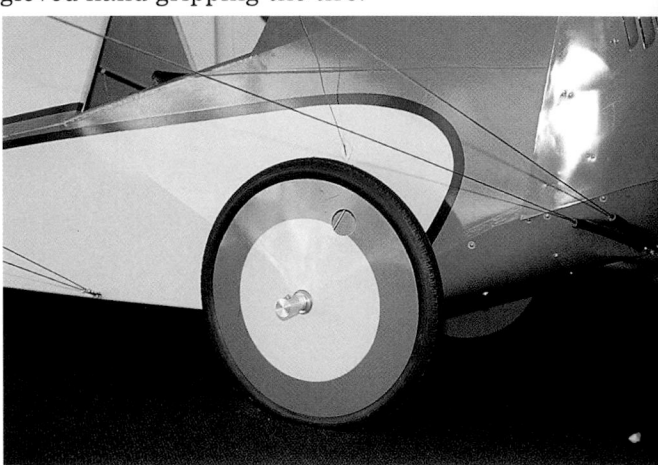

To solve the wheel and tire problem for the restoration of the Aeronca C-2 at NASM, an evaluation of the local conditions around which the airplane was manufactured provided the answer. This is a horse-drawn jog cart wheel, common to the area of manufacture in Ohio.

In the process of restoration, it became desirable to return this unique little airplane to its original landing gear configuration. Making a new one-piece axle was little problem since the retaining slots were still welded to the lower longeron. These

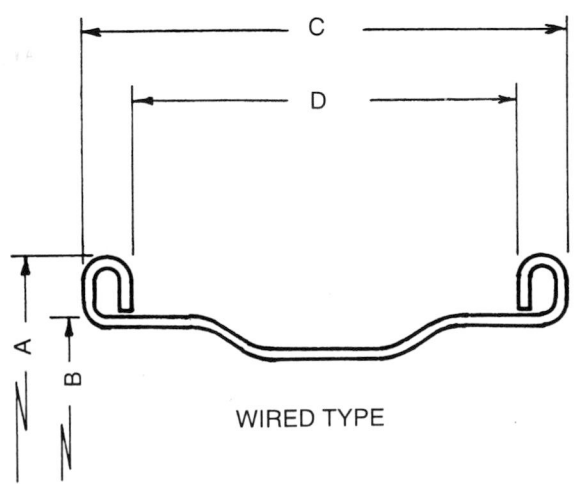

BEADED EDGE

WIRED TYPE

vertical slots allowed a minor form of shock absorption travel by the axle held to the down end of the slot by a bungee cord. But what about finding replacement original-type wheels and tires?

All that was known at this point was the outside tire diameter, also confirmed by scaling from photographs. A bicycle wheel-and-tire combination was thought to be a quick and proper solution, but this was not even close. Inquiries were then made with motorcycle dealers and tire distributors in various parts of the US. Calls were also made to Canada, and sources there in turn contacted sources in England, but with no success. The hope had been that if a tire of the matching outside diameter which had been determined could be located, finding a mating wheel would be an easy matter.

The problem was seemingly without a solution, and it was beginning to appear that both wheel and tire had long since been out of production. Then, thinking through the problem as it would have been when the Aeronca was built in 1929 in southwestern Ohio, a bit of inspiration solved the problem. This was horse country, and might the wheels be associated with horse-cart racing in that location? This search, which began locally with a call to a harness and saddlery shop, confirmed through a supply catalog that such wheels were used on jog carts for exercising harness racehorses. The wheels with tires were ordered and installed, matching all size references. The original type of landing gear for the C-2 had finally been found!

Kawanishi N1K2-Ja 'George'

A more recent experience came during restoration of the NASM's N1K2-Ja 'George' fighter. Since the end of World War II until it was acquired by NASM in 1983, the airplane was on exhibit outdoors at NAS Willow Grove, Pennsylvania. Over the years, the deteriorated original wheels and tires had been replaced with an undersized American set, and replacements for the correct size had to be found.

The original size of tires that were needed was 600 x 175 mm, also used on the A6M Zero fighter and perhaps others. This was little consolation, however, for where does one obtain this Japanese wartime vintage wheel and tire today? After some inquiry, a collector in Japan who had one set was located, but it had an exorbitant price attached. The owner admitted that the rubber had hardened and therefore was hardly suitable for this aircraft restoration need. The search for original tires went no further. An alternative that at least approximated originality had to be found.

There was the possibility that a suitable substitute could be located in the catalog of the large variety of wheels and tires used by US military aircraft. The recorded tire size of 600 x 175 mm for

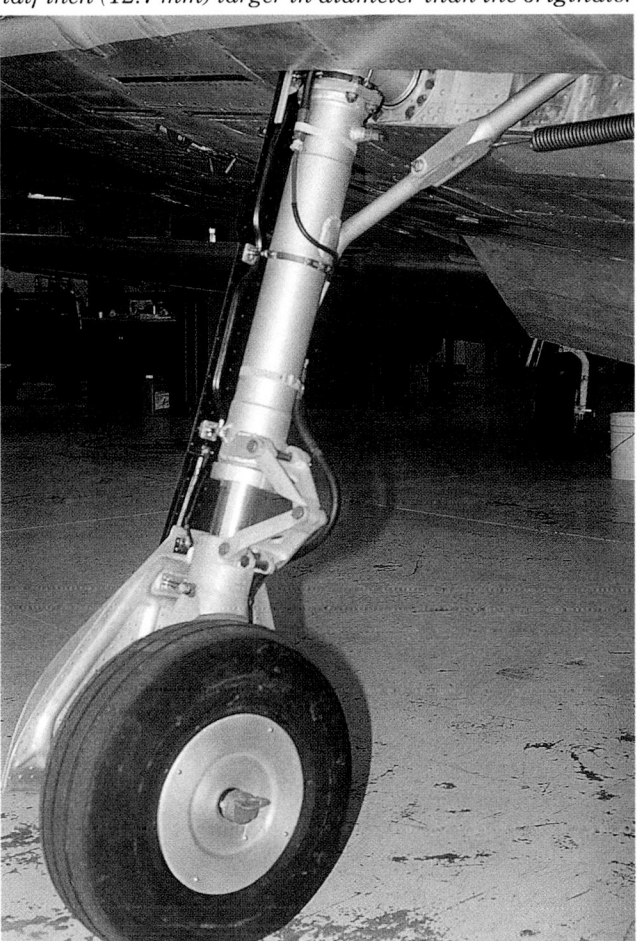

With some luck, reasonable substitutes can be found as wheel and tire replacements. This newly-restored Kawanishi N1K2-Ja 'George' is equipped with North American T-28 Trojan trainer tires which are only one-half inch (12.7 mm) larger in diameter than the originals.

the 'George' converts to 24 x 7.7 inches in American tire size. The catalog listed such a tire and revealed that these were used on the North American T-28 Trojan trainer. Both the 'George' and the T-28 had 11-inch (28 cm) wheel rims, with tire sizes seven inches (17.8 cm) wide, and the T-28 tire was a mere half-inch (12.7 mm) greater in diameter. That excess could be trimmed by a tire recapping company by spinning and cutting if it became necessary. How could we insist upon being any closer?

A very good set of used wheels and tires were purchased. Size-wise, they fit nicely into the wheel wells, so the problem was nearly solved. A sleeve had to be turned so as not to alter the original axle to fit the larger hub of the T-28 wheel. The brake band assembly was removed and retained as unused parts of this airplane since this unit would not fit into the T-28 wheel that used the disc brakes.

The wheel design was of little consequence since wheel covers had to be fabricated to conform to the appearance of the 'George' installation. Here again a curatorial decision and compromise was made in not removing the half-inch (12.7 mm) excess diameter of the tire, which would have removed the tire

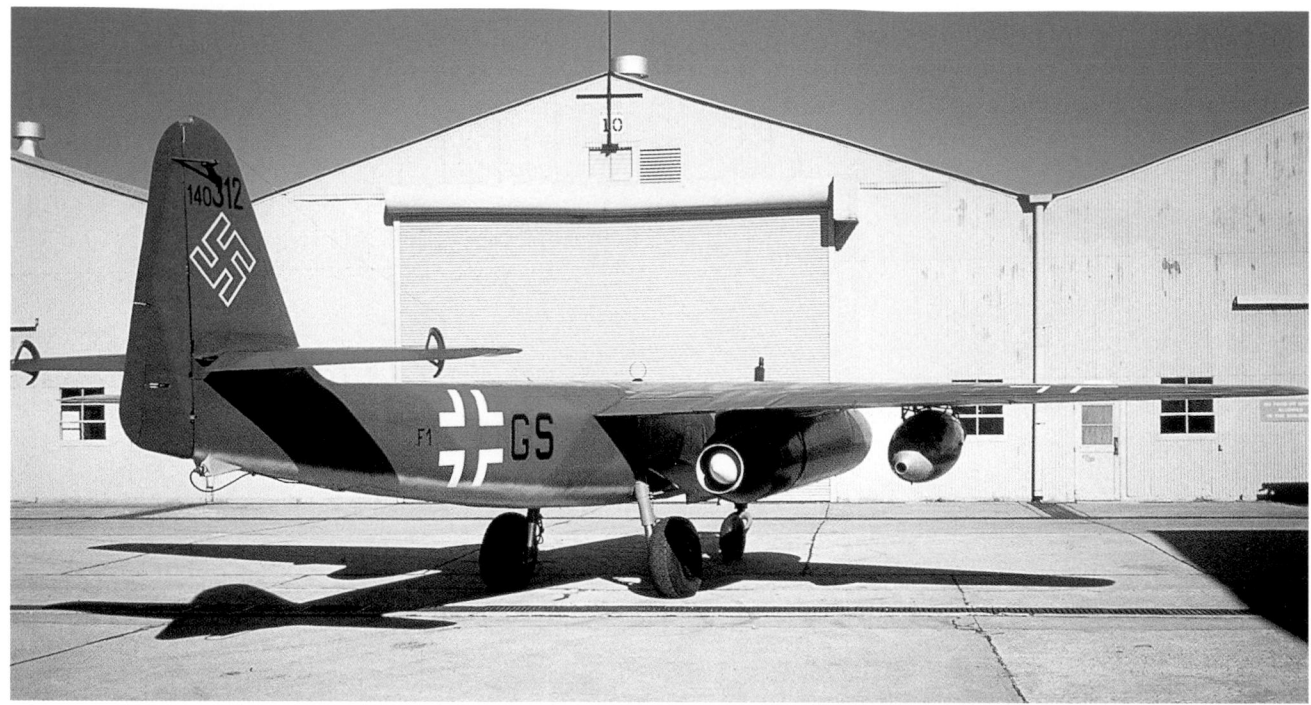

tread to make it like that of the original. For the sake of tire longevity, it was felt that this extra 'beef' may have a positive effect.

Arado Ar 234B-2 Blitz

Then there is the situation where there are no reasonable substitutes, as was the case with NASM's Ar 234B-2 Blitz. The airplane has a large-diameter extra-low-pressure tire that even tires for heavy industrial usage if trimmed down did not come close to. The original tires had hardened, with flat spots from being uninflated and carrying the weight of the aircraft for years. An attempt had to be made to salvage these tires.

While the laborious task of restoring the airframe was taking place, restoration technician George Genotti frequently massaged Armorall™ over the tires at periodic intervals. A slight amount of tire pressure was added at times to help reshape each tire. Armorall™ penetrates rubber and rejuvenates its flexing qualities. Some users regard it as a preservative agent along with its remarkable softening effect. On the other hand, some conservators have reservations as to how long this rejuvenation period may last before a rapid breakdown will occur. Normally, this potential breakdown point is long after the usefulness of serviceable objects and is of little consequence. But for a museum object this has a different meaning. Without more information on the long-term prospects for Armorall™, an answer to come only with time, there seemed to be no alternative but to use this softening agent on the tires.

As the restoration reached completion, the tires had nearly recovered in shape, texture and overall appearance. But serviceability was another ques-

NASM's restored Arado Ar 234B-2 Blitz had to retain its original tires since no suitable substitutes could be found. They were foam rubber-filled during this process in order to make them blow-out and leak-proof. Now, as solid tires, they can safely hold the static weight of the aircraft although it normally rests on jack pads.

tion, for the Ar 234B-2 was a heavy aircraft. Although it would be exhibited in the standard way by having landing gear supports in order to hold the weight off the tires, what if for some unforeseen reason the weight of the airplane would be placed on these tires? The casings would surely blow and there would be no replacement.

Although it is an irreversible process, something that museum curators prefer to avoid, the decision was made to foam-fill these tires. This process, developed for the military early in the Vietnam War, fills the tire with liquid rubber that hardens to the consistency of a solid rubber ball. If a projectile were to penetrate the tire, the military vehicle would not be disabled. The process has been used on selected USAF Museum and NASM aircraft since the mid-1970s, with good success so far. No adverse effects are expected, but only time will tell.

A special machine injects the liquified rubber through the valve stem. A metal tube is inserted through the top of the standing tire to allow the air to escape. Once the liquid begins to escape, the tire is filled and no air remains. The tube is pulled out and replaced by a simple sheet-metal screw to seal the hole. Then more liquid rubber is added under increased pressure until the prescribed pressure is reached. It is then capped off, and in time the rubber solidifies to a flexible mass. This makes for a very heavy tire by virtue of it being solid rubber. In the case of the Ar 234B-2, each wheel and tire now filled weighs 440 lb (199.7 kg)!

In time the tire casings are expected to be the area of first failures, since rubber is known to have a relatively short life expectancy. Care must be taken to protect aircraft tires while on exhibit from exposure to sunlight, along with minimal stress caused by the weight of the aircraft. Landing gear supports are a must.

For the Long Term

Recognizing all these problems associated with tires for museum aircraft, there are actions to take that will help alleviate some of them. In addition to the use of landing gear supports at all times, and even substituting alternate wheels and tires when moving these museum aircraft, having a set of spares on hand should be considered. Here is that reasoning.

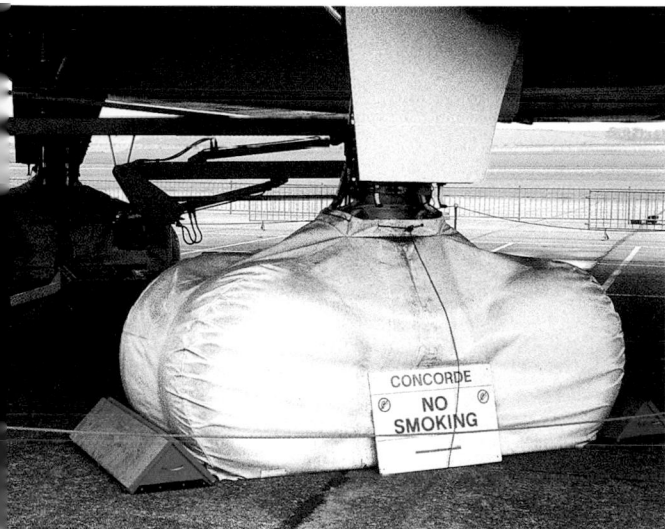

A more aggressive method of tire preservation on a static-displayed aircraft is this covering for tires of the Aérospatiale Concorde at IWM, Duxford, England. Canvas bags tightly tied at the top keep out rodents, dirt, and ultraviolet light.

From observations made of tires on museum aircraft that go back to World War I, tires kept in museum environments can be expected to remain serviceable for exhibit up to 75 years. Certainly there have been changes made in the preparation of the rubber and the molding process over the years that may affect longevity, but one aspect might cancel out another. This is a subject that conservators have little information from which to predict outcomes, for rubber is a relatively new material. But with each museum restoration, and the pain that accompanies finding a tire substitute for the project, a second set is normally acquired at NASM. This set is placed in the tire storage room in the hope that when the tires on exhibit are expended, at least another 25 years of life might remain in the

rubber of the second set. Consider a spare set of wheels as well, with the tires mounted on them. This will save undue stress in mounting at a time when frailty of the tire is beginning to develop.

This practice should not be limited to restored aircraft; it should be applied to all within the collection. But there are staff research limitations in terms of time as well as that of proper storage space, not to mention funds. Perhaps this can be given greater priority within museums. But for now, after the hypothetical 100-year time period has elapsed and the acquired tires have been expended, this problem must then pass to the future curators!

Tire Care While on Exhibit

The remaining portion of this chapter pertaining to tires may at first appear to be outside the scope of this book on restoring and preserving museum aircraft. However, considering the critical nature and relatively short-term life expectancy of rubber goods, the proper care of existing tires becomes a crucial element for present and future restorations of aircraft requiring these often irreplaceable rubber parts.

The storage of tires will be covered shortly, but first the proper care of tires while on aircraft in storage or on exhibit should be considered. It is here that the most abuse of these rubber goods takes place. We have already discussed the short time period in which replacement tires can be acquired. Therefore we must pay particular attention to those on hand by giving them the best care possible.

The most important thing that must be done for tires mounted on aircraft is to relieve their load

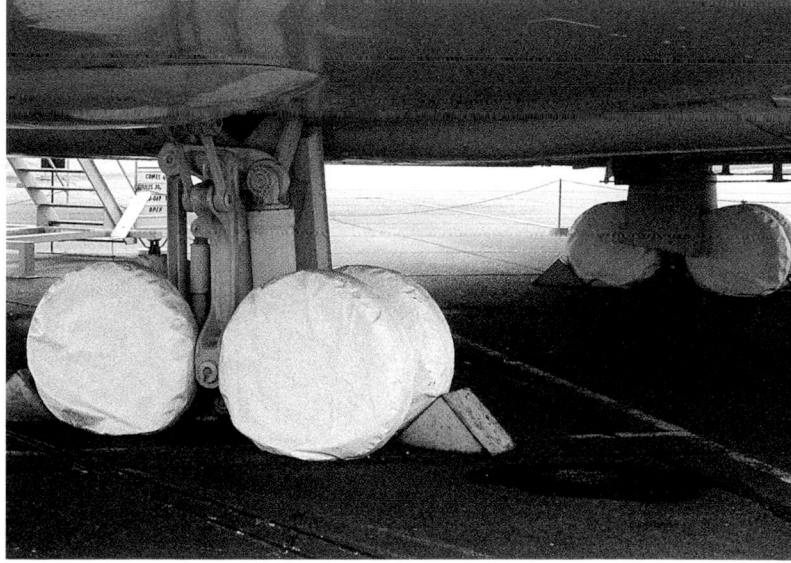

Not only are modern tires expensive, but their replacement will become more difficult. The de Havilland Comet 4 on exhibit at IWM, Duxford, England has its tires covered when not being used for special time periods of exhibit. These covers protect the tires against dripping petroleum liquids, the elements, sunlight and heat.

stress by placing the aircraft on jack stands. Ideally, these metal stands are fabricated to suit respective types of aircraft. In so doing, they need not be overly large and therefore can be inconspicuous. Normally they are placed under the landing gear which usually has provisions for a jacking point. A ¼ inch (6.3 mm) of airspace between the tire and floor is all that is needed in order to allow for floor cleaning.

By design, air museum buildings often have many windows to give the feeling of openness and space, the sky in which the airplane is designed to operate. But all this light has a detrimental effect upon museum objects, particularly upon rubber. Unknowingly, at certain times of the day or year, sunlight may directly strike the tires. If the museum is striving for the maximum life for these tires, a label panel or another object should be placed so as to shadow the tires while on exhibit. Deflecting as much light away from the tires as possible is important.

While aircraft are in storage as well as exhibited within the museum, hydraulic fluids and perhaps engine oil often drip on aircraft tires; this can severely damage the rubber. These fluids should be washed off first with alcohol and then with warm soapy water and dried thoroughly.[50] While the aircraft is in storage, protect the tires with a cover made of aluminized fabric. Far too often we see stored aircraft resting on flattened tires. Jack stands are a must, otherwise there is a frantic search for a replacement tire when it is time to exhibit such an uncared-for aircraft. Will the tire even be available?

With all these precautions that can be taken over the years in order to preserve authentic vintage tires, some of which may have even flown on historic aircraft, all the benefits of this care can be lost in a matter of moments for lack of sound planning. An example of this occurred when an aircraft was taken from its weight-supporting jacks that protected early Silvertown tires perfect in appearance and then set down on the floor in preparation to be moved. The sound of crushing hardened rubber and the sight of flattened split casings that occurred under the weight of the aircraft can never be forgotten. The tires were no longer usable even for exhibit and replacements are non-existent.

Normal practice should be that while the airplane conveniently rests on jack stands, remove the wheels and tires and replace them with substitutes that will allow the airplane to be safely moved. For tires after seven to 10 years on static exhibit, the rubber will begin to crystalize to some degree, though it is hardly noticeable initially. Any distortion caused by rolling or supporting the weight of the aircraft will cause rubber in this condition to

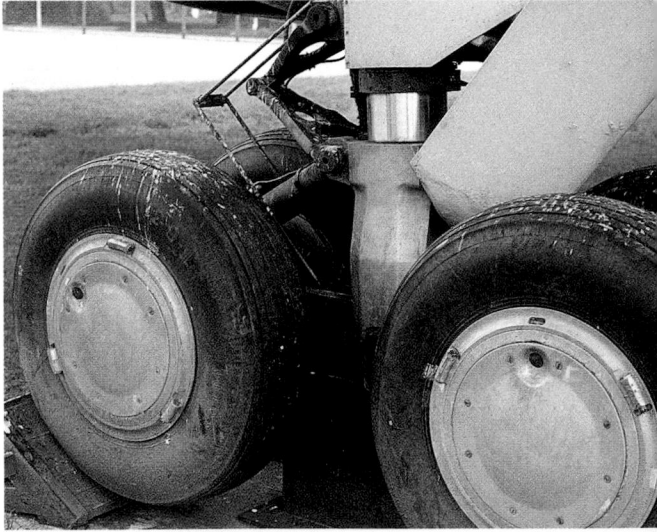

The outdoor exhibit of aircraft often develops into scenes such as this. Acid from bird droppings is more than harmful to rubber. Leaking fluids such as hydraulic fluids on to tires is frequently seen and very damaging.

Fixed-height landing gear jacks provide the first form of tire preservation. When moving aircraft, it is wise to either use a wheel-basket dolly, or substitute the wheels and tires with others for this process.

break down and eventually crack and separate, reducing its time for exhibit use considerably. The older the tire, the greater the hardening. Remember that German aircraft production during World War I used wooden wheels to move the airframes about until ready to be flown. Likewise, the use of substitute wheels should be a hard and fast policy when moving museum aircraft, requiring approved waivers for those few exceptions. The time and cost in changing to substitute wheels and tires can hardly be measured against the destructive use of vintage tires when moving airplanes.

Covering aircraft tires on aircraft outdoors is especially important. Recognizing that the tires of the Concorde, Comet and other aircraft at the Imperial War Museum (IWM) Duxford, England are not only expensive to replace, but in time will not be available, the IWM uses a system of complete envelopment or easily removable shields that are dispensed with during times of aircraft display.

Tire Storage

At the National Air and Space Museum, there is a separate Bally Box (a well-insulated metal storage building with sprinkler system) that contains tires only. This building has a controlled humidity of 40–45 per cent and temperature near 40°F (4.4°C). It is without windows and therefore the natural light problem is solved. The one remaining element of rubber deterioration is that of oxygen, and this can be partially solved by placing tires in black plastic bags and sealing them. One step further would be to evacuate the air from within the tire and replace it with nitrogen, and to do the same for the air within the plastic bag.

To avoid stresses on these tires when called upon for service, a spare wheel for the airplane would be nice to have on which the tire will already be mounted. This will help retain the shape of the tire.

The positioning of tires while in storage is the most difficult aspect. Tires should be stored in an upright position; but because of the variations in size and weight of tires, there is no one way to accomplish this for some, and with others it is difficult. Since this storage is long-term, the efforts to place tires correctly can be justified.

For the smaller tires, hanging them from wall-mounted brackets is considered best. To spread the weight more evenly across the tire bead, a metal leaf mounted on the bracket upon which the tire bead rests gives this a wider surface. For heavier tires, a trough-like support will divide the weight across two points rather than concentrating it all at one point at the bottom as the tire stands on the floor.

In all cases, a time-monitored once or twice a year repositioning of the tires with some degree of rotation is essential. Rubber will take on a permanent form if held in one shape for an extended period of time. These pressure distortions caused by standing or hanging of the tire must not be long-term. This periodic attention becomes a part of the museum conservation program.

A paper on this subject condenses the aspects of rubber storage that followed lengthy discussions on the various aspects of rubber. This paper[51] is quoted here in part for the valued guidance it provides:

Tires can only be stored efficiently if retained in their own storage facility. This insulated storage room for NASM-stored tires is maintained at a constant low temperature and humidity level. Most tires are on wheels for their intended type of aircraft. The wheels help the tires retain their shape and reduces stress by not having to be mounted when the time comes for them to be used.

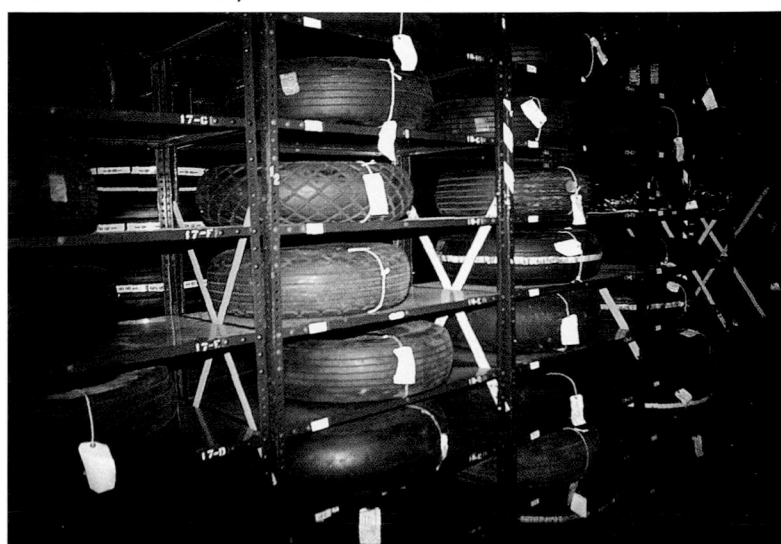

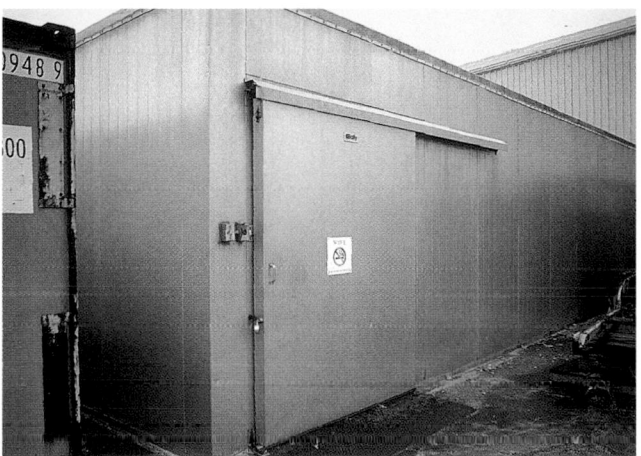

This Bally Box at NASM is dedicated to aircraft tire storage with its own controlled environment. Being windowless, it is without damaging ultraviolet light.

Additional Guidelines for Storage

In view of the inherent instability of rubber, it is perhaps worth considering the optimum methods of storing rubber artifacts. The prime consideration must be how to compensate for the inevitable hardening of the rubber. Rubber objects must always be stored or supported in the correct shape; it is important that the right shape be found since whatever is chosen could well be the final one!

Storage should be as cool as possible; a deep freezer would be an ideal location. All light, but especially UV, is harmful. All stress should be avoided (e.g. vehicles should not rest on original rubber tires and these should certainly not be inflated too much). Ozone sources such as electronic air cleaners should be avoided.

If oxygen can be excluded, the survival of rubber objects for several hundreds of years could be a possibility. However, this is inconvenient and expensive, necessitating sealed enclosures which are either evacuated or filled with an inert gas such as nitrogen; or submersion in an oxygen-free liquid.

Much has yet to be learned about the care and safeguarding of rubber. Before accepting the foregoing as the ultimate word on rubber preservation, it would be wise to explore this subject further when initiating a conservation program for rubber products.

This smooth contour tire fits on a split wheel held together with 12 carry-through studs. Museum Restoration Technician Joe Fichera is assembling the newly-restored wheel and tire for the Focke-Wulf Fw 190F-8 belonging to NASM. (NASM, SI 83-6878-8)

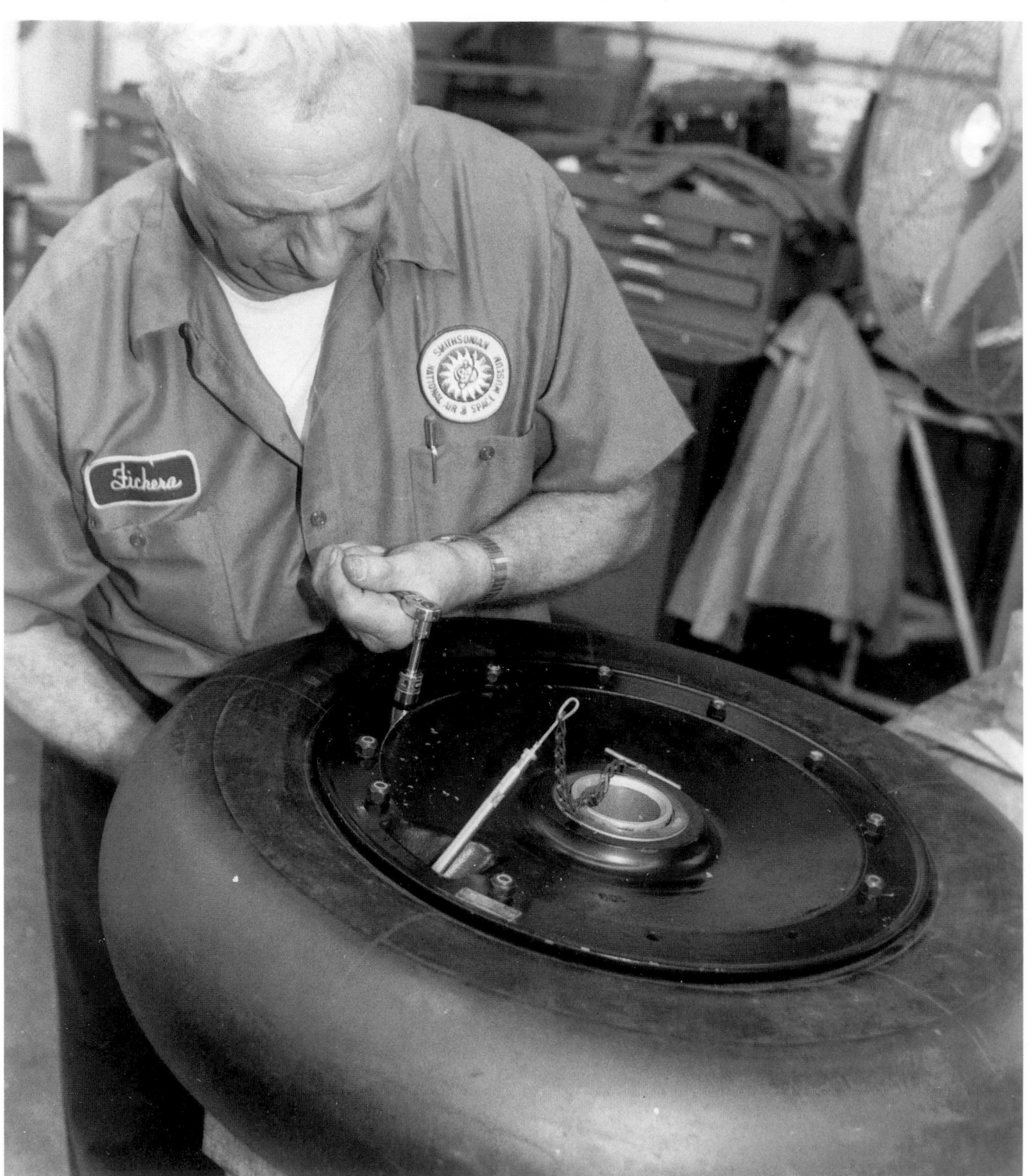

CHAPTER 9
Colors and Markings

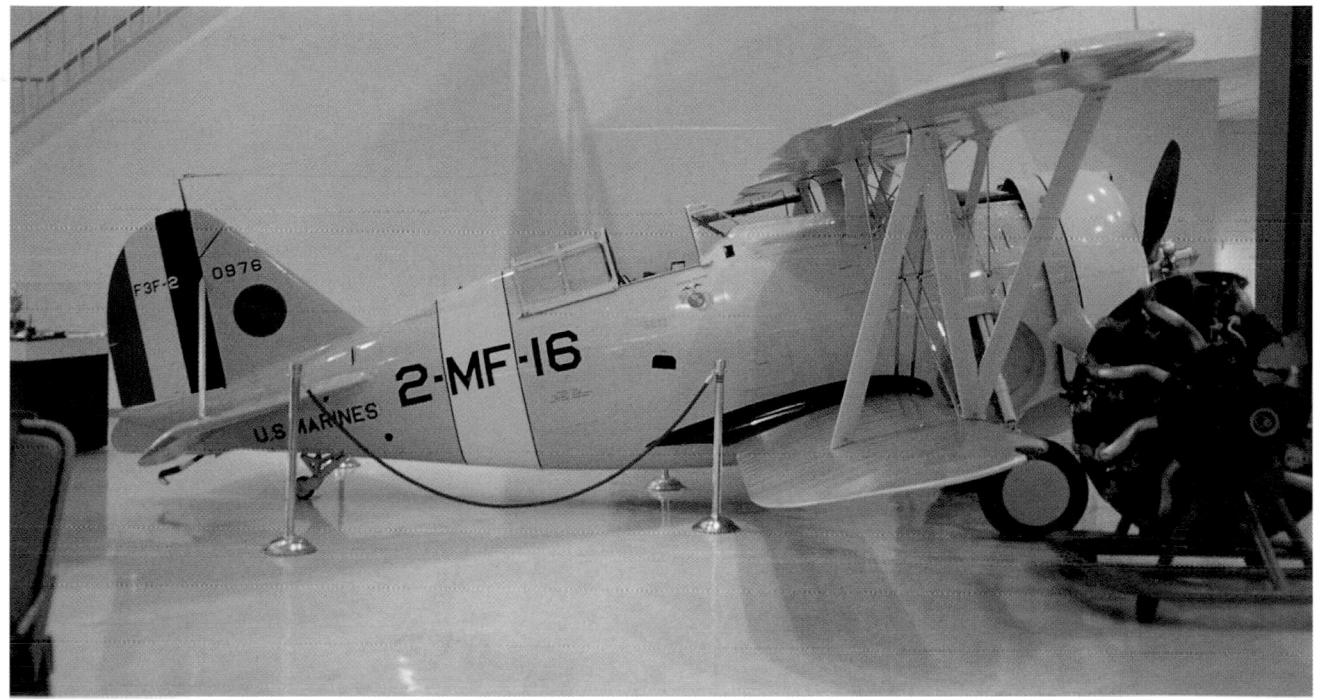

With the exception of demanding a perfect match of new paint to a damaged and repaired automobile, there is probably no other field involving paint colors and related markings quite so exacting as aircraft restorations and aircraft model-building. Advocates are almost fanatical as to exactness in colors used and the texture that they provide. Only those with a keen interest in and detailed knowledge of aircraft would detect a serial number placed one or two rivet distances too high or too low on the tail from that of the original. I welcomed this type of a challenge by reviewers of an aircraft when I was curatorially responsible, because I admit to being one of these sticklers for exactness in detail, which stems from my interest in model-building.

The extreme attention paid by many viewers of a newly-completed restoration to this outward appearance has its disheartening aspects as well. Is the primary effort of preserving, along with the attention to details and systems on the inside, fully

The challenging restoration of this Grumman F3F-2 began with its recovery from the depths of the ocean off the coast of California where it rested for more than half a century. Its rebuilding was intensive, all of which could have been undermined had the attention to painting detail shown here not been properly applied. Restored by the San Diego Air Museum, this F3F-2 belongs to the National Museum of Naval Aviation.

appreciated? Despite the importance of appearance, one must not be distracted from the primary objective of the project, which is the long-term protection of the aircraft; but if it doesn't look right on the outside, it probably isn't right on the inside!

Much was written in an earlier chapter on restoring metal aircraft about not disturbing the originality of paints, markings and materials except where necessary, even if to paint over them. What cannot be over-emphasized is the need for documentation of colors at the time the restoration begins. When possible, retain a sample of original paint on an unused part that one day may be the subject of laboratory analysis. One never knows what purpose the preservation of this information might serve in the future. Tracings should already have been made with locator points that record original markings and paint separation lines. Now we are at the point of painting the aircraft and putting all these details back as they were originally.

There is currently much uncertainty concerning the use of painting materials in compliance with new environmental regulations. Most references made here pertain to materials used before the establishment of some of these laws.

For aircraft exterior finishes, I have mostly been concerned with the appearance and longevity of the newly-applied materials. To match the content of paint with original materials is virtually an impossibility and serves little purpose. Chemically, the preparation process of materials such as paint binders is different from earlier times, when they were generally not meant to last. The restoration materials require a greater life span and color stability, causing the repainting process to be repeated less often. For the new exterior finish, lacquer has been preferred over enamels for museum restorations because the all-too-frequent handling and moving dings are more easily repaired.

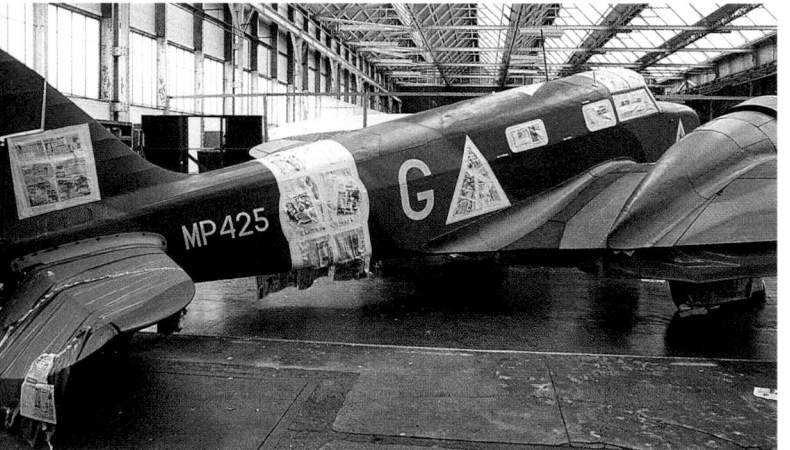

At the RAF Museum's Cardington restoration facility, this Airspeed Oxford has been masked for repainting. The Oxford served as an RAF advanced twin-engine trainer for pilots as well as for other crew positions.

Senior Conservator David Hallam made a very good point about this in a presentation concerning restoration finishes.[52] He recalled hearing the boastful remarks from a distant restoration team that their project 'contained identical paint in composition to that of the original' even though paints of greater durability could have been used. According to Hallam, 'It is unethical in [this] extreme to do anything that will confuse the public now or scholars in the future. Our work must not be concealed or deceiving but it should blend with the original material so as to create the image we wish to convey for exhibition and study.'

My feelings about paint primer surfaces are the same as for the paint. Regardless of whether a primer was used originally or not, I prefer the technician to use a primer that he or she is most proficient to work with in order to assure the best results. The objective in primer selection is to attain the longest life and appropriate appearance for the exterior finish.

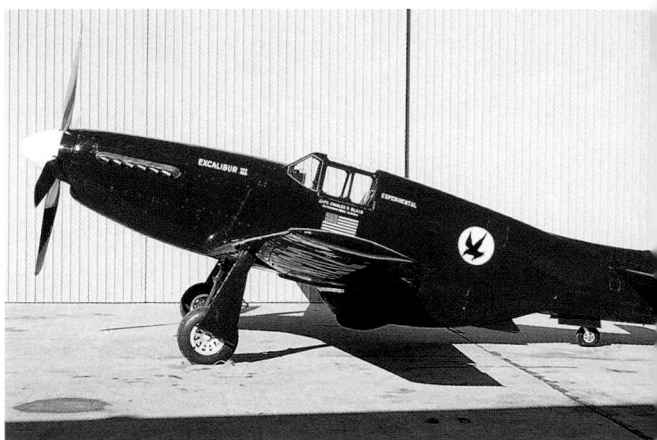

Had visual matching of colors prevailed, the bright red P-51C Excalibur III *could have been a muddy maroon color; original paint samples had shifted to that color. Careful analysis revealed that only one color on the market at first painting could have been used, as shown here.*

P-51C *Excalibur III*

Before getting into the details of this process, let me tell you of my experience early in my employment at NASM. Sometime in the early 1960s, before I arrived at NASM, the P-51C *Excalibur III* was under restoration. This is the Mustang that had been owned and flown across the North Pole in 1951 by Captain Charles F. Blair to prove a new form of navigation by sun lines. This interested National Defense planners because it demonstrated that an enemy could fly across these polar regions as a shorter route to targets in North America. Prior to making this flight from Norway to Alaska, Blair set a new speed record in this airplane by flying from New York to London in seven hours and 48 minutes — a record for propeller-driven airplanes of this class that still stands and may never be broken. Paul Mantz had been the previous owner, and this airplane took first place twice, and a second place in the coveted Bendix races. Mantz set a westbound transcontinental speed record just to return home.

Much of the success achieved by this airplane was the result of the modification to its wing, making it mostly a fuel tank, or 'wet-wing', for additional fuel to extend its range. In time, fuel seeped past the impromptu liner and severely corroded the metal.

In NASM's restoration, repair of the fuel-soaked wet-wing modification became so involved that the project was put aside while Blair sponsored a contractor to do this work outside the museum.

The restoration was started again about 10 years later at NASM, and was coming to a conclusion in 1977. Through the foresight of those involved at the beginning of the restoration, paint had been ordered to exactly match that which was on the airplane before its removal. What a fortunate happenstance! As a few of the components were being painted before final assembly, I was able to check the applied color against a sample of the red that still remained on the rudder balance weight. They matched perfectly. Achieving this exactness became a snap — or so I thought!

Fortunately at this point, Charlie Blair and his beautiful actress wife Maureen O'Hara made one of their periodic visits to observe the progress. To my dismay, Blair blurted out: 'That airplane was never that color!' In shock I wondered how could that be? I showed him the balance weight sample of red and assured him that the paint right from the can was mixed and matched before the original was removed from the airplane. It had to be the same. 'No way,' was his reply. 'It was red, not this muddy maroon.'

I asked Captain Blair questions as to what the red may have been matched to. He admitted that it was matched to nothing. In 1950, he merely wanted his airplane painted red, and told his mechanic to go to an aircraft supply house and buy red paint — simple as that.

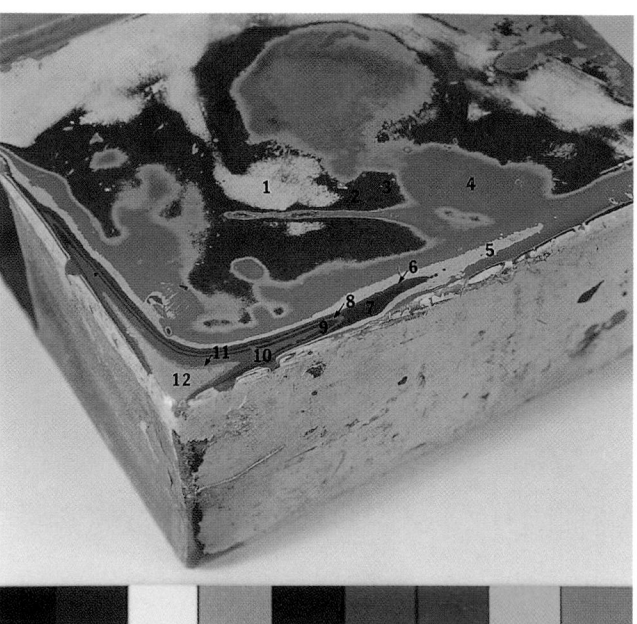

In order to document colors that were found when restoring P-51C Excalibur III, *this photograph with color correction bar and notations helped to record its past. This rudder counterbalance weight retained enough of the original colors to be analyzed when the restoration took place after 25 years. Sanding through the various layers of paint confirmed the sequence of events for this historic airplane:*

Color surfaces for N1202 (Munsell Color code equivalents):
1. White: tail stripe
2. Dark Red 2.5R 2/6: overall finish
3. Red 7.5 4/10: 1949 overall finish
4. Kelly Green 5G 4/6: shamrock for 1948 race
5. Light Gray N 6.5/: 1948 overall finish
6. Medium Gray primer surfacer
7. Red 7.5R 4/10: 1947 overall finish
8. Medium Gray primer surfacer
9. Red 7.5R 4/10: 1949 overall finish
10. Medium Gray primer surfacer N 3.5/
11. Zinc chromate
12. Bare metal

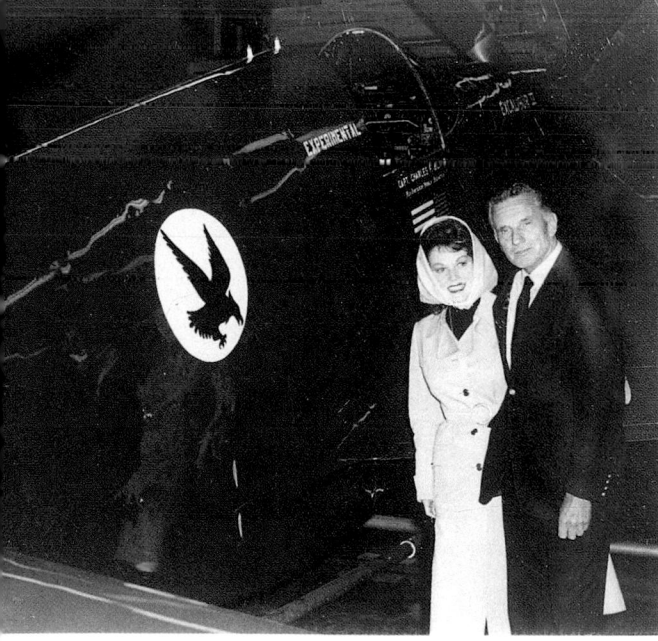

Standing beside the newly-painted P-51C is Captain Charles F. Blair and his wife, screen star Maureen O'Hara. Blair flew this Mustang across the North Pole from Norway to Alaska in 1951 to prove navigation was possible by fixes made from sun-lines to plot his route.

By now, the Randolph Products Company representative had been called in. He went back with the loan of the original paint sample to conduct an analysis with their spectrophotometer. After analyzing the wave curves of the pigments in this paint, the numbers matched perfectly the formulas used for Randolph Wine Red B-9164, also known as Stinson Red Q-1913. The only exception was in the visible difference of the original sample, which was decidedly darker. The aging effect of the oil base of the enamel had darkened the original paint almost to a maroon. What further cinched it was that this was the only Randolph Red on the market in 1950, and Berry Brothers had only one red at that time as well — and both products matched. What a difference in what became a bright red Mustang, to what almost became a deep maroon Mustang with a bluish cast and very little red luster!

143

Documenting Color

Reds are the most unstable of all the colors, and the example of *Excalibur III* is an extreme case. But this gave me an all-new perspective when it came to matching colors to the original. What constitutes original color? Is it the way the color is at the start of the restoration, or is it as it was when first applied; in this case, 27 years before?

Often a person involved in a restoration project will boast of his plan to retain the *original* paint and merely match it with new in the areas that need repair. This is an admirable approach in trying to preserve the original at hand; but such an effort may merely be continuing a color that has changed from the original. As time wears on, the old and new paint will shift at different rates and the effort will become more quilt-like. I am not aware of any restorations that ended up carrying through with this plan, and succeeded.

Through most of my experience, I recorded color notations with the Munsell Color System for one very good reason — this system was well-entrenched at NASM when I arrived! It continues to work well and is a system still recognized as one of the standards worldwide. The Munsell Color System consists of pages in a notebook binder, each page having many pockets which hold variations of enameled colors on small cards. Each color is classified in terms of hue, value, and chroma. A system of trial and error by placing different color chips to the color being evaluated usually results in a close or exact match, and therefore a color code to record for future use. This is a very expensive system to purchase as a complete set, although individual color samples are also available. (See Appendix F)

There are other very similar color systems like the one described, examples being Methuen, ColorCurve, Color Atlas, and Pantone, to name but four. These are inks on paper and are not considered to be as stable. The system most widely used by Government contractors and agencies, model-builders and those restoring US military aircraft, is the Federal Standard 595a and revised edition 595b color chip book and fans of color chips. These severely lack in range of samples for identifying colors, but when a color has a known value within the Federal Standard system, it is an excellent way of conveying and documenting this information. (See Appendix F)

A device recently placed into use at NASM is the Chroma Meter CR 200 colorimeter made by Minolta. There are other similar instruments on the market as well. This hand-held device measures colors electronically with its consistent built-in light source, and records the colors in one of four color identifying systems. Three of these systems were devised by the Commission Internationale de l'Eclairage: XYZ tristimulus values, YXY color space, and L*a*b color space. The fourth is the Munsell Color System which remains the recording measure for NASM.

Gathering color readings is now a simple matter. Darkened warehouse storage no longer presents a problem when comparing color sample chips. The problem is that not every reading made by the colorimeter is in a color chip form. For example, greens within each color grouping, or hue (i.e. G (green) GY (green yellow) range in sets numbered 2.5, 5, 7.5 and 10), leave much to interpolation as to hue. A reading may begin as 6.3GY, requiring an interpolation between color chip sets 5 and 7.5. Variation in colors between adjacent color chips is relatively small yet discernible to the eye. Regardless of the precision of electronic color measuring, it still comes down to visual color determination by comparing color chips.

Granted, the colorimeter reading can be taken to a paint supplier who is equipped with the latest technology in paint-mixing by computer input; but most suppliers require a minimum order of five gallons (19 ltr) of any one color mixed this way at a staggering cost.

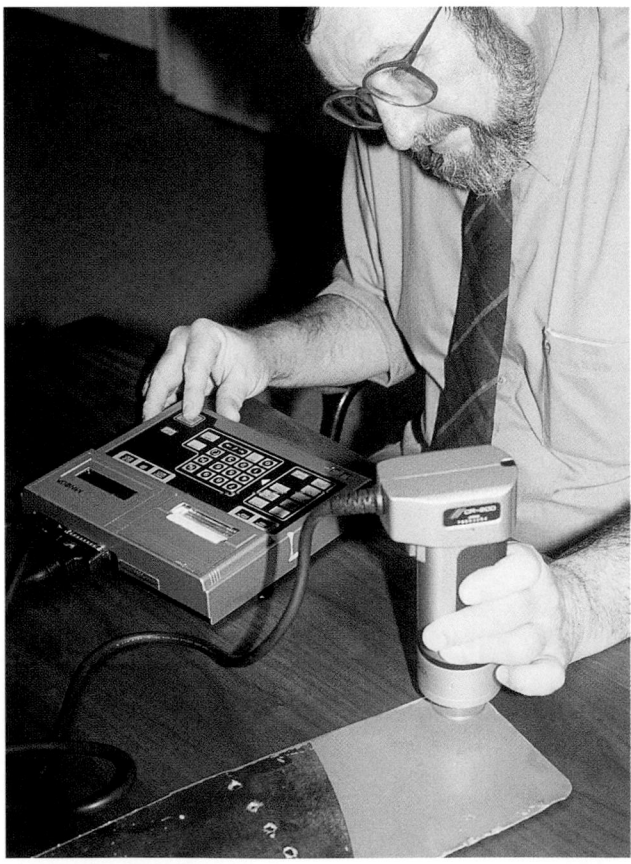

With this electronic device and consistent light source, colors can be recorded with great accuracy. NASM's Conservator Ed McManus uses a colorimeter to record the various values of green camouflage on the Aichi M6A1 Seiran under restoration.

Basically, it amounts to this: obtain your color readings and samples for record, then research what the color was originally from original sources, and match to that specification. For example, there is little or nothing gained by matching to a World War II color, regardless of how well-protected a sample appears to be. That sample is bound to have had some type of exposure to moisture, oxygen, and light in varying degrees over all these years, to say nothing of expected shifts in color pigments that are bound to have occurred over time. Hidden areas having original paint will have been affected the least. It is from these surfaces that readings should be taken.

There is reason to remain critical of colors and textures, recognizing the shortcomings of what is thought to be 'original.' The color to match to for a restoration would be that which is recorded in a stable color system that is identified as that original color. (See Appendix F for color and marking information sources)

From Those Who Know

There can be situations with some aircraft where finding the proper shade of colors, patterns and appropriate markings can become a difficult yet essential part of the restoration. Take for example the task of selecting proper shades and patterns for Russian aircraft that are becoming more often seen in Western countries. For American, British, German and Japanese aircraft, the right colors are fairly well documented and easily matched with some degree of authority. But for restorations made by Westerners of former Eastern Bloc aircraft, the problem is compounded. Where does one go for source information?

There are people who seemingly make a life study of this type of data — and we are lucky to have them. These are the aircraft model-builders mentioned earlier as being meticulous with every detail of this art. Draw upon their knowledge — use their source information and expertise regarding this very demanding subject of colors, pattern styles and markings.

It would not be surprising that such a specialized model-builder would make himself known to the restoration team as the project gains attention. If no one presents themselves, then ask around. Find out who is really good as an accurate scale model-builder. That person may not know anything about colors and markings of your particular airplane, but you can be assured that a truly skilled model-builder might have a library containing documents that will cover your type of aircraft, or know someone else who does. Use these references, contact the authors that come close to having covered the type of aircraft or military service you plan to represent. Most likely they will have

addresses of foreign sources they are in touch with that are close to this subject and are experts in the field.

For making a determination about color selection, the problem again is what was 'original'. No doubt there will be very little sound evidence with which to support these selections. You are now in the position of a model airplane selection judge to determine accuracy. The builder (in this case, the person supplying you with information) is the one who provides the background material in making color and marking judgments. This same technique will work for your project. Above all, document all aspects of your color and marking selection process.

Remember the basics when painting and marking Category III aircraft: select a photo (not necessarily color) as pattern to follow, do not depict a well-known and often-illustrated aircraft if in fact this is not that aircraft, and stay away from duplicating a plastic model kit. Your Category III aircraft should be unique and reflect accuracy in its presentation. If you have satisfied the fastidious model-builders, you have done your task well.

Exterior Markings

For exterior appearance, markings have a high priority. Colors are sometimes unsubstantiated; and black and white, and especially color photographs cannot always be relied upon for this type of record. But with markings, a photograph of the restored aircraft compared to a photograph of what it is supposed to have looked like will reveal any mistakes that have been made.

To prevent these errors from occuring as part of a restoration, examine photographs closely to make patterns to be applied to the unfinished aircraft before starting the actual painting. Once the patterns are made, take a set of pictures to show them in place. When comparing these pictures with photographs of an operational airplane of the type, irregularities can more readily be detected. It is much simpler to make changes in the patterns before painting is begun than to correct figures after the paint has dried.

Arado Ar 234B-2 Blitz

This method for markings development and verification was used on the Arado Ar 234B-2 that was restored by NASM, the only survivor of this advanced German World War II jet reconnaissance-bomber, four of which were transported to the US after the war. NASM's example was captured at Stavanger, Norway, and was part of II/KG 76. Upon reaching Freeman Field, Indiana, the airplane was made ready for flight-testing. It was the practice during these preparations that the paint be removed, taking with it the unit markings. No records or photographic evidence of these markings

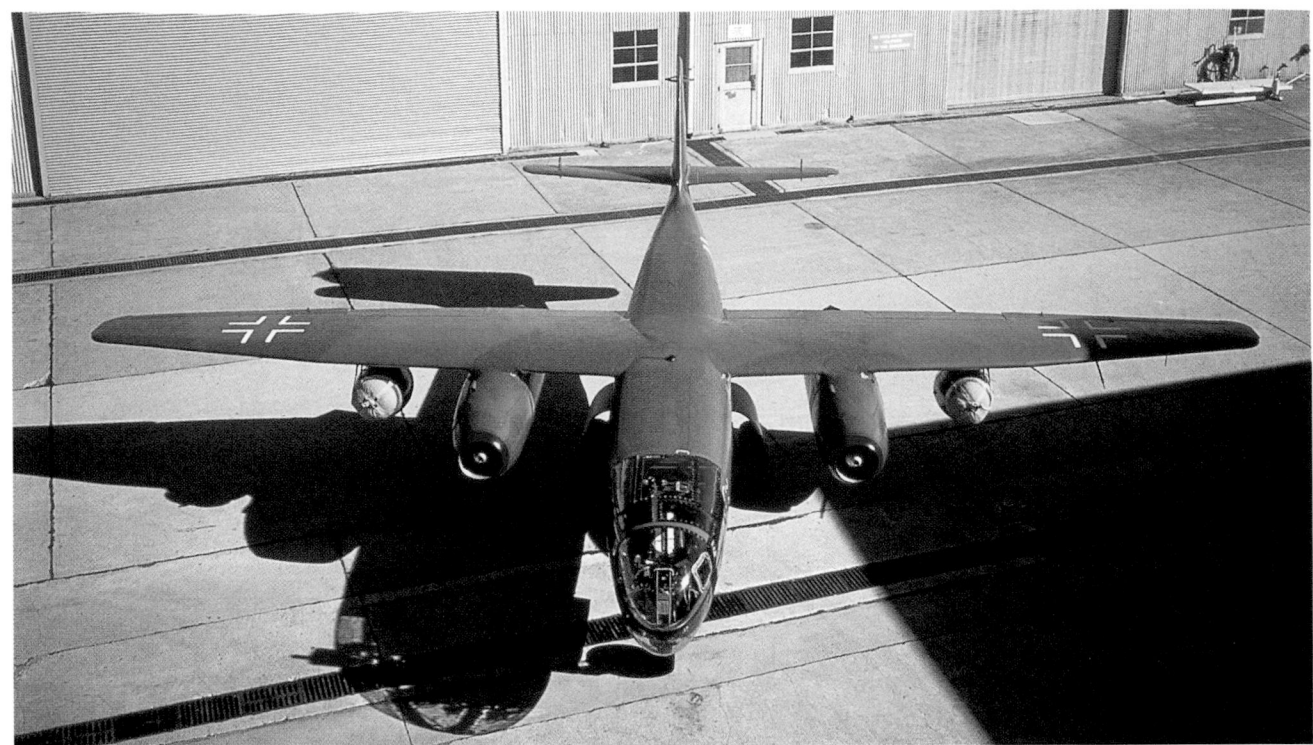

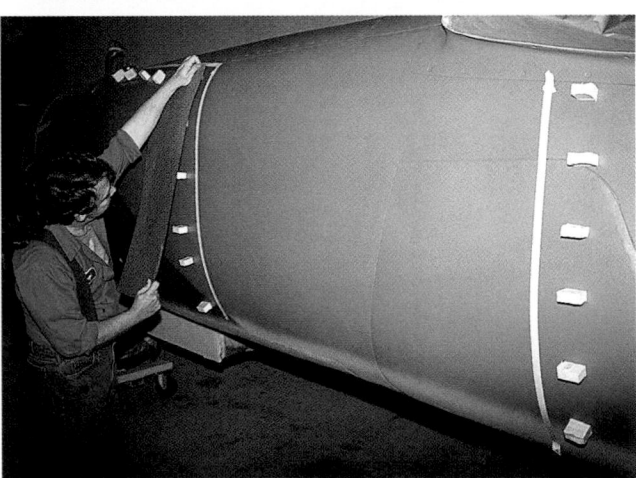

While this Arado Ar 234B-2 Blitz (Lightning) of NASM was being restored, its Werk Nummer *was found within the structure. This identified it among a group of these airplanes assigned to 8. / KG 76. 'F1' therefore was the unit code to be used and other markings were similarly determined.*

While holding a heavy rubber mat in place against the separation blocks, the masking tape was removed and the second color of the camouflage was sprayed along the raised mask. This provided an even, straight, yet feathered demarcation line.

The two-color camouflage of the Ar 234B-2 was applied in a rather unorthodox fashion. To provide a straight but feathered color separation, the color line was first plotted with masking tape. Two-inch (51 mm) spacer blocks were added and held in place with double-face tape.

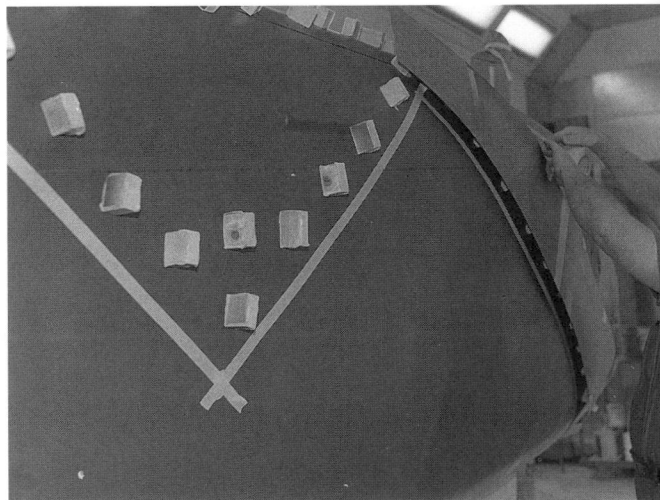

were made.

In this repainting phase, reference to the Curatorial Guidelines (see Appendix B) will show that research had already been accomplished that produced a suitable set of identifying code letters and numbers for this restoration. A representative picture had been designated to serve as the basic pattern aircraft since a photo of this actual aircraft was not available. The task now was to develop patterns of the figures that were to be placed on the aircraft, confirm their accuracy and size, and describe how they could again be positioned when it was time to paint.

This process more easily begins when the fuselage is resting in a normal attitude. This should be well before getting ready for paint, since repeated photo-taking and processing, with changes in pattern development in order to get it right, can be time-consuming.

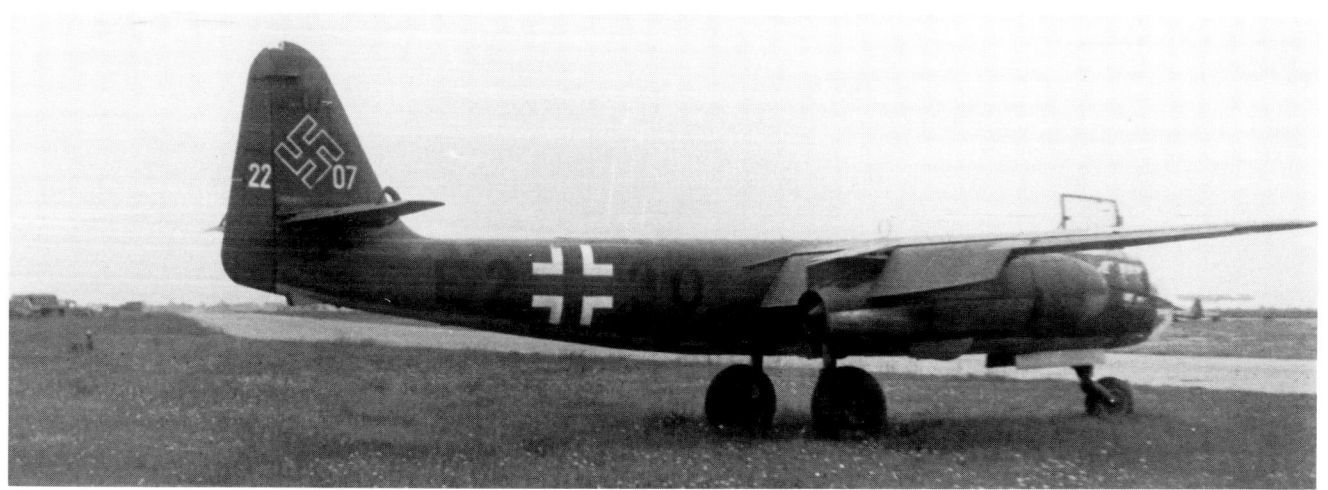

Operational photographs of Ar 234s helped confirm the location and sizes of markings that were otherwise spelled out in German directives. Prominent in this photograph are the location of the German insignia and swastika. (NASM, SI 79-7210)

Having made an insignia from craft paper of the specified size, it was taped into position to conform to operational photos with skin lines for reference. This and other photos were taken to compare marking positions with photos of operational aircraft. Necessary adjustments were then made and rephotographed.

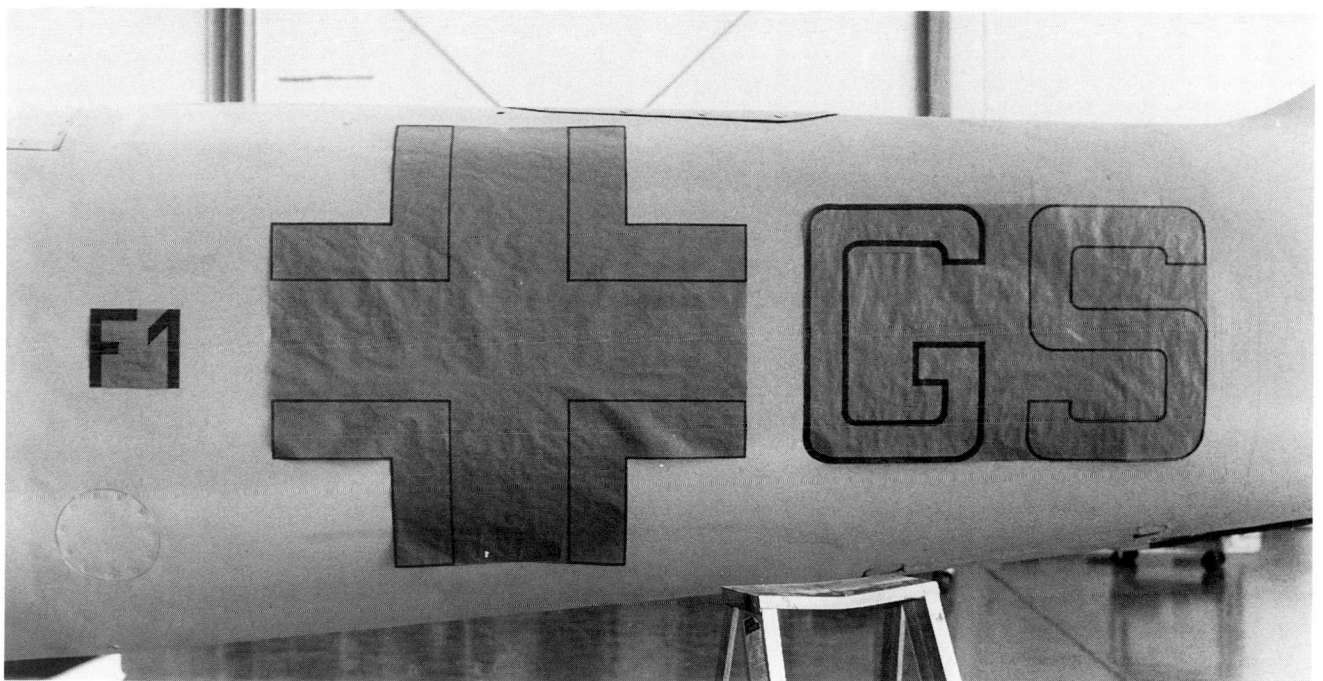

With the Ar 234B-2, it was easiest to start with the insignia cross. Once confirmed in size and design, the other figures were developed with this as a size reference. The references used for the size and placement of the more standard markings were found in *The Official Monogram Painting Guide to German Aircraft 1935-1945*, published by Monogram Aviation Publications and generally recognized as an authoritative source. Not only were the proportions given for the cross, but dimensions were also provided. This pattern was laid out on brown wrapping paper because it was convenient. Since patterns are generally large, by laying the paper on a tile floor, this provides ready-made grid-lines to aid with layout construction. Once the layout of each marking was confirmed, the lines were intensified with a felt-tip ink marker for photo clarity. The pattern was cut to shape and taped in place on the aircraft to confirm proportionally that the size was correct. With the first try, this worked out fine. When comparing with an operational photograph taken many years ago, it is amazing what details like skin and rivet lines can be detected from photographs with a strong magnifying glass. These reference points were used for placing the insignia pattern to match the photograph.

Sizes of letters were determined from operational photographs of similar markings in relation to the size of the national insignia. Normally these sizes equate to even number dimensions. In the example shown here, the photo reveals that the 'GS' is too large in comparison to pattern photographs.

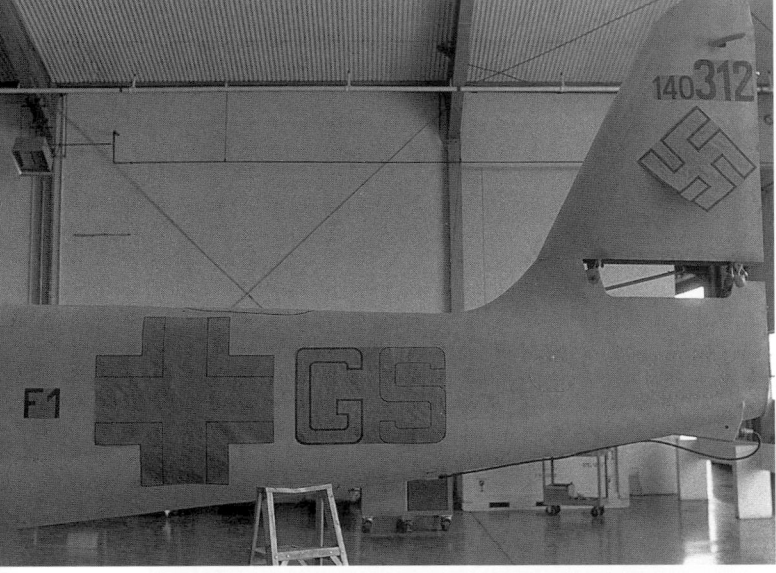

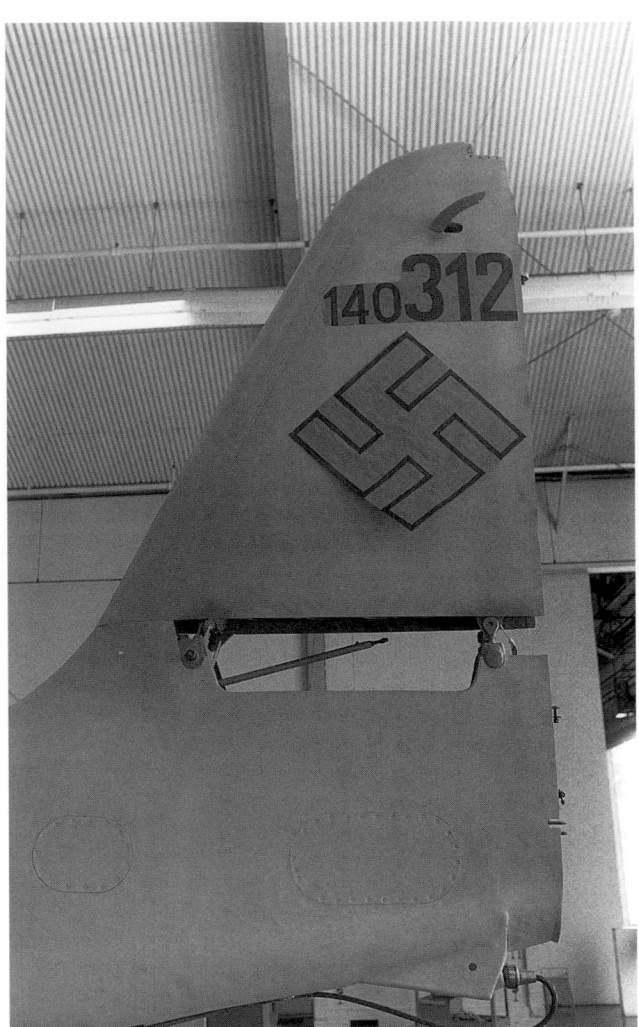

ABOVE:
Patterns of the tail markings were taped in place, photographed, and analyzed. Photo comparison with operational views revealed that the points on the '3' were incorrect and changes in the pattern had to be made. This was far easier than making adjustments after an incorrect number style had been painted.

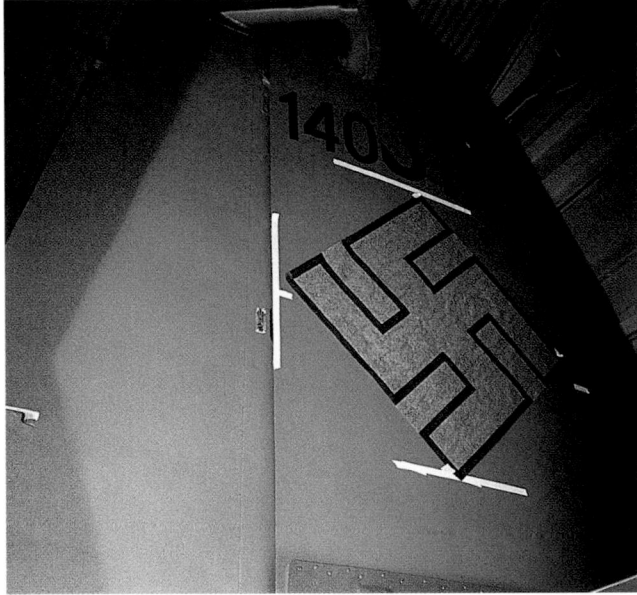

Once satisfied that the patterns were accurate, it became a matter of transferring those designs to the aircraft in final form based upon reference marks as to location.

RIGHT CENTRE:
With a full-size pattern already confirmed as to size and location, the task was greatly simplified by taping the borders and masking the fuselage insignia prior to painting. John Cusac defined the margins with masking tape while Karl Heinzel assisted.

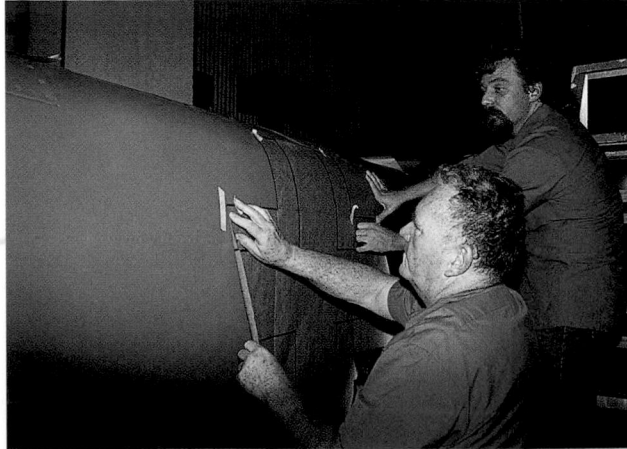

BOTTOM RIGHT:
The fuselage insignia became a simple pattern to apply to the Ar 234B-2 since this style of marking for this time period consisted of four white figures. This outlined the image of a cross that had no background color other than the existing camouflage.

148

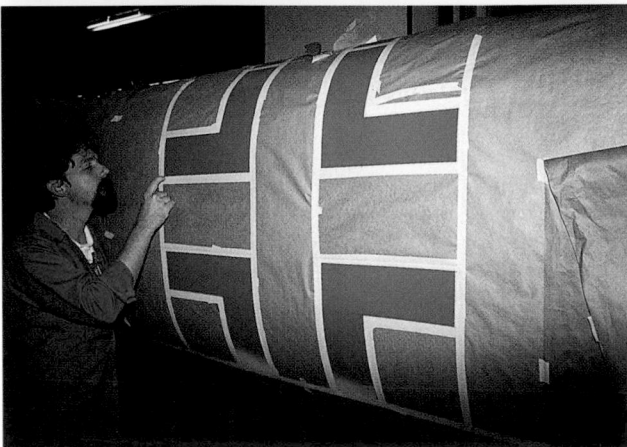

From an assortment of photographs of Arado Ar 234s the fuselage letters and numbers were developed through proportional comparisons with the national insignia pattern. A proportional divider is a handy drafting tool for transferring information from a photograph to the drawing board. It was here that two or three attempts at getting the right proportions for the letters were necessary. The second try, which at first looked right, was photographed, and only then did further irregularities show themselves. These were corrected, new patterns put in place, and photographed again.

It was at this stage that copies of these pictures showing the placement of the patterns, along with operational photographs were sent to reviewers. We select as many as five reviewers for this scrutinizing process. They are usually people we feel know the most about the subject, and certainly would be the first to be heard from if something appeared to be inaccurate in its final form. In this case, one reviewer noted an error in how the ends of the '3' in the *Werk Nummer* were turned when compared to an operational photo. At this point, such a change was easily made.

The photos showing the patterns in place are a supplemental reference to the dimensions taken previously for positioning the patterns. From here the technicians can easily take over the painting process without guesswork or fear of disappointment if errors are found too late.

F-100D Tail Markings

Another example using a marking layout was on the NASM North American F-100D Super Sabre 56-3440. This called for a change of tail markings to those it had while in combat in the Vietnam War. This airplane was obtained by NASM as a representative USAF fighter-bomber of the type used so extensively in that war. Its military service was more illustrious than just participating in combat. In an early test configuration, this airplane reached an unprecedented altitude of over 60,000 feet (18,300 m). When assigned to several fighter squadrons, '440 made four round-trip crossings of the Atlantic in support of several tactical deployments to Europe. During the aircraft's 21 years of service with over 6,000 flying hours, it flew in combat during five of those years.

Of the few photographs showing '440 while in service with the 3rd Tactical Fighter Wing at Bien Hoa Air Base, South Vietnam, only one clearly shows the earlier location of the serial number and code letters of 'CP' for the 531st Tactical Fighter Squadron. For this reconstruction, two photos were

Although a 'high-time' USAF 'Century Series' fighter, this North American F-100D Super Sabre retired from service in excellent condition. This is a typical Level 2 Condition aircraft that is ready for exhibit without needing restoration except for a change in unit markings to reflect its combat unit of assignment.

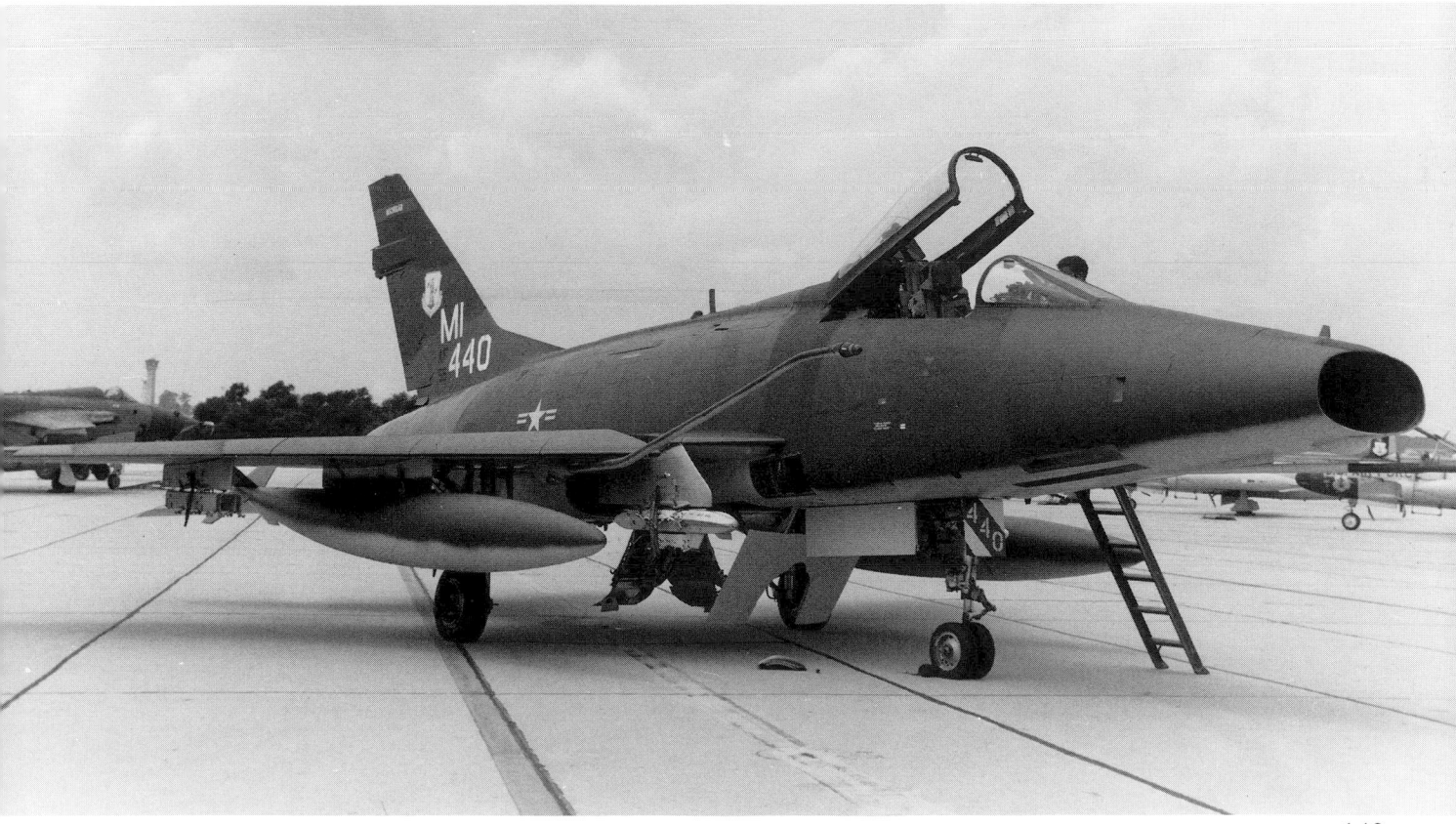

These are the markings on NASM's F-100D when it arrived from the Michigan Air National Guard for the collection of Vietnam service aircraft. The intent is to apply earlier markings worn by this aircraft when serving with 3rd Tactical Fighter Wing at Bien Hoa Air Base.

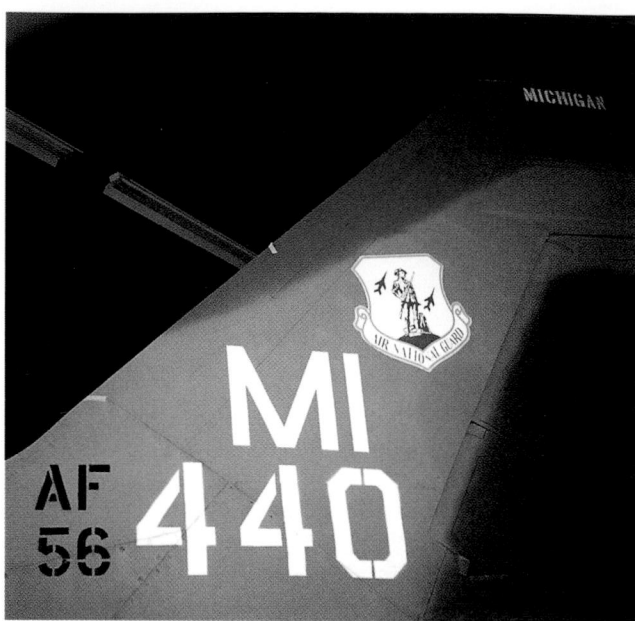

This is a method whereby marking sizes and locations can be verified prior to actual painting. With a photo of the aircraft showing the proposed pattern in place (top), and the markings being duplicated (bottom), extension lines from each photo have been drawn to the right. Dimensions X and Y are common in both pictures as being the height of the rudder. Proportional dividers confirm that the pattern must be raised so that the proportions will match that of the operational photo.

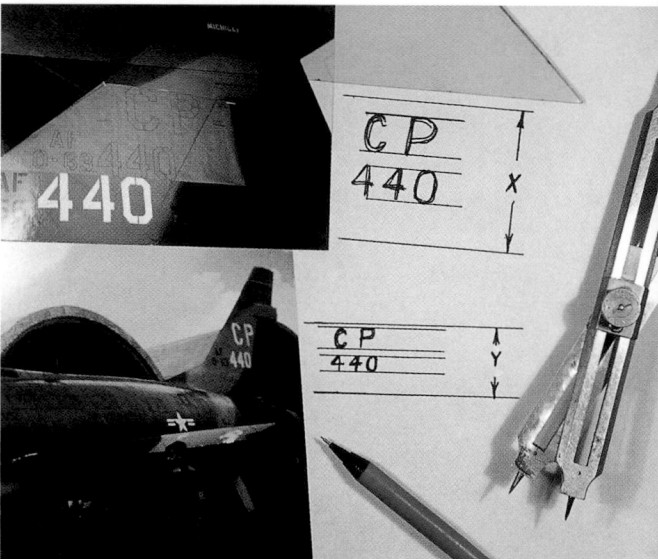

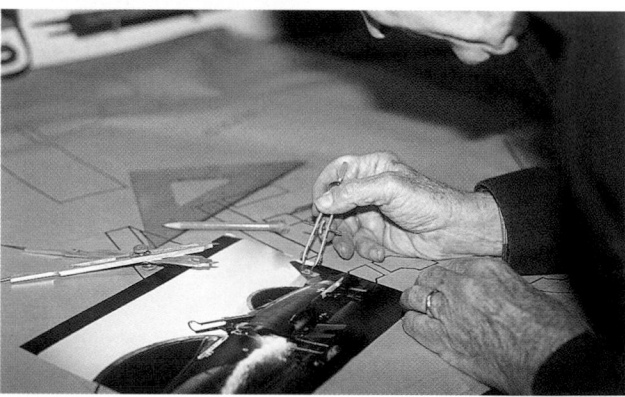

used: one as just described, and the other showing how the tail is presently marked with new patterns overlaid. These two photographs were taped down on the drawing board over paper on which this marking design was to be developed. Extension lines were drawn from these photos in order to work out the proportional sizes of the markings.

One dimension common in both photographs was the easily-measured height of the rudder on the actual airplane, which is 56 inches (142 cm). Extension lines were drawn from each of these photographs at the top and bottom of the rudder, marked X and Y. Now we had a basic proportion from these two photographs which we could use to scale other markings. Projecting parallel extension lines from 'CP' and '440' in the lower picture, we could establish dimensions for positioning by proportions based upon the rudder height. Air Force Technical Order 1-1-4 states that these letters and numbers ('440') for the 1960s time period were 24 inches (61 cm) and 15 inches (38 cm) tall respectively. In this case, the proportions confirmed these dimensions, but be aware of situations where the Technical Order instructions are not always adhered to in actual application.

Up to this point, the top photograph has no relevance but is used to check the accuracy of the pattern once it has been constructed and photographed as shown.

When projecting these extension lines on the top photograph to match those on the lower photograph, we were surprised to find that the '440' that was now on the airplane was not placed in the same loca-

tion as shown in the lower 1960s photograph. These too had to be reconstructed as a pattern and relocated. Again, only through comparison of photographs did this change become apparent. How awkward to be ready to paint — and find that things would not match up because short-cuts had been taken by not pre-planning on paper as just described.

Wrapping paper was laid on the fin and taped in place over the area where the letters and numbers were to be applied. We placed this paper on the same alignment as the existing markings. This was to aid with the pattern position reconstruction. Reference marks were made on the paper showing the boundaries created by the fin leading edge and the rudder cutout. These reference points were marked so that the paper could be returned again to this same position. Now the paper could be removed and taken to a work area.

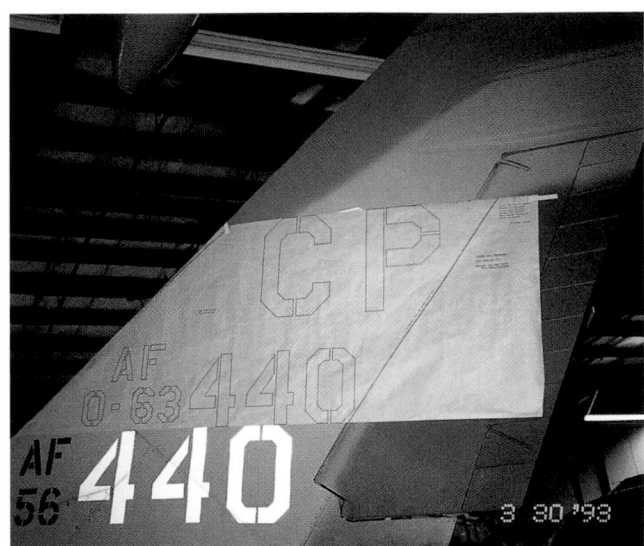

Once the pattern and its location have been confirmed, registration points are recorded so that the pattern can be used at a later time. Note that the current '440' is larger and lower than for the Vietnam markings scheme.

The numbers to be painted on the nose of this F-100D can only be confirmed by placing patterns of standard USAF-size lettering in place. Comparing these patterns with wartime photographs of the same aircraft will determine the correct size and location.

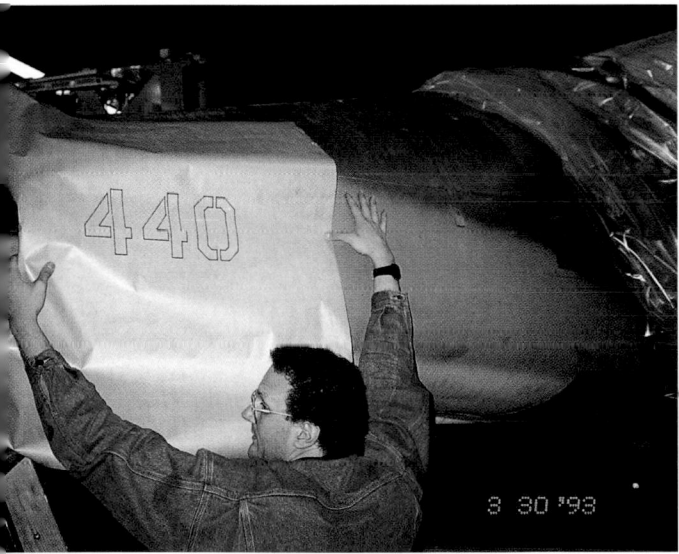

The letters and numbers were then laid out on the wrapping paper. To make the process easier, we first made these figures separately, then placed them on the wrapping paper in the locations that proportions from the exercise described with the lower photograph seemed to dictate.

The finished patterns were then photographed in place on the fin, then the resultant picture taped to the drawing board as shown. The extension lines when drawn showed a disproportionate vertical location of 'CP' and '400' in relationship with the rudder lines X and Y compared to the lower photograph. This was not detectable on sight, but when

seen in a photograph and with extension lines, the error became apparent. This was easy to see because the extension lines were not proportional in the two photographs; but with the use of the proportional dividers we could make an adjustment to the correct dimensions. The painting instructions to be followed for making new tail markings not only contained this full-size pattern of confirmed proportion and design, but accompanying written instructions gave the dimensional location as well.

These two examples point out the need to construct patterns, place and photograph them, and make checks in various ways to assure their accuracy *before* the painting is begun. This accuracy cannot be assured by 'eye-balling' without this check between comparison photographs.

Lockheed XP-80 *Lulu Belle*

Not all markings layouts can be correct according to Technical Order directives without altering history. An example of this occurred when NASM was restoring the Lockheed XP-80. This was the first in a long line of Lockheed fighters ranging from the P-80 Shooting Star and F-94 Starfire to the T-33/TV-2 and T2V-1 jet trainers, a total figure of over 9,000. From this prototype, Lockheed was firmly cemented into the post-war military market.

When tracing the markings that were to be duplicated during the repainting process, it became obvious that the national insignia was constructed improperly in all four locations on the fuselage and wings of the airplane. What seems to be a common mistake is that some painters extend the horizontal bar an equal distance below the horizontal center-

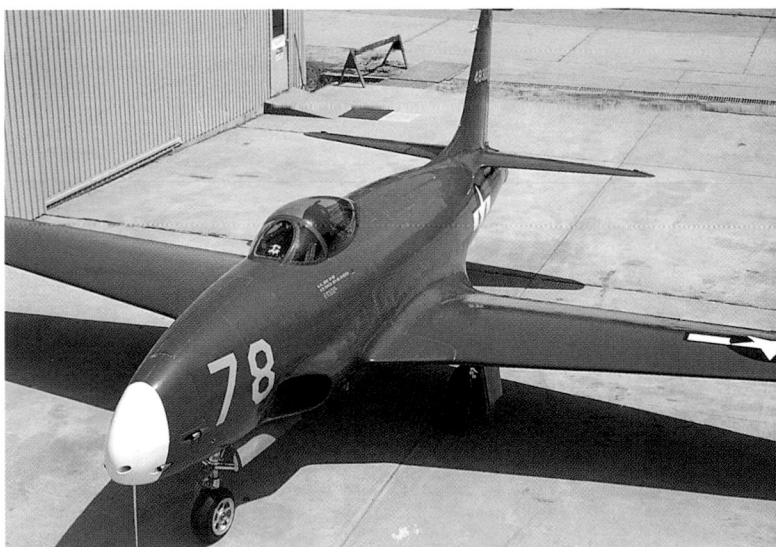

This is the grand-daddy of all the Shooting Star series aircraft, the Lockheed XP-80 that was nicknamed Lulu Belle *and* Green Hornet *during its flight-test period. The airplane was decidedly more green than the standard US Army color used on other aircraft. This is the roll-out picture when newly restored.*

The unrestored XP-80 shows the original but incorrectly constructed national insignia on the side of the fuselage. So as not to alter history during the restoration process, the same inaccuracies have been duplicated. Note how the original green turned to a brick red due to color shift.

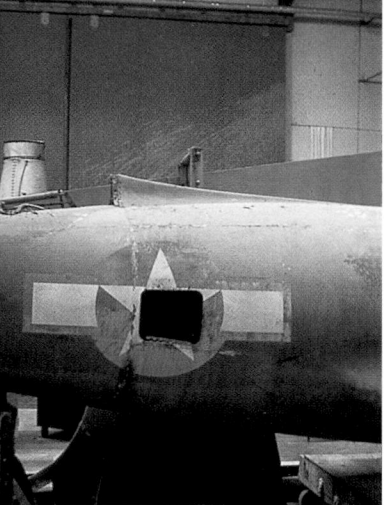 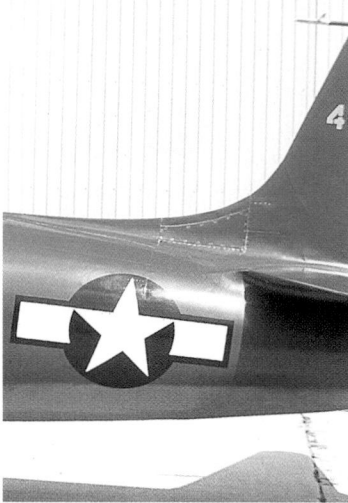

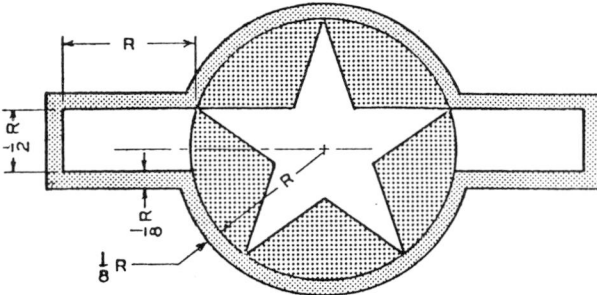

FIGURE 1.

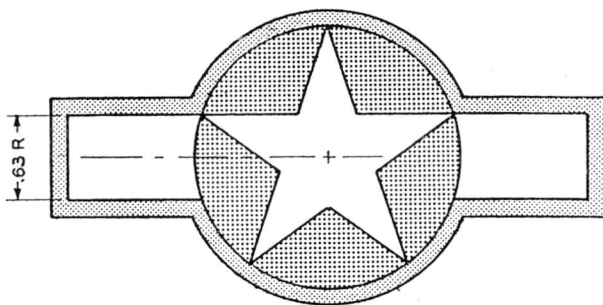

FIGURE 2.

line of the star-circle, instead of one-half the star-circle radius dimension downwards from the top line of the bar which is positioned by the points of the star. The bar is intended to be disproportionally above the centerline.

In this restoration, should the proper insignia have been used, or should it have been left as it was through its operational time period? The answer was obvious — do not change history, so the airplane rests on exhibit in NASM still wearing an improperly designed national insignia.

The restoration of the XP-80 brought about another interesting color problem. This airplane had been disassembled around 1950 and crated when the bulk of NASM's collection was moved from Park Ridge, Illinois, to the Silver Hill facility. When the time came to open its crates for the planned restoration in 1976, the airplane was not green as it was during its operational service life, but almost a salmon pink. There was hardly a trace of green remaining.

This was another example of color shift, like the red we spoke of earlier on the P-51C. Green camouflage aircraft like this and the P-38J Lightning also in NASM's collection, which were manufactured on the west coast, had a tendency to turn to this reddish brick tint. Conversely, examples from the east coast areas from different paint manufacturers normally remained more stable; the Martin B-26B Marauder *Flak Bait* is a good example. While this statement describes generalities, it also points out how inconsistent paints can be with regards to color shifts.

An interesting point came to light when preparing to paint XP-80 *Lulu Belle*. The airplane also had the nickname *Green Hornet* which signified

US NATIONAL INSIGNIA: The correct proportions for laying out the insignia are shown in Fig. 1. The most common error is to construct the height of the bar to be symmetrical with the centerline of the circle as in Fig. 2. Later insignia have both the border and field for the star in insignia blue, yet the construction format remains the same.

something unique or significant about its color. When questioning those who worked with this airplane, all confirmed that it had been decidedly green and not the US Army's standard olive drab. Investigating further, I was able to talk directly with the retired painter who had had the overnight task of having to paint the airplane to meet the next day's flying schedule. Tired from a long day of production-line painting of RAF Lockheed Hudsons, the painter and his crew merely moved their painting equipment containing that day's production paint to the Lockheed *Skunk Works* and painted the test aircraft. What they used was RAF green from the RAF sand and green shadow camouflage scheme. With that information it made the task a simple matter to copy that color for this restoration.

At the Fly-Ins

While attending a major fly-in one year, instead of admiring the restorations done with precision and making the usual record on film, I paid closer attention to those with improper markings. The photographs on the following pages show some of these inaccuracies.

What was it that brought about these strange combinations? Did the owner wish to create a montage collection of markings that represented the span of his military career on a single airplane? Or was it that the owner liked the colors and design and 'went for it?' Whatever the case, the owners were not shy about showing up with their unusual markings on airplanes having very high price tags before the markings spree.

A number of Piper J-3 Cubs appeared at this particular prestigious event. All were of the correct Cub Yellow (if there are any other choices of yellow), yet no two had the same — or correct — fuselage lightning stripe that matched the original factory application.

An example of incorrect markings is this Aeronca Champion that showed up at a major fly-in. Oddly, it had camouflage with a post-war (1947) national insignia and D-Day (1944) invasion stripes on the wing.

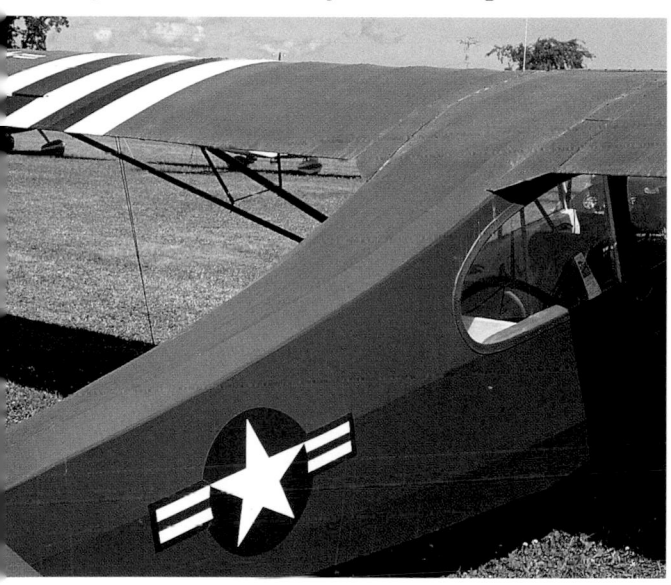

Marking errors become very distracting on otherwise well-restored aircraft. Great effort was put into this North American T-28 Trojan restoration, only to be marred by orange being used instead of red in the South Vietnamese Air Force insignia.

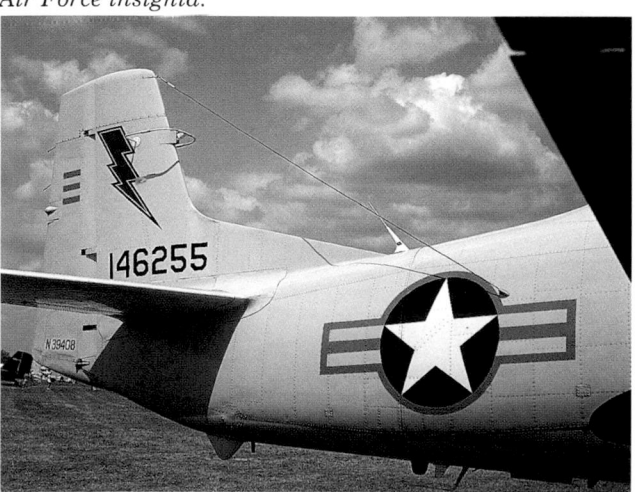

Check this modern interpretation of the US national insignia against the graphic which shows the correct proportions for its construction. This was an obviously intended stylization for this Taylorcraft L-2.

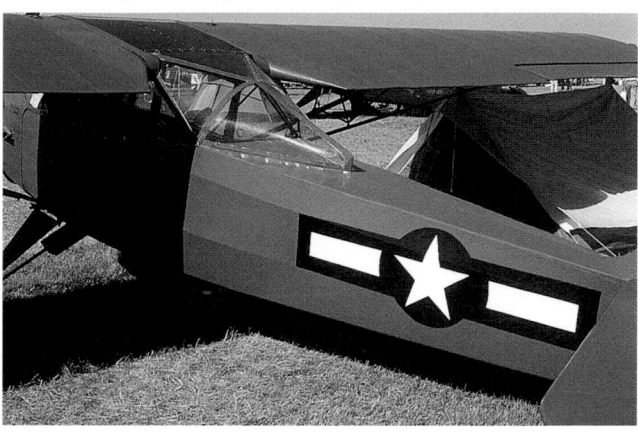

This mix of insignia conveys a lot of originality on the part of the owner. The wing insignia, although undersized is correctly constructed. So was that of the fuselage until the oversized bar was added, even extending above the point of the star. The US Coast Guard tail stripes are correctly constructed, but not appropriate for an Aeronca L-3. The blue field at the top of the rudder is undersized.

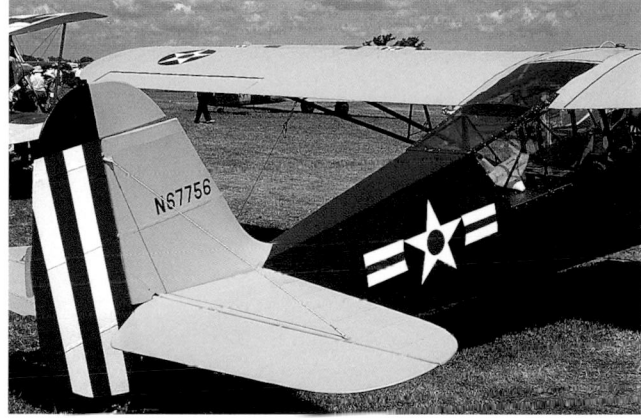

The best of two time periods is shown here with this Piper L-4. This wartime fuselage insignia was no longer used after June 1943; but it was not until 1947 that the USAF became a separate service and often applied their service name on their aircraft in the fashion shown here.

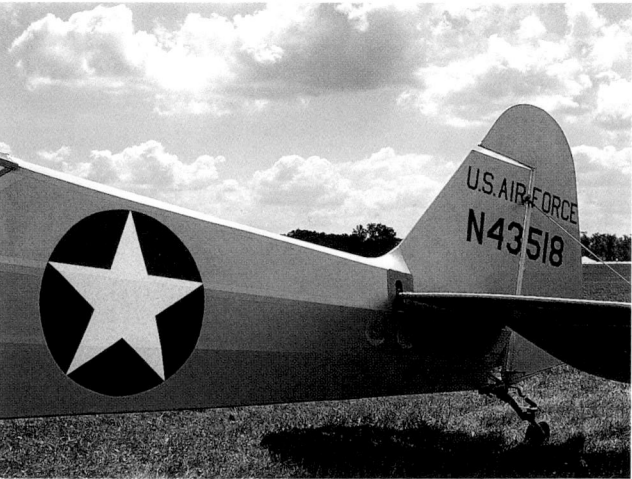

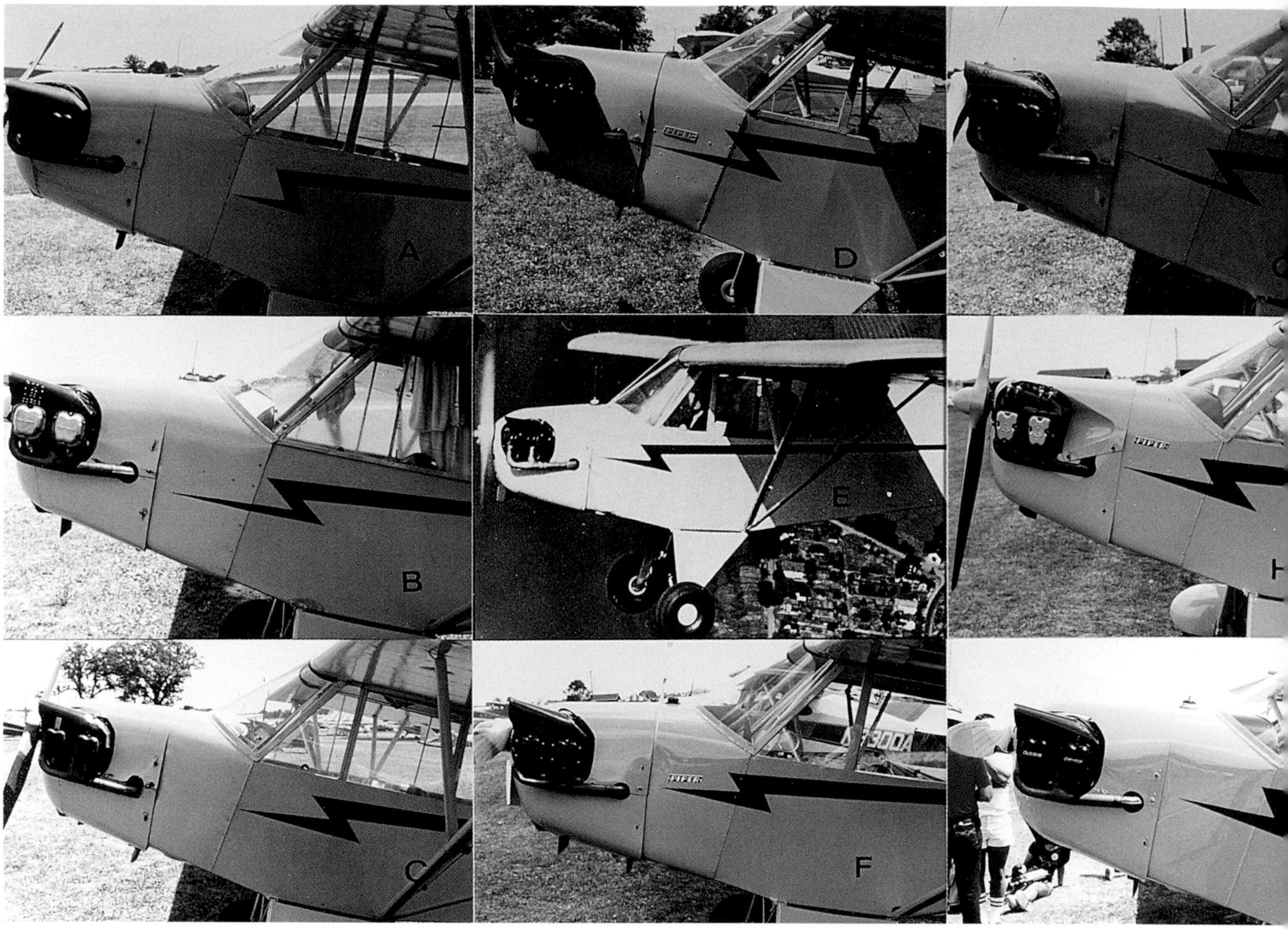

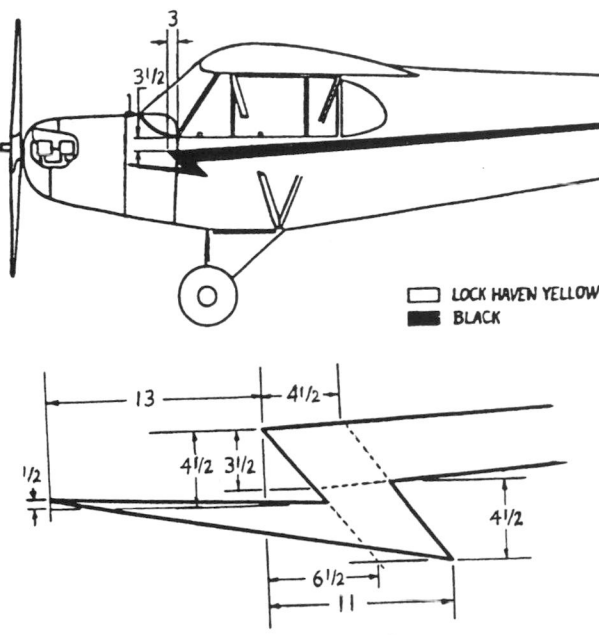

Piper J-3 Cub fuselage lightning stripes came in all styles at this fly-in, no two alike, yet there is only one correct factory format. The factory photograph in the center shows the correct lightning stripe.

☐ LOCK HAVEN YELLOW
■ BLACK

Factory-designed fuselage stripe for the Piper J-3 Cub.

Reversible Painting and Markings

Disturbing the existing original finish on part of the airplane is sometimes not advisable. Often these finishes or markings are regarded as historical and original material, possibly so because a famous person applied them. While being considered significant, their appearance may not be considered suitable for exhibit purposes. Here are two actual situations that have occurred at the National Air and Space Museum:

1. When restoring the Wright Flyer engine in 1985, we found it had an adequate coating of original black paint that had been applied by Orville Wright in 1927, but was now dull and chipped. Surrounded by a new white fabric covering of the airplane and renewed wood finish, the drab appearance of this engine would have seemed out of place.

2. The name painted on the B-29 *Enola Gay* was still in the original paint which had been given a fresh coat a few days after the historic bombing of Hiroshima. Chipped, scratched and worn thin with age and recent metal surface polishing, the name lettering needed to be repainted to restore it to original condition.

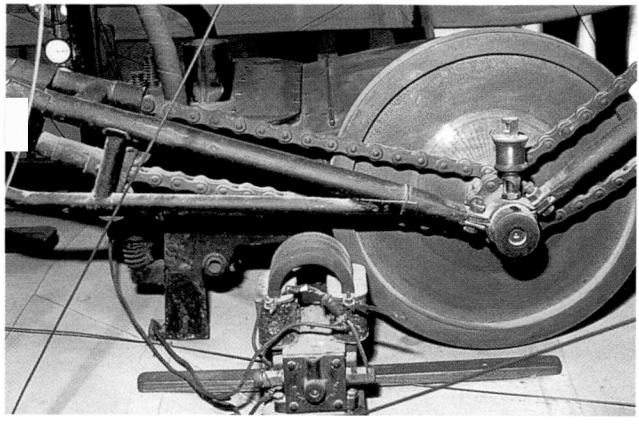

Original appearance need not be lost because of a restoration. The Wright brothers' engine exhibited on the Wright Flyer at NASM was in good condition except for the accumulation of dirt. Once its parts were cleaned and reassembled, the original paint applied by Orville Wright was kept intact.

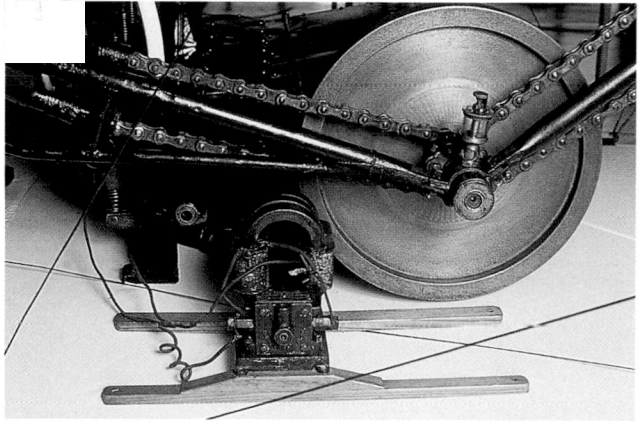

After reassembly of the Wright Flyer engine with its cleaned parts, it was given two coats of microcrystalline wax as a protective film. This allowed the original paint to remain, and presented a rejuvenated appearance that blends with the rest of the aircraft as a National treasure should appear.

To have painted over these surfaces in either situation would have ended possible access to the original paint for any future study or exposure. The solution in both of these situations was to apply a barrier coating of microcrystalline wax over the earlier paint. Once applied, a new coating of paint, such as a complete covering of the Wright Flyer engine, and new lettering over the old deteriorated letters of the name *Enola Gay*, provided the desired appearance. This process is reversible by merely directing a heat gun to the painted surface to warm and soften the wax undercoating. With a wad of cloth, the outer surface can be simply wiped away as thin membranes of paint, thus revealing unharmed the original painted surfaces and markings. Tests show that this does not alter the color of paint with the minor exception of the clear protective coating of wax that remains.[53]

The B-29 Enola Gay *carried historic markings relevant to its combat. The name alone identifies this to viewers as the airplane that dropped the first atomic bomb. Its wartime missions were marked with four black and one red* Fat Man *symbols on its nose, all heavily chipped at the start of this restoration.*

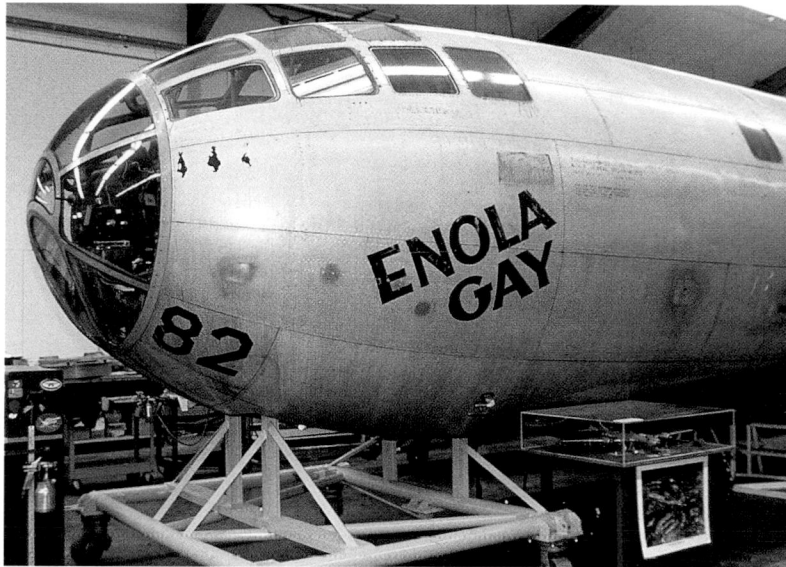

NASM uses Petrolite™ BE SQUARE 185 Hard Microcrystalline Wax that has a melting point of 195°F (90°C). The wax is prepared by first melting it to soften it, then mixing it with denatured alcohol to a light paste consistency. Two coats of wax are applied, being buffed in only one direction after each application to a smooth, hard surface. This one-direction buffing is an essential process for this type of wax so that it does not remain porous. The surface is then ready to be sprayed or brush-coated with either enamel or lacquer.

An interesting point to note is that lacquer could be applied over an enameled surface without the enamel being disturbed because of this wax barrier. Both types of coatings have adherence to the wax, and only when the surface paint has been broken would it readily peel away. Openings like this that may occur can easily be repaired by touch-up paint over the wax.

Of the two types of finish, the enamel is the easiest to remove because it is stronger and comes off in larger pieces than lacquer. We tried removing this outer layer with hot water as well as with swabs dipped in petroleum spirit with a high boiling point. Seemingly, the aluminum surface dissipated the heat too rapidly from these liquids and therefore heating the wax by these methods was unsatisfactory. Summer heat or sun should not affect this work since the wax has a melting point of 195°F (90°C).

While in actual practice microcrystalline wax has worked well as a suitable barrier for safe removal of an outer coating of paint, other separators may work equally as well or better.

Two-for-One

When restoring NASM's Boeing 247D twin-engine transport for the Transportation Gallery there were two sets of markings to choose from which had been applied to the one historic aircraft. For this gallery, the transport markings that were original for this aircraft as the 'first modern all-metal transport plane', were appropriate. However, this airplane was much more significant than a mere transport since it was also used in the MacRobertson London-to-Melbourne Race in 1934, and this should not be overlooked by exhibit requirements. Flown by Colonel Roscoe Turner and Clyde Pangborn, it had come in third in that race, quite a feat for a transport aircraft in an air race.

Knowing that this aircraft was to be positioned with the right side facing visitors, the decision was made to paint on the right side the original transport markings, and the racing markings on the left side, which was facing away from the general viewing of the transport gallery. No mix of markings can be seen from any one angle, and thus, the airplane represents both of the two most significant historic aspects of its operational service.

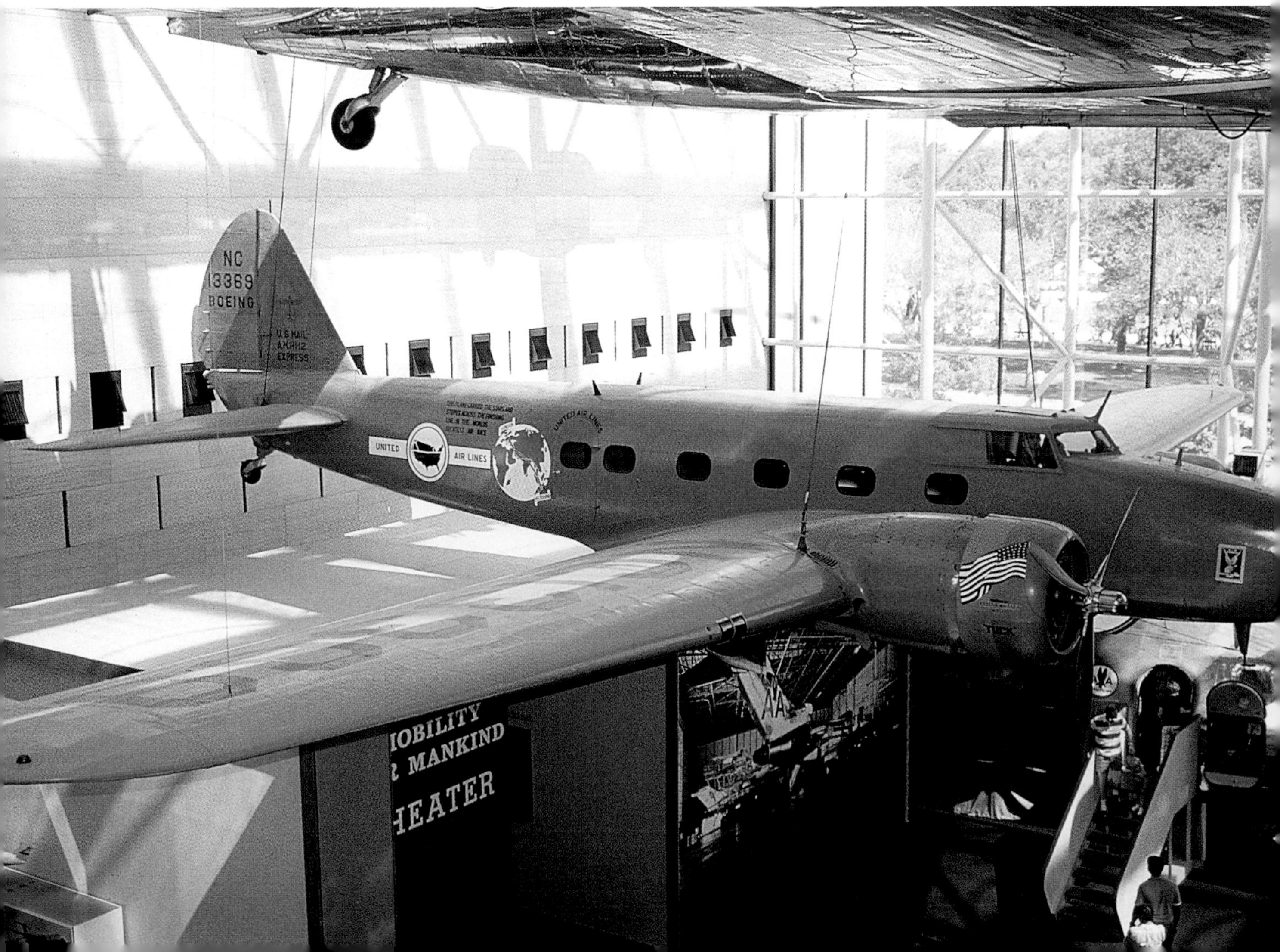

This Boeing 247D airliner at NASM was historic in more ways than one. As a type, it is referred to as the 'first modern airliner' and carries United Air Line markings on the right side as it had while in service with that company. It is displayed here in the Air Transport Gallery.

As an airliner, NASM's Boeing 247D also made history as a racing entry in the MacRobertson London-Melbourne Race in 1934, taking third place against aircraft designed for racing. As such, on its left side, not detracting from the air transport theme when viewed from the right, it has reproductions of its race markings used during that event.

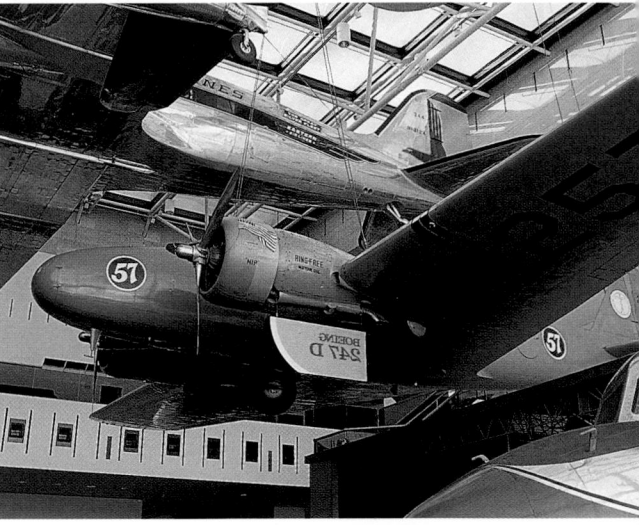

The same holds true with military aircraft of the Vietnam War period. In NASM's collection the Lockheed C-130A Hercules and the Douglas A-1H Skyraider not only served USAF units but Vietnamese Air Force (VNAF) squadrons as well. Since both air forces used the same camouflage colors and patterns, the plan now stands that one side of each will have its wartime USAF unit markings, while the other side will have VNAF unit markings, further documenting the actual operational combat history of these airplanes.

The P-51C *Excalibur III* would be good as a two-for-one painting candidate, having two distinct and important histories. Not only was this a two-time winner of the Bendix races and other race-setting records, but as *Excalibur III* in the same red finish this was Charlie Blair's mount when he flew from Norway to Alaska across the North Pole. This event that confirmed the feasibility of sun line navigation in polar regions where magnetic compasses are not reliable won for Blair the Harmon International Trophy in 1952. Had NASM acquired this airplane on their own, such a double-painting would have been appropriate; however, as a donation to NASM from Blair and Pan American Airways for the sole purpose of commemorating the polar flight, common courtesy and museum ethics prevailed in keeping the airplane in the one marking scheme.

All distinguishing markings had been painted out, yet careful paint removal brought out its serial number, 135332. Through this Bureau of Aeronautics number, its US Navy and USAF operational service could be traced. The 'FFA' uncovered on the tail confirmed service with the 514th Fighter Squadron of the South Vietnamese Air Force based at Bien Hoa Air Base. All markings were traced for future reference.

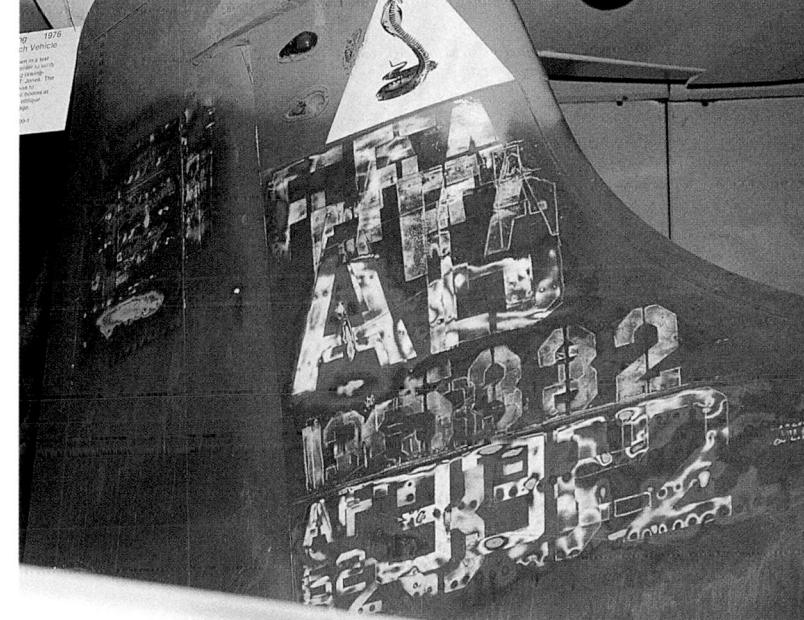

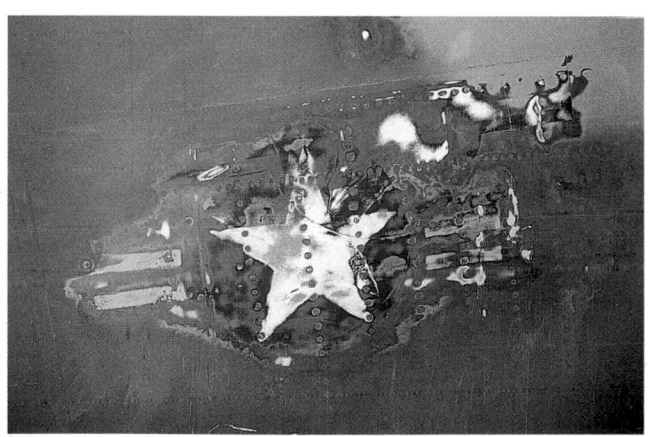

When the time comes to restore this Douglas A-1H Skyraider belonging to NASM, much of its history and marking details will have already been uncovered. Sanding through the layers of paint, the newly-discovered national insignia confirms that it once flew with the South Vietnamese Air Force.

This photo-engraved metal plate is the type used to iden-tify museum property by accession number, and to permanently record vital information about an aircraft. This placard pertains to the Douglas DWC-2 World Cruiser Chicago that belongs to NASM.

NATIONAL AIR AND SPACE MUSEUM
SMITHSONIAN INSTITUTION

DOUGLAS DWC #2 "CHICAGO"

Built by: The Douglas Company
          Santa Monica, Calif.
Manufactured: 3 March 1924
Manufacturer No.: 146
Air Service No.:   23–1230
Engine: Liberty 12, Model A
          By Ford Motor Co.
          Mfg. No. 1911
Accession No.: NAM 74
Catalog No.:   1925–8
Restored: 1973

First Aircraft to fly around the world.
   6 April to 28 September 1924.
28,000 statute miles, 175 days, 371.11 flying
   hours.

With the crash of the original flagship "Seattle"
   in Alaska, this aircraft crewed by
   Lt. Lowell Smith and Lt. Leslie P. Arnold
   became the flagship for the remainder of
   the flight.

Transferred to National Air Museum from
   U.S. War Department 11 December 1925.

CHAPTER 10
Finishing Up

This will not be the most popular chapter in the book, because it addresses the effort of keeping the records of the restoration, and that means dreaded 'paperwork.' But all the hard work just completed is more than worthy of making the effort to properly prepare documentation that will preserve this part of the aircraft's history. Most of the writing should already be done, so this is just a wrap-up of the final elements.

Mini Record

Since this book deals with museum airplanes, there will be an established accession system for accountability of museum objects. If not already in place, that identifying mark (Museum Accession or Catalogue Number) is probably attached to each artifact, and so should be attached to the airplane in a permanent, yet inconspicuous location.

Such a marking system was established in the 1970s at NASM and is known as the Mini Record. This is a metal placard, generally 3 x 4 inches (7.62 x 10 cm), similar in appearance to those often found in aircraft: black face with natural metal lettering. The data they contain is photo-engraved into the metal so that in the event of fire, there would be some chance that these identifying placards could survive where a painted or less hearty material might not. These plates are generally riveted in the vicinity of the cockpit or pilot seat so as not to be conspicuous, particularly from the outside.

These unobtrusive placards carry considerable information about the aircraft's identity for historical documentation. Generally, the information consists of the following:

Owning agency (museum name)
Aircraft nomenclature
Aircraft Identification numbers
Builder or manufacturer and date
Engine type and serial number(s)
Museum Accession (and/or Catalog) Number

Date received
Donor or source
Date restored (and other pertinent details)
Significance to the collection. (If this is a Category III aircraft, the significance of markings now applied and any changes to the structure should be described.)

The content and format varies with each aircraft because each has its own unique set of circumstances. In the case of NASM's Me 262A, for example, all through its restoration no trace of an identifying *Werk Nummer* could be found. All identifying placards had been souvenired after capture in its early life. To have left this conspicuous number off the tail would have been an incomplete marking condition. A fictitious serial was arrived at by picking one from a set of numbers assigned to

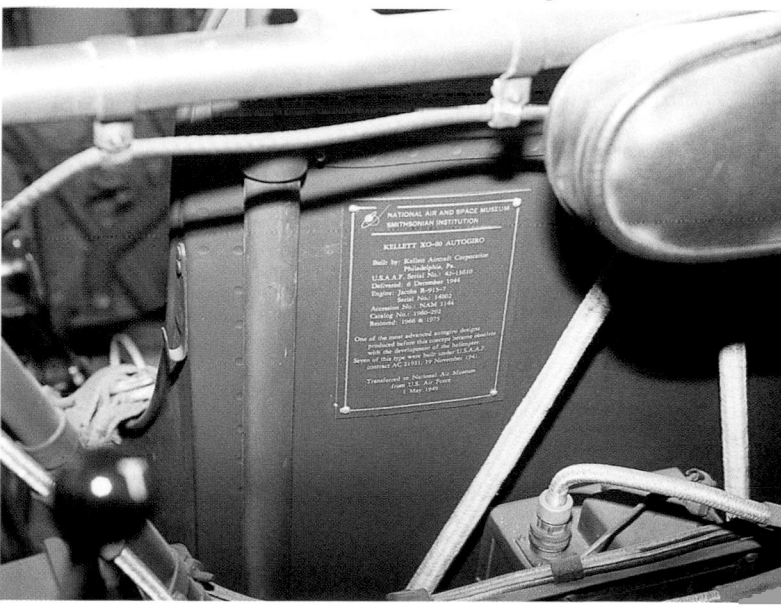

Metal-identifying placards, sometimes referred to as Mini-Records at NASM, are permanently attached to the aircraft in the general vicinity of the pilot's seat. This is particularly true with newly- restored aircraft. Shown here is the placard for the Bf 109G-6 / R3.

this model of Me 262. In the Mini Record, it states that the *Werk Nummer* is 'unknown,' then in the remarks the circumstances of the painted serial are explained.

In another case, the Hawker Hurricane currently being restored at NASM was used almost exclusively at a flying school, yet its purpose for being in the National Aeronautical Collection is to be representative of an RAF operational fighter. Because of the serial numbering system within the RAF, if it were marked with its assigned alpha-numeric serial, yet camouflaged as an aircraft in an operational unit, its identification would be out of context. Consequently, a correct type alpha-numeric serial will be selected that is suitable to the unit markings. On this permanent Mini Record, however, the true serial number will appear with an explanation for the exterior difference. This permanent form of identity attached to the aircraft avoids factual confusion. This is particularly important for properly identifying Category III museum aircraft (generic) so that colors and markings will not be taken to be authentic for that specific aircraft.

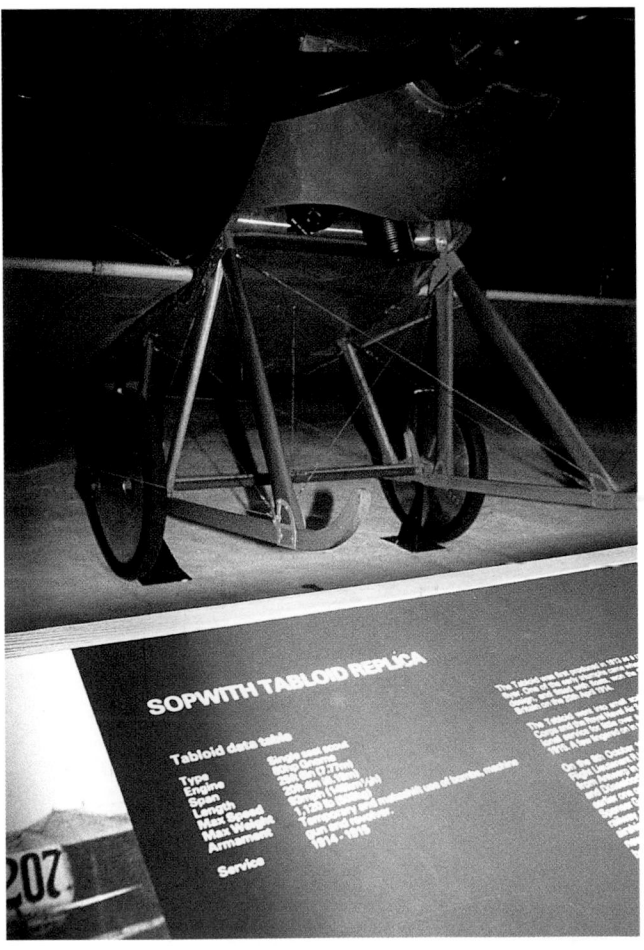

Museum staffs should not expect visitors to distinguish on their own what are original aircraft and what might be look-alikes. This aircraft label in the RAF Museum at Hendon, England clearly identifies this Sopwith Tabloid as a Replica.

Truth in Labeling

Museums may contain a wide range of aircraft categories within their exhibit areas. These can be original aircraft, reproductions, replicas, look-alikes, mock-ups and mock-ups *containing original parts* (if less that 50 per cent of the original structure (see Glossary). These identifying categories of each aircraft should be pointed out in the exhibit label and not left to speculation by the visitor. This is equally important for Category III aircraft when exhibited in markings that are not original to this aircraft, as discussed in Chapter 2. The significance of what the markings selected for this airplane represent should be explained. Builders of replica and reproduction aircraft should be recognized in labels.

Concluding Check-List

To conclude the documentation that is so necessary, here is a list of items that are deserving of attention:

1. Primary File: This is the general file containing the work contract, Curatorial Guidelines, correspondence, sub-contracts if any (along with relevant reports that were called for in contracts), brand names of material used, purchase records, photographs (other than for Item 4 below), etc.
2. Concluding Curatorial Report: This is very important and must be written now. It records various points that do not appear elsewhere, e.g. assembly and disassembly pointers, list of items still needing to be acquired, vendors involved for possible future purchases, summaries of man-hours, costs, start and stop dates, etc. This is the main document that will be referred to for all follow-on action. (See sample report in Appendix C).
3. Shop Activity Logs: Package as a separate identifiable file.
4. Progress Photographs: Organize for file as an appendage to the Activity Logs.
5. Periodic Reports: Place these chronologically as a separate file to serve as a summary of the project.
6. Drawings: This may be an oversize file containing structural drawings acquired, patterns prepared, and other outsize items.
7. Sort remaining aircraft parts from the project into what to keep for historical and technological purposes and what to dispose of. Tag for identification those items to be saved.
8. Consider a second set of new tires mounted on wheels for this aircraft, these to be stored in proper tire storage for future use.

Publish the Knowledge Gained

After all the work put into a restoration and the

major and minor discoveries that have been made, the knowledge gained must be preserved. There is no way that this can effectively be done without publishing it. If left unpublished, then all the careful analysis and determination of previous markings and history, etc., simply sits in a folder somewhere; and where might that be in 100 years? That irreplaceable knowledge can be lost in a small fire or a well-meaning 'I'll take this file home with me for the evening,' and it becomes lost forever. Even if these notes are preserved, they may not be legible or readable to someone 200 years from now, especially after the notes have been shuffled and pages lost. If the restoration is worth doing well, it is worth describing in one of the major aviation magazines or in a special publication. In this way the information is not only disseminated, but preserved.[54]

A number of museum aircraft restorations have been documented very nicely in this regard. One popular series of publications is *Famous Aircraft of the National Air and Space Museum*. The intent in 1978 was to prepare such coverage on each aircraft as it was restored. Unfortunately the series has become dormant after the publication of nine volumes. Articles that detail NASM restorations have also been published in *Wings, Airpower, World War I Aero*, and other periodicals.

Another, more recent example of this type of docu-

mentation comes from the National Aviation Museum in Ottawa, Canada. Their first publication in a series called *Profiles in Aeronautical History* pertains to the Curtiss HS flying boats and details their restoration and the knowledge gained from working with these craft.

These are a few examples of completing the aircraft restoration through documentation so that others can share in the knowledge gained.

Smithsonian Quality

Having restored the airplane to the best of everyone's ability, there is the enjoyment of admiring the quality of the work that has been labored on for months and years. The crowning compliment is the one that comes from a respected admirer of the project who pronounces that the work is 'Smithsonian Quality!' This is certainly intended to be the highest of complimentary comments.

But what defines Smithsonian Quality? Seemingly this has never been adequately described, yet we so often hear the term. Wishing to have the phrase defined when it comes to its use in relation to aircraft, what Smithsonian authority would one go to for the answer? Seemingly the senior curator for aircraft would be the logical person. Oddly, when asking this question myself, I was the senior curator at NASM of the Smithsonian Institution. The buck had to stop with me. Therefore, here is what I regard 'Smithsonian Quality' to be:

An aircraft that is as complete as possible with original, or original type of parts in every detail, not only externally, but internal systems, particularly

Aircraft need not just be 'beautiful' to be classed as Smithsonian Quality. An aircraft justly deserving of the title must be of original parts to the greatest extent possible, stable in preservation, and accurate in detailing among other things. This Grumman G-21 Goose is a good candidate for such a description.

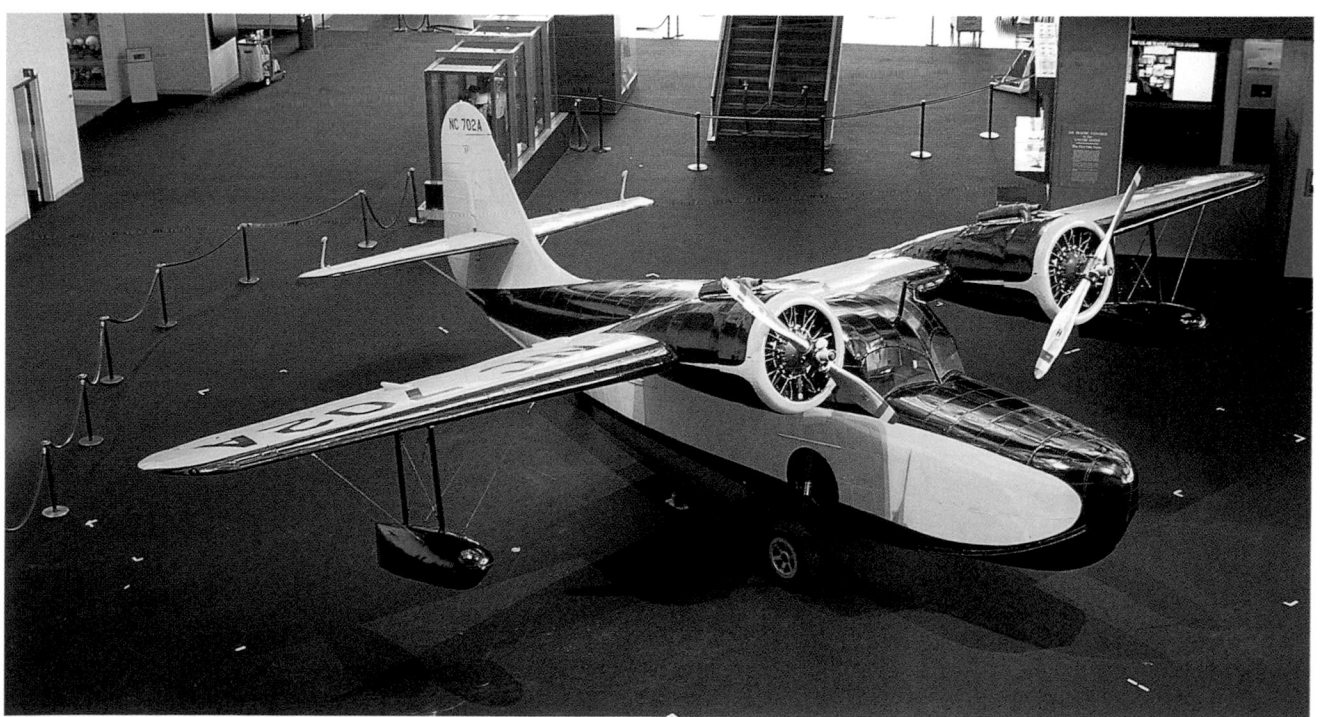

in the cockpit and passenger areas. The structure and the engine(s) have been properly and thoroughly treated to extend their life indefinitely in a museum environment. Colors used are matched to original specifications or color evidence. Fabrics are of a reasonable match or appearance to the original in textures, weave and designs. If a person knowledgeable of the subject has determined that little else is possible to achieve completeness and perfection in craftsmanship is apparent with the artifact, that is 'Smithsonian Quality.'

This judgement need not be limited to only Smithsonian staff with this qualifying technical and judgmental knowledge. This judgement could be expressed by anyone who understands the limits to which the object in question can be elevated for the purpose of attaining the elements of perfection just described. A number of aircraft meet this standard in museums throughout the world, not just certain examples within the Smithsonian's collection. When this perfection is not achieved, the fault often lies in replacing with new parts the old materials that could be repaired, preserved and retained within the structure as original; often not achievable with airworthy aircraft because of safety and durability concerns. Systems and cockpit detailing may not be complete as originally built to properly

document the technologies once found within this aircraft. Often the aircraft is improperly marked or of an odd paint color or texture. Too frequently, dirt or corrosion is ignored, leaving parts of the structure in an unstable condition.

In the final analysis, it is you as the restorer of your project who can best step back and make an honest judgement of your effort. Only you know of the detrimental shortcuts taken, or the extra effort that you went to when working on various parts that will help prolong the life of the aircraft. You will know that if by chance it is *you* who returns for judgement of your work after 300 or more years, what rating you might be given for your efforts! If you have that inner feeling of having accomplished near perfection, then no one need tell you that you have reached the ultimate by achieving 'Smithsonian Quality.' (But then, what real craftsman will admit to his own perfection?)

The interiors of Smithsonian Quality aircraft must be complete in as much detail as possible. Since this Grumman G-21 Goose restoration was a Category III aircraft made from many disassociated parts, it was configured to represent an early twin-engine corporate or executive transport of the late 1930s. Fabrics and appointments shown here bring out these details.

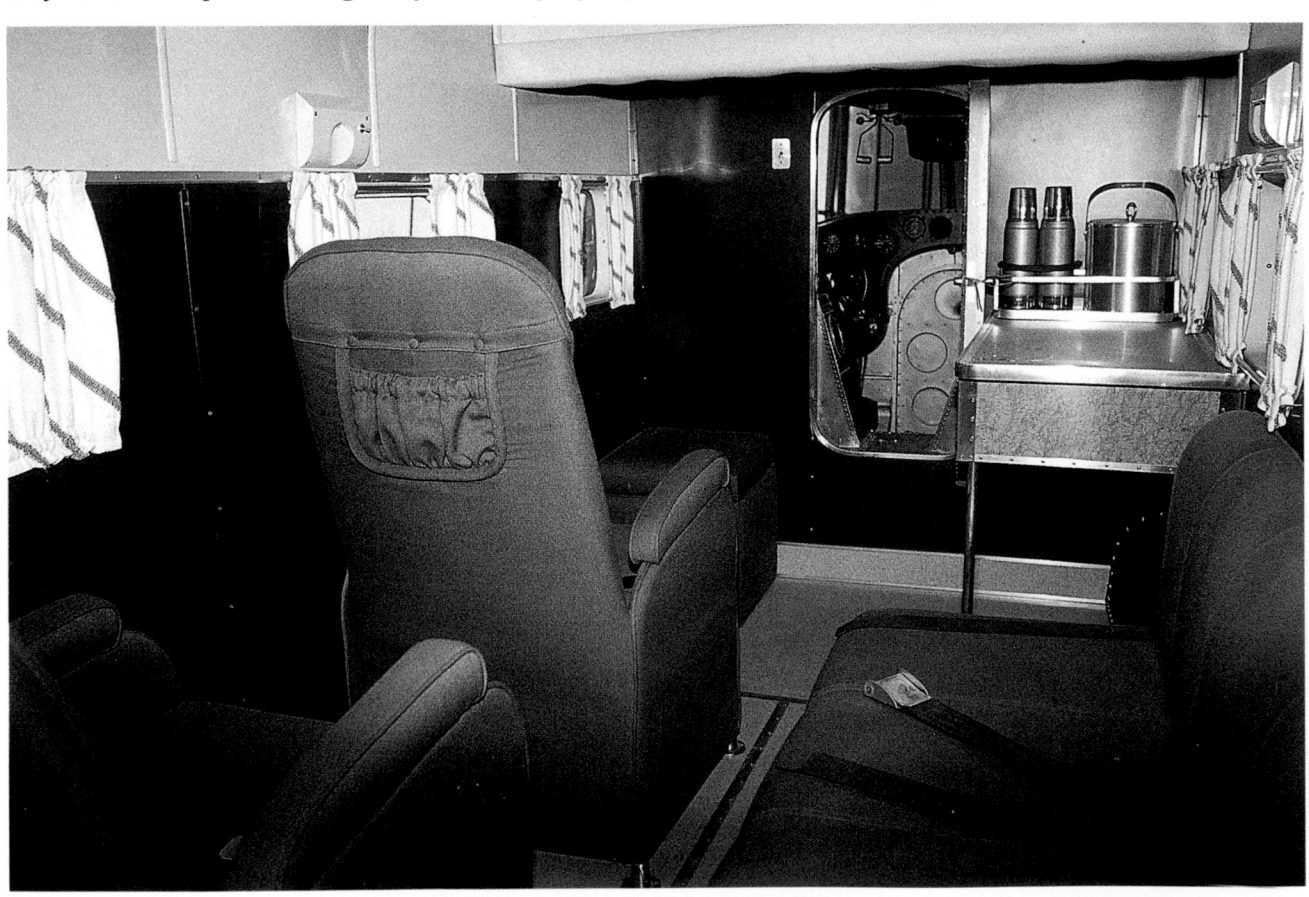

CHAPTER 11
Contracting the Project

Sometimes it becomes necessary or appropriate to have an aircraft or engine restoration done outside the museum. I have always had mixed feelings about doing this for fear of losing day-to-day curatorial contact with the project. It would be like a structural architect having to oversee his building being constructed in a distant city.

Fortunately, I was never confronted with having a Category I or II (historical or technical one-of-a-kind) aircraft restored outside NASM. My fear has always been that something could appear to be of little consequence to those unfamiliar with museum-type restorations, yet when seen by a curator it could be recognized as having historical importance. Unusual discoveries of any kind, if recognized, are just as important when found on Category III aircraft as well.

Advantages and Disadvantages
There are obvious advantages to having a restoration accomplished by an outside contractor. The museum's shop will always have a backlog of work, be it full restorations or maintenance of aircraft already in the collection and on exhibit. Having the restoration done elsewhere is one way to avoid consuming museum shop resources.

The quality of work expected from an outside contracting shop may be different from what they are actually capable of doing. Good intentions may be there, but it is often very hard to visualize that shop's actual capabilities. The shop being considered should be visited well in advance of final decision-making. Examples of earlier restorations produced by the shop in question must be looked at, and judged whether or not to be acceptable for what is expected for your project. Naturally this judgement is made with the assurance that the same technicians will do the proposed work. Being sure that the contractor can and will do the job that is expected is a major risk. One person must accept that responsibility.

When I reviewed restorations done at distant locations, the quality of work and my satisfaction were directly proportional to the degree of communication between me and the shop supervisor. When I did not hear from the project for a long time, I knew we were in trouble. The supervisor was answering questions his way and moving on rather than taking time to discuss it with me first. This is not to propose micro-managing, but rather to review only those aspects of the restoration that really should have a curatorial input and are not already covered in the guidelines. After all, the museum that owns the aircraft is the customer, the agency that needs to be satisfied.

The Contract
When a restoration to be done outside your museum is being considered, professionalism begins with the way the project is handled. Be up front with a signed contract that protects both parties. It places on paper exactly what both parties expect from one another. Its psychological effect is the commitment towards doing the job in a professional manner. The sound of a legal instrument such as a binding contract has some frightening undertones. Adherence to the contract is easier for some than having to consider the preparation of the contract. A sample contract that has stood the test of time for aircraft restorations is included in Appendix D. This can be copied, names of both the contractor and museum inserted in the spaces provided, and executed without the need of a lawyer, if both parties agree.

Never send an aircraft or engine out for restoration without clear written instructions, namely Curatorial Guidelines. Without these, what the contractor thinks the museum wants can be far from what is expected by the museum. Museum standards come in many different forms. Clearly-defined instructions must be identified as an attachment to the contract when executing the contract. Without it, there is no common ground upon which to agree the amount of work expected and the

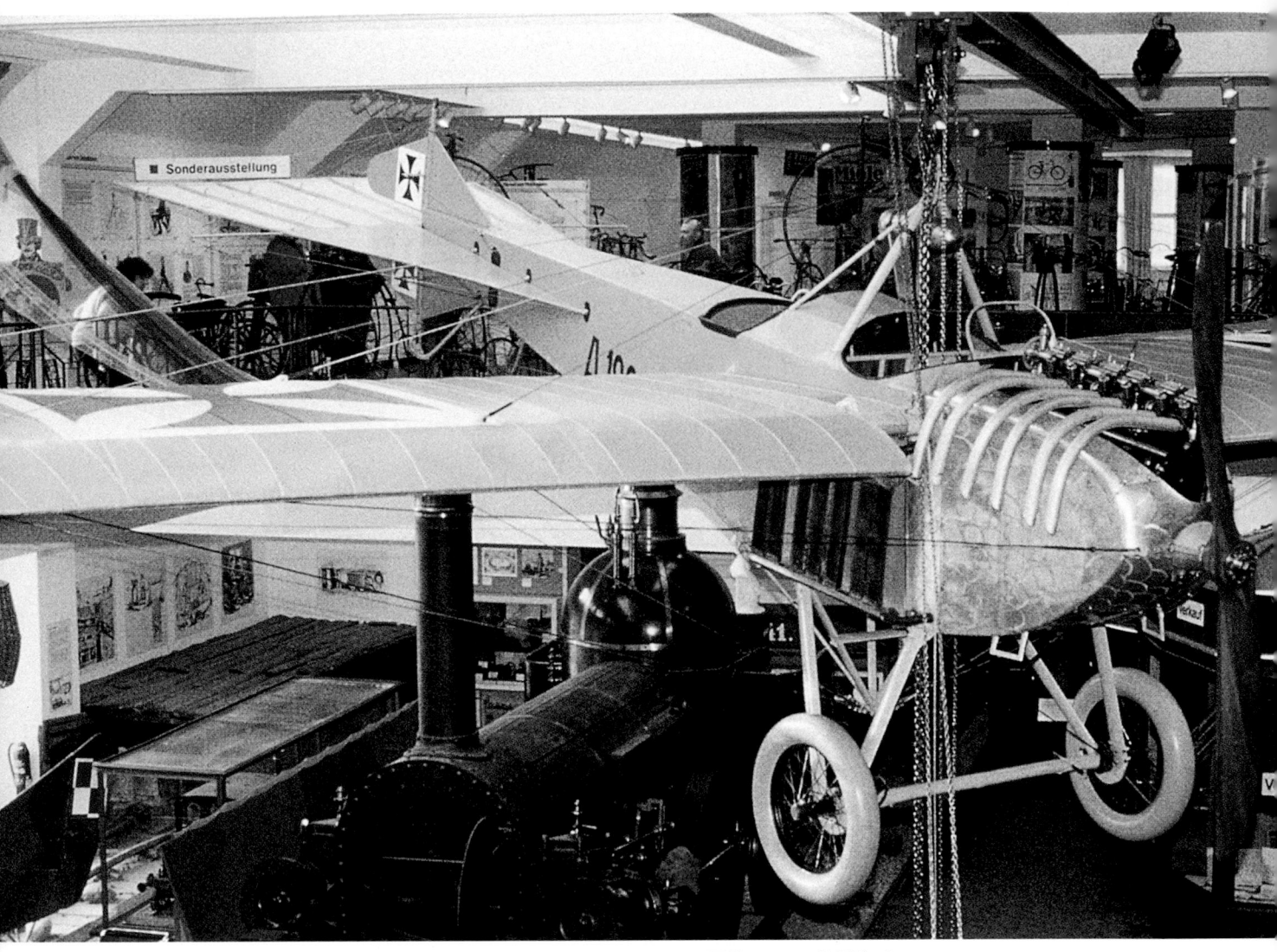

This is the Jeannin Stahltaube restored and displayed at the Museum für Verkehr und Technik in Berlin. This proof of the excellent workmanship by technicians still on the staff brought further contracts to undertake restorations for other discerning museums.

results to be achieved.

In Chapter 2 we discussed time estimation of man-hours and material costs in planning a project (see also Appendix E). It is with these figures that the contractor can evaluate his capability of being able to comply with the time allowed and quality of work expected. The prospective contractor should have plenty of time to read the contract and the Curatorial Guidelines and know what the museum expects. When the aircraft has been moved to the contractor's site is no time to re-evaluate the magnitude and complexity of the work that had not been evident beforehand.

Make it clear in the contract as to disposition of unused parts. If not stipulated, they may be found being sold on the street as souvenirs of the restored aircraft. Wisely, everything should be recovered.

Planned Visits

Aside from assurances that the contractor can do the job to the *quality* and *standard* expected by the museum — (think about that for another moment, are you sure?) — provisions must be worked out ahead of time for curatorial visits. Depending upon the distance the curator must travel to the restoration project, these visits can be costly, and who is going to pay for them? The best solution would be for them to become part of the contract. Usually the project has a sponsor with a given cash amount within which these trips can be budgeted.

Two curatorial visits a week to the curator's own restoration shop are not too frequent. When extended distance becomes a factor, the perspective must change. As frugal as one may try to be, four curatorial visits as an absolute minimum for an average project have worked out for me in the past.

The first visit should be soon after the aircraft is in the shop and the technicians are becoming familiar with the project and related parts. Questions abound at this point. The resulting guidance given by the curator sets the pattern of quality for the technicians.

The second visit would be at about the one-third mark, a time when the structure is still fairly well open and an assessment can be made of the interior and stability measures taken. For metal airplanes, this is before the skin is riveted in final closing, and for fabric-covered aircraft, before the new fabric is put in place.

The third visit should be when major elements are going together and the project is beginning to take the shape of an airplane. The final visit is when the end is in sight, maybe a month away. The airplane at this time is complete enough that you can point out closing details that you want accomplished to complete the project. This also allows time for making corrections or adjustments that will not affect the anticipated concluding date of the project.

Depending upon the magnitude of the project, time spent during these visits can vary from two to four days with each visit. These visits can either be an orientation tour of their facility (perhaps a 'smoke screen') conducted by the restoration team — if the curator will allow — or it can be one of mutual involvement, the latter being preferred. An agenda prepared by the restoration team leader before the curatorial visit takes place will make the most of limited time. Prepared questions from the team leader will focus attention on details needing clarification and the granting of approval for work methods ahead, rather than to only be shown 'the outstanding work being done!' The curator should have prepared questions in hand as well. During the first visit, for instance, a review of the Curatorial Guidelines will bring up points that need further discussion and clarification of what you as the curator expect.

Strangely, I would always come away from these visits with a longer list of things to do in support of the project, than the list I went in with. The questions are usually technical in nature, and require research when returning home. Checking on a part serial number to see if it is original equipment for this type of aircraft; asking for a color sample from within the cockpit of another museum's aircraft of the same type; comparing fabric samples from which to make the best choice (lab tests might be required); preparing graphics for having missing placards or decals made. Generally all little things, yet they require weeks of personal attention by the curator in order to have a restoration as complete as possible.

Some curators may be tempted to send an assistant or colleague on one of these visits. After all, some of these are exotic locations where the work is being done. This is foolishness, however, if the goals of these visits are to be achieved. It is like having a different doctor each visit to look in on your progress after major surgery. The working relationship between the contractor and curator is such that each depends upon the other for personal and professional support to reach a successful conclusion.

Another factor regarding these visits has other effects. Your presence as curator sends a message that the work that the shop is doing is important, if only because you have taken the time to be there. It is called 'showing the flag.' But the sincerity of the visit is an important factor, showing that the museum you represent is interested; in return, a top-notch restoration job will normally evolve. Direct involvement with the project by the curator during — as well as after — the visit is essential, otherwise one's presence might be viewed as a 'boon-doggle' trip!

A concluding thought in this regard is a review of something quite the opposite. I have seen aircraft sent to contractors, and for various reasons the museum representatives never looked at the airplanes again until the projects were ended. In every case, the results turned out to be unsatisfactory, leaving many disappointments, particularly in the area of preservation for longevity of the aircraft. Since the finished work now looks good on the outside, this brings about a reluctance on the part of the customer to go beneath the paint and do the neglected cleaning and corrosion control that the paint has covered up. Curatorial visits to these restoration sites would have caught these problems in time to be corrected.

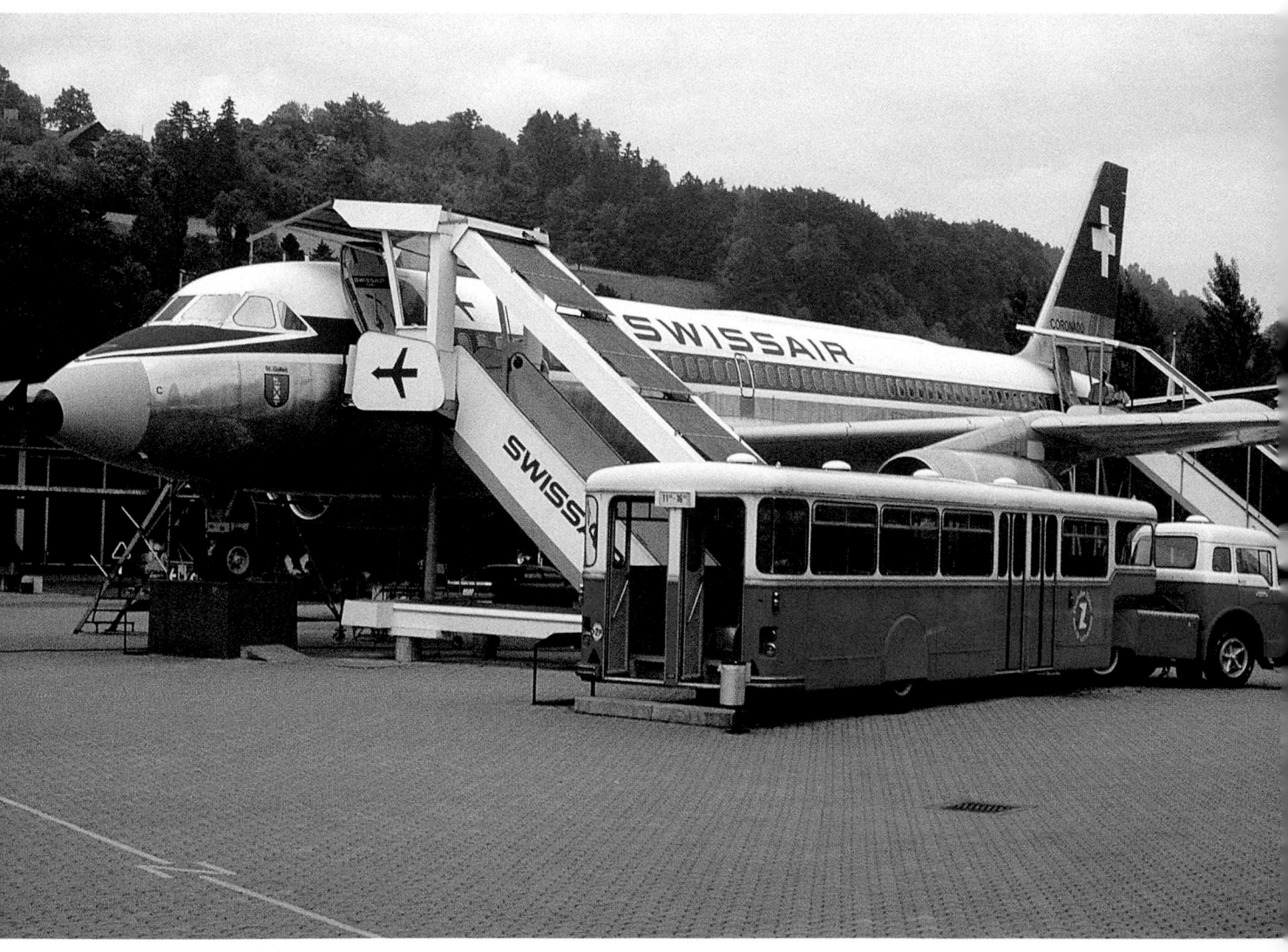

The Swiss Transport Museum's Convair 990A Coronado is a model example of an aircraft exhibited outdoors. It was planned from the beginning with as much care as a permanent structure. The passenger-handling vehicle is part of the exhibit.

CHAPTER 12
Preparing Unsheltered Exhibit Aircraft

Few air museums have the luxury of being able to exhibit all their aircraft indoors in environmentally-controlled conditions. However, subjecting an aircraft to the elements need not spell its early demise if proper means of preservation are undertaken.

To collect and display selected aircraft is the purpose of air museums in the first place. However, the disadvantages of exhibiting them outdoors become overwhelming if the best interests of the aircraft are not realistically planned for in advance. Recognizing and facing the problems at the very beginning, before accepting an aircraft, are often obscured by the allure and excitement of acquiring the magnificent airplane that is being offered or sought. Within a few short years, the wisdom of having accepted such a large aircraft that is beyond the capability of the museum staff and volunteers to maintain is often questioned. As a result, they must watch the elements overtake and produce a shabby, rust-streaked aircraft exterior that has anything but a pleasing and inviting appearance. Such an airplane soon becomes a liability to the museum, not an asset.

There are solutions, if the problems are properly addressed in a methodical, well-planned program for each aircraft. The cost can be high and much time can be consumed, and this must be recognized early. Airplanes have never been inexpensive, including those that cost the museum nothing to acquire. So often it is not the initial cost that must be considered, even when the airplane is free, but the continual upkeep required to maintain and support it. One measure of the professionalism and maturity of a museum is how this difficult problem is managed.

Perhaps only portions of the plan described here can be managed by most museums, but at least this description will address the issues to be considered. Four distinct phases can be addressed separately in aircraft planning considerations: the **acceptance transactions, aircraft moving, exhibit positioning**, and **recurring maintenance**. If each of these major phases is adequately dealt with, the airplane and the museum have a chance of a long and pleasant relationship.

The Preparation

One museum that has attained near perfection in outdoor preservation of several aircraft is the Verkehrshaus der Schweiz (Swiss Transport Museum) in Luzern. The museum first acquired a Convair 990A Coronado from Swissair in 1975 and moved it to the museum grounds. It was placed in the courtyard of the museum, and even today it looks as new as the day it arrived. The years of exposure to the country's extreme seasonal temperatures and conditions show little effect because of proper care. The air in Luzern has a high content of carbon and sulfur dioxides and nitrogen oxide, combined with high and low humidities depending upon the time of year and wind direction.

Despite these problems, the museum intended to have the airplane in an open environment, flanked by some of the support equipment associated with passenger transports, as aircraft of this size are seen. Had they elected to house this airplane in a building, it would not have blended in well with the other buildings or the openness they desired. One can wonder, however, which avenue — outdoor maintenance costs or building costs — would have been the least expensive to follow. Based upon the experience gained by the Swiss Transport Museum, here are some factors and guidance to consider before acquiring an airplane for outdoor exhibit.

The acceptance transaction is always the first issue to be considered, but perhaps it is not always addressed with the museum's best interests in perspective. If the airplane in question is an air transport being acquired directly from a major airline, the problems can be less cumbersome than if it is accepted after several users. Nevertheless, the benefits of enlisting the help of an airline that once used the type as an active and supportive

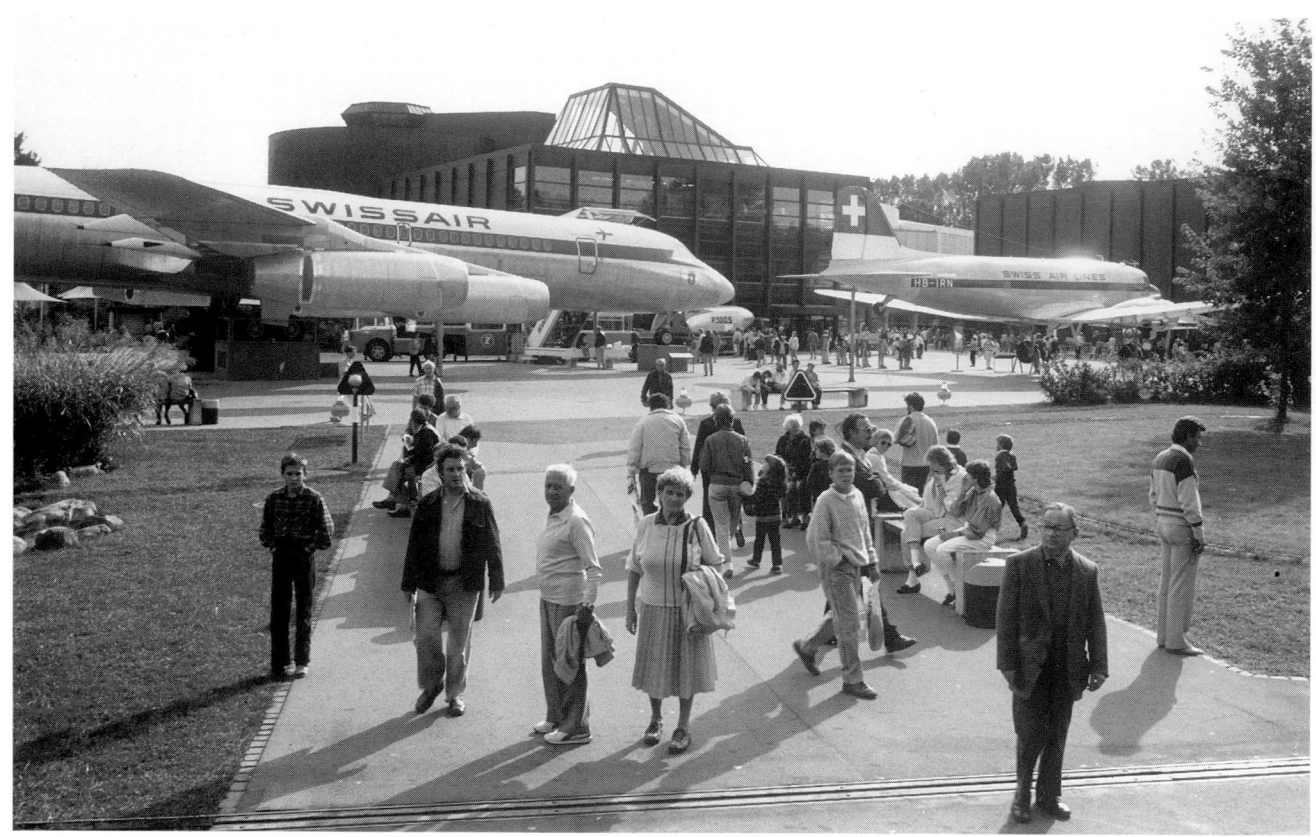

sponsor, should be recognized by both the sponsoring company and the museum. In the case of the Coronado, this airplane represents Swissair, the flag-carrier of Switzerland. The company was proud of this airplane and its service, and now it has high visibility in the company colors and the bold name on its fuselage that is seen by countless visitors to the museum.

It is essential to work out mutual agreements with the sponsoring company early in the acceptance phase. Preparation and maintenance support can most efficiently be done by the company rather than by the museum staff, always limited in number. During this early pre-acceptance phase, try to work out a written agreement concerning periodic support that the company will give to the airplane and the museum. Identify recurring work to be performed by the company. Set a time limit for this support, such as five years. This would be much easier for the company's management to accept than an open-ended agreement. If the museum exhibits this aircraft in that company's markings, a satisfied company would probably renew its agreement rather than see the airplane deteriorate with its name on it.

Whenever possible, enlist the help of the airline's maintenance facility to prepare the airplane before it is delivered to the museum. The importance of this was not recognized until after the Coronado was in place at the Swiss Transport Museum. It then became the responsibility of the airline tech-

A proud and active sponsor of the museum's Coronado, Swissair provides the material and manpower needed to maintain the aircraft as a shining symbol of the airline.

nicians to accomplish the entire project in the open while working out of tool-boxes at the museum location. It was estimated that 60 per cent of the preparation work could have been done at Swissair's maintenance facility under much easier, and less costly, conditions.

The airline's maintenance facility is the best place to check for, and to remove, corrosion. This is a must in any case in order to enhance the life expectancy of the airplane, a task which the maintenance facility is well-equipped to accomplish. Replacement with worn parts just because this airplane will not fly after its ferry flight is a false economy. Worn parts will not last as long, so false savings have been defeated. The airplane should be delivered in first-class condition, as the airline wishes it to represent its company.

The interior can be brought up to exhibit standards and configuration while at the maintenance facility. This is important if museum visitors are to be permitted to enter the cabin, especially since this is an important feature in the preservation of air transports. While some museums have resorted to placing Plexiglass walls along the aisle to keep visitors away from seats, this portrays an unnatural and more confining interior. Much depends upon the museum's location and its visitors, but a more aesthetically pleasing method is to have heavy clear

The air-conditioned passenger cabin is an integral part of the Coronado exhibit. Visitors enter from the front of the cabin and exit to the rear. Clear covers of 0.5mm PVC sheeting and rope barriers along the arm rests protect the seats.

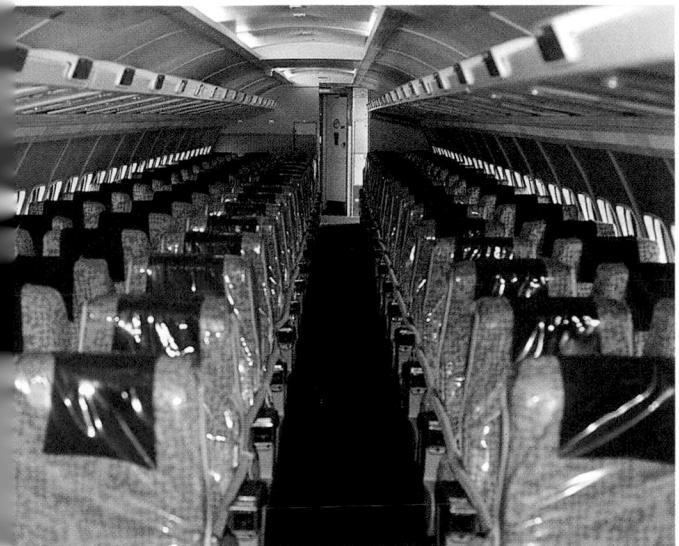

PVC sheeting for the seat covers along the aisle to protect them from hands as visitors move through the cabin. These protective covers will not last indefinitely, so a continuing source of replacements must be available. The need for other work to be done at the maintenance facility will become evident, depending upon the aircraft type.

Exhibit Placement

The next phase, **aircraft moving**, will be a problem that can only be addressed on an individual basis, but **exhibit placement** needs considerable pre-planning. A major reason for the Swiss Transport Museum's continuing success in preserving outdoor-exhibited aircraft is that ground support equipment is close at hand and has been dedicated to supporting these aircraft. Not visible to visitors is an underground room below the Coronado, hidden beneath the surface of the exhibit grounds. An air-conditioner with a 500 m³/hr capacity is in this well-lit and -ventilated basement. The outlet for this unit is connected unobtrusively to the airplane at the normal connecting point for a ground equipment air-conditioning unit. This

permanent installation maintains the aircraft cabin between 65-69°F (18-20°C.)

This feature not only makes it pleasant for visitors walking through the museum aircraft, especially on a hot summer day, but is important for other reasons as well. During the hours that the cabin doors are closed and airflow is restricted, more of the exhausted air is forced through the structural parts of the airplane, e.g. wings and fuel systems, cabin wall interiors, lower fuselage cargo compartment, empennage, etc. With the Coronado, the fuel purge-and-dump system is used to direct low-humidity air through the fuel cells and wing structure. Openings were made through closed parts of the structure to allow this gentle passage of air to take place. As a result, daily condensation and damaging moisture is prevented from collecting at all points of the structure's interior by the flow of cool dry air.

Also contained in the basement below the aircraft is a heavy-duty air compressor. When maintenance

The secret to the Coronado's successful preservation is the underground utility room located beneath the airplane. It contains an air conditioner for cooling and drying the aircraft interior and an air compressor for maintenance work.

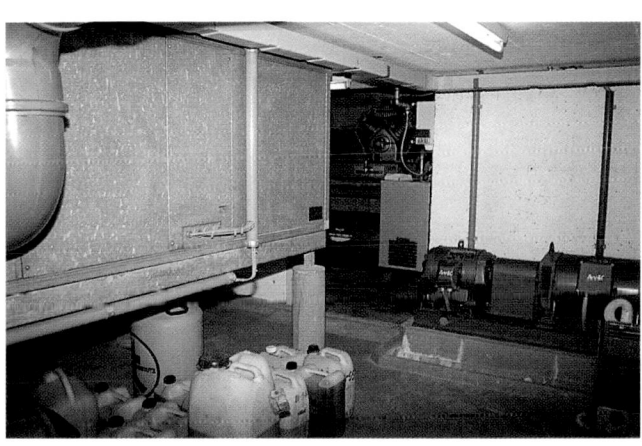

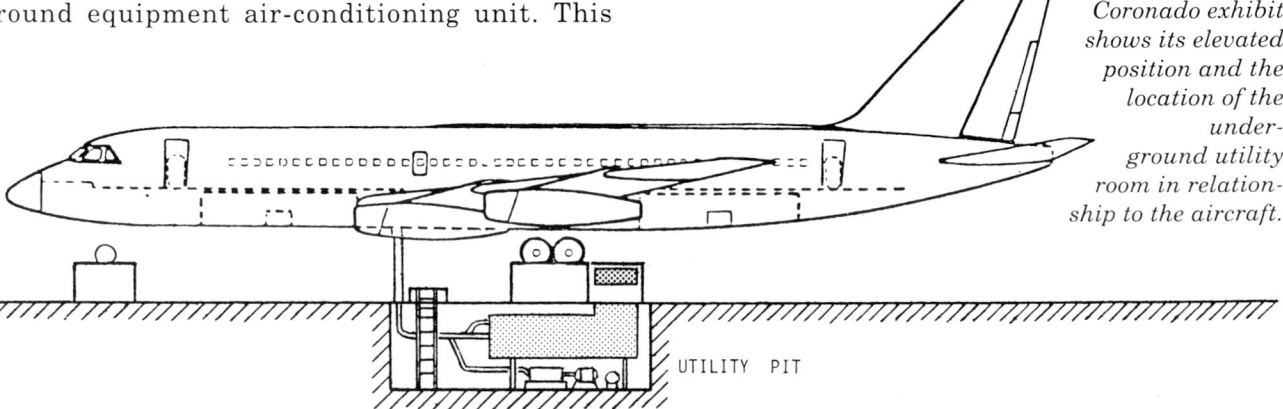

Profile of the Coronado exhibit shows its elevated position and the location of the underground utility room in relationship to the aircraft.

UTILITY PIT

work requires compressed air, which is often needed with any aircraft, the source is readily available. Concealed in this way, the resounding noise that the air compressor generates is muffled and not offensive to museum visitors, and is certainly less tiring for technicians working on the aircraft.

While considering these major expense items for the well-being of the airplane, a water line to the aircraft site should be included. An airplane needs its exterior washed frequently to keep it in exhibitable condition; therefore, the convenience of available water should be addressed early in the planning phase.

Where and how to locate the airplane is more of an exhibit's design function, but other factors should be considered as well. When making this selection, the airplane should be looked upon as a permanent fixture. Placement of the underground support equipment for an aircraft, for example, is a major consideration. This might be determined by the direction of strong prevailing winds. Pointing the nose into the wind is normal when positioning aircraft, but if wind is not a factor, consider the direction of sun exposure. Sunlight has a damaging effect upon the outside finish of an aircraft, and will affect one side more than the other. The angle at which the aircraft will generally be viewed by visitors may dictate some inflexibility in positioning.

How an aircraft rests on its landing gear needs special attention. When viewed at the distances outdoor exhibits can provide, an airplane does not look right if the landing gear strut travel has bottomed out, or worse, if one or more tires are flat. As with all exhibit aircraft, here again the need is

Since tires for the Coronado are relatively easy to come by, the aircraft rests on its wheels for added realism. Landing gear jacks could have been used to support the airplane's weight and enhance tire life. The cleanliness seen here is indicative of the way the entire aircraft is maintained.

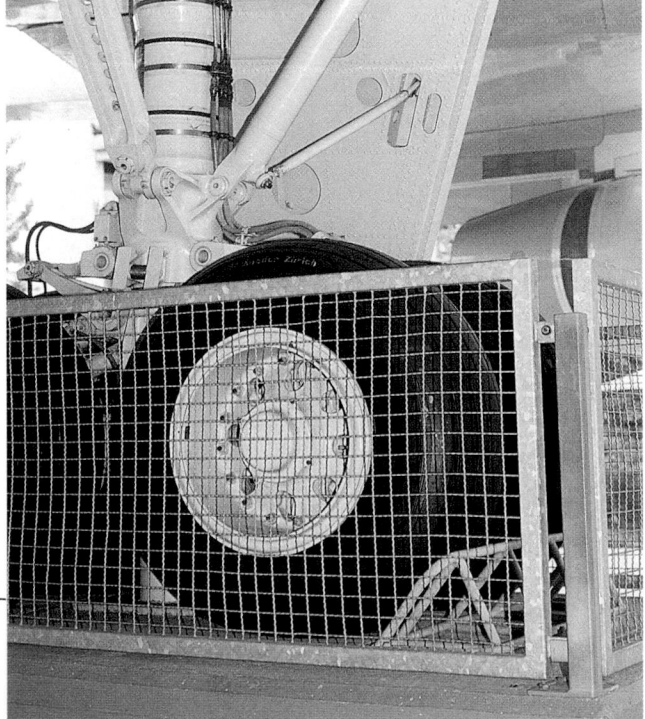

for an internal strut-spacer for proper extension and a beefy landing gear ground support to take the aircraft weight off the tires. If done well, these supports may also serve as anchors for the aircraft, avoiding the ugliness of tie-down cables.

Recurring Maintenance

With the airplane established on the museum grounds, the **recurring maintenance** phase begins with the preparation of the exterior to endure the rigors of outdoor exposure in the years ahead. Again, the technicians of Swissair are to be complimented for mastering the many problems encountered. Following their plan, once the airplane was initially prepared, a periodic process of working on certain areas of the aircraft surface in greatest need of attention began. The side facing the sun requires the most repeated attention.

For the Coronado, Max Widmer from the Swissair Technical Department has taken this recurring project as all but a personal undertaking. It shows in his workmanship. Each spring, at the end of Switzerland's winter snow, Widmer and an assistant depart the airline's maintenance facility in Zürich for a 10-15-week stay at Luzern. Their time is devoted to accomplishing many things that would have been best accomplished originally at the maintenance facility and, more visibly, working on areas of the aircraft needing painting or repairs. What they cannot accomplish in this time must be left until the following year. Nevertheless, this ongoing maintenance program is rigorously followed, and the excellent condition of the Coronado shows this.

Max Widmer can recite from memory a simple and logical checklist for these functions:

1. Clean by generally washing the airplane.
2. Remove any corrosion.
3. Paint inside surfaces with primer (at NASM, a clear coating is used on visible areas if not painted originally by the factory) and paint outside surfaces with appropriate color.
4. Apply corrosion prevention material on the inside of the structure.
5. Clear all cracks and crevices that are not securely filled, and seal all skin line seams on the top and sides of the structure, leaving lower seams open.
6. Ventilate structure where possible.
7. Inspect from time to time and prevent damage before it occurs.
8. Repair as needed.

Understanding most of these steps is rather straightforward, but some need further explanation. The Coronado is washed twice a year, in the spring and fall. Natural rain will not handle the

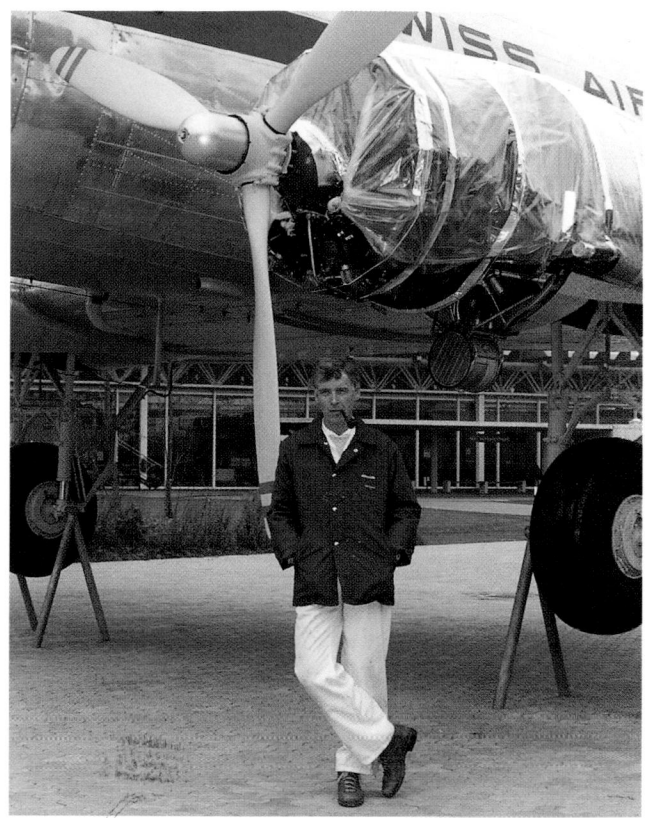

Swissair's Max Widmer (facing camera) is the master-mind and overseer of the preservation of the DC-3 (foreground) and Coronado. Aided by one or more assistants, he spends 12-15 weeks each spring performing routine maintenance on the two aircraft.

Sealing material (black caulking) is used to fill seams to prevent water from seeping into the Coronado. Steel screws in this engine pylon have been cleaned of rust and coated with putty-like material for a tight, waterproof seal. Aluminum tape covers large gaps and access panels.

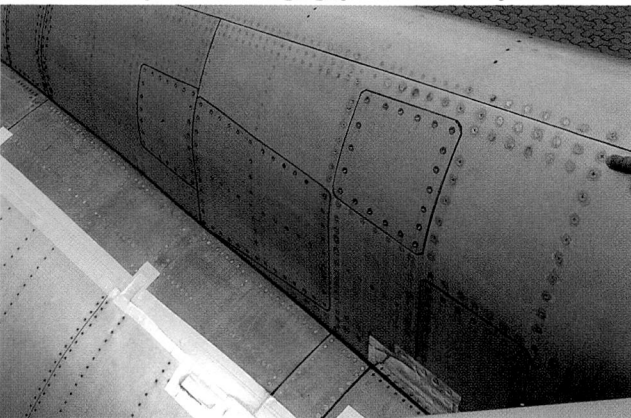

Pooling of water is prevented by the build-up of sealing compound where the external wing spar stiffener would otherwise prevent water run-off. Aluminum sealing tape covers the gap between the wing and the landing flap (upper left).

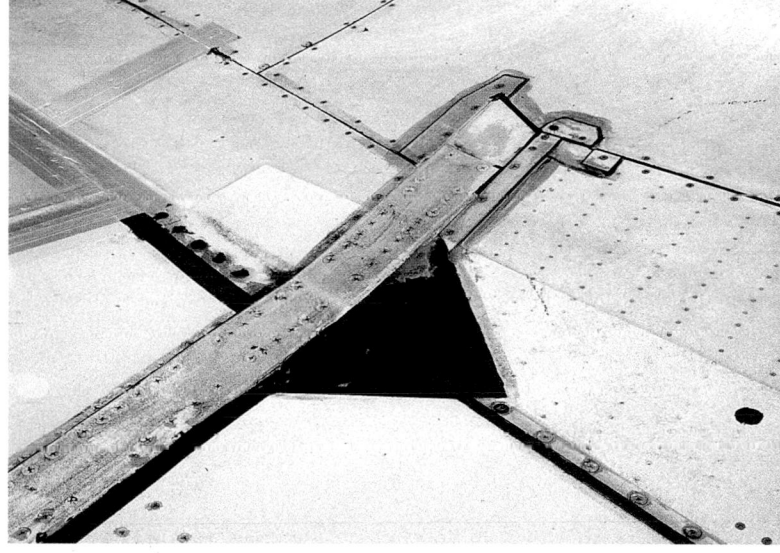

situation like a free wash as it did in earlier years. Not all the unsightly rust stains will wash off. To prevent them from recurring, steel items which cause rust stains were removed. Where possible on the Coronado, steel fasteners have been replaced with titanium hardware of the type used on Swissair DC-10s. When suitable replacement items cannot be found, the fasteners are removed and sandblasted for rust removal. This is followed by a normal galvanic treatment such as cadmium plating. Uncoated steel parts are coated the same day after cleaning with a rust converter primer; otherwise they would begin rusting overnight in Switzerland's humid night air, similar to conditions at many other locations around the world. When installed they are coated with a wet, putty-like material, which seals them in place and prevents water entry under the taper screw head and threads. Residue is removed with acetone and a cotton towel. The heads are painted again to match the surrounding area, which is normally covered using a paint roller. Cross-point screw slots that are missed are paint-filled with a small brush. This material does not permanently fix the screws in place, for they can be removed. All this is painstakingly time-consuming work, but the results are gratifying.

To help cut down on water streak lines on the lower surfaces of the aircraft structure, an area easily examined by visitors, artificial dams made with aluminum tape have been strategically placed. Rather than having a run of water go the entire length of a surface, leaving a telltale streak, the tape causes water to drip off at the point of contact.

Any access panels within the area worked on are opened for interior inspection. After corrections have been made, a coating is sprayed inside with a material containing properties which neutralize electrolysis action, or provides a thin self-healing coating that displaces moisture for the prevention of corrosion. New products of this type are always being improved upon; it is best that prospective users make their own determination of the best products available in their respective locations.

This view from under the Coronado's fuselage and wing fillet, looking out towards the wing-tip, shows an aluminum tape water barrier. Water running off the wing and around the trailing edge of the fillet drips off at the barrier, rather than following down the aircraft belly and leaving streaks.

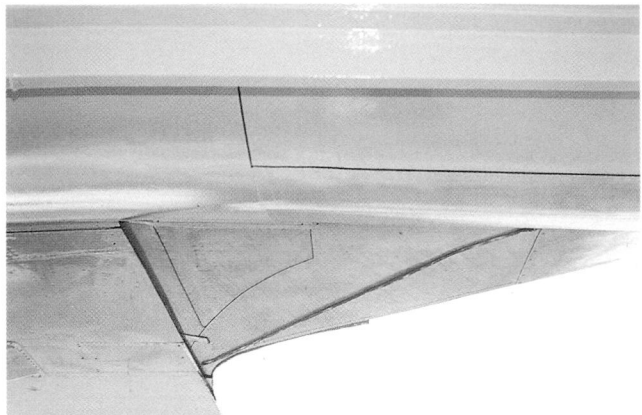

Internal coatings of this type are currently expected to last from three to five years. Be careful to remove any excess material that may be on the closing lips of access openings. This would serve as a barrier for the sealing compound that will be used when securing these covers.

It is of prime importance to seal the upper and side surface crevices from water. Not only does this prevent trapped moisture from causing corrosion and related deterioration, it also prevents water streaks from originating at these skin lines. This is a laborious, but rewarding, operation.

First, the skin mating lines are cleaned, using a tow-scraper to loosen embedded dirt and deteriorated caulking material. Then the seam is cleared with air pressure. When cleaned and dried, both sides of the seam are lined with masking tape, right at the edge. Using a caulking gun, a sealer is forced into the crevice. A putty knife (a steel rod, of ¼ to ⅜ inch (6.35-9.5 mm) diameter, bent to a spoon-like profile), or a more suitable trowel, smooth the seam surface, and the masking tape is then removed. What is seen just within the skin line is a very fine black line (white or other colors are available) that in no way detracts from the aesthetic appearance of the airplane. Initially this can be slow work, but in

the case of the Coronado, Max Widmer and a helper sealed 110 windows of this aircraft in four days. Once finished, it had a crisp appearance, and also kept water stain lines from reappearing under window frames after the stains had been removed.

Upper skin lines often overlap a lower surface. These must not be overlooked since, through capillary attraction, water does run uphill. To prevent moisture from entering these seams, they must be filled and smoothed as well. By masking the seam edge to be filled, the fill-line need not be any wider than one-and-a-half times the thickness of the lapped skin edge itself. Filled seams of this type, using the material described, can last from six to 10 years. But since climatic conditions vary, they must be inspected at least annually for cracking and tightness.

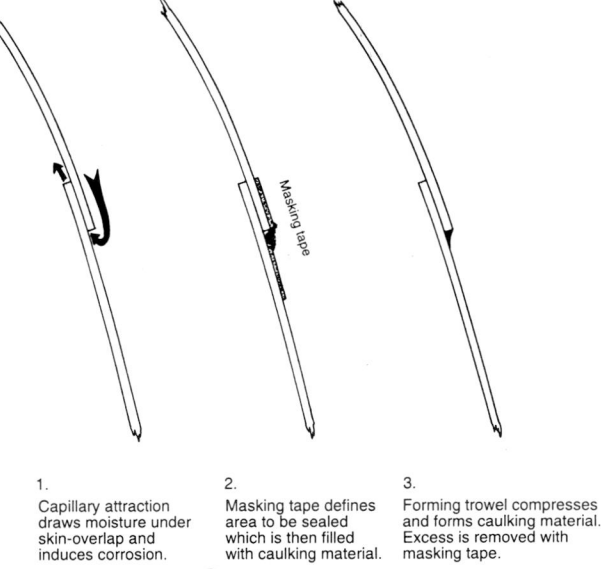

1.
Capillary attraction draws moisture under skin-overlap and induces corrosion.

2.
Masking tape defines area to be sealed which is then filled with caulking material.

3.
Forming trowel compresses and forms caulking material. Excess is removed with masking tape.

Sealing skin laps against capillary attraction of water.

Some cracks, such as gaps between flaps, ailerons, and spoilers on the wing, and between the elevator and horizontal stabilizer cannot be filled with putty. These are bridged with a high-grade aluminum tape in widths of one, two and three inches (25.4, 50.8 and 76.2 mm), and 120 mm (4.7 inches). One-inch aluminum tape is also used to close gaps around hatches and removable access panels, such as cowlings. This is applied like roof tiles, starting at the lowest edges, the next applied tape overlapping the lower one, and so on. Once all the areas are sealed, a final one-inch (25.4 mm) save-tape prevents the uppermost seal-tape from being forced away by ice and snow as it slides down the wings, stabilizer, and engine cowlings. Tape-ends are always smoothly cut with scissors, and all tapes are pressed into place with plastic-smoothers.

Normally, this tape will last for one year through the Swiss seasons, but the operation moves quickly once the skill of application is learned. It is essen-

1.
Cleaned skin opening to be sealed.

2.
Masking tape protects both sides of opening which is then filled with caulking material.

3.
Forming trowel is drawn along seam and presses caulking material firmly into skin opening.

4.
Excess caulking is removed with masking tape for finished seam.

Forming trowel made from ¼ to ⅜ inch diameter rod.

Method for sealing skin lines against moisture.

Air and water inlets are neatly closed and sealed to keep out moisture and birds. The bottom seams of the aircraft are left unsealed, so moisture inside can escape.

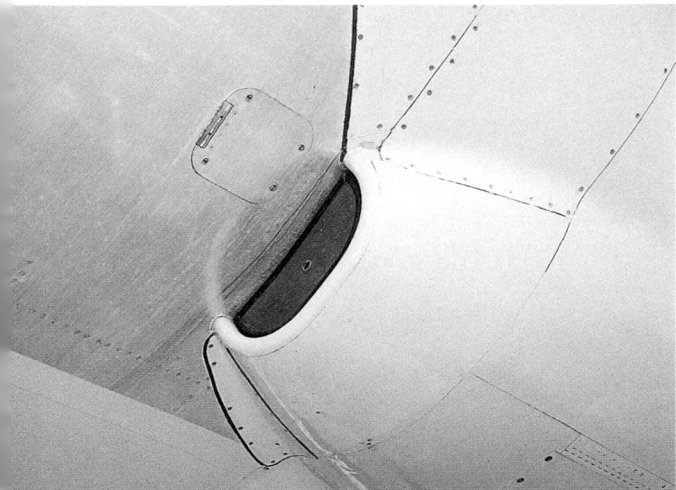

tial that earlier tape residue is completely removed with white spirit, nylon brush, and cotton cloth, and then degreased with acetone or chloroethene, before new tape is applied. The residue must be removed carefully and not accidentally distributed over the adjacent area. This is confirmed with the bare hand, for if residue remains on the aircraft skin, the surface feels sticky. Removal of any residue prevents corrosion and improves the adhesive qualities of new tape.

The paint on the Coronado oxidizes most rapidly on the south side, where sunlight is most intense. White residue from the paint has streaked across the red fuselage stripe, requiring repainting. This effect is much less apparent on the shaded side of the aircraft.

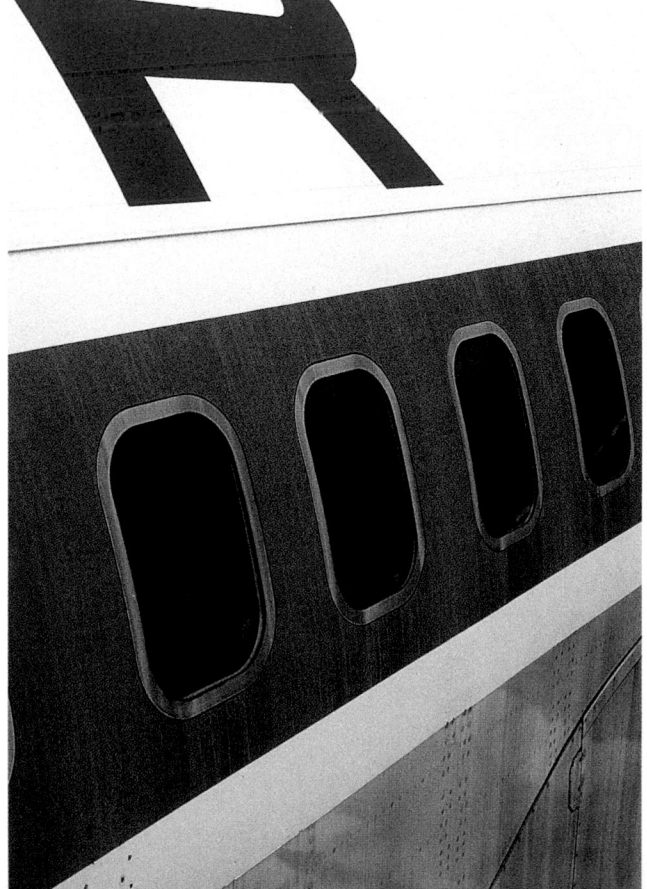

Repainting is a routine process and must be done for appearance's sake, *before* it is needed. While red is an exciting color on almost any vehicle, it is the most difficult color to maintain. In the case of the Coronado, the red fuselage stripe on the southern side needed repainting about every three years because of white paint run-off that will not wash off. On the shaded side, the same red paint that had been in place for 10 years was still in good condition. By concentrating on selected sections of the aircraft exterior rather than the nearly impossible task of addressing the entire airframe while at the museum, no more than necessary work need be undertaken.

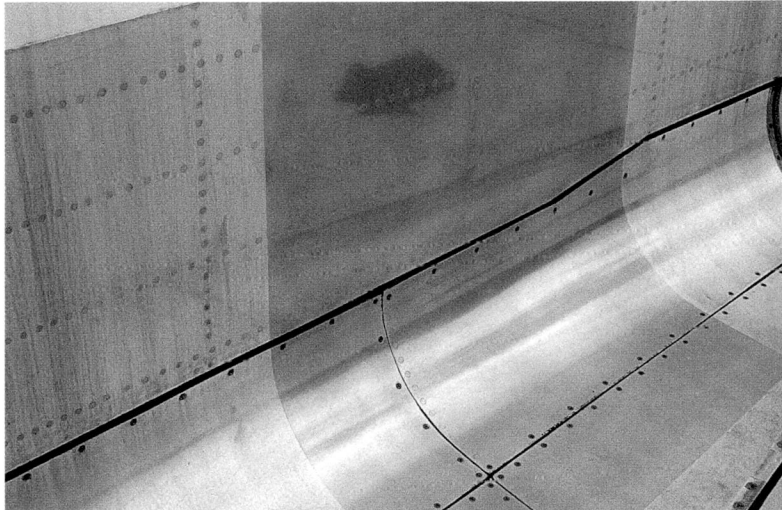

A panel of outer skin was coated with polyurethane lacquer to test its protective quality. Unprotected areas to the left and right show water streaks more readily. The lacquered surface reflects the egress arrow painted on the adjacent wing.

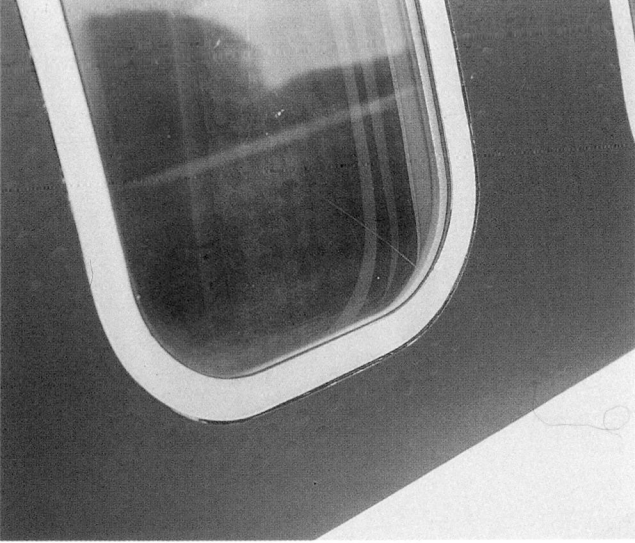

Window frames are normally made of steel, and without frequent attention they will corrode, causing rusty streaks beneath them. To prevent this, each window is carefully masked, then the seams are sealed with caulking and smoothed with a special tool.

The unpainted skin on the Coronado had taken on a leaden appearance rather than the once shiny aluminum surface. Good results for renewing this surface were obtained over a test section of the fuselage on the shaded side. The test area was prepared by first applying an acid treatment to the metal skin, followed by appropriate cleaners and primers before a clear polyurethane lacquer was applied. When conditions prevented spraying, a paint roller was used. From close-up inspection, rolling gives an uneven surface, somewhat like that of an orange skin, but it is not noticeable at any normal viewing distance. Max Widmer refers to this clear-coated surface as the 'wet look.' At this point, it should be noted that the glossy surface requires more frequent washing than bare metal, but the improved appearance makes it worth the effort.

Window Tint Film

Sun radiation through windows is another consideration, especially for cockpits, with their larger glassed areas. It is better to totally paint the windows to keep the temperature lower for the interior aircraft components. However, this gives a very artificial appearance. A reflective, yet transparent, window tint film had been applied to the cockpit windows of the Swiss Transport Museum's Coronado and Douglas DC-3. Max Widmer reported a marked reduction of heat in the cockpit of the DC-3 with this tinting material before it, too, was air-conditioned. This had reduced the cabin temperature from 132°F (55°C) average to 95°F (35°C) over a one-week summer average.

The main problem with applying window tint film to aircraft windows is that it will not adhere as well to these acrylic surfaces as it will to auto glass, for which it was designed and is marketed. It will adhere to aircraft windows initially, but over time it will begin to bubble because of the breathing qualities of acrylic surfaces used for aircraft windows. Where the situation warrants, remove the window frame and place the tint film on the window surface without removing the clear adhesive barrier. The film must be cut to extend beyond the window area. Reinstall the window frame, which now holds the film in place. As an alternative method, adhesive tape has been used to hold the film in place, but it releases the film over time because of the heat and the smooth film surface.

How Long Can it Last?

The visible results of the many phases of preserving the Swiss Transport Museum's Coronado, in place since 1975, are impressive, to say the least. But all good things must come to an end some time, and when that will be remains to be seen. Dr Alfred Waldis, President of the Swiss Transport Museum when the Coronado was accepted, was asked when he would expect the maintenance of this airplane would be overtaken by outdoor deterioration. He

The Swiss Transport Museum's Douglas DC-3 was mounted in flight attitude instead of its normal three-point static position. As a result, drain holes designed into the structure were ineffective and new provisions had to be made so water could drain from the aircraft.

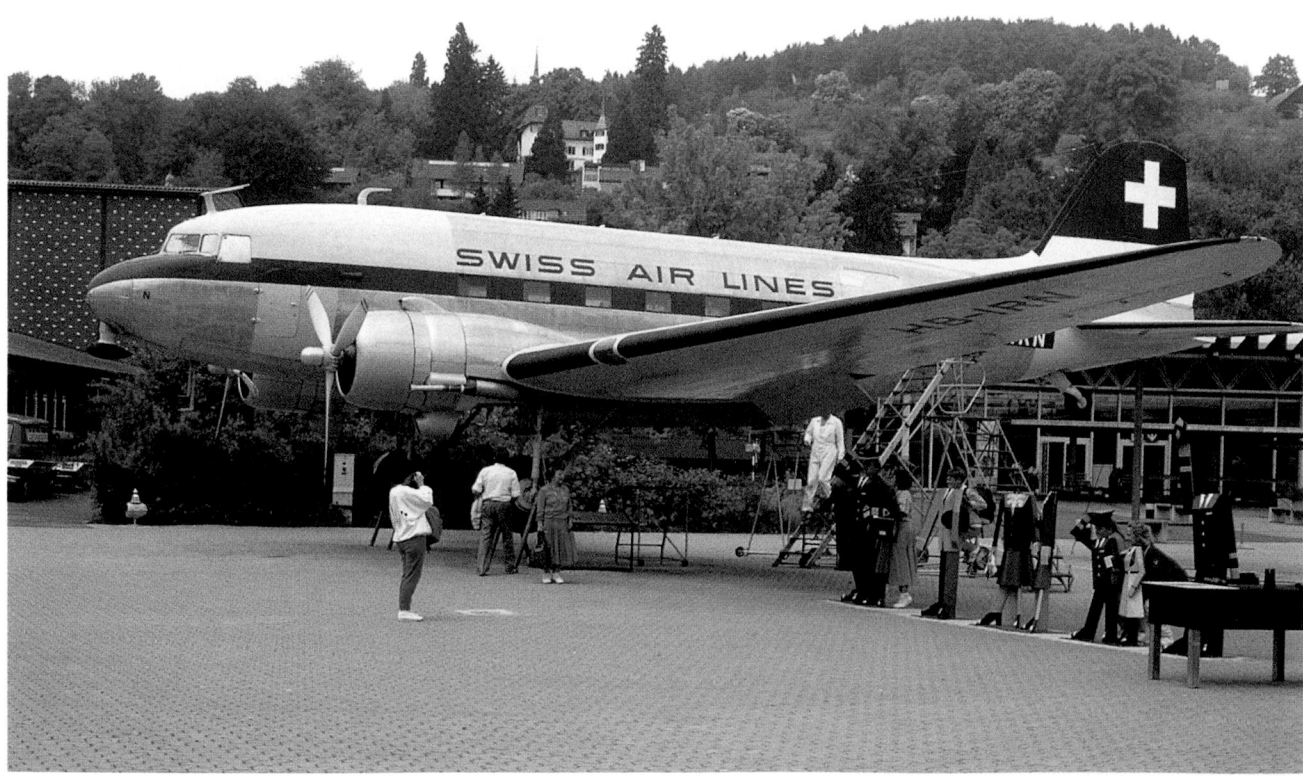

replied that he would be satisfied if the airplane could serve as an exhibit for a period of 35- 50 years. To do so would make all this effort worthwhile. After that time, a newer-generation airplane would be worthy of this exhibit location. With the removal of the Coronado, the cockpit and other technical components may be retained as separate, and more easily-managed, indoor exhibit items.

'This is not a bright future for such an airplane when other museums plan in terms of hundreds of years,' according to Waldis. 'But this is better than other alternatives, such as letting it deteriorate at its own natural rate or not having the airplane at all.'

The content of this chapter was the keynote presentation by the author at *The 1989 Tri-Service Conference on Corrosion*, held in Atlantic City, New Jersey, and was printed in the *Proceedings* of that conference, Vinod S. Agarwala, Editor, published by the Naval Air Development Center, Warminster, Pennsylvania 18974-5000.

Footnotes

1 Restoration Philosophy and Policy, NASM, Aeronautics Department, General File (May 1969), p.4.

2 Naval Aviation Museum (dedicated 8 June, 1963); Air Force Central Museum (1 July, 1956); and Smithsonian's National Air Museum (activated 1 August, 1947), later 'Space' was added (1966).

3 David Hallam is now Senior Scientist, Materials Conservation, Queensland Museum, South Brisbane, Australia.

4 Cultural Resources Management Bulletin, Vol. 17, No. 4 (1994), p.9.

5 See minutes of NASM meeting and attendees, 21 March, 1973.

6 Ibid.

7 B-17D *Swoose*, Far East AF; B-26B *Flak Bait*, 9th AF, Europe; B-29 *Enola Gay*, 20th AF, Pacific; JRS-1, Hawaiian Air Command.

8 P-38J, SW Pacific; P-39Q, South Pacific; P-40E, China-Burma; P-47D, Mediterranean; P-51D, European Theater; P-61C, (non- designated); P-63A, Russian AF; B-25J, SW Pacific.

9 *The Restoration and Preservation of Historical Aircraft*, International Association of Transport Museums, Yearbook 1, pp.98–103, by Cdr. Walter J. Tuck, RN (Ret'd), former Deputy Keeper, Officer-in-Charge, National Aeronautical Collection, the Science Museum, London.

10 Oral presentation at the 1988 International Association of Transportation Aviation Conference, National Aviation Museum of Canada, 26-30 September, 1988, Ottawa, Ontario, Canada. Title: Principles of Artifact Conservation and Exhibition, by James Burnham.

11 Extracted from *Proceedings Of The Inaugural Australian Aviation Museums Conference*, November 1-3, 1989; published by the Australian Aviation Museum Association, ISBN 0 646 01693 8.

12 Extra Super Duraluminum, similar in hardness to 24ST.

13 See Footnote 5.

14 Dr Michael A. Fopp, Director of the RAF Museum, provided most of the text used in describing this event about the Bristol Bulldog and related concepts.

15 *Air & Space* magazine, April/May 1990.

16 Imron is a high-quality modern paint finish; Loran is a modern electronic air navigation system (see Glossary).

17 *Albatros D.Va, German Fighter of World War I, Famous Aircraft of the National Air and Space Museum* series, No.4, by Robert C. Mikesh, Smithsonian Institution Press, Washington, DC, 1980.

18 Described in a letter dated 30 September, 1995, to the author from Dr Michael A. Fopp, Director, RAF Museum, Hendon.

19 Documentation of Aircraft Restoration Projects at the RAF Museum, by Air Commodore David F. Lawrence, Keeper of Aircraft and Exhibits, RAF Museum, Hendon, and Bruce James, Manager and Deputy Keeper, RAF Museum Reserve Collection and Restoration Centre, Cardington; published in *Stopping the Rot*, British Aviation Preservation Council, November 1992.

20 A method of splicing-in new material according to a prescribed standard.

21 A similar method of reinforcing and supplementing existing material has been used recently by the Australian War Memorial on their Mosquito aircraft on thick sections of balsa and plywood sandwich using an epoxy micro balloon filler.

22 Albatros, produced by the Signal Corp, US Army, historical film 1106, Reel 3, National Air and Space Film Library, Washington, DC.

23 Albatros D.Va, *Famous Aircraft of the National Air and Space Museum*, Vol. 4, by Robert C. Mikesh, Smithsonian Institution Press, Washington, DC, 1980. The new drawings are filed in NASM Archives.

24 Improved products are now used and will continue to change.

25 At the time of writing, Grade A cotton may be discontinued as aviation-quality material, but

as a weave of cotton material it will supposedly remain available.

26 Wright Flyer Preliminary Textile Report, by Mary Ballard, CAL 4566A, Conservation Analytical Laboratory, Smithsonian Institution, Washington, DC, 1985.

27 For the complete article see *World War I Aero*, No. 95, 1985, pp.70-73 and repeated in *The Canadian Aviation Historical Society Journal*, Vol. 25, No. 2, summer 1987, pp.41-44.

28 *The Aviation Pocket-Book for 1918*, by R. Borlase Matthews, Westminster, England.

29 *Canada's National Aviation Museum, Its History and Collections*, by K.M. Molson, 1988.

30 Lozenge camouflage: German Patent No. 308410, granted November 18, 1916.

31 Idflieg issued a letter (296651/17) to all aircraft manufacturers instructing them to use the new printed fabric available from the Augsburg Cotton Factory.

32 Idflieg Directive Tgb Nr. 300451 through the Proof and Test Establishment advising manufacturers of the new printed fabric for subsequent use.

33 Letter to the author from Dan-San Abbott, 9 November, 1995.

34 The French Section Technique and the Ministry of Munitions both quote an average dimension on the roll as [4ft 5 in] 1.35 m, whilst the firm of Aviatik quoted the specification as being 'not less than [53 in] 1,335 mm, and not to vary more than [0.8 in] 20 mm along the entire length.'

35 Most critics feel that the Museum für Verkehr und Technik in Berlin has had the most exacting lozenge fabric reproduced.

36 World War I German Aircraft Finishes, P.L. Gray, *Aero Modeller*, November 1957, p.604.

37 Ibid.

38 *Cleaning*, Crafts Council Conservation Science Teaching Series, Book 2, by Crafts Council, 11/12 Waterloo Place, London, 1984.

39 *Proceedings Of The Inaugural Australian Aviation Museums Conference*, 1-3 November, 1989, published by the Australian Aviation Museum Association, ISBN 0 646 01693 8.

40 Since the airplane would not have been flown in this condition, it was believed that this damage happened during American flight evaluation and therefore is not significant to its Japanese operational history. Such a repair was justifiable under these circumstances.

41 3M Spray Disc Adhesive, Part No. 51135, also available in brushing liquid form; generally an auto parts store product.

42 Extend™ is a tannic acid base protective coating over rusted areas which can be painted. See Appendix G for source.

43 Aircraft Propellers, War Department Technical Manual, TM-412, 5 January, 1944.

44 Ibid

45 *Building and Flying an Aeroplane*: A Practical Handbook Covering the Design, Construction and Operation of Aeroplanes and Gliders, by Charles Hayward, Chicago: American Technical Society, 1912, p.142 w/ills. TL670.H3X

46 The distance that the propeller would move forward after one complete turn if working as a non-slipping screw.

47 Color separations can be found in *Albatros D.Va, German Fighter of World War I*, by Robert C. Mikesh, Famous Aircraft of the National Air and Space Museum series No. 4, Smithsonian Institution Press, Washington, DC, 1980.

48 *Aircraft Tires and Tubes*, by Dale Crane, Aviation Maintenance Publishers, Inc., Basin, Wyoming, 1980.

49 *Aircraft Tires and Tubes*, International Aviation Publishers, (Jeppesen-Sanderson Training Products), Casper, Wyoming, 1985.

50 Ibid.

51 *An Initial Approach to the Stabilization of Rubber from Museum Collections*, by Miriam Clavir, assistant conservator at Pares, Canada, Conservation des Ressources Historiques, Quebec, 1980.

52 *Aircraft and Space Vehicle Treatment as Works of Art*, by David Hallam, Australian War Memorial, presented at NASM for Mutual Concerns of Air and Space Museums Seminar, March 1989.

53 *Microcrystalline Wax as a Paint Barrier and Separator*, Test Report by R. Mikesh, August 27, 1994, NASM Conservation Office.

54 Dr Kevin McCartney, University of Maine at Presque Isle, contributed many of the constructive thoughts for this section.

APPENDIX A

Wood-and-Fabric Aircraft Sample Restoration Guidelines

This is a set of Restoration Guidelines prepared at the National Air and Space Museum for a typical early wood-and-fabric aircraft. It is presented here to serve as a sample when preparing guidelines at the start of a similar restoration. Restoration Guidelines will differ as do the airplanes, so each one must be written separately. They should not tell the technician 'how to do the job', but what the end product is to be. To prepare this material, the writer must have an understanding of the work process ahead in order to describe for the technician the problems expected to be encountered and how the curator wishes to have them resolved. These instructions are for guidance and record only, and do not replace communication between the curator, technician and conservator. Perhaps more detail has been gone into than is needed by the technician, but by doing so, technical knowledge about the aircraft is recorded and is therefore more easily explored in advance of reaching problem areas.

RESTORATION GUIDELINES
BENOIST TYPE XII
Cat. No. 1950-79
NAM 666

The 1912 Benoist Type XII tractor biplane is being prepared for restoration. Because of its age, condition, and the fact that portions of the aircraft are missing, this machine presents very special problems. Fortunately, while considerable rebuilding will be required, particularly the fuselage, empennage, and control system, we should be able to answer most of the questions that will arise on the basis of photos, drawings and written descriptions. The following guidelines should be considered as preliminary only, since we can expect to encounter many additional problems when working more closely with the aircraft components.

Background

In the spring of 1912 Thomas Wesley Benoist (he liked to pronounce it Ben—oyst, but the more commonly accepted pronunciation is Ben-Wa) announced the completion of his firm's newest aircraft, a two-place tractor biplane. Powered by a Roberts six-cylinder, 75-hp engine, the machine was the first tractor produced by Benoist and one of the first 'modern' closed-fuselage tractors to appear in the US.

The Type XII, as the new machine was identified, corresponding with the year, had a wingspan of 35 feet (10.67 m); 45 feet (13.72 m) if the protruding ailerons are included). The gap between the mainplanes was 5 feet (1.52 m) and the chord was 4 feet, 9 inches (1.45 m). The aspect ratio was given as 7.3:1.

Perhaps five Type XII aircraft were produced by the Benoist shop over the next year. In December 1912 one of these 'craft, mounted on floats, made a much-publicized 1,973-mile (3,175 km) flight down the Missouri and Mississippi Rivers with Tony Janus at the controls. The other Type XII machines were sold to private exhibition pilots.

NASM's specimen (Factory No. 32) was acquired from its original purchaser, Edward Korn, in 1949. Edward and his brother Milton constructed the machine themselves in the Benoist shops in St. Louis, beginning work in March 1912. Completed on 20 May, it was flown soon thereafter at Anna, Illinois. Over the following year Korn filled numerous exhibition dates with the aircraft.

The airplane was also altered significantly during this period. The ailerons (warping, not moving ailerons) fixed to the outer forward strut at the midpoint were replaced by normal ailerons attached to the trailing edge of the upper wing.

On the morning of 13 August, 1913, the Korns crashed while flying near their grandfather's farm at Montra, Ohio, 20 miles (32 km) south of Lima. Five days later, Milton Korn died of injuries suffered in the accident. Edward, the pilot, was badly injured but recovered. The remains of the Korn Benoist were placed in storage.

In 1917-18 Korn turned the Benoist over to a group of manual arts students who rebuilt, but apparently did not fly, the machine. During the course of the rebuilding a number of alterations were made to the original Benoist design, particularly in the substitution of a fuselage and tail having a different configuration than the original. At least three of the original 13 wing panels have been repaired with different-sized material, and five panels are missing. All of these deviations are addressed in the appropriate sections that follow.

After the plane's reconstruction during World War I, the Benoist was broken down and stored at Korn Airport in Jackson Center, Ohio, three miles (4.8 km) east of the crash site. It remained there until it was moved in 1949 to the National Air Museum's facility at Park Ridge, Illinois, and finally to the Washington Area in 1951 to what is now the Paul E. Garber Preservation, Storage and Restoration Facility at Silver Hill, Maryland.

Our Benoist is an extraordinarily significant machine. It is a prime example of pre-World War I, US aeronautical technology. Most American aircraft produced during this era were direct copies of Wright, Curtiss or European machines. Benoist was one of the very few US firms building and selling original designs. One other Benoist exists of a similar tractor design. Our airplane, once restored to the original configuration, not only will serve to memorialize this influential company of tractor design airplanes, but represents the earliest example of Benoist technology we will ever be able to preserve. For this reason we will attempt to remove all of the later accretion from the Korn aircraft in an effort to return the machine to factory original condition.

Preservation and Restoration Requirements

This project must be undertaken with the intentions in mind that every component of this structure must survive for 300 years, or better still — indefinitely. This will require individualized treatment for preserving the various materials contained in this aircraft. Existing rubber and fabric must be removed and replaced, for these materials are considered expendable due to their relatively short life-span. Retain samples of these materials for reference purposes. All other parts must be repaired and retained within the structure wherever possible. When repairs of structural members that are often repeated throughout the aircraft, become excessive and cause the parts to loose their significance as being original, they can be replaced with new material. The reconstruction of these new parts must duplicate original construction techniques and material.

Wood can be best preserved if left undisturbed in its natural state and in a fairly stable humidity environment. Once this airplane is restored and not abused, it will closely achieve this status. Since the wooden structure was originally varnished, a light coat of spar varnish will again be applied. Over the areas where the wood fibers protrude when the varnish dries and can easily catch and hold dirt particles, these areas can be lightly sanded and a second coat of varnish applied if needed. This finish was originally applied to resist moisture from penetrating the wood when the airplane was in service. Now, as a protected Museum airplane, chances are that this varnish will not add to the life of this airplane.

(*Current note: Varnish is not a wood preservative, it is a water repellant. Therefore, in restorations of wooden aircraft, varnish is not applied over wood that was not originally varnished by the maker. In no case should polyurethane varnish be used as this seals the wood and does not allow it to breath evenly, causing stresses on the wood fibers and eventual breakdown.*)

Nails have become rusty and must be removed if this is possible without excessively damaging the surrounding areas. Ideally, it is desirable to rust-strip these nails and give them a phosphate coating so they can be used again in this structure as original parts. Where a near match with new cement-coated nails can be found, these can be used as replacement substitutes.

Unless undue damage may be caused to the wood, all metal parts must be removed from the structure for rust-stripping and preservation coating. This is an essential part of this restoration since rusted metal surfaces against wood, including steel bolts through wood, affects the wood and in time it becomes soft and pulpy and will rot. No harm will be caused by inserting a properly-coated bolt or nail into a hole around which rust stains are already present.

All metal will be treated according to instructions contained in NASM Chemical Processing Specifications, dated April 1979. (*Instructions contained in NASM CPS referred to here are not included in this book. The use of chemicals and processes change with experience and new materials that develop. The latest methods should be employed in restorations as described here.*) Before metal parts are reattached to the aircraft assembly, they will be painted or preserved with (*the latest clear-coating preservative, which was Rhom & Hass™ Acroloyd at this writing*), which does not alter its original appearance.

All repaired or replaced wood and metal parts will be appropriately marked (stamped) and dated in order to distinguish them from original parts should they be studied in the future.

An effort will be made to acquire Goodyear No. 10 rubberized fabric for recovering this airplane since this was the original material. After this fabric was attached to the aircraft it was coated with a thin layer of clear dope. If this fabric material is not available, the next closest match of weight and weave will be determined and acquired.

(*Current note: A cotton fabric, rubberized coated on one side, was specially prepared for this project by Archer Rubber Company, Milford, Massachusetts. This became a poor committee decision by not heeding the advice of the manufacturer. Insisting upon originality by having a rubberized coating, this latex has now turned brown as forecast and the covering must again be replaced. A more stable substitute covering should have been selected.*)

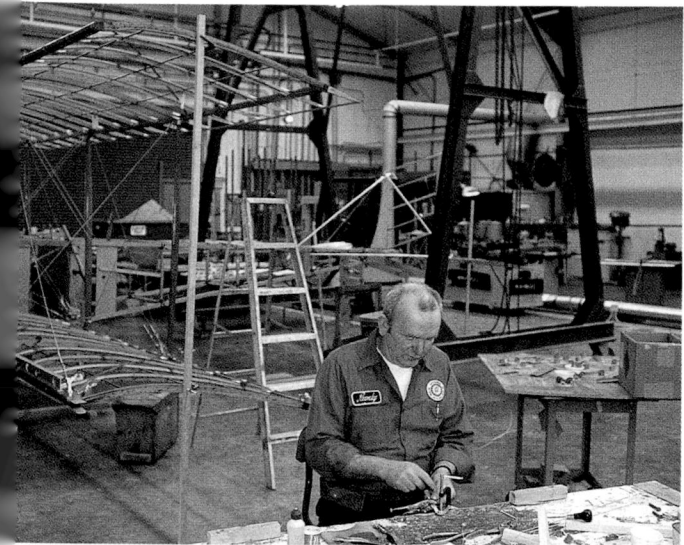

LEFT: *The construction of wood and fabric aircraft is an art form no longer practised except for restoration of museum aircraft or building replicas. The restoration of this Benoist Type XII called for the re-learning of skills for which there is little application in modern aviation. Here a special tool is being fabricated by museum technician Charlie Parmley.*

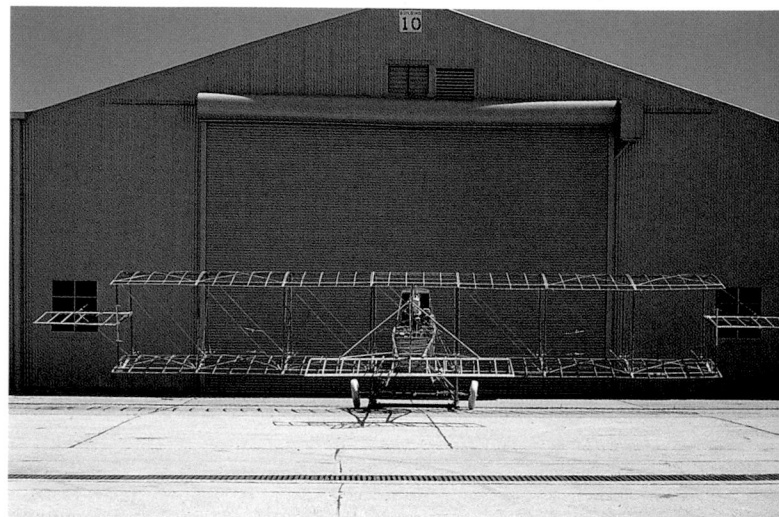

After the many assemblies of the Benoist Type XII were restored, they were assembled and new rigging fabricated in order to assure everything fitted properly before fabric surfaces were applied. This tail-on view shows the unusual mounting for ailerons that extended beyond the wings.

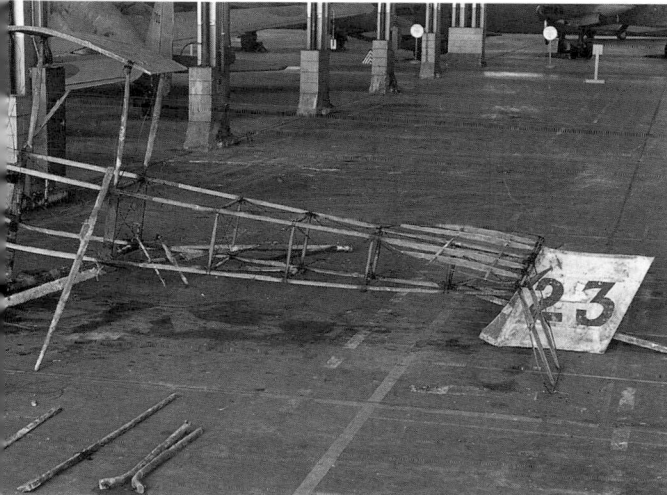

Shown here are some of the basic parts of the Benoist Type XII when received by the National Air Museum at their Park Ridge, Illinois storage location in 1949. Changes had been made to the fuselage structure sometime after the crash, yet these materials were used in the restoration when returning the fuselage to its original, flying design. (NASM, S.I. A-38712B)

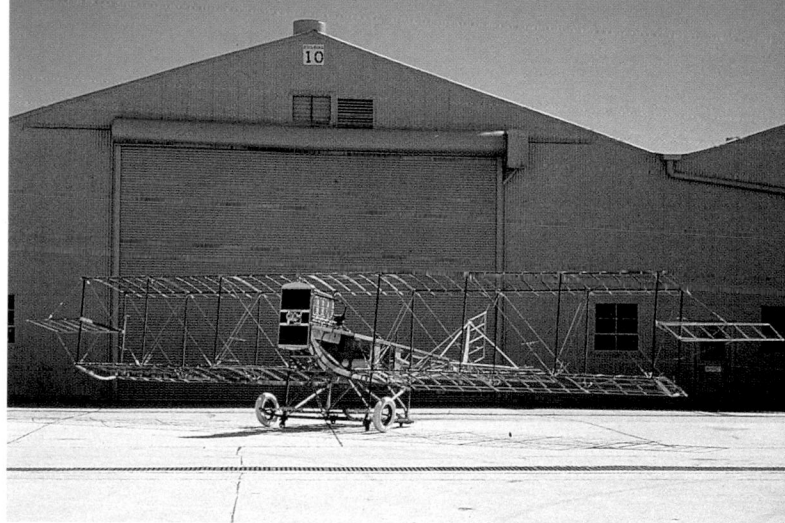

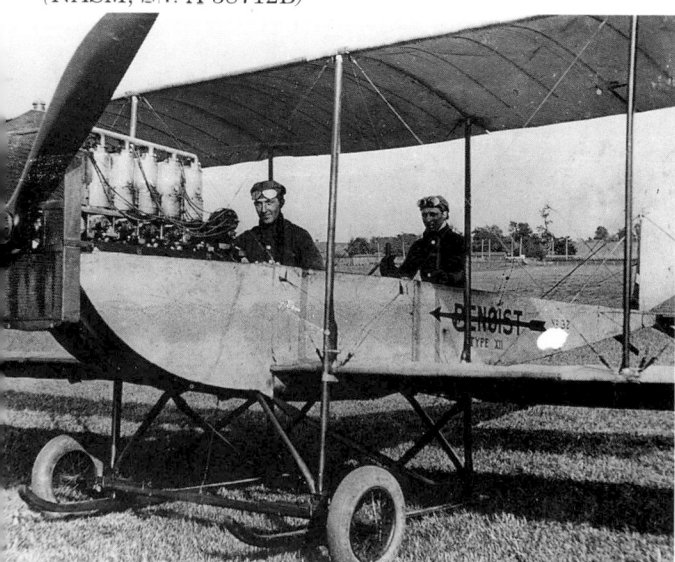

The radiator and propeller were not included amongst the parts of this airplane held in storage for several decades. Both components had to be redesigned from photos and notes for the former owner. Fabrication was contracted with firms highly-skilled in building these components so that their technology would be better preserved.

LEFT: *Only a few photos of the Benoist Type XII are in existence. This view was selected as the pattern picture since changes in certain details were evident in other pictures. The passenger in the front seat was in a noisy location behind this Roberts engine. (NASM, SI A-38724)*

A note of caution must be made here in regards to applying this fabric to the aircraft wings. The original wooden inch-wide material used on the wing trailing edge was very light for the tension of the fabric that was placed upon it. To prevent this strain again bending and breaking this lightweight trailing edge, the fabric must be applied without the normal amount of tension — only enough to keep it taut after the dope has been applied.

Another note of caution is also warranted. Ideally, the fabric should be attached to the aircraft in the same fashion as it was originally. Unfortunately, we have discovered that the tacks that were used have caused considerable damage by splitting wooden areas such as the lightweight wing ribs. When applying this fabric, technicians must keep in mind that this fabric will again have to be removed and replaced in the years ahead, long before the structure will deteriorate through the ageing process. Do not tack the fabric so firmly that damage will result when these fasteners are once again removed in future years.

General Configuration

After inspecting the existing Benoist parts, it became obvious that many changes had been made to the original configuration of this Type XII aircraft. The fuselage is totally different in shape to that of the original, the wing span was slightly reduced by narrowing the upper center-section to equal that of the fuselage width. This allows the lower wing panels to be attached directly to the fuselage without the need of short insert panels. The original strut-supported warping ailerons are on hand but so are the later trailing edge ailerons with modifications made to the outer wing panels. These outer panels have that portion of the wing aft of the rear spar removed to accommodate the four ailerons. Many wing struts and most of the landing gear struts are on hand. No item of the original tail has been retained, although a picture taken around 1949 at Park Ridge, Illinois while in storage show the rudder with these parts.

After evaluating the small degree of originality that remains of this Benoist Type XII, the logical question was raised as to how valid was it to proceed with this restoration, since the basic component — the fuselage — was not that of the airplane in question? To not restore this airplane would leave two choices; discard the components since major parts of the aircraft are missing, or return the existing parts to storage with no purpose for the future. The answer became obvious; reconstruct the Type XII now, using as many original parts as possible, for if not continued, the project may never be fulfilled.

The guidelines that follow are for preliminary planning, and although they can be used as a point of departure for this reconstruction, they can be modified as the project develops if warranted. Such deviations must be curatorially approved and become written amendments to this plan, which by this record serves as documentation covering this restoration. Adherence to original workmanship techniques, material, and component design will be assumed unless instructed and documented to be done differently.

Fuselage

A structural drawing for the fuselage will be developed for building an entirely new fuselage. (*Current note: This means that the curator will assure that this drawing is accomplished.*) The source for preparing this drawing will be the general arrangement drawings contained in *Aeronautics* magazine, page 62, 1912, along with sketches and a description provided in several letters from Dr Edward Korn to P.E. Garber, former NASM curator.

Some critical dimensions around the cockpit area can best be determined by reassembling the existing original landing gear to the lower wing structure with a mock-up of this fuselage section. Original parts on hand can then be placed according to their attachment fittings. From this mock-up arrangement, dimensions can be determined as an aid in preparing structural drawings and fabricating various components for the new fuselage.

According to Dr Korn's letter, he states that the 'barrel' turnbuckles and guy wires used on the fuselage we now have are not of the original type. Instead, 'spoke' turnbuckles (this is an unfamiliar term but may be the type which uses stamped sheet-metal parts, a type found with this fuselage) were used, and all guy wires were Roebling (perhaps a trademark) stranded cable. Cable attachment to the turnbuckles were wire-wrapped and then soldered.

To obtain turnbuckles that match this 'spoke' type described, may present a problem. Their size is also not known. An alternate approach can be to use the barrel turnbuckles that are now on the existing fuselage and fabricate cable guy wires as described. The metal fittings at guy wire junctions at the longerons and cross members of the existing fuselage will be used since there is little or no guidance to the contrary except in the area of the cockpit. Although not necessarily original to this airplane we are restoring, we are somewhat confident that this hardware was used on a Benoist-manufactured aircraft.

This fuselage is actually made up of three major components, all of which can theoretically be separated from one another by unbolting. The center-section consists of two one-inch (25.4 mm) spruce plywood rectangular bulkheads joined together by four 1¼ x 2-inch (31.75 x 50.8 mm) longerons approximately 46 inches (117 cm) long.

RIGHT: *It was from this single magazine drawing that the layout of the aircraft was developed, as were the missing components. (Aeronautics magazine, August 1912)*

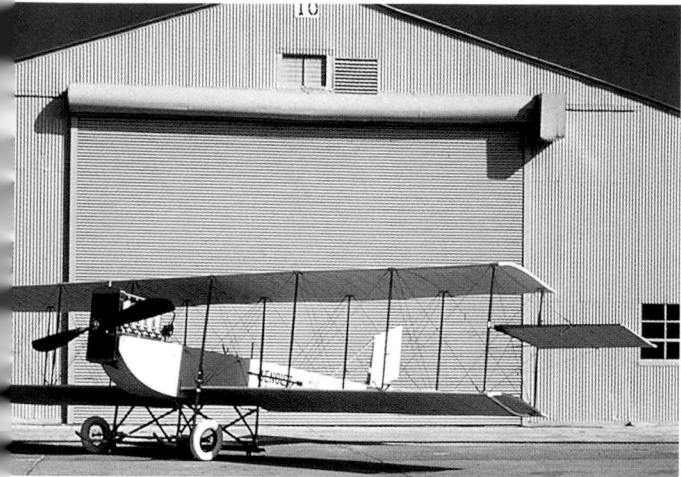

This fabric covering of the Benoist Type XII was rubberized in the same fashion as balloon cloth. By the 1912 time period of this airplane, the importance of air-proof fabric was better recognized in order to attain greater lifting power from the wings than from uncoated cloths of earlier types of aircraft.

The following set of drawings was created at the beginning of the project, based upon existing components, photographs and the Aeronautics magazine drawing. These drawings became the source for creating the missing components for the Benoist Type XII restoration. It is the responsibility of the curator to provide this technical material for such projects.

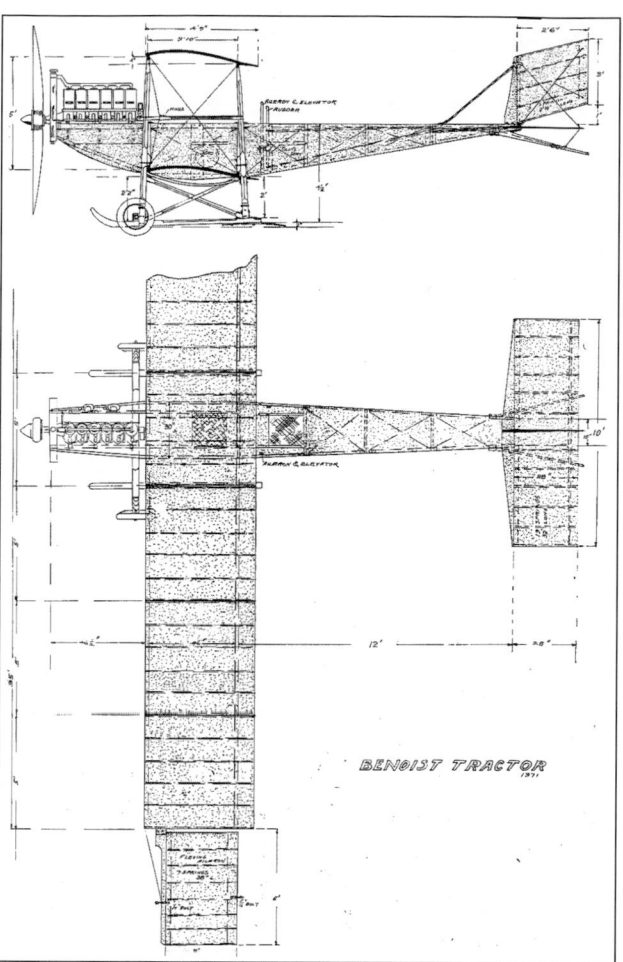

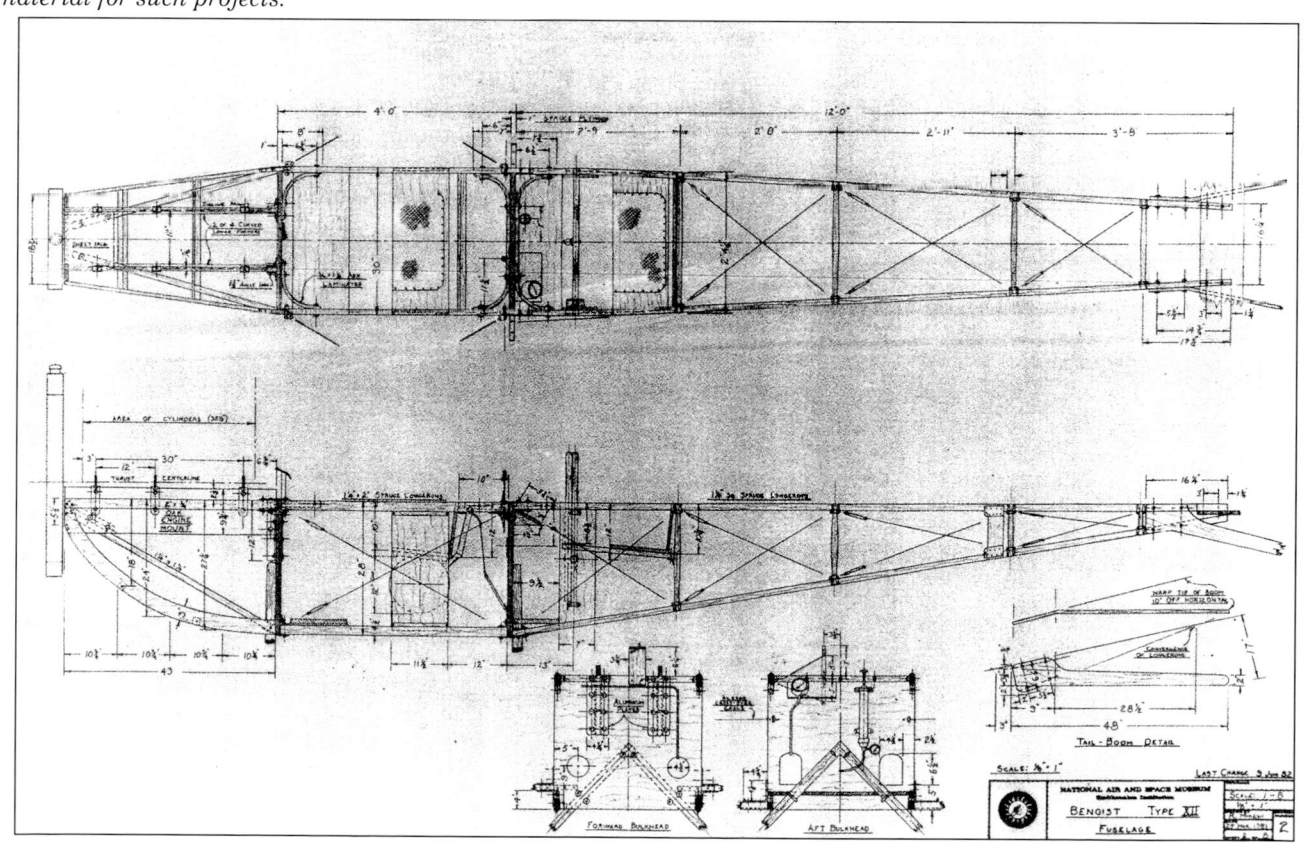

This is assembled with bolts joining these pieces together, with iron angles to form a box effect with four open sides.

The aft fuselage section is made up of four longerons and a series of spaces in between, with guy wires for rigidity. These longerons are presumed to be 1¼-inch (31.75 mm) spare since this is the size of the longerons of the fuselage that was included with this airplane. This dimension also matches the width of the material shown in Dr Korn's sketch of the center-section longerons. This aft-section is a horizontally-laid wedge-shape that tapers to the stabilizer and the only curve is at the area of the rear cockpit. The forward end of this assembly is bolted to the rear bulkhead of the fuse-lage center-section and reinforced with a curved wooden strap. The pilot is seated in the forward end of this aft assembly. (This places the passenger ahead of the pilot at a near center of gravity posi-tion which allows solo flight.)

The nose-section and engine mount are bolted to the forward end of the center-section. The only other curved piece to the fuselage appears to be a wooden, non-structural supporting member along the lower sides of the nose. This supports only the fabric covering of the nose to give it a streamlined effect.

The landing gear must be reconstructed from surviving parts to the fullest extent possible. Many are badly damaged, but once repaired and joined with the necessary new pieces of the landing gear that replace missing parts, sufficient strength can be attained. Note must be taken with these pieces to the effect of determining if paint (possibly black) had been used on these exposed wooden structural members.

The dried out 20 x 4-inch (508 x 102 mm) clincher-type tires can be removed (cut) from these wheels at an early time of this restoration. The wheels must be chemically derusted, preserved, and painted black after which time we will attempt to locate suitable white rubber tires or have them made for these wheels.

(Recognizing that NASM does not fly its aircraft, Donald M. Wimer of Goodyear™ Tire and Rubber Co. in Akron (in 1981) was kind enough to solve this problem. Having access to the original rims, he located garden implement tires that fit, removed the tread and coated them with white latex to visibly match the original tires.)

Cockpit

The cockpit of this airplane can hardly be treated separately from the fuselage because of its construc-tion. Therefore man-hour estimates for this area can be included with the fuselage estimate.

The focal point of greatest technological signifi-cance is often found in the cockpit area. Therefore this warrants considerable attention to accuracy and completeness in details.

A few of the items contained in the cockpit for control of the airplane are on hand and will be used. Simplicity of this cockpit is the first point to be noticed. Aside from the bench seat for the pilot, it contains two hand controls for flight. At the left, in the position where the throttle is usually found, is a control stick for rudder movement only, forward for moving the rudder to the right, back for left rudder. In the center front of the cockpit is another control stick with a universal movement. This operates the warping ailerons and elevator in the conventional manner. The pilot's heels rest on a floor board and the front of the foot extends into openings in the bulkhead. A foot-operated throttle is hinged on the forward side of this bulkhead to be operated by the right foot of the pilot. Two similar openings for the passenger's feet are also in the forward bulk-head. A left-right moving piece of Shelby steel tubing (term is not recognized) controls the magneto, to advance and retard the spark. The routing of cables can be determined from photographs. A 15-gallon (57 ltr) gas tank is mounted under the passenger seat. The shape and type of tank will be determined during the fuselage fabrication. The only instruments are a tachometer and clock that are mounted in the rear cockpit.

Engine

The Roberts six-cylinder water-cooled engine, Cat. No. 1959-79 of the type that originally powered this aircraft is currently on exhibit in the Early Flight Gallery. Its preparation for exhibit purposes is recorded as having been completed on 31 October, 1966. Due to this early date of work accomplish-ment, it is possible that only the exterior may have been restored and the interior may still require our normal preservation practices which have been raised in standard over the years. This engine will be removed from exhibit when needed for this preservation inspection and possibly will need addi-tional work before being installed in the Benoist aircraft. The other two Roberts engines belonging to this collection are four-cylinder.

The large radiator originally mounted on the Type XII is missing and was reportedly destroyed in the crash. Other radiators in our collection are not of this type having a center opening for the propeller shaft, although they are listed as Roberts radiators. Requests will be sent (by the curator) to other museums and sources in hopes of locating the correct radiator. Special attention must be given to internal cleaning and proper preservation of the radiator walls.

(Current note: None could be found, nor could draw-ings or dimensions be located for constructing the

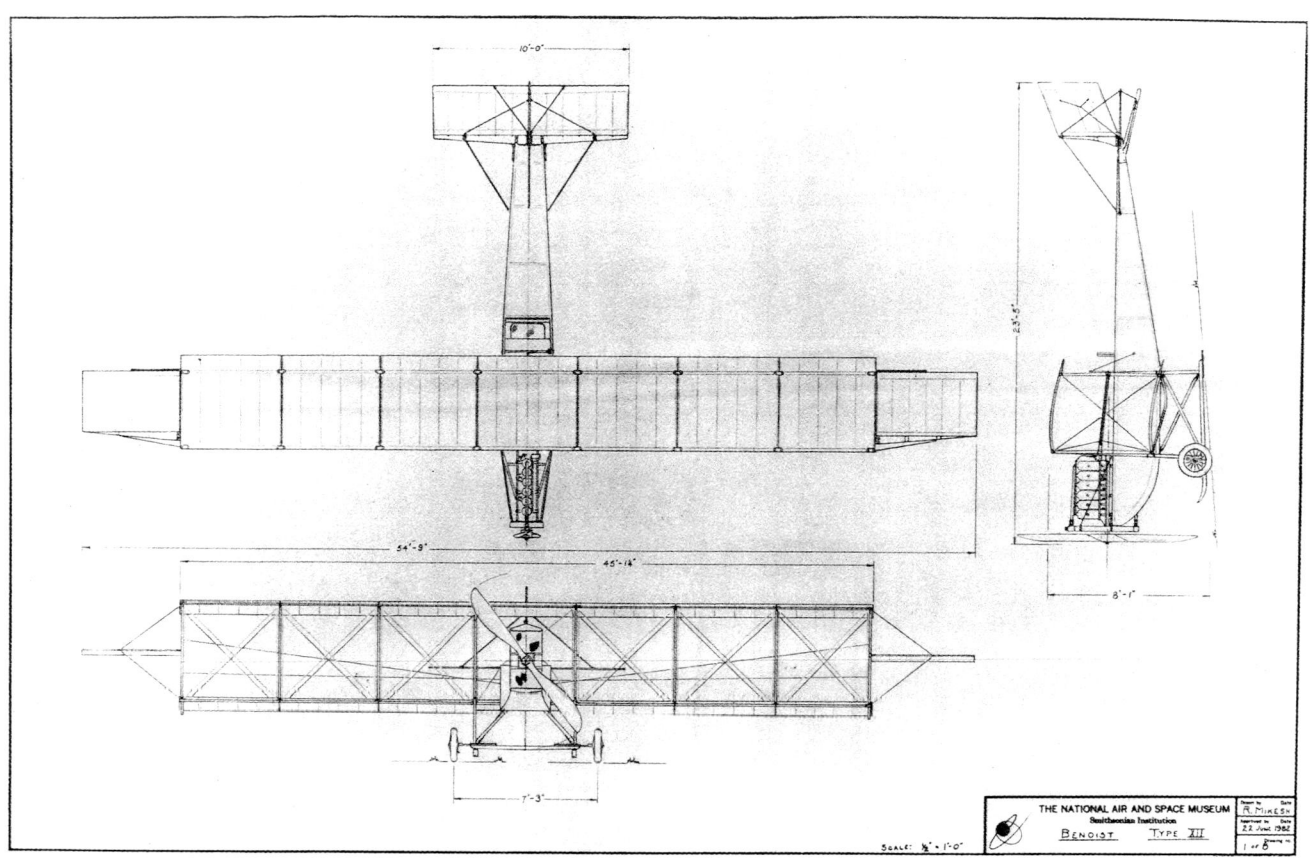

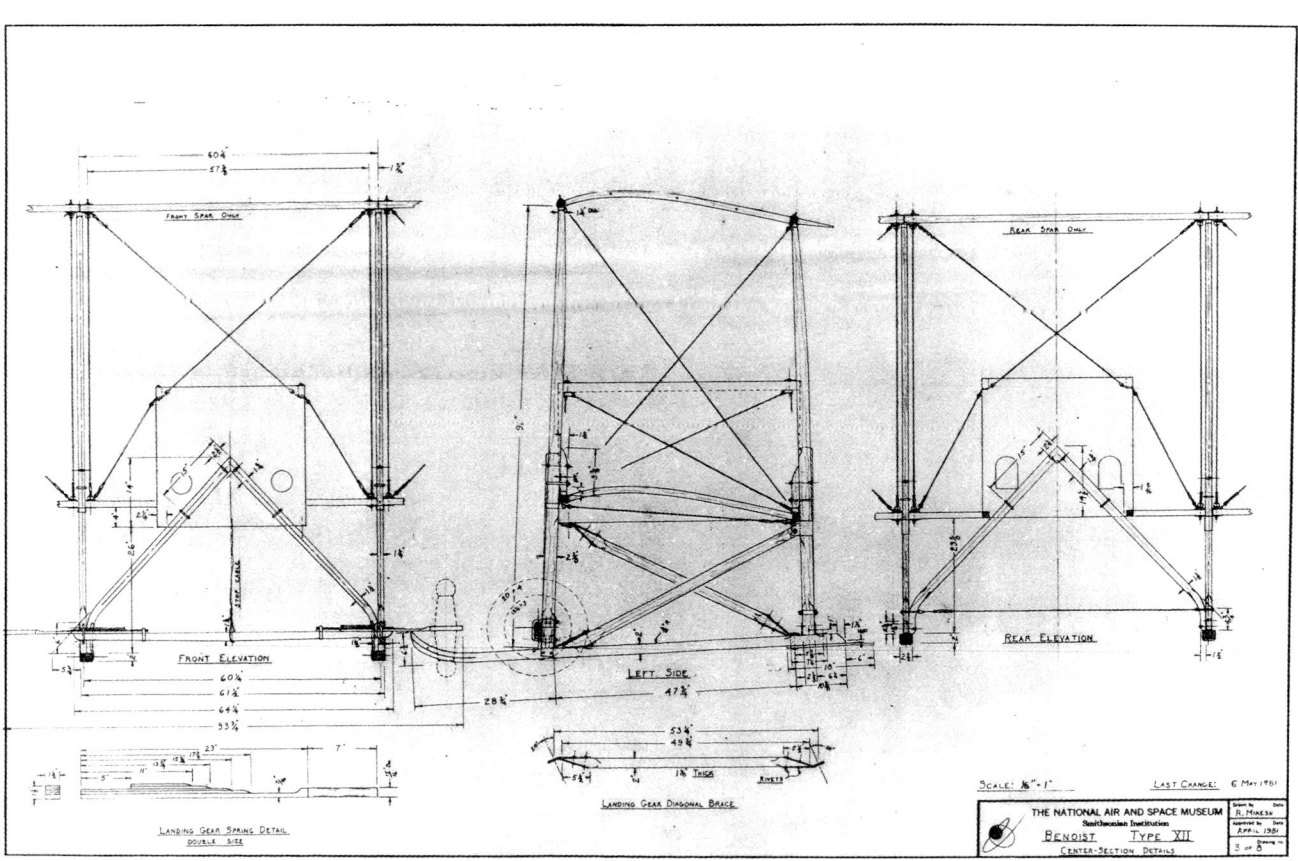

radiator. The curator made general format drawings of a radiator scaled from photographs and to fit known mounting parts. This fabrication was contracted to Neil Thomas, American Honeycomb Radiator Manufacturing Co., Staten Island, New York at a cost of $2,280 (£1,436) in May 1981.)

A study of the carburetor system for this engine will be made in order to determine the placement and connection of an air pump for a 2-lb (0.9 kg) pressure fuel system. A hand-operated air pump will also be required. The fuel system must be complete and contain the necessary components for operation although it may be impossible to determine if they were of the original type or not.

The propeller that was accessioned with this airplane will be checked with references to photographs to determine if this is the correct design. When the correct propeller is located it may be best to send it to a manufacturer of wooden propellers for this restoration.

(Current note: No propeller in NASM's collection was a close match to the one shown in photographs of this airplane. The curator scaled from these photographs and made a drawing of the desired propeller for exhibit use only. This new propeller was contracted for building by Chad Wille, St. Croix Propellers, Lake Oswego, Oregon for $685 (£432) F.O.B. in July 1981.)

Wings

The wings for this airplane are unusual by later standards in that they are made up of 13 five-foot (1.52 m) panels with two smaller insert panels for connecting the lower wing to the fuselage. Of the eight panels on hand, all appear to be original, but three have been repaired as evidenced by the wider trailing edge stringers and later brown fabric covering. The original trailing edge material was ¼ x 1-inch (6.35 x 9.52 mm) and replacement stock was ¼ x 1-inch (6.35 x 25.40 mm). The outer four wing panels have the portion behind the rear spar removed to form aileron-cutouts, when the wing was modified with having trailing edge ailerons. We have these ailerons but they will not be used for this restoration.

Before proceeding too far with wing restoration, each panel should be identified as to its position on the airplane so that it can be returned to that location. Since the wing strut support brackets are on the outboard end of each panel, this will serve for identifying left and right panels.

The modified outer wing panels can be returned to their original form by adding the rear portion of the ribs with trailing edge to the rear spar. These rear portions of the ribs were separated in the structure by the rear spar and joined with sheet-metal strips along the top and bottom. It should be noted that the design of this wing airfoil called for this trailing edge portion to be raised slightly in relation to the normal airfoil curve.

The condition of these wing panels range from fair to poor. Many of the lightweight pieces have warped and the laminated wing ribs have become unglued. In general, most of each wing panel will have to be disassembled, broken parts repaired or replaced, and reassembled once again. The five missing panels will have to be built, making sure to duplicate material and construction technique with that of the original parts.

The between-bay mounted ailerons have been saved. These consist of a rigid-member leading edge that has its root attached firmly to a fore and aft member between the front and rear outer struts. Its outer reach is supported by two guy wires. The aileron trailing edge is raised and lowered by a rocking 'T' bar which is moved by control cables from the cockpit. This assembly actually flexes in this action rather than being hinged, attached to its rigid leading edge by leaf springs. The members that appear to be ribs within these fabric-covered surfaces are made of spring steel with tapered oak strip facing that distributes the warping effect evenly along the aileron. The control surface actually warps into a curved surface rather than being rigid and hinged for deflection.

Only a few of the wing struts may be serviceable, but there are sufficient examples from which to obtain an accurate pattern.

Empennage

None of the original tail members remain with this airplane. Construction drawings will be developed from the general arrangement layout found in *Aeronautics* magazine since the basic dimensions are given there. The construction of these tail surfaces are dependent upon what is learned from the unusual aileron structure. There is no indication that the movable tail portions are hinged to the rigidly supported leading edges, but uses a warping action instead.

Control movement is unique in that there are no control horns or torque tubes. Direct pull for moving the surfaces is by control cables which are routed through lengths of tubing which also act as bracing members for the leading edges of the tail. Two components having the appearance of tail skids are actually supports for the elevator control cables. This is a fascinating system of flight control and it is of prime importance in this restoration to duplicate its originality as closely as possible from the study of photographs, Dr Korn's sketches, and evidence found within the two original ailerons.

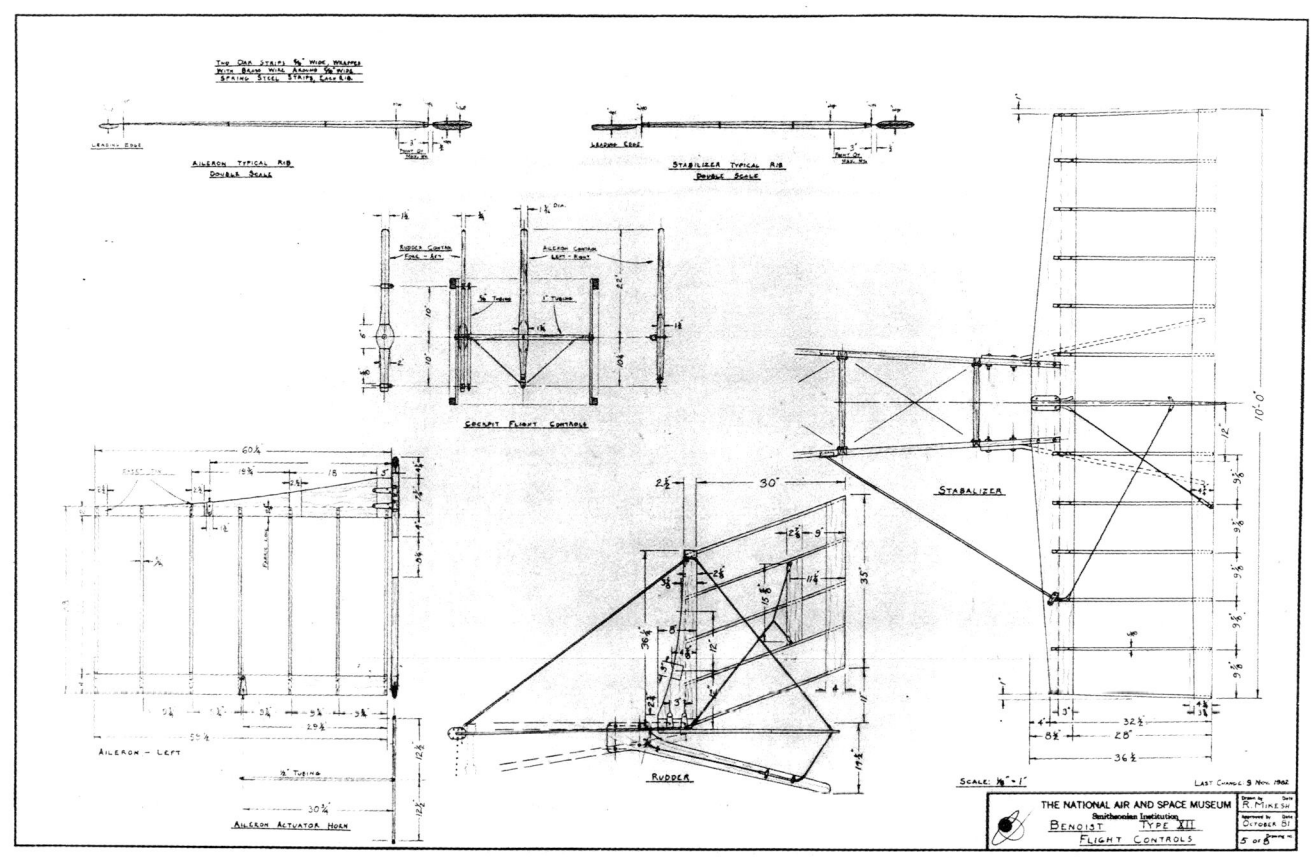

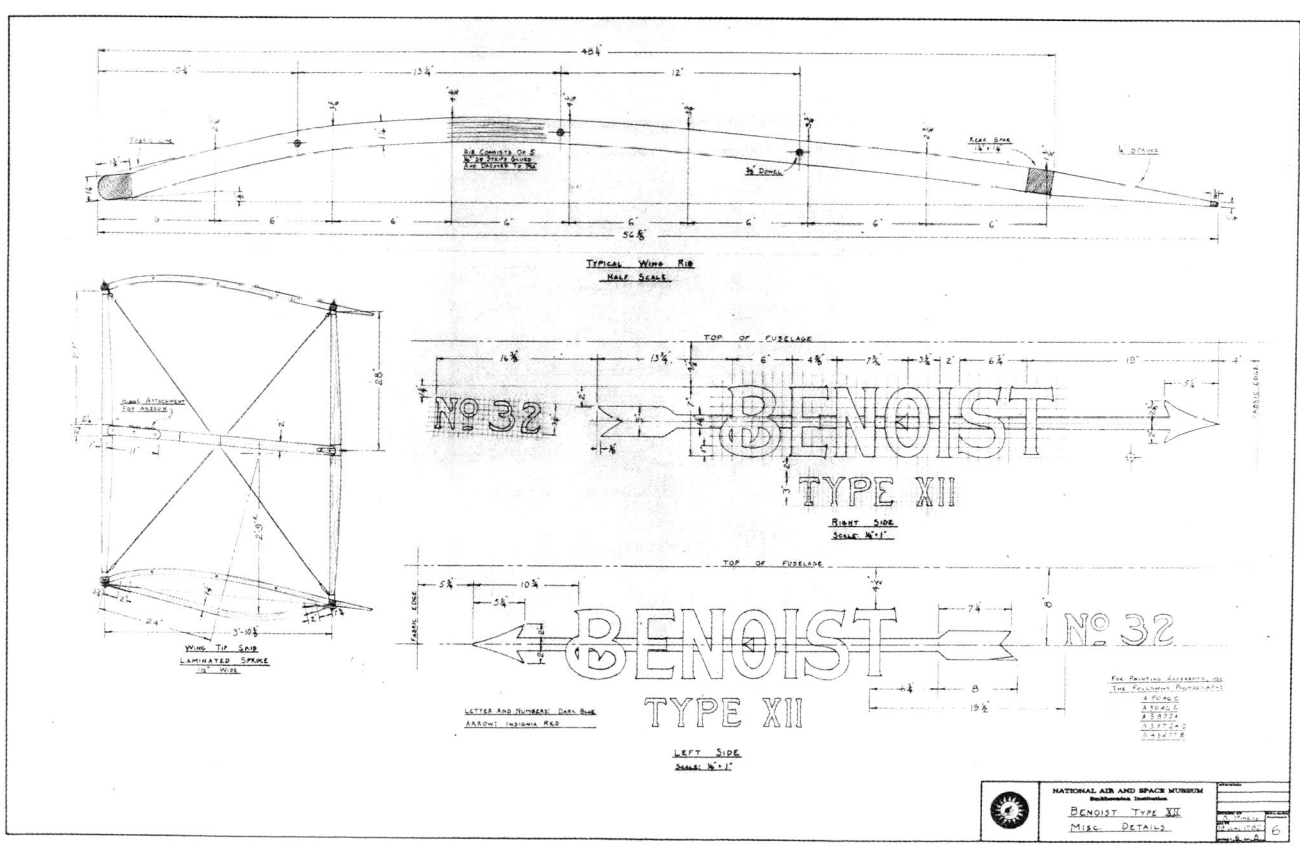

Paintings and Markings

The aircraft will remain in natural fabric color. Photos show that the exposed wooden portions of the aircraft are consistent in color, yet are darker than natural varnished wood. Further study may reveal what material had been applied to these portions of the exposed wooden structure. A decision on this will be made after closer inspection of the parts and examination of other reference material. (*Current note: No evidence of pigmented paint could be found, so this wood was left in natural varnished state.*)

The fuselage trademark will be on both sides of the fuselage, and a full-size pattern of this company design will be provided later. Colors consist of a red arrow going through the name BENOIST which consists of dark blue letters. TYPE XII, also dark blue, will be applied below the trademark. At the rear of the arrow feathers in dark blue is 'No. 32'. The number 23 will be hand-painted in black on the rudder. This number was added by Illinois State Fair officials in 1912. A pattern for this tail marking will be provided, based upon the photo of this rudder when seen at Park Ridge, Illinois while in museum storage. Colors to be used for the markings are:

Red: Federal Standard 595a 11136
Dark Blue: Federal Standard 595a 15102

(*Current note: The development of these patterns is a curatorial responsibility. Their accuracy as to shape must be determined by the curator which is done initially with correctable patterns. Once painted, no changes can be made.*)

Conclusion

As touched upon in various sections of this guideline, many of the mechanical and structural features of this airplane must be reconstructed as the project develops, in a form that is considered logical and practical. With the limited technical information that is available such as construction drawings, existing photographs, much must be left to the application of American know-how — and through this, the structure will probably be correct. This restoration will be a true test of American aviation pioneering spirit, now handicapped by jet-age technology.

Robert C. Mikesh
Curator of Aircraft
Aeronautics

Concluding Time and Cost Breakdown

Date started: March 5, 1981
Date concluded: Sept 31, 1982
Calendar time: 19 months

Phase	Man-hours	Cost (1981/82) $	£
Fuselage	1,142	13,715.72	8,640
Cockpit	41	512.50	323
Wing	1,138	14,118.60	8,895
Empennage	236	2,953.68	1,867
Engine	90	1,133.98	714
Final Assembly	48	616.32	388
Chemical treatment	2	23.42	15
Planning & Prog.	149	1,834.36	1,155
Total	2,846	34,908.58	21,997
Materials		4,582.28	2,886
Total cost:		**$39,490.86**	**£24,883**

Project Technician: Charles Parmley

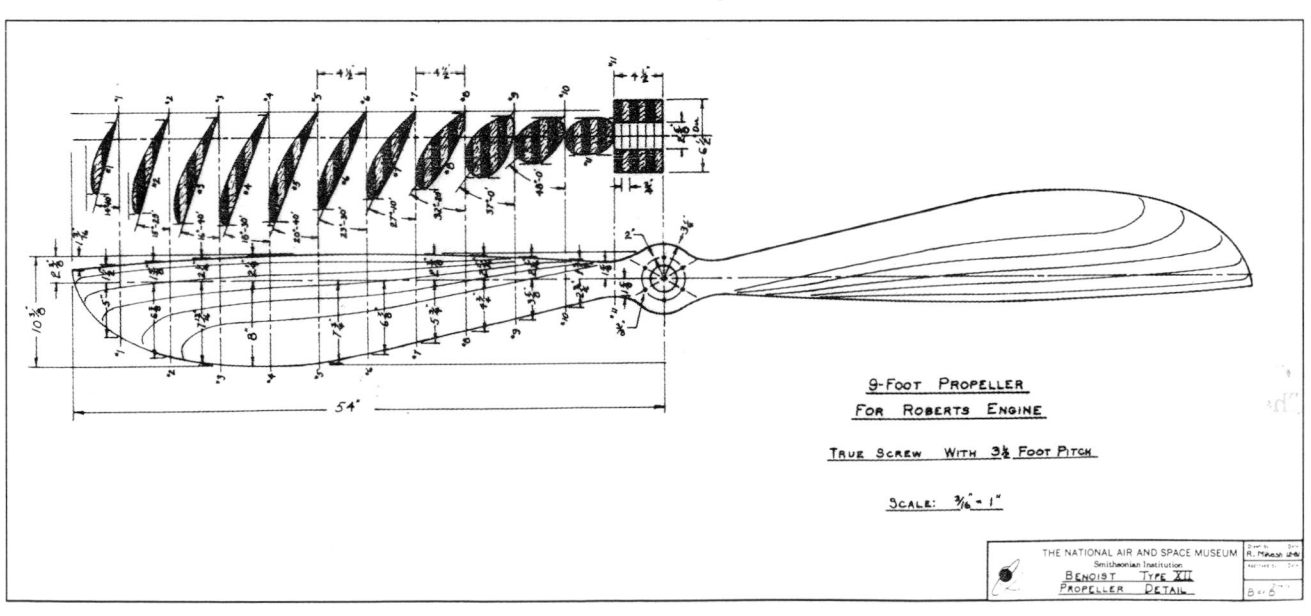

9-FOOT PROPELLER FOR ROBERTS ENGINE

TRUE SCREW WITH 3½ FOOT PITCH

SCALE: ³/₁₆ - 1"

THE NATIONAL AIR AND SPACE MUSEUM
Smithsonian Institution
BENOIST TYPE XII
PROPELLER DETAIL

APPENDIX B

Metal Aircraft Sample Restoration Guidelines

Restoring metal aircraft requires a totally different set of skills compared to that of fabric-and-wood aircraft. To assist those having to prepare Restoration Guidelines for an all-metal aircraft, the following is provided as a sample. It will bring to light some of the problems and issues that should be addressed when considering other restorations of this type. Materials recorded here are for reference only and should not be regarded as the best available, due to possible product improvements.

RESTORATION GUIDELINES
Arado Ar 234B-2 Blitz

Wk. No. 140312	(FE 1010)
Cat. No. 1960-312	NASM
1144	

The purpose of these Curatorial Guidelines is to provide the restoration technicians with a guide for achieving objectives in restoring the Arado Ar 234B-2. While some of the actions described here may be routine with many restorations, other details are unique to this aircraft, and therefore, become essential guidance to those working on this project. As a final result, these guidelines become a historical document that not only describes the condition of the aircraft at the start of the project, but serve as a record for the actions taken to achieve the restoration and preservation objectives. At the time of preparing these guidelines for the restoration, the Arado Ar 234B-2 project has been moved into the shop for closer study in order to determine and describe here, the degree of work that is required.

The paramount objective of this project, as with all other NASM aircraft restoration projects, is to ensure that every action is taken that will increase the life expectancy of not only the aircraft structure, but each of the components and systems as well. This Ar 234 is already the sole survivor of its type. Therefore, every assurance and safeguard for maximum longevity is essential.

Significance of the Arado Ar 234

The Arado Ar 234 Blitz was one of the great hopes of the *Luftwaffe* to achieve victory over the Allies during the waning years of World War II. It had a relatively short but illustrious career. The Ar 234 enjoys the position of being the world's first true jet bomber employed in combat and the third jet-propelled aircraft to see service. While this is its distinction in aviation history, it was not initially designed as a bomber but as a reconnaissance aircraft. It was in the reconnaissance configuration that the aircraft first became operational.

The Arado 234 jet reconnaissance/bomber went through a number of configurations during its short life which included a twin- and four- engine version. It was originally conceived in late 1940 to utilize the new jet engines that were being developed by BMW and Junkers. Work on the design began in 1941 at the Arado plant in Brandenburg, Germany. By 1942, two prototype airframes had been built. However, delays in engine delivery prevented the aircraft form flying until February 1943. The Ar 234 V1 made its maiden flight on 30 July, 1943, and was piloted by *Flugkapitän* Selle, who was later killed flying the Ar 234 prototype V2.

The Ar 234 was initially plagued with undercarriage operational problems stemming from the use of a jettisonable trolley gear for take-off and a skid for landing. It was not until 12 March, 1944, that the aircraft was flown with a conventional retractable tricycle landing gear. Concurrently, a four-engine version was designed and built. As prototypes V6 and V8, they flew on 25 April, 1944, and 4 February, 1944, respectively.

On the morning of 2 August, 1944, one of these aircraft, piloted by *Leutnant* Eric Sommer, took off on the world's first jet reconnaissance mission to photograph an area in Normandy held by the Allies. After over-flying the area at an altitude of 34,000 feet (10,370 m) to reach the French coast, Sommer then reversed his course, descending to about 1,700 feet (518 m), and photographed his area of interest at about 460 mph (740 km/h). The entire flight, which lasted for one hour, was a complete success. During this single mission Sommer was able to achieve more than routine German reconnaissance had been able to achieve in the previous two months.

It was not until 24 December, 1944, that an Ar 234B-2 participated in its first bombing mission. As a bomber, the aircraft's speed and altitude were traded-off for bomb load and operating range. For horizontal (level) bombing, a three-axis autopilot with a Lotfe 7K tachometric bombsight (located forward between the pilot's legs) was used. During the bombing run the pilot would unlock and swing the control column to the right, unloosen his shoulder straps, and lean forward to look through the sight. Photographic sorties were usually flown at a height of about 29,000 feet (8,845 m) utilizing two aerial cameras fitted in the rear fuselage.

Because of speed and altitude capabilities, the Ar 234B easily avoided Allied interception attempts as long as it maintained a relatively straight course. It was not until 24 February, 1945, that the first Ar 234 was brought down by USAAF P-47s, which provided the Allies their first close look at shattered remains of this type of aircraft.

Background of NASM's Aircraft

Soon after Germany surrendered on 8 May, 1945, aviation experts from the Allied nations set out to obtain as much information on as many undamaged German aircraft as they could find. It was possible that Japan had obtained this German technology and Allied forces could be met with radically new aircraft in the Pacific. An Arado Ar 234 was especially desired because of its advanced state in development and war record. Unfortunately, the Arado factory and test airfields were taken over by the Russians. This was offset, however, by the British finding at least 15 Ar 234s in good condition in the areas under their control. The British kept 11, two were donated to France, and four were transferred to the US; three to the USAAF and one to the US Navy. All of these aircraft were apparently operated by *Gruppe Stab*, the 6., 7., 8., and 9. *Staffeln*, 1(F)/5 and 5./KG 76 of the German Air Force. The NASM aircraft, Ar 234B-2, serial number (*Werk Nummer*) 140312, Air Force foreign equipment number FE-1010, was one of the three allotted to the USAAF. It is the only Ar 234 remaining in the world today.

The British found what would become NASM's aircraft at Sola airfield near Stavanger, Norway. After a close inspection, it was flown by one of a group of pilots that became known as 'Watson's Whizzers' under the leadership of Colonel H.E. Watson, USAAF. It was the responsibility of this group to gather these highly technical aircraft. After the Ar 234s made stopovers at Flensburg, Germany, they continued on to Melun, France and eventually on to Cherbourg where they were loaded aboard the British auxiliary carrier HMS *Reaper*.

On arrival in the US, the airplanes were reassembled at the Army Air Force Overseas Depot at Newark, New Jersey. In August 1945, NASM's eventual aircraft was flown to Freeman Field, Indiana, which was the Air Force Air Technical Services Command base for refitting these aircraft with standard American equipment for flight-testing. Upon completion and installing new engines (29 June, 1946), the airplane was flown to Wright Field in July 1946 and transferred to the Accelerated Service Test Maintenance Section (ASTMS), Flight Test Division at Wright Field, Dayton, Ohio, for flight evaluation. It remained

there until 1947, when it was moved to Orchard Place Airport, Park Ridge, Illinois (now Chicago International Airport).

On 1 May, 1949, the Arado Ar 234, along with many other military aircraft, was transferred to the Smithsonian's National Air Museum (NAM). These aircraft were eventually crated and shipped to NAM in the early 1950s. As far as can be determined from Army Air Forces Maintenance Inspection Records, Form 41B, the last flight of the Museum's Arado Ar 234 was on 16 October, 1946. From available data, it is presumed that the Museum's Ar 234B-2 was in the production run of *Werk Nummer* 140301–140360.

Final Configuration

The airplane will be restored to as near configuration as it would have been when operational during World War II when assigned to III/KG 76. Records provided by Manfred Griehl in his letter to NASM of 25 April, 1986, shows that this aircraft, *Werk Nr* 140312, was flown by KG 76, III, *Gruppe*, 8./*Staffel* from November 1944 to January 1945 and perhaps longer. This configuration will not only consist of appropriate camouflage and markings for this unit and time period, but suitable equipment such as wing-mounted rocket motors, bombsight, periscope, drag 'chute, and other components in the collection and appropriate for this type reconnaissance/bomber aircraft.

There will be no cutaway portions of the aircraft. All components will be able to be moved, i.e. flight controls, flaps, and landing gear but electrical power and hydraulic systems will not be the moving force. There are no known photographs of this aircraft while operating within the *Luftwaffe*, making it difficult to select the exact identifying markings used. Photographs of other aircraft within this unit will be used as patterns for general details of this nature. A letter from J. Richard Smith of 27 October, 1985, a noted German aircraft author and researcher, conveyed that 8./*Staffel* of KG 76 identification would be 'F1' in small figures to the left of the fuselage national insignia as verified by photographs. The unit color was red which was applied at the intakes of the jet engines and around the aircraft identifying letter. This color conforms with the standard of white, red and yellow being assigned in that order to the aircraft of the three *Staffeln* (flights) within a *Gruppe* (squadron). In this case, being the 8th *Staffel* of KG 76, the color is red, and the unit letter by a similar allocation system was 'S'.

Accepting these known marking standards, all that remained in question was the selection of a ship number. The letter 'G' was recommended by Mr Smith, since it is a letter that was not identified with a *Werk Nr* either in known photographs or

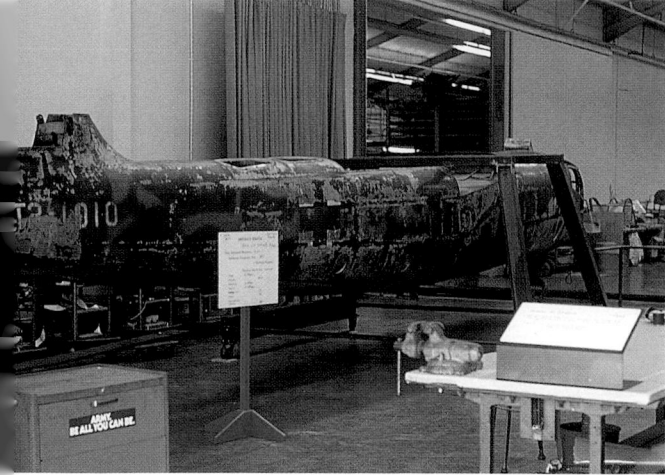

At this early stage of the Ar 234B-2 Blitz restoration, the fuselage was suspended from its support rack by the wing attachment points. Although much of the paint had chipped away during its years in storage, many areas were closely examined for color and paint samples that were carefully recorded for future reference.

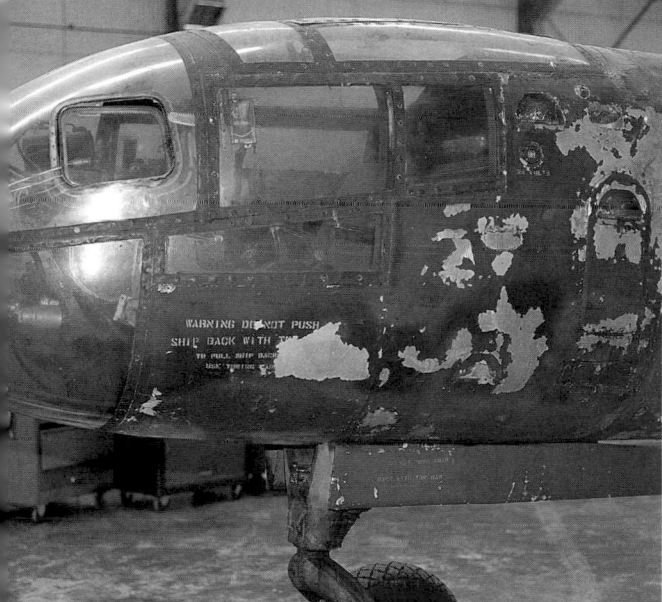

The Ar 234B-2 Blitz was a Category III airplane needing considerable attention to corrosion control, repair, and to be made exhibitable. Although made flyable for American evaluation after the war, many components had been removed from the airplane and American equipment added to the cockpit. (NASM, SI 84-2814-9)

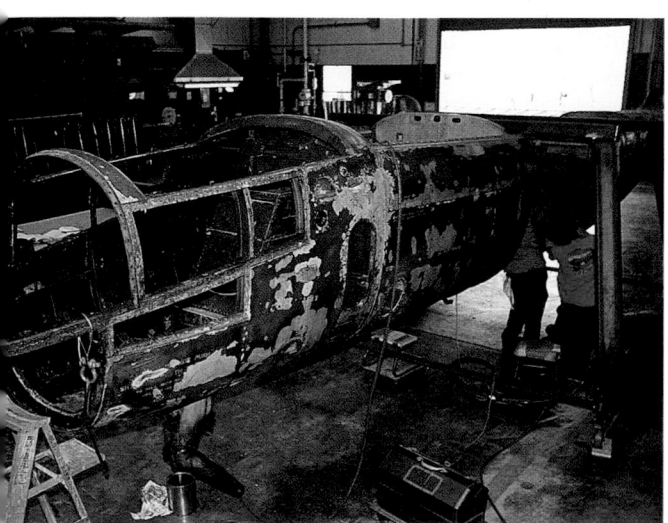

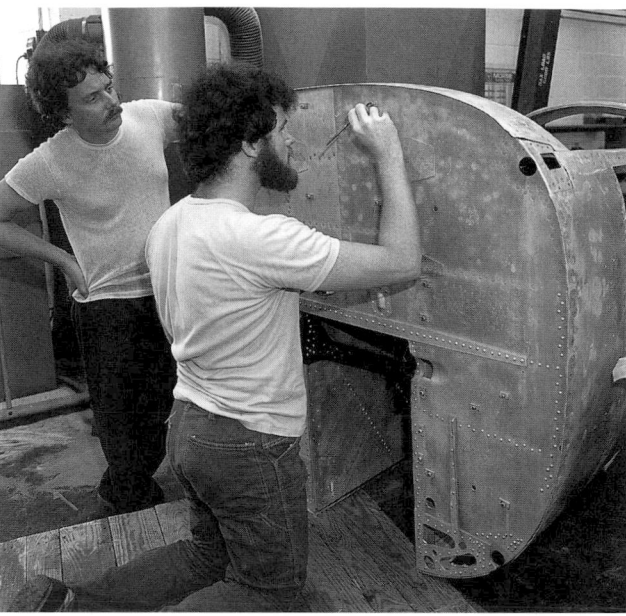

Visiting metal conservator from the Australian War Memorial in Canberra, David Hallam, had a special interest in various metals used by warring nations during World War II. Here he examines the back side of the Ar 234B-2's cockpit during the cleaning process. Karl Heinzel (at left) was one of two restoration technicians assigned to this aircraft. (NASM, SI 84-9433-11)

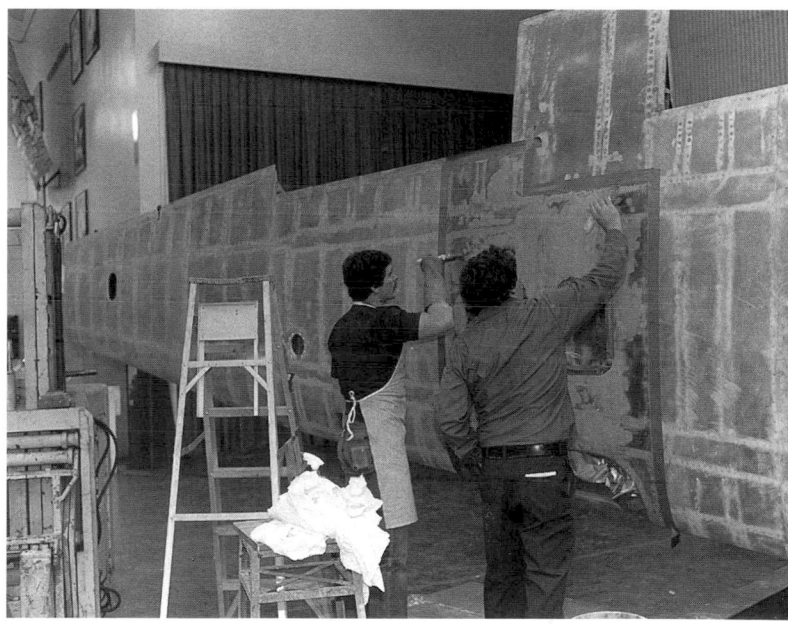

The restored wing of the Ar 234B-2 had skin depressions filled with body putty as was the case when the aircraft was manufactured. The original putty that was also flaking off, had to be removed in its entirety to arrest areas of corrosion that were forming. (NASM, SI 86-14172-21)

LEFT:
The nose section was nearly emptied of its many parts and had yet to be disconnected from the main section for thorough cleaning. Technicians are seen working in the wheel well which contained several dissimilar metals that had to be treated in place because of the way they were firmly attached.

189

written documents, yet is a letter within a group that would be used within a second *Staffel* of a *Gruppe*. This letter is to be outlined in the unit color red to the right of the fuselage national insignia, and appear again in a smaller format on the nose in all-red. The unit letter 'S' follows the 'G' on the fuselage sides.

Preservation Requirements

The most important aspect of any museum restoration project is to take all of the appropriate measures that will preserve the artifact to the maximum lifetime possible. There is no phase or portions of this preservation process that can be deferred since preservation measures taken at the time of this initial restoration will have the greatest effect on the life span of the aircraft. The ideal time to fully inspect the structure and to take every action possible to completely control corrosion and retard rust is while the structure is fully disassembled. In many areas of this structure it is necessary that permanently affixed skin panels be removed to ensure that the complete corrosion control process reaches all the surfaces of the internal structure. Instructions covering these processes are contained in the attached Chemical Processing Standards (CPS). Properly followed, as they must be, they will offer the greatest life expectancy methods of preservation that we know, to each of the parts of this aircraft.

Where parts of the internal structure are not painted, Magnus™ FF111 Clear will be applied throughout the structure as a protective coating. In areas of the structure where complete coverage cannot be assured, and the structure will be relatively sealed from outside access, anti-corrosion compound R-2000 will be used according to directions.

This restoration will require the repair of many parts and the remanufacture of others. Two rubber stamps, one for repaired parts and one for replaced parts, are provided. These rubber stamp impressions must be applied to these repaired or new parts to properly identify them for the years ahead as not being original. The date of work accomplishment must be added to these impressions with an indelible pen. Apply a clear coating over these marks to ensure their preservation over the years.

Before beginning work, an assessment must be made as to the degree of original paint finish that can be retained. Many of the interior components are in satisfactory condition that they need only be cleaned and coated with wax rather than to repaint. Follow this concept to the greatest extent possible. The exterior has been overpainted with American paint and bogus markings. Random surface wet-sanding is already underway in order to record original colors and their location. These are being recorded on a factory marking diagram in order to compare the actual color location to that of factory intentions. A paint layer search is in progress in an effort to find the painted *Werk Nummer* on the fin, and unit markings elsewhere.

Fuselage

This structure is particularly a major problem as compared to other metal aircraft. While basically an aluminum structure, major supporting components are made from steel and riveted in place in such a manner that to remove them would be a radical disassembly of permanently affixed structural members. While the preservation of these parts against further deterioration caused by rust is essential, it must be accomplished as best possible while remaining in place. The product Extend (basically tannic acid) will be used at major structural junctures, while blasting with walnut shells will be the primary method of removing rust on exposed surfaces. Glass bead blasting can be used on the more stubborn areas.

The normal chemical process of corrosion control for the aluminum surfaces will be followed. Disassembly of the fuselage into smaller units can only include fuel cell and landing gear removal, the detaching of the cockpit nose-section, and related plumbing and wiring. Each of the major attach fittings are of steel, and because of the problems already described, they must be watched closely in the years ahead to retard further rust as much as possible. Each steel fitting will be given a coating of Extend prior to painting with original color paint.

Cockpit

Aircraft interiors reflect much of the history for the state-of-the-art of flying for the time period of the airplane. This relates to pilot accommodation and methods for control with which to operate the aircraft. Therefore this area must be as complete as possible with every item that was originally installed. All of the American-installed components and related markings will be removed permanently, and replaced in every instance possible with the correct type of German equipment. Of greatest interest with this aircraft is that of the periscope for the pilot. The one in NASM's collection will be installed since none came with this aircraft. A housing for this periscope must be fabricated from a drawing scaled from photographs that will be provided. The original canopy pieces will be used. It appears that the discoloration can be buffed out from the surface of this material.

Components needing to be repainted will be matched in every instance to that of the original color.

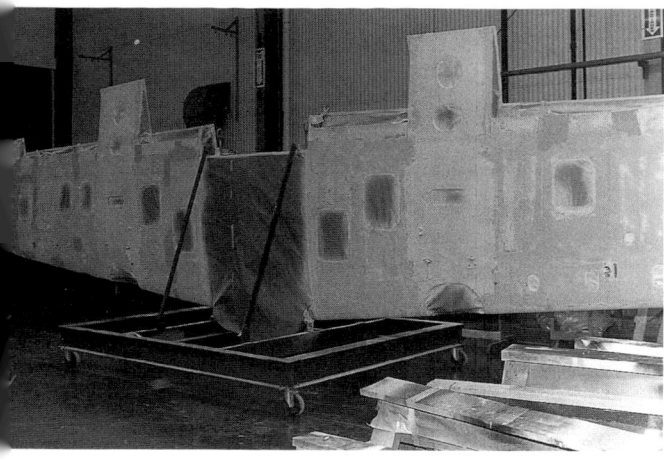

Access openings on the bottom of the Ar 234B-2's wing were covered and taped so that dust would not enter the wing during the smoothing and sanding of the body putty. Note the transport stand that provided safe mobility for the wing. (NASM, SI 87-2118-42)

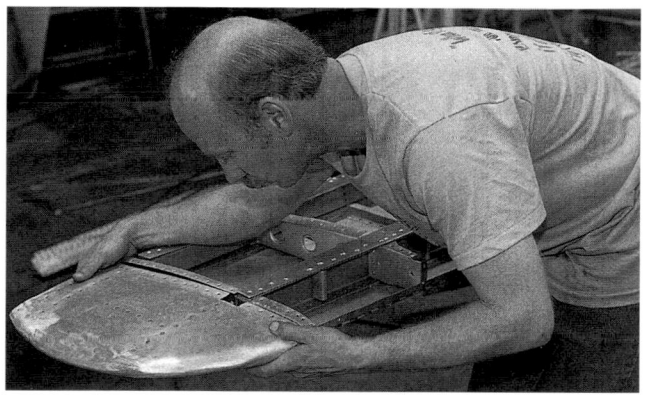

The tip of the Ar 234B-2's stabilizer suffered considerable damage while in storage and required major repair by metal technician Dale Bucy of NASM. The bottom skin layer was fully removed in order to properly clean the interior of corrosion. A clear protective coating was then added to interior surfaces. (NASM, SI 86-6704-29A)

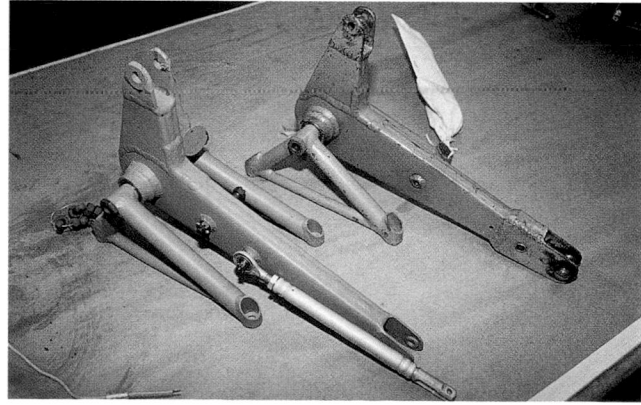

Shown here are two examples of both restoration and preservation. One flap actuator was seriously corroded and needed restoration attention; the other showed minor damage and could be left original after being cleaned and receiving a protective coating of wax, particularly to coat chipped-paint areas.

These record photographs of the Ar 234B-2's wing were taken as it came from the paint shop. All flaps and ailerons were put in place in order to have consistent and factory-like paint coverage. Very likely the airplane was originally painted when fully assembled. (NASM, SI 88-16585-34A and 88-16585-36A)

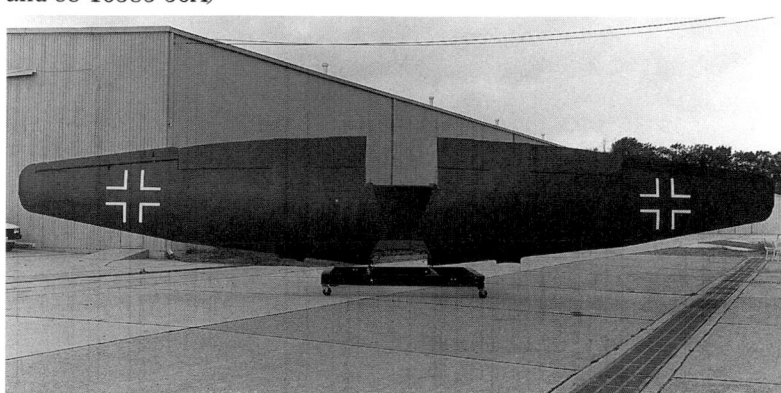

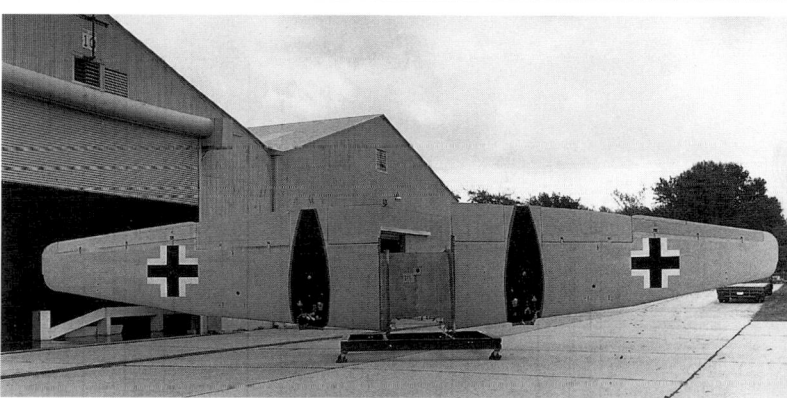

This is the eight-stage compressor rotor of the Jumo 004 turbine engine. Matthew Nazzaro carefully lowers the rotor into the housing of the engine during rebuild. (NASM, SI 88-8618-3)

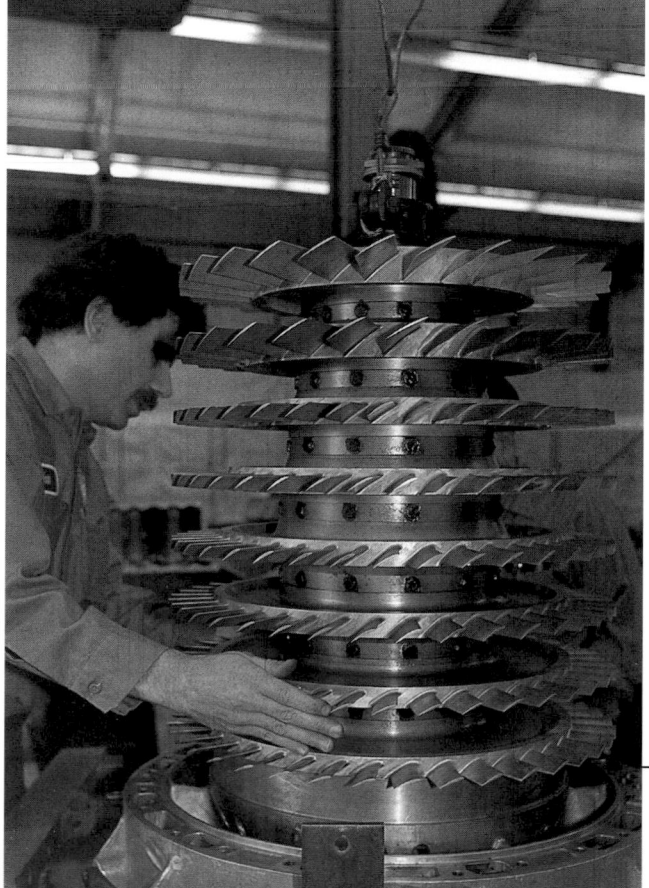

191

Landing Gear

Disassembly and cleaning of the many components of this landing gear will be accomplished in the usual manner. A spacer block will be inserted into all three struts so that the oleo will be extended to the point where it would normally rest while the aircraft is static on the ground. Jack pads will be fabricated to support the aircraft while in storage or on exhibit.

Tires will be rejuvenated to the best extent possible and used again on this aircraft. A search will be made as to the availability of replacement tires, and if available, a new set will be acquired now, and placed in controlled storage for anticipated future use.

(*Current note: Replacement tires could not be located. In order to prevent damage in the event that the weight of the aircraft was placed on these surviving tires, they were given a 'Tirefill' plastic foam treatment for permanent inflation.*)

Wing

The existing paint covering this wing will be explored by selective area sanding to see if any of the original German paint remains. Should this be the case, unit markings and identification may be revealed. Following this evaluation, all the paint will be removed in order to arrest surface corrosion that has appeared in several critical areas under this paint. While doing so, a record of body-filled areas will be noted for duplication prior to repainting.

There are many places on the wing where the skin was damaged during storage. When these panels are removed for repair, all other removable panels will also be taken from the wing to make its internal structure as accessible as possible for cleaning and corrosion control. It is here that some of the skin panels may have to be removed by drilling out rivets to gain access to closed areas. Use rivets of the same type when replacing skin panels and making repairs.

The structure of this wing may be like that of the fuselage in that many strong-points are made of steel and their removal from the structure would be more detrimental than to make an attempt to clean and preserve them in place. The product Extend™ will be used in these instances. Where it is practical to remove these steel parts from the structure for cleaning, they will be removed. Cleaning of these steel parts and seeing that adequate preservation methods are applied is a very critical factor to this restoration.

Engines

Engines installed in this aircraft are two Junkers Jumo 004B-1. Both engines now crated, are to be reworked to ensure that they are technically complete with all working components. They are to be cleaned, preserved, and painted as they were originally. The degree of teardown will be determined after the engines have been opened for inspection. This should be to the degree that the rotor can be fully exposed for inspection and coated with preservative. Bearings must be cleaned and permanently lubricated with Molykote™ FS-3452 Valve Lubricant. Other internal non-friction surfaces will be coated with CRC™ Soft Seal.

During this process, a list must be made of the part numbers noted on the various components such as starter, generators, pumps, etc. This will be included as a permanent entry on the records for this aircraft.

The exterior of the assembled engine will have matching paint to that of the original. A record of color shades must be kept in the aircraft files for future reference.

Both engines are to be installed in the completed aircraft.

Empennage

The same process as describe for the wing will apply to the components of the empennage.

All fabric covering will be Grade A aircraft cotton. This is a close match to existing fabric samples found on the aircraft structure. A check must be made of the existing covering in order to make a determination for being original German-applied fabric or American replacement. The original method for applying new fabric for this restoration must follow the techniques used by the German manufacturer.

Missing Parts

The aircraft must be inventoried in order to locate missing parts. Some items known to be missing are the periscope, all avionics, drogue 'chute and cable, booster pods, and bombsight. Fortunately, a Lotfe 7K bombsight is in the study collection and will be installed. PV1B sighting head (periscope), the BZA bombsight, a braking parachute with cable, and rocket pods (RATO) are also in the inventory.

The following items will be removed from the study collection and installed as needed in the Ar 234 during this restoration.

(*This listing is deleted here to save space.*)

Colors and Markings

Primer paint and fillers will be of modern materials that are most suited for this application. The aircraft will require considerable body-filling to duplicate the original filling that was done at the time of manufacture. Refer to notes taken at time of paint removal which records the more important areas of filling.

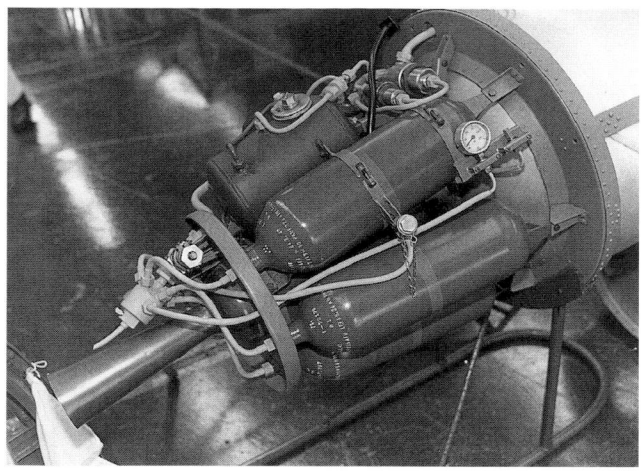

This close-up shows some of the details of the rocket motor for RATO assist. Of the two, this engine required a complete restoration and repainting because of corrosion damage. The second needed only to be cleaned and preserved, saving much evidence of original craftsmanship and material. (NASM, SI 88-14864-62A)

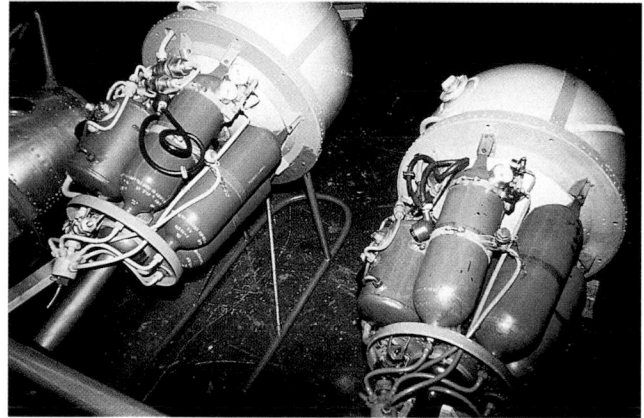

The best of two concepts were used during the attention given to the two rocket-assisted take-off (RATO) motors which were mounted under the wings. The worst of the two (left) was completely restored, preserved and repainted as its condition dictated. The less affected (right) was merely cleaned, leaving untouched its original paint which was given a protective coating of wax.

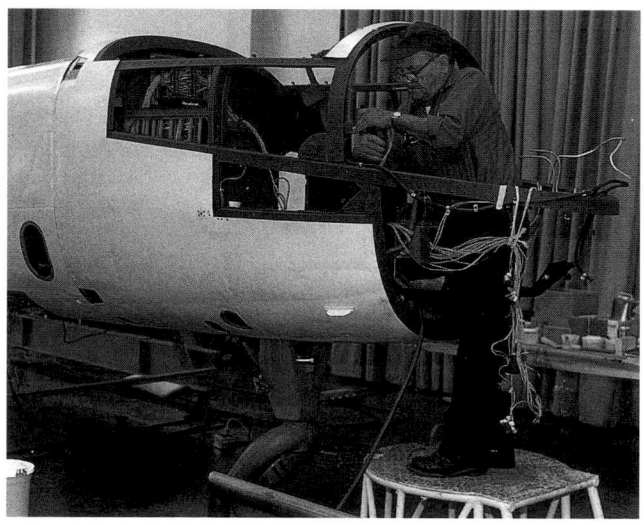

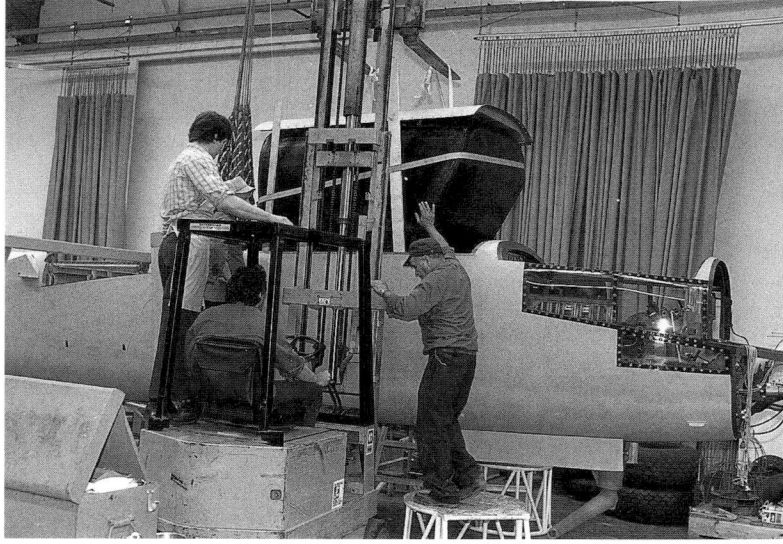

The main self-sealing fuel tank is carefully lowered into the fuel bay of the Ar 234B-2. Note that this fuel tank is attached to the top of the fuselage so that both are removed as one unit. (NASM, SI 86-4365-63)

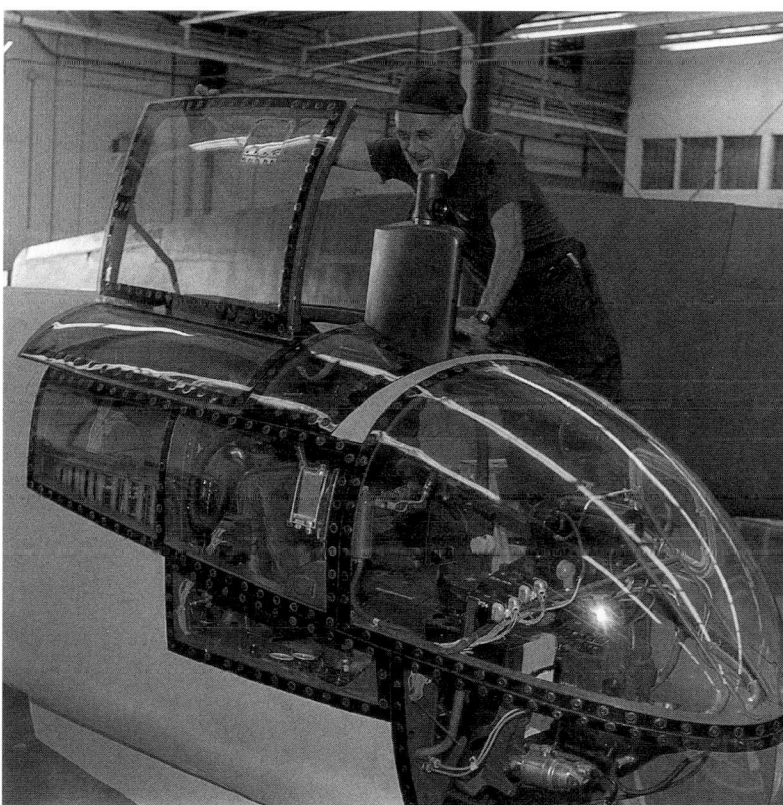

One of the final details added to the cockpit by George Genotti was the well-streamlined periscope to aid the pilot's rearward vision. The airplane was received without this device, however a periscope of the desired type was in NASM's collection. The fairing and mount were designed from photographs. (NASM, SI 88-16594-31)

LEFT:
The refitting of the cockpit areas was an intensive task. Since this was a small area for an airplane of this size, the area was dense with flight-related components. All had to be removed in order to thoroughly clean the structure and components of corrosion. (NASM, SI 85-13527-59)

193

The camouflage pattern for the Ar 234 will follow the lines shown on the attached drawings. This drawing was traced from a factory drawing recently found in East Germany, yet varies in some details from other published drawings. The traced drawing will be followed since it does not differ from color demarcation lines found in photographs and sanded sample areas on NASM aircraft. Demarcation lines are straight with angles, but not masked. Feathered edge should not exceed one-half inch. All colors will be flat finish in lacquer material, with a final coating of semi-gloss clear lacquer as a way of obtaining the original paint texture used on Ar 234s.

All other interior details that require painting will be matched as closely as possible to the original color found on that part. Where possible, clean, preserve and save as unrestored original parts.

Markings will be sized as follows, and placed in accordance to the drawings provided:

Top of wing:	1000 mm	White cross	(B6 style)
Bottom of wing:	1000 mm	Black cross	(B3 style)
Fuselage sides:	900 mm	White cross	(B5 style)
Swastika on fin:	600 mm	White	(H4 style)

The Museum's Arado Ar 234B-2 had nearly been stripped of all original paint at the time it was again repainted in the US soon after World War II. Selective sanding of the fuselage paint was undertaken in an effort to detect some of the original paint. Different colors were found, but for the most part, nearly all are believed to be American colors. All were small in area.

Location	Color	Munsell Color
Inside wing root	81 Brown-Violet	10GY 3/1
Left Nose	More yellow than 71	5Y 3/2
Left Nose	Buff, not 97	2.5Y 5/4 to 4/4
Bottom	Greenish-Gray	5GY 7/2
Cockpit	Close to 66	5GY 2/1
Wheel well	Olive Brown	2.5Y 4/6
Rudder post bracket	02 RLM	10Y 5/1

The above is included as a matter of record only.

Stenciling was standard on nearly all German aircraft but in different formats and usage by aircraft type. Since no reference was available for the Arado Ar 234 aircraft, stenciled notations will not be applied until able to be confirmed.

Robert C. Mikesh
Senior Curator for Aeronautics
Aeronautics Department

Colors to be used are as follows

Area	German No. Equivalent	Color Name	Munsell Color
Upper surface:	Color 81	Brown-Violet	5 GY 3/2
Upper surface:	Color 82	Light-Green	7.5GY 4/4
Under surface:	Color 76	Light Blue	7.5B 7/2
Rear of nacelles:	Color 22	Black	N2.75
Insignia:	Color 22	Black	N2.75
Insignia:	Color 21	White	N9.5
Cockpit:	Color 66	Black-Gray	N3.0
Interior structural details including landing gear	02 RLM	Gray	5GY 5/1
Main landing gear wheel wells:	(none)	Olive Brown	2.5Y 4/6

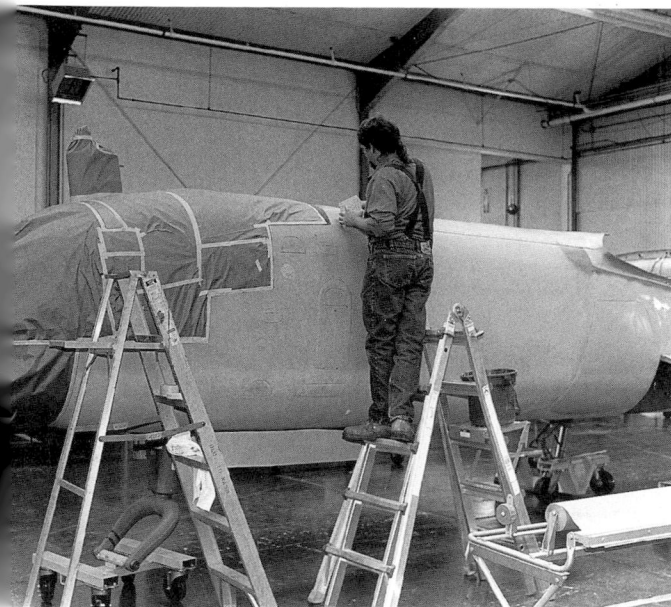

In preparation for painting, Karl Heinzel covers the Plexiglass areas of the cockpit. Note that the gray under-surface has already been painted in preparation for the layout of the two-color green and olive camouflage. (NASM, SI 88-17797-20)

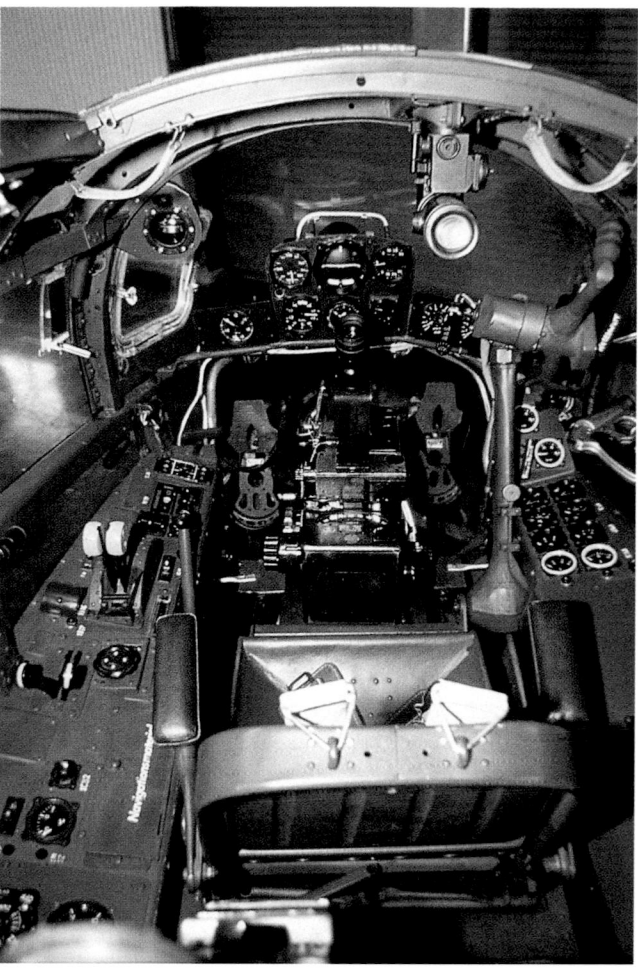

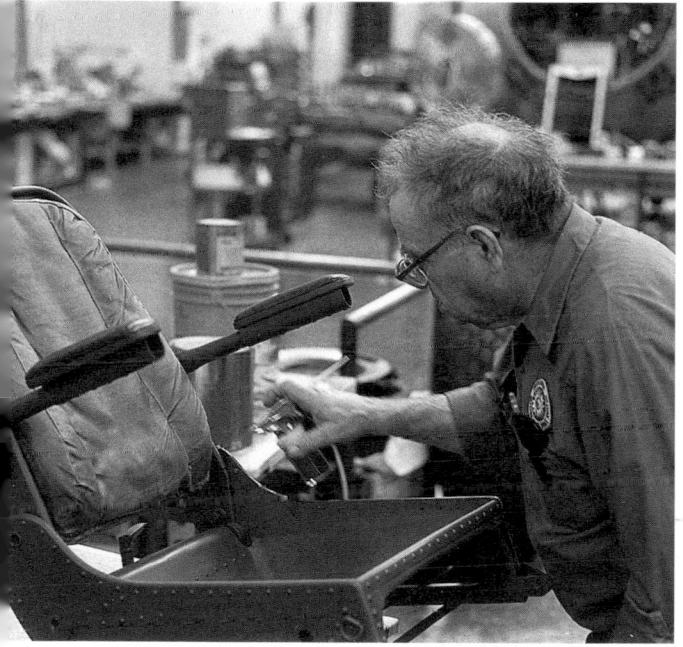

The finished cockpit is one that was comfortably designed around the pilot. As the single crew member of this twin-jet reconnaissance-bomber, the pilot served as the bombardier as well as photo officer. Having an autopilot, the control wheel is shown here disconnected and swung out of the way to the left so that the bombsight can be operated.

A final paint touch-up is given to the pilot's seat by restoration technician George Genotti. This was an elaborate, yet comfortable seat for this time period. It is noticeably small because of the restricted size of the cockpit for its one crew member. (NASM, SI 85-17689-49)

RIGHT:
The wing was attached to the fuselage long before having to be removed again for the painting process. The reason was that the wing-to-fuselage fairings were missing and the new parts required considerable hand-forming. The same held true for several fairings at the engine junctures. (NASM, SI 88-11227-2A)

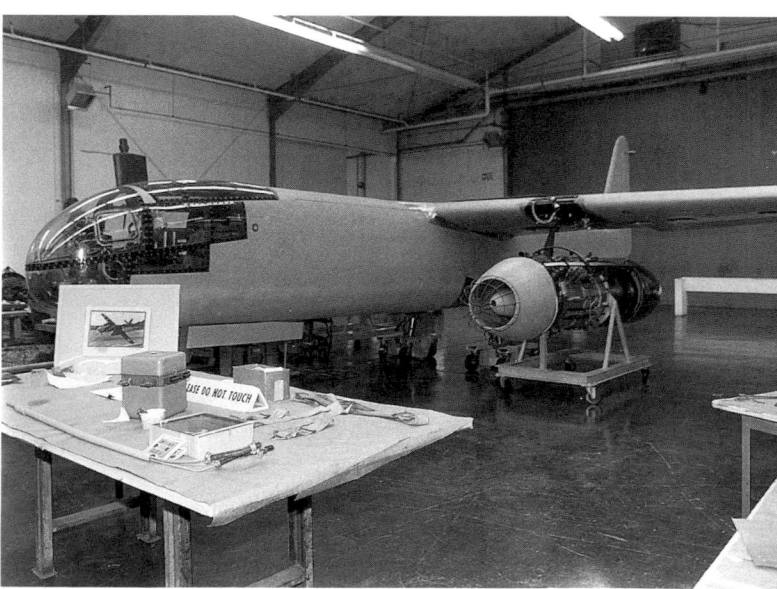

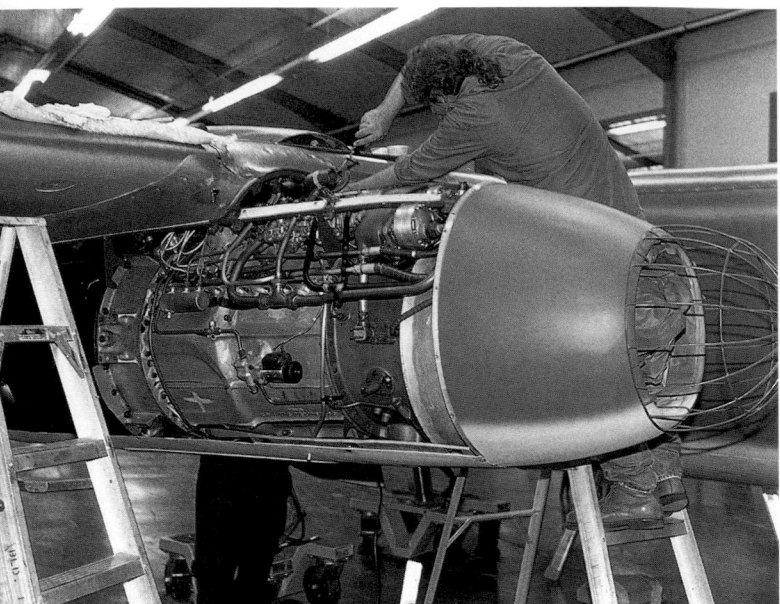

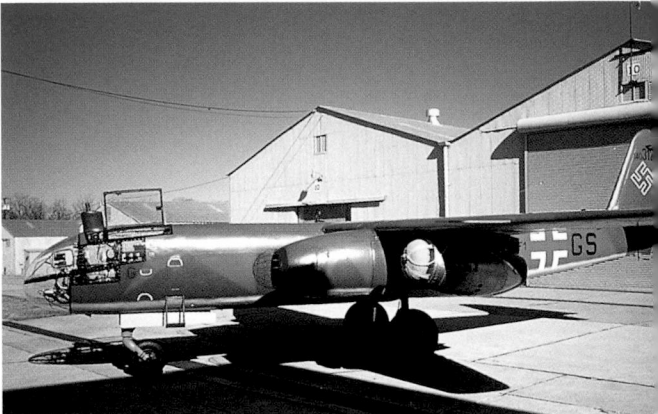

Completely finished, the Ar 234B-2 was moved out from the shop for a series of photographs. Note the periscope mounted above the cockpit for rearward visibility. Under the wing are jettisonable RATO rocket motors that, when released, each fall to earth with the help of a parachute attached on the motor's nose. Screens on engine noses are original and were for ground use only to prevent ingestion of foreign objects.

The Jumo 004 engines are attached to the underside of the wings. Engine cowling attachments had such close tolerances that there was no interchangeability. It was obvious that much handwork was done to enable the fitting of these panels. (NASM, SI 88-18664-65A)

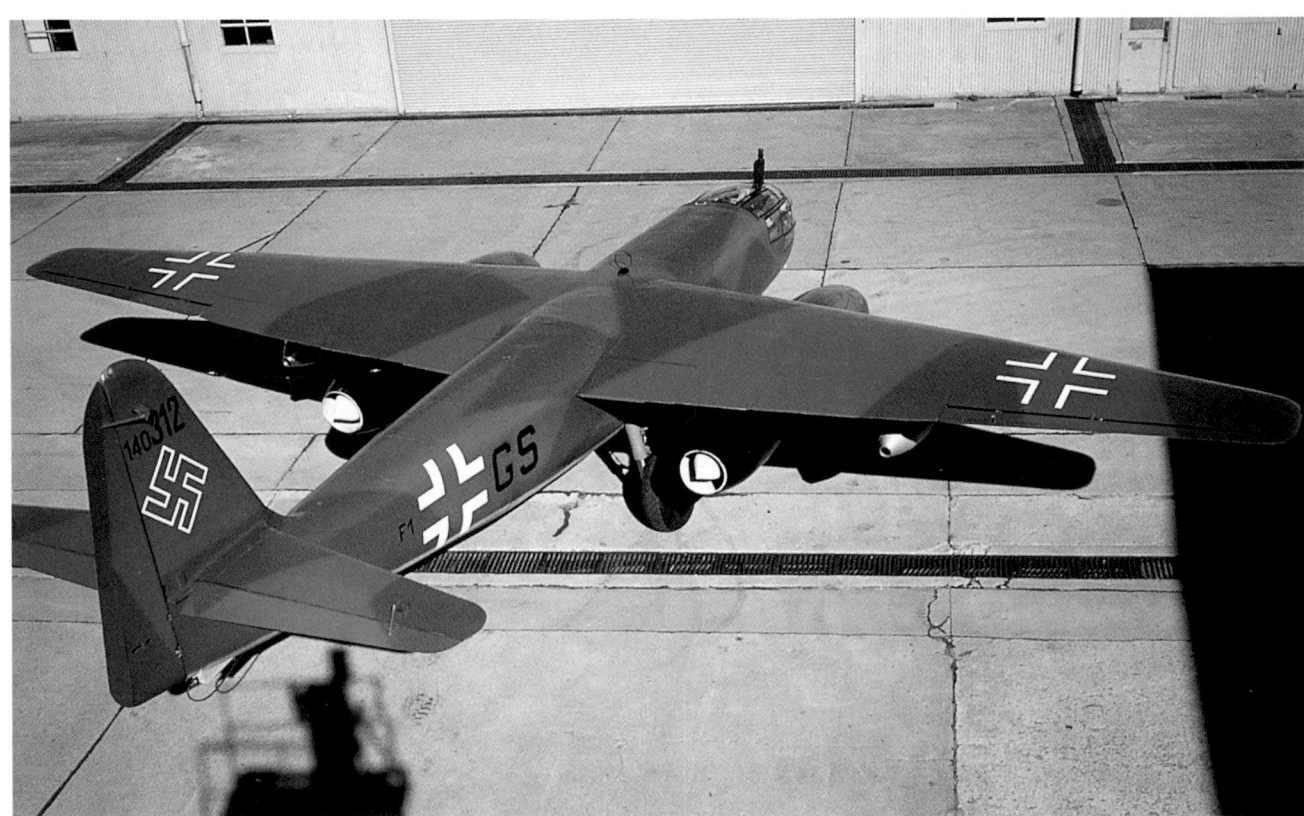

All but a few traces of the original paint had been removed from this airplane before being repainted by Americans soon after the war. The factory layout of the camouflage scheme was followed for this restoration repainting. Operational markings were developed from photographs of what was standard at the time and appropriate for the airplane's probable unit assignment.

APPENDIX C

Concluding Report Sample Covering Restoration

Many details of the restoration project are bound to be missed in the technicians' daily notes or visitation reports made by the curator. It is this concluding report in which these general details need to be recorded as a matter of historical record for the aircraft in question. As a sample, the concluding report for the Arado Ar 234 (see Appendix B) is reproduced here.

MEMORANDUM FOR: Aircraft Records File
SUBJECT: Arado Ar 234 Restoration
Concluding Report

Attention is invited to the excellent detailed notes that were made during this restoration by the restoration technician, George Genotti. He has covered every aspect of this restoration in fine detail. Many photographs of Polaroid type are also included in the file box covering this restoration that is kept in NASM archives.

These concluding remarks are of the type that would not otherwise be included in the Restoration Guidelines that were written before the fact, yet are of the nature to be of assistance to those having future access to this aircraft, be that of research, or disassembly for moving.

Disassembly/reassembly

To simplify the disassembly process for future moves of this aircraft, standard straight bolts have been used for joining the four attachment points of the wing to the fuselage. One taper bolt came with the aircraft. This served as a pattern for making the missing three, all of which are stored behind the pilot's seat.

Both engines and the two rocket motors must be removed for safety and to take the weight off the wing for movement. An electrical release mechanism disengages the rear pylon mount for the rocket engines which then swings clear. This can be tripped manually through the small opening at this point.

None of the wing-to-fuselage fairings came with this aircraft. All were fabricated as part of this restoration.

Engine cowling panels must be replaced in their same order for they are not interchangeable between engines. These were very difficult to attach since the attach-railings on the engines had been repositioned during the restoration, but it was also felt that poor fitting of the panels were the case in the beginning. All fairings are original, yet they look as though they were modified or repaired at the time of manufacture. An example is the material that was added on one that was necessary to complete the cover of the area.

Flaps must be lowered in order to remove the fairings between the inboard flaps and the fuselage. This is accomplished, though the access that has been placarded in English to show the location where a turnbuckle is installed for holding the flaps in the up position. Since these flaps are hydraulically actuated, they would otherwise rest in the down position.

The left jack pad within the wing is too far to the rear with comparison to its access opening on the bottom of the wing. The jack extension had to be set at its fully extended position in order for the jack to be slender enough to enter the wing and not interfere with the skin opening.

Placement and removal of the wing has been effectively accomplished with fork lifts and mattress pads.

Landing Gear

These tires have been filled with foam rubber and have supported the weight of the aircraft and rolled nicely at the time of this restoration. As ageing of the original casings continues, they may not be as resilient for this support of the aircraft. The use of wheel based dollies for any movement of this airplane in the future is strongly advised. With this foam rubber filling, each main wheel and tire weighs 440 lb (199.7 kg).

The nose gear will not retract without disassembly of the extension strut. This strut has an extender bar inside that holds the proper ground extension that in actual operation is contracted mechanically during retraction.

The main gear can be mechanically unlocked for it to retract. When opening the wheel well door for this process, do not extend the doors fully or they will lock in the open position, since this was a hydraulic process with a sequence valve system. To unlatch this door should it lock in the open position, this valve must be repositioned through the small opening which is a difficult process to do manually.

A low tire-pressure switch is on the left wheel only. When sensor points touch due to a low-pressure situation, a light illuminates in the cockpit. The wires for this system had previously been cut.

Engines

The left engine nose cowling was heavily damaged at some point during the storage and moving of this aircraft. Since others were in the collection, it was replaced by another nose cowling which was in better condition. Exchanges must have been a common practice while these aircraft were operational, and it appears that these nose cowlings are the same as those used on the Me 262.

The engine starter nose cones were not matched, nor should it be assumed that they were supposed to be. This dissimilarity was distracting since one was natural aluminum and the other had a green tinge. To avoid future confusion over this seeming irregularity, the right nose cone was exchanged with the one from our Go 229 which then makes a match for both aircraft.

During this restoration process, the rocket engine in the worst condition was fully repainted. The other engine was restored internally as well, but the outside surfaces were cleaned and protected with two coatings of microcrystalline wax in order to preserve the original paint and colors. Both engines are normally cowled when in place.

The tail cone for the left rocket motor has been specially spun for this project since it was missing from this engine.

Both parachute bags for these rocket motors have been fabricated for this restoration. They were copied from a German cargo parachute in the collection which matched photographs for those used on the rocket motors. Since only one parachute was available, this has been retained in the study collection, and therefore the inside filling is plastic packing fragments (peanuts) contained in a plastic bag. Clips holding the straps for release were fabricated without patterns.

Drag Parachute

A German parachute of seemingly the correct type was withdrawn from NASM's collection to serve as the drag 'chute. It was cleaned, and then packed by the parachute shop at Andrews AFB. It is installed with the ejector springs disengaged for safety purposes. To unlatch the ejector doors, access must be through the top of the fuselage to reach this door release.

Cockpit

The electrical power panel in the cockpit has all-new placards. These were designed and completed with reference to fragments that still remained and then applied with a decal process.

The bombsight was drawn from NASM's collection for installation in this aircraft. Since a mounting platform was not in the aircraft, this was fabricated from the use of photographs and graphics and fitted to the instrument. It is possible that this is lower than the original since the optic protrudes below the surface of the nose which is not evident in photographs of operational aircraft. The cover normally installed could not be used in this case, and is therefore stowed in the cockpit. It could only be installed if the bombsight were removed. The placard on the front of the bombsight is copied from the original that had all but disintegrated from age.

As was the plan from the beginning, the periscope was withdrawn from the Museum collection for installation in this cockpit. A mounting bracket was fabricated to suit the purpose and in no way is implied to match the original bracket. The streamline housing was then configured around the periscope and scaled from photographs.

The battery in the cockpit was thoroughly flushed for this restoration and terminals connected to prevent any possible charge build-up.

A fully new oxygen system has been fabricated for this restoration from technical drawings of this aircraft since the original equipment had been removed and replaced by an American system when the aircraft was prepared for flight evaluation. This includes new tubing, and the German oxygen bottle which was withdrawn from Museum stock.

Miscellaneous Observations

The dorsal loop antenna was made in NASM's shop to match photographs. There is question as to this having not been centered, for it may have been attached to a (24-inch (61 cm) approximately) round disc on the top of the fuselage which could have been clear plastic originally. This deserves further research.

The wire antenna installation is also questionable. Since the radio used within the Ar 234 is the same as that on the Fw 190F-8, that installation was closely followed. Picture frame wire was used since it was as close a match that could be found. Some fittings and insulators are not original.

Factory installation of the rear fuel bay was accomplished with explosive-type rivets. For this restoration, pop rivets were used instead.

To preclude the thought that sabotage was attempted when a black-handled screwdriver is one day found under this fuel bay, this was not the case. George Genotti dropped his screwdriver through the opening in the top of the fuselage and it rolled under this tank to the bottom of the fuselage when the aircraft was being reassembled in Building 24 at the Garber Facility in April 1989. Too much disassembly would have been necessary to retrieve the tool.

The only graffiti found on this aircraft during the restoration was a stick-man drawn with a pencil on the bare aluminum surface at the lower left of the left engine nose cone at the trailing edge. This has been preserved under a coating of clear epoxy primer that can be seen if the paint is removed and the primer is not disturbed.

It should be noted that at this early time in the construction of this aircraft, that all the flight controls were of the balance type around the hinge pivot point. This was done with counterweights.

None of the warning streamer flags and pitot cover now on this airplane are copies of original German equipment.

Robert C. Mikesh
Senior Curator for Aeronautics
Aeronautics Department

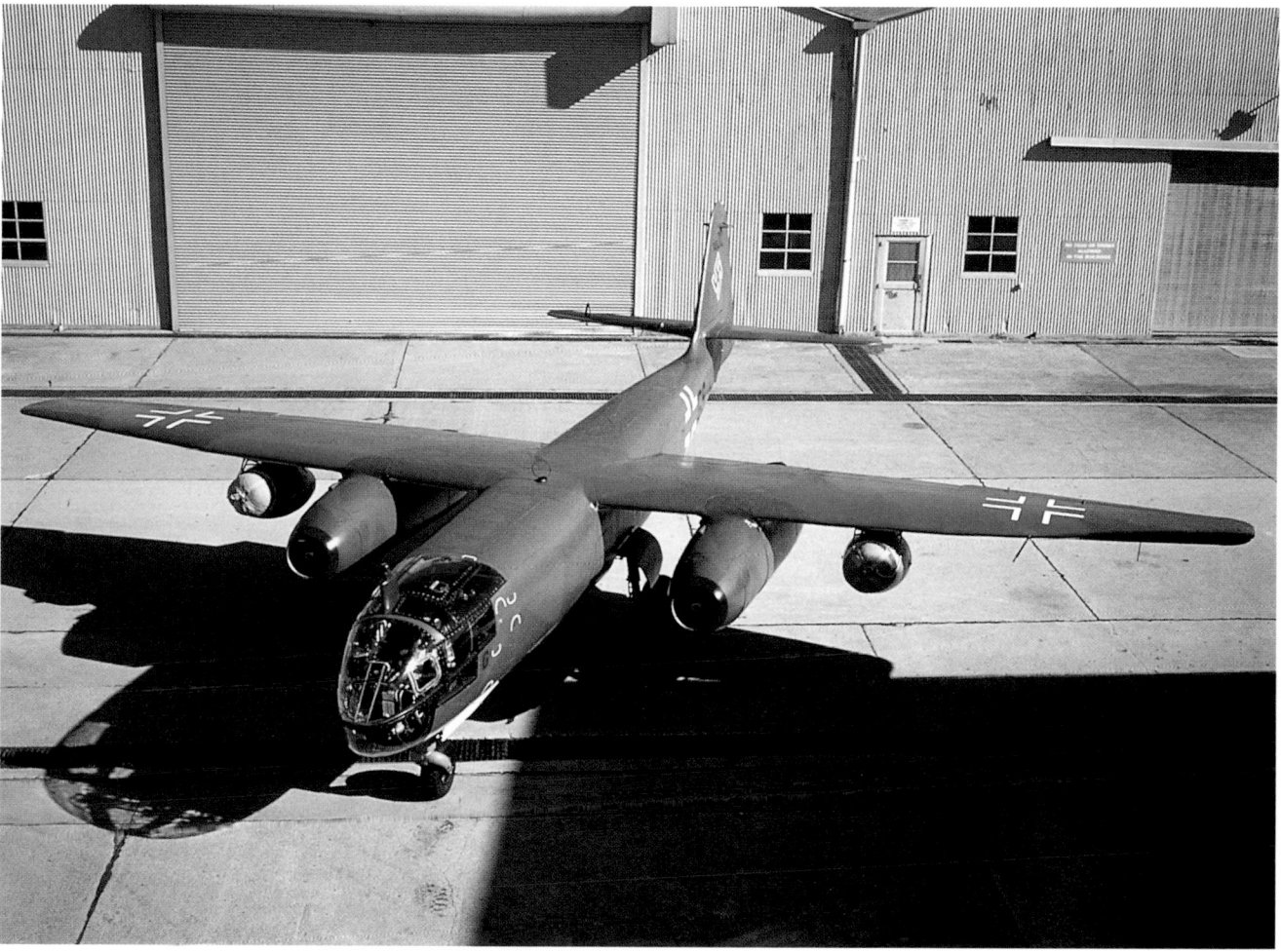

Record photographs are usually taken at the end of a restoration project such as this with the Arado Ar 234 in the NASM collection. Often a handicap is in not having a suitable location with unhibited backgrounds for picture taking.

APPENDIX D

Restoration Contract Sample

This is a sample contract that can be used between a museum that owns an aircraft and a contractor that intends to do the needed restoration of that aircraft. The areas enclosed in brackets [ ] are to have the appropriate information filled in. Normally, a document such as this is type-written double-spaced.

CONTRACT FOR THE RESTORATION OF THE [name aircraft] BELONGING TO THE [name of owner, give city] U S A ([give identifying serial or mark of object])

This Restoration Agreement is made _____, 19[ ], between the [*owner and location*], hereinafter referred to as the Museum [or a more specific short name], and the [*contractor and location*], hereinafter referred to as Contractor [*or appropriate short name*].

WHEREAS, Museum's airplane, the [*identify*] and its engine, hereinafter inclusively referred to as the Aircraft, is in need of restoration; and

WHEREAS, Contractor warrants that it has the experienced aircraft restorers, appropriate work shop facilities, restoration equipment, and the technical knowledge needed to reconstruct such an aircraft, and represents that it is capable of and desirous of performing the restoration required;

THEREFORE, the parties to this agreement, and in consideration of the mutual covenants and stipulations set out therein agree as follows:

CLAUSE 1. Contractor agrees to restore the Museum's Aircraft to the specifications described in the *Museum's Restoration Guidelines* [use actual title of this document].

CLAUSE 2. Contractor agrees to complete restoration of the Aircraft within, but no later than, thirty-six (36) months from the date it signs this agreement. Time is of the essence in this agreement. If the Contractor fails to perform the restoration of the Aircraft within the restoration period stated herein, subject to Clause 3, the Museum may at its election terminate the agreement.

CLAUSE 3. Contractor agrees to return the Aircraft to the Museum if the Contractor is unable to show evidence of at least 100 man-hours of work progress on the Aircraft over any six (6) month period, and/or is unable to complete the restoration within the restoration period as stated in Clause 2. A maximum extension period of six (6) months beyond three years from the date that Contractor signs this Agreement will be permitted at Museum's discretion, provided:

a. Museum receives written notification of Contractor's request for an extension of time sixty (60) days prior to the expiration of the restoration period;

b. Such notification states the cause of the delay and Contractor's ability to complete the restoration within the six month extension period.

CLAUSE 4. Contractor agrees to bear the cost of insuring the Aircraft in the following conditions:

a. While in transit from the Museum to the Contractor and during its return. While the Aircraft is in the custody and control of the Contractor, the Contractor agrees to cover all possible loss or damage up to the amount of value stated in Clause 4c. below.

b. The Contractor may pay the Museum to include the Contractor and these requirements under the Museum's own insurance program. In the event that the Contractor elects to provide its own insurance, copies of the certificates of insurance naming the [name of beneficiary] as a co-insurer and in a form acceptable to the Museum will be furnished to the Museum. Such a certificate must be received and approved by the Museum before release of the Aircraft. A conversion at a later date to an insurance company of the Contractor's choice can be made once it is approved by the Museum as suitable coverage.

c. Value set by the Museum on its unrestored aircraft will be $X0,000 during the first year, $X0,000 for the second year, and for $X0,000 during the remainder of the period the Aircraft is held pursuant to this agreement.

CLAUSE 5. Contractor agrees to bear the cost of handling and transporting the Aircraft from Museum to Contractor and from Contractor to Museum. Contractor further agrees to bear the cost of handling and transporting the Aircraft parts and equipment relevant to this project.

CLAUSE 6. Contractor agrees that it will not deviate from the specifications stated in the Museum's Restoration Guidelines (Attachment A) for the Aircraft without first receiving written permission from Museum's responsible curator, or, in that person's absence, from the [*state the title of the alternate person*].

CLAUSE 7. Contractor agrees that it will restore the Aircraft in a manner satisfactory and acceptable to the Museum, which shall be the sole judge of quality of performance. Contractor agrees to grant Museum representatives complete access to the Aircraft during the restoration period for this purpose. Contractor further agrees to make whatever corrections to the completed restoration deemed necessary by Museum's responsible curator, or in that person's absence, by the [*state the title of the alternate person*].

CLAUSE 8. Contractor agrees that all parts and materials acquired for this restoration that become a part of the [name aircraft] will not be removed from the Aircraft when returned to the Museum or any other location.

CLAUSE 9. Contractor agrees to maintain complete restoration records and good quality photographs, to provide copies of these restoration records and a selection of photographs to the Museum upon request, and to provide the Museum with written quarterly progress reports.

CLAUSE 10. Museum agrees to lend Contractor the Aircraft pursuant to the conditions set forth in the standard Museum Loan Agreement for an initial period of three years plus any unused portion of the thirty-six month restoration period, provided the restoration is competed within the time stated in Clause 2 of this agreement. Upon expiration of the initial loan period, consecutive one year loan extensions may be made by mutual agreement subject to the conditions set forth in the standard Museum Loan Agreement. [*or substitute for the last sentence above:*] Upon expiration of the initial loan period following the successful restoring the Airplane, this loan can be extended by mutual agreement to [*state time*] beginning from the time that the aircraft is received by the Contractor at the beginning of the restoration process.

CLAUSE 11. The Museum agrees to use its best efforts to provide the Contractor with parts for the Aircraft from the Museum's collection and to assist the Contractor in locating necessary parts not in the Museum's collections.

CLAUSE 12. Museum agrees to respond in good faith to the Contractor's requests for information and assistance.

CLAUSE 13. Museum further agrees to use its best efforts to have a representative visit the restoration site at least every [*time period. See Chapter 11 about this point*] to assess the progress and workmanship and to provide advice.

CLAUSE 14. In the case of a dispute, the matter will be resolved by the relevant curator and restoration supervisor, and if the relevant parties are unable to agree, the case will be submitted to the Museum's [*state position of authority*].

CLAUSE 15. The duty of performance may not be delegated nor the rights under this contract assigned without the written consent of both parties hereto. If the duty of performance or rights of this contract are assigned with agreement between both parties, the Contractor will be responsible for ensuring that all terms of this contract are adhered to. The Contractor must directly supervise all contract work.

CLAUSE 16. Nothing in this agreement is intended to, or shall be deemed to constitute a partnership or joint venture between the parties.

CLAUSE 17. Copies of this contract, and the Museum's Restoration Guidelines for the Aircraft, shall be available to and understood by every member of the Contractor restoration staff responsible for the restoration of this aircraft and its engine.

/s/ _____
[*Name of Museum*]

/s/ _____
[*Name of Contractor*]

APPENDIX E

Man-hours for Restorations

This listing of restoration times for Level 3 Condition aircraft of the National Air and Space Museum is provided as a measure for planning other restorations of similar type aircraft.

Concluding Year	Aircraft	Man-hours
1958	Wright EX *Vin Fiz*	2,000
1962	Lockheed Vega 5C *Winnie Mae*	3,557
1963	Fokker D.VII	2,760
1965	Northrop Gamma *Polar Star*	5,182
1969	Curtiss NC-4	22,633
1969	Loening OA-1A *San Francisco*	6,246
1974	Douglas DWC-2 World Cruiser	8,579
1974	Supermarine Spitfire	6,015
1974	Fairchild FC-2	6,218
1974	Messerschmitt Bf 109G-6/R3	6,128
1974	Pitcairn AC-35	1,672
1974	Piper L-4 Grasshopper	632
1975	Kellett XO-60 Autogiro	2,128
1975	North American F-86A Sabre	3,921
1975	Mitsubishi A6M5 'Zero'	6,305
1975	Macchi MC-202 (interior incomplete)	3,756
1975	North American P-51D Mustang	4,415
1975	Douglas D-558-2 Skyrocket	3,872
1975	Bell XP-59 Airacomet	7,491
1975	Piper PA-12 *City of Washington*	2,355
1976	Fokker T-2	8,851
1977	Aeronca C-2	2,334
1977	North American P-51C *Excalibur III**	6,119
1978	Lockheed XP-80 *Lulu Belle*	5,206
1979	Blériot XI	3,704
1979	Curtiss D	1,582
1979	Albatros D.Va	8,629
1979	Messerschmitt Me 262A	8,673
1979	Bellanca CF	2,200
1980	Vought F4U-1D Corsair	9,315
1980	Langley Aerodrome	3,797
1981	De Havilland DH.4	4,163
1982	Ecker Flying Boat	2,265
1982	Benoist Type XII	2,846
1983	Northrop N1M Flying Wing	11,513
1983	Focke-Wulf Fw 190F-8	13,604
1983	Nakajima J1N1-S 'Irving'	17,249
1984	Wiseman-Cooke	2,086
1985	Wright Flyer 1903	2,319
1986	SPAD XIII *Smith IV*	8,435
1986	Fowler-Gage	4,917
1988	Vought OS2U-3 Kingfisher	16,310
1989	Arado Ar 234B-2	18,600
1991	Voisin Voi.8 Bn.2	1,665
	Boeing B-29 *Enola Gay* (Begun 1984 and in progress, 1996)	

*Restoration begun by contractor but finished in-house by NASM (hours shown).

APPENDIX F

Sources for Technical Information

Aircraft Structural Drawings

The National Archives is a general source, yet a particular source for US Naval aircraft up through World War II.

National Archives
Washington National Records Center
4205 Suitland Road
Suitland, Maryland 20409, USA.

The NASM maintains drawings of many aircraft, both civil and military. They are a primary source for Waco and Fairchild aircraft. The NASM also has an extensive collection of aircraft manuals.

Archivist
National Air and Space Museum
Archives Division MRC 322
Smithsonian Institution
Washington, DC 20560, USA.

For early civil aircraft: regional FAA engineering offices are responsible for maintaining master drawings of aircraft certified for ATC approval type certificates in their area. Check through local FAA office for Regional engineering addresses.

For drawings and technical matters that relate to World War I airplanes and this general time period. Catalog is available.

World War I Aeroplanes, Inc.
15 Crescent Road
Poughkeepsie, NY 12601, USA.
Tel: (914) 473-3679

Sources for aircraft manuals and technical orders include:

Western International USA, Inc.
PO Box 771
Monument, Colorado 80132, USA.
Tel: (719) 481 2286

Air Caravan
PO Box 50727
New Bedford, Massachusetts 02745, USA.
Tel: (508) 990 8588
Some service for aircraft drawings available.

For assistance with restoration informational sources for British aircraft, begin with the following:

Public Records Office
Imperial War Museum
Lambeth Road
London SE1 6HZ, England

Royal Air Force Museum
Hendon,
London NW9 5LL, England

Color Systems

For Munsell Color System:

Macbeth Division of
Kollmorgan Instruments Corporation
405 Little Britain Road
New Windsor, NY 12553-6148, USA.
Tel: 800-622-2384
16,000 removable gloss color samples in two
books: $525 (£328)
13,000 fixed-to-page matt color samples in one
book: $475 (£297)
Color samples sold separately.

For Federal Standard 595 System:

Federal Supply Services Bureau
Specification Section
470 East L'Enfant Plaza SW
Suite 8100
Washington, DC 20407, USA.
Tel. (202) 755 0325
Fax: (202) 755 0452
(Call to confirm February 1996 prices and
availability of the following before ordering):

	$	£
595B Color Book, 611		
paint chips (½" x 1")	40.00	25.20
Complete sets, 886 paint chips (3" x 5")	200.00	126.00
(Additional new colors added)	50.00	31.50
Fan Deck, 611 paint chips (½" x 2")	35.00	22.00
Individual Paint Chips (3" x 5")	2.00	1.25

For Pantone Color Specifier (contains 747 colors with six examples of each):

Pantone, Inc
590 Commerce Blvd.
Carlstadt, New Jersey 07072, USA.
Tel: (201) 935 5500

Military Color and Marking References

Bell, Dana. *Air Force Colors, Vol. 1 1926-1942,* Carrollton, Texas, Squadron/Signal Publications, 1979

Bell, Dana. *Air Force Colors, Vol. 2, ETO & MTO 1942-45,* Carrollton, Texas, Squadron/Signal Publications, 1980

Bell, Dana. *USAF Colors and Markings in the 1990s,* Somerset, England, Greenhill Books, 1992

Smith, Jerry S. *ANA Standard Aircraft Colors 1943–1970,* Grass Valley, California, Modeler's Journal Publications. Rev. 1981

Archer, Robert D. *The Official Monogram US Army Air Service & Air Corps Aircraft Color Guide, 1908–1941,* Vol. 1, Sturbridge, Massachusetts, Monogram Aviation Publications, 1995

Elliott, John M. *The Official Monogram US Navy & Marine Corps Aircraft Color Guide 1911–1939,* Vol. 1, Boylston, Massachusetts, Monogram Aviation Publications, 1987

Elliott, John M. *The Official Monogram US Navy & Marine Corps Aircraft Color Guide 1940–1949,* Vol. 2, Sturbridge, Massachusetts, Monogram Aviation Publications, 1989

Elliott, John M. *The Official Monogram US Navy & Marine Corps Aircraft Color Guide 1950–1959,* Vol. 3, Sturbridge, Massachusetts, Monogram Aviation Publications, 1991

Elliott, John M. *The Official Monogram US Navy & Marine Corps Aircraft Color Guide 1960–1993,* Vol. 4, Sturbridge, Massachusetts, Monogram Aviation Publications, 1993

Merrick, Kenneth A. *The Official Monogram Painting Guide to German Aircraft 1935–1945,* Boylston, Massachusetts, Monogram Aviation Publications, 1980

Mikesh, Robert C. *Japanese Cockpit Interiors, Part 1, Close-Up 14,* Boylston, Massachusetts, Monogram Aviation Publications, 1976

Mikesh, Robert C. *Japanese Cockpit Interiors, Part 2, Close-Up 15,* Boylston, Massachusetts, Monogram Aviation Publications, 1977

Thorpe, Donald W. *Japanese Army Air Force Camouflage and Markings World War II,* Fallbrook, California, Aero Publishers, 1968

Thorpe, Donald W. *Japanese Naval Air Force Camouflage and Markings World War II,* Fallbrook, California, Aero Publishers, 1977

Headquarters, Department of the Army, *Painting and Marking of Army Aircraft,* TB 746-93-2, various dates

APPENDIX G

Vendor Information
(Covers most materials mentioned in this book)

Preservation Materials

Corrosion Technologies, Corp.
PO Box 551625
Dallas, Texas 75355-1625, USA.
  Tel: 1-800-638-7361
  Corrosion X

CRC Industries, Inc.
885 Louis Drive
Warminster, Pennsylvania 18974, USA.
  Tec. Asst. (800) 521-3168
  Tel: (215) 674-4300
  Fax: (215) 674-2207

CRC Industries Europe NV
Touwslagerstraat 1
B-9240 ZELE, Belgium
  Tel: (32) 52-45-6011
  Fax: (32) 52-45-0034

CRC Industries Australia PTY Ltd
9 Gladstone Road
Castle Hill 2154
Sydney, Australia
  Tel: (61) 2-634-2088
  Fax: (61) 2-680-4914

Loctite North American Group
1001 Trout Brook Crossing
Rocky Hill, Connecticut 06067, USA.
  Tel (203) 571-5100
  Fax (203) 571-5465
  Extend (rust converter)
  Duro Naval Jelly (rust remover)

Man-Gill Chemical (Magnus)
23000 St. Clair Avenue
Cleveland, Ohio 44117, USA.
  Tel: 800 627 6422
  Tel: (216) 486 5300
  Fax: (216) 486 1214

Matchless Metal Polish Co.
840 West 49th Place
Chicago, Illinois 60609, USA.
  VL417WM Liquid Nickel Buffing
  Compound

Oakite Products, Inc.
50 Valley Road
Berkeley Heights, New Jersey 07922, USA.
  Tel: (908) 464 6900

Rhom and Hass
Home Office
  Tel: (215) 592 3000
  Tel: (800) 846 7641
Chemcentral
  Tel: (708) 594 7000
  Tel: (800) 338 1205

Dow Corning Corporation
Dept. A-7032
PO Box 7604
Mt. Prospect, Illinois 60056-7604, USA.
  Tel: (800) 637 5377
  Synthetic lubricants

Special Fabrics

Testfabrics, Inc.
PO Box 423
200 Blackford Avenue
Middlesex, New Jersey 02846, USA.
  Tel: (908) 469 6446
  Fax: (908) 469 1147

(Former J.P. Stevens & Co.)
JPS Converter & Industry Corp.
33 Stevens Street
Greenville, South Carolina 29602, USA.
  Tel: 800 896 6926

W.L. Gore & Associates, Inc.
100 Airport Road
PO Box 1550
Elkton, Maryland 21921, USA.
  Tel: (410) 392-4440
  Gore-Tex Vapor Barrier

Deutsches Technikmuseum Berlin
Trebbiner Strasse 9
D–10963 Berlin
Germany
  Tel: 030/254 84-0
  Fax: 030/254 84-175
  Limited supply of lozenge fabric

Propellers, custom-made

St. Croix Propellers
5957 Seville Street
Lake Oswego, Oregon 97034, USA.
Tel: (503) 636 4153
Chad Wille, President

California Antique Aircraft Museum
Watson Propeller Division
PO Box 495
San Martin, California 95046, USA.
Tel: (408) 270-7509
Fax: (408) 270-5908
Guy E. Watson

Radiators, engine cooling

American Honeycomb Radiator Mfg. Co.
171 Highway 34
Holmdel, New Jersey 07733, USA.
Tel: (718) 948 7772
(908)946 8743
Fax: (908) 946 8457
Neil M. Thomas

Rome Turney Radiator Co.
109 Canal Street
Rome, New York 13442-0032, USA.
Tel: (315) 336 2200
Fax: (315) 336 3995
Wm. Lynch, President

Neil M. Good
56 Scituate Road
Mashpee, Massachusetts 02649, USA.
Tel: (508) 548 2555 (work)
Tel: (508) 477 1259 (home)
Woodworking also

Paint sources, aviation

Randolph Products Company
PO Box 830
701 12th Street
Carlstadt, New Jersey 07072-0830, USA.
Tel: (201) 438 3700
Fax: (201) 438 4231
Roger Lehnert

The Eastwood Company
580 Lancaster Ave., Box 3014
Malvern, Pennsylvania 19355-0714, USA.
Tel: (800) 544 5118

Fax: (610) 644 0560
Canada 800 820 9042
Aluma Blast
Other detail paints

Tires, antique

Coker Tire Co.
1317 Chestnut Street
Chattanooga, Tennessee 37402, USA.
Tel: 800-251-6336
Corky Coker
26 x 4 clincher available,
30 x 5 available, others.

Desser Tire & Rubber Co.
6900 Acco Street
PO Box 1028
Montebello, California 90640-1028, USA.
Tel: (213) 721 4900
Fax: (213) 721 7888

The Goodyear Tire & Rubber Co.
5088 Pine Tree Street
Forest Park, Georgia 300550, USA.
Tel: (404) 362 3611
Richard Brown

The Goodyear Tire & Rubber Co.
Goodyear Technical Center
PO Box 3531
Akron, Ohio 44309-3531, USA.
Tel: (330) 796 4378
Fax: (330) 796 3049
Tom Dwenger, Dept 461B

Lambrook Tyres
Lambrook Farm
Farway
Collyton
Devon EX13 6DL
England
Tel: (01404) 871 282
Tim Bucknall

Universal Tire Co.
987 Stony Batter Road
Lancaster, Pennsylvania 17601, USA.
Tel: (717) 898 0114
Fax: (717) 898 0949
Harvey Nauss
24 x 4 clincher molds,
30 x 5 molds, others.

Miscellaneous

Maryland Metrics
PO Box 261
Owings Mill, Maryland 21117
Warehouse: 6119 Oakleaf Ave.
Baltimore, Maryland 21215, USA.

Kenneth D. Wilson
2324 East Florida Street
Evansville, Indiana 47711-4812, USA.
   Tel: (812) 477 7176
   Custom cut stencil sets,
   history reports for:
   Stearman 75, all models
   Republic P-47 Thunderbolt
   Grumman F8F Bearcat
   North American AT-6, SNJ
   Ryan PT-20,-22,-NR-1
   Cessna O-1, L-19, OE-1
   US insignia, various.
   Other custom services for restorations.

3M Center
Building 515-3 North-06
St. Paul, Minnesota 55144-1000, USA.
   Tel: (800) 364-3577
   Fax: (800) 713-6329
   Tapes, adhesives, Scotch Guard
   abrasives, etc.

APPENDIX H

Propeller Markings
(Technical data provided by Harry A. Jay, Williamstown, Vermont)

For airplanes of the World War II time period, Hamilton Standard Propellers were the most widely-used propellers by all branches of the US military, and by many nations of the world. For that reason they constitute the most commonly encountered propeller when restoring the larger aircraft of the 1930s and '40s. Depending upon the condition of the propeller at the time of restoration, it is not uncommon for all external markings to have vanished, yet they are needed for completeness when rebuilding the propeller. The information contained in this appendix will help determine the correct stenciling and how it should be applied for Hamilton Standard Propellers.

Hydromatic Propellers

In order to keep up with the demand for propellers during World War II, United Aircraft Corporation licensed several companies to produce propellers and spare parts under contract for their subsidiary, Hamilton Standard in East Hartford, Connecticut. Final detailing when restoring a propeller will reflect one or more of these subsidiaries and therefore must be marked accordingly. It was not uncommon to find a mix of parts from different sub-contractors on one propeller.

When restoring a propeller to either new configuration or to be representative of one that had been reworked at a depot, the highly-visible stenciled data found on the cambered surface of each propeller blade must be reapplied. If the propeller is in such a condition that this original stenciling is not visible, this information can be reconstructed if one has an understanding of the data that is permanently stamped into the butt end of each blade. This will be in ⅛-inch (3 mm) numbers and letters on the shoulder of the propeller blades (see Fig. 1). Data to be found there include such things as blade drawing number (e.g. DWG. 6477A-0; the '0' signifying that the blade has not been shortened from its designed length); blade improvement (e.g. CHG.B); hardness of the aluminum alloy (e.g. AMS 4130); and manufacturer's number (e.g. MFG.No. NKAU3143), signifying sub-contractor Nash-Kelvinator. Inspector stamps that have unique designs for each of these manufacturers will also be found in this butt area of the blade. From this information, the correct Hamilton Standard decal can be selected as well as reconstruction of stenciled infor-

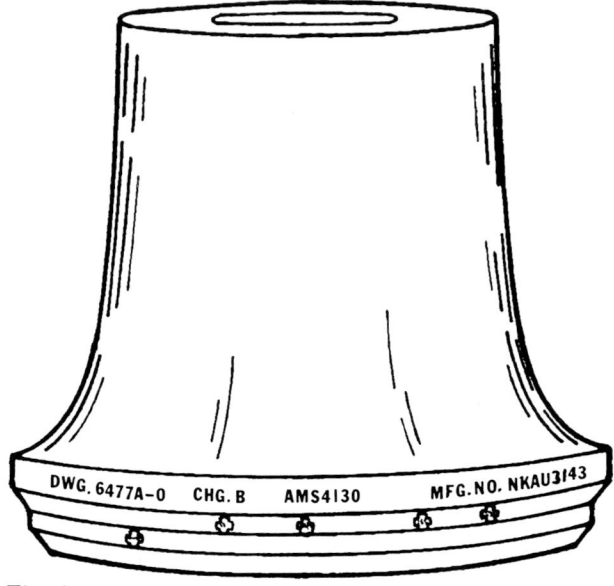

Fig. 1

mation for each of the blades. These inspector imprint-stamps and letter codes for the sub-contractors are as follows:

Hamilton Standard (parent company), Hartford, Connecticut. (Letter-coded 'P')

Nash Kelvinator Corporation, Propeller Division, Lansing, Michigan. (Letter-coded 'NK')

Frigidaire, Division of General Motors Corp., Dayton, Ohio. (Letter-coded 'F')

Remington Rand, Johnson City, New York. (Letter-coded 'RR')

Canadian Propellers Ltd, Longueuil (suburb of Montreal), Quebec, Canada. Contracted with United Aircraft to manufacture the Hamilton Standard Constant-Speed Propellers for training aircraft such as (AT-6) Harvards used by the Royal Canadian Air Force.

When new, Hamilton Standard propeller blades generally had data at varying locations in ½-inch (12.7 mm) white (sometimes yellow) letters and numbers seemingly silk-screened in a crisp format.

Anything added after acceptance was in ¾-inch (19 mm) yellow stenciled letters and numbers with exceptions being white. It was seldom that underspray to some degree did not occur. Format and positioning varied widely by sub-contractors. Therefore, positioning and content of this stenciled data must be based upon photos of the aircraft being restored. To help in evaluating what might barely be seen in photographs of stenciled data, a few known samples are given here:

A.A.F. SERIAL NO. 880-0   (B-17H)
PART NO. 6477A-0
ANGLE AT 42-20-88

BLADE DESIGN 6501A-0   (F7F)
PITCH HIGH 90
PITCH LOW 30

A.C.NO. 38-3577   (OA-9)
PART NO. 60853-12 (Controllable Pitch)
BL.SET.12 TO 23 AT 42 STA.
INSTALLED 8-23-38

DWG.NO. 6477A-0   (B-17)
SER.NO. NKAU3240
ANGLE,HIGH.88 AT 42
ANGLE,LOW.20 AT 42

DWG.NO. 6477A-0   (B-24)
SER.NO. F3888
ANGLE HIGH. 88 AT 42
ANGLE LOW. 16 AT 42

16 MIN   (This was often set apart
88 MAX   from the above block)

Propeller Hub Markings

When most Hamilton Standard propellers were new, there was often a decal about 2½ inches (63.5 mm) in length on the rim of the propeller hub. Since this application was not consistent, a restoration project could overlook this detail. (See Fig. 2 Item B)

At the midpoint between two blades on the hub, etched into the metal in ⅛-inch (3 mm) characters enhanced with Vulcan ink, is the following:

Manufacturer's Number: e.g. MFG-NO P90458, identical on both front and rear halves of the hub. (See Fig. 3 Item A)

Contract Number: e.g. CONT-2605 (See Fig. 3 Item B)

Model Number: e.g. 23E50-543 (See Fig. 3 Item C)

In translation the Model Numbers mean:
2 = major modification number
3 = number of blades

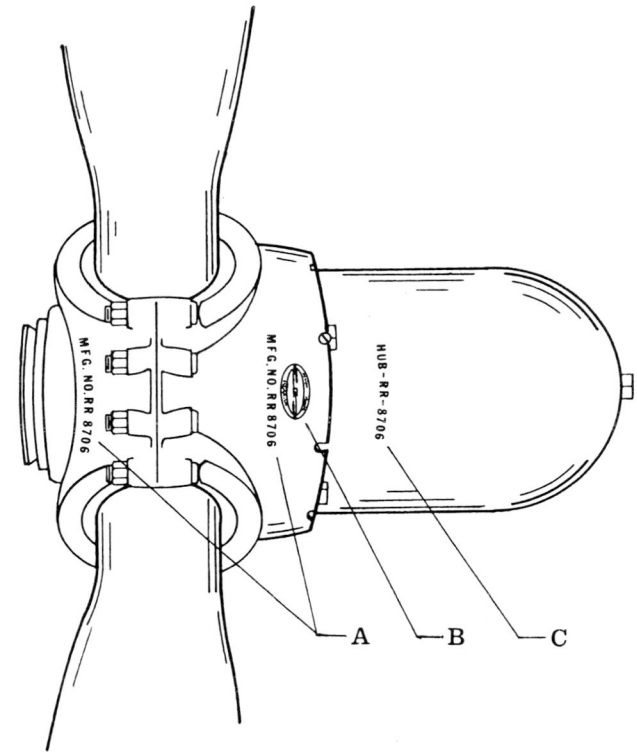

Fig. 2

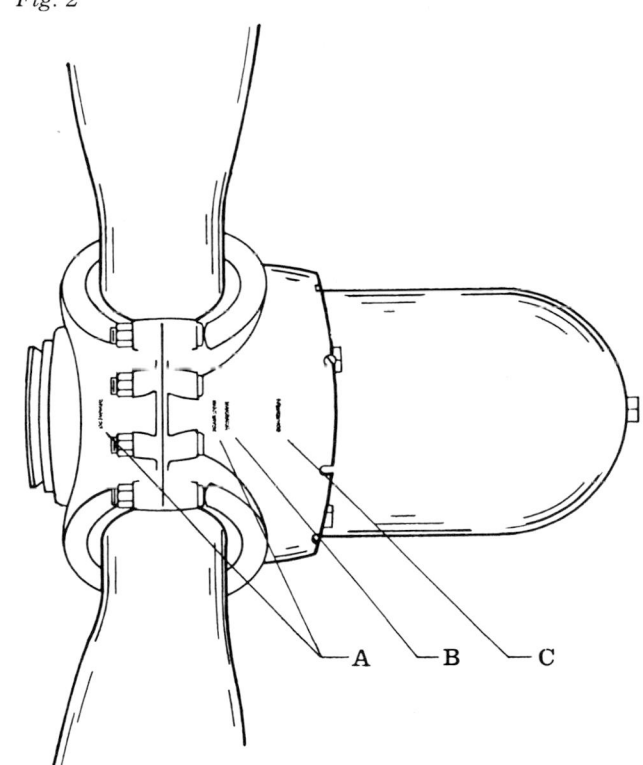

Fig. 3

E = blade shank size
(D: 3.2"; E: 3.4"; F: 3.9")
50 = prop shaft spline size
543 = minor modifications in the basic
      model

When new and after the zinc chromate had been applied to propeller hubs that were to be painted (for camouflaged aircraft), these etched identifying numbers were covered with a strip of ¼-inch (6.3 mm) masking tape. When the black lacquer had dried and the tape was removed, the numbers and letters remained visible through the zinc chromate in what appeared like pale yellow rectangles on the black surface of the hub.

Contrary to most painting directives, it was not uncommon for propeller hubs and domes to be left unpainted. For example, on unpainted airplanes like B-25 Mitchells, these shiny domes reflected (for those in the cockpit) the conformation that the nose wheel was in the down position for landing.

On these unpainted hubs, there are known cases where the MFG. NO. was stenciled in ½-inch (12.7 mm) black letters/numbers (yellow if on a black-painted hub) on the two halves (see Fig. 2 Items A and B) and occasionally on the dome as well (see Fig. 2 Item C).

Depot Marking Additions

Seemingly unexplainable was finding a PART.NO. stenciled on a number of B-17 and B-24 propellers and a few C-47s. This number actually matched the number given as the drawing number on the butt of the blade. This accounts for why most of these stenciled entries actually identify this number as the DWG.NO. Likewise, what is stenciled as the serial number (e.g. SER.NO. NKAU6258) will be found on the butt end as the MFG.NO. (See Fig. 1). The 'number' portion of this serial number painted on the blade surface was usually applied with an easily-changeable rubber stamp since the other portion of the markings remained fairly constant and warranted having a stencil. The 'AU' portion is thought to be a series prefix to the serial number.

Another marking variation was one found on civil aircraft when the propeller was natural metal. Normally the identification data previously described would be etched on with black ink. For ease when fitting the propeller on to the engine crankshaft, a red or black stripe approximately ¼-inch (6.3 mm) wide and two inches (51 mm) long was painted on the hub and dome. These were used for alignment of the holes in the base of the dome assembly with the locating dowels on the dome shelf in the hub. (See Fig. 4 Item A)

Propeller Manufacturer Trademarks

The number of propeller manufacturer trademark designs and variations is immeasurable. Because of these subtle differences among manufacturers, propeller specialists can determine much about the propeller if the original trademark can be seen. In a restoration it is therefore of great importance to preserve to the best degree possible what remains

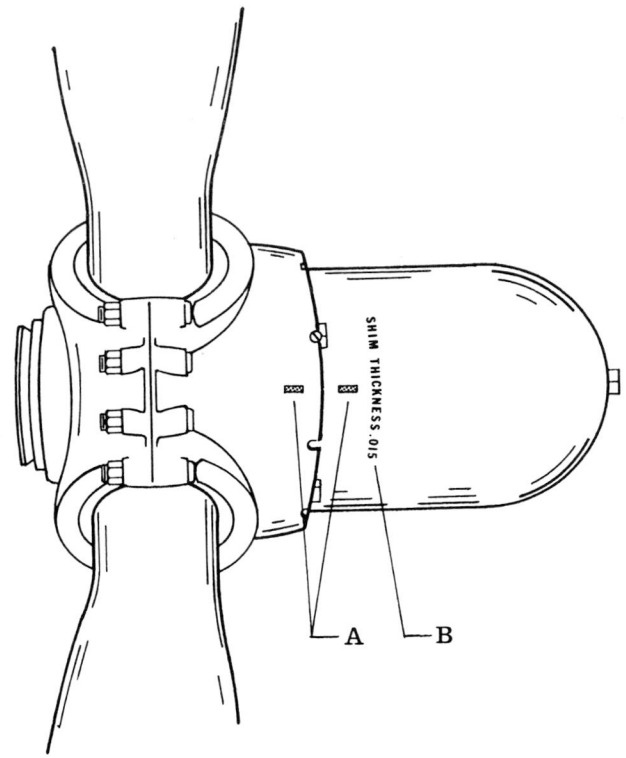

Fig. 4

of the original trademark decal.

The most noticeable error when restoring a Hamilton Standard propeller for a given aircraft is that of using a trademark decal for the improper time period. The overall design of the trademark decal remained fairly consistent, yet there were subtle differences for time periods and sub-contractors. A number of these are recent reproductions for restorations, but knowing the time period for which the aircraft is being restored to, matched to the proper design is essential when making a selection. The following pages show only a sampling of manufacturer trademarks at half-size that are identified as follows:

Fig. A: Hamilton Aero Manufacturing Co., Milwaukee, Wisconsin; circa 1920.

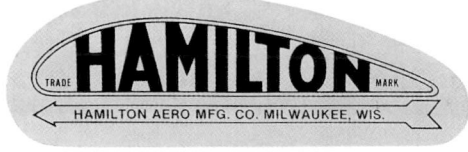

Fig. B: Standard Steel Propeller Co., Pittsburgh, Pennsylvania, circa 1927-29.

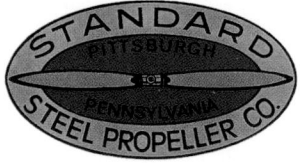

Fig. C: Modification of Fig. B with 'Co.' changed to 'Corporation'; circa 1929-1933.

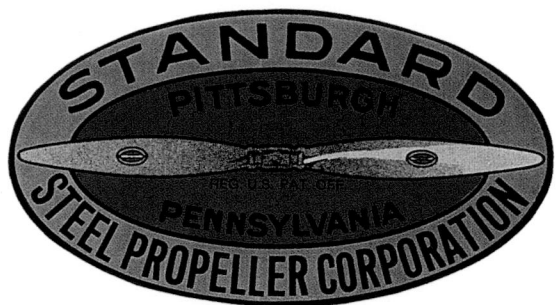

Fig. D: Curtiss Electric Propellers; circa 1940 and used throughout World War II.

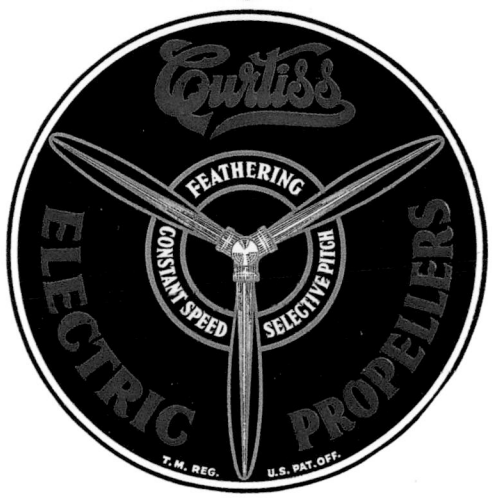

Fig. E: Sensenich Bros., Lititz, Pennsylvania; circa 1930s to around 1947.

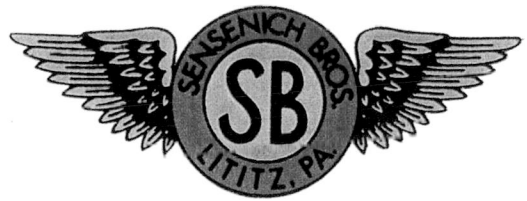

Fig. F: Sensenich Propellers, Lancaster, Pennsylvania; circa 1947 onwards.

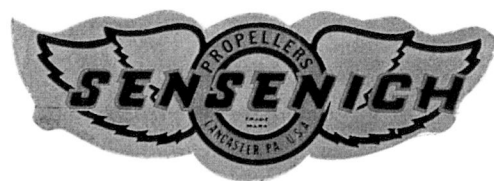

Fig. G: Hamilton Standard Propellers, East Hartford, Connecticut; beginning 30 June, 1936.

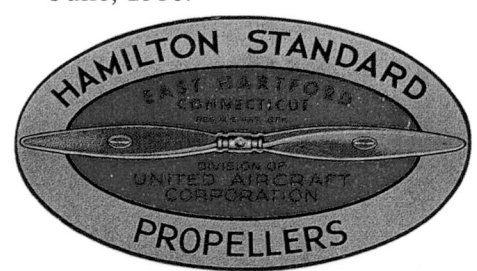

Fig. H: Hamilton Standard Propeller, Nash Kelvinator Corp., Lansing, Michigan; circa 1942. Sub-contractor decals used 'propeller' singularly while the parent company retained the word 'propellers'.

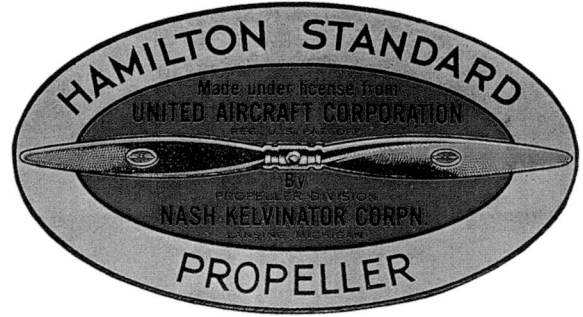

Fig. I: Hamilton Standard Propeller, Frigidaire Division - General Motors Corp., Dayton, Ohio; circa 1942.

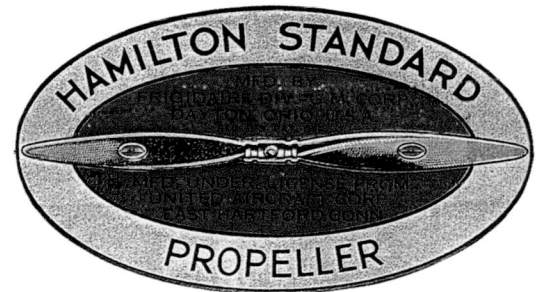

Fig. J: Hamilton Standard Propeller, Remington Rand, Inc., Johnson City, New York; circa 1942. Facsimile copied from a C-54 propeller blade.

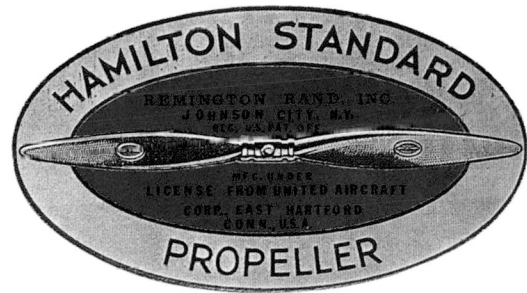

Fig. K: Hamilton Standard, East Hartford, Connecticut; used from 1940-52 which covered the World War II time period in addition to sub-contractors. Reproduction by NASM shown here.

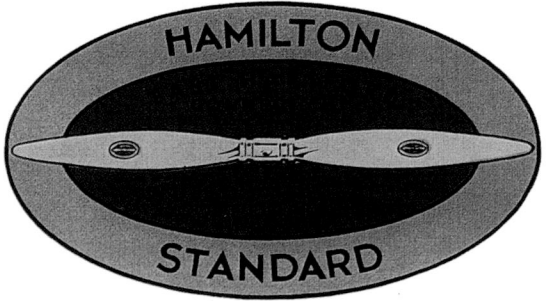

Fig. L: Hamilton Standard, Canadian Sales & Service Representative, Pratt & Whitney Canada, Inc., Longueuil, Quebec; circa 1961. Earlier versions (circa 1942) may have had 'Hamilton Standard' (top) and 'Propeller' (bottom).

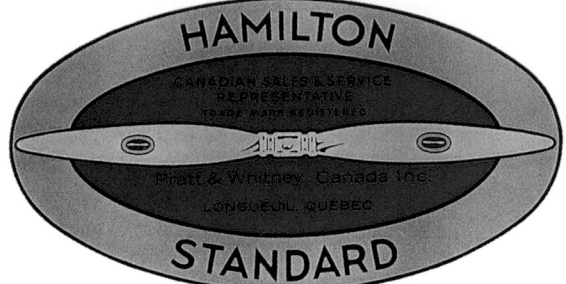

Fig. M: McCauley Corp., Dayton, Ohio; circa 1938 through World War II.

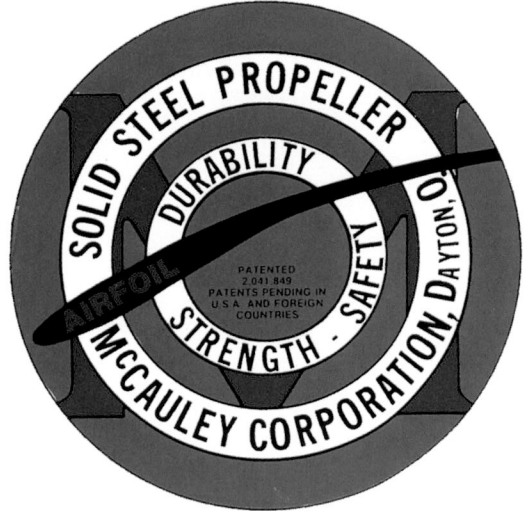

Fig. N: McCauley Corp., Dayton, Ohio; circa immediate post-war period of the late 1940s. (When decal is applied, the yellow becomes clear.)

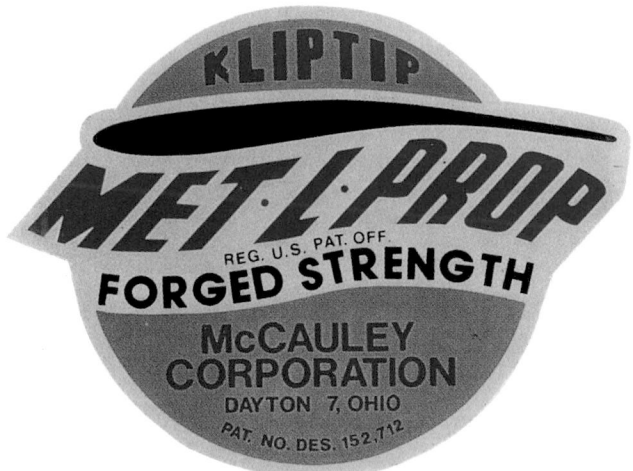

Fig. O: McCauley Corp., Dayton, Ohio; circa 1950s.

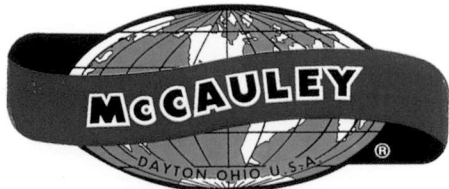

Fig. P: Curtiss Electric Propellers; a later version than Fig. D, replacing light blue with light green.

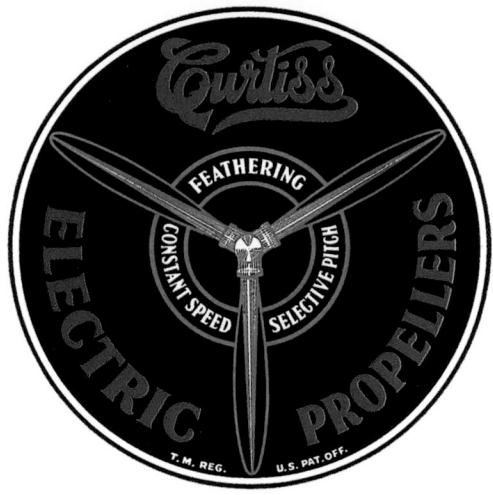

Fig. Q: Aeroprop, General Motors Corp., Dayton, Ohio; circa 1940s and '50s.

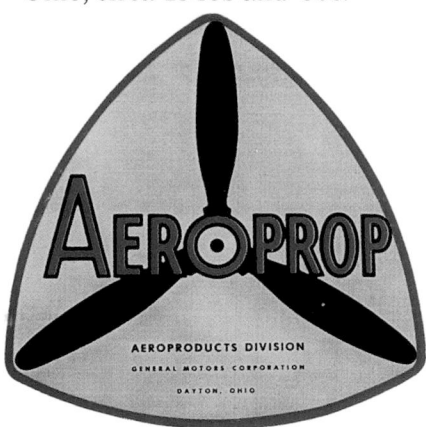

Fig. R: Hamilton Standard, Windsor Locks, Connecticut; circa 1952-69. Design change from Fig. K after the main plant moved to Windsor Locks in May 1952. The word 'Propeller' was eliminated when Hamilton Standard diversified into other products such as jet engine controls and environmental systems.

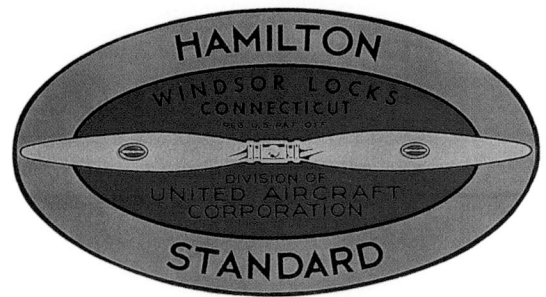

GLOSSARY

Definitions

This glossary represents terms that are used to greater or lesser extent by the members of the International Association of Transport and Communications Museums (IATM), Aviation Museums Group. These terms have been gathered or developed from several sources; some have stood the test of time, others are composites in order to create more meaningful terms relating to museum aircraft.

The need for standardized terms when describing the degree of originality of museum aircraft rests with that of meaningful labels as described in Chapter 10. The judgement of an aircraft ranging from being an original to that of a mock-up must not be left to the interpretation of museum visitors. Therefore a scale of importance for historic and technologically significant aircraft may be regarded in the following order:

> Original
> Restored Original
> Replica
> Reproduction
> Look-alike
> Mock-up

Occasionally an object will not fit a definition exactly, therefore compromises must be made when selecting the term that best describes a specific object. The terms listed above are described within the following with sources given where applicable:

Artifact: A man-made object which has historical importance. Normally, in museum usage, this does not include documents other than those which could be used for exhibit purposes. (AFM)

Conservation: As the technology of preservation, conservation is the scientific investigation of materials, the environment, and those things responsible for the deterioration of cultural resources. Its purpose is to limit the decay process and to prolong the existence of objects. (NASM)

Curator: The individual responsible for the professional management, selection, interpretation (restoration), accession, deaccession, exhibit and care of a museum collection. May be combined with directorial responsibilities. (AFM)

Economic Life: That period of an object's life during which it is in active service, whether performing its originally intended function, or other related use. (TIGHAR)

Fabric: The physical material of an object. (TIGHAR) (This usage differs from that of cloth material.)

Historical Aircraft: An aircraft which retains a meaningful degree of historical significance. (TIGHAR)

Historical Significance: An object's aesthetic, scientific, technological, and social merit assessed in terms of its:

* association with a particular historic event or individual.
* rarity as a survivor of its type.
* evidence of past design, innovation, style, construction techniques, etc.
* condition and extent of remaining original material.
* political, cultural, or spiritual significance to a particular segment of society.
* exceptional aesthetic qualities of form or decoration. (TIGHAR)

Look-alike: An artifact with a superficial resemblance to the original but made with different techniques and of different materials (AFM), that may include having an engine-type substitution and system modifications. (Example: A flying reconstruction of an early aircraft. This has greater technical value as a look-alike than that of a mock-up.)

Mock-up: A scale model, usually a full-sized imitation used exclusively as an exhibit prop and which cannot be termed as an aircraft. (Example: The exterior of a Sikorsky S-38 at the EAA Museum that was built for the express purpose as a theater on the inside.)

Original: A specimen that can be shown to be in the

original as-built configuration, or as modified by the user, that remains unaltered from the time it ended operational service. (Example: The *Spirit of St. Louis* is as received from operational service, with preservation care given.)

Preservation: The act of sustaining and maintaining cultural and natural resources that have been identified as significant and/or threatened and that warrant protection. (NASM)

Preventive (Passive) Conservation: Procedures and actions that serve to mitigate threats to collections. Unlike conservation treatment, which is often object-specific, preventive conservation measures are intended to provide basic care for most of the collection. Actions include monitoring and controlling the environment, ensuring proper storage and exhibit methods, good housekeeping, security, and proper handling. (NASM)

Professional: As regards museum personnel, an individual who commands an appropriate body of special knowledge and the ability to reach museological decisions consonant with the experience of his or her peers, and who has access to and acquaintance with the literature of the field of museology. (AAM)

Rare Aircraft: An aircraft of a type of which relatively few examples exist. Not necessarily an historic aircraft. (TIGHAR)

Reconstruction: Recreation of a cultural property or a part thereof, based upon factual evidence, but on little or no original material in order to promote an understanding of an earlier state or condition of a cultural property. (AIC) (Example: The terms Replica and Reproduction as described here can apply as well.)

Replica: A reproduction built by the builder of the original artifact in part or in total (AFM), and having substantially the same type engine and operating systems. (Example: The Gee Bee Super Sportster built by the New England Air Museum having technical supervision by Grandville Brothers' Chief Engineer Pete Miller. If the replica contains some original parts, it should be identified as a 'Replica with some Original Parts.')

Reproduction: A reasonable facsimile in appearance and construction of an aircraft made with similar materials, and having substantially the same type engine and operating systems. (Example: The building of aircraft with the use of salvaged parts as patterns for new material that would exceed 50 per cent from that of the original. This would be a 'Reproduction with some Original Parts.')

Restored Original (Restoration): An artifact composed of at least 50 per cent original components (by surface area or volume), and the remainder returned to accurate early condition made with the same materials, components and accessories. (AFM) (Example: The Wright Flyer is a restored original.)

(Note: Materials can be substituted when there is a need to differentiate for identification that of original materials, which do not alter the superficial appearance, and are reversible. Where reversibility is not possible it must be substantiated that the irreversible processes are entirely essential for the preservation of the object. (MAAS)

Restoration Technician: A craftsperson with the specialized skills and professional knowledge for returning an object to its original configuration in order to preserve its technology and historic significance.

ACRONYMS

AAM:	American Association of Museums
AFM:	Air Force Museum (actually USAFM), Dayton, Ohio, USA
AIC:	American Institute for Conservation
IWM:	Imperial War Museum, London, England
MAAS:	Museum of Applied Arts & Sciences, Sydney, Australia
NAS:	Naval Air Station
NASM:	National Air and Space Museum, Washington, DC, USA
RAF:	Royal Air Force (British)
SI:	Smithsonian Institution, Washington, DC, USA
TIGHAR:	The International Group for Historic Aircraft Recovery
USAAF:	United States Army Air Force
USAF:	United States Air Force
USS:	United States Ship

INDEX

Abbot, Dan-San 175
AEA Aerodrome No. 1 *Red Wing*
  79
  Aerodrome No. 2 *White Wing*
  79
  Aeronca C-2 132, 134–5, 202
  L-3 Defender 153
  Champion 153
Agarwala, Vinod S. 175
Aichi M6A1 Seiran 59, 141
Airbus A300 42
Airspeed Oxford 142
Akron, USS 16
Albatros D.VA 48–51, 65–77, 87,
  89–92, 128, 175, 202
Arado Ar 234B 37, 102, 114,
  136–7, 145–9, 197, 202
Army Air Force, US 26

BAC Concorde 137, 139
Beechcraft C17L Staggerwing
  28, 117
  Bonanza 43
  Model 50 Twin Bonanza 43–4
  65 & 80 Queen Air 43–4
  U-8 Seminole 43
Bell P-39Q Airacobra 43, 175
  P-63A King Cobra 132, 175
  XP-59 Airacomet 202
Bellanca CF 19, 54, 202
Bendix Air Races 142, 157
Benoist Type XII 61–3, 80,
  127–8, 134, 177, 202
Blair, Charles F. 23, 142–3, 157
Bleriot, Louis 61
Bleriot Type XI 37, 119, 202
Boeing XF6B-1 132
  247D 156
  B-17 35, 209–10
  B-17D *Swoose* 23, 175
  B-29 *Enola Gay* 28, 37, 126,
  154–5, 175
  367–80 23
  707 23
bombsight
  BZA 192, 198
  Lotfe 7K 187, 192
Bowers, Peter M. 71
Bradford, Robert 90
Bristol Bulldog 46–7

F.2B 42
Beaufighter 43
Bollingbrook 45
Bruce, James 55, 175
Bucker Bu 133B Jungmann 41
Bucy, Dale 108, 191
bullets 49, 99–100, 114
Burnham, James 31, 175
Byrd, Richard E. 22

Casey, Louis S. 10, 40, 90
Category for aircraft 22–31
Caudron G4 76
Cessna Bird Dog O-1, L-19 207
chemical processing 100–7
Cline, Garry 14, 65, 68, 71–5,
  101, 123
cockpit detailing 15, 39, 50, 57,
  70, 106, 111–2, 159, 162, 165,
  182, 190, 198
Collins, Michael 22
color documentation 144–5
Condition, Level of 31–6
contract 163–5, 200–1
contractor 200
conservation 11, 16–9, 34, 37,
  43, 51, 139–40
Conservation Analytical
  Laboratory, SI 64
Conservation Guidelines 37
conservator 11, 13, 16–8, 21, 34,
  36–7, 59, 64, 77–8, 82, 85–6,
  102, 141, 177
Consolidated B-24 Liberator
  209–10
Convair XF2Y Sea Dart 21
  990 Coronado 166–75
corrosion 18–9, 35, 39, 59–60,
  63, 70, 95–113, 119–22, 162,
  165, 168, 170–3, 175, 190, 192
Crosley Flying Flea 125
curator 7, 10–3, 17–21, 30, 36–7,
  40–5, 52, 59–60, 64–5, 83, 85,
  90, 93, 95, 98, 100, 112, 130,
  135–7, 141, 161, 163–5, 177,
  180, 182, 184, 186
curatorial guidelines 13, 36–7,
  41, 51–60, 98, 114, 146, 160,
  163, 165, 177, 187
Curtiss Aerodrome No. 3 *June*

Bug 79
A-1 19
D 202
JN-4 Jenny 72, 81
HS-2L 33–4, 161
NC-4 13, 23, 202
R3C-2 13
F9C-2 Sparrowhawk 16
P-40E Warhawk 35, 175
XP-55 Ascender 23
Glenn 80
Cusack, John 63, 92, 146, 148
cutaway sections 42

Dassault Falcon 20, 32
DeFiore, Joseph M. 70
de Havilland DH-4 14–5, 202
  Mosquito 25, 175
  Comet 137, 139
Dick, Ron, Air Vice-Marshal 47
diorama 9, 33, 47
Domenjoz, John 61–2
dopes & clear finishes 79–92
Dornier Do 335 114
Douglas DWC World Cruiser 22,
  158, 202
  O-47A 132
  XB-42 Mixmaster 43
  C-47 Skytrain 210
  DC-3 41, 171, 174
  DC-7 42
  DC-9 129
  DC-10 171
  C-54C *Sacred Cow* 115–6
  SBD-5 Dauntless 53, 121
  A-1H Skyraider 157
  D-558-2 Skyrocket 202

Earhart, Amelia 30, 36
Ecker Flying Boat 202
electrical wiring 113, 123
engine 119–125
  ABC Scorpion 125
  BMW 187
  Gnome 50 hp 119
  Junkers Jumo 004 122, 187,
  191–2, 196
  Nakajima NK9H Homare 121,
  123–4
  Nakajima Sakae 109–11

P & W R-2800 120
Renault 80 hp 125
Roberts 123, 128, 180, 182
Rolls-Royce Merlin 47, 118
Wright brothers 154–5
engine openings 124–5
explosive charge 114

fabric 10, 16, 19, 35, 37, 40, 55, 59–63, 71–93, 95, 100–1, 113–4, 120, 138, 154, 161–2, 165, 177–8, 182
Fairchild FC-2W2 *Stars and Stripes* 22, 202 203
Federal Aviation Administration (FAA) 29, 71
Feik, Mary 84
Ferguson, Reid 18
Ferko, Edward 71
Fichera, Joseph 2, 57, 62–3, 71, 104, 118, 140
fly-ins 152–4
flying museum aircraft 20, 45–7
Focke Wulf Fw 190F-8 57–8, 95–8, 104, 114, 140, 198, 202
Fokker D.VII 88, 90, 202
  F.VII 130
  T-2 202
  Super-Universal 132
Fopp, Michael 12, 16, 45, 175
Fowler-Gage 202
Frank, Heinz, Major 98

Gabreski, F S 24
Garber Facility 10, 17, 19, 43, 116, 152, 178, 198
Garber, Paul E. 65, 180
Garove, Francis P. 71
Genotti, George 106, 108–11, 113–4, 136, 193, 195, 197–8
Gossamer Condor 23
Graffiti 114–5, 198
Griehl, Manfred 188
Grosz, Peter M. 71
Grumman F3F Goblin 11, 141
  F3F Wildcat 23–4
  F6F Hellcat 9–10
  F7F Tiger 209
  F8F Bearcat 131, 207
  G-21 (OA-9) Goose 23, 161–2, 209
Guynemer, George, Lieutenant 82–3

Halberstadt C.L.IV 14, 93, 134
Hallam, David 17, 34, 102, 142, 175–6, 189

Handley Page Hampden 44–5
  Halifax 33
Harlow, Jean 78
Harmon International Trophy 157
Hawker Hurricane 25–6, 39, 47, 160
  Tempest V 31, 55–6
Heinkel He 219A 106
Heinzel, Karl 2, 9, 20, 62, 146, 148, 189, 195
Herrick Convertoplane 23
Ellsworth, Lincoln 33
Hollywooding 35
Horigan, Richard 49, 65–9, 71, 74–6

infra-red photography 96–7

Jay, Harry A. 126
Jeannin Stahltaube 135, 164

Kawanishi N1K1 'Rex' 113
  N1K2-Ja 'George' 20, 29, 53, 98–9, 111–4, 123–5, 135
Kawasaki Ki-45 Kai 'Nick' 55
Kellett XO-60 Autogiro 159, 202
Korn, Edward, Dr 180, 182

labeling exhibit aircraft 160
Lake, Paul 115–6
Langley Aerodrome 104–5, 129, 202
Langley, Samuel P. 129
Lawrence, David F. 55, 175
levels of aircraft condition 31–36
Lockheed 5-C Vega *Winnie Mae* 13, 23, 202
  5 Vega 36, 66
  10 Electra 30
  XC-35 23
  Hudson 152
  P-38 Lightning 13, 36, 126, 152, 175
  XP-80 *Lulu Belle* 151–2
  P-80 Shooting Star 202
  F-94 Starfire 151
  T-33 Shooting Star 132–3, 151
  T2V Sea Star 151
  F-104 Starfighter 42
  C-130A Hercules 157
  SR-71 133
Loening OA-1A *San Francisco* 202
look-alike 16, 125, 160
lozenge fabric 87–93
lubrication 108–9, 122

Luftwaffe 25, 187
LVG C.VI 89
Lyons, Michael 96–7, 104

Macchi MC-202 202
Macon, USS 16
MacRobertson London-to-Melbourne Race 156
Maloney, Edward 7
man-hours 38, 52, 57, 65, 73, 106, 120, 160, 164, 186, 202
mannequins 9, 10, 47
Mantz, Paul 142
markings 23, 25–6, 145–52
Martin B-26B *Flak Bait* 39, 152
McCartney, Kevin, Dr 176
McDonnell F-4 Phantom II 30
McDowall Monoplane 80
McManus, Edward 18, 144
McMillian, David R. 71
Messerschmitt Bf 109 17, 25, 29, 96, 202
  Me 262 36, 103, 114, 159–60, 198, 202
Mikesh, Robert C. 20, 74, 76, 175–6, 186, 194, 199
military aircraft 23
mini-record 158–60
mission, museum 24
Mitchell, Reginald J. 49
Mitsubishi A6M5 Zero 41, 45, 57, 101, 114, 121, 135, 202
mock-up 16
modified original 35
model aircraft 20, 30, 145
Molson, Kenneth M. 79–80, 175
museums
  Australian War Memorial 17, 37, 65, 71, 91, 175, 189
  Champlin Fighter Museum 24, 99, 111
  Confederate Air Force Museum 13
  Cradle of Aviation History Museum 24
  De Young Memorial Museum 73
  Deutsche Luftfahrt Sammlung 7
  Deutsches Technikmuseum Berlin 14, 42, 89–90, 93, 134, 164, 176
  Experimental Aircraft Assoc. (EAA) Museum 55, 125
  Flying Farmers Air Museum 24
  Henry Ford Museum & Greenfield Village 31
  Imperial War Museum 7, 137, 139

Jarrett Collection 7
Musée de l'Air et de l'Espace 7, 82–3, 88
Museum fur Verkehr und Technik (see Deutsches Tech.)
Museum of Flight 133
National Air and Space Museum (NASM) Natl. Air Museum 7–11, 13, 17–9, 21–3, 25–33, 36–43, 45–9, 54–9, 61, 64, 70, 77, 82, 84–5, 90–96, 98–102, 103, 105–7, 111–14, 116, 120–23, 125, 127–8, 134–37, 139, 140, 142–4, 146, 149–52, 154–57, 159–61, 163, 170, 175, 177, 180, 182, 184, 187–8, 190, 194
National Aviation Museum, Canada 33–4, 79–80, 90–1, 161, 176
National Museum of Naval Aviation 11, 13, 53, 114, 141, 175
New England Air Museum 24
Paul E. Garber Facility 10, 17, 19, 43, 116, 152
Planes of Fame Museum 7, 45
Royal Air Force Museum 12–3, 31, 33, 37, 42–5, 47, 49–51, 55–6, 125, 142, 160, 175
San Diego Aerospace Museum 11, 141
Science Museum 7, 30, 42–3, 47, 59, 175
Shuttleworth Collection 89
Smithsonian Institution 7
Strategic Air Command Museum 24
Swiss Transport Museum 41, 129, 130, 166–8, 174
US Air Force Museum 7, 13, 115, 134, 136, 175

Nakajima B6N2 'Jill' 33
    J1N1-S 'Irving' 54, 60, 105, 111, 115, 202
National insignia (US) 152
Navy, US 25, 30, 103
Nazzaro, Matthew 191
Neal, John 114
nitrogen 32, 133, 140
North American AT-6 Texan 207
    B-25 Mitchell 131, 175, 210
    P-51C *Excalibur III* 3, 23, 101, 118, 142, 144, 152, 157, 202

P-51D *Willit Run?* 26–7, 45, 103, 175, 202
P-86A Sabre 202
F-100D Super Sabre 32, 149–51
X-15 23
T-28 Trojan 135, 153
Northrop Gamma *Polar Star* 33, 202
A-17 Nomad 132
P-61C Black Widow 106, 175
N1M1 Flying Wing 14, 202
HL-10 23

O'Hara, Maureen 143
original specimen 11
outdoor exhibit of aircraft 166–75

Packard, Patrick H. 125
Padgett, Robert 105–8, 110–11, 120
painting 60, 95–8, 141–49, 154, 173
Pan American Airways 157
Pangborn, Clyde 156
Park Ridge, IL 43, 152, 177, 180, 188
Parmley, Charles 38, 64, 179, 186
parts, aircraft
    identification 56, 114
    marking 58, 106
    missing 60
    repair 58, 64
    storage 56
periscope, PV1B 192, 198
personalizing aircraft 30
Pfalz (Alb.) 67
photography 53–5, 112, 114, 160
Piper J-3 Cub 23, 117, 132, 153–4
    L-4 Grasshopper 153, 202
    PA-12 *City of Washington* 23, 86, 202
Pitcairn AC-35 Autogiro 23, 202
polishing 18, 115–6
preservation 7, 10–3, 17–8, 21, 31–6, 40, 47, 63–4, 68, 76, 83, 92, 100–3, 106–9, 111, 119, 121, 140, 142, 161, 165, 167–8, 182, 187, 190, 192
price vs value 44–5
programming 37
propellers 126–8, 176, 186
publishing results 161
Puglisi, William 71

racks and trunnions 57–8, 65, 70, 104–5, 109
RATO 192–3, 196
reconstruction 35
record keeping 40
Reese, William 19–20
Reiser, Jack 20
replica 11
reproduction 11, 35
restoration team 18, 59
restoration technician 10, 18–20, 36–7, 40, 65, 95–6, 100, 105, 136, 140, 177, 187
restored original 11
Republic P-47 Thunderbolt 23, 175, 188, 207
restoration guidelines 37,100
reversible painting 154
Rictor, Bayne 14
Roland (Alb.) 67
Royal Air Force 25, 26, 31, 46–7, 150, 152, 160
Royal Aircraft Factory BE.2c 125, 133
rubber stamps 58
Rumpler C.IV 90
Rutan Voyager 23, 32
Ryan *Spirit of St Louis* 22, 30
Ryan PT 207

Selle, *Flugkapitan* 187
Seversky P-35 132
Shortt, Alfred J. 80, 90
Sikorsky JRS-1 94
Silver Hill (see Garber Facility)
Siske, John 70
Smith, Richard J. 188
Smithsonian Quality 161–2
Sommer, Eric, Leutnant 187
Sopwith Tabloid 160
South Vietnamese Air Force 153, 157
spacer block 192
Spad VII 82–4
    XIII 23, 64–5, 82–5, 92, 202
Sperry Messenger 13
Stearman 207
Steinle, Holger, Dr. Dr. 85, 93
Stevenson, William 19, 74
Supermarine Southampton 37, 49–53, 57
    Spitfire 25, 47, 49, 202
suspending aircraft 41
Swissair 167–8, 170–1

Taylorcraft L-2 Grasshopper 153
technical materials 37

tires 129–40
Thiemeyer, Manfred 93
Thomas, Neil M. 183
Toille, Alan D. 84
trunnion 57–8, 65, 70, 104, 109
Tuck, Walter J. 30, 42, 175
Turner, Rosco 156

United Air Lines 156

Vehicle and Power Plant
   Restoration Planning
   Committee 22
Voisin Voi.8 Bn.2 202
Vought OS2U-3 Kingfisher 26,
   202

F4U-1D (FG-1) Corsair 13, 38,
   45, 47, 202

Waco 203
Waldis, Alfred 174–5
Waugh, Bob 70–1
Watson, H. E., Colonel 188
Watson's Whizzars 188
wax 18, 64, 103–4, 108, 112,
   114, 123–4, 155, 176, 190–1,
   193
wear rate 34
Westland Lysander 25
Widmer, Max 170–2, 174
Wilkinson, Stephen 47
Wille, Chad 184

Wimer, Donald M. 182
window tint film 174
Wiseman Cooke 202
work log books 55–7
Wright brothers 78–9, 129, 155
   Orville 59, 77, 154–5
   Flyer 13, 22, 30, 59, 64, 77–9,
   155, 202
   1909 Military 76, 129
   Model B 13
   Ex *Vin Fiz* 13, 23, 202

Zellers, Albert 90
Zisfein, Melvin B. 22